# PORTRAITS OF
# HIGH SCHOOLS

# PORTRAITS OF HIGH SCHOOLS

## A SUPPLEMENT TO *HIGH SCHOOL*: *A REPORT ON SECONDARY EDUCATION IN AMERICA*

## *Vito Perrone and Associates*

**THE CARNEGIE FOUNDATION FOR THE ADVANCEMENT OF TEACHING**

Library of Congress Cataloging in Publication Data

Perrone, Vito.
  Portraits of high schools.

    1. High schools—United States—Case studies.
I. Boyer, Ernest L. High School. II. Carnegie
Foundation for the Advancement of Teaching. III. Title.
LA222.B68  1983 Suppl  373.73  85–12809
ISBN 0-931050-27-8

Copies are available from the
PRINCETON UNIVERSITY PRESS
3175 Princeton Pike
Lawrenceville, N.J. 08648

# CONTENTS

# FOREWORD

## ERNEST L. BOYER

After more than a decade of neglect, education has become a top national priority again. It was high on the agenda of the 1984 presidential campaign. That same year, thirty governors organized task forces on the schools. So did hundreds of counties and school districts, superintendents, and school boards. Colleges and universities strengthened their relationships with the schools that provide their freshmen. Political, corporate, and education leaders have joined forces to bring about school improvements. Education matters once again.

This new concern for schools arose during a period of inquiry, examination, and evaluation that began with the release, in early 1983, of the National Commission on Excellence report, *A Nation at Risk*, and with a whole series of subsequent reports, including our Foundation's own *High School*. Americans became aware, as never before, of the strengths and weaknesses of their schools.

The portraits in this volume illustrate what the debate is all about. Prepared as a part of the research for *High School*, they enabled our Foundation to think vividly and concretely about conditions in our schools. They helped us to cut through the abstractions and code words in the professional education literature. Through the testimony and actions of youths and adults in real schools, and through detailed descriptions of representative institutions they give flesh and blood to notions discussed too often only in terms of the modes, means, and medians of statistical analysis.

Vito Perrone, Dean of the Center for Teaching and Learning at the University of North Dakota, was the leader of this project. He helped select those who visited the schools. He reviewed the detailed reports, searched for themes, priorities, and contradictions, and prepared a synthesis of what the observers revealed. His perceptive essay has been adapted as an introduction to this volume.

Why do we publish these high school portraits now? First, we want to share the richness of the reports that vividly document many of the major themes of *High School*. Only samples of the observers' significant detail could be accommodated in what is essentially a policy-oriented document. We hope that the complete portraits will demonstrate what able school teachers and administrators can accomplish when adequate conditions and encouragement are provided. We also want to share evidence of how poor practices and performance distress and damage teachers and learners and impair education generally. In preparing the reports in this volume, Vito Perrone and his associates have rendered a valuable service to our Foundation and to education. They are to be commended for their achievement. By sharing their work with the public now, we expect to add fuel to the national awareness of the importance of schools and encourage current initiatives for school improvement upon which the attainment of educational excellence so urgently depends.

ERNEST L. BOYER
President
The Carnegie Foundation for the
Advancement of Teaching

*Observers for the Carnegie Foundation High School Studies*

MARIANNE AMAREL
Development Research Division
Educational Testing Service
Princeton, New Jersey

ROBERT ANDERSON
Chairman
Program of Instructional Leadership
College of Education
University of Alabama
University, Alabama

MAJA Apelman
Mountain View Center for
Environmental Education
University of Colorado
Boulder, Colorado

EVA BAKER
Center for the Study of
Evaluation
UCLA Graduate School of
Education
Los Angeles, California

AMITY BUXTON
Director of Staff Development
Oakland Unified School District
Oakland, California

MARILYN COHN
Assistant Professor of Education
and Director of Elementary
Teacher Training
Washington University
St. Louis, Missouri

ANN COOK
Co-director
Community Resources Institute
New York, New York

ARTHUR DUNNING, JR.
Faculty Member
University of Alabama
Tuscaloosa, Alabama

KATHLEEN DEVANEY
Director
Teacher Centers Exchange
Far West Laboratory
San Francisco, California

B. DELL FELDER
College of Education
University of Houston
Houston, Texas

G. THOMAS FOX
Research Associate
School of Education
University of Wisconsin
Madison, Wisconsin

W. ROBERT HOUSTON
Associate Dean
School of Education
University of Houston
Houston, Texas

WAYNE B. JENNINGS
Principal
Central High School
St. Paul, Minnesota

E. JOHN KLEINERT
Professor of Education
University of Miami
Miami, Florida

SARA LIGHTFOOT
Harvard Graduate School of
Education
Gutman Library
Cambridge, Massachusetts

HERB MACK
Co-director
Community Resources Institute
New York, New York

Dr. Marlene McCracken
Associate Professor
School of Education
University of North Dakota
Grand Forks, North Dakota

ROBERT MCCRACKEN
Professor of Education
Western Washington University
Billingham, Washington

FRED M. NEWMANN
Professor of Curriculum and
    Instruction
University of Wisconsin
Madison, Wisconsin

RUTH ANN OLSON
Evaluation Specialist
Minneapolis Public School
    System
Minneapolis, Minnesota

ANNA D. STEFANO
Graduate Institute of Education
Washington University
St. Louis, Missouri

WARREN STRANDBERG
Professor
College of Education
Virginia Commonwealth
    University
Richmond, Virginia

CECELIA TRAUGH
Center for Teaching and
    Learning
University of North Dakota
Grand Forks, North Dakota

INEZ WILSON
Director
Chicago Teaching Center
Northeastern Illinois State
    University
Chicago, Illinois

# PORTRAITS OF HIGH SCHOOLS

# INTRODUCTION

## VITO PERRONE

This volume is intended principally as a supplement to Ernest L. Boyer's *High School: A Report on Secondary Education in America*. It is also, however, an effort by The Carnegie Foundation for the Advancement of Teaching to contribute to the literature of secondary schools—a sparse literature that, in general, lacks adequate descriptions of school practices. It contains thirteen of the fifteen school portraits prepared by scholar-educators associated with the Carnegie study of the American high school. These portraits were part of the rich information base from which *High School* and its recommendations emerged. Much of the descriptive narrative of *High School* that brought readers into the everyday life of secondary schools came directly from these portraits.

The portraits included in this volume were prepared by twenty-one experienced scholar-educators, persons with excellent observational skills and histories of thoughtful reflection about schools and the society. The schools selected for observation reflected a broad geographic distribution as well as diversity in regard to race, social class, size, and community. They were intended to represent, to as large a degree as possible, the larger universe of American high schools.

The observers—our scholar-educators—were asked to take special note of preselected Carnegie themes. These were: the contextual changes affecting the school, students, school goals, school climate, leadership, curriculum, teachers, teaching and learning, education beyond the school, and media and technology. But they were encouraged also to construct their own meanings, to prepare their portraits around the dominant issues that emerged in their particular schools.

The school observations were scheduled for twenty days. In many cases, however, observers spent more than twenty days. Although twenty days were not enough for a rigorous ethnographic study, they allowed, as it turned out, sufficient time for experienced observers to gain a significant understanding of the schools, their principal motifs, and the issues that confronted them. The observers were able to capture in important ways the life of the schools; they came away, in every case, with powerful impressions, vivid vignettes, and poignant personal statements.

The portraits presented here demonstrate the considerable variance among American high schools. While all popular descriptions—those ongoing attempts to characterize *an* American high school in singular terms—fit *some* high schools, they seldom describe, in any significant sense, *most* high schools. There is, for example, talk of violence and a lack of order, but these are not the characteristics of very many of America's high schools. There is also talk of too many offerings—a proliferation of courses—but in large numbers of America's high schools there are so few students and teachers that a paucity of curriculum options exists.

The observers presented to the Carnegie staff these school portraits—essentially their efforts to describe a closely observed, complex cultural institution—as well as their field notes (often far more extensive). Here, as already noted, we present only the portraits. In most cases, the portraits were longer than they are here. In my concern about space, I have taken the liberty of removing paragraphs and pages that, while interesting, appeared to extend a point already sufficiently made.

A brief comment about the methodology might be in order. Each of the observers was given an outline of the purposes of the Carnegie study, a descriptive essay relating to the Carnegie themes, and considerable information (catalogs, demographic information, and the like) about the school he or she was to observe. In addition, the observers came together for two days to discuss the themes and share with each other their particular styles of entering and observing schools. The sharing of individual experience in observing schools was particularly useful; it seemed to enlarge the range of possibilities for virtually everyone. Such questions as the following helped guide discussions relating to the themes: What behavior would cause you to believe that students were deeply involved in learning? How would you come to understand whether or not there is a sense of shared purpose in the school? What would cause you to say that the school is well integrated into the community? In addition to such fairly open-ended discussions, attention was given to several parent, teacher, student, and administrator interview schedules prepared by the Carnegie staff and related to the themes. It was suggested, however, that the observers adapt these materials in consideration of their own styles of interaction with others.

Subsequent to these sessions, I communicated with the observers by telephone, responding to questions, sharing the experience of others, and providing support. No guidelines were given for the preparation of the portraits. I believed that each observer should follow his or her own best instincts and style, recognizing in the process the overall purpose of the activity—informing the Carnegie study. As will be noted, the portraits are, as a result, quite different.

For this volume, the portraits are grouped according to the following geographic characteristics and specializations: urban, suburban, rural, alternative, vocational, and selective academic. The volume ends with a summary statement I prepared for the Carnegie staff. While not originally intended for publication—in that sense, it is not a carefully articulated essay—it might still give readers a further glimpse into the kind of work that helped form a base for The Carnegie Foundation's major study of the American high school.

# REFLECTIONS ON THE
# PORTRAITS

VITO PERRONE

As noted in the Introduction, these reflections originally were prepared for the Carnegie Foundation staff, principally to stimulate internal discussion and to assist Ernest Boyer as he thought about the general directions for *High School: A Report on Secondary Education in America*. Together with the portraits, they bring the field studies component of the Carnegie study to a natural conclusion.

## Urban Schools

Each of the four urban,* comprehensive, nonselective high schools we observed has been shaped by a unique history that parallels, to some extent, the history of many other urban high schools in the United States. With the exception of one built only thirteen years ago, they now serve different populations of students than was earlier the case and exist in neighborhoods whose characteristics have changed dramatically. All face complex challenges that many of the educational professionals within their walls find confusing and often unrelated to their particular training.

GARFIELD, located in the Midwest, serves principally the local neighborhood though it is open to students citywide. Built thirteen years ago, it is the recipient of a national architectural award. It now houses 2,000 students, several hundred more than intended. Eighty

* This summary includes all four of the urban schools making up the Carnegie sample. Only three of the four profiles, however, are included in this volume.

percent of the students, many from middle-class families, are black. The school from the outset has striven to be an academic school with high expectations and standards. Although it provides special education opportunities and some vocational courses, it concentrates its resources on the college-bound—55 percent of the graduating students. The school is heavily tracked academically, with almost all entry-level courses taught at several levels. There are honors courses and courses in advanced placement in most of the standard academic fields. At the apex of the curriculum, in advanced-placement courses and calculus, for example, white students predominate. In the lowest academic levels of the curriculum, the special education and basic tracks, the students are all black. While fairly obvious to observers, such divisions are not topics of discussion within the school.

SANDS, in the Southeast, served approximately 2,800 students fifteen years ago, 95 percent of whom were white and middle class. Today it serves 2,600 students, of whom 75 percent are Hispanic. It is expected that 80 to 90 percent of the students will be Hispanic by 1990. The Hispanic population, primarily, but not exclusively, pre-1970 émigrés from Cuba, is upwardly mobile, mostly middle class socially, and striving to be so economically. Sands was oriented heavily toward students preparing for college before 1970, and in 1982 it was much the same, though it experienced some difficulties during the seventies when the population changed radically. While it is academically oriented, offering several advanced-placement courses and boasting a substantial number of students with high SAT scores, the school gives increasing amounts of its resources to a variety of vocational job-training options to satisfy many of its students and their families. Spanish is the common language of the hallways and lunchroom, but English is mandatory in the classrooms. Americanization, an old theme in our history, is taken seriously at this school and receives little, if any, challenge. In the seventies, there were special ethnic studies courses and two special publications that stressed Hispanic culture. But these have fallen in the wake of budget problems and limited commitment among teachers and administrators.

DE SOTO HIGH SCHOOL, all white just a decade ago, is now 30 percent black. With an enrollment of 1,000, it has become the smallest school in this particular northern industrial city. As part of a desegregation plan, each high school in this city was to have a designated specialty and be open to students citywide. The specialty for De Soto, selected by the central administration rather than by those in the school, is finance and small business. But few of the students actually come for the specialization. They come because they live close by, have friends who attend, or because they "didn't get into their first choice school." Many of the teachers have been at De Soto for a long time—ten years or more—and they tend to view the school quite negatively today in comparison to its pre-desegregation years. A basic core of academic, vocational, and special education offerings are available. While the school caters most heavily to the needs of those not considering college, a limited college preparatory program includes one foreign language and very few advanced electives in social studies, English, science, or mathematics. Course proliferation, whether vocational or academic, is not the story of present-day De Soto.

VALLEY HIGH SCHOOL, located in a large, multiracial urban center in the West, has 2,400 students in grades ten through twelve, is overcrowded, and serves a lower socioeconomic population that is 69 percent Hispanic (of Mexican and Central American origin), 16 percent Asian, and 15 percent white. Located in an area noted for gang activity and violence, the school is considered neutral and safe. The student population has a transient quality. It has about 50 percent turnover during the course of a normal year. A fairly large number of students drop out of school each year. The tenth-grade class, for example, has 43 percent of the student population and the twelfth-grade class has 23 percent. Those who persevere into the twelfth grade generally graduate, with approximately 30 percent going on to four-year colleges and universities. Average daily attendance in Valley is 84 percent. That is considered very high in this urban school district. There is considerable emphasis on athletics and socially oriented clubs to maintain interest in the school. And considerable attention is also given to culturally oriented courses dealing with Mexico.

What are the commonalities in the four urban schools? All are relatively orderly—teachers and administrators are firmly in control. Although there is occasional vandalism or physical violence, these schools have to be characterized as safe, well maintained physically, and comfortable settings to be in. It should be noted, however, that in three of the settings the environment immediately *outside* the school can be very unsafe. Violence, crime, and drug-dealing are highly visible. Students, while occasionally overexuberant (as one might expect), tend to accept school rules and behavior expectations, generally show appropriate respect to teachers and administrators, and are responsible enough in classes to assure that a reasonably productive climate for teaching and learning can exist. Interestingly enough, most teachers and students in these urban schools are convinced that conditions are much worse at other schools in their particular districts or adjacent districts—that disorder is common almost everywhere.

In spite of the relatively positive conditions just cited, teachers and administrators, especially in schools other than Sands, feel that they are unable to do as well as they might because of the interference of their central bureaucracies. Teachers come and go in response to circumstances that are principally budgetary but also are connected to a variety of seniority and race-related factors. Administrators and teachers in the schools don't select their colleagues; they are assigned people. Often, they lose teachers they don't wish to lose. The uncertainties about staffing are enormously discouraging for everyone. Some classes in Garfield, for example, had as many as four different teachers in one semester. The kinds of independence desired for developing a curriculum are also not available. Proposed changes must go through a variety of offices far removed from the individual schools. Choice of textbook and materials is limited. Goals established citywide often have no meaning at the individual schools; policies developed at the central offices often appear inappropriate. While some of these difficulties are understood to be related to teacher-union contracts, the central bureaucracy is often seen as the school's enemy—as a defensive, conservative enterprise that seems to assure by its actions that the schools are destined to decline in quality.

In none of the settings is there much opportunity for professional growth. Teachers, for the most part, feel isolated, having relatively few professional contacts with educators in the colleges and universities or in other schools. This is the case even though prestigious universities are very close to all of the schools. In one, the university is only blocks away. Teachers are not challenged to discuss curriculum intensively. They have little time, given their schedules, to meet formally or informally with their academic colleagues or with curriculum advisors. Opportunities for professional development that might take a person away from the school are restricted by central office rules and regulations. If teachers wish to attend a professional meeting, it generally costs them a day of sick leave and they must meet all of the related costs. While there are enthusiastic teachers in all four settings who inspire young people and gain personal satisfaction from their lives as teachers, they are outnumbered by teachers who, while meeting their minimal obligations, are not enjoying themselves much.

Teachers in these urban schools are, by and large, better educated than those in the rural schools. Most of them hold at least a master's degree. Many have graduated from the larger state universities and selective private schools that are generally diverse in their student populations and program offerings and offer intellectually stimulating environments. A majority have gone through urban high schools themselves, typically during a time when the urban schools were catering even more to a college-bound population. They generally view the high schools they attended as being better than the schools in which they are teaching.

Unlike the rural settings in which the school is possibly the only place where young people can gain substantial intellectual stimulation and social interaction, the schools in these urban settings compete with a wide range of other sources of exchange. The urban streets are full of alternatives. In the settings we observed, high school students—as many as 60 to 70 percent—hold part-time jobs. Consequently, school is not the central focus of attention for the majority of these students. This shows up, in part, in the relatively small student turnout for social activities and athletic events. For example, at Sands, a school of 2,600, only about 200 students would be expected for a football game. In all of the schools, there was comment on how "school spirit has declined."

Students speak positively in all of the settings about the opportunities for meeting students of races other than their own, acknowledging that this is less possible in many of the other high schools they know about. Significant interaction of students across racial lines, however, is not particularly extensive.

Parents are not particularly active in any of the schools. In most cases both parents work. In the case of one-parent families, a prevalent circumstance in two of the schools, the one parent is working and/or bearing the burden of several other children. At Garfield, the Parent Advisory Council is rather active but white parents are in the majority (sixteen of twenty-five). This is hardly representative of the student population. In the Hispanic settings, parents view the school as a center of authority and tend not to be deeply involved in any formal manner, even though they are intensely interested in the education being provided.

Students seem to be quite practical in their orientation to school. They expect to receive the help necessary to be reasonably successful in whatever tests are required—whether these be local or state competency tests or college admissions tests such as the SAT or ACT. Teachers often commented that students asked about their assignments, "Will this be on the test?" In Sands, enrollment in an elective vocabulary course—designed to assist students with the State Literacy Test and the SAT—is very high. In contrast, because very few students consider world literature important for the foregoing purposes, enrollment is very low. Efforts to encourage problem solving, inquiry and classroom discussion of an open-ended variety are discouraged, teachers say, by students whose motivations are overwhelmingly practical in a fairly narrow sense.

Tracking is very heavy in all of these urban settings. In contrast to the suburban schools, however, the upper tracks are typically made up of students who read *at* what is described as grade level as opposed to students who are *far above* the average.

Homework depends upon the particular class and its level, but, in general, little homework is assigned. At Garfield and Sands, students in college preparatory programs are likely to receive from eight to twelve hours of homework per week. At DeSoto and Valley there might be two to five hours of homework per week for those in college preparatory programs. In part, this acknowledges that large numbers of students work. But it also relates to the fact that many teachers hold very limited expectations of students.

One important lesson emerges from the portraits of these four urban schools. And it could, undoubtedly, be extended to students in all of the schools. The students are, for the most part, teachable, desirous of an orderly environment, interested in and caring about social relationships, generally responsible, searching for or solidifying an identity, concerned about fairness, and wanting those in the schools to care about them as individuals. In this sense, they are more like high school students of the forties and fifties. I say this because so much mythology has grown up about how different young people are today. In urban communities, in particular, there is a belief that young people—especially because of their great numbers, those in high schools—are to be feared. This fear is even more apparent when large numbers of the students are black or Hispanic. In contrast to such attitudes, in all of the urban settings teachers and school administrators, while often concerned about the learning skills of many, described their students as pleasant, personable, and teachable—"nice kids."

One cannot observe these urban high schools without a strong sense that they are struggling with enormously complex social issues. The issue of race is especially potent. The schools are trying to be models of integration in a larger society that continues to make the reality of integration difficult. Nowhere else does integration work as well, or are people as serious about it, as in the schools. The isolation of the schools from colleges and universities, business and industry, and public community services and their resources is an impediment. Those within the schools need more contact with such resources. Large numbers of students have learning difficulties. But specialized resources are limited and, as budget declines become the norm, these resources may even disappear. These urban high schools are attempting to be comprehensive, promising many job skills. But their resources for such a task are limited. It may even be unrealistic for these high schools to promise, as they tend to, programs that provide entry-level training for very many specific employment fields.

## Suburban Schools

The three suburban high schools we observed are adjacent to large cities and are influenced greatly by their urban environments.* In contrast to schools in more recently developed suburban communities that are an hour or more away from their related central cities, these schools are in older, close-in, suburban communities. In one suburb,

* Portraits of only two of the suburban schools are included in this volume.

70 percent of the housing is of the multiple-unit rental variety. It looks much more like the city to which it is attached than the next rung of suburbs.

What are the principal distinctions between these high schools and those in the large cities to which they relate as well as to the urban schools we observed as part of this Carnegie study?

They tend not to have large black populations—12 percent being the largest proportion. Asian students tend to be the largest minority in these suburban schools. In no case is the overall minority population greater than 30 percent of the total. It should be noted, however, that in two of the three settings, minority student population has expanded significantly since 1970, when there was virtually *no* minority population.

Socially and economically, these schools have a larger middle-class base and place considerably more emphasis on college preparatory programs than schools in the cities. Fifty to 70 percent of the graduates of these schools are expected to enter colleges and universities; many of them plan to enter prestigious schools such as Harvard and Yale.

Approximately the same size as schools in the cities, the suburban schools experience similar financial difficulties. They face, as well, an increasing number of students with learning difficulties and limited academic interests.

CALVERT is located in a Middle Atlantic suburban school district with more students than there are in Boston. With an enrollment of 1,400, small for the district as a whole, it sends most of its graduates to colleges and universities.

Because of a decline in student population since 1977, when it had 2,000 students, there is great fear that Calvert will be closed—judged to be too small to function efficiently or effectively. While it is essentially a middle-class school, its minority and poverty-level student population is growing, and ove·all student interests are changing. But given a lack of school-based decision-making, constructive responses to the changing circumstances seem difficult, if not unapproachable.

SEQUOIA, in the Northwest, is the smallest high school in a suburban district whose overall school population has declined substantially since 1975. Destined to close in 1978, parent and teacher pressure was great enough to force the school board to keep it open. This faculty-parent coalescence is viewed as an important event. But beyond this effort, parent-teacher interaction tends to be insignificant. More homogeneous racially and economically than the two other suburban schools observed, Sequoia is only now receiving a small minority population.

Sequoia is also facing extreme fiscal pressures owing to the unique legislation surrounding school finance in the state. In addition, it has to respond to a number of state mandates regarding basic skills. Each of these factors impinges substantially on curricula and teacher-student morale.

ROSEMONT,   serving 2,000 students in the Northeast, is the largest of the suburban schools we observed. It is also the most diverse racially, socially, and economically, and the richest in terms of curricular offerings and opportunities. In many ways it is more similar to the selective academic schools we observed than to other suburban or urban schools in our sample.

A long history of excellence in its academic and arts programs continues to give Rosemont a constructive base in its changing circumstances. But this same history contributes to tension because more students than ever are struggling academically. Functionally, two schools have developed, causing considerable discomfort for many within the school. Of all the schools we observed, Rosemont has the highest level of parent involvement. As a community, Rosemont takes education seriously and actively supports the high school.

Teachers in these three suburban settings are experienced—the norm being well above fifteen years. They tend to have at least a master's degree. In this sense, their educational levels are higher than those of teachers in the rural schools and similar to those in the urban and selective academic schools. Teachers at Rosemont and Sequoia express considerable delight about being in high schools that they consider the best, the most interesting, and the most academic, in their respective states. However, teachers at Sequoia share with their counterparts at Calvert, and many urban schools we observed, considerable frustration about the current state of their schools. With the severe shortage of fiscal resources, class loads at Sequoia have increased substantially over the past four years and course offerings have declined. There were seventeen courses in English five years ago; now, there are only four—all basic courses designed to assure that students will satisfy the basic skills requirement. Without opportunities to teach courses in their special areas of interest, enthusiasm among the English teachers, for example, is relatively low. Much of the attention of the math department is directed toward preparing students for the basic skills tests, draining resources and enthusiasm.

Within the basic courses, students are separated by ability although the content tends not to be different. Art and music offerings have been cut because they are not viewed as critical to the school's mission. Vocational education, never large, remains underdeveloped. The athletic programs, especially important at Sequoia, continue, however, to thrive.

Teachers at Calvert seem somewhat dispirited. They feel pressures to limit course offerings and to gear basic courses in each academic area toward a common set of objectives that can be measured by countywide competency tests. Seeing decision-making about curriculum occur at the county level, they do not assume a great deal of responsibility for the school's academic programs, but there is a strong belief that circumstances are changing and that they need to respond differently to their particular students.

Because the serious vocational activities take place at a central location and with an accounting system that takes students off home-school rosters when they attend, there is a belief among the vocational staff and many academic teachers at Calvert that students are discouraged from enrolling in the more intensive vocational offerings for fear that any further shrinkage of enrollment will force the school to close.

In both Sequoia and Calvert, there is a great deal of emphasis on order and control. Once open, both campuses are now closed. In part, this is an outgrowth of early- to mid-seventies concerns about drug use and perceived misuse of the freedom of an open campus. Teachers in both settings tend to resent the time and energy spent on control. They do not see it as really necessary or constructive in promoting morale. Drug use is viewed by faculty and students in both settings as declining.

In all three of the suburban schools, students are viewed as a strength. They are seen by teachers as generally responsible, willing, motivated, interesting, and pleasant. Teachers like them—in contrast to much of what is printed in the popular press. Students at Sequoia and Calvert are favorable in their overall responses to their lives in these schools. They are pleased to be where they are rather than at other high schools in their respective districts. They do not, however, find their academic programs to be particularly challenging. A majority believe they are ready for bigger challenges. There is not a great deal of homework (two to five hours per week) and much of what is expected in classes has a routine workbook orientation. Inquiry teaching, problem-solving, open-ended explorations are encountered infrequently, if at all.

Rosemont, on the other hand, is different. There are 300 courses in the formal curriculum at the "basic, standard, honor, and advanced-placement" levels. The foreign-language department offers courses in eight languages; there are fifteen courses in music, six in dance, and five in drama. In light of the growing resource constraints, the Rosemont faculty is being pushed to decide which courses are absolutely essential. For students in the honors and advanced-placement courses, expectations are high, and the teaching is thought-provoking, inquiry oriented. While no stigma is attached to teaching basic and standard courses, and many of the finest teachers in the school teach courses at these levels, there are expectation differences. Minority students tend to cluster here, posing a dilemma for a thoughtful faculty wishing this school to be democratic and just, educative in the highest sense for everyone—the 30 percent not going on to further academic schooling as well as those who plan to continue academic pursuits. Nowhere in the high schools we visited were faculty as thoughtful about curriculum, as involved in course development, as intensively interactive about issues of teaching and learning, as concerned about the school as a democratic, justice-based environment as at Rosemont. But, within the urban-suburban cluster of schools we observed, *none* were as free of external constraints on curriculum, teaching staff, administrative practices, and uses of community resources.

In regard to leadership in the suburban schools, a variety of administrative personnel—assistant principals responsible for discipline, student affairs, and curriculum, department heads, house masters, assistant house masters—support the principals. The principals, though, tend to be quite different in the ways they carry out their roles. The principal at Sequoia, anxious to retire after twenty-nine years of experience, is hardly visible in the school. He is known by few students. Described as pleasant by teachers, he is not viewed as a curriculum or instructional leader. The assistants at Sequoia are so busy keeping up with day-to-day management that they, too, are unable to provide any instructional leadership. The principal at Calvert is directive, anxious to implement an instructional-management program, notably responsive to the dictates of the central administration, and not very sophisticated about involving teachers in decision-making. He circulates a great deal of paper, but depends on his assistants for most face-to-face contact with teachers and students. Neither of the foregoing principals could be characterized as particularly reflective or sources of intellectual leadership. In this regard, they are similar to most of the principals we encountered.

The principal at Rosemont, now in his second year, is quite different. Supported by an array of other administrators, he encourages teacher decision-making about curriculum, decentralization in regard to student issues, and schoolwide discussion and consensus-building about purposes. He is quiet, thoughtful, and intellectual. He likes his job, is enthusiastic about Rosemont students, teachers, and parents. Unlike the principals touted in the "effective schools" literature, he is not highly visible in the building, standing in the front door greeting students as they enter, walking the hallways, monitoring the lunchroom, and so forth. That is not his style. He is viewed, however, as an intellectual, educational leader.

## The Rural Schools

The three schools studied appear representative of those that fill the rural landscape.

ARCHER HIGH SCHOOL is located in Uniontown, a small community in the rural South, that was more active in the past than in the present. Jobs and shopping—the mainstream of American social and economic life—now exist elsewhere, 30 to 40 miles away. Court-mandated desegregation in this community, as in many other rural settings in the Deep South, has resulted in the development of private academies, leaving Archer with a population that is 97 percent black. While, on the surface, education is acknowledged to be important for the future well-being of young people here, the setting itself provides limited intellectual stimulation and access to the larger social or economic culture. For a significant part of the population, life goes on now, as it has for a long time in the past, without very much education of consequence.

PRAIRIE VIEW, in the upper Great Plains, is even more isolated than Uniontown. Seventy miles from the nearest town of substance, it exists on the edge of an Indian reservation and is shaped in many ways by the historic, often volatile, interplay between native and white cultures. The high school in Prairie View, considered large by the students, has 170 students, half of whom are Indian. Education is seen principally as a vehicle for leaving the community. This presents a challenge for the school, which exists in the community and is influenced by the community's insular values. It represents, as well, a psychological burden for the school's students, who understand that they must leave the community or face a difficult, possibly limited adult life.

RIDGEFIELD, a midwestern community, is, like many small towns within a 50-mile radius of large urban centers, in transition. Long a small rural community, it has recently absorbed a substantial blue-collar urban population in search of a different, nonurban lifestyle. A small school of 180 in the mid-fifties, it has become a school of 1,000. Although the expressed values of the community continue to be those associated with rural America, the school has many of the problems associated with suburban bedroom-community schools, but is without their sophistication or resources.

What kind of response would these three rural settings give to the question, "What is the purpose of a high school education?" "Preparing young people for selective colleges or the state universities," a purpose for the selective academic and suburban schools included in our sample, would not be central in any of these three settings. Social concerns, on the other hand, though defined a bit differently in each of the three, would likely take a more dominant place in the response.

What are the commonalities? In all three settings, the teachers had roots in their communities, having graduated from the schools they were currently teaching in, or having come from communities similar in size and background. In addition, these teachers completed their basic teaching degrees and certification requirements in the same, or similar, types of colleges—essentially the more nonselective, noncompetitive, public state colleges rather than selective colleges or the principal state universities in their regions of the country. The alma maters of these teachers generally lack diversity in terms of students and programs and are limited in terms of intellectual and material resources. While often providing an adequate education, they are not typically regarded as institutions that hold high expectations for academic achievement. There is, then, a quality of homogeneity among the teaching staffs in these schools. In some ways—for example, by instilling a sense of the values of the communities in which the schools exist—the homogeneity is a strength. But it also tends to limit the potential quality of the students' academic learning and the possible expansion of their social and cultural horizons.

Teaching vacancies occur regularly in these districts, but, in spite of the proclaimed surplus of certified teachers, these schools do not receive large numbers of applicants. Prairie View, for example, receives, for most academic openings, no more than one to five applications. And these tend to come from teachers very much like those already there. In special fields, such as speech pathology or learning disabilities, where the potential applicant pool is relatively small, Prairie View is not likely to receive a single applicant for a posted vacancy. (In contrast, vacancies in an urban or suburban school would produce several hundred applicants.)

While the popular press suggests, on occasion, that a proliferation of courses of questionable academic value has contributed to a deterioration of the schools, these rural schools offer, for the most part, only basic, traditional, courses. Advanced-placement courses do not exist and there are very few elective opportunities. A student who wants advanced study in mathematics, science, computer technology, foreign languages, art, drama, or music will not find these schools adequate. Such shortcomings limit, in a number of significant ways, the postsecondary options available to many of the students in these schools. At the moment, for example, such fields as computer science, mathematics, and engineering promise substantial job opportunities.

These fields, however, may well be beyond the backgrounds of many students from these rural schools. Few of these students are likely to go into college-level calculus, physics, and chemistry with sufficient confidence to compete successfully with those whose high school programs are richer.

One of the three schools, Ridgefield, is close enough to a community college to have a number of vocational options available. But that is not the case for the other two, where, although some vocational opportunities exist, they are enormously limited.

Students with difficulties handling the reading and writing needed to function at minimal levels in the high school curriculum (and in all three settings the numbers appear large) do not have the systematic support they need. Teachers wish there were specially prepared individuals in the schools who could work directly with such students.

Taking into account the difficulties of many of the students, a significant number of teachers in the academic areas have altered their expectations. Consequently, reading assignments are minimal, little writing is demanded, and much of the class time is consumed by teachers reading to the students or providing information at relatively simple levels. In all three of the rural settings, teachers make accommodations to assure that most students can and will complete minimal requirements. The trade-off for minimal expectations appears to be regular attendance and reasonable deportment on the part of the students. Little, if any, homework is assigned. Teachers prefer to provide time in class for reading, completing worksheets, answering end-of-chapter questions, working on math problems, and the like. They do not believe that students, by and large, would complete very demanding homework assignments or that parents would support them if they regularly expected and graded homework. They believe that parents' expectations, in regard to academic learning, are not particularly high. And there is little evidence to suggest they are wrong.

All three of the rural schools are orderly. Students tend to be courteous and to accept school rules. Vandalism, when it occurs, generally is not attributed to students in the schools.

Interactions between teachers and students are fairly informal and unstressful. Teachers generally enjoy their interactions with students and students tend to find most of the teachers supportive and friendly:

"Concerned about them as individuals." The schools fulfill a major social need for the students. In contrast to having "nothing to do at home," the schools provide important opportunities to be with friends. They also provide a large number of social outlets—athletics, clubs, dances, lyceums—that have few, if any, counterparts outside of the school.

If the students in the three settings were asked to evaluate their respective schools, they would, for the most part, respond positively. While many would like the schools to be academically and intellectually more stimulating, they feel, nonetheless, that it is possible for students to acquire a reasonably good education even in the schools as they are, if they assume the necessary initiative and responsibility.

Teachers are reasonably satisfied, even though they do not perceive these schools to be intellectually challenging. They do not, on the whole, question seriously their practice, discuss educational philosophy or purpose, conceive of themselves as curriculum developers, or debate the curriculum and the interrelationships among courses. They receive very little external challenge. Their interaction with educators beyond their respective communities is limited. They would like to have a larger professional life, but it is difficult to attain in these settings.

Teaching practices within each of the schools have much in common; there is a sameness about each day, as though the teachers do not know how to make use of diverse teaching strategies, or, possibly, that they don't believe that trying to alter their teaching strategies to introduce fresh ideas and materials, to place more responsibility on the students, to give attention to inquiry or problem solving, and the like, would make much difference in student motivation and achievement. They seem to fear that such efforts might only create unwanted tensions. Many of the teachers saw "sameness in the day" as helpful in classroom management as a kind of safety net for security.

Principals are quite visible in these schools. They interact with students and teachers and attempt to be problem-solvers in relation to schedule conflicts, student difficulties, and the like. They do not tend, however, to be deeply involved in curriculum issues, accepting in this regard considerable teacher autonomy without providing leadership to stimulate very much curriculum activity. They have backgrounds similar to those of the teachers, and do not view themselves as skilled intellectual or academic leaders.

One often reported hallmark of rural schools in America is a high level of parent involvement in the school. This may exist in many rural communities, but it is not the case in these three settings. Parent involvement is limited, and personal knowledge about the schools' academic activities appears to be fairly low. Parents do, however, attend athletic events and are vigorous supporters of the home team.

Teachers tend to know the parents—can identify them by name. They are involved together in many social and economic activities that occur in the communities. But this involvement does not translate into substantial levels of parent-community participation in the nonsocial aspects of school life.

In the rural communities, teachers play fairly active community-service roles. They provide leadership in programs such as scouting, community recreation, and alcohol and drug counseling. They also often serve as town representatives and commissioners. They have important skills that are needed in settings that tend not to have significant numbers of other college-educated people available. In spite of these community-service roles, however, teachers do not feel as respected as they would like to be—in part, they believe, because they are paid so poorly. Teachers in all three settings quoted people in town as saying they didn't understand why anyone would want to be a teacher. Such attitudes were clearly painful. A significant number, possibly a third of the teachers, would like to be doing something other than teaching but do not feel adequately prepared for alternative employment.

Many of the foregoing characteristics have, I suspect, a somewhat negative quality. It would be unfortunate if nothing more were conveyed. The young people who come to these high schools seek a supportive social environment, a place where they can learn more about themselves, test out a variety of lifestyles and skills, share adolescent trials with others, and consider what they wish to do with their adult lives. A high school has to accommodate such interests if it hopes to be at all successful. While it is possible for a school to devote too much attention (time, energy, resources) to these kinds of concerns, it is not really possible to concentrate exclusively on rigorous academic learning and not acknowledge the critical importance of these social-relationship needs.

The rural schools attend fairly well to social-relationship matters. And teachers, principals, and counselors see positive results from many of their efforts. If they saw similar results from the energy they put into academic/instructional activities, they might be persuaded to expend even more effort on them. There are times, however, when their attention to social-relationship issues connects with academic programs. For example, in all three of the schools, there is concern about the quality of personal interactions among students. A good deal of what counseling teachers do is related to such issues as fairness, respect for others, and support of those students representing the school in sports. Such efforts undoubtedly help create a climate where academic activities are indeed more possible. In Prairie View, for example, there is a recognition that the potential for Indians and non-Indians to interact is higher within than outside the school. Teachers and school administrators genuinely desire these interactions to be based on mutual respect and understanding. Such interests have resulted in Indian cultural days, mini-courses in Indian crafts, literature, history, and language. In Ridgefield, courses such as Minorities in America and World Religions represent efforts to help students understand the differences that exist 30 miles away, a recognition of the significant racial and religious biases that exist within their community. At Archer, there is a conscious effort to build racial pride among the black students and there are also activities designed to promote intercultural/interracial understanding. In all three settings, there is evidence that such efforts are productive and help create a climate where academic learning is possible.

There are a number of differences in the three rural settings that have a particular historical base. In Prairie View, for example, very few Indian students went to the high school before 1976 and very few of those who did remained through graduation. Today, a majority of the high school students are Indian, a majority of these students graduate, and about 30 percent go on to college (though the number going beyond the freshman year is negligible). A school that was not particularly attentive to Indian students a short time ago now puts a good deal of energy and resources into programs designed to assist Indian students and to promote greater intercultural understanding.

While some people in the school would like to see more tracking that would keep the most academically successful students together for math, science, literature, and language (especially beyond the first year), there is a recognition that to do so could, at this time, create socially unacceptable levels of segregation within the school as non-Indian students are currently the most successful students academically. This is a complex issue that can't be decided outside this particular setting.

At Archer, the politics of desegregation coalesce in such a way that resources available to the school are minimal by national standards. Those with the principal resources don't send their children to the public schools and don't support the provision of adequate resources. It might be easy, I suspect, to suggest that this shouldn't particularly matter, but it is, nonetheless, difficult to come to terms with the fact that most whites send their children to private schools because they do not believe their children will receive a good education in the "desegregated" public school. Those at Archer feel, as a consequence, understandably defensive and unsupported.

Ridgefield also has its uniqueness, three distinct diplomas being just one of many possible examples.

## The Alternative School

NEILL HOUSE, the alternative school we observed, is located in a large midwestern city. It is small, with only 67 students in grades nine through twelve. A product of the more radical sixties, it serves, in contrast to its early population, which was white and middle class, a student body that is 37 percent minority, with native Americans in the majority.

Although in size it has qualities of many rural schools, there are few other similarities. Once a symbol of rebellion against the existing order of schools, heavily political, parent-controlled to as large a degree as was possible within a public system, idiosyncratic in relation to curriculum, casual in its concern about standards, and defensive about its status, it is now more highly structured, less political, less radical, less insular, and more confident.

Whereas textbooks were anathema a decade ago, teachers now use them and offer formal courses. For a significant number of students, Neill House has become a school of last resort. In this regard it serves as a safety valve for the system. For many other students, it is a place to use a well-developed sense of independence and responsibility more constructively. For some, it is a half-way house where drug counseling is available, or a setting that won't provide too much hassle to an individual who has, for all intents and purposes, dropped out of school but hasn't reached the legal age of sixteen. In its current state of diversity, it matches the social and racial composition of most other high schools in the city.

Academically, Neill House tends to have extremes—students who are particularly able and those who are struggling. The size of the school and its overall ethos is supportive of a high level of individualization and its requirement of competency rather than course units for graduation provides a corollary flexibility in curriculum. These qualities serve a majority of the students quite well.

Nonetheless, for students interested in courses such as chemistry and physics, for which laboratories are needed, almost nothing is available. Mathematics is also limited, as are foreign languages and all of the vocational fields. To try and make up for the deficiencies that exist, external volunteers are sought to teach certain specialized courses and, more recently, students are being encouraged to do some of their work in other high schools and local community colleges. Few students, however, use these systems to gain more intensive experience in traditional academic fields. They are more apt to make use of a variety of community resources to pursue experience in the arts.

Budget difficulties prevent the school from making more use of the community for its instructional programs. In this regard, the school, though an alternative, is subject to citywide formulas that leave it impoverished in relation to its needs. Nonetheless, Neill House makes greater use of the community for student learning than any school we observed.

Teachers at Neill House are younger than the average age of the overall teaching population in this school district. None were at the school in its earlier, more radical days. Teachers now end up at Neill House because they have tenure in the system and need to be assigned to schools where openings exist. Many have said yes to Neill House because they have commitments to its philosophical directions, but others have accepted Neill House solely because alternatives were less attractive to them. This is a marked change from the beginnings when teachers were recruited *for* the school and its philosophical directions.

Teacher turnover has been high over the entire history of the school. Administrative turnover also is high. There have been five principals in eleven years.

Teachers are expected to be independent in relation to curriculum, teaching what interests them most while attending to the diverse learning needs of the students. They interact easily with the students; relationships are friendly and courteous. In contrast to the school's earlier days, when students were deeply involved in decision-making, teachers alone now set the standards. Student rights is no longer a dominant theme.

While teachers exhibit a high level of caring, instructional practices are fairly traditional, and expectations for student performance are not particularly high. No homework is assigned; there are no grades. Both issues were decided early in the school's history and have not been debated for a long time. Students express interest in increasing the level of challenge in the school, but they clearly prefer life at Neill House over the schools they would otherwise attend.

Parents continue to maintain involvement in the school, though the patterns of involvement are changing. For example, parents are no longer equal partners in the decision-making that relates to budget and staffing. Along with their sons and daughters, they would like the school to provide more academically, but they seem willing to accept Neill House even with its academic limitations. Such acceptance says a great deal about how negative they are about the larger regular high schools in the district.

## Vocational Schools

The vocational schools we observed are radically different from each other in almost every respect. *Carver*, in a large southwestern city, is a magnet vocational school that offers a full high school diploma program. *Sage Area Vocational School* is a decentralized set of facilities in the Rocky Mountain area offering specialized programs to students who attend twelve different high schools in six different districts encompassing urban, suburban, and rural communities. The Sage Area

Vocational School serves its state's wealthiest and most academically successful school district as well as one of its poorest and academically least successful districts.

Both schools are similar to the kinds of vocational schools that exist in many different parts of the United States.

Carver High, in the Southwest, was originally organized in 1970. At that time, it had 1,500 students and was integrated racially, reflecting to a fairly high degree the overall racial composition of the schools in the district. By 1976, the school had a population of students that was 20 percent white, 35 percent black, and 48 percent Hispanic. In 1979, after a new facility was completed at a location several miles from the original site and in an essentially black community within the city, the population in the school changed rapidly. By 1981, the school's black student population had increased to 75 percent, the white population had declined to below 5 percent, and the Hispanic population declined to approximately 20 percent. Total student population declined to 1,000. In contrast, the Sage Area Vocational School has virtually no minority population.

Carver is an orderly school, and a job-oriented ethos is dominant. This means that teachers and students dress neatly—a tightly administrated dress code is in effect—and are courteous. (Neat dress and courtesy are talked about as hallmarks of the employment market.) The building is clean and free of grafitti, indications that students respect the building, its equipment, and its purpose. Equipment in most of the trade areas is up to date, a feature not typically found in America's vocational schools. Its purposes are straightforward—to provide students with job skills. Serving predominantly students from lower socioeconomic classes, the expectations are that the students will go upon graduation to blue-collar jobs and will not pursue additional training.

There is little talk at Carver about colleges or non-blue-collar options. Academic course work is aimed at minimal basic competencies. There are no foreign languages, and there is no math beyond second-year algebra, which is taken by fewer than 5 percent of the students. Those who teach the academic courses feel like "second-class citizens" in this environment. They have little interaction with the vocational teachers, little sharing of perspectives about students or skills. Their teaching is very traditional, generally uninspired. Homework is not assigned; expectations are low. The trades, vocational business, and home economics are the fields that count here. The teachers in these areas tend to be skilled tradespersons vocationally certified to teach their trades and skills. They stress *learning by doing*, individualize their instruction, and seem attentive to the students. While they wish the students had better reading and math skills, they believe they can still teach the minimal job skills that students will need. More good teaching was observed in the vocational courses than in the academic courses. Teachers in the vocational areas appear confident and develop much of their own curriculum. In the academic areas, teachers tend to rely on standard school district outlines.

Students at Carver are there because they have chosen to attend. Those in the school do not view Carver as a dumping ground for the least able—a view fairly common in the vocational programs of comprehensive schools. (The "dumping" view pervades thinking in Sage.) Because Carver's goals are so firm and the options so narrow, the school has a homogeneous quality. But one wonders whether, at this stage of their lives, young people should be locked into a job orientation and, correlatively, locked out of the broad options that exist in our culture. That question surfaces occasionally at Carver but is never pursued very seriously.

There is no athletic program and nothing in the arts. Clubs, all related to each of the vocational programs, are numerous and part of the school's job-oriented acculturation process.

There is a great deal of faculty turnover at Carver, especially in vocational fields, where outside job opportunities at much higher pay exist. In contrast to those in the vocational fields, academic teachers feel undervalued by the community. They tend to be discouraged. There are virtually no in-service or staff-development opportunities of consequence, yet teachers express numerous needs related to their teaching efforts.

The Sage Area Vocational School is different. It was organized six years ago as a way of sharing vocational resources to cut down on the costs while increasing vocational curriculum opportunities. It has students for only a part of the day, generally for a two- to three-hour course; hence, it is a part-time effort. Students have to maintain complicated transportation schedules in order to participate. They often find such schedules too difficult to sustain beyond a year. While there are elaborate structures for governance and counseling in each host high school, few of the counselors (who have many *other* responsibilities) appear to have a very high level of knowledge about the various vocational offerings. There is a suspicion among vocational teachers that many students are encouraged to attend Sage in order to get "easy" credits to complete high school. This, in fact, might be true.

Vocational teachers are also concerned about the relatively small number of students who continue into second-year programs, the heart of their efforts. They lament the students' limited reading and math skills, believing that these represent serious limitations to any significant vocational education. This concern would seem to be a good one for the faculty members in the vocational school and in the host academic schools to address collaboratively. But there is virtually no interaction. The vocational teachers do not have working relationships with teachers in the host high schools. They are, it seems, worlds removed.

There are some important benefits to the way the Area Vocational School is structured. Students from six different school districts, for example, come together for a part of each day. Given the diversity of the students, socioeconomically and experientially, this has to be constructive. Stereotypes, held fairly commonly, are challenged, and students' human-relations experiences are enlarged.

The teaching in the vocational setting in the Area Vocational School has an apprentice-journeyman quality. It is moderately paced, carefully organized, and tailored to the diversity of student interests and experience. Students are effectively engaged in ways that they suggest is not common in their work back in their home schools.

## Selective Academic Schools

The two selective academic high schools in our sample are located in large cities, have long and honored traditions, and exist to serve exclusively the most able of the public school students in their particular communities. White, middle and upper middle class two decades ago, they are now more diverse, a response to the changing demographic patterns of the public school population in these communities as well as to the pressures of the 1960s for enlarged educational opportunities for minorities and the poor. There is, and likely will continue to be, pressure on both schools to accept even more minority students, even though both are well beyond an optimal capacity of total students now. Though they are more diverse than ever before, the belief persists that these schools still serve students of privilege. The West Coast school, *Brette High*, is now 70 percent minority, principally Asian, predominantly Chinese. Almost 3,000 students are enrolled in a facility originally built for 1,800. The East Coast school, *Jenner*, is approaching 40 percent minority, predominantly black and Hispanic, and also serves 3,000 students. In both settings, teachers and administrators feel their resources are being stretched much too far.

As one would expect, there are many similarities in these two schools. In both, students are very serious academically, viewing their performance as important to their admission to a selective college or university. Virtually all of the graduates of these schools—close to 99 percent—go on to colleges and universities. They expect to be prepared well to take the SAT and to do sufficiently well in advanced-placement courses to receive college credit. In this regard, the expectations have a strong utilitarian quality. Such expectations are met quite well, though meeting them creates tensions for teachers as they consider curricular content and approaches to teaching.

Even though academic expectations for the students tend to be high, teachers in both settings suggest that the students are not as able overall "as they used to be." Aging faculties in both settings seem to share considerable nostalgia for those earlier years. At the same time they acknowledge their good fortune in being at Brette and Jenner.

The teachers have been in these schools for a long time—most have been there well over fifteen years—and many are thirty-year veterans getting close to retirement age. They came to Brette and Jenner before the demographic changes in the schools occurred and they are predominantly white. They were recruited originally for their academic interests and intellectual qualities; almost all hold masters' degrees, many hold Ph.D.'s. Large numbers are graduates of the schools where they now teach. They view themselves to be at the top of their profession, in the kinds of schools they value. There is concern in both schools that replacements for existing faculty members will be of lesser quality, assigned from the excess pools of teachers with seniority from other district high schools. There is justification for this concern.

Budget pressures are keenly felt by teachers. Classes are getting bigger; materials are becoming less plentiful; and fear of layoffs is growing. Cutbacks in resources in the two schools are, for the most part, rather demoralizing. Surprisingly, budget cuts are *not* viewed as challenges in any constructive sense, or as catalysts for rethinking programs or utilizing staff differently.

One gets a strong sense of continuity and tradition in both schools that, in large measure, can be traced to the stability of the teaching staff. But there is also stability at the administrative level. While there is a new principal at Brette, he replaced a twenty-year veteran. The principal at Jenner also is relatively new in this position but has been in the school for over twenty-five years and is only the third principal in the school's forty-five-year history.

As rich as these schools are in relation to curricula and teacher backgrounds, teachers in these schools share with their colleagues in virtually all the other schools we visited a sense of professional isolation. There is very little interaction across disciplines and very little systemic, ongoing discussion about teaching and learning.

Brette and Jenner are enormously diverse in terms of curriculum. Small colleges tend to offer much less. Both schools have rigorous requirements for academic study in science, math, English, social studies, and foreign languages. And within and beyond these areas there are numerous electives. Students are enrolled in from four to six *solid* subjects each semester with a homework load that averages two to four hours each day. The days for students are *very* intense. Honors and advanced-placement courses abound and are at the apex of the curriculum. At Jenner, there are advanced-placement courses in thirteen subject areas. Both schools give considerable attention to advanced-placement efforts because such programs are considered an important reason for the existence of these schools. But the pressures to assure that students do well in advanced-placement examinations also mean that the courses have a particular pace, cover a fairly narrow range of literature, and maintain a heavy dose of advanced-placement-style examinations. Teachers do not experiment much in these courses. Because of the class size requirements in advanced-placement courses, basic courses tend to be larger and more difficult to manage.

Jenner has a math and science orientation; hence, its rich elective array—principally for students in the last two years—is in math and science. Brette, on the other hand, offers a rich array of electives across *all* areas of the curriculum. It is especially attentive to the arts, an area that is not only not stressed but rather neglected at Jenner.

The curriculum at both schools, while diverse, is accompanied by instructional patterns that stress information acquisition. There is some, though not a lot, inquiry teaching, speculation, focus on ideas. There is little differentiation in most courses in what students are expected to do. This is not to suggest that the teaching is unimaginative or uninspiring, however. The quality of teaching is high, though fairly traditional. The stress on information acquisition is buttressed by frequent examinations—one per week per course seems the norm. Students seem always to be preparing for tests—memorization being a critical skill. At Jenner, the principal is pushing inquiry-oriented instruction very hard; and teachers do, indeed, talk on occasion about inquiry teaching and greater differentiation in their instructional styles. *But*, there is concern that such directions might bring a decline in advanced-placement and SAT scores. There is a reluctance to take any risks. Students complain about the emphasis on memorization and the pressures of testing, but also acknowledge that they are being prepared well for the SAT.

In both schools students are viewed as a major strength by teachers and administrators. They are teachable, and are seen as capable of succeeding at these two schools and in college. They tend to be enthusiastic about learning, and seem willing to invest long hours in study. Many make enormous sacrifices to attend these schools, especially in relation to travel. While pragmatic and fairly conservative in this sense, they also have a playful, imaginative quality that comes through in their literary journals, newspapers, and extracurricular (at Jenner) and co-curricular (at Brette) activities. They also are positive about the diversity of the schools they attend. This is particularly the case at Jenner. Social and academic interests merge at many points. Clubs that grow out of the academic interests of students and faculty abound in both settings.

Both schools share with other high schools in their respective cities an antipathy toward their central bureaucracies. Teachers and administrators feel burdened by increasing pressures to conform to city-wide norms and expectations, as well as to respond to persons and groups that are far removed from the schools and are insensitive to the schools' unique qualities. Because resources are handled centrally and by formula, the special needs of these schools generally go un-recognized. Brette and Jenner have 95 percent average daily attend-ance, as opposed to the 70 percent that prevails at most of their sister high schools. This provides greater pressure on staff, facilities, and libraries. Because they offer intensive academic programs, their de-mand for library resources is high, but this is not reflected in any special allocation. With 99 percent of their students planning to enroll in a college or university, the counseling and record-maintenance demands are enormous. Yet the number of counselors is based on citywide formulas that don't take these different circumstances into account. In Jenner, the need for faculty to come together for curric-ulum planning and student advising is great, but the central office has instituted citywide policies on "instructional time" that make the needed scheduling impossible. In both settings, the central offices have instituted a number of mechanisms to counteract absenteeism among students. For Jenner and Brette, these directives are time-consuming and burdensome—student attendance is just not a prob-lem. Both schools want more room and support for independent decision-making.

Both schools are viewed as safe. This is one of the reasons that interest in them is so high. Violence and lax standards are seen by students and parents, as well as Jenner and Brette faculty, as being fairly common in the *other* high schools. Interactions among students and between students and faculty are friendly, courteous, positive. These are caring communities in which all parties take considerable responsibility for the enterprise as a whole. The indifference that characterized some of the settings we visited is not present. Brette, more than Jenner, stresses the personal development of students and encourages active student participation in governance, providing nu-merous opportunities for student-initiated activity, especially in the co-curricular program. Students and faculty alike take pride in their respective schools and are especially solicitous of their schools' rep-utations.

Although it is itself safe, the environment beyond Jenner, especially, is *not* considered safe. Students at Jenner are pretty much kept in the building to prevent problems. And a security force is present to keep out those who are not associated with the school.

In most respects, these high schools offer what most of us would like in a high school program serving *all* young people. While neither has a vocational education program, they are centers of high expectations with generally caring teachers who like what they do. They also provide course offerings and activity programs that support a diverse set of interests.

# PART I

## URBAN SCHOOLS

# 1

# GARFIELD HIGH SCHOOL

## G. THOMAS FOX AND INEZ WILSON

Garfield High School stands smack in the middle of one of the largest cities in the United States. Just a few blocks north of the school it is black and white, poor, high-rise, and tough. A few blocks to the south it is black: middle class, poor, and rich, an integration of class but not of color. A half mile west, away from the water, it is very depressed, a place not to be a stranger. The immediate neighborhood of Garfield, however, is different. It is integrated in color and social class, but perhaps not so much in lifestyle. This is a section of liberal America, with a major private university close by, and proximity to the cultural and business center of the city that appeals to its condominium owners. It is an artistic and scholastic community, traditionally identifying itself with academic culture and liberal attitudes, and recently (in the 1970s) priding itself on its racial integration. Although daytime robberies and purse snatching are common neighborhood events, the present pride of its residents is their hard-headed, nearly irrational determination to survive.

Walk around the neighborhood and you will find tree-lined streets; small green yards; comfortable-looking, three-story dwellings with porches and bay-windows; and an occasional five- or six-story red brick high-rise with courtyards and iron gates. Nearer the water, there are twenty- or thirty-story high-rise condominiums and large, stone-front houses with wrought iron gates. A shopping center across the street from the school is three blocks long. There are large parking lots, closed streets, and fancy shops. You can sip wine at a plant-filled restaurant there and watch chess being played under the trees of a quiet square. Raised train tracks separate the school and the shopping center from the high-rises and the waterfront properties. Many bus lines weave around the school and the shopping center and through the neighborhood.

## The Site, the School, and the Principal

Garfield occupies an open space nearly as large as the shopping center. Coming from the lake through the viaduct under the railroad tracks, one sees the school building on the far end of an open field. The macadam playground with its basketball standards looks like a small afterthought in the flat green expanse protecting this side of Garfield. Few trees break our view of the building, a four-tiered zig-gurat with wings. Since the eye never really settles anywhere, let's start at the top level of the ziggurat: a rectangular, shining metal box housing the heating and cooling equipment. The next two levels are brick, each in step form. The ground level of this four-tiered central section of the high school is hidden by the two-story glass and metal causeways that link the ziggurat to two-story wings on either side and create a pair of modest courtyards, with grass and trees visible as one passes from section to section. The wings are brick with a series of vertical concrete slabs that outline narrow windows. A third wing connected by a second-story causeway extends toward the water. This is not, technically, a part of the school; it houses offices of the ad-ministrative staff for one of the city's subdistricts. It took us more than three days to understand this architecture while walking to the school and spending our time inside its halls.

Some community members and a university professor were in-volved in the school's plan, but the teachers and the principal of Garfield were not. The building won an architectural award for school design, and, as its administrators, teachers, and students point out repeatedly, it has thirty-seven double outside doors. With mock praise, the principal says, "This building would have made a lovely little junior college." She goes on to say that that is probably what the community and its academic design committee members wanted. It is a picture of what the residents would like the neighborhood and its school to be: safe, pleasant, academic. Now, twelve years after it was finished, and with over 2,000 students (more than it was designed to hold), the building still looks good. The halls, rooms, and lockers were painted last summer, and, except for a few broken and boarded windows here and there, the building is extremely well kept.

Garfield first opened in September 1966, in an old, stone junior high school on the same grounds. For three years it was housed in this relic augmented by enough portable classrooms to hold 1,100 high school students. In 1969, the faculty and students moved 100 yards south to its award-winning permanent residence. (The old junior high building is still there, by the way, without the portables. It's now an experimental school, kindergarten through eighth grade.) Mrs. K. has been Garfield's only principal. We are told by the teachers and parents that Mrs. K. is committed to educating children and has succeeded to the extent success has been possible. In the early years she hired an extremely competent staff; in the middle years, she did what she could to remove or transfer the more incompetent staff assigned to her from the central administration; and in later years she has ingratiated herself to those in the central office who count when it comes to gaining support and a few extra privileges from the system.

Mrs. K. is not an imposing figure nor an engaging personality, but these qualities are irrelevant to running the show. She is an older woman with a round pink face and a determined, thin smile, which curves up when she has said something that she wants to sink in. With us, she is confident and open; in a meeting with her 114 faculty members, she is quiet until the questions stop. Then, she answers them directly while protecting her faculty. In large student assemblies, she is not visible. She uses her faculty advisory committee as a line of communication to the rest of the faculty, and relies heavily upon two recently assigned assistant principals to carry out disciplinary and programming responsibilities.

Two years ago, Mrs. K. broke her leg in many places. For a year, she said, she ran the school from a wheelchair, barely missing a day. She is tough and determined in a quiet and dignified fashion: a tribute (if you make such connections) to her own training in a private girls school in the city. She lives quite a distance from the school, getting up at about 5:30 A.M. in order to beat the traffic and arrive at school around 7:00 each morning. She is one of the last to leave, taking well over an hour to get home each night. There are those who express concern about Mrs. K., about her health and her ability to deal with the school in the central system game as it is now played. After our twenty days in Garfield, however, we cannot understand their worries about Mrs. K., but we can understand the worries about the school.

*Introductory Remarks on Some Themes and Lessons Learned by Two Visitors at Garfield*  Garfield is a school that works. With its thirteen-year tradition, it is one of the best academic institutions in the city. This reputation is supported by relatively high SAT scores and advanced placement of its students into colleges, by daily attendance rates of over 96 percent during the past year, by a newspaper that wins national awards, and a mathematics team that "beats the pants" off elite suburban teams. Students consider Garfield to be essentially different from other high schools in the city, parents consider Garfield to be the major alternative to benign neglect or worse in other city schools, and its teachers consider Garfield to be one of the few high schools in the city where teaching is what teaching should be: working with kids who care about learning and class performance.

This is not to say that Garfield is free of problems. In fact, a visitor gets the impression very quickly and very often that teachers, parents, and students believe the school is struggling, slowly but surely going downhill. The most serious problem, expressed in personal terms and frustrating tones, is that no one feels in control of his destiny. None of the teachers, administrators, students, or parents, feel that there is much they can do to stem a slide toward mediocrity. The important issues like curriculum, teacher employment, instructional support, and professional reward are not in the hands of those in Garfield nor in the homes it serves.

What unites all those directly involved with Garfield is a common enemy. Parents, students, teachers, and administrators share a deep distrust of the central office of the school district. Blame was seldom aimed at close range; rather, it was loaded like artillery shells and fired toward a largely unseen enemy camped nearer the city's famous skyline.

Our biggest problem in understanding what it is like to be in Garfield is to appreciate its reputation and performance while identifying the realities of its reported decline. To understand this problem, one must recognize, first, the grip held on the school by the central district office, and second, its isolation from the rest of the educational profession at large. These two facts help explain our feeling that, when we visited Garfield, we were stepping aboard a well-constructed ship that could do little but bob on waves over which it had no control.

The first problem is politics. The belief is that schools in this city must be controlled by the central office if education is to stay in favor with the political powers of the city. The teachers' union is a direct partner in this centralization process. It can share the limited spoils as well as protect the teachers from capricious central authorities. The second problem was expressed by teachers as the lack of professional respect for them and their work. This is not only a problem within the hierarchical morass of the school district itself, where distrust by those at the "bottom" (the teachers) of those at the "top" (the administrators) required the protection of a union contract as well as strong and sensitive local school administrators, but *it was also expressed in terms of the educational profession at large*. The local university, for example, taught the teachers (and some of the best of their students), but it did not talk with them. In terms of in-service training and their own professional development, teachers expressed not only dissatisfaction but a sense of extreme isolation from more favored members of the educational profession. If they went to professional meetings, they had to use sick days and pay the costs out of their own pockets; if they went to in-service programs they were often talked down to by misinformed informants; if they went to courses, they were treated as if they were limited and unaware practitioners of a science or an art they didn't understand. Teachers at Garfield were only too aware of the difference between their professional opportunities and those of such educators as the teachers at the university six blocks away. Furthermore, they recognized that their own teacher organizations did little but make that difference more evident. If politics was the sea upon which Garfield bobbed and drifted, professionalism was the excuse for systematically removing the school's rudder and navigation devices. Real professional wisdom, they were repeatedly expected to acknowledge, was held by educators working some place other than Garfield.

A third major problem revolves around the nature of adolescence in the early 1980s. Although we are both parents and educators of similarly aged children, we had much to learn about the high school student of today, especially the student of color in our large cities.

For better or for worse, we found the adolescent at Garfield to be not that different in attitudes, intellectual focus, understanding, and concerns than we and our peers were a full generation ago. The wonder and fear of adolescence, it seems, are far more powerful than we had anticipated, the differences in our circumstances and lives notwithstanding. Our own remembrance of fundamental anxieties about social acceptance and unanswered questions about sexual development were as much the primary focus of the students at Garfield as they were among our own friends in the 1950s. The central point, however, is our *misinformation* about high school students of the 1980s, about their social sophistication, advanced sexual development, and general worldliness.

This misinformation about the high school student is related to central district politics and the professional isolation of the staff. The less that is known about the high school and the adolescent and the less respect that is accorded to those who work at Garfield the greater is the power that can be transferred to and assumed by a central authority.

Fear is the basis of that power. The fear of the super sophisticated, sexually developed, and socially aware high school student feeds both the bureaucratic centralization of authority and the professional isolation of those who work most closely with these teen-age adults. What must be done, we began to realize more and more in our visits to Garfield, is to replace the fear rhetoric that supports such power and isolation with facts and accurate assessments of circumstances.

Thus, we have arrived at our final point. The primary step for any improvement of Garfield is to open some of its thirty-seven outside doors to the general public. Before the grip of the central district office will be loosed, before the supercilious look of the university toward the school can be challenged, the fear and misinformation about the student clients of the school must be dispelled. The amount of misinformation about students, especially about students of color in our large inner-city schools, must be reduced before education at Garfield can be expected to continue in the direction of quality that the teachers, students, parents, and administrators want.

So far, we have referred minimally to those in authority at Garfield. We began with some understanding of the current research on "effective schools" and the role of school leadership. We believed, with so many others, that the school itself is where the ultimate responsibility for educational success and failure lies. We were shocked by how wrong that perception is for Garfield. To assume that Garfield is where the critical educational decisions are made only exacerbates the tremendous problems we saw.

Before moving on, we wish to repeat the lessons that were most powerful.

Lesson one is that much of Garfield's educational program is out of the hands of those who work there. Instead, more direct control is held by those in central office positions whose decisions are predicated on large-city politics and whose power depends upon the general public fear of adolescents, particularly adolescents of color or with non-English-speaking parents.

Lesson two is that the educators at Garfield, the teachers and the administrators, are not only on a professional limb, they sit on a different species of tree than other educators. Professional educational opportunities are unevenly distributed and the professional respect accorded to those who work in high schools by those who don't is small.

Lesson three is that adolescents, particularly metropolitan adolescents of color, are systematically misunderstood by our sources of information. They are not necessarily the super-sophisticated, teenage adults whom we have been educated to fear, mistrust, or wonder at. If we can remember some of the concerns we had as high school students, we can begin to hear them.

Lesson four is that high school policy and control will not change until the general fear and misunderstanding about high school students is reduced. If Garfield is to advance toward its goal of academic excellence it must understand students better, know teachers, and describe its program in realistic terms to its political constituency.

To understand Garfield, one needs to understand that the arrangements between the political forces of the city and the central school authorities have not changed much over the past twenty years. The schools have always been run by a central authority with delineated hierarchical lines of responsibility. Except for the wave of community fervor in the late 1960s, there has never been much community involvement in the schools in this city. This school district has always been a well-protected bureaucracy. Its only relationships with the community have been with the well-oiled machinery of political bosses. Recent conversions to "citywide" and magnet schools with no neighborhood boundaries could move them farther from the community and from local parental involvement.

Garfield was not around twenty years ago, but its teachers and administrators see a real change over these years in the nature of community involvement. In the late sixties and early seventies, when Garfield began, there was active parent and community involvement in the school. Many Garfield educators refer to this period as "the revolutionary" time. Much of the fire of this involvement has sputtered out, we are told, but the school Parent, Teacher, Student Association council meetings are still relatively active. PTSA's paid membership includes about 25 percent of the families, and the Go-to-School night is normally packed with nearly 2,000 parents.

A November parent-teacher conference day, however, indicates a major development: the bureaucratization of school-community relations and the reduction of the range of decisions local schools and their parent groups can make. The PTSA of Garfield, along with 90 percent of the teachers, had agreed to spend a full day on parent-teacher conferences. It wanted to change the social atmosphere of Go-to-School night to a working relationship between teachers and parents that would focus on the students' school performance. The school district authorities would not permit this plan to be implemented because it would mean a day with no students in the school and thus loss of state revenues for a day. The PTSA and teachers agreed, therefore, to substitute a long afternoon-evening session for individual teacher-parent conferences from approximately 4:00 P.M. to 10:00 P.M. Two weeks before that event was to take place, it was effectively squashed by a district-wide ultimatum that that date be used to distribute report cards to all parents. The afternoon and evening, which had been so carefully planned by Garfield parents and faculty, turned into chaos.

The real authority of Garfield, in the eyes of its community and public, is probably greater now than it ever has been. Few question its status in the lives and career expectancies of students, few ask penetrating or potentially embarrassing questions about its instructional program and educational practices. Nevertheless, Garfield is a beleaguered institution. It is beleaguered by its own central administration and school board. It is bullied, questioned, intruded upon, invaded, and assaulted by the higher authorities of the bureaucratic structure. No one in Garfield feels free of criticism or able to act because of the policies, rules, and regulations and their consequences on the actions, image, and performance of the school. "Get off my back" is the common plea of nearly everyone we talked to in Garfield— its administration, its teachers, its students, its parents. And they are not talking about public opinion, or even about general professional criticism. They are referring specifically to the central authorities of the school district. As public accountability is administratively pursued by the school district, bureaucratic control gets worse.

## Climate

People are comfortable at Garfield. There are pleasant conversations in the halls before and after class, in the teachers' lounge, in the cafeteria, in the department offices, often in the central office. The general feeling is that the teachers and students at Garfield know and like each other. Students kid around with each other, and, at times, with the teachers (and vice versa). We should not infer that this atmosphere of good humor and friendly interaction prevails, but, generally, those at the school consider it an oasis of tranquility and peacefulness. As one teacher said with quiet conviction, "This is the way teaching should be: I wish all teachers in this city could teach in a school like this."

The students think the school is theirs. Some of the greatest administrative problems at Garfield arise when non-Garfield students enter the building during school hours. Early in the fall, a ninth-grade boy opened a door to a stranger who then robbed him at gunpoint. To the administration, serious problems often occur when the "community," those outside of the school itself, enter the school through one of the thirty-seven outside doors. It is the high school that is considered safe and tranquil, not the outside community.

One reason Garfield attracts unwanted attention from outsiders, we are told, is its reputation for having pretty young women as students. School dances can be difficult occasions. At one recent dance, a number of coats and purses were stolen by a small outside group that scaled the building and entered windows on the third floor. At a homecoming dance one of us attended, there were six plainclothes policemen as well as a few uniformed policemen near the door. Still, some cars were vandalized. Thus, there are very few dances at Garfield. The administration does not want to (or feels it can't) cope with the problems caused by "outside agitators."

This "defend the palace" mentality is not shared by the students, but they appreciate it. When we asked students about their ID cards, for example, we were told that the cards are needed to identify those who do and don't belong at Garfield. Students appreciate the safety the cards claim to guarantee. We got this response from students who don't wear their ID cards as well as from those who do, and we got it even though the ID cards have stimulated serious animosity and haggling between teachers and students in the hallways and at the classroom doors.

Once we "belonged" in Garfield (we each had our own ID card), it was a hell of a nice place to be. There are more than seventy student clubs at Garfield, most of which meet after school and are supervised, with no compensation, by teachers. There is a very fine newspaper and a full range of sports teams for girls and boys. The best sports are tennis, swimming, and soccer. The football and basketball teams are not anything super, and their players are not accorded the extreme respect that is so often stereotypical in primarily black schools. Homework is expected and turned in by nearly everyone.

Students just do not seem to be angry. Even in our first few days of visits to Garfield, when we saw pointed challenges by teachers of students' rights to be in the halls ("Let me see your pass! That's not a pass! Did you write this?"), students just blithely and quietly let the challenges pass. At their homecoming pep rally (the only one in the fall), the sarcastic admonition by a vice principal because they were too active and noisy getting seated in the auditorium, did not affect student enthusiasm and good spirits, nor was it a topic of conversation after the rally.

We were given two reasons why this climate of good feelings was so prevalent in Garfield. One reason was the students themselves. Garfield was their school, and they wanted it to be comfortable and open for enjoying each others' company. The second reason was the history and image of Garfield. In some ways, the students were living up to the image of the school that had been given to them: the image of a serious academic institution where politeness and performance were expected.

This image, of course, was both a problem and a boon to those at Garfield. The image made it difficult to address certain underlying problems because acknowledging that such problems existed would hurt the school's public image.

Thus, individual teachers could express their concerns about the academic program for the average student at Garfield, but little would be done about it in a public or systematic way. A vice principal could refer to race relations and the need to address racial attitudes, but found little could be done about that. The students and parents could complain about the inordinate amount of work accompanied by fairly low grades in certain courses (especially in math), but would get little response other than a reference to "standards." We left with the recognition that as nice and as friendly a place as the school was, its reputation also was a major self-inflicted flaw. It made it difficult to publicly address problems privately recognized in the school.

## Students

Almost everybody at Garfield—the teachers, the administrators, the counselors, the coaches, the janitors and maintenance people, the security policemen, the parents, and even the students say that "most of the students at Garfield are such *nice* kids!" And they are. Within our first few days at Garfield, we were struck by the students' good-humored deferment to the nervous authority exerted in the halls by the teachers, their open enjoyment and friendliness to each other, their quiet application in the classroom, and their comfort and naturalness with us.

The dress of students at Garfield is strikingly handsome and co-ordinated—"preppy" is the term these days—with much care given to what is worn. For some students, it is glamour nearly every day. Some of this attention to clothes diminishes in the upper grades honors classes, where many Garfield T-shirts and sweatshirts are seen. We also saw many bright-red school jackets, with Garfield on the back, worn by both boys and girls.

Students' pride and attention to the school and to their own image goes deeper than the clothes they wear. Many students talked about the role of school and the values of work and its just reward. They were achievement oriented. Hard work and competition are prerequisites, they told us, to success. They spoke of the importance of grade-point averages and were well versed in university requirements for high SAT and ACT scores. One of the first things most students wanted us to know was that Garfield is different from other high schools in the city. Garfield is better; it is a school where students are expected to work, and they do. It has an atmosphere for schoolwork that other schools they had attended do not have. Many also feel that they are supported by their teachers, whom they described by using words and phrases like "caring," "fair," "expect you to compete and try to be the best you can," "expect you to shine."

Some students, however, argued against this special image, saying that you can get just as good teaching and just as good an education elsewhere. But, they added, getting a good education in a different school might be harder.

This brings up an opinion that was expressed at Garfield by many of the teachers and others who work there. That is, how good the kids at Garfield have it, how fortunate they are to be at this school. Some students seemed to believe this themselves, that they had comparatively "lucked out," but many students challenged this view. Many teachers expressed concern that Garfield's comfortable environment was too unreal, and that the students would suffer when they left to face the challenges of the real world. This was discussed with sincerity, but often with racial overtones. Students were viewed as overprivileged at home and in school. Some teachers saw this as potentially detrimental to the students, fearing that when they left Garfield they would not be prepared for the racism they would surely encounter. Black teachers extended this idea further and were concerned that the black students at Garfield did not know that blacks had to *work harder* and *be better* in order to achieve what whites achieve more easily.

One passionate and extremely articulate challenge to the "how good the students have it" theme came from a student in a senior English class. She was outraged, she said, at the mechanical nature of the instruction she was receiving. All the attention on textbook learning, the absence of intellectual discussion and analysis, the dependence of the teachers on an external outline led her to conclude that this was no real education at all. She wanted to see some excitement about learning; she wanted to be taught by people who were obviously excited about learning themselves; she wanted something better than the mechanical regurgitation of questionable facts. She hoped, she said, that the intrinsic qualities of learning would be experienced in college because she felt she was missing it here. Perhaps, she surmised, college would be different—going to classes three days a week rather than five, and having more freedom for study and living. But she would have none of the image of Garfield as an exciting intellectual haven, where all those under its roof were fortunate just to be there. No student in her class challenged her viewpoint, other than to say that there were a few teachers at Garfield who were excited about what they were teaching, and who communicated that excitement to the students.

Another student viewpoint that challenged the "lucky you" theme was not as articulately stated, but was more generally shared by one whole class, a ninth-grade social studies class described by the Garfield tracking system as an "essential" class. "Come and see the other side of Garfield," we were told by the teacher. The students liked the idea of having no class that day but they didn't particularly want to talk about themselves. Nevertheless, in a few outbursts—some arguing with each other, and some saying, "Okay, let me tell you how it really is"—the general view was that *they* certainly did not feel lucky to be at Garfield. Some enjoyed their vocational courses, but not that many vocational courses were offered. All hated the way their math was taught. Most thought they were getting the short end of teaching, curriculum, and care. There were protests about unfair treatment by the administration, and stories of friends thrown out of school for what these students considered minor infractions while more favored students guilty of major infractions went undisciplined. They also said that some of their own classmates made it impossible for the teachers to teach them, or for the majority of the class to learn. The few who expressed some gratitude for being at Garfield did so on the grounds that it was integrated. "I wanted to go to a school that wasn't entirely black," said a black girl in a no-nonsense tone and with a smile, "and here I have made a few white friends and mix with whites in class. I wouldn't get that at other schools." Some of the other students nodded their heads.

Talking with this class reminded us that, as much as we tried to observe and see the "whole picture" at Garfield, there was a group of students unheard from. They were observed in the reading lab, in basic and essential courses, and in the vocational education sections, but they were not the students who usually volunteered to talk. These students were mentioned by the administrators and teachers when they described special programs designed to upgrade students' skills. "There is no place for average students at Garfield," said one parent. "Special Ed, okay; genius, okay, but the run-of-the-mill, work-a-day student is left out." A counselor mirrored this feeling. "Simply put, we don't do enough for the regular kid; smart ones get more. What then of the below-average student in the basic and essential tracks?" A vice principal wondered what would happen if the best teachers were given the slowest students at Garfield for a year. One of these "best teachers" wondered the same, and expressed some desire to give it a try.

For many of the students, this invisible aspect of their existence goes well beyond academics to their own teen culture. In response to a question about which students were the most popular at Garfield, small groups of students would say, "The seniors and the athletes," or, "A combination of good-looking kids and athletes." They suggested that the "smart kids" weren't necessarily popular, unless it was within their own group. More important was the implication that the majority of students were not so blessed with either "popularity" or with special academic attention.

Over 80 percent of the students at Garfield are black. Its official estimate is about 70 percent because that figure conforms better to federal guidelines for integration. The principal, among others at Garfield, tries to point out that the racial figures do not represent the variance and integrated nature of the students' families; their ethnic lineages, which are far richer than simple classifications of "white," "black," or "other" allow. Parents are concerned about the figures because they want the school to exist; they see Garfield as an oasis of educational opportunity for their children. For the students, Garfield is integrated: for white students, this means being in the minority; for black students, it means knowing some white students. In the halls, classrooms, teams, clubs and pep rallies, even on the homecoming court, the kids seem to have accommodated to the integration ratio of 80 to 20 very well. In our conversations with the students, we got comfortable and sophisticated answers to questions about race. "For thoughtful people," one student said, "it is the engagement of minds that is important, not the color of the skin." On the stage at a homecoming pep rally, the one white lineman received nearly the biggest applause when introduced; the king of the homecoming dance is white. Even more telling is the lack of cliques in the classes. As visitors to over sixty classrooms and a variety of other events, including hallway encounters (which are *very* important to the students), we never saw clear black-white groupings.

But, as we are told primarily by the parents and administrators, there is more than meets the eye. One mother said, "There is no social thing for them [white students] at Garfield. They are intensely conscious of being in the minority, a new experience. . . . I would like to see Garfield more racially balanced." Another mother spoke to the reason few whites are enrolled. "One of the greatest problems at Garfield is people's perception of the security problem. Lots of parents are antsy because they think it's dangerous because there are so many blacks. I think it's mainly that so many blacks in one place scare people. My son has black friends and he has no problems."

One vice principal told us there were indications that racial tensions do exist. The white students sit in one spot in the cafeteria and generally leave their places a mess. The vice principal thinks this is done in protest of their minority status. There is one bathroom that white students know better than to enter, for there is, we were told by some black students as well as the vice principal, a small group of "thugs," blacks who, for historical reasons, hate whites in general and will do what they can to protect certain turf. We were warned before attending the homecoming dance that no whites would come, not because of their classmates, but because of neighborhood problems in the parking lot outside the school. All were pleased and proud, however, that a number of whites actually came to the dance and stayed. Later, a parent told us that this was done with great care and planning by the white students who decided to go.

We also found an answer to our question about why we saw so many C's and D's in honors classes—consistently so over two or three years for some students. Honors classes can be entered voluntarily, and some white students stay in them because the classes are primarily white.

Thus, race and integration are addressed by the students (and sometimes by their parents). Sometimes students' racial attitudes are more sophisticated, aware, and informed than those of their elders, sometimes not. The issue is an open one for the students: they can and do talk about it to a black visitor and a white visitor with comfort, experience, and a refreshing lack of abstract rhetoric. But it is still an issue that one of the vice principals would like to see addressed directly through a specially designed interpersonal program he has seen in other schools. The problem, he says, is that not enough adults involved with Garfield want to admit publicly that race is an issue.

This brings us to the adult view of the high school student. One of the first questions asked and answered by the adults around Garfield was: Are these students different from students of twenty years ago? Some teachers thought so. There was a general call by some teachers for students to be more like they used to be. Many thought that today's student was less responsible, too relaxed, and too impatient with what they called "the learning process" than previous generations. There were parents, and other teachers, who did not agree with this description. As one parent put it, "Some values are as important now as before. Punctuality, responsibility, and initiative are as much in demand today as before. . . . We shouldn't always be looking back. . . . Too many things have happened; the world is different." A teacher who had attended the old neighborhood high school and had spent her teaching career in schools in this area describes the student body this way: "These kids *are* different from other generations. They have the same problems, but they have had to deal with more at an earlier age. They have to learn to cope and live in *this* world *now* and they do a good job of that!"

In response to a teacher's probing for the value of intrinsic learning and the role of competition in their classes, the students' general response was, "Yes, there is some competition at Garfield for grades, but it is nothing compared to competition we feel in our social lives here!" Now that, and the resulting discussion about their primary fears about acceptance, reputation, and image in the eyes of their peers, we could firmly recall from our own high school days. When we were writing notes in the Garfield library, a girl came up to us, introduced herself and said, "You're never going to find out what Garfield is really like, because Garfield is really like a small village where *everyone* knows your business, especially your social life, and rumors are as important as fact." We knew what she was talking about because we could remember our own high school days. This small-town simile reminded us also of a student union meeting prior to the homecoming dance. Seventy-two students attended and spoke as if in a village hall.

Again, as we were talking to a class of seniors, just before the bell ended the class period, someone mentioned a sex education course they all had to take in their sophomore year. We couldn't tell if the course was mentioned in a positive or negative light, so we asked the next class we talked to, a class of juniors, about this sex education course. The initial response was about what we would have responded at their age: "Oh, all it does is tell us what we already learned on the streets." But the response shifted quickly when a girl said, "It was the best course we have had here at Garfield; although much of this we sort of knew before, it was good to have a deeper and more public understanding about what is happening to us as we are developing." That triggered a number of comments on the course, the fact that it was co-educational, and the general feeling that they benefited from and were appreciative of the increased understanding they gained from that required course. That, too, was a response and an admission we could see ourselves and our high school peers making thirty years ago. Sexual sophistication was not claimed by these students, most of whom, by the way, were standing around the homecoming dance floor for hours before getting into the swing of things, much as we remembered doing years ago. Adolescence, in short, was a period of life we shared with them.

This brings us to the last point, which we think is critical. Many of the media-fed views of adolescence are contradicted by the students at Garfield. We won't emphasize this point here, other than to state unequivocably that the most important step in understanding high school is to take time to listen to students. Our understanding of adolescence is perhaps more distorted by the media than is any other critical feature of high school. This includes those adolescents who have chosen to stay in schools as well as those who have chosen not to. The views of adolescents are not being heard above the noise of the popular media. We can take a simple example. Yes, the students said, there are a few nuts our age who have guns and knives, and freak out on drugs, but it's no big deal. Most of us aren't that way. Yes, pills and marijuana are available here at Garfield, just as they are anywhere now. But there is a choice. "We're not in a drug culture, we're not forced by peer pressure here." A few days after this conversation, there was a "drug bust" at Garfield. A few students smoking marijuana were caught by plainclothes policemen outside the school during lunch hour, and it made the front page and the evening television news. After that, our talks with people who were not involved with Garfield pointed to one thing only: that is the school where the kids were arrested for drugs.

Now, some months after our visits to Garfield, there are two impressions of the students that stand out. The first impression is of seriousness. "You know," one of the seniors told us one day in the office, "late fall is the worst time ever for us seniors. It's then that we find out what our chances are for getting into the college of our choice, or into any college. Our future depends on that and we're really anxious, all of us—more anxious than we've ever been in our lives." The second major impression was the student awareness of the institutional contexts of their lives. The one set of attitudes, besides their experiences with and views of race, that sets these students on a different level than we were at their age, is their sensitivity to and acknowledgment of the power and role of institutional organizations. In describing Garfield to us, they felt it necessary to discuss the central office, school board, and school district. In analyzing their own future aspirations, attitudes, and values, they included their judgments of where present and future power lay, and of the nature of the job market, in terms of who makes the fundamental economic decisions that affect jobs. They considered their own status, sometimes in terms of race ("You know if you're black, you have to be twice as good to get the job"), almost always in terms of economic background, as they discussed their plans for the future. They took institutions and organized wielders of economic power seriously—although none, perhaps, were viewed quite as seriously as Garfield itself, a place in which they and their parents placed considerable hope for furthering their own economic well being.

## Teachers

"I have no control any more," the principal said, referring to central policy, "but we have a core of super teachers." She continued, "We have had five weeks of school and, already, fifteen new teachers have come in and fifteen have left because of bumping [teachers with seniority removing other teachers]. It's really extreme this year; with three a week, it's a whole new ball game. The teachers are demoralized, they're scared to death they will lose their positions." To complete this thought about her faculty, she said with reasonable pride, "I get rid of about three to five bad teachers every year. But it is *so* time-consuming it's unbelievable. Each year, mostly through inheritance from somewhere else, I get three to five inept teachers. What makes them inept? They don't care."

Parents agree. First, they acknowledge the good teachers at Garfield, and second, they deplore a seniority system that sustains bad teachers and transfers them from school to school. While we were at the homecoming dance, a parent said:

> You know why I like Garfield? It is a no-nonsense school. Teachers expect the child to work here; and, more than that, they care about the child. My daughter's music teacher, for example, checks up on how she is doing in her other courses, and she talks to her about her other courses. Yesterday, before the first grading period, I decided to call all her teachers, and they were all available and interested in talking to me. It's not that my daughter is that good in class, always. She has had some troubles in school. But she has always been able to work out the troubles because the teachers can explain what they are doing and because they obviously care. As a parent, you know something is right when your daughter is getting up early and getting you up early so she can get to school. Before Garfield, I had trouble getting her out of bed; now she gets me up.

The other side also is described by parents, but they do not hold Garfield responsible. Instead, they cite the few "bad teachers" as an example of how the central authority and the union assure the powerlessness of administrators and parents. One told us:

> My daughter has had one problem teacher each year. We must stop the politicization of the school system and the unionization of teachers. . . . There is continuation of bad teachers, seniority rule. I'm very bitter about incompetent and unfit people being kept on or being given other jobs. It just drives me up a wall. The administrators and parents have no power.
>
> I would like to be able to kick out bad teachers and get new ones and get past the union. The union riddles the system with bad teachers. It's one of the strongest. We can't fight it. I am a union person, but this union is no good for the schools. Garfield is lucky in getting good teachers only because Garfield has a good reputation in the city. Good teachers want to

come and stay. Relatively speaking, we are better off than most high schools in the city.

I'm satisfied with the quality of teaching at Garfield but I would like to see the community and school have more say so about decisions made for their school. . . . My child has had a few bad situations with teachers [but] the administration has no control.

As mentioned earlier, Garfield students had very definite ideas about the qualities of their teachers. Most often, the teachers were described by the students as supportive and caring, but also demanding.

For an outsider, visiting the classrooms at Garfield and talking to its teachers can be impressive. As friendly and open as the teachers can be in conversation, it is intimidating to us to hear students ask them, "What does '$x^{2/3} + y^{2/3} = 1$' look like?" Most visitors, whether or not they had calculus twenty-five years ago, don't know. Likewise, we felt humbled when, in a regular physics class, we heard questions like: "You have been told the initial velocity, the rate of acceleration, that it is constant, and the time of the acceleration. Write an equation to tell us how far the object has traveled." In an English class that was analyzing some of our favorite poets, or in a social studies class where law was critiqued articulately, we realized that we would have to work to catch up with the students, to say nothing of the teachers. Thus, when we talked with the teachers, it was with a deeper appreciation of their special knowledge. We spoke to them as subject-matter specialists, while we tried to probe for and understand the educational concerns and experiences that they considered most critical and memorable.

One of the first things we learned from the teachers at Garfield was that they were dissatisfied with what they knew (in spite of our admiration), and, more specifically, they were outraged at their lack of educational opportunities to know more. Some emphasized subject matter, but many referred to participating more in the educational process itself, in attending professional conferences, forming professional liaisons, having dialogue about instructional practices.

Talking with teachers at Garfield left impressions of real commitment, intelligence and concern. The commitment was evidenced by such incidents as:

A science teacher handing out detailed breakdowns for each student's grades and work performances for the semester, all done, we found out later, on his home computer, which he had programmed for this task.

Math teachers unsuccessfully trying to get a bus for the school's thirty-member team from the central administration, and continuing to provide the transportation themselves, often returning home as late as two or three in the morning.

An English teacher showing me her students' themes, which she called lousy and disappointing, but on each of which were extensive comments, corrections, and analyses requiring at least an hour for each theme.

A music teacher (who says she's at school until 5:00 P.M. every day), who has written a textbook and curriculum guide for her class and directs the students in school operas and symphonies.

An art teacher, with a special interest in photography, who bought his own materials and built eight darkrooms in his classroom.

A vocational education teacher, who regularly scavenges for felled trees because the budget cutbacks have left no money to buy wood.

A home economics teacher, who must not only pick up the groceries for class work but must pay and wait to be reimbursed by the school.

Although money was an issue, especially for departments whose supplies were consumable, it was not, we kept hearing, the major issue. Professional respect, recognition, and opportunities for their own professional development would go a long way toward sustaining them. These teachers were not talking as know-it-all experts or as subject-matter specialists who happen to be teaching in a high school. They were talking as professionals who are interested in their work and have a need for dialogue and discourse in order to develop more coherent professional views, richer professional backgrounds, and more satisfying professional practices. They raised their own questions and doubts about the educational process, about how their students learn, about the form and format of the curriculum, about the educational life of their students, and about their institutional status. In current educational lingo, many of the teachers we talked to at Garfield expressed a need for their own professional development. This was not, they pointed out, "in-service" as defined by the school district, where time is usually spent improving administrative details or meeting in citywide groups to review the curriculum guidelines.

Nor was it "staff development" as defined by faculty in universities and schools of education who, so often, are only too willing to confer their expertise on the teachers. Instead, it was staff development as professional dialogue, discourse, and inquiry. It was a call, sometimes stated explicitly by the teachers, often implied, for some of the same opportunities for analysis and discourse that we investigators had. To us, it seemed like a reasonable request, but one that held little possibility of being answered by the school district, by their own teacher organization, by the local universities, or by the educational profession at large.

Professionalism, then, is a major issue for the teachers. It is an abstract notion that captures many of their concerns about their work and their ideals about the practice of teaching. Teachers were sometimes cynical in describing how they were rewarded. One teacher, for example, said, "There is no appreciation of those born and innately qualified to teach. We are all grouped together when rewards are given. In this situation, people don't produce more than they have to. If you can keep order, then you get the student misfits." On the other hand, many teachers had developed their own systems of sustaining themselves professionally. Some were very proud of their work and accomplishments. They spoke of the courses they had designed in response to student and department needs—not frivolous and trendy courses, but courses designed to improve students' performance or expand the knowledge base. These teachers often spoke of avoiding "burnout" by recognizing that when things became monotonous they had to make a point of becoming more creative. They also spoke of their affiliations with professional organizations and their continuing advanced study as ways of sustaining a feeling of professionalism. As for rewards, most teachers indicated they derived satisfaction from seeing youngsters thrive and mature. "My reward," said one, "is seeing young people go forward, seeing them become total citizens." "To have students succeed," said another. Similar remarks were often made by teachers at Garfield.

In contrast to these sustaining features of their work, were the menial tasks and duties expected of them, tasks that took time they could better use for instruction or planning and that reduced their self-image as professionals. The majority of these tasks were what teachers viewed as clerical, baby-sitting, or security-related. The mounds of paperwork included reports, hall passes, absence slips, and program changes. Study hall duty was seen as an irritant and hall duty was considered obnoxious. Some teachers offered suggestions to solve the problem:

> We have more busy work because the computer [downtown] wants something. We spend a lot of time on ID's, passes and cut slips. We should brick up some of those doors.

> I would like to use my duty periods for tutoring, have the kids guard the halls like at T. High School. They don't do it here because they don't want kids in the position of being the security force.

> People in charge of teachers are more interested in promoting organization of the school. Clerical work should be done by clerks. The office should handle tardies and cuts; we should have computerized programming.

In addition to the paperwork, teachers referred to the central policy (worked out with their teacher organization) that rewarded seniority rather than teaching excellence, and that impaired the quality of Garfield in the teachers' eyes. Even teachers who supported the union's accomplishments and thought tenure was "good," felt uneasy about the retention of poor teachers. "Tenure is good," one union representative said, "but after so many transfers, poor teachers should be terminated. Teachers should have to take courses to upgrade their skills. Administrators should *observe* teachers."

Equally erosive of teachers' self-image are the critics of school practice who have gained public favor while being safely removed from school practice. "Isn't it nice," one teacher said as he turned his back to us, "that you were able to find some interesting work." A parent concurred, saying, "I bitterly resent people who tell us how to do things if they haven't been there."

Enough of our trying to paraphrase the teachers' comments about their work. The following are remarks made by some of the 110 teachers at Garfield.

> We have teachers here who can't teach, but there is nothing that can be done. [A union representative.]

> There is lots of rumor here and not much communication. We've got some problems with the office downstairs. One problem is that they are advocates of the parents, which, in turn, decreases our sense of professionalism.

I am no longer excited by teaching. Entertainment is expected. It's a visual society now, not verbal. Besides, the reality level of kids is just not acceptable. I can't even bring up racial issues. We're substitute mothers, fathers, and clerks. Everyone is expecting teachers to do too much without doing anything well. Intercom systems are a pain. Burnout is *with* us. Union meetings are hysterical. They just have to take schools back to instruction. [A white teacher.]

We are professionals and, like other professionals, we get attached to our clients and they to us. It is nearly impossible to keep this feature of professionalism when you are being moved willy-nilly from school to school. Not only are you insecure, but you keep having your professional ties broken. Soon you just decide not to have ties at all—that is when you stop being a professional.

I'm getting damn good pay. I wish it were for twelve months instead of for nine, but in my mind I am well paid, and I give time to doing it well. I work at home until early morning, sometimes, but I'm not complaining. That's my job and what I get paid for. [A science teacher.]

Two weeks ago, we lost our best biology teacher because she had only six years' experience. No one cares about the teaching performance; it is now irrelevant. Why? Because of the union and the central office. Who is going to give up seniority in the union? And who in the central office is going to stand up and look for answers? Science has never had that much emphasis at Garfield, but now . . .

This is the best high school I have seen, and I have been teaching in seventeen of them in this city. The kids have kept up the school so well, the halls and lockers are in such good shape and it's such a nice place to work. I'm glad I'm here. Visit my class anytime. [A substitute teacher.]

I've just heard of a job at a high school [one of the major competitors of Garfield] that would be ideal. You would teach two courses and the rest of the time you would be the director of this international baccalaureate program. I can't get the job out of my mind. It would be so *exciting* to build a new program like this and have the time to do it right!

There have been some crackerjack, great, great teachers at Garfield and other schools in this city, but many of these teachers are now gone. Many were women teachers, you know, older women teachers for whom teaching was the major professional outlet. Some, like Mr. T., are black men for whom the same could be said. No longer is such job discrimination prevalent, though, and no longer are there such excellent women and blacks who go into teaching. Also, the system gets some of the best ones down and they leave. They go elsewhere in education or out of education entirely. [The teacher then gives two examples of good young women teachers who said "to hell with teaching" and went on to become lawyers in town.]

There are some rewards to teaching, you know. Like kids who come back to see me after six, seven, or eight years; students who are the fourth or fifth child from a family. I have had children from one family, where the father is a Nobel Prize winner in physics and he sends his children to Garfield. That says a lot to me. What really keeps me teaching, though, is the productiveness of my work on the newspaper. Every two months or so, the kids and I can see a product from our work. Teachers and parents and students come up to me and the kids and praise us, or at least talk to us about what we did. This never happens with teaching. It's too bad, isn't it, that the students don't have more opportunities for this kind of productivity in their years of schooling.

You know, I think Garfield is the best an inner-city school can be. Not that the staff or the circumstances are perfect; in fact, I'm sure the staff was better eight years ago, when I first came to Garfield. I never saw such professional, such smart people in my life when I arrived here. Of course, many of those have left, a few have stayed here, and a few new ones have kept Garfield going. When you think about it, this school is *resilient*. I don't know exactly why, except it must be many things together—the parents, the kids, the teachers, the administration, tradition. Yep, resilient is the best word to describe Garfield today.

Two years ago I was teaching in another high school close by, and I was ready to quit teaching. I was taking real estate night courses until I was bumped and put into Garfield last year. What a difference! This is what high school teaching should be. It's too bad other teachers can't see this and experience teaching in a school like this. When you're being confronted by the kids daily, challenged and verbally abused, you begin to hate the kids and to just look forward to completing the day. That's when I realized I couldn't stay in teaching all my life; it was awful. Let me tell you, I love this place. Here at Garfield, the teaching is fun, the kids are nice, good kids. You can do something here and see teaching accomplished. It's the way things are supposed to be.

We are like the Indians. They took the land and gave us a candy bar. Our program here at Garfield supports academics. Our woodworking funds are used for other programs. We get the kids who can't add or read. Garfield is two schools, one for the college-bound and one for the forgotten kids! [A woodworking teacher.]

## Notes from a Day at Garfield

Ed. Note. The following section consists of notes taken by Tom Fox during his first full day at Garfield. The day begins just before the first hour and ends in the evening after a PTSA meeting. These notes are included to share more directly the actual experience of visiting this high school.

A STUDY RESOURCE CLASS. I enter a room that I thought was the mathematics department office and it turns out to be a learning disabilities room (the map on the student folder is not up to date). One student is there with a teacher when I arrive a little before the starting time of 8:05. Another arrives soon after and a third arrives a few minutes after that. The first two students come in with no fuss or bother, they sit down at their desks, bring out their pencils and papers and get down to work naturally. One is getting whispered directions to a test from the teacher. The third student comes in agitated over what he says are false rumors about his missing second-period class yesterday. The teacher questions him, gets complex answers that suggest all his absences were excused, but the teacher never really believes much of the story because his teacher, obviously, has told this teacher differently. She remembers it's the student's birthday, congratulates him and things quickly quiet down again and all three get to work.

It's a small room with no windows, three teacher desks, five small tables, eleven chairs and two student desks facing the wall. There is a large list of Murphy's laws on a file (e.g., "Everything that can go wrong will and at the worst possible time"), and on the blackboard is the following: "vocation = jobs; vacation = trip." I am told by the teacher that this is not a class but a "study resource," a place where kids who have trouble with school can go for help. Students are assigned to the study resource, but don't receive any credit. There are five assigned at this period. In addition to help, there is assessment and (yearly) reassessment of the kids (she shows me the file starting with elementary school assessments and identifications of learning problems). A fourth student comes in late, says she overslept, takes off her coat, opens a book and starts to study. The teacher is talking quietly to one of the boys about home, other courses, other teachers. It is quiet here, the three guys are working, but not too hard. They have bright-red school jackets on with the name of the school on the back and very nice athletic bags with them. The girl is humming, looking over her notes, and asks the teacher to help her by testing her on pronouns and adjectives (she will have a test on these later this morning). The teacher sits down and works with her. The guys relax when they finish, fold their arms and stare straight ahead. The bell rings and all quickly gather their things and leave smoothly.

THE MATH DEPARTMENT ROOM. I go one door down from the small resource room for learning disabilities and find the math department. It's much longer than the resource room and a little wider, filled with eleven teacher desks and some bookshelves and files. All eleven math teachers (three men, eight women) are here at this time. I find out that the school day has been scheduled for the teachers of each department to meet together one period each day. There are a number of students in the room, each talking to a teacher when I come in (the students leave with the bell). A parent is sitting, talking to a teacher for some time after the bell. The thought occurs to me that the teachers may seldom get a chance to talk together (even though in the same room), but about the time the thought occurs it is proven wrong. The chairperson (a woman whom I later got to know, respect, and like very much) gets up and addresses them all with a few announcements and then a discussion begins on a meeting of state mathematics teachers to be held later that month. Seven of the eleven teachers choose to go, even though the expenses are theirs entirely, and they will have to take a sick day to do so (it will take place on a Friday and Saturday). The talk is about room and driving arrangements (it's over 100 miles away), but it turns more animatedly to the agenda and nature of the topics to be covered as well as to the camaraderie at the conference and the people to be met. Some teachers have never been to the state mathematics meeting before. A few of the older women recall that there is a local mathematics club that until just a year or two ago was for men only.

Looking around the room, it appears even more cluttered and cramped than at first sight. There are bookcases and files and piles of textbooks on wheeled carts between the teachers' desks, and bookcases and cupboards against the wall, one with a dead fern on it. All the teachers, I notice for the first time, have ID tags. There is one telephone in the corner farthest from the door. Before and after the discussion on the math conference, Mrs. H., the chairperson, spends some time trying to find a bus for their math team. They're proud of their math team; it beats the elite suburban teams in competitions.

The problem is they have thirty kids on the team, and the "meets" are outside of the city. It's difficult to get enough private transportation to take them all and bring them back (usually in the early morning). But, Mrs. H. tells me, she has had no luck in getting school board approval for a bus. She has called a number of people in authority who won't take the responsibility. This morning it is the police she is calling for approval. (A week later, after more days of calling, I find out she was unsuccessful. No school bus was or will ever be supplied for the math team.)

One of the math teachers is an Indian, a Sikh with turban and trim beard who has said nothing to anyone but has been attentive to the discussions going on while grading papers at a desk in a corner of the room under the dead fern. The phone rings, and it is for him. He goes to the phone slowly (it's across the room) and the discussions hush as he identifies himself, listens, acknowledges something in a low voice, softly hangs up the phone and returns to his desk, saying nothing to anyone. After sitting down, he looks straight ahead for a while before getting back to his papers. The next hour, I am told that I have just seen a teacher "bumped" from his job. He is the fifth math teacher to be bumped in five weeks, and was here himself for only a week. One math class has had these five different teachers in five weeks! (Later that day I see him saying goodbye to the assistant principal. He had just called his wife and is telling the vice principal that he has really enjoyed being at Garfield and would like very much to return. He asks her if she thinks that may be possible and gets no response, only an embarrassed silence and a head being turned away from him. He leaves with no more words and no goodbyes.)

A TALK WITH THE MATH CHAIRWOMAN. Mrs. H. is a woman with an active mind and a forceful personality. She looks matronly; talks directly to a topic with little hesitation. She begins our conversation (which started late in the period with all the math teachers and continued through the next period because it was her planning time) by referring to the relationship between the local university and the school. The school used to have and appreciate a number of student teachers from the university, but lately, she says, they are lucky to have one a year. "There is little money for the program and only a few student teachers." She mentions, matter-of-factly, that the last master's candidate teacher the school had was a male whom the university had requested be placed with a male teacher (she never learned why). Otherwise, the only contact Mrs. H. has had with the university, other than her getting her degree there, was with a research project done in this school by a Ph.D. candidate.

Mrs. H. explains more of the school mathematics program to me. The math team, she says, began last year, but, in addition, they have had school math contests, and an equations club that meets every week. It's the only math team in the city, by the way, and she refers again to the difficulties she has had with their transportation and the frustration of trying to get a bus for their trips with no authorization, money, or help from the board. While talking about the high reputation of the math department, she proudly states that *all* twenty-two of the students who took the calculus course last year not only passed the advanced placement test, but all but two had the maximum score, an unheard-of accomplishment, when most schools can brag about one or two passing the advanced placement tests. (Passing the test means that the student gets college credit for the course.)

Along with the high math achievement, however, are statistics and problems at the other end of the spectrum. Mrs. H. tells me that the math department has received much criticism as well as praise because of the number of failures in some classes. Although the average of failures in all the math classes is about 12 percent, the average for Algebra 1 (the freshman course) is 21 percent with some classes being nearly as high as 50 percent. The problem, she says, is homework. Much is assigned and expected to be done. If it isn't done, the student fails because the homework is a significant part of the grade.

Teachers have tried inventing many new classes, Mrs. H. says, for kids to get their necessary math credits in high school while learning something and enjoying it. But it hasn't always worked. Problems include the lack of an appropriate text, the need to produce their own materials, and the difficulties in predicting what will get the students involved (last year's emphasis on tax forms, for example, didn't work). This year, the course is titled Survey Math and includes a history of math concepts, the use of calculators, consumer math and problem solving. Because it is a course designed for (and by) this school only, they need a special number from the district for the course to be included on the students' transcripts.

Math classes, she says, are held all over the school, with teachers teaching in different rooms throughout the day. Any extra activities are all done by teachers on their own. The math teams, the equation clubs, the in-school math contests, even the placement exams at the beginning of the year are all done on volunteer time. In addition, the placement tests are designed by the teachers themselves. The teachers buy paper with their own money and are responsible for repairs of their mimeograph machine (which is broken now).

What is so discouraging, Mrs. H. says, is the lack of attention to the professionalism of teachers. There is so little respect or support given by the educational system, the school board, the school or the general public to the teacher as a professional that many times each year she considers dropping out entirely. "There have been some crackerjack teachers, some great, *great* teachers at Garfield and other places," she says, "but many of these teachers are now gone."

I asked Mrs. H. what she would tell someone who wants to know what high schools are like. "They're not all the same," she answers. "Tell others, parents especially, that if they want to know what a high school is like, *go* there, because different high schools are different."

The bell rings and I have four minutes to make my next class: I want to see what the calculus class is like and then to see other math classes in later periods. I am amazed that we had over fifty minutes to talk, that it was so natural. I'm not surprised that I liked talking with Mrs. H. nor that I wished I had more time to get to know her better.

THE CALCULUS CLASS. The first high school class I enter is calculus. I don't expect to be intimidated by the content, but I'm still concerned about my reception around the school. There are seventeen in class including one black male and four white girls. These students are dressed in jeans and old shirts, not nearly as neat as most of the students I have seen in the halls of Garfield. The seating is likewise casual; students sit in rows of movable desks with six students in one row and one in another, changing the direction of the desks as they get in. They go over the homework, each student looking at his or her paper as the problems are solved on the board. One student is still wondering why there is so much attention to the algebraic notations and simplifications of the functions given in their book, and the answer is given in terms of it being essential to the next few steps in understanding the derivatives of functions.

A problem is put on the board, a question for thought overnight, the teacher says. The question is: What does '$x^{2/3} + y^{2/3} = 1$' look like? No one has a ready answer although a few try some half-hearted ones, which are dismissed without a word. Not only do I not know the answer but I don't have any idea of how to find it out, other than doing some plotting on a graph. A test is given. Each "row" of students is given a different set of four problems. Everyone gets down to work right away with some finishing within a few minutes, others taking the full fifteen minutes left in the period. It's a dull-looking room with clean walls, a little writing on the desks, and a few pieces of paper on a bulletin board that suggest this room is mainly used for English classes. There is a relaxed feeling between teacher and students, with some kidding going on between them, but there is also obvious attention to "getting the job done."

The calculus book is a large one. It reminds me that Mrs. H. mentioned that last year the calculus books were being stolen, and she couldn't figure out why. Later she found out. It was because kids want to be seen on the bus carrying a calculus book, not a general math book. After class I asked the teacher why algebra seems to be emphasized in this introduction to calculus rather than geometry. The answer, he says, is that it is not exactly his preference but that the advanced placement exam is oriented to algebraic notations of calculus problems and to problem solving. "Basically," he says, "I teach to the AP test."

A GENERAL MATH CLASS. I enter the general math class just before the bell. There are twenty-one students here, all black. The topic is long division with two-digit divisors (e.g., $25\sqrt{790}$). After the bell rings, the door is closed. A student walks into the room, but the teacher stops him; he doesn't seem to have his ID card or a correct pass for coming in late. The teacher tells him to go get one. He leaves. Later there is a knock at the door and the teacher opens it slightly, takes a look at what the student hands her and says, "This is no good. You heard me before; get an ID or a pass!" Sometime later there is another knock. This time the teacher doesn't open the door but looks through the window pane at the "pass" and tells him to move on.

About fifteen minutes before the period ends, the guy finally has the right pass, comes in with his large backpack, sits down, brings out his book and pencil, looks at the homework assignment on the board, but doesn't copy it. He starts to ask the girl next to him questions about the work.

The content of the instruction is obviously not what one would think of as "high school work." It's a "refresher" course in math (with a big black textbook) for kids identified by poor scores on the placement tests. No student says, "I know this stuff." It seems to be a challenge and everyone does the work—quietly. At the start of class, homework is handed in (about two-thirds of the students have done it; the third that didn't do it is mostly boys). The teacher has the kids name the terms (divisor, dividend, quotient) and reads off the answers to the homework problems. A few examples are shown on the board, then a new set of homework problems is given. The rest of the time is spent by the students doing the homework at their desks with the teacher going from desk to desk, helping where necessary and occasionally making some general statements to all ("Remember, show your work always").

There is no kidding between teacher and student in this class (there is some between students). The teacher is a very serious, no-nonsense person who seems to care that the kids do the work and understand it. As she goes around the class, she talks quietly to those who didn't do their homework. Toward the end of the period she spends some time with the student who had so much trouble getting into class, admonishing him for not doing his homework, making up a schedule for handing it in, and making sure that he understands how. The students in this class are dressed very nicely (with much more care than the calculus people). Many have very fancy briefcases, leather satchels, athletic bags hung over their shoulders and filled with books, pencil cases, papers, etc. There are thirty-five desks in the room, in rows spaced widely enough for a teacher to walk through easily. The teacher's desk is placed in front.

A SURVEY MATH CLASS.  This course is designed by the teachers for those students who would not take algebra but need a math course to graduate. The topic today is different ways to multiply multiple-digit numbers like $386 \times 4187$. The method being learned is taken from early Egyptian times, and a special grid is used. It's a livelier class than either of the previous two, with much more interchange between the teacher and the students and among the students. The students greet me openly, ask who I am and why I'm here. The girl in front of me is by far the most active, talking to me and her friends, combing her hair, lending pencils, borrowing pencils, paying, it seems to me, no attention at all to the examples being done at the board by the class. There is quite a bit being done at the board, and many students (and I) think it is rather interesting to find the patterns and see the early Egyptian process work. Some students ask specific questions to make sure they understand, since they will be doing problems for their homework. At the bell, the girl in front of me puts away her brush and pencils and with great satisfaction blurts out for all to hear, "Hey, I've learned two things today!" I believe her, but how she did it, I have no idea.

LOOKING AT STUDENT TRANSCRIPTS. I'm in the office now, looking at student transcripts. We were told earlier that it would be difficult, because of the lack of clerical help, to get copies of the transcripts, so I thought I would just take a look at them to see if they contain anything interesting. I'm not expecting much; transcripts are a poor indication of high school life. But I find them captivating and surprisingly personal and touching. At first I ask for twenty of them, spread over the four classes, then I ask for twenty more, picked at random.

The first thing I notice is that the honors grades are often very low. Not only are there many C's and D's in honors classes, but there are students who receive these grades over three years' time and still stay in honors. The explanation of this could be praiseworthy—that is, that there are no guarantees for student grades—but I wonder what else is going on? It's interesting to me that a few bits of information— name, address, age, mother's and father's names, place of birth, date entered school, from where, transcripts sent to where—are stories in themselves. The rudiments of these teen-age lives suggest beginnings in faraway places, some family break-ups, long distances to travel to get to this school, and hopes for the future through more schooling. None of this is my business, of course, and it's perhaps because I'm such a transient stranger that sentimental feelings arise. But they do, and that is interesting to me; transcripts didn't mean a thing to me when I was a teacher.

There is another story to be seen in the pattern of grades. R.F., who transferred from a university lab school two years ago, has gotten mostly C's; C.H., who has flunked Italian, gets A's in typing; C.L., who had an F and D's in ninth-grade algebra, took math through trigonometry in her junior year (FDDD, DCDD, CCDC)! She also took sciences during this time and has done OK. J.M. scored very high at the end of eighth grade on math tests and very low in reading: from B's to D's in English, A's in law and accounting, A's in honors algebra, but D's in geometry. F.H. had lots of failures in 1980 and 1981, not many earned credits, and is now listed as a junior at eighteen years old. Will she finish? Why does she stay around? Then there is B.G., who has had all A's in her two years here, including classical piano, or D.J., who started out with A's in Spanish and now is getting D's. You don't see many absences on these transcripts, a day or two per year at the most (K.I. is an exception, with over thirty days absent and three courses flunked in 1981).

These transcripts show eight levels of courses, each identified on the individual student's transcript: S = special education, B = basic, E = essential, R = regular, N = non-level, H = honors, T = honors telescoped, and A = advanced (or college level). I wonder, when I look at such minimal information, just what the trends and tracks mean for the young people whose names are in front of me.

A PTSA COUNCIL MEETING. It's a brisk fall evening. I walk to an iron gate, up the steps, and into the glass-doored foyer of the first-floor apartment in a large stone house three blocks from the school. I am here for the PTSA (Parent Teacher Student Association) council meeting, which meets once a month. I have been told to expect about twenty people and that the main topic will be planning for the November open house. Mrs. K., the principal, had told us quite proudly that the parents were changing the school open house from a social meeting between parents and teachers to meeting for discussion between parents and teachers of individual students' progress in school. "They want the time to be more informative and worthwhile."

As I walk in I am greeted warmly by the hostess and others who have come a little early. Mrs. K. is there and obviously has told them who I am ("You must be the Carnegie man"), and of her invitation to me to attend the meeting. The council meets once a month, the PTSA meets much less than that. As we stand in the living room, waiting for the others to arrive, I am told with pride and directness by one of the parents, "This is the forum where real direct and candid discussions take place about Garfield." I find this to be very true.

Everyone has arrived (we are twenty-three), and we arrange our-selves on the chairs and couches in the living room and porch sitting area, with the president of the council and officers against one wall and the rest of us more or less facing them. The people here represent the community: white, black, Oriental, Spanish. Many seem to know each other well, all are comfortable. The president is an older black man, large in stature. He has been president for some years. There are men and women, one teacher, Mrs. K. (the principal), an assistant principal, and no students. The meeting begins with minutes from the last meeting, reports on finances, budget, memberships paid (333 so far, a good number), and announcements of special events such as the homecoming football game and dance and a community confer-ence. There is some discussion on the budget and its line items. For example, one parent argues for money and a line-item position for special education materials. She wants at least $50 and gets $35.

The discussion then turns to the major topic of the evening: the plans, purpose, and structure of the school open house in November. One of the first discussions is about the fact that the group had wanted a full day and evening for the open house, enough time for all the parents to speak to individual teachers about their children. In a straw vote, nearly 100 of the 110 teachers responded positively to the idea. So did the parents. But the school board would not allow it. Why? The kids would miss a day of school, which would mean the district would miss state money. No one likes this interference with their plans, but they move quickly to alternatives that will make it possible for parents and teachers to talk about individual students. Included in the discussion is the need for a general PTSA meeting, membership sign-up, and sales of items (such as school T-shirts) for special pur-poses. After discussing a variety of possibilities, it is decided that a late afternoon and evening meeting is about the best they can do. They decide the open house should be from about four to nine, with the membership meeting at the end of the evening. Discussions on the mechanics, the timing, and the problems of moving efficiently through so many parent-teacher conferences takes a lot of time, and a committee is eventually named with volunteers to work out the details.

It's getting late and the teacher leaves, but there is more on the minds of those present. The president recognizes the chairman of a parent committee looking into school security problems and he asks for another parent to speak. She has something to tell us all, he says, looking around to all of us, but focusing on Mrs. K., the principal. The parent (white) begins to speak, quietly at first and then with more passion as the momentum of her story unfolds. She has three sons at Garfield, a senior, a sophomore, and a freshman. On the third day of school, her freshman son was held up at gunpoint inside the school. The parent takes pains to tell the story as plainly as possible with a clear focus of where she does and does not place some blame. She recognizes, for example, that thirty-seven outside doors are a problem. She explains that a buddy who was with her son had let in the guy (black) who robbed him. The thief came to the door, asked to be let in, and "being nice boys," they did. She blames herself and her son for his carrying over $100 to show off in school (he had earned the money in a summer job, was just paid, and wanted others to see it). She doesn't, she says, blame the school. Things like this can happen.

She refers to her fourteen-year-old's trauma when he stared into a pistol barrel in his first week of high school, no less. But, as she describes it, the horror story began after that. She first questioned the security policeman, who was stationed full-time in the school (he has since been replaced). He blamed the kids and did nothing (from her viewpoint) to pursue the assailant. She thought the school administration listened, but didn't act in terms of (a) calling for an immediate replacement of the security policeman, (b) getting the police actively on the case, (c) helping them identify who the assailant was, or (d) doing more to make the school secure. But by far her greatest concern is the lackadaisical attitude of the police to the case. As she describes it, it took many, many phone calls from her to various police departments and persons over weeks of time before she was certain they were pursuing the case with some attention.

Up to now, her story was heard with absolute attention by all of us. As she began to mention the police department, however, others began to interrupt, give advice, and offer similar experiences. The lack of police response, the message that there are many other matters much more pressing to the police than armed robbery in school, the bureaucracy of the system, and the ways in which that system is so difficult for the public to deal with, *especially* the passive bureaucracy with rules and procedures and endless lines and loops of authority are everybody's villains in this story. The victim was not blameless, and the school, where the armed robbery took place, was held partly responsible, but the lack of interest, the hesitant response of the city bureaucracy was too much for either the storyteller or her listeners to take without outrage.

The case is still pending; the boy is now going to lineups. All the parents are furious, but it is a helpless outrage they express, a recognition that it is a system that must be dealt with the way it is; changing the system is out of the question. There is a brief discussion of safety and hassling within the school itself, of ID tags, and similar matters. The young assistant principal gets up and with some emotion suggests that perhaps the parents and community are partly at fault, not for the incidents as they occur, but for the kids' laid-back, don't-get-involved attitude toward the incidents. He cites instances of home robberies in broad daylight, where neighbors, not wishing to get involved, don't even call the police. The same thing, he says, is happening in Garfield. The kids don't report incidents. They, like their parents, don't want to get involved or don't want to be labeled a snitch. It's a tough statement to make here since no one in this room has, up to now, had a finger pointed at them. It's also at least a little off the mark, since the incident, as far as I know, was reported.

The talk soon turns to other concerns. One parent makes a very articulate plea for more discussions with the students, more humane talk about adolescence, about what it means to be an adolescent, about the ways in which certain codes made by kids themselves and their peers are followed. The teachers, she says, should spend more time with the students, talking about how to live in a community, about the social aspects of living. "Can't we free up the day a little for talk beyond academics?" she asks. A few others support her concern, but quickly turn to other things like the lack of a swim coach, and the lack of cooperation by the athletic director in finding a swim coach. The principal responds in general terms, but acknowledges the criticisms and concerns while, at the same time, protecting her staff from blame.

The meeting breaks up late in the evening, after eleven. It's cold now, walking back to the hotel. For a PTA meeting, this was a barnburner. Issues were raised with experience, concern, and passion. Where is the parent apathy I've been hearing about? It wasn't in that room of twenty parents.

Early in the meeting, I was asked to speak to the group about our study, which I did, and I answered some questions (i.e., How was Garfield picked? What about the other schools? The entire study?). I mentioned that their views would be important for this study of Garfield. A paper was passed around so those who were interested in being contacted could provide their names and phone numbers. I have over a dozen names on the list, not including the president, who said, "Call me."

## Goals

Where does one look for the goals of a high school? We had to go directly to the students, parents, and teachers of Garfield. Although forming school goals was evidently a very serious activity from the district's perspective, the products were frustratingly general or inappropriate. This was expressed by the administration and teachers of Garfield, as well as by us visitors.

Earlier, in the fall of the school year, all principals in the school district were brought together for a two-day workshop with the specific purpose of establishing school goals. Mrs. K., the principal of Garfield, brought one of her assistant principals with her. They, with all the other principals, produced a list of eight goals. Four of these goals were clearly inappropriate for Garfield. One dealt with student attendance rates; since Garfield has always had over 95 percent attendance (at or near the top in the city), the attendance goal at that level was easily achieved. Another goal referred to teacher attendance, which not only was not a problem at Garfield, but the stated goal of no more than 7.5 percent absences turned out to be less than the number of sick days allotted to teachers in their contract. A third goal concerned student discipline, which has never been a problem at Garfield. A fourth goal called for the design and implementation of a specific master plan for parent and community participation in school affairs. This goal, too, was considered by those at Garfield to have been successfully met by the school since it already had an organized group of parents (the PTSA council) who were active in school affairs. In fact, it was pointed out, the community and parents were largely responsible for the school design.

The one goal that those in Garfield felt fully applied to the school was to prepare students for higher education or to enter the work force. Of course, this goal was too general to be of any help. Thus, although goal-making was an important concern of the school district, the results formalized through the district workshop were neither overdemanding nor effective for Garfield.

When we talked to the parents, teachers, and students, three primary goals were mentioned: (1) preparation, (2) critical thinking, and (3) developing a sense of community. Preparation was the only goal referred to by everyone: teachers, parents, and students. For the parents and students we talked to, preparation meant one thing: to enable each student to compete for positions at colleges and universities that would provide more satisfying life chances. Garfield, from most parent and student viewpoints, was to prepare the student well for more education and training.

Teachers also readily spoke about preparation, but not with the uniformity we heard from the parents or the students we happened to talk to. Although the teachers, like the parents, felt that the goal of preparing students for future schooling was being accomplished quite well in Garfield, they worried about two aspects of this goal. First, some teachers expressed a great deal of skepticism about the educational ambitions of a significant proportion of their students. As one teacher put it, "I feel that middle-class students are motivated to go to college—their parents tell them that's the goal. Even kids with minimum skills have college as a goal. Many students, then, will end up having to work who won't be prepared." The principal also expressed this concern when she mentioned that nearly 85 percent of Garfield students went on to college, but she doubted that that was in the best interest of all of these students.

Another side of the preparation goal was the preparation of students for the world of work. A few parents and students were concerned that Garfield best served the "bright" students who would go on to college. The deepest concerns were expressed by the teachers of the vocational and business-oriented subjects. These teachers saw their goals as preparing their students for careers commencing after high school graduation. They prepared their students by introducing them to different trades and tradespersons, and by providing students with supervised work experience in order to ease their entry into the work force. Their concern was with Garfield students who do not or should not go on to college. From these teachers' perspective, Garfield was moving away from being a comprehensive high school and toward becoming primarily a college preparatory academy. Vocational and business education will be phased out, they predicted, and become part of a different city school whose theme is vocational education. They seriously questioned the commitment of Garfield to the goal of preparing students for work. Although the principal fought for a comprehensive high school, and offered the thirteen special education programs as evidence of her commitment, some parents and the vocational education teachers were worried that "comprehensive" meant special attention to those on either end of the spectrum, but little attention to preparation for work.

We also heard expressions of deep concern that Garfield should adopt a goal of student critical thinking. If the goal of preparation was expressed as outward-focused and on the future, this second goal was expressed as more intrinsic to the student as an individual. Parents especially spoke about the development of rational, disciplined thinking—an ability to critically analyze situations—as a necessary major goal. And they were concerned that this goal was not being met. As one parent put it: "You know a major difference between school before and school now? People now take algebra to learn algebra! Can you believe it?" Included in the meaning of critical thinking was the students' ability to critically appreciate learning and personal experience.

Some teachers expressed similar concerns, but not with the same conviction evident in their concerns for preparing students for future schooling. One teacher, for example, presented the idea of the intrinsic joys of learning to his class, and the students treated the idea as something foreign and rhetorical. Talking with another teacher about how much we had forgotten of the content of classes we had had in high school (and college), she said, "That's to be expected.

What we are really aiming for here at Garfield is critical thinking and the appreciation of learning." When we asked her if she thought the schooling at Garfield, with its forty-minute classes five days a week would support such a goal, she hesitated and said, "Actually, it doesn't, does it?"

We saw an interesting example of how the teachers tried to reach their twin primary goals of college preparation and critical thinking. The International Baccalaureate Program is housed in Switzerland and administers a battery of tests to students from a variety of countries. Those who pass these tests are automatically accepted by European universities. A number of high schools in the United States have participated in this program over the past five years, and Garfield (along with another city school and a number of other high schools in the area) was considering seriously the possibility of joining the program. Although Garfield already had a strong advanced placement program of its own, what attracted its teachers to the International Baccalaureate Program, we were told, was the possibility of being treated differently by the school district.

Four teachers representing the math, English, science, and social studies departments attended a long introductory two-day session outside of the city at their own expense (except for registration fees) to learn more about this program. The teachers left Garfield just before their final class period at 2:15 in the afternoon in order to make the 4:00 P.M. starting time for the workshop. The workshop went until eleven that evening. The next morning the sessions began at 7:30 A.M. and ended at 6:00 P.M. The four teachers were not only at Garfield teaching the next day, but they were revising a written analysis of the strengths and weaknesses of the International Baccalaureate Program for a presentation to the principal. They presented their findings and recommendations to the principal the following afternoon after school.

The teachers' presentation included one of the finest pieces of critical work completed in an extremely tight schedule that we have ever seen by anybody. They pointed out, for example, the overprivileged nature of the program (bad) as well as the requirement for a philosophy of thought course (good). They pointed out the dependence on testing (bad) as well as the emphasis on the disciplines of inquiry (sometimes good), and the overall focus on a well-rounded education (good).

There were two things that impressed the teachers most. The first was the high quality of public school people (about 400) who were at that meeting. "It made you proud," said the chairwoman, "to see so many intelligent people who were teaching in public high schools." The second was the potential for the district to remove programmatic and professional restrictions on Garfield. It appeared to the teachers, for example, that administrative support of this program could mean that the teachers who were involved in the International Baccalaureate Program could: (a) substitute one more period per day for planning, (b) make a different kind of school day, where both teachers and students of the program would have the afternoon for planning and work required by the program, or (c) substitute work on this program for extraneous duties, such as hall or cafeteria monitoring. Further, the hiring and retention of special teachers could be expected at Garfield if they were to adopt this program, whereas it wasn't possible at all without it. In other words, what was expressed, time and time again, by these four teachers in their discussions of this demanding program was that it might give them some leverage to meet the basic goals they already had in terms of college preparation and in terms of critical analysis.

A third goal, expressed primarily by parents but also by some of the teachers and administrators at Garfield, was to prepare students as citizens of a democracy. One parent at the October PTSA council meeting, for example, urged eloquently and passionately that Garfield seriously pursue a goal that she felt was particularly relevant to developing adolescence: the goal of fostering a sense of community and social responsibility. It was a goal, she felt, that was in some conflict with the idiosyncratic, independent, and autonomous directions of adolescent growth, as well as the school's focus on academic excellence. Thus, it was a goal that had to be made explicit. It could not be achieved through the subtle ways that school administrators said were being pursued. Likewise, she argued, the school was the appropriate place for such a goal to be pursued because the school was a social community far more than was, say, the family. A counselor at Garfield expressed a similar concern. "Schools must help these kids find direction in life," he said. "We have an obligation to make students politically and socially aware, to show them how politics and society relate to them and their community." Some teachers mentioned helping students "to know their responsibility in society," "to have goals and values," "to function in society," "to acquire life skills, such as becoming informed consumers." Many teachers spoke to the need for students to function in the society as well-rounded or total persons. A physical education teacher, reacting to what she felt was a lack of appreciation for her department, said, "I say that our goal is to send out more knowledgeable students than came in—including physically." An assistant principal referred with similar commitment to instilling more care for school as a community, more sense of responsibility by the students and the faculty for making a community and an institutional setting of which they could be proud. He talked, for example, about a race relations program that had been given in his former school, which he thought would be particularly appropriate and effective for Garfield. The social and community problems of the school, he indicated, were purposefully hidden by those who felt Garfield should rise and fall on its academic reputation alone.

In summary, Garfield is not burdened with too many goals. It is burdened with innocuous, formally stated goals constructed under the auspices of the district's central office. In discussions with parents, teachers, students, and administrators three major goals stand out: postsecondary preparation, critical thinking, and the development of a sense of social community. Under consideration is the issue raised by some parents and teachers about the school's relevant preparation for all students—of preparation for work as well as for more schooling. Combining college preparation and critical thinking is difficult at Garfield, primarily because of the consequences of current central administration or state policies. Likewise, the pursuit of a social community, of developing a sense of social responsibility within Garfield, is also found to be very difficult because of certain policies. Examples of such policies are the regulations of class periods (for example, forty minutes every day every week), state funding by daily attendance rates, and the nature of college advanced placement tests. Programs that hold promise for reducing the hold of these policies on Garfield will be considered very seriously, even if they come from Switzerland. That a school of Garfield's reputation and performance cannot pursue even three fundamental goals because of the restrictions of current education policy is absurd but true. Most agree that the reason this is true is because of the overriding emphasis on college and university preparation. Ironically, this attention not only reduces the possibility for work preparation, it also reduces the possibility for supporting critical thinking and developing a social conscience as well.

## Curriculum

As in most high schools, curriculum at Garfield is a complicated topic. Even if we begin with the simplest definition of curriculum—the courses taken by the students—it is not all that easy to define. The graduation requirements are: four years of English, three years of social studies, three years of math and science (two of one and one of the other), one year of art, one year of music, and four years of physical education. There is also a ten-week consumer education requirement (satisfied in a number of departments by courses such as business, mathematics, and social studies), and requirements of two-year sequences in the "electives." Graduation requirements, of course, are only the tip of the curriculum iceberg. Complexity increases as we try to understand what these requirements mean in terms of courses offered, or what they mean in terms of the programs of individual students. In this section, we will describe the curriculum by referring to four strategies used by the teachers and administrators of Garfield to accommodate the complexity of a comprehensive high school for two thousand students. These four strategies include tracking, scheduling, departmental autonomy, and the redesign of departmental course offerings. Admittedly, this is only one way to consider the curriculum at Garfield. It emphasizes the adults' views of the curriculum, and, more specifically, focuses on problems that are associated with the curriculum offerings at Garfield High School.

Although we were initially told that there was no tracking at Garfield, it became apparent that there was at least a great deal of differentiation in the nature and difficulty of courses. There are three classifications of courses that are below the average level: special education, basic, and essential courses (in that order). There are two classifications at the average level: regular and nonlevel. There are three classifications above the average level: honors, honors telescoped, and advanced (or college level). The course classification scheme is most prevalent in mathematics, but is also present in science and in English. It is minimally used in social studies and not at all in other subjects like gym, art, music, or vocational courses. (The business program achieves somewhat the same result by screening students and accepting only those with an average overall grade-point score and three teacher recommendations.) Just how rigid these eight classifications are for individual students we were never able to determine. Figures on this, we were told, were few, just as there were few figures on most questions asking for numbers. One teacher had no doubts about tracking at Garfield and its effect on students. "There are successful and unsuccessful students in this school . . . there is status and dignity attached to any tracking program."

Thus, it was very clear that in some subjects, such as mathematics, there were tremendous differences in the content, teaching style, and student enrollment in the various classifications. As we described earlier in our notes, we literally went from calculus to arithmetic in two periods, the latter having all black students, the former having all white students except for one black. Moving from one level course to another seemed unlikely. For example, although we were told that the reading lab was designed to help students advance after ten weeks, a teacher working in that lab told us that, in practice, it seldom happens because of the difficulty in effecting program changes at Garfield.

This brings up scheduling, which, at Garfield, is an extremely thorny issue for teachers, student counselors, administrators, as well as for students and parents. Scheduling individual student programs at Garfield is a nightmare. The teachers who are responsible for the students' programming, the "activity" (or homeroom) teachers, are very disappointed in the inefficiency of the process. Complaints include the difficulties they have in programming individual students, the time involved in the process, the length of time before the schedules are confirmed, and the inaccuracies in the confirmed schedules. The office personnel (including the assistant principal responsible for programming) are no happier with the programming system. Everything has to be done by hand; the teachers make mistakes in programming some students; and the crunch times in programming are hell in terms of repetitive, boring, and time-consuming clerical work, with no clerical support. It is simply a horrible system for programming and scheduling students' classes, with no computer support at all.

It is not too surprising that the most significant conflicts between the administration and the teaching faculty involve student programming. Although the teachers often blamed the problems on the personality of the vice principal in charge of programming, just as much blame could be placed on the inefficient and backward nature of the process and the corresponding lack of computer support. Everyone agreed, however, that this was one problem that needed to be, and could be, resolved with more attention and support. The support everyone referred to was computer support, something that the district central office had, but that Garfield had to do without.

The third strategy for organizing the complexity of the curriculum is to develop autonomous and independent departments, collections of teachers who can design and revise certain curricular features of their own subject-oriented programs. This was done so effectively at Garfield that it was seen by the teachers as a real curricular problem as well as a curricular solution. The problem was fragmentation, the lack of interaction between the departments, the lack of an integrated curriculum. Part of this fragmentation is physical because each subject area has its own departmental office. The presence of these departmental offices and the scheduling of common preparation periods for teachers every day considerably help the individual departments make cohesive and consistent policies of their own. It certainly does not, however, support interdepartmental communication. This departmental autonomy instills some departmental competition (for example, about SAT scores), jealousy (about the tracking system used in the math department, for example), and animosity (about the singular responsibility felt by the English department, for example, for the writing and library research skills of all the students).

The strong departmental system of Garfield also seems to produce idiosyncratic characteristics in each department. Mathematics, for example, considers itself to be professional and tough, constantly reviewing and revising courses and content in response to student needs. Teachers in the language department, which has suffered some loss of good teachers, emphasize their attempt to maintain standards and avoid departmental fragmentation: "We do things uniformly so that it doesn't matter which teacher you get." In contrast, the social studies and science departments are not as cohesive. In social studies the teachers are skeptical and independent. The science department, where each teacher has his or her own office rather than a department office, has had recent difficulties protecting some of the department's better teachers from being bumped from the school by those with more seniority. English has devised three years of a common curriculum as well as a variety of individually created minicourses in much of the senior year. The relatively small departments of art and music are left to themselves, and operate mainly through personal entrepreneurship for materials, support, and recognition.

Although the vocational teachers felt left out of the school's mainstream, within their departments they were strong in the belief that they formed their own curriculum. "We have a lot to say about the design of programs," one shop teacher told us, "even though we structure the programs within the Board of Education guidelines." Teachers in the physical education department strongly affirmed that they made many curriculum decisions. "It's easy to design curriculum in this school. The concept of bringing new ideas is accepted, where our discussions are two-fold: student benefit and teacher interest." The home economics teachers also said that they had the freedom to make curriculum decisions, and illustrated this by informing us that they will add a second food service course next year in response to recent job opportunities available in that field.

This brings us to the fourth strategy for handling a complex curriculum: designing and revising within the departmental framework. The mathematics department is an interesting example of how this strategy works because it has received the most parent criticism and has also tried to respond and revise its own curriculum repeatedly. A large percentage of students at Garfield flunk their mathematics courses (over 30 percent in some classrooms), but students at the school also have the best record for general college placement tests (for example, SAT scores) and advanced placement of graduates in college. In addition, the department has a large and powerful math team, and a variety of popular mathematics clubs. As a department, then, it is more complicated than the fact of having black students in arithmetic and white students in calculus suggests.

The teachers acknowledge the failures in their classes, but maintain that the failures and successes in the mathematics program are attributable to the same demand: tough requirements for daily performance. Parents, however, attribute the failures of their children to something else: inappropriate teaching methods and curricular focus on the content and not on the child. There are several accounts of ongoing discussions with the math department on this issue. One parent, after concluding that there is no place for the average student at Garfield, said:

> One problem I saw was in my daughter's algebra class last year. Fifty-four percent of the students were failing and the teacher refused to assume any responsibility, so the PTSA formed a special committee to discuss the problem with the math department.

Another parent who is concerned about the honors and accelerated courses and the low grades produced there, said:

> Last year, the parent committee met with the math department chairperson because of complaints from parents about the high number of failures. The question we put to them was, "Are you teaching a course or students?" Their answer, I think, was that they were teaching courses. They said that the courses were designed for the gifted and they had a lot to cover. . . . So, I told my son to stay out of honors, take the regular courses.

This same parent, however, gives high praise to the same department because, "My daughter stayed in honors and got a D, but at Southern University she was fourth in math in a class of five hundred students. It looks like Garfield was a good experience." An unconvinced parent gave us her opinion and her solution:

> I'm not happy with honors math. Some dodos think kids are in a doctoral program. I took my kid out of honors because I saw the program as almost punitive. They were penalized for being bright. In regular classes, he gets A's and B's instead of C's.

The mathematics teachers conscientiously respond to the problems and failures of instruction by redesigning the lower level courses. There have been a number of changes in the content, structure, and timing of these courses—courses that are essential for satisfying state graduation requirements. One course, for example, is divided into four sections: the history of mathematics, the use of calculators, consumer math, and problem solving. The sections of this course have been changed and revised, dropped and added over the years in a kind of trial and error, planning and evaluation process. They have worked at finding appropriate texts for these sections or in designing their own texts. It is a course that needs its own special number just to be recorded in the school district's ledger.

This personal attention and professional investment in the curriculum is also shown by the entrance exams in mathematics given before the school year starts. These exams are designed, given, graded, and analyzed by the mathematics teachers entirely on their own time before school begins. The tests are used to determine which students should appropriately be placed in which mathematics programs. This includes identifying students who may need remedial courses (identified by Garfield as "basic" or "essential" classes) covering arithmetic skills that should have been learned well before high school. Some parents are not impressed. One parent acknowledged that the test ensured that the students were tracked properly, but she emphasized that the parents want to work something out so that the tracking is not harmful to some students.

> Some parents have asked teachers to explain why they are not reviewing math with the ordinary freshmen students. Our concern is with the ordinary child at Garfield. The school never had a middle; it always had bright kids, and it doesn't do well with the others.

Many teachers expressed similar concerns, but they had little opportunity to go beyond their focus on curriculum to investigate and analyze their teaching. There just does not seem to be much chance that the parents' questions about teaching strategies can be effectively addressed by the teachers at Garfield. Given the lack of resources for curriculum analysis by the teachers, we are impressed by the ways in which they have tried to acknowledge and respond to their problems.

## Teaching and Learning

The instruction in Garfield classrooms reminds one of a time long past. Desks are lined up in front of the blackboard. The teaching-learning periods are still forty minutes long. Report cards are now "course books," and homerooms are "divisions"—but each still serves its usual purpose. Students are tracked in academic subjects and grouped homogeneously (to the extent this is possible); *how* a subject is taught as well as *what* is taught often depends on the "track." Course content is divided into discrete units to be covered in certain blocks of time, and students' successes are measured by their performance on pop quizzes, tests, midterm exams, term papers, and final examinations. As we have said before, Garfield is a good school, with many concerned teachers, ambitious and attentive students, involved parents, high attendance rates, high SAT scores, and a large percentage of college placements. When a visitor stands back and tries to analyze the teaching practices at Garfield and the nature of the learning approaches brought to the classrooms, however, there is little that is memorable.

Classrooms at Garfield are not dull places; they are always filled, after all, with twenty-five to thirty teen-agers. These students enliven any forty-minute period—even when they are attentive to what is going on and hand in their homework. There are enough possibilities for interaction between teacher and students and among students to make the period interesting and allow teachers and students to enjoy themselves at their work. For an example, a student comes a little late to a physics class, with her tennis racket in hand. She is besieged by questions and playful bantering about the performance of her team as she moves to her workbench. Another example: it was the morning after the Sadat assassination and a student asked his social studies teacher what she thought of the event. The teacher shot back: "Don't attend parades."

Regardless of the banter, teaching at Garfield is a practical means to learning, and learning at Garfield is a practical means for gaining entrance to more learning, which is intended to lead to a professional position. When we asked students what was expected of them, we found that some sense a difference between preparing to compete successfully for college and an intellectually stimulating education. Some think intellectual stimulation should happen in the classes they are taking now. Others hope to find it in college. For example, the Afro-American History class was instructed to read an especially provocative article on why slavery was essential to the economy of England and then immediately to take an open-book test on the article. A student in the class told us, in utter frustration, "This book is okay but it's not self-explanatory, you know. We just read. Sometimes I'm not sure I understand it all." The topic of slavery, by the way, was never discussed in terms of its meaning to the students (all black) in the class.

Some students describe what makes a good teacher and an enjoyable class by expressing their desire for intellectual stimulation:

> Some people want you to learn their point of view. They should encourage you to think.

> I like U.S. History best because there's more to think about, more discussions, not just out of the book.

> English is best because the teacher covers the subject in depth. Lots of discussion. I dislike classes where the subject is just covered and then tested.

Of course, with over one hundred teachers at Garfield, our observations revealed a variety of teaching practices, ranging from very exciting to awfully dull. We attended one memorable English class, which included a pithy discussion and penetrating analysis of the poetry of e. e. cummings and W. H. Auden and a captivating ten-minute exposition of Freudian ego and id theories. There was also a fascinating music appreciation class where students in small groups played instruments, tried out a composition, engaged in animated discussions on a musical theme—all at the same time and all, somehow, under the strict supervision of the music teacher. The integration of discussion with the musical activities spoke volumes to an observer about the meaning of music education.

But there were other classes where the teaching was extremely mundane. In one such class, division by two- and three-digit divisors was being taught. In another, students were learning how to subtract fractions. Perhaps that is unfair. How do you teach such skills to students who have somehow missed getting them over previous years, when it was expected of everyone? Did they never get taught, or did they never learn? Regardless of the answer, the teaching at Garfield was no different than the teaching one would have expected these students to have received some years before, when it didn't take hold.

There are a few places in Garfield where the teaching just looks awful. One example is the "reading lab," where each student who tests below a certain reading level sits in a study carrel, answers work-sheet problems, and goes to the teacher to get the answers checked. There is no further analysis of specific reading problems; no questioning of the results of the one failed test by alternative performance; no attention to the process, expectations, and consequences of reading other than as a set of low-level drill and practice skills necessary to get on to more serious matters.

In the main, however, we saw places where teaching and learning hummed along efficiently. The calculus class moved smoothly with discussions on the homework problems, a quick pop quiz, some pointed teacher questions about the next day's work, and some organization of future problem-solving strategies, all within a forty-minute period. As the calculus teacher confidently says, his subject matter blends well with the required forty-minute daily meetings with students. Likewise, the chemistry and physics classes, though more restricted by time than mathematics because of laboratory exercises, appeared to move along after only a month or two of school. In chemistry, the students knew what was expected of them, and, with little extra time for teacher introduction or housekeeping chores, got right to work on the demonstrations at hand.

We were a bit shocked to hear that the lower-level general science course is taught with little laboratory demonstration, but we were impressed by the nature and level of discourse on, for example, the structure of the atom. In the lower-level English class, the discussions and analyses of good short stories seemed especially well structured by the teacher and the students in spite of the tracked "level" of the class. A major semester-long course on writing a research paper, on the other hand, seemed unusually ragged in the range of engagement and performance when students were given a rather open-ended but serious challenge.

In our twenty days at Garfield, by far the greatest intellectual intensity was seen in a seventh-grade mathematics class. This was a large class of over forty students who were not "leveled." The teacher approached mathematics as a fundamental dialectical activity, an activity requiring verbal interaction. He demanded creativity and individual intuition as students wrestled with algebraic notation and meaning. The seventh-grade students were excitedly engaged in their own personally constructed strategies and arguments, with the teacher doing all he could to keep up with the various approaches and making sure the arguments and explanations were between the students, as well as between himself and the students. We couldn't help but leave that classroom wondering about the challenge these students would give to the high school program they will confront in a year or two.

That seventh-grade mathematics class helped us understand the remark of a teacher who had taught a common lesson in anthropology to seventh graders and to eleventh graders in the same week. She couldn't believe the difference in the level of discussion. In all cases, she reported—questions, analyses, applications to other situations (including their own), and arguments over differing interpretations—the seventh graders were far more engaged intellectually than the eleventh graders. And intelligence, she was quick to point out, had nothing to do with it as far as she (or anyone else) could tell. Both the seventh- and eleventh-grade classes had been identified as "high performance" classes. There is enough there to ponder, but no one in Garfield has the time to ponder, which brings up a major point about teaching and learning at Garfield.

There simply is no time or professional circumstance available for discussion of real questions about teaching at Garfield. Some teachers can take time to analyze and review curriculum (such as math or English course offerings), or invent new social studies courses like women's studies. Content can be pursued by staff members on their own or in some in-service programs on special curriculum topics. Teaching and learning, however, the twin spirals in the educational tower, are just too difficult to tame or to understand, to analyze and to discuss, given the other "professional" demands on the teachers. The casual pseudoscience of educational research certainly won't help the thoughtful teachers at Garfield address their own acknowledged shortcomings, failures, disappointments, and unanswered questions about the teaching of subject matter, skills, and appreciation they want the students to experience. The requirements of their own teaching mitigate against their chances to understand and reconstruct their own art and science of teaching.

All teachers at Garfield know this. Some ask for more assistance from the local university, but most realize that few professors there wish to be engaged in the quicksand of discourse on classroom practice. The point is that almost no one cares about teaching and learning, no matter where one encounters the educator.

That the problem at Garfield may be one of circumstance and

opportunity (rather than intention) can be argued by noting the similarities of teaching styles within the departments. Science is organized and knowledgeable, more concerned with the algebraic and symbolic triumphs of modern science than with its more pedantic experimental or skeptical nature. Social studies are taught as a serious source of platitudes with the teacher as expert, of generalizations as unchallenged idiosyncratic truisms about human nature, yet with dialogue, discussion, and student questioning as expected ingredients in learning. Human predictability is the unwritten law that determines how one explains human behavior, and cynicism is the appropriate response to most human actions. Anything that serves both is to be doubly appreciated. The English department treasures the artist's sensitivity for a story well told, but it has the touch of a plumber in introducing the writer's craft to students. The English teachers also, justifiably, feel put upon because they must develop the one tough skill (writing) that all other disciplines continue to rely on. The mathematics department is riding high in its advanced courses, but quickly acknowledges the difficulties of ensuring that all its graduates have the basic skills. And the average student somehow gets lost between the stars and the mire.

Of course, we're not being entirely serious in these descriptions of whole departments, but there is enough commonality within departments to suggest that having departmental offices in Garfield has some effect on *how* (as well as *what*) the students are taught.

Finally, there is the major question of who gets the best teaching at Garfield. The answer is predictable—the most favored students get the best teachers—but no one feels good about it. A vice principal wonders what would happen if all the best teachers took the slower classes for a year. A chairperson speaks about a minor paradox: advanced students' work requires much more time for a teacher to grade, but the less advanced students need more personal attention. The paradox arises when one considers who should have smaller size classes: the advanced or the less advanced students? By the later grades, the question of who is *really* expected to learn is answered within rigid and narrow boundaries—even to the extent that advanced physics students are allowed some opportunity for laboratory work that the average students aren't.

There is some personal attention for some special kids. Those who are having difficulties (and have been so identified) meet for an hour a day in an almost one-to-one manner with a surrogate teacher. But even this conscientious response to instructional responsibility highlights our basic theme. At Garfield, not much attention is paid to what may be the heart of the matter: the teaching act itself. Remedial work is approached with the student as the problem, not with the teaching strategy as the problem. In math, where 30 percent may flunk a course, teachers blame the students for not doing their homework, while students and parents argue that they have tried to do the homework but have not been successful. There is enough talent, intelligence, and concern among those who work within the walls of Garfield to address some of its interesting and perplexing pedagogical problems, but teachers don't have the time, nor, by definition of their jobs, the responsibility. As we have pointed out in other sections, those who may have the power to alter these job specifications—the system administrators and the union (with the local university by default)—have reduced the importance of teaching to the point that it is not even a consideration as to whether one keeps his or her job.

## Media and Technology

Oh, the wonder of it all! As visitors to Garfield, we could entertain fancy thoughts about the possible contributions of modern technology. Just think what computers and the microprocessing chips could bring to the students and teachers of Garfield. Instead of typists working on broken keyboards, there would be word-processer operators preparing for the new marketplace. Instead of draftsmen, there would be young computer scientists perfecting computerized draftsmanship. Instead of dull, tedious lessons in reading labs and basic math classes, there would be self-correcting and interactive computer programs that would better engage the students and free the teacher to work with individuals, bringing meaning to what is being learned.

Such fanciful imagining of the possible contributions of technology is misleading. As the principal says, "The first thing you must remember is that we work in a business that is bankrupt." Nearly all the clocks in Garfield tell a different time. We use these clocks as a symbol of Garfield, where time is hardly ever *now*.

There are nearly no materials in the art classes. Clay is out of the question; colored pencils and crayons are passed around instead of paints; paper is used on both sides if it can be found. Buses are not available for the mathematics team, and difficult to find for many school activities. Broken windows are not repaired for months because there are so few central office maintenance persons available who can replace them. The library is a pleasant place to be, but because of its limited supply of books, it can't be used as a resource for the students; they go to the public library instead. Student programming is done by hand for two thousand students, a task that demands huge amounts of a small professional staff's time and generates considerable animosity between teachers and administrators because of the inevitable inefficiencies. In these circumstances, considering modern media and technology for Garfield may be interesting, but its financial problems place it in a much different world, where basic supplies of a generation ago would be appreciated.

There is some technology in certain places. Thanks to one teacher's ingenuity and determination, there is a photography class with rooms and equipment for developing color and black-and-white film. There is a computer class with the only computer facilities and terminals in the school. The instruction of the teacher and the engagement of the kids are impressive, but even here there is little paper for computer printouts so they must print on both sides of the paper. Furthermore, with a limited number of terminals, half the class must share a few terminals while the other half works on programming, and the teacher must literally run from one to the other when his help is needed. The equipment for the sciences seems fairly adequate. The chemistry lab and equipment are not up to date, but at least there are chemicals and a workbench for all the students. Students put out a good newspaper with quality photographs and printing as well as pointed editorials, and few sensitive spots at Garfield are left untouched. The printing, however, is done outside the school.

The impact of television on students' lives is minimal: they're too busy with homework, their social lives, and work. Besides, it's too boring. Their greatest contact with modern media and technology is the "boom-boxes," the fancy radios and tape decks that one sees on the streets.

All in all, however, to talk about high technology in Garfield when windows can't be replaced, buses aren't available for the math team, materials aren't available for art classes, seems to be a bit academic. It would, of course, be very much appreciated if Garfield was better prepared for the technological future. But it would take some outside intervention to make that possible.

## Summary: The Community and Education Beyond Garfield

Those involved with Garfield realize that the world outside is not a particularly good place to be. They understand that there are private interests to be fought, large bureaucracies to be encountered, foolish exercises of authority to be circumvented, and concentrations of political power to be distributed. In a sense, that is the good part, compared with the violence in the streets and homes, or the racism experienced nearly every day by students at Garfield and their families. Along with these not very sentimental views of the world outside is the overriding acknowledgment that, at this time, it beats existing alternatives. You don't have to like it to prepare to enter it, and that is where Garfield comes in. If Garfield works well, it will prepare its students to achieve and perform in this world, to compete and eventually find professional jobs where their work will be appreciated and worthwhile. Perhaps we should remind those who sit in easier places that these are high goals, goals that the parents and students realize will require hard work and drudgery.

Garfield faces problems as it prepares students for the economic realities of American life. We have already described two in other sections. The first is the anonymity of Garfield in the school system. Although it has attendance and performance numbers that place it first in the city, there are other high schools in the system that get much more attention and fame. We have said it before: if there were one feeling that could be said to unite all the parents, students, teachers and administrators, it would be their dislike and distrust of the central office. We are suggesting here that the systematic denial of Garfield's performance is tied closely to its being a middle-class black high school. The city's best-known school is nominally integrated but still exists primarily for whites and technically gifted others. A sister school to Garfield exists on the opposite side of town, but that school is populated by both the more affluent and the poorer; a showcase of bootstrap strategies. Garfield is just what it appears to be: a school that is servicing its growing middle-class black population quite well. It demonstrates the self-sufficiency of that population, which is attractive to neither the conservatives nor the liberals in the city.

The second problem that has been mentioned before is that Garfield is a harbor of safety in a sea of great danger. Violence is not a characteristic of the school. When violence happens it is almost always a result of the outside world walking through Garfield's doors. Garfield is a safe place to be, the outside world is not.

This brings us to the third problem Garfield faces in relating to the outside world; the attitudes of adults toward the students at Garfield. Within our first half-hour at the school, we were taken aside by a concerned teacher and told that "the students have it too good here." We heard that same message, repeatedly, from teachers, the maintenance people and occasionally parents. At all times, the views expressed were that Garfield was somehow either better than the students, or a much too protective environment for them. Comparisons were made with the "real world" out there: the unfair, racist, competitive world of private interests and powerful authorities that would grind away gentility and disregard performance. Though the emphasis differed, these views were held by adults of both races.

The concern, as expressed by whites, was about the outside world and what it would do to students once they "really" entered it. From their perspective, a certain toughness and guile were necessary if a black were to compete successfully and survive in the world of professionals. They didn't think that gentle and hard-working Garfield provided that inner strength (and, for some reason, they didn't think it was provided elsewhere). They didn't see this as a racist attitude; in fact, just the opposite, they considered this an acknowledgment of others' racist attitudes and an expression of their concern for their students' welfare. The view that somehow any black professional had to be stronger or more mean and tricky than her or his white counterpart showed the misunderstanding of much black experience just as much as it showed genuine concern.

Black adults, on the other hand, could say, "These kids just don't know how good they've got it: they have a rude awakening in front of them," and mean something quite different. As conversations continued in this vein, the reference was to their own experience in that outside world. Often, black adults did not have a school like Garfield to look back on, and they regretted that the students did not understand that fact. They were expressing a concern that their own experience in becoming a black professional and a successful black parent was going to be lost to the next generation. The pride in what they had accomplished wasn't going to be heard or understood by anyone other than their own peers.

We can sympathize with both adult points of view, white and black, while, at the same time, we regret the racial message being given to the students. If you are a black seventeen-year-old experiencing a good high school and looking forward to a real opportunity to enter a professional future, then the message says: "You are both lucky and foolish." It is a message that comes from the adults' understanding and experience with the world outside of Garfield.

Although Garfield is not strictly a neighborhood school, it has a definite "community" of parents spread around the city. They were doing what they could to make sure that the school "worked" for their children. There were Parent Teacher Student Association advisory council meetings once a month. These meetings were attended by about twenty parents, the principal, and some teachers and were occasions for wide-ranging and candid discussions on serious topics such as school security, grading, parent-teacher conferences, and the support of extracurricular activities. After attending a session, we were impressed not only with the depth of discussion but with the attempts made to resolve problems during the meeting itself. We were also impressed with the obvious build-up of trust and mutual concern. These are people, black and white, from a wide range of economic situations, some with a great deal of formal education, others with little, who now know each other pretty well and are all pulling for the same thing: making sure that Garfield is the best it can be for their children.

An example of their concern for communication between teachers and parents was the restructuring planned for the traditional Go-to-School night. Considerable time and effort went into designing a day when teachers and parents could talk in some detail about each student, but, at each step of the way, the central office of the educational system insisted on a revision of the plans. Eventually, from the parents' point of view, the effort became a shambles because of a district-wide rule made just two weeks before the parent-teacher meetings were to occur.

Talks with parents were conducted over the telephone. Always interesting conversations, they often lasted more than an hour. As we have indicated in a previous section, one theme of these talks was the need for a no-nonsense school staffed by concerned teachers who cared personally for the students. By and large, the parents felt they had such a school and wanted to express their appreciation. Another theme was that too many academic demands were being made on the students without attention to equally important instruction in living in a democratic community and ensuring that students received a rich variety of teen-age experience. Parents' concerns were that content was being overemphasized by the teachers at the expense of enriched teaching practices or the pursuit of other values. Race, as could be expected, was not ignored. White parents, particularly, talked about the nature of their children's experiences as the minority race, and cited reasons, for example, for insisting their children remain in "honors" courses although, obviously, they were having trouble making the grade. At the same time, they were supportive of the school and of the extra challenges they felt their children had to encounter as a minority. Black parents, on the other hand, seldom referred to race, other than to acknowledge that Garfield was the one school they felt they could send their children to and feel comfortable about the classroom instruction they were getting.

In many ways, the students prized the extended community of Garfield. With more than a little pride, they referred to having friends from around the city now—friends from their own neighborhoods and friends from Garfield. In a city known for its enclaves, this was a significant personal claim their parents, for example, probably couldn't make. They pointed with satisfaction to the integration of their sphere of friends and acquaintances. This, too, in a city of tremendous black-white distinctions and little social integration, was considered a personal triumph of sorts, regardless of the percentage of integration, and regardless of the race of the student.

The administration of Garfield, in the persons of its principal and a young assistant principal, was also trying to build up cooperation between the community and the school. Despite reasonable pressures to do just the opposite, the principal insisted upon Garfield being a "comprehensive" school, a school that served a range of students—including those who had been identified as learning disabled or behavioral problems. Included in thirteen extra programs for special students, was a home outside the school where dropouts, and particularly disaffected students, could live, get help, and receive an education far from the walls of Garfield but still under its protection (for funding) and with its diploma. The principal was extremely proud of this home, of the thirteen separate programs, and of her commitment since the beginning to make the school a place for those who are often forgotten by the system as well as for those who are prized by the system.

The teachers generally were not as involved with the community. Many lived in the community; many responded with alacrity to parents with questions and concerns about their children; but few really went to the community or invited the community to participate in the educational programming of the school. Some teachers posted lectures on related topics at the local university and encouraged their students to participate. However, some teachers considered the public to be the enemy of their professional status. One teacher, for example, stated that, in his mind, the school administration had become the enemy of teachers because it was now supporting the parents.

The cause of this we/they syndrome between teachers and the general public is *not* Garfield itself but rather the local media. Nearly every day or evening of our visits to Garfield there was at least one major story about the schools in the newspapers or on television. All of these stories were basically negative. For example, there were articles about the high schools in the city not being accredited because of a lack of contact time per day for students. Drug busts were reported, and up-and-coming journalists who visited the high schools wrote about how changed they are now (ten years later) and how different the students are. These views are nearly always irrelevant, wrong, or terribly misleading in regard to Garfield, and the faculty of Garfield feel wrongly accused. Perhaps the major lesson to be taught by Garfield is that the image of the school given by the local media is wrong.

An interesting sidelight to the public image of community and school cooperation is a current widely publicized district-wide program in which large local businesses are linked to individual schools to pursue a particular theme. One business, for example, has pledged $20,000 to one school for aid in instructional typing, another is sponsoring a school to encourage it in computer programming. In Garfield, a school where one would think local businesses would jump to make a contribution, there is no action at all. When asked why not, the principal reported that the arrangements were not being made between the schools and local businesses. Instead, local businesses were expected to report an interest to the central school district office, and the district office, in turn, would identify the recipient school. So much for significant involvement of businesses in Garfield. The small businesses surrounding Garfield, on the other hand, do what they can by buying candy for the school's funding drives or by placing ads in the school publications.

As disappointing as the lack of significant involvement by local industry in Garfield is, the attitude of the university nearby is more disheartening to educators. Some of the most quoted and respected research on teachers, on teaching, and on learning emanates from the pens of its famous professors, but there is no dialogue between them and the educators at Garfield. As we have said before, some teachers from Garfield take classes there, a few fondly remember the work for degrees gained there many years ago; a handful of especially gifted students take classes there; one university-based research project took place in this school; and a student teacher or two per year is sent to the school by the university. For this, the faculty and administration of Garfield are immensely grateful, speaking with due respect and gratitude for these professional crumbs. To us, as outside visitors, the university's lack of involvement doesn't make much educational sense. We know it happens everywhere, and we don't hold the professors at the university personally responsible. In our talks with them, they express interest in Garfield, but they have other, wider professional commitments for a book, an article, a research project to run in the pursuit of a university commitment to academic excellence. Unless a different attitude and closer relationships are drawn within its professional community, we see little chance for educational improvement in the school, and perhaps only more distance between university excellence and school practice. Professional dialogue, an ideal pursued by this university for half a century, is what we looked for and what we failed to find.

In our search for interactions between the communities served by Garfield and the school, we found a particularly interesting enigma. There is one person in the school who, literally, stands above the rest. He is about six foot eight, thin, with regal bearing and an articulate interest in all that is going on. In the teachers' lounge he tries to engage the teachers in discussions on the political events of the day, in competing philosophies of justice, or in recently published literature. He is a poet and a learned man, perhaps the most learned person we encountered in Garfield. After some days of seeing him in the halls, at the dances, in the cafeteria, or in the teachers' lounge, we finally asked him what department he was in. The man is the security guard. He has been a security guard at Garfield for six years. In response to our question, he says, yes, he is happy in his role; he enjoys the atmosphere and especially his relationships with the high school students. There probably is not a better example of the relationship between the literacy and understanding of the community and the educational performance of the school. This elegant, self-taught, intellectual security guard is another indication of the respect that the black community brings to this school.

In the final analysis, however, Garfield is not viewed as an end in itself but as a means to something more important—acceptance in a university and a diploma that is really critical for a worthwhile job. Thus, nearly all at Garfield look to the future of its students. In a school where visits by recruiters from the best-known colleges and universities in the country are announced over the loudspeakers daily, it is clear where Garfield stands. It stands as another stepping stone on the path to a professional job in that outside world.

# 2

# SANDS HIGH SCHOOL

## E. JOHN KLEINERT

$S$ands High School is on the outer fringe of a major metropolitan community experiencing a heavy influx of Hispanic families. By 1981, just over three-quarters of the school's students were first or second generation Americans of Hispanic families. Seven years before that, the figure was 46 percent; twelve years before, 10 percent. When the school opened in 1963, the figure was just under 5 percent. Population projections for the area served by the school indicate that it will likely yield a 95 percent Hispanic school population within ten years.

Total enrollment at Sands High School during the past decade has remained relatively stable. Minor school attendance boundary changes and the opening of two new high schools in the area have resulted in an enrollment range that peaked at approximately 2,800 students in 1979 after a low of 2,250 right after South High School opened in 1974. Since the opening of nearby Sunset High School three years ago, Sands' enrollment has steadied at between 2,600 and 2,800.

Latest figures show that more than 80 percent of the school's seniors have attended Sands all three years. This is a high figure for a city that features rapidly shifting populations.

Fifty-five percent of the teachers who were on the faculty at Sands seven years ago still teach there.

During an era of conservatism and retrenchment, it is not surprising to discover that the curriculum of the school has changed little during the past decade. The tendency toward specialized courses, common in the sixties, has given way to more basic offerings—few new courses have been added, and several unpopular or esoteric electives have been dropped. As the school's English department chairperson said, "This school changes slowly, almost lethargically, in regard to curriculum and policy change; but it reacts quickly to real problems. This is probably a reason for the high degree of discipline in the school."

Regarding the acculturation of the young Latins, a teacher said, "I've noticed whenever I convene a new class at the beginning of a semester I go through the printed roster of first names like, Sergio, Juan, and Alfredo. I say to them, 'If you want me to call you something else, let me know and I'll jot it down on the sheet.' A large number raise their hands and tell me to put down Paul or Al or John." While most teachers have similar experiences, a few perceive a drift toward greater ethnicity as the school approaches 80 percent Cuban-American. One said, "If we teachers let up just a little bit this would be a Spanish-speaking school. When teachers don't remain vigilant, the spoken language between students in the classroom soon lapses into partial Spanish. The language carry over from home to school is inevitable."

To an observer, it does seem that use of the Spanish language is assumed when asking directions on the street, visiting a residence, and even shopping in some of the local shops. The school may be the only place in this community where English is the predominant language.

Conversations between students in classrooms and hallways were often observed to be either in Spanish, or a combination of English and Spanish, even when the speakers' families had been in this country from ten to twenty years. Some of the teachers wonder if the school can maintain English as the primary language (outside of classrooms) if the ratio of Hispanic to non-Hispanic students increases beyond the present 3 to 1, as is expected.

Although the shift from a mostly Jewish to Latin culture in the community has been accomplished with relative ease and grace, it would be a mistake to assume it hasn't created difficulties for a few. A longtime non-Hispanic resident said, "There are certain people here who just resent the difference of language and culture; many believe the newcomers are not making as much effort as they should to become more American." He went on to say, "I don't think the problem is as great as it was three to four years ago when there was a 'white cracker' element attending the school from nearby Bluewater—of course, now Bluewater is mostly Latin."

The fact that the school has a preponderance of Anglo teachers has caused no discernible resentment among the Hispanic parents. Many of them say they prefer Anglo teachers so that their children will have to learn English. The evidence shows, in fact, that the Cuban parents think the school is doing a very good job. They like the fact that discipline is better there than in most other schools. This doesn't mean, however, that they wouldn't like more Hispanic teachers than there are.

Non-Hispanic parents who are active in high school affairs lament the difficulty they and school administrators encounter when attempting to engage Hispanic parents in the official parent group, the Citizens Advisory Council. One noted, "The reticence of the Latin family to question, or offer counsel, is why, after eighteen years, we finally had to abandon our Parent Teacher-Student Association (PTSA) at Sands last year. We could not get enough people to turn out for the meetings."

As for the remaining body, the Citizens Council, only nine of the twenty-eight members are Latin—a ratio less than half that of the student representation.

Watching them finish their lunches in the cafeteria, a young teacher comments on the insularity of some of the Latin students: "Their social lines are almost entirely within their group; they mix little with the Anglo population. They don't have to; they are the majority." However, she sees changes in the Hispanic girls. "They are changing their attitudes toward the traditional male Latin role. Their dating patterns are becoming more American. Chaperones are not as common now. Occasionally the girls will date Anglos, but they'll probably marry Latin men. They won't, however, be the same kind of wives their mothers were."

From extended observations and interviews, it was quite evident that the young people of this high school don't demonstrate the contentiousness that was so characteristic of students during the early 1970s. They seem much less involved with drugs and less indifferent to authority, more concerned with earning both creature comfort and recognition. One teacher describes them as "Episcopalian" in attitude and posture. "There is that kind of exhibition of moral rectitude, a posturing of upper-middle-class in them," he says with a smile. Style and manner does seem to be very important to these youths. They dress well and speak with an earnest intensity. These qualities are perhaps most true for those students who are in the college preparatory courses, but this concern with pride and bearing was also evident among the rest of the student population.

## Four of the School's Important People

Dan Stoner, principal of Sands High School, assumed his post in 1975, shortly after the heart attack and sudden death of his predecessor, James Meyer, the stern, quiet man who had opened the school twelve years earlier. Meyer was a reclusive leader who usually made major decisions by himself, or with the counsel of a few close staff associates. Highly respected by students and faculty, he was also feared by many because of the distance he kept and the authority he wielded.

Stoner came to the job as an experienced secondary school principal. He had been principal of the city's Central High School for nine years, a period during which this inner-city school changed from a small, all-white institution with an enrollment of 1,200, to a desegregated school of 3,800, with a two-thirds black enrollment following the flight of the white population in the community around the school to the suburbs. It is to Stoner's considerable credit that these transformations were handled with so much skill.

Easy going and friendly, if somewhat unassuming, he was accepted quickly by the Sands faculty and students who liked the accessibility he offered. An army veteran from a family that had lived in this community for several generations, Stoner has been in education since graduating from the state university in 1956. Before becoming a principal he was a mathematics teacher, a guidance counselor, and an assistant principal at both junior and senior high school levels.

When asked about the most critical purposes of his school, Stoner paused and thought for a minute or more before saying, "They are to provide a healthy balance of the three A's—academics, activities, and athletics; to provide an attainable and practical education for non-college-bound students; and to provide a strong curriculum for the college bound." He added that his school's greatest success has been with the first of these purposes, that of offering a balanced program. He is particularly proud of the impressive involvement of students in the many extracurricular activities of the school and in the boys' and girls' athletic programs.

Asked about weaknesses in the program, the principal spoke of deteriorating formal lines of communication between faculty and administration, citing the recent faculty council arrangement set forth by the teachers' union as an example. Although he feels that informal communication at Sands is good, he laments the disappearance of the *old* faculty council, which was elected entirely by the faculty and held regular meetings. The present arrangement has membership partially appointed by the union, and agendas that tend to be adversarial. Further, he regrets the lack of vocational facilities in the school. Since the advent of a modern vocational-technical center in the county some four years ago, vocational students have to be bussed many miles away from their high schools to attend classes. Because many choose not to take the long round-trip bus ride, and the extended school day it causes, this has reduced enrollment in vocational programs at a time when the principal feels that they are especially needed.

"Robert Westin is a super student." That is the way he was described by one of his fellow seniors at Sands. Robert is at the academic summit of his class, in line to graduate as valedictorian if his grades hold up the last two semesters. He is president of the high school's Key Club, a member of five school honor societies, a National Merit Scholarship semifinalist and chairman of the Student Council Judicial Committee. He plans to study computer science at a university next year. Clear of eye, calm of demeanor, serious and concise during an interview, it was quite evident that he was very satisfied with Sands High School.

Asked what he attributes his success to, he did not hesitate an instant before answering, "My parents. I am the fourth of six children who have all been successful, so far. I have wonderful parents. They always urge us to do our best, and whenever we have any problems they are there to talk to us." Inhabitants of the area before the recent influx of Hispanics, the Westin family has seen no reason to move as so many of the other native families have. Robert feels this has helped them all to become better and more capable Americans.

Discussing drug problems among the young, he admits that they have affected some of the students at this school, but he says drug usage is much less prevalent at Sands than elsewhere and that it peaked a year or two ago. He believes much of it is the result of peer pressure, and that this is especially true for the students who aren't as involved with school life.

Regarding young people's attitudes toward authority, Robert said, "There is more respect for teachers and parents here. Most teachers have an easy time maintaining their leadership in classrooms; only the few who act like they don't care that much about their students have difficulty."

One of the first staff members a visitor is likely to meet when he walks about the grounds of Sands High School is Joe McBride, the roving and watchful assistant principal responsible for a reasonable and orderly school environment. He is omnipresent in hallways, cafeterias and lavatories, in parking lots, and on the campus surrounding the buildings. McBride carries a walkie-talkie and uses it frequently to send and receive messages between himself, the principal, and other assistant principals. He has a craggy look about him, his face is weathered and his figure is solid.

His venerable appearance is frequently softened by a smile and a youthful twinkle of the eyes. He speaks softly and intelligently while looking straight into the face of his listener. After watching him at work with young people, one senses kindness and character as well as vigilance.

He is in the school parking area every morning at 7:10 A.M., walks the public areas of the school during lunch hours, and moves about the walkways at dismissal time. Except for the "small percentage of students who are persistent problems," the students seem to know him and feel comfortable in his presence. In our discussions with dozens of Sands teachers, his name was mentioned invariably in explaining this high school's citywide reputation for orderly student behavior and respect for the rights of others.

Joe McBride has been assistant principal at Sands since 1966, when the school community was 95 percent white American. For these fifteen years, while the names he knows the students by gradually changed from Harold, Carol, and Linda to Antonio, Jesus, and Maria, he has been the conscience of the school, the guardian of the rules for student behavior. When asked to comment on the behavior of high school students in recent years, McBride said,

> The percentage of problem kids in this school has increased from three to four percent in the 1960s to ten to twelve percent today. The increase is based on lowered moral standards in families, I think—the parent's atti-

tudes regarding honesty, discipline, and things like that. It is no different these days in the Latin families than it is in the American ones. [Continuing, he said,] I don't think we have as many drug problems as we had a few years ago. Attitudes are what have changed. Young people don't like authority. They don't want to be told what to do. They want to challenge or debate their infractions! Don't get me wrong; most of the kids are great, but there are increasing numbers of them who take advantage of their rights while ignoring their responsibilities.

Parents are generally cooperative with the school, but they are overprotective. Some don't want their kids to walk to school, they drive them even if it is only a few blocks. If the kid comes in late enough times that we have to contact them they say, "It's my fault, I didn't wake him up." They appreciate what the school does for the child, but they want us to go out of our way to overlook his behavior when he breaks the rules. It didn't used to be that way.

Regarding disruptive classroom incidents, he says,

We administrators and teachers have got to stick together on this. We can't let a teacher be in a classroom with three or four chronic troublemakers and still expect him to teach. This is what happened in places like New York where the system stood back and let kids run teachers right out of classrooms. This is ridiculous. There is no way we're going to let that happen here.

"One of the biggest changes I've noticed in students of both ethnic groups is that they are less motivated toward the future," McBride said. He explained that their absorption with part-time jobs and regular income for spending money, at the expense of the kind of serious education high school students pursued ten to fifteen years ago, is part of the whole society's insistence on instant gratification. Their unwillingness to defer rewards in favor of greater preparation for the future is, he believes, to the detriment of our educational system and to the nation's future.

One of the few Sands faculty members who is of Hispanic heritage is Ofelia Hernandez, a member of the social studies department. Her story tells something about both the recent history and the current curriculum of this school. Hernandez, one of a small number of Hispanics in the school at that time, graduated from Sands High School in 1970. Her father is a painter, and her mother is a teacher of Spanish literature, with a doctorate from the University of Havana. The family moved from Cuba to South America in 1952, then to the United States in 1959. Her grandparents on both sides were Basques who had, in their time, emigrated to Cuba from Spain.

After the Hernandez family had lived in the city for a few years and "Ofie" had reached high school age, her mother determined that she should go to Sands High School because of its academic reputation. They did not live in the Sands attendance area, so they sold their home and purchased one within the school's boundaries. They did not do so, however, before Mrs. Hernandez had inspired other Cuban-American families in their old neighborhood to make the same move. Ofelia Hernandez says: "Their entire motivation was to obtain the best American education possible for their children so that they could be absorbed into the best of their new country's culture. Most of the Cubans who came to Sands High School in those days had moved here solely because of its reputation."

The young Cuban-Americans in this contingent were among the first Latins to enroll in this school. Hernandez remembers that these boys and girls were determined and highly motivated. The academic competition, especially from the Jewish students in the school, prompted them to work hard and get good grades. They set a tone, Hernandez believes, that still exists for nurturing friendly and accepting relationships with members of the existing culture around them.

After graduation from high school, Hernandez went to the state university and graduated from there seven years ago. That fall she was hired by her old principal to begin teaching United States Government. She believes the school is as strong as it ever was and explains: "The faculty is the reason for the school's strength. Teachers were carefully and skillfully selected by both the original principal and his successsor. Many of the best of them are the veterans who set the standard for good teaching for the ones who have followed."

In regard to the ongoing local struggles over bilingual-biculturalism, she says she reacts more like the native American teachers. "I make it mandatory that students speak English. I am a strong believer that when you're in the United States you speak the native language."

Does she feel lost halfway between the native Americans and the Cuban-Americans because of her family's influence and her strong belief in, and history of, being "Americanized?"

Not really. I can be Cuban when it suits a need—if they need somebody Hispanic for a token or something. I consider myself American. I've lived most of my life here. There was a time when I felt like I was in neither world. I feel comfortable now in both worlds. At home, I speak Spanish to my father and English to my mother.

Beginning her eighth year of teaching, Hernandez admits that last year she had some flashes of fatigue not unlike what is called teacher burnout. Operating with the energy she does, the thing that seems to keep her going at the performance level she requires of herself is being able to regularly experience new challenges.

[Each year] Dan gives me something new to do. This year, it has been the honors government course. The first year I was here, one other teacher and I coached all the girls' sports—seven of them! Then I took over publication of the student Hispanic culture project, *Legado*. After that it was other new courses, and different student activities. I hope I never run out of new things to do.

## *Student Life*

The Sands High School campus is surrounded by lush green, neatly trimmed bushes near well-swept walkways. The buildings are freshly painted, the windows are clean, and the surfaces of the hallways glisten with the daily care the maintenance staff gives them. Compared to the clutter and the rush of the nearby thoroughfares, the school is a restful park.

The school day begins at 7:30 A.M. Following the first academic period of the day, there is a twenty-minute homeroom. Each homeroom has about thirty students and represents, as one teacher put it, "the family unit of the school; the opportunity for teachers and students to relate to one another in a context less formal than the classroom." Most of the 120 teachers have a homeroom responsibility. After homeroom, there are five more 55-minute periods, interrupted midway by a half-hour lunch period.

At 2:15 P.M. life quickly changes for the students as the formal school day ends. Three different things may happen: one quarter of the students remain at the school and participate in the rich and varied student activities program, including sports, clubs, or performance groups; almost half of them go to part-time jobs that begin in the afternoon or early evening; the remainder go home or elsewhere to use the rest of the afternoon for individual pursuits and responsibilities.

A resident who lives within a block of the school says:

> I was worried about living this close to a high school when we first moved here a few years ago. I've heard what it is like in the vicinity of most of these schools—drifting groups of kids who are skipping classes, smoking marijuana, and racing engines. It is nothing like that here. Those school people, the principal and teachers, really keep the lid on Sands. The only kids you will see lounging around outside the school buildings are usually supposed to be there and are waiting for a ride from their parents.

Many first-hand observations confirmed what this woman said. The outside of the school, the width and breadth of its lawns and playing fields, is serene and well ordered. The only action is during that frenetic period ten minutes before the school day begins, and a similar period after the final dismissal bell. During the latter time, Officer Gable of the Metro police force is on hand to tame the spirits of the energetic student operators of the TransAms and Z-28's as they depart. During these entry and exit periods, as well as throughout the day, fights, harassment, or even distracting horseplay is rare. Yet, normal adolescent exuberance is clearly present. What distinguishes the behavior of these high school students from that observed outside other high schools in the area is said by the teachers to be a kind of respect students have for the building and what it stands for. Asked about this, a junior boy said,

> Sands has always been different from the other schools in the city. Two of my older brothers went here, and they felt the same way then. The reason is Mr. McBride. Don't you see him walking all over the place? You couldn't get away with anything if you tried. Everyone knows this and they like it this way. We're proud of this school.

Again speaking of Assistant Principal McBride, a senior boy said, "He puts a lot into this school. I come by early in the morning, late at night, on Saturdays; he's always here." Another said, "I think he lives here! This is his school. If you are a Sands student he cares about you." Another said, "In our peer counseling class we put him in the 'hot seat' one day and asked him the hardest kind of questions, like

'How do you feel when you have to report trouble to a student's parents?' He answered all our questions. He told us he likes dealing with people's problems because he believes everyone should have a chance to become a good citizen, and most only need the right influences around them."

A large number of the juniors and seniors drive their own cars. About 60 percent of these students were found to have regular part-time jobs as well as automobiles they were paying for. These two phenomena are closely related. Of those students who do not work after school, a third or less will find a parent at home this early in the afternoon. Both parents in the majority of families have full-time jobs. However, another family member is usually at home at this time. Extended families are common among the predominantly Hispanic population. Aunts, uncles, or grandparents often live under the same roof.

On relationships between the Cuban-Americans and the non-Hispanics at Sands, a boy from a Jewish family that has lived in the area for twenty-five years said:

> I have as many Cuban friends as I do non-Cuban; lately I think even more. Because of sports, I've gotten to appreciate how close their families are and how much they enjoy things.

Another said:

> I still have trouble with them sometimes. They talk Spanish too much and get so involved talking to each other in the hallways between classes that you can't even get through.

This kind of reaction was fairly common, although most admitted that the two major ethnic groups within the school tend to stay within their own groups for social and unstructured school activities. Friction was observed to be virtually nonexistent between Hispanic and non-Hispanic students, but close friendships or dating patterns that bring individuals in both groups together appear uncommon. Most of the Cuban-American students at Sands perceived no difficulty of any kind regarding group relations, a perception that prompted one teacher to say, "Yes, that's because those kids belong to the dominant culture here, and they know it!"

With the emphasis in recent years on staffing schools so that faculty ethnic representation exists where the student body has a specific ethnic characteristic, it was interesting to note that only 12 percent of the Sands teachers are of Hispanic origin, although 77 percent of the student body is. Neither teachers nor students nor parents reported any strong dissatisfaction with this. The general reaction of the majority of Hispanic parents is that they want their children to learn English and to learn how this country works, whoever teaches them. The teachers, Hispanic and non-Hispanic, say the only problem for Anglo teachers is not being able to speak Spanish to those parents who can't use English well.

A senior Cuban-American girl who is active in sports said, "We have fairly good school spirit among the students here. It suffers from the fact that our football teams haven't had much success lately, and we do run into problems when people get a little mad at others because they're speaking in a language they can't understand."

Discussing socialization between groups, a boy who is a member of the school band said,

> Some of the Americans and the Cubans date each other, but it is not common. There are no particular problems associated with this except that some of the Cuban parents still insist on chaperones whenever their daughters go out with a boy. Americans are not used to this. Sometimes there is resentment by the Cuban boys when a popular Cuban girl goes out with a non-Cuban. As a result, the popular kids usually end up staying within their own group.

Addressing the issue of relations between students at Sands, counselor John Popovich says, "They're getting along pretty well. You always have an element here that says, 'Oh, he's Cuban,' in a derogatory way, or, 'He's a redneck.' But the vast majority are getting along very well." However, he said that it is much harder to bring the student body together now. "There has been a change in the attitude toward sports the last few years. Attendance is much less for our varsity football games. The Cuban attitude toward American football is less than enthusiastic." Since, in the early years, the football schedule had been a focal point for school spirit and cohesion, the loss of major interest seems to have left a void that has only partially been filled by the extensive Sands student activities program. The latter, complete as it is, tends to allocate student interest among many dozens of school enterprises; this results in more total participation, but little whole-school commitment, and the school spirit that comes from the focus of many students on a single school effort. Popovich says,

> We won't have a hundred students at our next football game. Our Booster Club doesn't attract parents like it used to when we had a larger population. The change in ethnic composition of the school over the years has affected the unusually high degree of school loyality that Sands was well known for. Then it was centered about sports, especially football in the fall.

The young people in school now seem to be much more interested in their part-time jobs outside school. There was general agreement among the teachers that the lives of teen-agers today extend to a larger world—a world far beyond the school—than they did before so many owned cars and TV's.

Above a side door leading into the school cafeteria is fastened a small embossed plastic sign that says, "Teachers' Line—Students Welcome." I asked Principal Stoner about it. Although it had been there for years, Stoner was not aware of its existence. Teachers said they recollected no instance where a student had entered the line, but they agreed that students could if they wanted to.

An appointed committee of students and teachers surveyed student attitudes about the school during the past year. Using anonymous questionnaires, they learned that more than three-quarters of the student body felt they had either "good" or "excellent" relationships with their teachers, and that a like proportion were "proud to be at Sands High School." Only 18 percent felt that ethnic differences limited the relationships they had with other students.

In regard to the helpfulness of teachers, approximately one-third of the students thought that their teachers were not as available before and after class as they should be, that they didn't share and discuss test results with the class sufficiently, that they weren't fair and consistent with students, and that they didn't tolerate expressions of students' diverse opinions. Viewed another way, of course, two-thirds of the students appear to be satisfied with their teachers on these issues.

This survey included more than twenty items concerning student welfare, and only those cited indicated some degree of dissatisfaction. Some teachers speculated that the one-third who were unhappy with the fairness and availability of teachers were the ones who may be at the lower end of the grade scale; others agreed there has been some slippage as the school faculty has grown somewhat older, and perhaps a bit less patient.

Student attitudes about their school, relationships between students, and interactions between cultures were probed during several discussions with students while they were attending their regular classes.

The amount of homework in the college preparatory levels at Sands averages one to two hours per week per class. It varies considerably from one class to another, depending more on the particular teacher than on the course. Most students are quite happy that homework assignments are no greater than they are.

Asked about their perceptions of student behavior at Sands High School compared to behavior at other city high schools, virtually all students believe that students at Sands are more responsible and respectful of authority. The reasons they most often gave for this situation were: (1) the absence of significant poverty among the families of their community, (2) a smaller proportion of students involved in any kind of drug usage, and (3) the respect for authority often characteristic of the Cuban family.

Defending the tendency among the students (Hispanic and Anglo) to group up and stick together in the unstructured social settings of the school (hallways, cafeteria, and parking lots), students indicated that people their age always like to have their good times with those most like themselves. The Cuban students said they would spend more time with native Americans if their parents were not so conservative about dating and other evening activities. "My parents don't like the liberal ways of American teen-agers, so it is hard for me to get permission to go out at night unless they know that I'm with kids whose families they know," was the way one Cuban-American girl put it. "Besides," said another, "you want to be with someone who is compatible and likes the things you like; it's not just the fact that our parents make us take a chaperone along. But I'll admit, most American boys refuse to deal with that."

Although the students are generally optimistic, they are not particularly idealistic about their future. There is less reliance on college as the only future for them. The Hispanic students, if they do go to college, will likely go to a local university because their families and they, themselves, tend to prefer remaining close to home. The percentage of students attending colleges has been declining. School officials estimate that between 50 and 55 percent of the graduates in 1982 actually began postsecondary college level programs. That figure is down from the 60 to 70 percent range which prevailed throughout the late 1960s and early 1970s.

"School leavers," the current euphemism for dropouts, are increasing at Sands High School. During most of the 1970s the percentage of the student body that would normally drop out of school during the year hovered in the 6 to 8 percent range. During the 1979–80 school year, 10 percent left; during 1981–82, 342 students, or 13 percent, left school. Lack of interest was the reason given by 88 of those students, while 205 said they left to take a full-time job. School officials suggest that the trend "is part of the increased Cuban-American influence, which stresses working at an early age and the importance of economic independence."

The occupational specialist at the high school, whose primary duties are to locate jobs for the graduates of Sands and for the school leavers who drop out before graduation, estimated that more than 60 percent of the student body currently has some kind of regular part-time job outside the school. "This figure is higher than it has ever been because of the increased desire of young people to have some degree of financial independence," she said. "This is generally because they want to support their automobiles, pay for nice clothes, and enjoy the many pleasures of urban life. The parents encourage their children to have jobs."

## Leadership Style

The style of leadership that characterizes the administration of Sands High School is primarily established by the principal. Stoner is not a strong believer in the usefulness of committees that meet regularly and have the fixed kind of agendas common in educational institutions. He believes in group decision-making, but feels it works best when the individuals in the group are able to interact informally, coming and going to confer as needed prior to reaching consensus. As a result, he chairs no standing committees, although many of them exist in the school. He attends few of these meetings, preferring instead to make sure that everyone finds him available to talk with on a moment's notice. His door, literally, is not only always open, but his associates are often in his office, getting quick assistance with daily problems.

The principal describes his leadership style as eclectic. "I use various techniques, tools of the trade, depending on the situation," he says. "I started various programs here, and I started by talking *with*, not *to*, my teachers, then sending them out to look at programs in other schools. If I'm trying to start something new, I try to think of it as farming—plant the seed of an idea, work it with fertilizer and water and hope—get my staff to know it's their idea, too, then get out of the way."

Although there has been a strong teachers' union for a long time, it is noteworthy that Stoner has never had a grievance filed against him in either his six years at Sands or during his nine-year tenure as principal of Central High School. He has some difficulty, however, with the concept of each school's Faculty Advisory Committee, a body that was recently transformed into a quasi-union group by a new system-wide policy that requires half its membership to be appointed by the union. In the past, the committee was strictly a teacher-elected group. The way it is constituted now has, he feels, changed the scope of concerns and affected the attitude of good will. "They tend to see the trees and not the forest. As an administrator, I am paid to see the forest. I've got to have a global perspective, but I've also got to be able to see each tree as the teacher does," he says. He believes it may have become more of an adversarial group than it was, "a factor that inhibits the open communication that used to be evident."

Stoner is not a principal who walks the hallways daily and regularly appears before the student body at assemblies and pep rallies. Many Sands students are juniors or seniors before they recognize him. As he perceives his role, visibility is not as important as working behind the scene to help other people who are dealing directly with the students.

He had this to say about his handling of ethnic group relations:

I started as a high school principal at Central. When I began it was a small, all-white high school. During my nine years there I saw it mushroom to a desegregated high school with three times the enrollment—two-thirds black. When I left it was an *integrated* school. That's one of the things I'm proud of.

Speaking of the Cuban-American students at Sands, he says, "I think there is an identification by them with the mainstream of our traditional American culture. The kids in the hall speak Spanglish, shifting in and out of English." Stoner sees the Latin families as being proud to be Americans and believes that the school has no problems associated with any collision between Latin and American ways.

Faculty reactions to Dan Stoner's form of leadership were most typified by a math teacher who has taught in two other local high schools:

> I can't find fault with this school's administration. The biggest advantage for me teaching in this school is just that—the administration. They treat you like a human being. You're here to do a job and you're trusted to do your job properly. If you don't, you hear about it. Until then, you're assumed to be O.K. I think most of the teachers feel this way. Turnover is very low here. Teachers throughout the system know about this school and many would like to transfer here.

Teacher turnover is, indeed, extremely low at Sands. Last year it was 5 percent. It has averaged 6 to 7 percent over the past ten years, a figure well below the system average. As evidence of the school's attraction to veteran teachers, over 90 percent of the faculty is tenured. None of the 120 teachers are in their first year of teaching, and the majority have been in this school seven years or more.

Reacting to a reference to the school's reputation for good student discipline, the principal said,

> I have a hard-headed ex-Marine sergeant who runs my physical education department. At the beginning of each year the boys and girls are all required to do certain exercises—weight lifting, jump-rope, and the like—before they are allowed to participate in the classes. At that time the classes are run like a drill unit. They are given complete instructions and they go out and are given close-order drill. It culminates just like it does in the army with competition between platoons, and those kids will bust their guts trying to be the best. I honestly believe that department, the way they take those tenth graders through the paces at the beginning of the year, and the resulting attitude that is set the first few days of the fall, has a lot to do with the maintenance of discipline in this school.

The administrative-line relationships in Sands are typical of most large urban high schools. Under the principal are three assistant principals, each with fairly well-defined responsibilities.

Although he has a number of other tasks, Joe McBride is primarily responsible for the "orderly and productive behavior" of the 2,600 students who make up the school's enrollment. A second assistant principal is in charge of the guidance division of the high school, and a third is responsible for the curriculum and the coordination of the instructional program.

The latter assistant principal appears to serve in the capacity of a nominal executive principal. She is the one who carries out special and urgent tasks. Newest and youngest of the assistants on the staff, she is a former high school English department chairperson who was appointed to her present position within the past year. She coordinates the work of the department chairpersons. Extended observation indicates that she serves as the voice of the principal: issuing directives, reviewing teacher lesson plans, chairing committees, transmitting messages, fielding complaints. With Stoner's style of quiet, in-the-background leadership, this assistant is the mobile representative of the chief administrator to the teachers and the program. She spends an hour or more a day in conference with the principal, taking instruction, listening to advice. While Stoner deals with the unending directives, memos, and reports required of his office by the district and system-wide school headquarters, she is carrying out his directives and receiving reactions to them. Because they operate closely together and communicate clearly with one another, most teachers say that the situation appears to work to the benefit of the staff and the school as a whole.

## Faculty Morale

Discussing his typical school day, guidance counselor Popovich, like many of the other administrators and special staff people at Sands, says he starts the day on the run.

> At seven-fifteen I go over my mail and messages, then start seeing students. I call them down according to which of them have made requests for me the day before and which I need to see because of a problem or task related to them. A lot of it has to do with making sure they are in the right classes, some of it has to do with testing—checking records to see which kids have had certain tests, which haven't, which have to take them again—that sort of thing.

During this typical day he says he will see twenty to twenty-five students. "The time with each will depend upon the problem he or she has. Many require only a couple of minutes. Eighty percent of these contacts are usually student initiated. Almost all of these are Hispanic students. I'm more likely to have to call for the American student in order to see him." Normally, in addition to the students, he will see two or three parents each day. "I don't speak Spanish, but only three or four times a week will I have to call in a translator because the parent can't speak English." Popovich indicates that language problems are easily resolved since several of the nine women who work in clerical jobs in the school's main office (of which the guidance cubicles are a part) are Hispanic.

After joining the faculty in 1978 as a biology teacher, John Popovich became one of the school's six counselors a year later. He had been a junior high school science teacher and counselor. Like the other counselors in this high school, he is responsible for scheduling and guiding 450 students. As a special, secondary assignment, he acts as test chairman for the school.

This personable, buoyant young man grew up near Pittsburgh. He first came to the local university on a football scholarship, graduated from there in 1971, and began his teaching career in the local public schools. Married, and the father of a young son, he is one of several football coaches.

When asked if he is as happy working at Sands as he was at the other schools to which he previously had been assigned, he quickly replied,

> Oh, much happier. The last place was a battleground—a very rough school, a very rough neighborhood. They had a mixture of students there who just hated each other—one-third black, one-third Cuban, one-third Anglo. Sands, from administrators down to teachers, is run the way a school should be run. We are strict on discipline. Kids are well behaved.

Without exception, every teacher interviewed cited the superior discipline and order of this school compared to the others with which they had experience or knew about. Some cited occasional behavior problems at Sands, but invariably qualified those problems by saying how much less frequent and less serious they are here.

Although broad agreement existed concerning order at this school, opinions differ as to the principal's leadership methods and the relative contentment of the teachers.

Regarding staff morale at Sands, one of the school's veteran teachers stated, "I think that this school has one of the best working climates of any school in our area. Teachers, for the most part, feel good about teaching in Sands. They are relaxed; they're not hassled in this school. They don't have people looking over their shoulder every five minutes. On top of this, the student body is a pleasure to work with. They are polite, well-behaved, and responsive kids." This teacher, who works with both upper and lower ability levels, said, "I have respect for Dan Stoner, both as an administrator and as a person. I think there are many people in this building who don't realize how fortunate they are to have him as their principal."

One of those who sees some problems related to Stoner's quiet leadership methods confided:

Teachers are unsure of the chain-of-command. They don't know where to go when they have a problem. Dan needs to clarify who among the administrators we should go to when we have questions and need decisions. The trouble is that people here don't want to complain. They are afraid of being transferred or of being considered inadequate. They realize this is the best school around, but they see how it could be better.

The teachers' union doesn't have the strong influence on principals that it used to have. I know Dan is proud of this school and its achievements, but he doesn't remind the teachers that he knows they are the ones who really make the school work. I'm sure he feels that way. He comes to some of the games to back the kids. Most principals won't set foot in a gym! The players are elated when that happens, and it makes a coach feel good that he cares enough to come. If he would just get out of his office more, people would find out how much he cares. Many students don't even know who he is.

Another teacher said:

The morale of the faculty is not as good as it used to be. There is a lack of face-to-face communication here, not only between administrators and teachers, but between teachers and teachers. We have very few meetings and little chance to get direct information from—or ask questions of—our principal. We all need more direction. You know, if you don't know what your boss wants, everybody ends up going their own ways and school unity suffers. However, I think the biggest problem is that, compared to the old days, too many of our teachers are failing to do the extra things they used to do.

A sizable majority of the faculty, representing most of the divisions and departments within the program at Sands High School, seemed to be extremely satisfied with the working climate of the school and the style of its principal. On the faculty are a dozen teachers who taught at Sands in its early years, transferred to other schools in the system for several years, then finally requested transfer back to this school. They are among the most adamant in expressing their satisfaction with the working conditions at Sands. During interviews, the following reasons were most frequently given for the school's favorable atmosphere.

The seriousness and sincerity of this school's students are remarkable in an era characterized by apathy among this age group. Perhaps because of their Hispanic culture, and the challenge of succeeding in a different culture, they tend to be more determined to learn and succeed than other young people.

The school administration demands, and gets, good performance from teachers and, in turn, provides more stability, resources, and trust to them than is provided in most schools.

The school's venerable assistant principal for student management enforces a level of student behavior which is (a) the envy of most of the other high schools in the region, and (b) defies previous assumptions about inevitable adolescent behavior in large group settings. He has set this standard, and enforces it, with tact, friendliness, and good humor.

The physical plant is kept clean and well equipped at all times. Its appearance conveys a clear message of order and productivity to all who see it. The physical environment at Sands helps to cast the aura of success that is associated with this school.

Usually, experienced teachers of teen-agers will list "student discipline" as one of their first priorities when listing the attributes of a good school working environment. Since Sands' reputation for student behavior historically has been good, teachers were asked what factors other than the presence of Mr. McBride account for this. A science teacher said, "The student body has always come from the middle and upper-middle social classes. It did when it was predominantly Jewish; it still does now that it is comprised of Latins from upwardly mobile families."

A social studies teacher added, "There is a respect for authority in the attitudes of these families. This respect is missing in most high schools."

Another reason given was that, from the beginning of this school eighteen years ago, the faculty has been older than most. The first principal staffed the school with handpicked mature teachers; turnover since then has been low and, as a result, the average age of the faculty has increased.

There is very little discussion among teachers of "burnout," though a math teacher in his thirties and father of several children shared the following:

> I've liked teaching during most of the fifteen years I've been at it, but there have been a number of times when I thought I needed to get out of it and find a new challenge.
>
> Now I'm kind of trapped. My salary is above $20,000 for a ten-month year. If I go into anything else, I'd take a considerable cut. What I used to do—my release valve—was to take a different job in the summer. I was a carpenter's apprentice. One year I worked sanding and painting the solaria in a hotel; another time I worked with a fellow in extruded aluminum— we put together cases for holding signs advertising tourist attractions.
>
> Each summer I would try to do different things outside of education. Now I can't do this in the summer because I can't make half the salary outside that I can teaching summer school. But still, I need to get away from the classroom at times.
>
> I can keep on going, however, because I'm lucky enough to be in a school where it's easy to be a teacher.

## The Educational Program at Sands

After years of local prominence as an "academic" school where the traditional disciplines were emphasized, the basic curriculum is now being tested by the school's newest classes of young students. A counselor at the school says,

> There is a gap between the expectations of the curriculum designers and schedulers, and the capabilities and interests of the students. Many of our students need more electives and options in the required sequences, es-

pecially more work-study programs; otherwise we will see a continued loss of interest in school and more focus on outside work by our students.

One of the school's department chairpersons says,

The curriculum has remained constant and rich over the years, but interest in it—as evidenced by the downtrend in enrollment in the academic electives—has sagged as student motivation and teaching quality have dropped during the past several years. Burnout and disillusionment have affected some teachers; absenteeism among students is up and school spirit is down. Part-time jobs have taken the place of elected enrichment courses for many.

A teacher at Sands who has lived in the area all his life, sees no deterioration in spirit and optimism among the young, but he calls for a shift in emphasis by the high school:

I don't think the city is going to the dogs. I don't think the kids are going to go out and become irresponsible adults. I think we're at the point where schools should take the emphasis off college preparation and put more resources into job-oriented programs. Society needs fewer college graduates and more tradesmen, anyway. Young people are more and more interested in finding something they like to do, and then going to work at it right after high school. We should do far more to encourage this at school.

A Jewish teacher, who was part of the original faculty, made the following observation about the curriculum and the changes in the student body since the early 1960s:

I find very little difference teaching here now from teaching here in 1963. We've replaced middle-class Jewish kids with middle-class Latin kids, and I find that the motivations, parental attitudes, and their goals are very similar. These Latin kids want to go to college to earn a good job—they have very well-defined objectives, as the Jewish students of 1963 had; they know what kind of job they want or what they're going to major in at college. As a result, they want very practical, relevant instruction here. If I stray from what looks like something that will be of use to them on the SAT exams, they let me know. If they can see the application of an assignment, they will do it.

The World Literature elective course was dropped because there was not enough interest in it. The students no longer want courses that are only intellectually stimulating and exploratory. They want elective courses that will either enhance their getting a job right after high school or will supplement their English course so that they can score better on tests and get into college. Look at the enrollment in our vocabulary elective course—260! They break down the doors to get into that.

## The Purposes of the Educational Program

As part of the prologue written for Sands High School's Curriculum Guide, seven items were cited as the school's statement of objectives. Three of them were related to the humanization of students:

To provide substantial and varied learning experiences that will facilitate life in a multi-cultural, changing society

To develop programs that are consistent with student interest, abilities, and potential

To encourage each student to know his worth and to use this sense of worth to productively participate in the school and the large community

Three more of the objectives were related to the socialization of students:

To provide a body of learning that will encourage the cohesion of the student body, while encouraging an appreciation for the diversification of the multi-cultural community

To provide an atmosphere of cooperative interdependence among faculty, community, administration, and student body

To encourage the student to understand his rights and responsibilities . . . in the development of policy and practices at Sands . . . and in the larger environment

The seventh objective was directed at the students' economic and utilitarian future:

To teach skills . . . that will enable the student to function both effectively and affectively in a changing society

Since students and faculty were largely unaware, or couldn't remember these official school objectives, they were asked what they perceived the school's purposes to be.

Teachers tended to stress those purposes related to humanization in the curriculum. Lew Heilberg said his main function as an English teacher is "to help students to develop their rational capabilities for determining right from wrong, to discover who they are, and to help them develop cultural and ethical standards." In order to enable them to learn these things, Lew believes a teacher must focus on real life problems, and apply discernment and rationality to them. "These are what I call survival tools," he said. He went on to state that there are absolutes and these must be taught. "There is a cultural and ethical body that binds us all. A culture requires that this body be taught. A society must not disintegrate into randomness, as Yeats said in one of his poems. There is a repository of wisdom, which we all must ingest."

Another teacher perceived a more practical purpose in the current program saying, "Our job is to provide the foundations of basic skills to students new to the American culture, and to provide cultural understandings that will bring the Hispanic and Anglo closer together in this community." She used the words *mainstreaming* and *Americanizing* in reference to students but also explained that she favors a patient and sensitive approach by the school, one that shows respect for the Hispanic culture.

One of the science teachers, in discussing his perception of the purposes of Sands High School, summarized views expressed by many of the teachers at this school.

> Most of all, we need to get young people ready for the real world. This means giving them the academic background they need if they're headed for college, and the right habits and work skills if they are going to look for a job. In both cases they need to get from us the ability to cope with life. This means first learning how to use their own system of values, how to be involved and work effectively with other people, and how to get the most out of life for their own sense of fulfillment, because that last, after all, is what keeps us all going.

School purposes were the topic of a meeting of six student council officers from Sands High School. They were asked to consider what they thought the school was trying to do for them during their three years under the influence of its teachers and curriculum.

For a while, these seniors discussed what they thought they actually got out of their school years. Mentioned, for example, were such varied outcomes as "opportunities to learn responsibility," "preparation for college," an "education for life," "a chance to meet people from other cultures." Then they turned to the question at hand, what the school's objectives appeared to be. Using as clues the methods their teachers used, the way they tested, the rules of the school, the way the administration seemed to function, they finally agreed on four purposes they thought Sands High School had: (1) to provide academic experiences in order to prepare students for advanced study; (2) to help students learn to cope with the major problems of life; (3) to teach students how to get along with other people; and (4) to teach students how to compete in a free and competitive society. These purposes, as they were perceived by the students, seemed to be of a much more pragmatic nature than those the teachers saw.

The group then discussed the last goal, one that all agreed was perceptible, but also a little surprising. They spoke of the intensely competitive grading system, "that damned curve," which they thought most teachers used relentlessly. The students all admitted that that is the way the world is out there, but they wished it weren't. They all felt it was proper that the school emphasize this. However, after the meeting, one said privately that the American stress on winning, on being "Numero Uno," makes this educational approach mandatory.

When asked about school purposes during a hallway exchange, a student who is not in the college preparatory program said, "The school is here to keep you off the street and out of trouble until you're old enough to get out there and deal with it."

## The Curriculum

Each student is a member of one of three clearly distinguishable academic subcultures at Sands High School. The segregation of students who are in the differing groups occurs in most areas of the curricular and extracurricular program. Only in athletics and in the untracked required courses are there exceptions to this.

During their three years at Sands all students must complete 36 semester credits. Of these, 20 are required, the other 16 can be chosen. Six must be in English, four each in mathematics, social studies, and physical education, and two in science.

Four programs are available to students: college preparatory, business education, vocational education, and general studies. The curricula for these programs vary from one another only insofar as the students' 16 elective credits are deployed. In the college preparatory program, it is advised that the student add two years of foreign language, one of science, and a semester of typing. In business and vocational programs, specialized courses fill in the elective blanks. In general studies, no restrictions on the use of electives are given.

Most of the required courses in the major disciplines are tracked according to tested ability level. English is taught at four levels each year, biology at three, social studies at two, and mathematics according to the sequence chosen.

The three divisions of students can be discerned by examining the current enrollment figure for these courses. In English, the lower two ability tracks, remedial and level one, enroll 41 percent of the student body; college preparatory and honors English enroll 59 percent. In the required science course, biology, a virtually identical ratio separates the ability tracks (40 percent/60 percent). In mathematics, 48 percent are taking, or have taken, Algebra I, a sine qua non for college plans. When enrollment in these various courses and tracked sections is crosschecked, it is evident that students are in learning environments with their own levels most of the day.

The honors students form a small elite. Most of them are members of two or more honors classes, some as many as five. All college bound and highly motivated, they tend not to be engaged in demanding part-time jobs, but they are almost all vigorously engaged in the diverse student activities program, usually in several activities, including honors clubs. Membership in this highly talented and promising group numbers only about 7 percent of the student body—approximately 180 young men and women.

Those in the college preparatory—but not honors—sequences form the most numerous and diverse group. They represent about half of the total student enrollment at Sands. Ethnically, they are representative of the population as a whole. Many of them have part-time jobs; others are involved in clubs or sports at school. Few are able to work and engage in the school's activities programs.

If there is an "average" student at Sands it would be difficult to designate him or her to any of these groups—certainly not to the honors group, nor as a member of the college prep group nor as a student who is part of the remaining 43 percent of the school's enrollment—those who are pursuing the general (30 percent), vocational (10 percent), or business (3 percent) curricula. The latter, the non-college-bound students, are generally, but not always, the ones who are found in the average or remedial sections of the required courses. Most of them go to jobs right after school, and very few of them participate in the activities programs. They do have contact with the other segments of the school population when they engage in athletics and in a few of their required courses where students are not separated by their scores on a standardized test.

These two large groups, and the one small group, were observed to function quite independently of the others. Members, friends, and the effect of the school on each of them, were seen to be largely determined by their placement in designated sections of courses meant to deal with them at their respective levels of ability. This comprehensive high school, thus, is a collection of several schools under one roof, each school composed of young people whose academic work and future orientations contrast vividly with that of the other schools.

The usual array of teaching departments exists at Sands High School. There are the five academic areas that contain the courses colleges like to consider when they look at student applicants' grades. In addition, there are physical education, business education, vocational education, industrial arts, art, music, and home economics. Since all of the latter, with the exception of physical education, tend to be elective, it is of interest to note that, among these additional areas, total student enrollment at the school is highest in business education and industrial arts, areas of study offering directly applicable job skills. It has to be noted that this statement refers to course enrollment, not program enrollment, thus reflecting students' elective choices at Sands. Almost half of all Sands' students are enrolled, at a given time, in a course from one of these two departments.

In all, there were ninety-three different courses being offered at the high school in the fall of 1981, twelve of which were tracked for high-ability students. Several aspects of the curricular offerings at this high school merit special comment. The school has earned its reputation for having an excellent honors program. Advanced placement and honors courses exist in all five major academic disciplines. In addition, the mathematics program is exceptionally strong, offering no fewer than nine courses above the level of introductory algebra.

The English department's elective course, Vocabulary, a no-nonsense demanding program of study, is elected by almost 30 percent of Sands' students before they graduate. Students apparently prefer this kind of practical offering to World Literature, which was the most popular academic elective offering of a decade ago.

Eighty-seven percent of the total enrollment in social studies courses is in the two required courses, U.S. History and American Government. Only three other courses are offered by a department that traditionally has been one of the major sources of electives in most high school curricula. Surprisingly, no courses in ethnic studies are offered. The following breakdown of enrollments are of interest.

### ENROLLMENTS IN JOB-RELATED COURSES

| | |
|---|---|
| Vocational shops | 286 |
| Work-study programs | 308 |

### ENROLLMENTS IN ACADEMIC COURSES AT UPPER TIP OF CURRICULUM

| | |
|---|---|
| Algebra II | 296 |
| Chemistry | 183 |
| Physics | 77 |
| Calculus | 18 |
| Spanish III | 77 |
| French III | 48 |

### ENROLLMENTS IN OTHER ELECTIVE AREAS
### (percentage of school enrollment)

| | |
|---|---|
| Industrial arts courses | 20 percent |
| Art courses | 15 percent |
| Music courses | 11 percent |
| Home economics courses | 7 percent |
| (13 percent of school's female enrollment) | |

Of particular interest is the fact that in the fall of 1981 only 22 percent of the student body at Sands High School took a foreign language course: 10 percent took French; 3 percent took Italian; and only 9 percent took a Spanish course. At this high school, with its Hispanic majority enrollment, only 12 percent of the school's Anglo students studied Spanish, and only 8 percent of its Cuban-American students took the special Spanish courses designed for them.

## Teaching

One of the elective courses Ofie Hernandez teaches is called Close Up/Legal. The first half of the year is the Close Up section, a government lab in which students with a high degree of interest in government participate in several county-wide programs and government-related activities. The second section, Legal, includes court observing and interviewing of jurists and state prosecutors. In the legal course, students go out into the community and experts come to the school, as the workings of the criminal and civil judicial system are studied. Simulated and real-life problems and case studies are used.

Recent guest speakers in the Close Up course have included Janet Reno, head of the County State Attorney's office, Judge Farino from the Civil Court and Judge Goderich from the Criminal Court. The students themselves are responsible for choosing, inviting, and arranging the visits of these guests. The course culminates in a trip to Washington and a visit to the U.S. Congress.

Evaluation of students in this class is based on a contract system rather than on testing. To carry out the terms of their contracts some of the students worked on the plans for a U.S. congressman's annual Labor Day picnic, some worked for campaign staffs of local officials who were up for re-election in the fall—all "hands-on" experiences. Thirty-three students from all three grades are in the course. Two or three are in honors courses, some are athletes, some are normally average or below average students in their other academic work. What brings them together is an interest in discovering how the system works out there.

"There is so much demand for this course we could schedule more sections of it," Hernandez said. "I would teach more of them if Dan [Principal Stoner] would let me. But he needs to see that the required courses are covered." One of the projects students worked on in the past was getting the street that runs by the school named Ram Road (for the Sands Rams). They went through the whole legal and political process and were successful in getting the Metro Commission to rename it. Another project awhile ago was running the re-election campaign of a local congressman. They were his committee and they handled the whole thing.

To keep the students interested and working in my regular government classes, I renamed the course Soap while we were studying the Constitution. The kids are so into soap operas—especially *General Hospital*—that I ran the course like one. Each day I would end the class on a note of suspense so that the story about the Constitution was a series of dramatic events, each resolved only by tuning in the next day, or by going home and reading about the event to find out what unfolds. It was like a game to them that would tease them enough that they would go home and read the book so they could find out what I was going to say the next day.

For instance, the other day I was teaching about The Great Compromise. I role-played, acting out the events leading up to it, but I stopped just before getting to the compromise itself. By the next day everyone in my class could tell me all about what finally happened. Every one of them went home and read about it.

Commercial jet liners can be seen through the closed windows of the classroom as they make their graceful descents to runways Nine Left and Nine Right at the Metro International Airport, just far enough north and east of the school to preclude the sound of the big engines interfering with the voice of Miss Fowler, a teacher of English and department chairperson. Miss Fowler enthusiastically lectures on Kafka and *The Metamorphosis*. This twelfth-grade college preparatory class of fifteen students listens attentively, interrupting her occasionally with questions. Few take notes; earlier she had given them a ten-minute quiz composed of four questions related to their most recent reading assignment. They all wrote furiously until the time signal to stop was given. All of them, quite apparently, had read the assignment.

Afterwards, during a discussion in the cluttered but comfortable departmental office, Fowler and several of the teachers talk about student motivation. The coffee is hot, the teachers loquacious. "It is not a problem here; these are pragmatic kids," one of them says. "If they think what you are teaching them is going to help them pass the state tests or make college freshman English any easier, they'll learn it." But what about the 40 percent who aren't going to college next year? "We have to teach to practical outcomes. They know that their jobs are going to require skill in reading, speaking, and, sometimes, writing. Most of them, or their parents, are new to American culture. They still see education as the key to their upward mobility. In recent years, many native Americans have become cynical about what school can do for them, but not at this school because of the pervading optimism of the Cubans. It rubs off."

Teachers come and go in the small room. The duplicating machine clacks away. Members of the discussion group change as bells ring. "Students aren't so interested in the general rap session in the class-room anymore," says a male teacher in his forties. "If our academic subjects got boring I used to motivate them that way, but now they get restless if I try to get them into a topic of general concern. They want to get on with the assignment." Is this a return to a more con-servative era among young people, as during the Eisenhower years of the 1950s? Heads nod as one teacher says, "It is definitely different than it was in the sixties, and it's not entirely because the ethnicity of the school has changed. A lot of it is that today's young adult has seen what drugs, family breakups, and joblessness can do to people, and they want no part of it. They are much more serious."

Later, a young woman teacher adds, "You can see their seriousness outside the classroom, too. Watch them in the cafeteria and at school events. Adolescents are growing up faster. They're world-wise. Here, we have to see to it that they don't become world-weary."

The teacher allows several minutes to pass after the bell signals the start of the class as he finishes dealing with some of his students' individual questions at his desk. During this time the other members of this tenth-grade general (non-college-bound) mathematics class en-joy the opportunity to carry on relaxed conversations with each other. Then, Mr. Bizzaro, a teacher with twelve years of experience, whose assignment at Sands also includes three advanced courses of Algebra II-Trigonometry, begins with explanations and demonstrations of sev-eral kinds of decimal operations. Although he doesn't stop for fifteen minutes, students remain watchful, listening carefully.

When a quiet conversation does break out between a pair of girls in the class, he applies to the guilty subjects a mild visual fix and a moment's silence. The distraction ends and is not resumed.

Problems out of a workbook are assigned for in-class work. A few minutes are granted for release of youthful energies—the buzz of talk, some standing up and sitting down—then everybody goes to work and Bizzaro walks the narrow aisles helping individuals when they need it.

He is all business—no jokes, anecdotes, or light-hearted banter; but he is also responsive and sensitive to his students. The atmosphere is that of a working business office or newspaper room.

This class is officially called Individual Mathematics Study. Until this year it was run on a "systems" approach, where students were tested on particular skills, given individual work on the skills for which they were found deficient, then tested again. The cycle was repeated, skill after skill. Sands High School dropped that method last year. Now, although the title remains the same, the course is taught in a more traditional manner. Bizzaro said he doesn't know why the method was changed or why the many materials needed for it are no longer supplied. He indicated that he thought it was a good way to teach math.

Students in this class are mainly those who are academically in the lower 50 percent of their grade in school. Their mathematics scores on standardized tests, and their previous performances in math courses in junior high school, are the criteria for placement in the various levels of math classes at Sands. Individual Mathematics Study is the course taken by those who have had trouble with math and who are probably not in the college preparatory track. They accomplish two things by taking this course, Bizzaro explained. "They are completing one of the two years of math required for graduation, and they are getting ready for the quantitative section of the State Assessment Test, first given in May of their tenth-grade year."

It was evident in talking with the students in this class that they liked both the subject and the instructor. "I never liked math, and I don't do very well at it, but this class is O.K. I'm learning what I need to know for the test," said one boy who sat in the back. As is true for most "general" track students at Sands, the ability range within the class is wide. This is why some teachers of these courses preferred the systems method. Bizzaro uses a large paperback workbook and devotes at least half of each class to assigned work from this book so that he can spend most of his time with those who need it.

Throughout the discussions with teachers pertaining to those sections of courses that are tracked for the non-college-bound students, the age-old problem of how to get those students to take homework seriously appeared to have been written off as unsolvable in today's environment. Most general mathematics and "level one" English and social studies teachers no longer give homework assignments, relying instead on supervised study time within the classes themselves. Here students do whatever reading is necessary and also complete a host of work sheets. In all three of those disciplines, teachers report that only 10 to 20 percent of the students will bring completed homework assignments to class. The reasons both students and teachers gave for this is that they know they aren't going to college, and their out-of-school jobs take up too much of their time; in short, their priorities reduce school work to school time only.

Teachers report that it is also becoming more difficult to depend on completed homework from college preparatory students. Their commitments to part-time jobs and relaxation or peer activities during after-school hours appear to be gradually overtaking their willingness to study at home. The consensus among the faculty is that two hours of homework per course per week is about the average assignment in most of the college preparatory academic courses at the high school.

Even as homework demands have declined, most teachers continue to believe that the department curricula are just as strongly geared toward academic achievement as they ever were. In social studies, European History was dropped, and the enrollment in World History is way down from previous years, but the school has two advanced placement sections of American History. The main difference in quality now is reported to be the students' attitudes. Although the aspiration level of the students at Sands appears to be well above the average for area high schools, young people generally seem not to be as internally driven to succeed academically as they might once have been.

## The Demise of Two Innovative Programs

As the school's instructional program has returned to its more traditional pattern, following some flirtation with varied courses and electives in the 1970s, at least two noteworthy approaches at Sands have been given up. The IMS (Individualized Mathematics Study) basic math skills course described earlier was changed back to a traditional, text-centered course from the most recent "systems" teaching approach. Principal Stoner explains: "Some of the original teachers who set up IMS math left the school." He characterized them as particularly dedicated to, and gifted in, this approach and it was difficult to find replacements for those who left. Secondly, the program required large classrooms capable of handling 100 students, and the school has never had adequate provision for that. Building remodeling was not considered because of the general trend in education away from "open-space" arrangements and back to individual teacher control of self-contained classrooms.

Finally, there was growing parental resistance to a teaching method that put so much emphasis on independent study with only occasional one-to-one contact between teacher and student, and concern about possible discipline problems in a setting with so many students in one place. (Stoner did not believe that discipline was, in fact, a serious problem.) An additional factor cited was teacher reluctance to continue to deal with the clerical and management tasks required by such a test- and exercise-focused curriculum. As a result, Stoner and the mathematics department agreed to return to the traditional method of instruction.

The other example of an abandoned innovative program is the case of *Legado*, a course based on the folkway concepts of *Foxfire*, which until this year was most recently taught at Sands by social studies teacher Hernandez. While taking this course, students produced a Spanish heritage magazine featuring stories, poems, and essays illuminating special aspects of life in the region.

Originally, it simply traced Hispanic influences in the area. Then the format was changed to include not only Hispanic matters, but also the general history of the region, so that it would appeal to both cultural groups of students, Anglos and Cubans. It was quite successful, but it was terminated because the school could not afford to allow the instructor a second hour of teacher planning time for it. "It was consuming all of my time and I needed another period for it," Hernandez said, "I understand that this couldn't be arranged, but I regret having had to give it up. We tried to get it funded by the government, but that program budget had been cut."

This interdisciplinary experiential learning project was started in 1978 by the librarian, Rosemarie Ferry, and a social studies teacher, Marsha Shafer. It utilized social studies research techniques. Students enrolled in the course attempted to preserve the skills, customs, traditions, and attitudes of the Hispanic culture through photos and interviews with people in the area. During the first two years, *Legado* students started an Hispanic archives collection and published a bilingual magazine, the latter to be used as cultural resource material to support the Spanish instructional program in the local area schools.

A community advisory board was formed and various faculty members acted as consultants. The formulators of this course of study saw it as an opportunity for education in the best sense of the word, as not only preparation for life, but participation in life itself. The community became the classroom. Students explored the rich and diverse culture that has emerged in the area as a result of the interaction of two traditions, and they attempted to document this community's fascinating and changing character.

In essence, as an innovative addition to the curriculum, *Legado* attempted to deal creatively with the growing polarity that has occurred in the community as a result of the rapid change in ethnic make-up of the area during recent years. As Ferry stated at the time, "Differences in languages and custom are superficial. Even though our heritages are diverse, we share a common humanity and home. We are shaping a common history. We hope *Legado* will promote mutual respect and understanding . . ." In the three years of operation, three stunning editions of *Legado*, replete with photos, poetry, essays, and special features illuminating the most captivating and beneficial of Hispanic influences, were published. Several students who had taken the course and participated in the production of the publications agreed that it was one of the most memorable experiences they had ever had, that they had learned more during their work on *Legado* than ever before in a course of study.

In spite of its enormous success, it perished because of lack of funds and a priority system that puts elective courses, no matter how successful, below required courses. The publication costs of *Legado* were borne the first year by the school system's bilingual program. After that, the school applied for a federal assistance grant and did not receive it. The students and teachers struggled through two more issues by scrambling for funds through the combined efforts of Stoner and student pleas for private assistance. This year it proved to be too much of a burden on the school's reduced budget allocations and the decision was to give it up rather than reduce it to a diluted version of what it had become.

The result was that the curriculum at Sands High School returned to what it was before the influx of Hispanics into its community and school. Except for the sections of English as a Second Language and several bilingual classes of American history and introductory biology for students who are still having trouble with English, the written curriculum reveals no sign that the student body is primarily Hispanic.

Although regretting the loss of *Legado*, teachers at Sands generally accepted the situation. Most expressed the belief that the first order of business for citizens new to this country is to learn the native language, and the second order of business is to learn and adapt to the predominant culture. Next in priority, according to general sentiment, is that they retain respect and knowledge of their own culture. Just as educational conservatives believe sex education, driver education, home economics, and personal adjustment should be taught at home, these educators feel that the cultural values which reflect their heritage and are perceived as important to Cuban-Americans should be the responsibility of the neighborhood and family, and should be taught at home rather than at school.

One non-Hispanic teacher said:

> There is so much fragmentation and divisiveness in this city. Schools have got to bring the cultures together, and we can't do that with ethnic study programs. We found that out in the seventies when we tried all those black studies programs that ended up increasing aggravation and hostility between blacks and whites in the very institutions where they were supposed to heal conflicts. Where are those programs now? They were counterproductive, and were allowed to die for the lack of funds.
>
> This city's problems with multicultural issues have been 90 percent black-white, not Hispanic-Anglo, even though we have more than twice as many Hispanics as blacks. The Cubans have been willing to buy into our cultural values in the marketplace, while retaining their own culture at home and in their neighborhoods. They have made this work for themselves with tremendous success. Our schools would be retreating into recent social history if they pushed this Hispanic culture thing at the expense of courses in the basic skills of communication and mathematics, and in American government and history.

This refrain, in other forms, was heard again and again. In most cases, the words were spoken without rancor or bitterness but with an obvious sense of relief about perceiving one obvious truth in a world today so full of ambiguities and uncertainties. I wondered if their views would be so dominant if most of the teachers were Hispanic.

## Work Experience

In sharp contrast to the cultural abstractions of *Legado* in the educational program at this high school are the pragmatic applications of the school's work experience programs. These programs are the most sought after—and difficult to enter—at Sands.

Represented by five separate groups, they are offered by the vocational department as opportunities for students to gain valuable experience in the world of work outside the school. Jobs in the community's business sector are selected by faculty; students are placed in these paying jobs for two to six hours per day; the school provides supervision along with related classroom work; credit toward graduation is awarded.

If a student participates for three years running, he or she can gain as many as six of the required 36 credits toward graduation by working at a job. Currently, 306 students are enrolled in these programs. Several hundred more would like to be enrolled, but cannot because of state requirements on the number each faculty member can supervise. A decade ago, these programs enrolled no more than 70 students.

The positions and companies are carefully selected to ensure that the student is receiving useful training on the job, rather than performing rote chores. Because of the increased desire of students to earn money while gaining credit toward a diploma rather than take courses at the school building site, many more would like to be admitted to these programs. The vocational department selects students with two groups in mind: those who are most sincere about going into a related occupation immediately after graduation, and those for whom this program will give encouragement to stay in school rather than drop out and seek a full-time job.

In the tenth grade in 1981–82, 74 selected students at Sands High School elected the Work Experience Program. They go out to jobs each weekday afternoon. Their jobs require twenty to twenty-five hours of work per week and are meant simply to introduce them to employment experiences in the business world. In DCT (Diversified Cooperative Training), offered in the eleventh grade, and DCT II, offered in the twelfth grade, there are currently 132 students assigned to jobs related to their occupational preferences, jobs that might be representative of the type of work they will enter after high school. CBE (Cooperative Business Education) is offered to 25 senior business curriculum students who are interested in business office training. Available to another 37 seniors is the Job Entry Program, whereby, if they have completed all course requirements for graduation, but still need semester credits, they may work at a job full-time. Finally, a marketing and merchandising program is serving 38 upper class students who are in specialized training for DE (Distributive Education). These jobs are in business that sell and market products.

These work-study programs now enroll 12 percent of all Sands High School students for 50 percent of their current academic credits—two daily hours for on-the-job work, and one hour for the related class. One hundred seventy of these students are seniors; therefore 20 percent of the students in their last year of high school are spending a significant portion of the school day working at a supervised job in the business community.

## The Extracurricular Program

During an interview with senior student Robert Westin, he said, "The main purposes of Sands High School are to help prepare students to enter the field of work they prefer, and to teach them to become a part of society and the world through helping them learn responsibilities." He went on to say that the latter is done through the school's organized activities program. As an important part of that program, he said, "There are six honor societies here. Each has a tutoring program for its respective discipline—English, mathematics, science, languages, social studies, and general. Each society has two or three honor students on duty after school three afternoons per week. Students having difficulty, or wishing to move ahead in a particular subject come in for tutoring."

As president of the Key Club, Westin organizes these tutoring services, and he states that forty to fifty students come in for tutoring each day. Teachers sponsor these societies, but stay in the background and allow the student leaders to run the program.

In fact, the whole scope of student activities—the organized, formal program of clubs, service societies, interest and performing groups— appears to be uniquely important to Sands students and staff. Jackie Eades has served as full-time activity director since Sands opened. She reveals no sign that her energy or enthusiasm for her job has been diminished by this long tenure.

Eades reports that over half of the members of the large faculty of this school is involved in active sponsorship of one or more activity groups. Most of the groups require extra time. There is no extra pay for this and, though the principal, Dan Stoner, strongly urges faculty participation, she says most do it because they enjoy it.

Attractive and vivacious, she is a compelling role model for the dozens of students who crowd her work area throughout most of each school day. Good natured and light-hearted, she is in motion most of the time, telephoning, receiving messages, conferring with club presidents about policy, service group members about agency visits, faculty sponsors about trips, drama and music teachers about production dates, facilities, and promotions. The bulk of her contacts is with students. Eades says,

> I see my job as that of a teacher. Kids are growing up in a difficult time. I wouldn't want to be a teen-ager right now. I try to help them learn to get along with others, to handle responsibility. Most of all, I want to influence their character development in a good way.

Of all the myriad groups she works with, which does she enjoy the most? "Student Council. I am their advisor. It keeps me involved with the school as a whole, and it affords me contact with cross-sections of students. It's very rewarding to me."

Eades is optimistic about the latest groups of young people with whom she has worked.

> They are becoming more concerned with adult approval again, more involved with their families and a wholesome social life. But there are so many decisions they have to make now that children before didn't have to confront so soon. Jobs, drugs, sex, and peer relationships create so much confusion. Parents are much less involved with their children's school activities than before, and this adds to the students' sense of anxiety about growing up so soon.

Although many teachers at Sands give generously of their time for the student activities program, Eades regrets the trend she has seen toward deterioration of professional attitudes, a lack of willingness to work with students beyond the academic schedule of classes. At present, 1,089, or 42 percent, of the school's students are members of at least one organized, regularly scheduled, teacher-sponsored activity at the high school. This number does not include students involved in the athletic program. When sports participation figures are added, the number rises to 63 percent, an astonishing figure in a school this large during a proclaimed era of self-preoccupation and alienation, particularly among adolescents.

Many of these students are involved in from two to four activity groups each. This activities program has made the majority of students at this school feel that they are integral, productive parts of the institution and that their learning experiences extend out from the classroom.

### EXTRACURRICULAR PARTICIPATION FIGURES (1982)

| | | |
|---|---|---|
| School Enrollment | | 2,630 |
| Clubs | | 1,328 |
| Interest clubs | (24) | |
| Honor societies | (12) | |
| Service clubs | (4) | |
| Drama | | 78 |
| Music | | 263 |
| Student Council and governance bodies | | 328 |
| School publications | | 71 |
| Cheerleaders | | 67 |

## Athletics

Bill Mihm is one of a core of "plankowners" at Sands, teachers and administrators hired by James Meyer, the original principal when the school opened in 1963. Mihm took the job of Athletic Director, a position he had held previously for four years at another city high school. Historically, in this sports-minded city, this has been regarded as a very important high school position. The original principal was not unaware of this, but, in his effort to start this school as a serious institution that would balance attention to mind, spirit, and body, he encouraged Mihm to build a wide variety of both boys' and girls' sports so there would be breadth of student participation. To keep varsity sports in perspective, they avoided the usual policy of allowing athletes to use their last academic period of the day for the beginning of team practices. Although this change restricted total practice time for Sands athletics, it signaled to students and staff that studies came first.

This kind of perspective has been part of Mihm's outlook since he began his career. Eighteen years after starting the athletic program in this school, he continues to work tirelessly for the total development of the youngsters who participate in sports. Currently, 18 percent of the student body are members of one of the twelve girls' or thirteen boys' interscholastic teams during the year (10 percent of the girls and 23 percent of the boys). Many more than this are engaged in the large intramural sports program at Sands High School.

Mihm says, "In recent years, our varsity teams have been about in the middle of the all-sports rankings for area high schools; before that we were usually in the upper third." There is no regret in his voice as he cites this. He then says with obvious pride, "Talk to Dan Stoner about how we've been first, second, or third on average SAT scores among county high schools the last few years."

Talking about changes in the school since its beginning with a predominantly Jewish and WASP student body, he says the differences are few, and most of them reflect the general changes that have affected youth since the early 1960s. "They are more conservative; they want to get out of school earlier so as to get started in a job." He believes they're just as ambitious as they've ever been, although he admits to a few differences attributed to the Latin culture: "These kids are more work-oriented, they don't feel as much prestige in being an athlete. Their parents may not be as involved with their kids' school experiences as the other parents were."

## The Peer Counseling Program

Several years ago, when the human relations movement was still strong, each of the city's high schools had a peer counseling program, which was supported by a special allocation of funds. However, during the past six years, these special counseling programs have slowly been pushed out of school budgets. Today, only a handful of the city's high schools have an active peer counseling program staffed by a full-time specialist. These schools have retained the program only because their principals were willing to sacrifice other parts of the school budget to keep it. One such principal is Sands' Stoner.

The staff member in charge of Sands' peer counseling is Betty Davis, an educator with twenty-five years of experience in the local public schools, five of them as part of the citywide human relations team that was responsible for assisting schools during the tense post-desegregation years. Her husband is a social studies teacher at Sands. Her students, who see their group counseling units as a form of extended family, call her "Mom," and him "Dad."

She describes her program as being composed of two parts. The first is a class called Peer Counseling, which is offered one period per day. It is an elective activity for those who take it, and its purpose is to introduce students to the principles of group counseling, the range of problems adolescents face, and to provide skills necessary for them to moderate the group sessions, which are offered to the student body at large. These group sessions form the second, and larger, part of her program. They are the actual peer counseling classes that occur every period of the day except for the first, at which time the trainers-to-be are taking their course. The students who attend these sessions are part of what Betty Davis calls Growth Groups, and they come from two sources: those referred to the program by the guidance department and by Mr. McBride because they have demonstrated some form of behavioral problem at school, and those who sign up for a series of sessions because they want to learn how to deal better with some issues affecting them or their school.

She also encourages teachers to schedule whole classes for individual or serial appearances in the program room. For these occasions, she provides facilitation and processing of class interpersonal issues with the participation of both students and teacher. About ten of the school's teachers have attended with one or more classes thus far. She hopes to interest more teachers in the program as time goes on.

Students who are members of the Growth Groups are enrolled for one period per week over a four- to six-week time span. The cooperation of their teachers is essential, since they must excuse the students from regular classes each time they participate. Davis uses her own considerable humane and persuasive qualities to maintain enough good will so that they will usually approve their students' requests. This part of her job is particularly important, she explains, because of an inherent skepticism on the part of classroom teachers toward what goes on in group counseling sessions. Over the years, she has largely solved this problem by keeping the sessions productive, requiring each participant to be active, and working toward improved understanding and capabilities.

The reputation of her program within the school is good. Teachers' fears that students may sign up for Growth Groups just to get out of classes are allayed by the added understanding they have seen in their students who have participated, and by their control over the approval system that allows students to attend.

Currently, there are twenty-two students enrolled in the peer counseling training class, and about 130 students attending the Growth Group sessions.

Speaking of the personality development of the young people she deals with, Davis said, "The Cuban students are having to come to grips with their emerging value system, and often they are finding that these values are different from those of their parents. It is a struggle for them to stay loyal, yet hold to their own developing value systems, but most of them do it."

The groups under her leadership have been successful, according to many of the students and teachers at Sands, in turning around some of the young and disaffected people who were sent to peer counseling as an alternative to school suspension. These "discipline cases" make up 30 to 40 percent of the membership of any given Growth Group and, through the expert and kind influence of Davis, the supportive guidance of peer leaders, and the encouragement of fellow participants, many of the adolescents with records of troublemaking during their previous school years have found adjustment to school easier.

Participants in the program seem to become permanently attached to it after their initial sessions have ended. They form a large group within the school, with Mrs. Davis and her room full of beanbag seats and soft colors, as the focal point. On any day, after the last class is dismissed at 2:15 P.M., one of the busiest areas of the school becomes Davis's rooms as students stop by to chat.

## Student Achievement

In spite of the good reputation of Sands' instructional program, most of its teachers say there has been a perceptible decline in the average level of academic performance in recent years. Most agree that this decline is more related to the widespread and general decrease in academic proficiency of young people throughout society than it is to the shift in ethnic composition of this high school. The usual reasons were offered—increased adverse effects of TV and the resultant diminished reliance on print media, social unrest, and emphasis on outside activities, especially work.

This fall-off, however, has not affected the relative standing of the school in the several areas where comparisons with the Metro area's other twenty-three high schools can be made. Sands is one of seventeen Metro high schools that offer the advanced placement program. Sands' reputation for having an exceptional program for honors students is borne out by the fact that it ranked second among these schools in the number of students who took advanced placement examinations last year—138. In the number of National Merit semifinalists last year, Sands, with six, did better than all other area high schools but one.

Sands led county schools last year in its average scores for the three major sections of the Stanford School Achievement Tests. The year before, only one high school averaged higher. In both years, this school's students scored highest on the mathematics and the writing sections.

Perhaps most important of the standardized tests are the state's required tests in communications and mathematics. The passage rate among Sands' students (a three-year average of 99 percent in communications, 87 percent in mathematics) was second highest among the Metro area schools in each of the past three years. This can be considered especially significant in light of the fact that this school has one of the highest proportions of first- and second-generation Americans in the county.

In spite of its academic success, the school's most striking achievements may be social. Sands High School has moved into the 1980s with its image of productivity and cohesiveness just as strong as it was during its successful first decade. The former student body of highly motivated young Anglos has given way to an Hispanic population whose families are new to America, but the school's countywide reputation for excellence as an ordered and purposeful social institution remains intact and unblemished.

If tranquility were not too passive a word to describe the vibrant and engaging young men and women at this school, Sands could be described as an island of tranquility in the troubled sea that is the metropolitan area. Most of the urgent problems faced by this community today—violence, drugs, disaffection—are reflected in some measure within the metropolitan area high schools. Sands is, in most respects, an exception.

# 3

## DESOTO HIGH SCHOOL

### FRED NEWMANN AND G. THOMAS FOX

DeSoto High School rises high above a neighborhood of small single-family dwellings with modest front yards and just enough space between them for narrow driveways on one side and small walkways on the other. It is an established community with one-and-a-half-storied houses about fifty or sixty years old and, by contrast, trees that are young and scrawny. A freeway cuts through the neighborhood. There is a zoo close by, and a major league ball park adjacent. A finger of the city, jutting out into two more affluent and long-established suburbs, it is a white, blue-collar area that has never been politically powerful in this large midwestern city.

Directly in front of DeSoto is a park occupying at least two large city blocks, including macadam playing areas, a small wading pool, softball diamonds and tennis courts, a baseball diamond, a grass football field and a brick blockhouse with rest rooms. On the long side of the school is a grassy open area with a few mature trees and benches at the upper end. On this cool October day, toilet paper dangles from these trees and has been there since homecoming week. In back of the school an outside track rings a football practice field.

Opened in 1932, DeSoto is a solid, brick, three-story building with regular long columns of recessed windows separated by large vertical sections of bricks. From a side view, the columns of brick and windows resemble a temple. Five enormous sculpted stone and metal entryways extend at least two-thirds up the face of the building. Steps leading up to these entrances are dark gray marble. Each of the entryways has multiple opening doors. They are a dull green, wooden, with wire chain-link mesh across the upper half to protect the glass.

Beyond two sets of doors with a few stairs between them, the entryways lead to a foyer containing a set of trophy cases. The case on the left commemorates one of the first astronauts to go to the moon, the most famous graduate of DeSoto High School. Opposite the astronaut exhibit are the school trophies, a modest lot, with wrestling and debate supplying most of the hardware within the past ten years. Set in the marble floor in the middle of the foyer is a mosaic depicting DeSoto life. Although the tradition is to never walk on this mosaic, tradition is trampled on many times a day. On a column near the mosaic, a commemorative plaque honors students of DeSoto who were killed in World War II. The plaque was found in the storage room by the new principal last year. When she asked why it wasn't up, she was told it would only be vandalized again by the students. She had it polished and put it up anyway, and is proud (while some teachers are surprised) that it has stayed up for over a year now with no trouble. She would like to put one up for the Korean and Vietnam War veterans as well.

## Context

DeSoto was scheduled to be closed by the central administration four years ago. With about 1,000 students, it was then the smallest high school in the city. It included grades seven to nine as well as the three grades of high school, and served the white neighborhoods that surrounded it. Under a court order to desegregate the schools, the district organized a plan calling for the voluntary assignment of students to specialty high schools. Under the plan, each high school would have a specialty, such as computer programming or arts and the theatre, that would attract interested students. Each student in the city would then have a choice of schools with certain standards (quotas) to maintain racial balance in each school.

The DeSoto community organized to keep DeSoto open. In the end, DeSoto was saved, but another smallish neighborhood school, about the same size as DeSoto but in a black neighborhood on the far side of town, was closed against the strong protests of the city's black community. The wounds from these political battles are still felt. Some of the black students, for example, speak of the terrible reputation of DeSoto in their neighborhoods.

A solid and obviously proud offering to the neighborhood fifty years ago, DeSoto now hangs by a thread. Few seem confident that the school will continue to stay open. In the teachers' eyes, the thread is linked to only one source: the central school administration. If the central administration wants it, it will remain; if not, "It will be cut just like that." In the eyes of neighborhood parents, the thread was initially spun from an unexpected community protest and political pressure on the school board. Some of the active parents, however, have mixed feelings about the result of their victory. Changing DeSoto High into a citywide school has tempered their enthusiasm and seems to have lowered their esteem for the quality of the school. In a city where racial strife has made national news, the successful integration of DeSoto High staff and student body is visible and a source of some satisfaction, but many wonder about its costs in educational quality.

Invisible is the strong feeling of teachers, parents, and even the students of DeSoto that they have been moved around in place and circumstance by policies of the central administration of the school district. A major source of strength is DeSoto's comparatively small size: 1,080 students and 72 teachers. The small size gives DeSoto's constituents hope that the school can be personal, informal, and autonomous—features they believe are constantly endangered by the policies of the larger school system.

## Climate

What is it like to be in DeSoto High School?

Physically, DeSoto has several "climates." The outside doors, either without glass or with glass covered by steel mesh, show signs of abuse barely hidden by the dark green paint. The halls inside have gray tile floors and are lined by lockers covered with many coats of light brown paint. No conspicuous graffiti or vandalism, except for writing on the desks and scars in the bathrooms, mar the building. Some of the offices and rooms have richly aged wood trim, bright cabinets, and tables. The boys' bathrooms, locked during several periods, are a gloomy gray and brown, with no towels ("they would be stolen or burned"), and felt-pen graffiti on the walls, embellished occasionally with shaving cream. In contrast, the cafeteria's bright yellow walls and small tables seating eight people create a cheerful atmosphere. Lunch periods are well supervised, and students seem to respect the facilities, although faculty report finding dozens of forks, spoons, and the like in the trash can. The library is spacious and carpeted. It houses 12,000 books in high wall shelves and five-foot shelves that break the open space into areas for study. Small tables are equipped with pastel colored chairs. An average of about ten students, usually quiet and on task, are there each period.

SCHOOL COMMITMENT AND PRIDE. A major priority for the principal is to build school spirit. There was, on our first visit, a Monday morning pep rally to celebrate the previous Friday night football victory. The entire student body honored the team in the school auditorium with cheers, songs, short speeches by the coach (who described contributions of specific players in particular parts of the game) and students. The principal, greeted by some booing, praised the team and the student body as she gracefully accepted the game ball.

A few weeks later, several assemblies and special events punctuated homecoming week, honoring the football team and featuring student performances by the band, cheerleaders, pom-pom girls, drill team, a jazz combo, rock group, dance group, a special "dress-up" day, a parade, election and recognition of homecoming court, and the homecoming game and dance. If school spirit is to be measured in decibels and participation in events like this, DeSoto showed impressive commitment.

School spirit notwithstanding, sports teams have a difficult time attracting enough players (the varsity football team had only twenty-one members, girls basketball can barely fill one team). A junior in her first year at DeSoto starred last year on the best girls basketball team in the city but refused to go out for the team at DeSoto because it had only five or six players and lost so many games. A male student, with aspirations for professional football, started on his former school's team, but wouldn't go out at DeSoto because of the team's poor record. In spite of boisterous pep rallies, few spectators attend the games. A former cheerleader reported that she had cheered at some football games with no more than a dozen fans in the stands. A pom-pom girl mentioned that as she carried her pom-poms to school on the bus one morning, an acquaintance asked her where she went to school. Too embarrassed to say DeSoto, she mentioned another school with the same colors. This year's homecoming football game attracted about 400 students, and the team's 6-0 victory produced joyous celebration. DeSoto's struggling teams "play their hearts out," according to one coach. The small number of students and staff who struggle together show a commitment to their respective teams, if not to the school as a whole.

Some students show their commitment by contributing to the daily maintenance of the school, or working as volunteers in the library and main office, or by being part of the stage crew, or helping with audio-visual equipment. The student council sponsors service projects such as food donations, but there is no official student involvement in school policy-making, rule enforcement, or judicial proceedings.

Staff members vary in their commitment to the school. A dedicated core of about twelve teachers and administrators speak enthusiastically about DeSoto, their goals, and activities. They work overtime with students and staff in modifying curriculum, developing competency tests, meeting with students and their parents, raising funds, and inventing new projects to boost the spirit of the entire school community.

There is considerable evidence, however, of staff apathy and even demoralization. Most teachers leave the school promptly at the end of the last period. (The union contract provides that they can be required to attend only one department and one full faculty meeting per month.) In their lounges, teachers can be observed sleeping, playing cards, sitting silently; some grade papers or phone parents of absent students. There is little conversation even at lunch. Complaints about students and other teachers or administrators are frequent, but discussions of curriculum, pedagogy, or how to improve the school seldom occur. Nevertheless, a number of teachers show impressive personal commitment to students in their courses (one teacher made several phone calls trying to find employment for a student in his shop class), and over 70 percent indicated in a survey that faculty responsibility for students, beyond teaching courses, should be increased.

The general lack of pride and enthusiasm for the school appears to arise from constant reminders that the staff has little control and, therefore, finds it difficult to consider the school "theirs." Mandates from the central office have changed the student population and the curriculum. Teachers are assigned to the school or "bumped" from it without regard to their wishes or the interests of the existing staff. Decision-making within the school proceeds through an informal process, rather than formal channels that empower all constituents.

Within this environment there are some pockets of committed students and faculty who do work cooperatively in small groups. These are described by participants with considerable enthusiasm. The office education and distributive education programs, for example, involve students in group activities such as fund raising, banquets, and trips. Program teachers meet students' parents and show special interest in students through supervision of their work experience and helping them find jobs after graduation. A human relations committee participates in workshops with students from other schools, runs dances, and discusses human relations issues at DeSoto. In addition, there are the more traditional activities such as the debate team, musical productions, the newspaper, and athletics.

PERSONAL CARING AND COOPERATION. DeSoto is generally a friendly place. Students and staff are pleasant toward one another. Staff on hall duty do not need to ask students for ID's, because they know them by name. Even while trying to move students through the halls or disciplining them, staff members engage students in friendly banter and gossip.

At one pep assembly, a good deal of booing greeted Mr. T., assistant principal in charge of discipline and director of athletics. He ignored it, urged support of the football team, and placed this in the more general context of support for the whole DeSoto family. Mr. T. emphasized the importance of support for all sports and all academic and nonacademic endeavors. In a later interview, he identified his major goal as the creation of a sense of family within the school, the breaking down of cliques. A few years ago, he told us, blacks, whites, greasers, jocks, and brains were highly divided, even entering the school through separate doors. Now they come in the same doors.

One of DeSoto's major challenges has been to make racial integration work in a school that was previously all white and is now 65 percent white, 35 percent black. Teachers and administrators believe much progress has been made, and continues to be made, in small steps behind the scenes, not through visible programs such as in-service or special parent committees. The Student Human Relations Committee is supervised by a black teacher with special responsibility for human relations in the building. A white teacher in charge of homecoming this year made special efforts to operate an open election for homecoming court. Students voted in homerooms for prince and princess in each class, along with king and queen for the school. They elected blacks as junior and senior princes and homecoming queen. The sophomore prince was of Hispanic origin. Several teachers expressed pride in the integrated homecoming court.

DeSoto has about twelve black teachers, and its black and white assistant principals work well together. Some staff members perceive a strong division between black and white staff, but most do not. Most staff members seem committed to improving race relations and are satisfied with DeSoto's progress, but there is some insecurity, a belief that their progress remains a bit fragile. Fortunately, teachers reported, a large fight between blacks and whites early in the fall was started not by DeSoto students but by outsiders from a predominantly white neighborhood known for racist assaults against black students. News of any student fight is heard with apprehension because of the fear of interracial strife. Students, black and white, generally agree that race relations at DeSoto are positive. A black faculty member remarked, "A few years ago if kids were messing around in assembly you could never expect a black or white kid to tell someone of the opposite race to straighten up [without starting a fight]. Now this can happen and the kid will be supported by responsible kids of either race."

Fellowship and cooperation among the staff as a whole are hard to find. Teachers complain about colleagues who fail to enforce school rules, participate in meetings, or help students. There are also complaints that some teachers have lighter workloads. Some divisions appear drawn along the lines of old-timers vs. newcomers, the committed vs. the apathetic, academic vs. vocational orientation to curriculum, black vs. white. In the fall, a teacher broke up a student fight while other teachers stood by without helping. One teacher suggested that the whole staff could benefit from human relations training. Another recalled that when she first came to DeSoto, they had social gatherings among the fifty faculty members, lending cohesiveness to the school, but they don't have these any more. One example of communal fellowship is the tradition, praised by many, of teachers bringing food to share each Friday in the faculty lounge.

Fragmentation among staff, however, does not preclude special acts of caring between faculty and students. During an assembly, a student announced that it was a special day for a special teacher, and they had a present for her. It was Mrs. D.'s (an English teacher) birthday. Responding to thundering applause and cheers, she came to the stage and tearfully accepted the gift saying, "Is this what I get for yellin' at you kids all these years?"

ORDER AND SECURITY. Teachers and administrators are preoccupied with maintaining order. There is little comment about—or fear of—students attacking or abusing teachers, but incidents such as student fights, smoking, or stealing balances from science labs cause concern. Major problems for teachers, however, are student attendance and tardiness.

The student handbook is seven single-spaced pages of general rules and regulations including, for example, the daily schedule, use of the elevator, attendance policy, immunization, and two pages of discipline procedures (a student may be suspended for failing to show an ID, for using profane language, for destroying a Form 72 card—a teacher report on discipline). Students generally agreed that school rules were well known, but felt they were often not enforced fairly—"Some kids could get away with a lot and other kids were picked on." Students have no formal role in making school rules, in enforcing them, or resolving disciplinary disputes.

Disciplinary actions are usually taken by administrators (who often carry walkie-talkies) either on the spot, when they observe rule infractions, or in response to reports—72 cards—filed by teachers. Several teachers complained about slow response from administrators, one of whom received about three thousand 72 cards in the previous year. Sitting in the main office one day, we saw four students suspended in about forty-five minutes and two parents waiting to have their children reinstated. Usually, discipline problems were handled courteously, but occasionally we heard sarcastic remarks ("Here comes Sally. She must be in trouble again. We could expect as much from her.") One student, dismissed from class for wearing a hat, missed several classes while waiting for an administrator to sign his 72 card.

Administrators respond to one interruption after another. Mr. G. explained:

> Generally I am working on four things at a time, but I know my priorities. I may have two students in my office to reinstate. I get a call there is a fight on the third floor. I shove the students out of my office, lock the door. As I run upstairs, a teacher confronts me, holding a student by the collar, upset about his behavior. I must ignore her to get up to the fight. By the time I reach the third floor, that teacher informs me the situation is under control. All this effort, and what have I accomplished? The two students I started with are still not reinstated, and other teachers had to deal with their unauthorized presence in the hall. Another teacher is upset because I couldn't respond to her discipline problem. I didn't even settle the fight on the third floor.

Later, he said, "I love this school; I love my job; but I just don't have time to talk."

Although the potential of chaos lurks beneath large student gatherings, the staff remains in control. At one assembly, in the midst of much rowdiness during a student-led pledge of allegiance, Mr. I., the band director, hurried to the stage and expressed his anger that the students had failed to conduct the ceremony with care. He demanded that the pledge be recited again. "We're going to stand to say the pledge of allegiance over again, and do it right. Now please stand . . . I pledge . . ." The students cooperated and completed an orderly recitation.

Students who enroll in DeSoto must sign a "contract of mutual understanding" that enumerates responsibilities of school personnel: for example, "To provide a quality education for every student . . . , to treat all individuals equally . . . , to enforce rules and regulations"; responsibilities of students: "To meet minimum competencies in English . . . , to demonstrate respect of authority, property and rights of others, to have the necessary materials for every class including an assignment notebook . . ."; and of parents: "To support the rules and regulations . . . , to see that the student attends school regularly . . . , to encourage your children to be well-groomed . . ." The contract is also signed by the parent/guardian and principal. Ideally, the contract establishes mutual obligations that can be continually invoked in dealing with problems among students, staff, or parents. Apparently it is signed and filed, but not subsequently used. The principal explained that it is not her policy to dwell on rules that cannot be enforced.

## Goals

The official goals of DeSoto High are described in handbooks for students and parents, emphasizing a "strong basic program in a caring environment." The curriculum is aimed toward competency in basic skills relevant to a variety of careers, with a specialty program in finance and small business. Extensive opportunities for career exploration and work experience in the community are offered, along with "strong academic emphasis" for students intending to pursue education in technical schools or colleges. The school's low enrollment facilitates individual attention: "At DeSoto a student is not just one of many, but a unique person."

How did these goals evolve? For several years, the school operated as a small, white, neighborhood school, grades seven through twelve. Affirmative steps to integrate the city's schools in the late 1970s, along with declining enrollments, led to threats a few years ago to close the school, but parents and others campaigned to keep it open. District administration instructed the staff to design a specific program that would serve an identifiable, citywide student population, and not just those from its traditional neighborhood feeder schools.

Constraints imposed by central district policy frequently affected DeSoto's efforts to develop its set of goals. Administrative and union restrictions prevented the school from selecting a new staff appropriate to a new program with a different overall mission. Staff transfers were possible, but generally the school's goals were expected to be tailored to the existing staff philosophy and professional training. Previously, the district had established special programs, such as performing arts, data processing, or college-bound programs, for other high schools, but DeSoto was not allowed to duplicate any of these. Except for some limits on racial balance, no meaningful admission requirements could be exercised; DeSoto had to accept any student in the city who applied. After a team of teachers and administrators at DeSoto had developed an extensive competency-based program (including systematic diagnostic testing, individualized placement, and remediation), the central administration denied support. Furthermore, they required DeSoto to change its specialty to a "developmental" school, whose description by the central office baffled DeSoto staff.

The previous principal directed much of the goal-setting process, relying on an appointed team of teachers and administrators. Issues were discussed among faculty, and input was sought through departmental lines, but major decisions were made by committees or individual staff persons, not by official voting of the entire staff. Since the adoption of the current official program, several new teachers and a new principal have been assigned to the school.

The current set of official goals may well be an imaginative response to the realities of district politics and staff relations within DeSoto, but they do not inspire a focused, unified commitment. Some staff members (for example, the principal, the person in charge of developing the competency-testing program, the person leading the career-education program, and staff in the specialty areas of finance and small business) strongly endorse the official goals. Yet many others are strongly opposed to the career-education emphasis and competency testing. Staff members generally affirm the importance of a caring environment and responding to individual student needs, but several also consider that this is impossible to do for many students in this particular school. An estimated 50 percent of staff members perceive a lack of clarity and consensus in DeSoto's goals; several feel they are aimed in too many different directions, try to serve too many interests. An administrator described the program as "rag-tag," but was committed, nonetheless, to "making it work."

Students know about career emphasis, but they never mention this or any other special program—such as finance specialty, work experience or competency in basic skills—as a reason for choosing DeSoto. Usually they mention such factors as living in the neighborhood, having friends who go there, or, most frequently, the fact that they didn't get into their first-choice school. They frequently mention the friendly atmosphere of a small school as one of DeSoto's main strengths.

Trying to be both a career-oriented (finance and small business) and comprehensive school creates problems. Not more than one-third of the seniors are enrolled in the career-oriented program. To meet the needs of other students, college prep courses and other courses (for example, industrial arts, music and art) must compete for resources. Even within career orientation, courses compete for students (office education vs. distributive education vs. real estate).

Staff members differ fairly widely in their educational philosophies. Some maintain that a specific career orientation is particularly appropriate for DeSoto's students. Others believe that students at this age are not capable of making informed career choices, that they need a broad, general education prior to undertaking career responsibilities. Staff members note that work-experience programs that take seniors, and some juniors, away from school in the afternoon, deprive those students of valuable course work and after-school activities. That also hinders school spirit, and deprives younger students at school of older role models. While a pragmatic case is emphatically made for DeSoto's goals (based on students' motivation, ability, economic resources), it does not reflect unified focused faculty endorsement.

The goals of a school reveal themselves not only in official statements describing the organization's instructional mission, but also in the personal intentions of key staff members. When asked about their priorities for the school, administrators did not emphasize the specific instructional programs, but spoke of building school spirit, maintaining order and continuing progress in race relations.

## Curriculum

Staff members describe the curriculum as aimed mainly at the needs of students who are not bound for college. The required tenth-grade course in careers encourages students to plan immediately for the world of work, including whatever further education may be necessary. A career center provides computer-processed information on a variety of professional fields, the educational background required for each profession, and the specific institutions that offer training. Ideally, students select courses in the eleventh and twelfth grades that are consistent with career preferences identified in the tenth grade. Seniors are encouraged to leave school in the afternoon to participate in various forms of work experience. Of the 1981 graduating class,

24 percent intended to go to college, 15 percent to technical and trade schools, and the remainder to full-time work.

Courses are organized into Carnegie units (usually 1 course for a year equals 1 unit), with 18 units required for graduation. Of these 18 units, the following are requirements: social studies, 4; English, 3; mathematics, 2; science, 1; physical education, 2; career education, ½; driver education, ½. DeSoto exceeds district graduation requirements in mathematics, social studies, career and driver education, and also requires students—except seniors—to carry 6 to 7 units per year. Most graduating seniors complete from 18 to 20 units, but several earn 23 or more.

Ninth- and tenth-grade students spend much of their time in common required courses, with the following typical schedules.

Ninth Grade: English 9 (general course in English usage, with emphasis on writing), urban citizenship, algebra or math concepts, physical science, physical education, two electives.

Tenth Grade: English (two courses selected from seven options), world history, geometry or vocational math, career education and driver education, physical education, two electives.

Electives increase in the eleventh and twelfth grades, where course work and on-the-job placements are offered in office education (typing, accounting, record keeping, shorthand); distributive education (retail selling, marketing, merchandising); and a specialty in finance and small business (banking services, real estate, small business management). Directed by DeSoto teachers, each of these programs requires course work in grades eleven and twelve, along with twelfth-grade job-placement in the afternoons. About 60 of the 180 seniors were enrolled in the three programs combined.

As alternatives to the business-oriented programs, students may choose other forms of training and work experience beyond school. The EPIC program (Educational Participation in the Community) places students in non-paid service work in schools, hospitals, and nursing homes. Several of the approximately twenty students enrolled saw this as an introduction to careers in social service. In addition, the vocational education counselor placed students in the following diverse programs.

| Programs | Estimated Number of Seniors Placed in 1980 |
|---|---|
| The City Area Technical College | 45 |
| Work Experience (scattered placements not connected with DeSoto course work) | 30 |
| General Education Degree (special program to gain high school equivalency diploma) | 15 |
| Health Careers (program sponsored by the district) | 2 |
| Specialty Programs (offered by other high schools) | 6 |

The nature of students' work and learning in these placements is described later, but it should be recognized here that the greatest attention is given to job-entry preparation rather than to four-year college or university programs.

Students interested in academic preparation for college can pursue additional course work in English, social studies, mathematics, and science. But offerings in these areas are limited. For example, the four-year requirement in social studies includes three specifically required year-long courses and only four half-credit electives, from which two must be chosen in the fourth year. Spanish is the only foreign language offered.

DeSoto has no official system of tracking. Special education students (about 140) have separate programs, but for the student body at large, ability grouping occurs only in the placement of students in *subjects* that represent different ability levels. Algebra, for example, demands more mathematics ability than does math concepts. Within a given subject, however, such as algebra or urban citizenship, classes are not programmed according to ability level. Teachers occasionally mention the problem of dealing with diverse students within a class (especially in reading levels), but their most frequent complaints are the generally low level of student motivation and talent, not the fact of diverse abilities within classes.

COMPETENCY TESTING   In the fall of 1981, DeSoto launched a program of competency testing in English, social sciences, mathematics, and science (the district requires only a reading proficiency test). The tests, constructed by the DeSoto staff to reflect the actual curriculum, are scheduled yearly. Students who fail to meet passing criteria are supposed to be placed in remediation programs (though these arrangements are presently vague). By 1985, DeSoto hopes to secure district approval for a notation on diplomas indicating which of the tests have been passed. Since the tests are administered as part of normal courses, students are largely unaware of the program. Teachers vary in their support, but, in general, the commitment to the competency-testing program seems tentative. Mr. B., the faculty coordinator who put much effort into organizing the program over the past few years, is realistically concerned that teachers may not cooperate, that the tests themselves may not have good psychometric properties, that proper remediation may not be arranged. It remains to be seen whether the testing program assists students and teachers.

COUNSELING   Where does the student turn for guidance in planning a program from among about 120 courses offered? The obvious place is the guidance office, and some students see this as a valuable resource, "if you get the right counselor." Many, however, find better help in the career education course, the career center, homeroom, or through teachers who take special interest in them. Of the four white male counselors, three have general responsibility for the student body; the fourth specializes in work experience and vocational counseling. The three counselors try to see each of their 360 students twice per year, and students must secure counselor approval for their class schedule and changes, which often occur when students don't get along with teachers. Some students will also visit a counselor to discuss emotional or family problems.

Beginning in 1981, each counselor stayed with a student through the student's career at DeSoto (previously, students changed counselors each year from the ninth to the twelfth grade). How, in fact, ninth graders select their programs, or which criteria counselors use to dispense advice (ability testing, student aspirations, parents' desires, students' previous records) is not particularly clear. There is no coherent system of periodic assessment and programming for each student.

Counselors are busy—meeting with students, testing, making phone calls—and are frequently out of the office. At eight o'clock one morning, a parent sat with her child in the guidance office, waiting to see a counselor. None were present, explained the secretary, because they were giving some tests that morning. Soon, one of the counselors appeared. After being introduced to the parent, he confirmed the situation. "We're tied up with testing this morning. I couldn't see you until eleven o'clock," he said, and hurried into the hall. The parent said she couldn't wait until eleven o'clock and left with her daughter. The tests, as it turned out, were mandated by the district, but DeSoto counselors did not use them in any significant way in their advising.

Counselors report that their large caseloads prevent thoughtful, consistent attention to each student. One counselor believes the department itself is disorganized and fragmented. Another believes the curriculum offers too many options and keeps students so busy that rational planning is impossible. Several students commented that counselors spend so much time with kids in trouble that the average student gets little help. A group of minority students, however, praised one counselor for organizing the college-bound students' club. It meets periodically to inform minority students about college entrance procedures and special opportunities to help them prepare for college.

We heard substantial student and faculty criticism of the guidance department, but almost all students believed that if they really needed help on an important problem, there was at least one adult somewhere in the school they could turn to and trust. Homerooms usually remain intact for four years, and although they are not officially designated to fulfill the guidance function, several homeroom teachers use this time to develop close relationships with students to help them with program decisions and to monitor their grades and progress in school. Selected teachers throughout the school—for example, in the career programs (office education, distributive education, banking), industrial arts, or coaching—take an active interest in some students' futures.

## Internal Decision-Making

Curriculum policy at DeSoto has evolved through an informal process, with the principal making final decisions. The whole faculty may discuss certain issues in meetings or in-service sessions, but they do not vote formally to influence any aspect of the DeSoto curriculum. Such graduation requirements as four years of social studies and one year of science, or the required career information course for tenth graders, for example, were instituted without any formal faculty endorsement.

The principal seeks faculty advice through a building committee of elected representatives. It meets about twice a month, but deals primarily with logistical issues (student locker keys, parent conference schedules, field trip forms), and student discipline policy (handling of the 72 cards, hall sweeps, when the classroom doors should be locked, whether to establish a "holding tank" for tardy students, lack of administrative response to teachers' problems with students). A main function of the committee is to express faculty complaints and to represent the union's position. While a grievance was pending regarding athletics, it was necessary to remind teachers not to assist in any way in the performance of these duties. Conversation in the committee is informal, but minutes are written and recorded (usually on a single sheet).

Departments are required to meet after school once a month. The meeting we visited dealt primarily with logistical issues (the times and places for showing a film), although some discussion occurred on the desirability of ability grouping. Departments vary in their cohesion and the extent to which they take collective action on curriculum issues. Our general impression, however, is that little meeting time, either for the whole faculty or for the individual departments, is devoted to discussion of curriculum policy.

This is not to suggest that faculty members don't care about curriculum. Teachers express strong opinions on such topics as the balance between high quality general education versus specific vocational courses, the need for more integration and cooperation among separate vested interests within the curriculum, the value of the newly required career education course and newly implemented competency testing, and the process of counseling and advising students. These matters, however, appear to be aired only in private conversations among colleagues, not in public or group forums. It may be more comfortable to avoid professional conflict in the teachers' lounge or in department and faculty meetings, but this leaves important issues unresolved, or resolved only by administrative fiat. The absence of public discussion and consensual resolution appears to undermine staff commitment to the collective enterprise.

Faculty are divided about the necessity for more formal faculty input into policy-making. Several, including the principal and key administrators, believe an informal approach to consulting and feedback works best. Others regret the lack of systematic faculty participation. While it is widely agreed that most faculty would be unwilling to invest much additional time in deliberation on school policy and governance, the majority of teachers reported they wanted more participation.

## Students

One of us followed Ray, a sixteen-year-old sophomore, for a full day. The account of that day follows.

> In the course of the day, Ray changed, in my eyes, from an embarrassed, reticent, slight, fuzzy-faced kid in a faded black T-shirt to an articulate loner who took pains to take care of me. At the end of a class, he would hurry out the door without me, but would wait in the halls to make sure I could follow him.
>
> By the end of the third period, he called his older brother over to introduce us. "Good," his brother said, "maybe today you'll go to all your classes." Ray didn't answer, but a period later he couldn't go to class because his 72 form hadn't been signed by an assistant principal. This was the fourth day in a row that he missed that class (because he had worn a hat), but he didn't seem concerned when he first told me. He did, however, put on a long-sleeved shirt over his T-shirt before reporting to the assistant principal. During the forty minutes in which we both waited for the form to be signed, he became increasingly agitated and nervous, tapping on the door, looking through the window to the office, snapping his fingers.
>
> Before I met him, I knew, from the transcript handed to me the night before, that Ray was a sixteen-year-old sophomore who had earned only 3.5 credits out of 6.0 credit hours taken at DeSoto High. Later I was told by one of his reading teachers that he was "learning disabled." In that reading class, Ray was doing exercises from a 1959 edition of *Breaking the*

*Reading Barrier*. The assignment was to identify statements as being either true or false. His teacher approached and asked Ray to read out loud. He did pretty well except for making words like "sickly" into "sticky." He didn't seem to pay much attention to the task. Then the teacher noticed something wrong. The sentence in question was: "All people who study hard get good grades." Ray had marked it true, and the teacher obviously disagreed. "Haven't you studied hard and not gotten good grades?" she asked. Ray replied, "I've never studied hard, so I don't know." After the class the teacher told me that she had never seen Ray pay so much attention to his work. "You should shadow him every day," she said. "He'd be a different kid."

He was a different kid in an area technical college class that he attends every afternoon. In transit there—getting a sandwich, walking to the bus stop and waiting for the bus—he was much more talkative about DeSoto. He lives close; his brothers have gone there; it was a good school until integration. Some of the blacks, he thinks, don't care about the school.

He also talked about his future. He plans to get his diploma and work in an auto shop. He ticks off the credits he thinks he'll need to graduate in two years.

He talked about his friends and interests. He has friends all over town, likes bike racing, has a dirt-trail bike of his own that he is working on and races.

He also expressed concern for me, for how I would get back to the school, and he arranged to take me to the bus stop during a break in his class.

The biggest change in Ray, however, was seen in the classroom itself. He was involved, engaged, and thinking all the time—talking with his class-mates, asking questions of his teacher, and trying to work out the problems he had given himself. The class focused on small engines, but the process and intent was investigative, scientific, and highly engaging. Ray's partner (and his best helper) was black.

So who is Ray? I think I know him a little better after that day, but is he the taciturn, nearly sullen resister at DeSoto, or is he the committed, highly engaged and involved student at the small-engines class at the area technical college? And Ray is only one student at DeSoto.

According to Mrs. Y., the art teacher, "Each kid has a million personalities at this age; you don't know which one will arrive when." The question of who will arrive when can be taken literally as well. Truancy at DeSoto is high, but many of those who do arrive get up before 6:00 A.M. each day to catch a 6:30 A.M. bus that arrives at school in time for the 7:45 A.M. homeroom class.

Students often express both pride and shame in the school. Many students praise their valuable friends in school, some good teachers, and especially the small size of the school, while also feeling ashamed of DeSoto's reputation. Some students comment on the high level of school spirit, others say there is no school spirit at all. The ninth graders, according to juniors and seniors, have the least school spirit, and yet the ninth graders seem most upbeat about the school, their teachers, and their classes. Seniors who have been at DeSoto for six years (they were junior high students there when DeSoto was a grades seven through twelve school, and all are white) identify themselves as the last ones to *really* care about DeSoto. These same seniors also complain most about the school's deterioration because it is no longer a neighborhood school, and they are the most critical of the student body, the administration, and the teachers. Comparing the more up-beat views of the ninth graders with the critical views of the seniors, there is no reason to believe school spirit is on a persistent decline.

When students are asked what a good teacher is, the typical response is, "Someone who cares for you as a person." If asked what this means in terms of classroom instruction, they will describe a teacher who goes step by step, slowly, who makes sure that everyone in the class understands each step before going on to the next. This is a view of education that many would label as "mechanistic." For these students, learning is a slow, accumulative process, where progress is gradual but assured if you understand each step entirely. Students appear to tolerate and respect work sheets, but not open-ended questions. Most importantly, they feel that teachers should never leave a student behind, because if they do (and by student accounts many do at DeSoto), then a student may never catch up and can become hopelessly lost in the course.

Students express mixed feelings about their teachers. Nearly all feel they have at least one teacher a year who is good, who cares for them, to whom they can go, and in whose class they feel comfortable and "successful."

Students' views of fellow students of other races are generally positive and open. It is acceptable to discuss integration, race, friendship, and racial conflict at DeSoto, and the students' responses to such issues are usually thoughtful. They mention race relations as a problem in the city, and in many other schools in the city that are nominally integrated. A black girl in a small interracial group spoke with no apparent animosity of a core of black "toughs" who just come to school wanting "to do to all whites what has been done to their great grand-parents." Generally, the students, black and white, view DeSoto as a relatively safe school with few racial conflicts and almost no large-scale confrontations. They agree there are some bad whites around the neighborhood who will gang up on young blacks when they see a chance.

When black kids are asked about race in DeSoto, the typical response is, "It's not bad here, it's almost good. I have a few white friends that I probably wouldn't have if I had gone to other schools in the city." The small size of the school apparently helps. Students speak of race and friends in personal terms: "She is a good friend, you know, because she doesn't put on airs one way or another, she is herself and we can talk one-to-one. "Some white students complain (perhaps parroting their parents): "I'm not against integration, mind you, I just don't see why we can't have neighborhood schools, that's all." And some black students identify certain teachers as being "racists."

The most serious conversations, concerns, anxieties, and hopes of students at DeSoto focus on future employment. They like working. The idea of a job is a good idea, much better to most than the idea of continued schooling for the sake of learning. They are worried.

The major concern in almost all the conversations we had with students, including Ray, the sophomore described earlier, was that no jobs would be available after they graduated. What would happen to them?

Most of the older students at DeSoto work after school. About half the seniors participate in special work-study programs, and many more are employed by fast-food places and other minimum-wage establishments. Many of the students like this work. They find some satisfaction being in the real world and earning money. Although they work primarily to have spending money, not to pursue career steps, the work experience often stimulates their concerns for schooling. More than once, students told us that after having a job, they began to look at school more positively in terms of how their studies could help them in their future jobs, which they described as grocery store clerk, auto mechanic, factory worker, or telephone line repairman.

Students who express the deepest worries about DeSoto High are those who plan to go to college. They are a minority. Many of the guidance counselors and teachers believe DeSoto would benefit if there were more college-bound students, but those who are college-bound seriously question DeSoto's academic quality. "I wonder what is going to happen to me because I went to DeSoto," said a black senior girl, drawing nods and comments from the rest of the small group (both black and white). "I have had such a limited education here compared to my friends at other schools. I want to go into nursing, and I've had almost no science to speak of and hardly any math. I know I'm not going to score well on the national tests, so how am I even going to get into college? And if I do get in, how am I going to compete with other students who got so much more education in high school than I did. I tell you, we here at DeSoto who want to go to college have been cheated."

### Teachers

Teachers at DeSoto High judge themselves to be both the strongest and the weakest features of the school. When asked about DeSoto's greatest strength, teachers responded: "There is still a nucleus of dedicated, sincere staff members—at all levels—who are determined to make this school work"; "[There are] ten to fifteen teachers whose dedication holds the school together"; "The majority of the staff are fine professional educators and really care about the success of their students."

In response to a question about DeSoto's most serious weakness, teachers responded: "Sadly, there is a large group of staff members which either doesn't care or doesn't have energy enough to work with the other group [that does]"; "[There are] teachers who are not even bodily present for assigned duties, are only physically present for assigned duties, are destructive to students via racist/sexist or simply cruel attitudes and behaviors, or [in the case of some males] are overtly seductive to vulnerable females"; "Some teachers are real leakers and often appear to be out to 'get' the students."

Seven teachers were particularly memorable and contributed significantly to our understanding of DeSoto High School. Along with many other teachers at DeSoto, they expressed their concerns about teaching, their ideas on what is right and wrong with DeSoto, and their individual styles of coping with the conditions they were experiencing. We introduce them in the following vignettes.*

*Mr. N.*  Within our first two days at DeSoto we had nearly a dozen encounters with Mr. N. and they didn't diminish much after that. He is a metal technology teacher, short and stocky, with nearly unmatched bursts of energy, an emotional and forceful delivery, and a friendly and open manner.

Our first encounter with Mr. N. was in the hall. He approached us that first day, identified himself, and began talking about kids. "They have no respect for teachers or authority at all," especially black kids. "Heaven knows what our fathers and grandfathers did to their fathers and grandfathers; now we're suffering the consequences. I don't blame them." He quickly assessed society: "It's all going downhill"; the school: "There just isn't the support we need, so few of us faculty even care." About his commitment to teaching, he says, "I have one hundred and twenty grades to make out in five days, each takes about half an hour to do it right. You tell me, how am I going to do that the way I should?" He says his work load has affected his marriage: "I'm working till early in the morning these days and over the weekend, and my wife doesn't understand it. 'What's wrong?' she says. 'Can't you do that at school? You're not being paid doctors' fees, you know.' She needn't tell me!" In the cafeteria that day, he saw kids throwing their forks in the garbage pail along with the food they didn't eat. "I just couldn't take it any more," he said, and then described how he rolled up his sleeves, put his hands in the garbage pail and took the time and effort to pull out 76 forks! "I had to wash my hands, up past my elbows, three times," he continued, "before the smell went away." Mr. N. hurried along at our sides, telling us about the absences of students—how it's one thing to be absent from English class, but when a kid is absent from his metalworking class, maybe he has missed a lecture on the safety measures for the next project. The kid can lose a finger or a hand and then who's responsible? "I tell you," he says, "it's a never-ending battle." He promised to see us again, because he had more that we should hear.

Mr. N. was true to his word. One day before school, about 7:30 A.M., he came up to me and began: "Everybody these days wants something for nothing, you know. No one wants to work, but they want the best and they think it's owed them. I tell you our society is just going to hell, no one knows the meaning of work, work has no positive value at all." He explained these comments further by exclaiming: "My wife won't go back to work. I tried to talk her into going back to work but she won't do it." He went on about how they both wanted to take trips and looked forward to retirement,

* Some of these vignettes were written in the present tense (with some reference to the thought of the interviewer) in order that the reader can better share the experience of the interview.

but have no money to enjoy either. He then left quickly to get to homeroom on time.

He was a toolmaker for many years before he became a high school teacher. He said toolmaking was good money, but it was too lonely and routine. He liked people too much to be happy doing that all his life, so he went to night school and tried a few things like insurance and real estate, but ended up with teaching. And he loves it. It's working with people all the time, the kids, and it draws on what he knows well. If you sit in on his class, you see a teacher who cares. He takes time before class to explain and demonstrate to students a tool that they won't be expected to use in this class, but that he thinks they might find interesting. He gives them responsibilities in class and expects them to work together and produce. He is interested in their work, gives it his utmost attention, measures it carefully, and speaks to the kids personally and individually about their work. He carries pictures of former students, of their products, and awards won. He finds his metalworking students jobs, and keeps in contact with them well beyond high school. He is proud of his own work, showing it off at the same time as he shows off the work of some of his better metalworking students. He has a display at the local teachers convention, has spent considerable time planning for the display, and, with professional pride, explains and shows why his projects, designed for his classes, differ from other projects given in textbooks or normally used in metalworking classes throughout the city. He proudly shows a variety of large machines, pointing to one metal press, for example, that he bought for $6,000. In short, he's committed, he's personal with the kids, he cares about them, and he is involved with the content of his courses. He likes *teaching*, and he has the energy to continue to keep trying to teach what he knows to kids.

But even in class, there is something wrong. During a class, he told us that blacks don't know what work is, that they really don't want to work, especially with their hands, and that they have no role models to follow. Yet, three feet in front of us were two black students out of only six who are in class. One of the blacks, a girl, was obviously the best metalworker in the class of ninth graders. As she pounded on her chisel, Mr. N. asked her if she was going to continue in metal technology. Yes, she answered quietly, she was going to take Metal Tech 1 next year because she likes it. Mr. N. was delighted—and then made a remark about her cooking for her brothers or boyfriends.

An older boy, perhaps a senior, came into the room and was told to leave, but then Mr. N. brought him over. Mr. N. said he likes him, had him in a beginning class a few years ago, but that he didn't take any more metalworking classes. He then asked the boy why he hadn't continued, and the boy said, "Because I wasn't all that interested in metal." Mr. N. responded excitedly: "See, I told you, these kids go on if they're interested, if not, there's plenty more for them to do!" Mr. N. asked the student what he was taking and the answer was "work experience." What that meant, we were told, was washing dishes, but for pay and two high school credits. The student said he enjoyed it, it was money, after all, and besides he was becoming a cook, too. Mr. N. asked him if he lived with his parents and the student replied that he lived with his mother. Mr. N. responded, quickly, "See what I told you? First it's two, then it's one, then it's going to be no one interested in him. The country is going to pot. I don't know where it's going to end. At least my kids have two parents and they listen to me, even now that they're out of high school! It's so important," he said to the student, "that you stay in school and get that degree." The student agreed. "That," they both said together, "is the ticket to advancement."

*Mr. O.*  Mr. O., a tall, unassuming young man with a master's degree in education, is working for another master's degree in counseling. He has finished his graduate courses in counseling but needs to spend a year as an unpaid intern. He and his wife (who also works) don't think they can afford that year without pay. "When you come down to it," he said, "counseling is depressing job. You work with the bums, the irate parents, and you can't really help the kids because of so much red tape." The trick, added Mr. O., is to get certified in as many areas as possible, to be employable no matter what comes up.

Mr. O. doesn't get as close to his students as Mr. N. We observed a physics class of twelve students, for example, where he passed out papers and stayed behind his desk while the kids worked first on a quiz and then on a work sheet. He talked to them, giving them the answers and explaining the problems where necessary, but always kept his distance.

Quietly, as the students took a quiz, he introduced us to the classroom by saying, "Isn't this (referring to the room, desk, etc.) depressing?" He then showed us the chemical storage room: "You want to see something *really* sickening?" Later he asked, through another teacher, that we visit him again after school. It was late in the afternoon of our last day of visits to DeSoto High when we talked again. He was sitting alone at his desk. The first thing he wanted us to know was that he had been nervous in the class we had visited. He was worried that his nervousness was visible to us, but we assured him that it was not and he relaxed a little and talked about himself and teaching.

"When I entered through the door of this room for the first time," he began, "I was as depressed as I was in getting on the plane to Vietnam. The doors on the cupboards and workbenches were all torn apart, the equipment was all broken, there was even broken glass around the room. Then I went to the back storage room for the chemicals and it was even more depressing. It took me weeks of many hours a day before I even got the room to look like this." (It's still a pretty drab room, with dirty dark-tan paint on the walls and little else except a large water-stained periodic table high up one wall near the door.) "There are so few possibilities for science here. With the curriculum scheduled as it is, for example, the seniors can't take chemistry because it's given in the afternoon and most of the seniors have a job then. In the labs, I have $20,000 of equipment, but most of it is broken. I have little money for equipment, no acceleration timer, the pulleys are busted and broken. There is no experiment where all the necessary equipment works. If I had more modern and working equipment, I would have more experiments and lab work. I know the kids want it that way, and so do I."

We asked about funding. "I'm not sure where the funds come from for science, whether it's from the principal, the science director for the schools, the district, I don't know." There was a pause before he continued.

"In DeSoto High, you know, there aren't that many kids going on to college, so there aren't that many kids motivated to take science. Maybe there is something I can do to make science more appropriate to them. I've been looking for textbooks that do that, and I have found one, a new textbook that relates physics to industrial arts.

"It's a depressing kind of situation, really. The kids are okay, the salary is not so bad with the summers off, but I just don't have the facilities to do my work. Sometimes I think I would just like to transfer to the new high school across town, the one just built a few years ago, but it's so difficult. Every science teacher in the city wants to go there. Every year, it seems, they allow us less and less money for items and the items cost more and more; so little can be bought. Some days, when I leave this place, I'm up, but some days it's so awful. I'm not sure I have more up days than the other ones, though.

"I've been thinking, what else can I get into besides teaching? You know, as teachers get older, the disciplinary problems get worse. I've had twelve years in teaching now. I started out in a junior high school in the inner city in the late sixties. Each day there my stomach was in a knot before getting to the front door of the school. It was a terrible place and a terrible time. Girls would be fighting, boys would be fighting, at times the whole school would be fighting with knives, clubs, you name it. I'll tell you this: I was drafted to go to Vietnam that first year, and I was happy to be drafted! The school system offered to have me deferred and I said, 'No.' You see, I wasn't prepared for that school at all. Schools of education don't help; it's all on-the-job training. I was happier, I felt safer, had less anxiety and fear in Vietnam than I had in that junior high. It's the truth. In that school, every day I was under tension, it was a constant battle. At least in Vietnam, there were times to relax, times when you knew you were safe, when you weren't *always* under tension.

"Middle schools are so much tougher to teach in than high schools, there is so much more fatigue.

"You know, a couple of weeks ago I saw Mr. C. walking down the halls, and he was walking around here happy as all get out, and I was wondering why. Why would he be so happy? Whistling, saying hello to people, things like that. I couldn't figure it out. Now I know. He took early retirement and he was retiring in a month!"

*Mr. L.* Mr. L. has taught at DeSoto High for thirty-two years. He was the head football coach until three years ago, and the math department chairman until last year. He still teaches Advanced Math II, the most advanced math course in the school. The course is mostly trigonometry and algebra. The day we visited, they were doing angular velocity and momentum problems using the formulas

$$\frac{D}{180} = \frac{r}{\pi}, v = rw, \text{ and } s = r0.$$

He told us earlier that this was his best class and that these students were the top ten in the senior class. As top kids, he said, they're average. The students were working on the problems at the blackboard. The two girls in the class worked alone, sometimes listening to the boys talk together. One girl was pushed aside for another boy, who came in late. She had to erase her work, and, for the rest of the period, tried to reach over a filing cabinet to get to her part of the blackboard. Only five students were present (there was a senior meeting that adjourned late). Mr. L. began the class by saying, "That's all right, we don't have that much exciting anyway." He invited us back to talk during a computer programming class, where, he said, the students would be working on their own. Here is some of what he had to say.

"For a good part of my thirty-two years here, DeSoto High was the best high school in the city. All the kids knew that, and educators came from around the country to visit this school to see how good schools are run. Now there are just so many interruptions. Like kids staying over in one class to take a test and then coming late to this class. The first ten minutes of any class now is pretty bad; but I'm just too tired to complain any more. Historically, DeSoto High has always been the smallest school in the city. When the school had grades seven through twelve it was a great situation because the kids were really our responsibility. After all, we had them for six years! For those kids who went on to college, we used to have all their college grades posted in the front hall, and that was good. Teachers used to run down there and check on the work of their former students; that's the way it should be. We used to have about 30 percent of the kids at DeSoto go on to college. Although this was always a middle class, blue-collar neighborhood, there were aspiring parents who supported the school. We had honor study halls and we were nationally famous for them. These study halls were in ten classrooms, each with fifteen students and no teachers.

One student would check around between the various study halls, but that was it. It was a cadet system of students, with captains and a general who, at the time, were the only ones [policing corridors]. Only one teacher was responsible for all this. Now there are teachers all over the place.

"The kids are no different now. Just three years ago they called me 'sir' on the football field. I know if I went back to coaching, they'd call me 'sir' again, and we'd do well, too. No, the students haven't changed. What has changed is what the administrators and the teachers allow.

"Coaching football was always my first love, but I left it because there was no appreciation for the work that you put in. For years, I *lived* that sport for three months, working late, planning, scouting other teams. My wife couldn't wait for me to get out of that. You know, although we were always the smallest school and the smallest team in the city, ten years ago we were number one in the state. But there was no administrative support in a thousand different details. Finally, it was just too much. At one time, I coached gymnastics here from six-thirty to eight in the morning. For a few years, I also coached basketball for no pay—and no thanks. They just don't realize that the coaches can be a great rallying point for school spirit. Do you know, in this building there are five coaches who quit and now don't coach? There is no return for your investment; all there is is disenchantment with the whole thing. And it's not just sports. We used to have a talent show here, a real big thing, and the kids were *good*. We'd have it for two nights, but that stopped about ten years ago.

"Now I'm one of those who isn't involved. I've removed myself. If I hear a commotion in the halls, I just close my door and call downstairs for help. I stay right here, hide in my room, and don't get involved any longer. As far as the courses I teach go, they're not much. Computers are the big thing now, so I teach this introductory course in computer programming. I went to summer school a few years back to get the training to do that. Years ago it was Sputnik, now it's computers. I can teach better courses than I teach. I *like* algebra, but we don't teach that much of it any more.

"Things are different now; the younger teachers' expectations are different now. I had assumed you had to wait to teach the better courses, the advanced courses. It was a matter of seniority, you know. But now that is not the case much. The women in this department wanted advanced courses and I fought it for a while, but they got support and I didn't. So I resigned my chairmanship this year. Now I waste my time teaching general math, though I could give so much more in higher, more advanced courses.

"Years ago, I used to be proud of the quality of the school. I wanted my children to go here. But no longer can I say this. As it is now, I would not permit my children to go to this school. I can't imagine how we can get North Central accreditation, given what we do here now. And this has happened quickly, like in the last five years or so.

"I can't see things improving, either. There was remodeling here at

DeSoto High about five years ago, and even that was done horribly. The design of the gym and bleachers were all botched up, and you can't even get a car into the new auto mechanics room. What killed us was when they made us a non-neighborhood school and then gave us all the fragmented programs. They're even doing insurance here. Everything is picked arbitrarily. The kids? It looks like some of them were never in a classroom before in their lives; they have no discipline at all, they just walk to the windows at any time during class to look outside, and then they wonder why they shouldn't. There are just so many interruptions. We used to have a rule—no announcements, no passes; now look at it. My buddies here are retiring now. Mr. C. is taking early retirement and leaving before Christmas. I still have ten years to go; I don't really know how I'm going to make it. What about going to another school? Why? They're all the same, we're all in the same boat."

## Mrs. H.

Mrs. H. is the office education and typing teacher. She has taught for thirteen years and is an impressive person—direct, honest, confident, concerned, organized. We talked with some of the employers to whom Mrs. H. sends her senior office education students, and they are impressed. One personnel manager in the largest and most modern bank building in the central city called her students "consistently the very best I have ever seen in the city; I wish they all were like that." She was surprised and very pleased to hear that—she must not be getting these comments directly.

Mrs. H. talks seriously and with commitment about the work-study programs at DeSoto. One of her concerns is the emphasis on recruiting the required number of students for a program (not enough students, no program), rather than on the quality of the students. She acknowledges that she is talking competition here because there are a number of programs that compete for the same students at DeSoto. In office education, she is very concerned about the quality of the students and the standards of the program. Sometimes, she believes, there is misselling at DeSoto—for example, when a junior is given a job, which is against the rules in these programs. Her own classes, however, are larger now than they have ever been. There are 26 juniors in her introductory course and about 20 in her senior course. She says five of her office education students this year are boys—a breakthrough, because the guidance counselors steer the boys away from office work. Not long ago, for example, one boy wanted to take shorthand but the guidance counselor wouldn't let him. "That's not a boy's job, that's a girl's job," he was told. Last year the guidance office didn't want to accept a student as class valedictorian because she was in office education! (Which, as Mrs. H. points out, was only one credit hour on her transcript.) We ask her why the counselors would act this way. She answers quickly, "Because they are all men." Then she grins and says, "So are you."

Mrs. H. goes on to describe her office education course with its prerequisite (Typing I) and syllabus. We are impressed and find it interesting, and say so. She replies that the kids seem to enjoy it, but, getting serious, she tells us the content is inherently boring. The seniors are interested because there are no books (the introductory typing class is mostly from a textbook). They like their work in electronic calculators, but not in data processing because of its emphasis on book instruction. They complain that the teachers won't help them, and they have trouble comprehending from reading alone. She returns to this problem later, and hopes that Mr. B. and others involved in competency testing (and teaching) will be successful. In English, math, language, and reading, her students just don't have the skills, the basics, says Mrs. H., and so she's teaching them these basic skills in office education along with the rest of her syllabus. "These kids today have really missed out," she adds sadly.

Mrs. H. came to DeSoto eight years ago, after being "excessed" from a different school. A few years before that, she had turned down the same position at DeSoto because of its small size and because of its poor reputation in the black community. For a few years, she was nearly the only black teacher at DeSoto. After teaching in other schools, Mrs. H. says, "You wouldn't find a better place to work than DeSoto. It's small and there aren't as many hassles as you get in larger, more impersonal schools. That doesn't mean it's perfect, not by a long shot." For example, DeSoto is the only school she knows with no coordination between the specialty areas and office education or distributive education. She mentions other schools with large specialty programs in banking and computing that feed their students into the office education courses. In DeSoto, what you have, says Mrs. H., are six different programs in competition for kids. At one time, she did help teach the real estate kids office education on her own preparation time, but she doesn't any more. "What can the kids do in real estate," she asks, "other than office and clerical work? Surely, they can't sell houses!" When she came here eight years ago, she thought DeSoto would be like the other schools, where office education is a culminating course rather than a competitor of other specialized courses. But it isn't, she points out again. "Who is responsible for this?" we ask, and she responds, "Now I am not sure. Just yesterday, I heard you talking to Mr. B., who I thought was responsible for this at DeSoto, and he said he's not, that the central office is. But that doesn't make sense either, so now I don't know."

Mrs. H. talks about her students with warmth and enthusiasm. Her joy in teaching comes from the kids and their response to her. The kids, she says, will do what you expect them to do. If you don't expect them to work, they won't. She refers to the ninth graders, new to DeSoto, and the need to be very clear about the work that they are expected to do outside class. She gives the example of one who has been arrested for robbery a couple of times and who would have been taken from DeSoto and placed elsewhere.

Instead, she gave him an ultimatum: "You come to class every day and do your work or out you go. Even if you are sick, you call me every day." Now, two months later, he is the best one in her class, is there every day, does his work, and likes himself better. Mrs. H. enjoys the kids "because," she says, "they have a lot of energy."

Mrs. H. shows me some letters from former students. One is working and taking night courses at the local technical college; another has worked for a few years and is now paying her way through law school; a third is taking medical technology. Although she likes the students, the parents, and the teaching, she doesn't like the travel in her job. She visits the parents of each student in the summer, for an hour or more, telling them about the program and what their child can expect from it. She visits the students on the job, seeing each one every five weeks or so. She travels around the city to find job placements for her senior year students in office education. Some places, like the large bank we visited, have had students for years, but some she starts new each year. She mentions that she has trouble placing some of her poorer students because she must be honest with the potential employers. After all, she points out, "I must deal with them all the time, and my credibility is on the line." She cites a student we have met, a girl with irregular attendance, as an example. At first, this created problems, she said, but now the girl is fine and has really matured in a few months at her work. In general, she has no problem with the students' attendance, either in class or in their jobs. They must call her if they are going to be absent from either. She acknowledges that office work these days is looked down upon; the pay and status are low. So she encourages her students to continue their education, to look for ways to improve themselves through more education, and through job applications.

When we asked about her own education, she praised her high school teacher. "I had good training," she says, "especially in high school." She still corresponds with her high school office education and typing teacher each year. She paid her own way through college by using her office secretarial skills. "When I went to college," she goes on, "I wanted to be the best office education teacher there ever was." Mrs. H. then smiles her broad smile and says, "Now, wasn't that naïve?"

*Mrs. Y.*   Mrs. Y. is an art teacher, the first teacher in DeSoto this year to display students' work in public places, like the front-hall display cases, for all to see. We enter her art class, and are impressed by the color in the room, which makes it very different from all other classrooms at DeSoto. In addition to artwork pasted up on the walls and bulletin boards, there are large colored papers with designs pinned on a line stretched across the room in front of the windows. The room has large worktables with four to six stools per table, three potting wheels, three large garbage pails full of clay, a supply cabinet, and a supply room behind the teacher's desk.

We begin by talking about her students' work in the display cases. She says the kids love it, and they fight for the chance to have their work shown. She then mentions that kids have trouble staying after school, and she doesn't ask them to any more. Once, last year, she kept two ninth graders after school—two of the nicest guys she knows, black, good kids, who were to work with her on a special project. After completing the project and leaving her class, about an hour after school, they were beat up and slashed across their foreheads right outside the building. She stays after school, cleaning up and getting ready for tomorrow, but she no longer asks or expects the kids to stay. The neighborhood is not safe.

Mrs. Y. hasn't always been in art. Although she started in art at DeSoto about twelve years ago, she was bumped from her position by a teacher with more experience. Since she liked DeSoto and had a minor in English, she decided to stay and teach English literature and composition. Teaching English was satisfying, but when given a chance to teach art again this year, she jumped at it. Art is her first love. The chance to teach art again at DeSoto arose when the teacher who had excessed her was excessed by the principal. Now Mrs. Y. must pick up the pieces, reorganize the stockroom, get more kids interested in art again, resolve problems that accrued over time. But she isn't complaining. She wants to stay at DeSoto, no matter what kind of extra work she gets. She likes the class, she likes the kids, and she loves art: "Each kid seems to have a million personalities here, but they produce in art."

Her interests in the students and in art join in her intent to have the kids enjoy seeing their work and appreciate their constructive accomplishments. One of the problems with this, Mrs. Y. cautions, is lack of engagement in art. "English was different," she emphasizes, with the certainty of her experience. "Both the kids and their parents took English more seriously." Her students' lack of engagement, their propensity to stay laid back, she feels, is somehow different from student attitudes when she was in high school. She points out that this is more true of the whites than the blacks. Some of this she attributes to drugs, which she knows to be a very serious problem for a few students in her class. Mrs. Y. has worked closely with one girl's homeroom teacher to see if they can help her out of drug dependency. Mrs. Y. gently but firmly admitted, however, that the girl knows Mrs. Y. thinks drugs have *no* place in one's life, and so the girl doesn't allow an open relationship to occur between them.

Another thing she finds so different is the students' lack of patience with anything less than perfection. If anyone makes a mistake in an assembly, Mrs. Y. points out, there is huge commotion and derision. It is as if the kids expect to be fully entertained and the entertainment should be professional and perfect. I asked if this attitude also affected her students' art, and she said, "You bet it does." Among other things, they don't like to be assigned projects in art. Often they want to do their own thing. So, in one of her classes, she gives them Fridays "to get that burning idea they want to let out on paper." Sometimes it works; sometimes only fluff comes out, of course. There is an unrest in these kids, she finds, an unrest and disquiet that is so different from her years in high school. It is their basic distrust and concern with the establishment, with each other, with themselves. They just can't seem to have peace and quiet with themselves. It's almost as if they have to be fidgety and unsettled because that is how they are inside.

Mrs. Y.'s twin sister, who teaches art in an established suburban community near DeSoto, has it much easier. Her sister has only to mention, for example, that it would be nice to have some more paints in the class, and the next day some of the students will bring a fancy collector's box of forty-eight paints. Although Mrs. Y. has good administrative support and reasonable art supplies, she says she is lucky if kids bring their own pencils.

Not many parents came for teacher-parent conferences. She notes that most of those who did come were black and were from some distance away. One came by bus and had to go by bus to another school that same day. Not many of the neighborhood parents came at all. But that, she says, is not much different from the way it has been at DeSoto since before it became integrated.

One very important thing to Mrs. Y. is administrative support. "It makes all the difference in the world that the principal thinks art is an important aspect in the high school curriculum, that she shows a real interest in what the kids produce, that she doesn't use or see art as just the dumping ground for poor students." She would like to increase art enrollment so that another art teacher would be necessary. She would kill, she emphasizes with a huge smile, for a sculpture class.

Sculpture is what *really* excites her, but, this year, not enough students signed up. Perhaps early next spring, before students choose next year's courses, she will actively recruit students, take them down to the art museum, introduce them to real sculptors so that they will appreciate, and sign up for, sculpture. One problem here, she says, is all the senior work programs. "Our program at DeSoto trades work for art! They have all their lives to work in jobs, and here they can do art for free!" But she realizes that the students want or need the money, that they see work as moving into the real world, that work is more attractive to them than the disciplinary problems and hassles of school. She still thinks the kids lose in the long run.

Not many, maybe none, of these students continue in art after graduating from DeSoto. What is sad, she says, is seeing real talent going to a factory. Also, the specialty school for the artistically talented in the city attracts the really talented and highly motivated students away from DeSoto. Although it is good for the kids in the long run, it does take away one of the joys of teaching: working with real talent and ambition in your main area of professional interest. Some students come back, and that is important to her. One student from eight years ago, for example, comes back pretty regularly. "It's funny," she says, "often it is those with whom you always had running battles, those with whom you seemed not to get along at all, who are the ones who return and look you up."

Mrs. Y. developed an interest in right brain/left brain research and is pursuing that interest in some of her teaching. This interest did not come from an in-service or university course. It was flamed by a book she read. She uses exercises from that book in her classes, but adds that they haven't been very successful with the students. Drawing from unrecognizable outlines and shapes rather than labelled or easily recognized forms does not appeal to them, nor does she see them applying their "right brain" to other artwork. "That's okay, I'll keep trying," Mrs. Y. says firmly.

*Mr. G.*   Mr. G. is an officer in the city's teachers union. He is in his mid-thirties, and he looked tired the few times we saw him. Mr. G. has a good reputation as an English teacher, and he coaches DeSoto's crackerjack debate team. The team is undefeated this year, and has more trophies in the trophy case than any other team except wrestling.

We begin to talk about the union. His style is not tired at all, his delivery is measured and confident.

"What about the union? Let's start with an example, with an ironic example from a few years ago. In my first two years of teaching I was an absolute failure. I tried unusual things—you know, open classroom kinds of activities and philosophy, ideas that I had built up in college—and I bombed in the classroom. I tried things that could fail, and they did, but nobody really seemed to care. So I was able to work things out for myself. The irony is that today I wouldn't have the opportunity to fail and to continue teaching. If I entered teaching today, and made the same mistakes I did then, I wouldn't last the year. The administration would can me.

"The union is good for teachers. It's needed and it helps, because there is such a dehumanizing atmosphere and attitude in schools. The problem of teacher surplus, the process of excessing teachers, of bumping them based on seniority, is, perhaps, something that can't be solved. Also there is little curricular focus these days because it seems we are on a plateau. There is little more we can do with the curriculum. All we can do is go down, and we do because of burnout. Personally, I'm not burned out, but there are days, maybe one or two in a year, when I call in sick and all I do is stay in bed all day, doing nothing. The faculty, quite frankly, needs psychological support. And the union is talking about providing this support in a city teacher center. Let me give you an example. Let's say a teacher gets assaulted—it happens you know—but there is no psychological support to help get him or her back in the classroom. Or what about human relations in general, between teachers or between teachers and kids? Human relations can't be done in a single group meeting, there needs to be more follow-up, and there needs to be an individual focus.

"What the union really handles, most of the time, are problems in human relationships. Fifty percent of the grievances we handle are really between teachers. The union spends most of its time trying to resolve problems between teachers, but it must grieve the principals to do that because there is no official liaison between teachers. Most people don't understand the teachers' perceptions of teachers unions. The top priority of a union, from a teacher's point of view, is to protect his or her rights. Pay, salary—what the newspapers always write about—is about third or fourth on the teacher's list. For teachers, the number one concern is solving communication problems. Grievances are basically human relations problems, communication problems. We talk about defending the contract, but really we're into resolving human problems, not legal problems.

"This is a strong union. Ninety-eight percent of the teachers in the city belong to it, so we do represent the teachers of this city. Does the union have a black-white problem? Yes, it does, because the majority of the rank and file are white and not as liberal as many of its leaders. We have some problems that are unnecessarily made into black-white problems. The seniority system for lay-offs, for example, wouldn't really affect the black-white staff ratio, but the arbitrators felt a racial quota system had to be put in anyway, for the future. So you get a white teacher who, not knowing the facts, thinks his or her job is less secure because a less senior black will take it away, and that just isn't going to happen. More serious, of course, was the black-white problem during the teacher strike five years ago, when the few who crossed the picket lines were black and the rank and file over-generalized. Some schools still suffer the consequences of that racial misunderstanding, but DeSoto doesn't. Racial problems are getting better in the union—slowly. They've got to, just like they've got to in our society."

He then discussed teaching and his debate team. "Why do you see so much textbook teaching and so much emphasis on work sheets? The answer is simple. I throw out open-ended questions to the kids and I get no response. But I hand out work sheets and they respond. So what do I do? I hand out work sheets. The kids here have a mechanical orientation to learning. There is no real concept of thinking, no understanding of independent thought. Maybe it comes from the family. These students have always come from blue-collar homes, tuned-out situations, situations where thinking, executive decision-making, for example, is just not a part of life. A teacher becomes frustrated with that mentality and, instead of changing it, begins to reinforce it. After all, how much frustration can you take?

"The debate team is the best I ever had, mainly because of one individual. He is proof that you can get a good education here if you pick and choose your courses right. He's been offered a scholarship to the University of Chicago and was real disappointed in being in the ninety-third percentile in his SAT's. What about the blacks on the debate team? When there was no integration, there were only white schools in debate competitions. After integration, you find that most good teams will have some blacks on them. The reasons are that their culture is oral—much of the street games are verbal—and they're quick thinkers. The best forensic team, for example, is at East, and they are mostly black. But it is also the worst school academically in the city. In debate, however, reading is more central. I put the worst readers on the team in the first affirmative, I put my best readers in the negative. I recruit like mad, and it's like squeezing blood out of turnips. I'll talk to fifty to sixty kids and maybe thirty will be interested. Then fifteen will drop out after a meeting or two. By the first tournament I have ten kids.

"I work hard on the debate team, I really put myself into it. I put in a lot of time and a lot of effort, but it is good for me psychologically. I give assignments, I look for materials, I beat my brains out, and I think, sometimes, what am I doing this for? But the nice thing about the debate team is that the kids are *motivated*, and you'd be amazed at what motivation does for some kids. And for us teachers, too. No teacher should have only classes of uninterested students, students who are just getting by. My salvation as a teacher is my debate team; they are why I am not burned out. I can take a ninth grader of average reading ability, and by the twelfth grade he or she will be doing work equal to postgraduate work! Each of these kids must produce the equivalent of a master's thesis on a topic; you should see the quality of their research into the problem. That's where much of my pride is—in the work of the debate team."

*Mrs. E.*   Mrs. E. is a delight to talk to. She begins our conversation by asking why it took so long for us to get to her. After a few minutes with her, we wonder, too. A small woman with tightly curled white hair, she exudes pep, enthusiasm, and ideas. She has taught at DeSoto for about twenty years, after working for NBC television in New York City "in the pioneer days of national TV, the fifties."

Before working at NBC, she received an Oxford University fellowship as a Shakespearean scholar. She loves England and Europe, has taken students there nearly every year since she has been at DeSoto. She makes a mean trifle once a year for the faculty, coaches the pom-pom girls, is the senior class advisor, and the English department chairperson. An interesting comparison could be made between Mrs. E. and Mr. L., the math teacher and former football coach. Both are old-timers (she is older, he has taught longer at DeSoto); both have been chairpersons; both have been coaches; but she is still involved, he isn't.

Mrs. E. loves film-making and theatre. More than that, she loves to see kids make films and do theatre. She teaches a media course the second semester of each year with ninety-five students, juniors and seniors, in three classes. The students make TV commercials of their own, planning and writing the script, putting in the sound and music and sound effects, executing the camera work, and putting it all together. They show [their results] in class, to friends, to other schools, and to some [friends of Mrs. E.] who work in television. "You just don't know how much work the kids put into them," says Mrs. E. "In fact, until they do it themselves, they don't realize how much work goes into what they see." Many of her students have won awards for the films they made at DeSoto. She describes one film that, with no words, but with music and juxtaposed shots of animals and people in everyday activities like eating and walking, compared and contrasted their habits and behavior. Another award-winning film was on death. The students filmed the inside of the mausoleum across the street from DeSoto High. Some of Mrs. E.'s former students now work in television and radio. One is the current president of the communication guild of the state, and she emphasizes that many others throughout the country have made media their vocation. Mrs. E. has taught this media course for fifteen years. The English department chairman initially vetoed her proposal for the course, but the principal overruled him and allowed the media course to be offered.

Mrs. E. also teaches theatre and drama, and at one time was the director of the city's children's theatre. This year, she is working with the college-bound students' club to dramatize to younger classes what certain college-oriented themes mean: class placement and ACT's, for example. She describes in delightful detail a production of *The Hobbit*, with webbed feet, a great dragon, and all, that her students wrote, costumed, and produced a few years ago. Students do much of their own script writing, costume design and make-up, and they have performed for other schools, nursing homes, and children's hospitals on themes such as "Don't be a *litter* bug," or the students' own adaptation of *Raggedy Ann and Andy*.

"It's great to see the kids in a different light," she says. "It is good to give of yourself where there is so much for them and you to learn. And the kids remember those experiences years later." Not only college-bound kids take theatre. More than twice as many students take her media course each year than go on to college from DeSoto. Many of her best theatre students don't go to college after graduation. They stay involved in theatre, and may attend college later.

"You know," she continues, "there are still college-bound kids at DeSoto, and that is good for the program. It's not just a dummy school like some teachers think." She refers to the brilliant star of Mr. G.'s debate team, and also mentions a class period of the previous day. "I wish you had been there. You could see what I mean when I say all these kids are capable of in-depth thinking. I was asking them the age-old question of life and literature—you know, does life reflect literature or does literature reflect life? They had fascinating answers, and it turned out to be an exciting intellectual dialogue." She worries about the attitudes of some who think that DeSoto has a lot of stupid kids. She doesn't. She thinks, basically, the kids haven't changed that much over the years. It is the new teachers about whom she worries the most, because they seem to her to be the ones who teach most mechanically.

I ask her about her love for Shakespeare. How much Shakespeare do the kids at DeSoto really experience? She explains that they're introduced to quite a bit of Shakespeare, from *Romeo and Juliet* in ninth grade to *Hamlet* in twelfth grade. What she'd like to see is more Poe. She describes the English curriculum as a four-year program with required courses in the fundamentals of English, composition, and oral communication. Myth, folklore, and science fiction are courses the students can enter upon recommendation of a teacher. The problem, she says, is that so many new students keep entering DeSoto and the teachers don't know if they should be taking these more advanced literature courses or not. The school is going to start soon to give all new students a reading test and an English test.

Mrs. E. also discusses the competency-testing program. She worked on the English competency tests herself and is quite proud of them. "You've got to get them," she says, "and see for yourself. I think we've done a darn good job." She was the first teacher to speak of the tests with pride. The vice-principal thinks that they are inadequate, and Mr. B. apologized for their crudeness, while at the same time distributing them and keeping track of them. The principal says, "Let's use them and see where it takes us." But Mrs. E., the media person, film-maker, and theatre expert, is proud of them. She thinks the competencies should be central to some of the English courses, but she also tries to tell the teachers that they should not just teach to the competencies. Now, after trying the first tests out, she thinks that perhaps there are too many competencies for the ninth graders, but she has worked with the English teachers to redesign them for next year. The tests are now graded by the teacher, but she hoped that the second batch of competency tests would be graded by a scantron and then recorded in a gradebook. The subject supervisors at the central office, she says, have been involved in the design of these competency tests, and have followed the DeSoto plan and format with much interest. They are thinking of using them in all the high schools. The reason she values the competency tests, said Mrs. E., is that they emphasize critical thinking skills, not just recall.

On the topic of faculty, she mentions that when she first began teaching at DeSoto, there were fifty on the faculty and only eight women. They had social gatherings then, and that was important to the cohesiveness of the school. They don't have social gatherings any more. It's difficult for teachers to get together now, even on school time. The teachers used to have only classes, preparation, and lunch duty. Now, because of school board policy, they have attendance and hall duties, and there just isn't time to get together. The principals also are different now, she says. They may be better now, but they don't have the power. The old guard were really tough men, and these schools were their kingdoms.

"I love to teach these kids," she declares. "I could have done other things in my life if I had wanted to. I still have people from television coming up to me, but teaching is my vocation." We observe that the school must sell itself to kids and parents but that the students at DeSoto seem uninvolved. Mrs. E. explains that she wanted the kids to get involved in talking about DeSoto to other kids, but that the guidance department didn't want it that way. They wanted to do the "selling" themselves. "It's really too bad," she says. "Kids can really talk to kids." She describes an idea—making a video tape of students telling other students how to study. It's important that they talk to each other, she insists. We attribute student passivity to television, but Mrs. E. admonishes us: "You *must* know, that radio is the medium of adolescents, *not* TV." She continues to explain that kids talk most about radio personalities and music and that the talk shows, patter, and music of radio is more in tandem with the moods and rhythms of teen-agers than is television. "These kids are fine. All we have to do is give them a chance." She recalled that in her twenty years at DeSoto she has given only one Form 72. She laughs, "And I didn't even know how to make it out."

Mrs. E. describes her old classroom, one that was hers until the past year. It had a stage, panelled walls, and used to have ornately carved pews. It was a beautiful room to teach in, she remembers. Besides theatre, she used to teach a humanities course in that room, with thirty-five students taking the course and a number of DeSoto teachers auditing it. That humanities course ended a few years ago when the new curriculum was designed for DeSoto. She really misses that classroom and making it hers.

There are some other changes at DeSoto that get her down. One is the effect of having a specialty school for art and drama where the best theatre students now go. Although she wants all the kids in DeSoto to experience theatre, film-making, and media, it hurts to lose some of her potentially prize students. The specialty school has offered her a teaching job, but she has repeatedly turned it down. She isn't certain, though, how long she can keep turning it down. The idea of teaching especially motivated and talented kids is attractive. The more she thinks about that possibility and her present working conditions at DeSoto, the more she thinks she just might take it. That, she knows without saying, would be DeSoto's loss.


## Teaching and Learning

We observed classes in English composition, mythology and folklore, urban citizenship, U.S. history, chemistry, physics, biology, algebra, geometry, physical education, typing, career education, distributive education, human relations, chorus, and metal technology. The classes were small, often with less than fifteen, rarely more than twenty students present.

Instruction usually proceeds according to specific tasks assigned by the teacher. In academic subjects, students typically work individually to complete work sheets, and then recite answers to the whole class as the teacher evaluates accuracy. Generally, the whole class follows the same activity; we observed no instances of students working in small groups or on independent research projects. Some students in the library appeared to be working on reports, and, in an English class, a teacher held conferences with individual students about their essays. Individualized activity occurred in music, industrial arts, and business education, but rarely in the basic academic subjects, except for special education students whose programs are highly individualized.

Most classroom activity seems to call for minimal cognitive competence. The emphasis is primarily on simple recall: "What were the provisions of the Treaty of 1763?" "What was Heracles' fourth labor?" Or application of an idea: "Write a sentence that uses a simile," "Given the symbol for an element, use the periodic table to find its atomic number." Occasionally, students are asked to develop explanations for phenomena: "If we release ammonia in one corner of the room, why is it possible to smell it in the opposite corner?" We never observed a school situation in which students worked together in a sustained way to solve a complicated problem, nor a situation in which the answer to a problem had to be seen as tentative, with reasonable arguments made for a variety of solutions.

Work sheets occasionally stifled careful thought. One exercise instructed students to list occupations where people work "with things and objects." A student commented that almost any career, from plumbing to medicine to politics, could qualify under this description. He began to question whether any answer could actually be ruled out as wrong. The teacher indicated an awareness of the problem: "Generally, this would refer to working with machines, but you have a point." She ended the discussion with the advice, "Don't think too hard about it; just put down what comes to your mind."

We rarely observed teachers guiding students through a systematic inquiry process, but many of the assigned tasks did involve complex activity. In a class on media, students wrote their own plays, movies, and commercials, and shared them with one another for critical analysis. A lab experiment in biology using an egg to demonstrate osmosis required eye-hand coordination and comprehension of abstract concepts. Producing chisels to specification in the foundry demanded complex motor coordination, perceptual judgment, and a high level of concentration. Occasionally, students demonstrated subtlety and humor. Asked for an illustration of simile, one student wrote, "My English teacher is like school in the summertime . . . no class."

Most activities in community agencies involve low levels of skill, a good deal of routine work. They demand accuracy, care, responsibility, and good human relations, but the tasks, such as transporting patients in a hospital, filing checks in a bank, photographing records in an insurance company, are relatively simple. Work-experience supervisors testify almost unanimously that students need no special language or numerical or cognitive skills to perform good work at their agencies, just a willingness to work and cooperate. Some community-based work does include complex activity. A student who took phone orders for appliance parts had to know how to translate nontechnical customer language ("I need one of those knobs in the box on my air conditioner") into technical charts and numbers; a student tutoring young children had to anticipate the knowledge they brought to a task and to pace the learning accordingly.

Students speak highly of their community-based work experience and classes at the technical college, finding the nonschool settings more interesting and useful. Learning in places outside DeSoto is perceived as more legitimate, we speculate, largely because the adults or teachers there escape the pervasive, distracting responsibilities for custody and discipline that befall teachers in the comprehensive school. In the nonschool agency, you get on with the work or are dismissed. The school, however, works hard to retain students so they can be properly socialized for adult behavior, and this creates interruptions in instruction because of disciplinary actions (dealing with tardiness, student misbehavior in class), or assemblies, or testing procedures that take students from class, or schedule changes in the length of class (half of the teachers reported adverse interruptions in more than one period per day).

Classes at DeSoto last forty-seven minutes, with eight periods during the day. Ninth and tenth graders typically take six or seven classes, leaving a period for lunch and possibly a study hall. Seniors typically take only four or five classes, and leave school in the afternoon. Because of problems in monitoring students during free time, staff members try to program students into as many classes as possible, but they also realize that seven classes is too intensive a schedule for many students. Students need free time, some space during the school day, but traditional study halls are hard to manage. An attempt was made to provide for individualized, supervised study in an "intervention center," as an alternative to study hall, but this has not been implemented. Some students work as volunteers in school during free time. Betty, for example, is a tenth grader who worked one period in the library and one in the office. She took five courses but did not need a study hall because she could finish most of her work in class.

Most students do not carry books to and from school, even though a majority of teachers expect students to do from fifteen to thirty minutes of homework per night per subject, which, for six subjects, could involve from one and one half to three hours of homework. Most students reported that in most classes they were not challenged and were not doing their best; that they do less than one-half hour of homework per night for all classes. (A majority of teachers reported that they themselves spent more than an hour per night on school work.)

Students usually remained on task, but uninvolved. We also witnessed a contrast in highly engaged activity. In physical education, students played vigorous volleyball, unsupervised by adults, while some students cut their bowling class. In chorus, students gathered around the piano, singing robustly with their teacher for thirty minutes, while in history, a teacher pleaded for students' attention. In one English class, a student used some spare time to practice a speech, and received helpful feedback from classmates. In another, five of the twelve students sat the whole period without any materials for completing their composition assignments. In a third, a student began to read aloud her essay on what she did over the weekend. Half way through a long list of activities, she stopped short, saying, "This is boring. I quit." In areas such as art, music, industrial arts, media, business education courses, we found several students approaching their work with concentration, self-direction, and enthusiasm. There seemed to be more apathy in academic subjects.

If learning is to be measured by standardized tests, citywide data in reading and mathematics show DeSoto to be below city norms, which, in turn, are below national norms. If learning at DeSoto is to be measured in grades, spring 1981 records show that 25 percent were A or B, 20 percent C, and 53 percent D or failure.

## Technology

DeSoto High School, thanks to the school district, has perhaps one of the most sophisticated and complete sets of computer print-outs in the country. There are eleven different print-out reports on each student, covering subjects that range from family background to class schedule. These reports are supported by a full-time data processor for this school of 1,100 students. The variety of information available on individual students can be impressive, but no one at DeSoto tried to impress us with it. Few seem to use it, because it seems irrelevant to assisting classroom instruction. When we asked for information on the students we were to follow for a day, we received a print-out for each student telling us about credits taken, credits earned, grade-point average, and course schedule (though not up to date). However, when we asked for cumulative data about the school (number of absences, number of daily suspensions, number of students per class, number of students new to DeSoto each year, number of students from the neighborhood), administrators were too busy to find any. Even with a computer and a full-time data processor for this school, cumulative data had to be constructed "by hand" or from memory.

We found "high technology" in a few classrooms; it was conspicuously absent in most, including the science classroom. The banking room contains about a dozen computer terminals, where keypunching, word processing, and certain types of basic accounting are practiced by the few students who take the banking course, and occasionally by office education students.

The metalworking laboratory is full of machinery, with a separate section for a classroom, tiered like a small theatre with the teacher's desk as "stage" and students' desks on each tier. About thirty large metal-machinery tools stand like thick robots in the shop section, along with the same number of vises on a weathered table along the edge of a large window. A wall from floor to ceiling with glass windows nestled in beautiful (at one time) woodwork separates the shop from the classroom.

One large piece of machinery, a foundry, is operated by six fourteen-year-old students. As the fire blazes in the foundry, the students manipulate the gases to increase and decrease the intensity of the blaze. These six students, shorter than most of the machines, could get lost in the forest of machinery, but they know what they're doing. They put a steel section in the foundry, bring it out red-hot and bang the hell out of it with sledge hammers to make a chisel. It all "must be done to specification," Mr. N. tells us. The real purpose of these projects is to introduce students to the tools of metalworking, to learn to work according to specifications, and to make something useful.

With some pride, Mr. N. pointed out the equipment in this room. Over the years, he has bought a number of new tools with federal vocational funds; last year, for example, he acquired a metal press that cost nearly $6,000. Mr. N. opened up a box packed with cotton and carefully unfolded a shiny brass replica of a cannon with spoked wheels, swivels, a hollow and finely shaped barrel. About a foot long, it feels solid and smooth, and sits heavily in the hands. The boys who made the cannon worked on it a full year in Metal Tech 2.

The saddest place to look for technology at DeSoto is in the chemistry and physics laboratory. It has old black-topped science workbenches, the kind we all remember from high school, with gas jets sticking out, heavy drawers, and an electrical outlet on the side. For demonstrations, there is a large workbench with a hood in the front center of the room. Except for this, there are few signs of the equipment one would expect to find in a working laboratory. The chemistry and physics classes at DeSoto are largely equipment-free; teachers rely primarily on work sheets and textbooks.

One teacher said the old tables really get him down. It would take $20,000 to replace them, but he knows the district has new ones that were moved to a warehouse from a school that was just closed. He adds, "There is not an experiment that I can have the kids do, because for each experiment, there is some equipment that is broken."

Our best example of technology, the scientific method, and student/ teacher engagement in analysis occurred in a class on small engines at the area technical college. The small-engines classroom had some worktables in the middle of the room, and, on one side, wire cages with iron-framed doors and padlocks were filled with engines in different stages of disassembly. Tools were stored in a large cupboard separating the tables from an open work space.

There were eleven students, including one white girl, five black males and a Puerto Rican male. Each was working on an engine, trying to start it. They pulled cords and feathered the chokes. Some engines began to sputter and vibrate, soon leading to a steady bam, bam, bam; other engines took longer to start, while the exhaust fumes rose from the vibrating engines and a strong smell of gasoline permeated the room. Students hunched over these motors for hours, using screwdrivers to fine-tune the chokes, fixing the gas lines, repairing magnetos, testing out the spark plugs. Often, a motor would die and they would try to start it again. They worked together much of the time.

The instructional emphasis, the teacher explained, was on the scientific method. After they learned the engine well, having taken it apart and put it back together, the teacher asked them to see how much they could change the behavior of the motor. They were to try out various adjustments of the primary components and describe, in their notes, the range of characteristics of their engine. The teacher talked about hypotheses, anticipations, observations, and conclusions. He showed us the notes the kids had written in their media folders. In describing the students, he said:

> I'm told that kids in high school are bad, but I'll tell you: these kids are beautiful. Every one of them is more than good. They help each other. They're responsible. They work. They're conscientious. They listen. Some are real talented in engines; some aren't. But they all put out. I love it. And you know, the kids come from all over the city, but our attendance rate is over ninety percent. Sometimes I wonder, should I believe what I read about high school kids today? All I see are good kids.

Thus, the one area that actively engaged students' minds in inquiry and analysis was the technology of small combustible engines, not the technology of information processing. The technology of these engines was treated as a question mark, a process to be understood and fiddled with, changed and manipulated in order to see what happened, to see if one could predict what would happen next, and to see if one could make it happen that way again. Textbooks, work sheets, computers, and television weren't utilized in such a way in any classes at DeSoto High School, except, perhaps, for film and theatre in Mrs. E.'s English class.

## Community

Where is DeSoto's community? Located on a peninsula west of the central city, surrounded on the north and south by two different municipalities, and serving a citywide student population, DeSoto's constituency is geographically diffuse. The homecoming football game was played several miles from the school at another school's stadium. About 80 percent of the students travel more than two miles to school, many requiring bus rides of up to one hour, but city bus service is convenient.

The former seventh- through twelfth-grade school could be considered a relatively cohesive neighborhood institution, but the school now has difficulty finding its community. A parent-teacher-student advisory committee was created to give input to the principal on school affairs. Present at one evening meeting were the principal, a teacher (Mr. B.), and two parents, both alumni of DeSoto. The two educators were on time at 7:00 P.M. One parent arrived at 7:30, another about 7:50. The principal raised the question of how to spend some funds available in a human relations budget along with another issue of increased graduation requirements proposed by the district. Discussion ranged from the use of human relations funds last year to buy bullhorns, to the need for more secure locks on the lockers, to students' writing on the desks, to last year's ethnic week being too long, to how students get accurate information about jobs, to how to remediate failures on competency tests. No official recommendation was made on either of the two main issues, but one parent strongly suggested that students have some say in allocation of the human relations funds. The principal said she supports the committee as a vehicle for parent input, but believes that only a few parents care enough to become involved. The principal feels that generating more parental involvement from a wider cross section of the student body is impossible because of the geographic diversity and lack of commitment or time of the largely working-class population.

School was closed for a parents' day, with all parents invited to come to talk with teachers. Teachers said they expected to see no more than half a dozen of their students' parents all day (most teachers are responsible for more than 100 students). During the day it seemed that about one-third of the teachers were engaged with parents about half of the time. We talked with five parents, most of whose children were ninth graders. Generally, they had a positive impression of the school. Often they came to ask the teacher for advice about what to do with their child who couldn't seem to buckle down and study. In a businesslike manner, teachers described to parents the students' performance and behavior in class. Parents did not criticize or challenge teachers, although a few expressed concern about the policy of sending students home on unofficial suspension for being tardy to class (the policy was abandoned later in the fall).

Through its work-experience program, DeSoto maintains extensive ties with community agencies. In visits to the technical college, a hospital, a bank, a savings and loan institution, a retail parts department, an insurance company, we learned of cooperative relationships between teachers and agency supervisors. Some of the programs, such as banking services and real estate, have their own advisory committees of business people. Most of the students, who work for minimum wages, complete their programs successfully and many agencies will guarantee students entry-level jobs.

Each high school in the district has a special patron business institution. DeSoto is to be assisted by an insurance company, but its program has yet to evolve. Last year, the company distributed free tickets for a selected number of students to such functions as concerts and the United Negro College drive banquet.

## Conclusion

Our description of DeSoto conveys contradictions—between symbolic goals and persons' actual experiences in school, between staff with different levels of involvement in the school, between students with different expectations for school, between the school's attempt to meet simultaneously the realities of district politics, to provide individual professional autonomy for staff, and to create a unified sense of purpose for the school. Most apparent to the reader may be the contradiction between the content of individual teacher portraits, which represent complicated, thoughtful, and apparently committed professionals, and the aggregate picture of school learning that we have drawn as fragmented and in many ways superficial. From our point of view, the greatest challenge for institutions like DeSoto is that of permitting apparently well-intentioned professionals to fulfill their commitment for students rather than having them continually frustrated by contingencies of organized corporate life.

PART  II

SUBURBAN SCHOOLS

# 4

# ROSEMONT HIGH SCHOOL

SARA LAWRENCE LIGHTFOOT

The town of Rosemont carves a triangular shape into the neighboring city. It is bordered on three sides by a major urban community and on the west by Norton. Its proximity to the big city and the easy movement across town borders give Rosemont a mixed image. Some consider it an urban community and even boast of its cosmopolitan spirit, lack of pretentiousness, and streetcars that can take inhabitants into the middle of the core city in fifteen minutes. These people enjoy the relative safety, affluence, and status of Rosemont along with the bustling, heterogeneous, sophisticated character of city life. They can "have their cake and eat it too." In some ways, they feel more fortunate than their neighbors to the west, who live a more suburban life isolated from the mood and tone of the city. There are other Rosemont citizens, however, who cling to the suburban, protected image and who underscore the differences in status and style between Rosemont and the city. They identify more with the habits and values of the people in Norton, Woodside, and Lafayette, and they discourage their children from thinking of the city as a neighboring playground. Depending upon whom you talk to, then, Rosemont is described as an urban or a suburban community, but in each case, the description is filled with pride.

## Urban and Suburban Images

For people who see Rosemont from afar, it has a homogeneous image of affluence and prestige. The prevailing image of Rosemont is based on stereotypes of Jewish people. The community is seen as largely Jewish, with the characteristics often associated with successful

Jews—a commitment to education, an aggressiveness about business matters, protectiveness and a heightened concern for their offspring, a sense of entitlement in relation to schools and other community institutions. The townspeople are also seen as enlightened and liberal, protective of civil liberties and resistant to the reactionary cultural and political trends. As with most stereotypes, this portrait of Rosemont is largely inaccurate. It misses the mark partly because it exaggerates and caricatures the qualities of a group of people who express a broad range of styles and characteristics, and partly because the community is not nearly so uniform with regard to religion, ethnicity, and social class. The homogeneous image lags far behind the heterogeneous and diverse reality, and often seems to obscure the great changes that are occurring in the community and to diminish the efforts of many who work hard at adapting to social and cultural shifts.

In fact, the emphasis in students' and teachers' remarks is on diversity. High school students speak of the many groups that form the school, of reaching out beyond racial and religious boundaries, of cliques that inhibit friendships with other kinds of kids. The teachers speak of searching out pedagogical strategies and curricula that would be appropriate for a broader range of students. And beyond the walls of the school, a visitor to the park can see an old Chinese grandfather dressed in a simple gray cotton suit caring for his young grandchild. Next to them on a park bench is a recent Russian immigrant woman, head tied with a peasant scarf, dressed in layers of sweaters, who is bending over her son protectively. The child looks all-American in his blue-and-white warm-up suit. Neither adult speaks any English. The offspring play with each other using the language of very small children, interspersed with Russian, Chinese, and English.

An elderly woman in the supermarket, dramatically dressed in a silver fur jacket, black velvet slacks, plentiful face make-up and a bouffant hairdo, complains that the town has changed for the worse. "It used to be a real community of like-minded people . . . and now I don't feel safe walking the streets in the late afternoon." Her comment is inspired by the actions of a black teen-age boy who darted in front of her at the check-out counter. When he zoomed in front of her with a racing-car squeal and a smile, she pushed her cart with great force into his thighs and backside. He responded, with a wider grin, "Old lady, you're crazy!" The woman had sought my alliance when she spoke of the deteriorating neighborhood. Despite the image of privilege and stability, therefore, townspeople must cope with diversity and change.

Rosemont is a town of 55,000 people. The diversity of the town is reflected in the wide range of income among residents, ranging from a median income level of $9,949 per family in the central village area to $23,021 in South Rosemont.

Some Rosemont residents, weary of the inaccurate image of affluence, point to places like Dale and Lafayette where "real wealth" resides. In Dale, the landed gentry own large parcels of land and keep their horses in private stables. Their riding gear is impeccable; their horses are beautifully groomed. In Lafayette, zoning ordinances protect citizens from the threat of close neighbors. Creative, modern homes of redwood and glass look out over magnificent vistas, and two-hundred-year-old houses, perfectly restored and cared for, nestle comfortably in the wooded landscape. A few years ago, no black families lived in Lafayette. A single black boy, adopted by a white family, suffered taunts and abuse from his schoolmates as he rode the bus to school. The parents of all the children involved were horrified. The episode did not match their liberal image of themselves. Many Rosemont "liberals" compare these towns when they assert that theirs is a heterogeneous town of "real people."

As a matter of fact, rental units account for 72 percent of the housing market in Rosemont. With an increasing trend toward condominium conversion, there is a very low (2 percent) housing vacancy rate. Forty percent of the housing is under rent control and 7.5 percent is subsidized. There is a continued demand for assisted housing with about 400-low income family units at present. The economic base is predominantly residential. Less than 1 percent of the land remains vacant. The industrial base of the town is divided into three business categories: wholesale and retail trade; finance, insurance, and real estate; and services.

But when Rosemont residents refer to the "real world" quality of their town they usually are not commenting on the economic base, but on the population shifts that have become increasingly visible. A list of the ethnic groups that form the town's citizenry reads like an idealized melting pot—Asians (including Chinese, Korean, Japanese,

Vietnamese), blacks, Hispanics, Israelis, Russians, Irish, and East Indians. Although the population of the town has remained relatively stable over the last decade (with a 6.2 percent drop, from 58,689 to 55,062), the minority population has increased more than four times (from 695 to 3,110). The numbers of blacks have increased from 487 to 1,060; those of Spanish origin from 656 to 1,162, and Asian and Pacific Islanders from 1,379 to 2,662. Many residents are proud of their town's willingness to reach out to strangers and believe that the reputation for receptivity has encouraged the increasing numbers of minorities. Others worry that their town may not be able to absorb the influx of foreigners without losing its sense of identity, stability, and order. And an increasingly vocal minority resists the changes and fears the repercussions of diversity. This latter group feels besieged, intruded upon, and threatened by the growing number of minority faces.

Incorporated in 1705, Rosemont is an old town with a rich history. Many of the fine, stately homes built in the eighteenth century have been restored and identified as historical sites. Some nineteenth-century sites are being rehabilitated, often with federal assistance. Townspeople are proud of the robust and sturdy architecture and seem to want to restore as many of the old buildings as possible. The old parts of town, with majestic single-family dwellings, are in sharp contrast with the more ordinary apartment buildings and two-family homes that crowd next to one another in less affluent areas.

South Rosemont, the section of greatest wealth, has many opulent homes, with long circular driveways, hidden behind protective walls. There is an emphasis on privacy. Mercedes purr along the winding roads and joggers enjoy the stillness and solitude of early-morning runs. After the first snow of winter, a path made by cross-country skis is barely visible across the smooth white landscape.

A few miles away, in Rutledge Square, the town sends out its plows immediately after the first snowfall to clear the streets for safe driving. Soon the pace of life resumes. People bustle among the shops and offices, and the snow becomes a dark city-brown. Life in this part of town moves at a different pace from the protected enclave of South Rosemont. Moving in and out of the stores, one is likely to see elderly, widowed women, large Irish families, a group of Chinese adolescents, a young black boy being pulled behind his big dog. Rutledge Square is the major business district of Rosemont, with several drugstores, fruit markets, shoe salons, a movie theater, fast-food spots, and an amazing number of optometrists selling hundreds of styles of glasses. There are stores that appeal to sophisticated tastes: a very expensive women's wear shop that sells designer originals; a chic French restaurant that has a fine wine list and an irresistible pastry tray; and a lovely shop for home furnishings that has original ceramics, jazzy dinnerware, and subtle tapestries. And there are shops that serve the ordinary needs of people: a well-equipped hardware store, a shoe store specializing in orthopedic models, a modestly priced clothing store for men and women, a deli, and an F. W. Woolworth. There are excellent delicatessens, a Japanese gift shop, a large health-food store, and a fancy cheese store, where customers get expert advice in selecting the right cheese. There seems to be something for everyone. The center of Rosemont's business district is lively and diverse.

As one moves away from Rutledge Square, the town becomes residential. Collections of stores, usually serving the everyday needs of people, are found grouped throughout residential areas. There is a growing business enclave close to Rosemont High School that serves the immediate neighborhood but also has begun to attract people from other parts of town. Most people come to this area to buy pastries, cakes, and bread from the Tour Eiffel Bakery, an establishment some describe as "the best bakery in town." Others come to poke around in the very large, well-stocked hardware store, where you can find everything from roof shingles to car antifreeze, to contact paper for kitchen shelves. The rest of the shops on this corner reflect the emerging mixture of styles and needs. A Chinese laundry is squeezed in between a twenty-four-hour food market and a used-furniture store. Next to the bakery is a shop that claims to have fancy antiques. Across the street, there is a laundry, a custom tailor, a shade store, and a delicatessen. A short distance down the street, but within easy view, is the Rosemont Public Library—a stately brick building with a newly constructed wing that blends nicely with the older structure. A large statue of a man on horseback guards the library entrance. Just down the hill is Chester School, one of the largest elementary schools in Rosemont. Like all of the other elementary schools in town, it has a distinct identity and reputation.

Chester School is only five blocks from the high school. Between

Chester and the high school there are a few brick structures of several stories that used to be comfortable apartments and now are advertised as deluxe condominiums, and mostly large, wood-frame houses painted in pale New England colors. The houses are two-family dwellings with well-tended gardens and lawns and newly painted shingles. They appear somewhat crowded. Given their scale and elaborate detail, they seem to ask for more space than the few yards on either side for driveways and hedges. In a big, old rambling house there is a nursery school with an elaborate wooden climbing toy in the front yard. When I arrive in this neighborhood midmorning I hear shrieks of laughter from young children coming down the long slide. A father arrives at the nursery school with his daughter in a backpack. She is dressed in a bright gold turtleneck and Oshkosh overalls, which seems to be the uniform for both boys and girls on the playground. Two blocks away and around the corner from this lively scene is Rosemont High School.

When classes are in session, the high school is quiet. On the morning of my first visit, it is early fall and feels like back-to-school weather. The air is crisp, the breezes fresh, and the trees are beginning to turn orange and yellow. A boy carrying books walks toward the school, casually kicking the fallen leaves. On the long green field in front of the school, gym classes are being held.

Athletic coaches wearing light windbreakers and whistles, stop the action occasionally and offer suggestions for improving playing skills. Young male bodies move up and down the field in an uneven game of soccer. Some are awkward, even afraid of the ball; others are reticent; still others appear more proficient and engaged in the game. On an adjoining field, boys and girls play touch football. Neither of these gym classes has attracted athletic types. The involvement of students ranges from disinterest and boredom to mild pleasure. The atmosphere is slightly lazy and gym teachers do not push their charges to compete. None of the edge and vitality of competitive sports is evident. At the other end of the long green expanse is a playground for children that includes a handsomely designed jungle gym, swings, and benches. Bleachers and a basketball court separate the playing fields and the children's playground. While I am watching the gym classes work out, three- and four-year-olds from the nearby nursery school arrive at the playground. The fourteen children, with two teachers supervising their activity, attack the climbing toy and swings with energy and exuberance. Their obvious enthusiasm and high energy is in sharp contrast with the self-consciousness and studied casualness of the adolescents at the other end of the field.

Three buildings form the high school—a main building, a recently built athletic building, and an old brick structure that is in the process of being renovated for industrial arts classes. The renovations are well behind schedule. The money budgeted for construction has already been depleted, and no one seems to know if the building will ever be occupied. The athletic facility houses the swimming pool, dance studios, well-equipped locker rooms, wrestling rooms, basketball courts, offices and classrooms. Like many modern structures it is difficult not to get lost in the maze of doorways, stairwells, and passages.

The entryway to this building is one of the favorite places for "jocks" and their entourages to "hang out." Basketball players, tall and lean, stand in front of the gymnasium. They "shoot the bull" with each other and sometimes can be seen practicing their "moves" against invisible opponents. Many of the players are black, impeccably dressed in casual clothes, and often carry expensive-looking duffle bags. The football players also gather outside the gym, but they are harder to identify. They come in assorted sizes and shapes, although some match the stereotypic image of brute and brawn. The jocks have a private language that is hard for a stranger to decode. They gather in small circles and talk about "scores, moves, and fakes." There are often a number of girls hanging around the edges of these circles, rarely entering into the jock exchange, but choosing instead to gossip with one another. The girls tend to be special friends, often "steadies" of the athletes, or cheerleaders. During my visits I rarely saw young women athletes gathered outside the gym and often wondered whether they had favorite hangouts or a private language.

The main building, built in 1949, is a three-story brick structure. It is solidly built, with the classic academic symbols. Heavy, stately columns, three on either side of the center door, support a wooden overhang upon which is printed Rosemont High School. There is a narrow circular driveway, no longer in use. On the right side as you face the building are several steps that lead to bright-blue doors of the old gymnasium. On the left-hand side is the entrance used most often by students, teachers, and visitors.

One can also enter the building through a courtyard. My footsteps echo as I walk across the courtyard cobblestones. As I face the back of the quadrangle, there are two sets of steps, one on my left and one on my right. Groups of students are sitting or standing on the steps. On the stairs to my right, five boys sit one next to the other in a straight row. Their conversation is minimal, and, with their heads down, what they do say is delivered to the ground. Occasionally a loud crack of laughter ricochets off the inner walls of the building before silence settles back into the courtyard. A more fluid group of boys and girls occupies the left-hand steps. Individuals enter and leave the building. Some gather in twos or threes as they sit or stand talking to one another. Their mood appears serious, and their conversations focused. Like the front of the gym, the courtyard stairs are favorite hangouts for students. After a few days at the high school, I become familiar with who is in charge of what territory. At first glance, it appears that the stance and style of the groups assembled in the courtyard are different from the jocks and their friends outside the gym.

Inside, the smell of years of chalk dust that has sifted down between the planks of the old wood floor remind me that I am in school. As I walk through halls of light brown and golden-colored bricks, institutional green and pale blue walls, low ceilings, and narrow walkways, it feels as if I am walking back in time. The bathrooms—free of graffiti and amazingly clean—feel almost antique. The low-hanging, dim lights have recently been replaced by more modern flourescent ones that have less character but offer more light. But the heavy wooden doors on the stalls, the brass latches, the occasional marble, decorative features, and the black and white tile floors, have survived the decades beautifully. Rosemont High is comfortable and old feeling—free of the sleek lines, open spaces, and bright lights of many modern school structures. Over the generations, the building seems to have been used with care; there are no signs of neglect or abuse. An elderly woman, who cleans the building every afternoon, expresses affection for it. We run into each other in a women's faculty room that is full of old and shabby furniture. With a strong Irish brogue she says, "This is a cozy corner. I come here for my cup of tea every afternoon. Don't you like the musty smell?"

Although the sights and smells of the school are almost anachronistic, the people and action are strikingly contemporary. Like the town of Rosemont, the tone of the school is reflected in the combined images of an urban and suburban school. It is not crowded by tall city buildings or surrounded by the clamor of traffic and commerce like most urban schools. The scale of the building in relation to the surrounding landscape gives it a gracious, almost stately, quality. The doors to the building are never locked during school hours, and there are no bars on the wide windows. No school guards stop you in the halls to inquire about your reasons for being there. Rosemont High, therefore, has the relatively safe and secluded appearance of many suburban schools, but it does not have the sprawling, opulent appearance that often characterizes them. There are no large parking lots reserved for teachers' and students' cars. Everyone competes for parking space along the nearby neighborhood streets, along one side of the green field in front of the school, or in the precious few spaces around and behind the new gym. The streetcar that stops a few blocks away from the school connects Rosemont with the city and adds to the urban tone of the place.

When students begin to pour out of the school at the end of the day, one immediately senses a mixture of students that is rare in any high school. Some look like stereotypes of suburban affluence and others have the style of more guarded, sophisticated city types. There is neither the uniform dress that I have seen in many high schools nor is there a Rosemont "look" that is distinctive. A diminutive Chinese girl, dressed in black slacks and a purple windbreaker and carrying an orange backpack that seems half her size, heads for her ten-speed bicycle, unlocks it, and speeds away. Two studious-looking girls with long straight hair and pale skin walk away from school very slowly. They are deep in conversation. One carries a cello, the other an oboe. A group of stocky, wide-shouldered boys talk loudly as they pile inside a green pickup, tune the radio to a blaring rock-and-roll station, light up cigarettes, and squeal away from the curb. A tall, lean black boy, smartly dressed and smooth in gait, has an arm wrapped around a shorter, pretty black girl. They walk away from school without seeming to notice the crowds of students swirling around them, alone together. Not only are the students diverse in color, style, and dress, one hears many languages spoken—Spanish, Chinese, Russian, and English in its myriad forms.

## A Rich Diversity: Confronting Realities

No matter whom you talk to about Rosemont High School, the first thing mentioned is the diversity of the student body. Faculty, students, and administrators seem to want to correct for the outdated, anachronistic image of the school as an elite suburban enclave. Bill Kennedy, the school's headmaster, says enthusiastically, "People used to say diversity was a weakness. Now we are saying diversity is a strength. This is an important shift in orientation for faculty, students, and the community." A prominent black faculty member echoes Kennedy's optimism. "Rosemont is a special place. I've never seen a better mixture of kids. You've got a little United Nations." A thoughtful, pretty sophomore who sits next to me in history class tells about the enlivening quality of diversity. "I went to a strict, Catholic elementary school, where everyone was the same; [it was] very protected and very sterile. When I first came to this school I felt afraid of all the different types of kids. But now I feel *challenged* by all the different groups and much less afraid." But even those who assert the great advantages of a multiethnic school admit the tensions and conflicts among the groups. Says one new arrival to the school, "This is a very cliquish, very separatist place. . . . I don't know where to break into the circle. . . . For every friend I make, there is an enemy."

There are 2,100 students in Rosemont High School, with 20 administrators, 150 teachers, and 40 adults in other professional capacities (e.g., guidance counselors, social workers, career counselors, and the like). Thirty percent of the student body is minority, the largest minority population being Asian (including Chinese, Japanese, Korean, Indian, and Iranian in significant numbers). Twelve percent of the student body are blacks, half of whom are from the central city's Metropolitan Educational Opportunity (METRO) program and half indigenous to Rosemont. Class divides this group. Most of the METRO students come from working-class backgrounds, while their Rosemont peers tend to be offspring of professional, upper-middle-class parents. Says the headmaster, Bill Kennedy, "Historically, they have been pressured into behaving as a group" despite their differences in background and experience. Another observer, who is close to both groups, claims that the divisions between METRO and Rosemont blacks are unfortunate but inevitable. "Rosemont blacks *naturally* take on the feelings, attitudes, and ways of the kids they've grown up with. I call it elitism. It never flares out in the open. There are no fights between them . . . but it bothers me. Maybe I'm at fault. Maybe I want black folks to be *too* close."

Forty percent of the students are Jewish, largely from upper-middle-class families. The Jewish population in the school is declining as parents become worried about the increasing diversity and about what they perceive to be a lowering of standards. Kennedy claims that there has been a noticeable migration of Jewish families to the more distant and protected suburbs of Newton, Lafayette, and Conway. For the most part, the elementary schools in Rosemont still enjoy a superior reputation and continue to attract the offspring of high-powered, academic-minded citizens. But the high school no longer has its old appeal as an elite school. Parents who have the resources and who are concerned about status and standards have begun to search out private schools for their adolescents or are moving to more homogeneous towns.

The remaining 30 percent of the population reflects a mixture of white students from a variety of social classes and ethnic backgrounds. One visible and identifiable subgroup of students from this last category is Irish Catholic and working class. Known as the Point kids because they are from the High Point section of Rosemont, they are long-time residents of the town. Most of their parents were students at Rosemont High; some of their mothers work as secretaries in the school; and the fathers "keep the town running" as policemen, firemen, sanitation workers, and mailmen. The Point kids are 10 percent of the student population and have a reputation for being tough. "Historically, they have battled with whatever group is lowest on the totem pole" says Kennedy. Their current competitors are the black METRO students from the city, who, they claim, receive more attention and resources than they do. They view the black kids as advantaged interlopers and often take out their feelings of deprivation and rage on this group. A teacher who has worked closely with the Point kids for a decade offers a different analysis of their hostility. "They feel this school really *belongs* to them. . . . They have always felt resentful of the upper-middle-class Jewish kids whose image forms the public stereotype of the school. But the Irish kids feel the privileged

Jewish kids are unavailable to receive their hostility—in some sense they are invulnerable—so they take out their anger on black kids."

The diversity of the student population is additionally heightened by the presence of numerous language groups. One hundred and ninety students, about 10 percent of the population, speak English as a second language: they represent more than 55 languages and come from 25 countries. Some of these students speak very little English and have great difficulty communicating with their teachers and peers. An increasing number of Russian Jews, recently immigrated from their homeland, speak no English and require special attention and expertise. A three-year, federally-funded bilingual program, called Project Welcome, seeks to reach out to the new arrivals and offers support and guidance.

Beyond the special program for foreign students, the school curriculum seeks to be adaptive to their needs. U.S. History for Foreign Students is a good example of a social studies course offered for new arrivals with limited proficiency in English.

The teacher is a woman in her mid-thirties. Her wavy red hair hangs nearly to her waist with a coiled braid gathered on top of her head. Her pale skin is lightly freckled, and her light brown eyes sparkle. The classroom is arranged so that all the chairs form a circle. Meredith, as she has introduced herself to me and is called by the students, refreshes their memories concerning the day's lesson. "Today we'll hear from the Committee on Leadership." It seems that the class is divided into six committees. Each committee must report back to the entire class, and all of the students must reach consensus before proceeding to the next committee report. The idea for this course belongs to two teachers, both of whom are in the classroom. Although Meredith is the one teaching, Robert Hall, her co-teacher, is in the room observing the action.

Meredith asks Kay, a Korean girl, to sit front and center of the group and give the Committee on Leadership report. Meredith smiles at Kay, leaning down toward her, and coaxes her to begin reading. She speaks gently with warmth and soon Kay begins to read from her report. Meredith writes Kay's points on the board. Kay comes to a word that she tries to but cannot read. She stops. Smiling, she looks into her lap, shaking her head back and forth. Meredith moves quickly to her side and reads the word quietly to Kay. As she moves back to the blackboard she says, "It's all right, Kay, you're doing just fine." Kay's smooth oval face is framed by black hair that falls in soft, sculpted waves to her shoulders. Her lips frame the words before she speaks them in a soft, tentative voice.

Another student walks into the room and stops to talk in Spanish to two other students sitting at the edge of the circle. Meredith moves toward him, motioning him to sit down. While this is going on, Kay is trying to read point four. After the boy is settled, Meredith walks over to Kay and apologizes. "Kay, I'm sorry, I missed that. What was number four?"

When all points are on the board, Meredith says, "I think I understand Kay's points. Let me repeat them." She checks with Kay when she is unsure. The committee has developed seven recommendations. Meredith says to the class, "What questions do you have?" Silence in the room. "Does everyone agree that we need a leader?"

One boy questions why only the representatives of the six committees get to choose the leader. Meredith is listening intently to him. She leans gently over Kay. "Kay, do you think you can explain your committee's reason?" Kay just shakes her head, her faint smile looking more fixed. Meredith turns back to the student. "Norris, why don't you develop your reasons for another way of selecting a leader." The room is silent. She asks, "Does everyone understand the issue? No? Let me draw a diagram." Most of the students face the board and appear to listen.

There are four Venezuelan students. I am able to locate them by their orientation to one another in the room. One of the two girls asks a question. "Can one of the representatives be a leader, too?" Kay says, "No." "Why not?" asks Sophia. "Just tell me why not." Kay begins to respond, but stumbles on a word. She seems to shrivel in her chair. She shakes her head back and forth. Meredith moves close to her. "Kay, just take a deep breath. It's hard, I know."

One of the Ethiopian students offers yet another alternative. Meredith works hard to keep the choices in front of all the students by writing them into her diagram. She watches the students' faces carefully and moves quickly around the room, touching students gently.

Lugo points to the diagram saying, "I don't understand very much. Will you explain?" "Will you explain?" is a phrase that Meredith uses a lot to encourage students to amplify their responses. The students seem to have picked it up and use it in their questions to her and to each other. Meredith speaks clearly, slowly, and patiently. She leans forward, urging words out of the students.

"We need more opinions from some other people. Lenora, what do you think? Would you please give me your reasons? This is not just a vote, I'm looking for your opinions."

A second Ethiopian student, a tall, thin young man speaks very softly. Meredith is by his side in a moment. She asks him to speak louder for all to hear. "I can't," he murmurs. Meredith urges, "Speak to Sophia across the room." Meredith leans down, "I know you speak quietly, you always do." She smiles fully at him. "Okay, you speak to me and I'll shout it out for you."

There is no talking among the students. They shift in their chairs so that there is an occasional creak. One of the Venezuelan girls exchanges flirtatious glances with Lugo on the other side of the room. Lenora is dressed in pink—pink sweat pants, pink socks, pink sneakers, and a pink shirt under a pastel blue sweater. Her make-up is dramatic, and she is singing to herself, keeping time with her head. Meredith barely touches her shoulder. "Lenora?" Lenora stops her rhythmic motion.

As class breaks, the Venezuelan students speak in Spanish to one another and the Chinese, Korean, and Ethiopian students likewise seek each other out for a few moments of easy conversation. For Meredith, it has been an energetic session. She has moved among the students, watching them carefully, helping them to frame their words, assisting them in whatever ways she could. In a later conversation, she turns the same full, warm smile on me and says, "I can't help it. I get a kick out of the students. I like them."

When people speak of ethnic and racial separations at the high school, they are usually not referring to the nationality groups represented in U.S. History for Foreign Students. Rather, they are speaking about the more entrenched groups—the blacks, the Asians, the Jews, and the Irish. Luke Simon, a social worker who is revered as "The Saint" by students and faculty alike, has been intimately and unflinchingly involved in the "interracial stuff" since he came to the school fourteen years ago. He has carefully watched "how this community receives strangers," and his observations indicate the great progress and the profound resistance to mixing among the groups. He remembers that when he first came to Rosemont, the Irish kids would cast aspersions on "those fucking Jews." The Irish resented the abilities and aggressiveness of the Jewish students and responded with "territoriality and physical prowess." Fourteen years later, Simon feels that the school is much more of a melting pot. "The old Jewish liberal spirit still exists. . . . There is good will for people and strong commitment to the philosophy and goals of public education." As minority groups grow in size and visibility, the school has had to find ways of adapting to their presence. Simon underscores the emerging tensions. "As the number of black kids has gotten larger, this has become more *their* place. . . . There continues to be a small core of resistance . . . status games . . . and old-timers still resist surrendering their town to newcomers." However, given the severe territoriality of a decade ago, Luke Simon finds these reverberations promising. "I'm very optimistic . . . I don't feel as much tension as I used to. . . . There are always lots of kids who want to take risks to reach out and know other kinds of kids, to cross the barriers."

Simon is wary of stereotypes, categories, and myths about groups. He knows the danger of static, dogmatic perceptions and recognizes the great variations within groups. When I ask him to characterize the ethnic and social groups in the school, he flinches at first and then risks the misunderstandings and inaccuracies of speaking in global terms. He is not the kind of liberal who says everyone is the same. He is a tough realist who recognizes the humanity in all people but perceives the striking cultural differences in style and values. Perhaps he believes that facing the differences and admitting the separations are the first steps toward tolerance and acceptance. I am impressed by the insight, pragmatism, and daring of his characterizations:

> Irish kids screw themselves. . . . They have directed their energy into a negative tradition, shut down their horizons. . . . Are they going to always have these attitudes? We should try to challenge the way they feel . . . help them to see the beauty in other people. . . . I think this is their last chance, and ours, to help them.
>
> I feel out of touch with the Chinese kids. We don't see many of them in our roles as social workers. They just don't get in trouble. . . . They seem to invisibly move through the building. . . . They must have a rich private life. Their publication, *The Inner Voice*, speaks about their mode of expression.
>
> The black kids are spiritually and physically together. They are as one— not just in a hostile way, but in a supportive way. They don't want to be messed over. If anyone is the target still, it is the black kids. For people who grow up needing an enemy, they are the great, visible target. . . . But that is being gnawed at from every possible angle.

The differences seem extreme, but they grow less pronounced with each year. School seems to be a good setting to work out hostilities, to straddle barriers, and to test the assumptions of stereotypes. Says Simon poignantly, "Sometimes Rosemont High School has to deal with the waves of tension coming out of the city. At times I've thought of this building as a sanctuary . . . away from the more painful street stuff."

The racial and ethnic cleavages are exaggerated by the long established "leveling" system. Although almost everyone claims that students are not tracked, there are four definable levels of instruction:

basic, standard, honors, and advanced placement. (Some departments, like social studies, have three levels: standard, honors, and advanced placement.) Students are assigned to these levels through an elaborate combination of self-representation and choice, parental preference, testing, former grades and standing in elementary school, and counselor evaluations. The guidance department describes the placement process as judicious, careful, and flexible. A student who is not faring well in an honors class, for instance, can move to a standard-level class without embarrassment or humiliation. The shift is made with the consultation of teacher, parents, and student, and the effort is coordinated by the guidance counselor. Many students I spoke with talked about the ease of entering and exiting from one level to another and the coordination of judgment that makes that possible.

A parent, who is a school psychologist working in a neighboring suburb, marvelled at the responsiveness of Rosemont's guidance department. "There is communication and availability. . . . When I had anxieties I could get a response. . . . They are always there." When her daughter, a sophomore, felt pressured by the demands of her advanced placement courses, a collective decision was made to move her to honors sections, where she is now thriving. The counselor, housemaster, relevant teachers, and parents met with the student to consider the options, and a decision was made that seemed to respect all voices and satisfy most needs.

Another mother, who works as a secretary in a local business, tells a less positive story about negotiating with the guidance office regarding level placement. In the beginning of the year, her daughter, a "bright but manipulative" senior, was having some difficulty mastering the material in her advanced placement mathematics course. She complained to the counselor that the work was too hard and received permission to move to an honors-level class. A form was sent home for parent comment and signature, but this mother felt the decision had already been made. "I felt powerless to change the course of things. The counselor never asked me about it *before* the plans were set in motion. My daughter followed their plan. Parents should have more power in these decisions." The experience of exclusion hit this mother very hard. She felt that parents have a knowledgeable and different view of their children that the school should take advantage of. Decisions should be based on collective evaluations, and parents should have a prominent voice. "I know my child is an operator. She needed to be pressed into working harder, not given the easy retreat to another level." She spoke of the lingering feeling of subtle discrimination against working-class parents. "Maybe if I was a lawyer instead of a secretary they would value my opinion more highly. . . . Maybe they don't know I'm a college graduate."

These mothers of achieving daughters both viewed the leveling system as flexible and responsive to individual needs, but had different perceptions of the decision-making process. To one, the process was careful and systematic; to the other, it was careless and impulsive. Although many people who defend the leveling system point to the movement it permits, most teachers, parents, and students recognize its static, separating effects. The advanced placement classes are filled with ambitious, articulate students from privileged backgrounds. They are safe from the contaminations of the more mediocre students and can expect to receive a superior, even creative, education. The minority and working-class students are disproportionately represented in the basic and standard levels. For instance, there are one hundred METRO students and the large majority of them are in basic-level classes. Seventy METRO students received D's or E's on their grade reports during the third quarter of last year. These are not students who have recently transferred from public schools in the city. They have been in the Rosemont system since kindergarten, and their failure cannot be blamed on the negative, oppressive environment of an inferior school system. Kennedy claims that these striking differences in achievement patterns have been ignored for too long. "Now they *must* be confronted. We must face the realities." He underscores the point more dramatically. "There are two schools here. I have two children in this school and they have no idea of the range of problems I deal with up here. Theirs is the suburban school, smooth and peaceful . . . and then there is the other school rumbling underneath all the time. . . . The challenge is to bring these two schools together."

A more ardent critic of the leveling system describes it as "insidious and discriminatory." An upper-level administrator, she is the only one I spoke to who claimed that students are "tracked." "The initial assignment is critical and it occurs in elementary school. . . . It completely determines what the student will come away with. . . . Some students come into school, get lost in a nonacademic life . . . do nothing, learn nothing . . . just hang around for four years. If you go into A.P. classes, you're not going to find black students . . . and no female students in A.P. science classes. . . . Maybe some of that has changed recently." Despite the school's liberal rhetoric, there are only a few faculty who recognize the contradictions between "a just and democratic community" and the leveling structure. In her view, the accepted stratification is related to preserving the image of excellence and elitism in the midst of major shifts in the student population. "As I speak to students, alumni, and teachers about Rosemont High School, I hear a recurring theme—RHS is constantly compared with schools such as Harvard. The references are almost interchangeable." These images are important to parents and students of high status, and comforting to some teachers whose self-image is linked to old visions of an exclusive education.

One distinguished old-timer echoes these sentiments. He has been at Rosemont High for more than two decades and enjoys teaching advanced placement courses in the dry and laconic style of a college professor. Many students, bored by his delivery, are pleased with his assumption of their excellence. He brags that his A.P. students can enter any elite college and excel. "One of my friends who teaches at Amherst said, 'Hey, you guys at Rosemont are putting us out of work.' " Nostalgic, weary, and a bit timid speaking about his negative responses, he describes the inevitable tensions between diversity and excellence. "Maybe I am not supposed to say this, but, definitely, standards are lower than ten years ago. . . . They try so hard to include everyone, to keep everyone involved in the school, and that's good— industrial arts, cooking classes, and such; they have courses in *everything*. But the quality, well, I would not vouch for that." He wonders out loud about the limits of inclusion. "I don't know whether you've heard about these problems from others, but there are now a whole bunch of kids from Southeast Asia who are fifteen, sixteen, and seventeen years old and they've *never* been to school. They are illiterate; can't read in their own language. And there are increasing numbers of Russian students. Some are very talented. Others are impossible. They get here and don't know what to do with all the freedom." The veteran's voice trails off. His attitude seems to combine a deep longing for the old days and genuine puzzlement about how to face today and tomorrow with integrity and fairness. With some apology, he admits that teaching is no longer a joy. There are too many persistent struggles and unanswered questions.

Just as there are some teachers who can only feel inspired by the brightest students, there are others who intentionally choose to teach the basic-level course. One English teacher has an excellent reputation among her colleagues precisely because she is capable of teaching well at all levels. Says one admirer, "We all knew that she was extraordinary in working with the articulate bright kids. Their facile minds could play with ideas. But then she managed to do a bang-up job with a bunch of basic students and we said, 'Now we *know* she is a fine teacher.'" An energetic and committed science teacher chooses to teach basic biology. "I love it," he exclaims. "It doesn't mean they get watered-down biology. What I teach they get in standard and honors. But it means that I have to work harder." A black scientist, he is determined to attract young black students into the sciences. "It is my personal crusade."

At Rosemont there does not appear to be the negative stigma attached to teaching low-achieving students that one finds in most tracked schools. Occasionally one hears derogatory comments about the basic students, but mostly these remarks are couched carefully and designed not to offend. Sometimes they grow out of a teacher's feelings of frustration about "making a dent" or "communicating." But one also hears faculty complaints about the more privileged, high-achieving students, who are occasionally accused of being overly competitive, indulged, and uncreative; fearful of losing their lofty position.

Group differences and boundaries are most clearly visible in the cafeteria. Students and faculty point toward the cafeteria when I ask about the "culture" of the school. It is here that the natural inclinations of students are allowed to flourish. One is struck by students' "groupiness," the variations within groups, students' understandings of why separations exist, and by the ways in which some of them try to cross boundaries.

During the first lunch period, I sit down with Marion, a senior who has recently run for school-wide office, and three of her companions. Marion is sitting with three other seniors, a blond girl and two dark, curly-haired boys. In the course of the conversation I learn that these four students are enrolled in honor and advanced placement courses. I ask the students about school pride. Peter Rosenberg leans across the table and says, "It's not cool to have school spirit. For about ten years there's been no spirit, but it's making a small comeback now, right Marion?" Peter is a thin, nervous person. He pulls apart a brownie he is eating and rolls the small pieces into balls in the palms of his hands. His hands are always moving. He is either tearing his brownie apart and rolling it, or twisting his fingers. He leans in close to talk to me, but nervously checks his companions for validation. He tends to defer to Marion when she is inclined to answer. Having just run for school office, Marion has a lot to say about school pride and spirit. She states emphatically that "RHS is just like college." She explains, "The courses are just as hard, the teachers are just as smart as at college." The blond girl to Marion's left has long hair that sweeps the table top when she leans toward me. She also talks with intensity. "Yes, it is just like college. I know that because last year in chemistry I had a student teacher and he said that we used the same book they had in college." Marion says, "This is a great place to see and get to know all kinds of people—Russians, Chinese, blacks, Jews." The two girls look at Peter and Jason. The blond girl says, "Truthfully, Peter, if I'd gone to private school I probably would never get to know Jews and here I am friends with a Jewish person." Peter says, "My brother goes to prep school and he really misses out. You know, everyone is white." Marion says, "My brother goes to prep school but he's better off there. He just can't control himself. He'd have trouble here." I ask why he'd have trouble here and she answers, "He's not as tolerant as I am about people." I say that it does seem to me that there are lots of different people and I tell them my observations about the student groups who occupy different steps in the quadrangle. All four students lean over toward me. Peter, twisting his hands . . . tells me about student cliques. "Of course there are cliques. There are cliques everywhere." He lowers his voice, "Behind you are the jocks. Over there," he points his head briefly, spinning back to face me, "are the preppies—white preppies, black preppies, and Chinese preppies." The pace of the conversation is frantic. All of the students are trying to talk at once. The subject of cliques is of interest. They explain that ethnic groups more or less hang together, but there is lots of mixing. I have noted that every fourth table seems to have a heterogeneous grouping of students. Jason says, "If you think the students are separatists, you should see the teachers, they're even worse." (Later in the day, when I mention that observation to two teachers they both agree emphatically. They are surprised that the students have noticed.) With the lunch half-hour almost over, the tone of the conversation is not simply animated, it is hyper. These students are active in Rosemont High School student activities, they recognize and appreciate the standard of academic work expected of them, and they want to put the best face of RHS in front of me—the stranger. Yet their curiosity about the ways students and teachers stratify into groups, "exclusive groups that are almost impossible for a new person to break into," leads them to expose what they see as a possible weakness of RHS. Peter grabs my wrist. "All of the groups are exclusive. Of course there are always some exceptional people who can break into any group, but that's rare. Mostly people just like to stick to a group."

In the second lunch half-hour, I ask two black girls if I can join them. Both smile shyly up at me and move their books to make space. One of the girls explains that she's late for class and must leave. She speaks with a lilting, rhythmic accent that I'm told later is Haitian. The young woman I face has a pensive, pretty face. She tells me that she is from Africa, from Ethiopia where her parents still live. She moved to the United States over two years ago to live with her older brother and sister. She was first enrolled at Bradford High School, which she hated. She explains, "The students at Bradford come to class with their tape recorders. They wear headphones while the teacher talks and they make noise all of the time. Rosemont is much better, it is serious. The students here are very serious, and that's good." Bahai explains that she came to America to get a good education. "That's why Rosemont is the best place to be," she says with certainty. When I ask if it was easy to meet people at Rosemont, she says, "Yes, it is most easy to meet white students. The blacks know we are different. They know we're African and think we're racist." I say, "That must be hard for you sometimes." She replies, "Yes, it is hard for all of us who are not American blacks. It makes us feel hurt." Later, when I talk to a senior who is an American black I ask her about the foreign black students. She explains that foreign students tend to stick together and not mix much with anyone. When asked how welcoming Rosemont High School students are to foreign students, she says, "I guess it's hard to incorporate new people into your group, especially if you've known these friends all your life. You don't make the effort. Not that we shouldn't, but we just don't."

For an hour and a half, the two rooms of the cafeteria are full. During the whole lunch period, teachers walk singly through the rooms. They are unobtrusive and generally ignored by the students. Occasionally a teacher will stop and chat with a table of students and then move on. The students settle among the rectangular, round, and square tables as if by routine. Most students tell me, "I always sit at this table." The underclass students move like flocks of swallows. They arrive in large groups, chattering and squawking, and settle en masse around three rectangular tables. The juniors and seniors tend to move more slowly and in smaller groups—in pairs or even singly. In the first room, black students occupy six rectangular tables against the folding partition. In the next room, Asian students occupy three rectangular tables set end-to-end. In both rooms are tables with black and Asian students, but the territory seems to be bounded for others.

## New Leadership: Change in Philosophy and Style

Dr. William Kennedy introduces himself informally. "Hi, I'm Bill Kennedy." His dress matches his casual greeting. He wears a loosely fitting light blue sweater, slightly rumpled dark trousers, and walks with a weary gait. His gray-black hair is tousled and he runs his fingers through it often as he furrows his brow to think. Kennedy's tired look is deceptive. When he begins to talk about things that are important to him, the energy and enthusiasm shows in his intense eyes. He thinks out loud as he says, "I don't know if this is what you came for—what you want to hear. Why don't you just let me go on? Stop me if I go too far off the track." But nothing is rambling about his comments. They are organized, perceptive, and contemplative. He is surprisingly open and self-critical, and doesn't have the guarded reticence of many school administrators.

Kennedy has been at Rosemont High for only a year. He came from a principalship in New Hampshire, where he enjoyed a challenging but easy life heading a school of six hundred and fifty students. "I liked it there very much. My kids were in good schools. . . ." Occasionally, during his decade of tenure in New Hampshire, he was tempted to sniff out other jobs, but he had no real intention of leaving. He was comfortable. However, the challenge of Rosemont was seductive. "This is the *only* school in the country I would have left New Hampshire for," he says enthusiastically. The attraction lay in the combination of the critical and interesting problems facing the school and the resources available to respond to those problems. He saw it as an "urban" school shaken by major crises, but he also saw a community committed to its salvation. Several months earlier, he had been called to apply for a troubled principalship in the city, "But I wasn't that crazy." The complacency and homogeneity of the more affluent suburban schools also did not interest him. Rosemont lay somewhere in the middle of these two extremes. It had big-city problems, but a cushion of money and positive sentiment that could challenge the difficulties if used wisely and bravely.

Long known for its fine academic standards, Rosemont High had deteriorated in the decade before Kennedy arrived. Built in 1854, the high school had enjoyed a reputation of stability. Since 1854, there have been only nineteen principals. Most of them had long tenures;

one stayed only for a year before he was elevated to the superintendency. The school's reputation as a solid, abundant institution still lingers, even though the image is long outdated. Although Kennedy points to the troublesome seventies and the "authoritarian" leadership of his predecessor, Joseph Lombardi, he does not view himself as the sole guiding force that got the school back on track. "You know, from what I'm telling you, you might be thinking that everything was rotten until I came. Then things suddenly got better. But I know you are too perceptive to believe that," he says to me.

Lombardi had been a teacher in Rosemont for a long time before he became principal. He had enjoyed the school's fine reputation and supported the high academic standards. But as the population of the school began to shift and the cultural norms of the community were transformed, he proceeded as if nothing had changed. He ignored the new diversity of the student population, claiming, "Everyone is the same and must be treated the same." The teachers and administrators seemed blind to the eruptions of violence, episodes of racism and human indecency. Says Kennedy, "If you were walking through the courtyard and some kid pulled a knife, you tried to avoid seeing it." During the first two months after Kennedy's arrival, there were sixteen serious fights. "My head was in a different place. . . . I wasn't used to this. . . . I felt scared."

But more shocking than the fights were the complacent responses of faculty to the violence. "They seemed to see it as part of their job to break up fights. They didn't seem to be angry." In talking with the faculty now, Kennedy discovered that they, too, were frightened and angry, but had not felt that it was legitimate to express their rage. In some ways, they were ignoring the profound troubles that surrounded them by pretending that fights did not disturb them. Kennedy challenged their pretense of complacency. "I would not accept breaking up fights as part of my job. I would show those kids how angry I was." Soon the "crackdown" began. Students were not allowed to congregate in ominous groups or bully fellow students who wanted to pass through blocked doorways. When there were violent incidents, parents were brought in immediately, and teachers expressed their outrage to the student and his parents. The new expressions of anger seemed to have an effect. Many students were shocked by the expression of feelings and the seriousness and intensity of their teachers who had seemed not to care so much before. Parents may have been embarrassed by the public outrage, but seemed comforted by the attempts at bringing a new order and safety to the school. Since the opening of school a month ago, there have been no fights yet this year. The norms appear to be shifting, and memories of last year seem to have transcended the summer sojourn.

The violence among students had often been associated with episodes of racism. A fight would break out between a black kid and an Irish Catholic kid and ripple throughout the school as other groups would choose sides. In the late seventies the violence against black students had become so severe that their parents took action. Says Kennedy, sympathetically, "It was not easy for these Rosemont parents to confront the School Committee. They were risking their relationships to neighbors and friends—their place in the community." The parents formed a group called Concerned Black Citizens, and they began to meet regularly to talk about the racist tone of the school and the violent assaults against their youngsters. They met denial from Lombardi, who refused to admit there was trouble, and reticence from the School Committee, who took a protective attitude toward the principal. As the violence became more flagrant and visible, as the parent group grew in numbers and sophistication, the School Committee could no longer ignore the charges. During one School Committee meeting when Lombardi was under attack from the black citizen's group, the committee "just let him hang there, swinging in the breeze." Soon after, Lombardi left.

Everyone talks about the sharp contrasts between Lombardi and Kennedy. Lombardi was "authoritarian, dominating, theatrical," and Kennedy is "low key, soft spoken, thoughtful." Lombardi was "visible, definitive, and uncompromising." Kennedy is "invisible, contemplative, and ambiguous." No one had any difficulty understanding and interpreting Lombardi's actions. Many claim to have difficulty comprehending the motivations and intent behind Kennedy's behavior. Some faculty allude to differences in style related to their ethnic origins. Lombardi had the flare and drama of Italians, and Kennedy the restraint and seriousness of his middle-class Irish upbringing.

Even though some express a nostalgic wish for the clear-cut messages of the old regime, I spoke to no one who wanted to have Lombardi back. Most agree that the problems grew to be too complex and tangled for the straightforward, dominating leadership of Lombardi. The seventies required a more flexible, subtle, and questioning style that did not fear change. Even though everyone seems to have recognized the need for a change of leadership, there is a lingering affection for their old leader. In one voice, people praise Kennedy and speak caringly about Lombardi. Their affection for Lombardi springs from their long association with him, from his genuine commitment to the school, from his outspoken protection of his faculty, and even from his human vulnerabilities. Paradoxically, one senses that his aggressive and charismatic style made him more open and approachable than the more sophisticated stance of his successor. "Lombardi let it all hang out," says one veteran teacher. Another claims, "With Lombardi, it was what you see is what you get." When he got in trouble, many teachers recognized his weaknesses and limitations but identified with his fate.

The connections to Lombardi remain. His shadowy presence makes it difficult for some teachers to fully respond to Kennedy. One administrator, who is strongly approving of Kennedy, explained it this way, "By the end of his reign here, Joseph had successfully alienated almost everyone. He was a man who had been loved and feared, but his departure was weird. No one understood it. One day he was just gone, and there was no way to say goodbye. . . . We never really severed the relationship and his presence is still deeply felt. . . . No one says, 'I wish Joseph were here,' but it was difficult making the transition."

Just as some faculty experienced more comfort and protection with Lombardi's "autocratic" style, many told me of the liberation and autonomy that Kennedy's leadership permits. Raved one teacher with an excellent reputation, "I love him. He is just wonderful—the best thing that has ever happened to this school!" Said another, in slightly more restrained tones, "Bill followed a witty, energetic, articulate, and very authoritarian headmaster who gave orders and told everyone what to do . . . but Kennedy is low key, sensitive, and secure. He won't take that position. . . . Lots of people have trouble with that, but I think he is wonderful. . . . Let me tell you something he did the other day. One of the guidance counselors, who was well loved by everyone, died of cancer. Kennedy got on the P.A. and talked about the sadness, the separation, the loss, and the anger we feel at being abandoned by her . . . and the kids really got it; the teachers got it." Tears came to the storyteller's eyes as she recounted the incident. "I think it is because he is a runner," she says smilingly. "We runners have great inner strength and lots of patience."

Those who express boundless admiration for Kennedy's personal qualities also tend to speak positively about his views on leadership and power. Kennedy is outspoken on the subject. "I have always found that the more power you give people, the more responsibility they take." He is eager to dismantle the hierarchical arrangement of roles and relationships in the school, and is trying to create a school structure that will increase the sense of community (a word he often uses) and participation among students, faculty, administrators, and staff (that is, custodians, cooks and secretaries).

Soon after his arrival, Kennedy established the Fairness Committee to deal with disciplinary problems. Students and faculty sit on this committee, and their recommendations for action, made to the administration, are binding. There are no empty gestures; this is real power and decision making. Kennedy hopes that, over the years, the Fairness Committee will increase its scope and become like the judicial arm of the school—not merely responding to incidents of crisis but also creating policy.

This year a new and important experiment is being initiated. The Town Meeting will become the major decision-making body of the school. With eighty representatives from all parts of the school community, the Town Meeting will establish the beginnings of a democratic structure that gives participating members an equal voice. Kennedy speaks about the new innovation with enthusiasm—recognizing the vulnerabilities of an open system and the inevitable problems of initiation and growth. Five years from now, he hopes that his role will be reduced in scope and resemble the executive branch of government. "They can take *all* the power, for all I care."

Kennedy's strong allies among the faculty share his vision, recognize the risks involved, and offer their good will and support. Others share much of his philosophical orientation but feel his methods are unfocused and unrealistic. One supporter spoke about the hazards of transitional periods. "No one knows who is in or where the power is. Kennedy's signals are sometimes mixed. . . . He seems to want it, then he doesn't want it—so everyone spends so much energy trying to figure him out." This observer told about Kennedy's ambivalence toward power (despite his rhetoric to the contrary). Last year, when they were searching for a department head, he claims Kennedy designed an elaborate and cumbersome process for the review of candidates. After many rounds of interviewing, the Search Committee proposed three names for his consideration. Kennedy did not like any of the names and chose the candidate that he had favored all along. "He was unwilling to relinquish power."

Many faculty seem to recognize that Kennedy's "mixed messages" are an inevitable part of the acclimation process. "Kennedy is working out a style in relation to the school. Half the time I'm invigorated by his approach, and half the time it drives me crazy." But they also recognize their wish for a visible, lofty leader. "He wants to come across as a normal person, but some people have trouble with a normal person as headmaster. No matter what people's inclination toward Kennedy, everyone seems to agree that this period has ushered in a great deal of uncertainty and shifting ground. There is a self-consciousness about actions and responses; a searching to find out where one stands in relation to others; a "staking out of territories and protecting of flanks"; and the optimism and fears that always go hand in hand with change. Everyone is trying to figure out the puzzle as the pieces get rearranged. At the center of the puzzle is Kennedy, a man with a well-articulated vision but, some say, a measure of ambivalence.

## The Town Meeting: Shared Power

The Town Meeting at Rosemont is designed to approximate Lawrence Kohlberg's notion of a just community. Convinced that moral development and growth can only thrive in a context that supports shared power and responsibility, last year some Rosemont teachers and administrators wrote a grant proposal that recommended the Town Meeting as a way of altering hierarchical relationships in the school. The Town Meeting, comprised of students, faculty, and staff would have the authority to govern Rosemont High School within legal constraints set by the state and in concert with the headmaster and the School Committee. This was not to be a vacuous form of student government or an empty gesture that camouflaged old patterns; it was to be a real attempt to change deeply rooted patterns of power and decision making. The proposal was funded and the day before I arrived, in early October, the project director was chosen to lead "the experiment."

Steve Smith, a recent graduate of a prestigious local university and a disciple of Lawrence Kohlberg, arrived with a realistic blend of skepticism, commitment, and hope. Despite the fact that many teachers shared Kennedy's enthusiasm for the process and supported his commitment to the goals of democracy and equality, many were reticent to become overly optimistic, and others were suspicious of motivations and purpose. Some teacher complaints were focused on the choice of Steve Smith. "He looks like a typical Ivy Leaguer—his language and style are wholly academic," said one. "An insider should have been chosen for this position. You have to know the school intimately in order to do this job," said another. But the dominant concerns of skeptical and resistant teachers seemed to be related to their views of the Town Meeting form as an administrative and decision-making structure. The most adamant faculty complained that the Town Meeting was a way for Kennedy to avoid the demands and liabilities of leadership. "He is afraid of power, afraid to be the bad guy," said one teacher, who admitted her penchant for conservatism, order, and certainty. But other, less critical voices, worried that the Town Meeting was based on a wrong-headed view of school culture, values, and norms. In their view, schools do not work best as democracies. Not only is shared decision making wildly inefficient, but it leads to ambiguities of power that make everyone unsure and uncomfortable. Clarity of roles and defined authority structures, they argued, are liberating, not oppressive; they support, rather than undermine, communication. In addition, these teachers believed that adolescents may not be ready for wielding power and making informed decisions. "My greatest worry," said one sympathetic but wary teacher, "is that Town Meeting will degenerate into the student government I knew in high school; be a popularity contest; stand for all the wrong values. It would be one thing if this had been an oppressive environment for students, but the kids have always had a voice, always felt cared for, always had their piece of the power. Why are we making all these changes in a system that has worked well?"

The elections for Town Meeting are to be held in early October.

During the week before the elections, posters and leaflets begin to appear, plastered carelessly in the hallways. Most are written on colored construction paper without much attention to precision or aesthetics. The great majority of the candidates do not appear to have made election posters or canvassed their peers for votes. A few posters have the practiced script of careful sign makers, but these tend to advertise freshman candidates for office. One enthusiastic and very earnest freshman boy has slick publicity material that appears to have been professionally produced. Perhaps he has not yet learned that it is not "cool" to try so hard, to appear to want it so much. Some of his classmates seem to be embarrassed by his vigorous attempts to get elected. The upper classmen seem half-amused and slightly scornful of his obvious enthusiasm.

The election speeches are given in each of the four houses: Maple House, Windsor House, Browning House, and Stevens House. With five hundred students in each house, they serve as major subdivisions of the larger school. All of the students and faculty attached to each house gather in large meeting rooms (the cafeteria, the student-faculty lounge, the old gym, and the auditorium) to hear the speeches of the candidates. There is a mood of anticipation and excitement as five hundred students crowd into the gathering places one Tuesday morning at 10:00 A.M. I am struck by the crush of bodies and the volume of noise that fills the room along with a sense of order and control. At no time do I fear violence, or even chaos. More importantly, the teachers in charge do not seem worried about outbreaks of disorder. Their attitudes are calm, affable, and restrained as they urge students to be seated anywhere they can find space—on chairs, on tables, on window sills, and on the floor. Once everyone is settled, members of Windsor House listen to Housemaster Selma Hill make the introductions: "Welcome to the first annual Town Meeting campaign session. . . . We have well qualified, eager, articulate members . . . a crowded field. Each candidate will tell you why you should vote for him or her. Voting will take place tomorrow in my office. You will be able to vote for two candidates in each grade, eight total. . . . There will also be at-large representatives if there are groups who feel that they are not being fairly represented."

The Browning House election meeting, held in the cafeteria, follows the same general pattern, but the atmosphere is a bit more informal.

The housemaster at the microphone has the easy good looks of someone who fits in. He has reddish blond hair, thinning at the top, a wide and frequent grin, and dancing eyes. He banters with the students who cheer him and boo him excitedly. The candidates assembled, his tone changes slightly as he begins by saying, "The people here in front of me are running for Town Meeting. They will be allowed to speak for one and one-half to two minutes. I ask you to please be attentive and polite and to listen carefully to what they say. This is an important decision you're making. You'll be able to elect two people from each class in Browning House." He jokes, "Now, let's see, that's four times eight or—" There's no answer from the audience. He points to his temple and shakes his head. The students laugh uproariously as he says over their noise, "That's what we like, an informed electorate." He waits for quiet. "If you are Chinese or black or Irish or Russian, or any other ethnic group, and you don't think that your group is represented by any of these candidates, please speak to your headmaster. We all want representation." With a few more introductory comments, delivered in a respectful and an accepting way, he introduces the first speaker: "Ms. Marion Best." Marion has shoulder-length hair, parted in the middle. Her slightly freckled face is serious as she asks: "Is there school spirit and school pride among us?" The crowd murmurs a hushed, "No." She moves ahead with her recommendations for increasing both spirit and pride. She says, "We should use the house system as a melting pot where students of all ages and backgrounds could get to know one another." To illustrate how much she cares about RHS, she says, "I cared enough to postpone getting my braces removed until after this speech and this election. I'll end up wearing them three more weeks than I had to." The applause seems genuine, the calls from the crowd supportive.

The next senior speaker is a blond pony-tailed girl. Her face is somber as she approaches the microphone. Joyce Hart is wearing a lime green turtleneck with a rag sweater and a single strand of pearls. She gives her political experience, but no platform.

The third senior to speak stands up, squares his shoulders and ambles forward. Brad has dark hair, parted in the middle, an athletic build and a popular following of girls who yell, "Yea, Brad." He doesn't have a prepared speech. He tells me the next day, when I am watching the soccer team practice, that he thought seniors would speak last so he was going to write the speech when the first three classes spoke. "Hey," he begins. He waits, looking at the crowd. They laugh and the second-row girls yell. "Listen, I'm not going to stand up here and give a speech, I just want you all to know that I'm here to represent you." He rambles on with apparent ease and ends by saying, "I just want you all to know that any of us would do a good job, except for Mark Stein." The students laugh and the teacher moves to the mike to introduce the last senior speaker: Mark Stein.

Mark has a head of brown curls and the same muscular, athletic build as Brad. He moves to the mike with a serious face. He nods toward Brad and says with deadpan delivery, "That's a real tough act to follow, Brad." The students love it and whoop and laugh. Without cracking a smile, Mark waits for the noise to subside and gives a short, clear speech with obvious poise and confidence. Finished, he smiles and walks directly to Brad. Placing his hand on Brad's head, he ruffles his hair and moves on to his own seat.

The four seniors finished, the juniors begin. Anthony Doxiadis is introduced. He is a heavy, dark-haired young man with a shadowy mustache on his upper lip. "I'm going to be different than the other candidates. I represent the right wing. I'm a conservative. Not like the left-wing candidates who are running. I support limiting property taxes and that makes me different." The crowd moans, but Anthony persists, "I think we need some conservatives on Town Meeting." He makes a mental jump, "I don't want people running after me, telling me what to do all the time. I'll tell you what to do, if I'm elected." He steps away from the microphone, the first speaker to get little applause.

Myrna Rosen scurries up to the microphone. Her wavy brown hair bushes out around her shoulders. She straightens her pink turtleneck and Fair Isle sweater, firmly grasps her speech, and charges into the text. She speaks rapidly without looking up. "I would not be a passive candidate. . . ." Each sentence trips over the next in rapid succession. She finishes, takes a deep breath, receives her applause and returns to her seat.

Roger Duke is introduced. A tall, slim young man with a short Afro walks to the microphone. His handsome black face slowly spreads into a contagious smile, "Hello, I'm Roger Duke." The students return his laugh. The audience seems to ease into Roger's sincere delivery. "I'm a person who wants your ideas for this Town Meeting. And I want to help this committee work." With one hand in his brown corduroy pants, the other is free to gesticulate. He thanks the students for listening and gets an enthusiastic applause.

The fourth candidate's introduction is the first to be greeted by audible hoots. A low "Hey, Jean" rolls forward from the back of the cafeteria. A short, sturdy Jean Goodwin seems to ignore the hoots, which die down almost as quickly as they began. Her square shoulders seem broad in the navy blazer she is wearing. In a stern voice she informs the students that she has experience, dependability, and good judgment. She levels her dark glasses on the bridge of her nose as she looks out over the audience. The gesture seems staged, almost as if her speech told her to pause and survey her audience. Jean finishes her speech and receives some applause.

The housemaster who is acting as the emcee perhaps feels the boredom in the cafeteria. He tells us, "A bulletin from election central reports that teachers will not be able to vote for students." His announcement is greeted by huge applause and whoops. He raises his hand to calm the students.

"But I must tell you, that means no students can vote for teachers." He claps and they boo him with high spirits. He introduces the first sophomore.

Betsy James reads her speech so quickly she simply can't be understood. Her racing, quiet voice blurs each word into a stream of words, and no one from the middle of the cafeteria to the back can hear her. The noise of the crowd increases substantially. Students turn to talk with one another, laughing, poking, teasing one another.

Matthew Miles follows Betsy. A straight, slim blond-haired young man, he says, "I come before you an honest politician." The audience laughs hard and interrupts his speech with applause. Seeming unruffled, Matthew continues his speech with seriousness, clear enunciation, and a loud, clear voice. The students have become more attentive now that they can hear the speaker again.

The next two speakers, Donald Turner and Joan Spielberg both have written speeches, which they read with clear, loud voices.

The last sophomore to speak is Jennifer Howell. As she walks to the microphone a supportive male voice in the back yells, "Yea, Jennifer." Without acknowledging her fan, Jennifer pats her long blonde hair, which is pulled back. Her pretty smile flashes as the light reflects from her braces. When she finishes her speech, she grimaces and hunches back to her seat.

Sammy is the first freshman speaker. A large, overweight boy, Sammy lumbers to the microphone. He wears a yamulka and clothes that seem to belong to a fifty-year-old rather than a fifteen-year-old. The gray pants are held tight at his waist with a belt and he scuffs his shiny black leather shoes against each other as he speaks. "I'm Sammy, and I'm not going to say very much." A voice in the back of the room yells, "Good." Sammy scuffs harder. "I'm a good leader. Those who know me know that." The students laugh. Sammy grins back at them.

The second freshman has his own cheering squad. They have pinned campaign cards on their clothes and all of them clap long and loud when their candidate, Zachary, is introduced. An impish face framed with bright orange curls faces the students. His supporters cheer his silence and his speech with equal zeal. He says, "Not many critical issues have been raised today." His fans respond, "Right." For a couple of minutes, campaign fever infects the audience.

The next speaker is a young black man. Martin is a round, somber-faced boy, who says of himself, "I am a man of very few words." Like Zachary, Martin also has a cheering squad sitting near the front. He directs his speech to them and they respond enthusiastically.

The audience is growing more restless. Pairs of Chinese boys at the next table are playing some game on a piece of paper they keep passing between them. The freshmen boys behind me are jostling each other and whispering loudly. A teacher in a gray suit joins their table. A youngish man, he looks directly at the boys, straightens his tie and settles into his chair, ostensibly to hear the rest of the speeches.

A small-boned blonde-haired girl whose name is Betsy begins: "Flash! Thirty-two teachers, two secretaries, thirty-two students announce. . . ." She catches their attention and the room becomes silent as Betsy reads her mock news flash. She finishes and looks up and introduces herself by name again. She completes her speech with clarity and poise. The students seem almost surprised that they were caught up into Betsy's fantasy flash. They applaud her speech with enthusiasm.

The last speaker is a short black girl. Under five feet, she needs the microphone lowered. As the housemaster-emcee attempts to lower the microphone, some male voices yell out, "Where is she? Where'd she go?" With the microphone adjusted, Nicole presents her platform, step by logical step. A clear speaker and the last speaker, Nicole receives a lot of applause.

On the following Friday, during homeroom period, Dr. Kennedy announces the winners of the student election over the public address system. In a voice that sounds reverent and deliberate, he expresses the seriousness of the new community enterprise. "I have the privilege of announcing the winners of the Town Meeting election. Thanks to everyone who participated in the process. . . ." In the homeroom where I hear the announcement, students show little interest in the news. Most of their conversations continue uninterrupted, despite the protestations of the teacher, who urges them to listen carefully. A few students listen for the names of their friends and show visible disappointment when Kennedy does not mention them. Out in the hall, after homeroom period, there is some buzzing about winners and losers. The victors receive congratulations from friends—"Way to go, man"—while the losers quietly accept bemused condolences. But the victories and defeats do not seem very charged. Perhaps the prize is not highly valued.

The moderate enthusiasm among students seems vigorous compared to the lack of interest among teachers. Departments were to select faculty representatives to Town Meeting. For reasons of reticence, skepticism, and overwork, teachers declined to become involved in election proceedings. To most, the Town Meeting was a high-risk venture that many teachers feared would demand more time and energy in their already overcommitted schedules. In most departments, teachers were asked to volunteer for seats on the Town Meeting committee. By the time of the first scheduled meeting, the faculty representation was below the designated numbers. Those teachers who volunteered their services tended to be vocal supporters of the new system ("The few who always get involved and do all the work"), or people who greatly admired Kennedy.

The first Town Meeting showed all the signs of a beginning experiment. There was the rhetoric and optimism of the leaders followed by restraint and reserve on the part of the members. There was disorganization and lack of direction as people wondered who was in control and who had the power. And there was confusion about roles, agendas, and purpose as everyone struggled with the self-definition of this newly formed group. Teachers appeared more tentative and tense than students, probably fearing they had more to lose. Steve Smith, the project head, expressed ambivalence in his every move. He needed to grasp the reins in order to move the group forward, but he did not want to create the impression of unequal power and authoritarianism. To one observing the awkward process, there were feelings of empathy for the pain and fears connected with change and admiration for those willing to endure it.

> Dr. Kennedy stands before the first Town Meeting assembled in the faculty dining room. "This is an important day, if not an historic day. Rosemont High School opened in 1854. In the 1930s we initiated the house system, which was the first of its kind in the country. Rosemont High School has introduced many firsts. I will predict that the concept of a Town Meeting for a large high school is another one of those firsts. I understand that you have some questions. Will the Town Meeting run the school? Who's in charge, now that we have changed our system of governance? First, don't worry that no one around here can make a decision. We're going to see power shared in this school, though. The reason why it's important that decision making be shared is because we're not an army here. And we're not at war. If our lives depended on immediate decisions, we'd have a different decision-making system. Very logically, the process of decision making in a school should be established where all aspects of the school are subject to review. People must accept that this is a school where agreed-upon regulations will be supreme, not idiosyncrasies of individual men or women. Better decisions are made when a lot of people are involved. That's my basic conviction and what my experience has been."
>
> Students are listening indifferently. They seem more interested in checking out who else was elected to Town Meeting. Recognizing each other across the room, they exchange smiles, small waves. The teachers and staff seem more intent on Kennedy's comments.
>
> He says, "I promise you that a priority for me is to provide release time

to all the staff involved in this process of Town Meetings. Students, if you desire that credit be awarded, we may work that out as independent study. You'll have a budget—money. Money is now available to repair vandalism in this school."

Looking around the room I count seven black students and two black staff. There are no Asian students, but one Asian staff woman. It's difficult to evaluate whether or not Town Meeting is representative of the RHS student population.

Kennedy says, "You have the authority to review and to make recommendations to the School Committee, to the state department of education, if necessary. In this room we will disagree, argue with each other, but if we can go to the outside boards as a united front, we stand a better chance of being heard." He has a list of issues he thinks Town Meeting will have to address. "We have an AWOL [Absent Without Leave] policy at Rosemont High School, which some believe is applied differently by different teachers. You will have to deal with that. Dope policy—in my opinion anyone under the influence of either alcohol or drugs should be reported to the police. Guardian Angels want to come and recruit here. Some of us question that. Is it appropriate? What do you think? Litter and vandalism—what can be done? Methods of discipline are open to your scrutiny. Student-faculty lounge—perhaps there should be pinballs, maybe supervision [murmured agreement in the room is loud], maybe we should put furniture in there."

In his final comments, Kennedy tells the Town Meeting, "We want to show that a large metropolitan high school can be run democratically." He introduces Steve Smith, who, Kennedy says, is working full-time on Town Meeting under a federal grant.

Steve Smith is standing in the center of a circle of Town Meeting participants. The students are getting a little more uneasy, but they remain polite—looking at Smith as he speaks, refraining from talking among themselves. He says, "I'm sorry that I will be doing so much speaking during this first meeting. This will not happen as we get ourselves organized. I have worked for the past several years with schools experimenting with democracy. I've worked with smaller schools, but I bring a faith and a confidence that this will work out. One of my jobs here is to work with this group to help in any way I can. I will take on a coordinating role to help the committees as they're established. People all over the world are looking to see how these democratic structures work in large, metropolitan high schools." He says, "I am most interested in issues of school climate. I would like to be taping all of these meetings because we will be doing some future training and tapes are invaluable for that. Number two, we'll have a permanent record and, number three, we'll be able to help other schools interested in setting up a democratic structure. So, I would propose we do tape our meetings."

A student asks, "Could we stop the tape if we wanted to speak off the record?"

Smith, "Well, that's an issue. We could discuss that."

A short, student-dominated debate of ten exchanges ensues. Smith terminates the debate, saying, "We could have two votes: first, a general policy. Will people be in favor of taping? He asks for a show of hands. There is unanimous approval of a general taping policy.

"The second vote, I would like to put off," he continues. "If there are matters that should be kept private, we'll discuss that as a special issue as it arises."

He looks at his watch. "I promised I would get all of you out of here by two fifteen and we still have several agenda items." Students and staff look at their agendas. "I need volunteers from this group. First, Dr. Kennedy wants five students to represent Town Meeting to the School Committee." A faculty member interjects that according to state law the school needs two seniors, two juniors, and one sophomore to sit in on the School Committee. Smith asks that students who are interested in volunteering, raise their hands. A discussion on how to resolve the large number of volunteers with the five places takes place. Finally, Smith is able to say: "I think we have three different approaches and I suggest we vote. We can have lottery by class, ballot election, or we can use rotating members." The discussion is still confused and it's 2:15. Smith simply asks that all interested students and staff sign up after the Town Meeting with one of the students.

He is rushing a little. "I would like to see volunteers to be on an agenda committee for the next few Town Meetings. I would especially like people with experience working with Town Meetings to help out on this. We could meet in the faculty lounge after the meeting."

"Thirdly, we're going to have a half-time assistant who will be the town manager. We need people to serve on a screening committee. Students and staff are needed to do screening as soon as possible. We'd like to interview next Monday and make a hiring decision later in the week. Would volunteers for the screening committee stay here after the meeting?" A short round of questions from staff on whether they can have release time ends this meeting.

Everyone rushes off. Steve Smith must be reminded of similar beginning attempts to change entrenched patterns and structures in other schools in which he has worked. His comments to me a few days later express both patience and weariness. He knows it will be an uphill battle to build trust, confidence, and a sense of community. He knows, also, that pessimism and optimism are both appropriate emotions. The odds of failing are at least equal to the possibilities of success.

## A Sense of Community

Rosemont's student population is divided into four houses: Maple House, Windsor House, Browning House, and Stevens House. "They were designed to be like the houses of Harvard and Yale," many faculty explain. They resemble the houses of Harvard and Yale only in a structural, bureaucratic sense. Houses create smaller communities with which a student can identify and affiliate. But at Rosemont they are not intellectual frameworks, nor are they communities that inspire loyalty and commitment. Although some students I talked with said they had vague feelings of affiliation with the houses to which they belonged, they did not speak of the houses as places of connection and solace. Faculty, administrators, and students seem to agree that, as they are presently organized, the houses serve little more than as organizational functions, and many express a wish that they could have more force in the life of the school.

Five hundred students are randomly assigned to each house, except that siblings are always assigned to the same house. This makes it possible for parents to build relationships with a single house, even if they have more than one child in the school. It also makes it more likely that younger siblings will feel more familiar and comfortable in houses in which their older brothers or sisters are already ensconced. The houses are administered by a housemaster, a full-time position, and an assistant houseteacher, a part-time position. With the recent statewide budget cuts, related to a referendum limiting property taxes, the houseteacher is now required to teach three courses along with his administrative duties. Before this year, houseteachers taught two courses and had more time for administrative work. The responsibilities of housemaster and houseteacher appear to be negotiated by the incumbents. Housemasters certainly have the ultimate authority and accountability within the house, but houseteachers play prominent roles as disciplinarians, advisors, counselors, interpreters of school policy, advocates for students in relation to other faculty, and negotiators with parents. Their roles often overlap as teacher and master work in concert, collaborating with and supporting one another. From the students' point of view, it is better to have two, rather than one, authority figures connected with the house. "If you don't like one, you can approach the other." Usually one adult seems to be more available or responsive than another to particular students and this allows for some choice.

Everyone agrees that since Kennedy's arrival, the housemasters have been permitted more power and autonomy, but it continues to be an administrative, not an instructional, role. Mr. Barclay, the master of Browning House, describes his increased authority. "With Lombardi, the housemasters were like lieutenants. The metaphors were very male, very military. . . . But Kennedy has opened up the door for housemasters. Browning House students are *my* students. I can make all the decisions about them." And to watch him in action, one sees a person with a wide range of responsibilities and tasks. The job does not seem glamorous. His office is functional, cluttered with papers and books, empty of aesthetic expression, and open for people seeking attention and help. Barclay is in perpetual motion, always trying to figure out what is in need of the most attention and what might be delegated to someone else. Within the first few minutes of our conversation, he responds to an irate parent who is calling long distance from Canada and wants to have a conference with Barclay as soon as he returns to town. Next, he speaks briefly with a boy we pass in the hall about some housing he has located for him. "That kid has a lot of strength. He is a reformed alcoholic; his mother is dead; and his father's a gigolo. In order to survive, he needs to move *away* from his father." In consultation with his counselor and social worker, Barclay has been trying to organize alternative living arrangements. His contact with the boy is a brief but very caring exchange. His arm is wrapped gently around the boy's shoulder and he seems, for a moment, like the great protector. Next, my conversation with Barclay is interrupted by a student helper in the house who says that two Hispanic boys need to be enrolled in school and they only speak Spanish. Barclay is on the phone trying to track down a Spanish-speaking student who can serve as translator. The duties are far-ranging; the pace is hectic; the relationships with students seem almost parental. There is no time to get wrapped up in status-maintaining behavior. In order to do his job, Barclay is easily accessible, has an affable style, and a clear respect for students.

Even though the role often seems overwhelming, there are limits that are defined by the structure of the house system. Although counselors and homerooms are affiliated with houses and faculty have house assignments, teachers identify with the departments of which they are a part and see them as the primary educational settings. Says one housemaster self-critically, "Houses really have no identity. . . . They are a superficial overlay. . . . Departments and houses often find themselves clashing over their educational role. . . . Housemasters are very often seen as separate from the educational function and I see this as a flaw." Inevitably, the housemaster must be responsible for the overall functioning of the house, attendance, conferences with teachers and parents, and working with the counselors in the house. This means that housemasters must sometimes assume a distant, supervisory role, and become less passionately involved in the fate of individuals. A female housemaster talks about shaping the role to fit her temperamental style and philosophical inclinations. "My role is more the heavy . . . counselors are more likely to function as advocates . . . but since I can't function as a heavy, I try to function as a role model. . . . I try to make kids feel responsible for their own actions in a way that is educative . . . to help them grow. . . . Additionally, I think it is important for people to see that a woman can function in an administrative position and still have womanly qualities. Before I was appointed to this position, there were only male housemasters . . . disciplinarians who had a cut-and-dried approach to the function. . . . I consciously tried to broaden the job to match my temperament and to enhance the school. . . . I wanted kids to see this as a warmer place." The tone of the house is largely influenced by the style and orientation of the housemaster. Through his or her own person, the atmosphere and norms get shaped and the relationships to students become established. One housemaster describes the tone she tries to develop. "I see kids as emerging adults. The more dignity and respect you give them, the more it will come back to you." Although many recognize the housemaster role as critical and of high status, there is also the feeling that it is cut off from the real business of schooling. Taken seriously, the challenges and responsibilities of the role are overwhelming and endless. Always confronting problems, always negotiating compromises, always orchestrating human resources, there is little opportunity for self-renewal. One housemaster, who is not eager for additional responsibilities but is eager for a "substantive challenge," says, "I would like to teach . . . develop a course. That would enrich my life."

In contrast to the houses that are experienced as partial communities, the School Within a School emerges as a real community that embraces the lives of its inhabitants. The School Within a School, or SWS as everyone calls it, is an alternative, "democratic" community of one hundred students and five teachers. Tucked in a fourth-floor corner of the school, SWS has a dramatic identity and strong reputation as a "different place." The nature of the difference is a source of some discussion, mixed interpretation, and much stereotyping.

Twelve years ago, when SWS was organized, it seemed a natural outgrowth of a more general cultural trend toward progressive, collective forms of education. Rosemont, like many other enlightened high schools, saw SWS as a response to students' needs for choice and as an effort to recognize diverse philosophical and pedagogical stances in education. Immediately, it was seen by most outsiders as a place for the "far-out," nonconformist kids, a refuge for the crazies and outcasts. "You could tell the SWS kids because they all dressed like hippies, had long, straight, dirty hair, and smoked a lot of dope." The SWS kids were feared and disdained by their peers as their reputation became larger than life.

SWS survived the criticisms and assaults of the wider community during its early years, and no longer appears to be a major threat to nonbelievers. With a twelve-year history and a very stable faculty, SWS is firmly entrenched. The stereotypes linger, but they do not stand up against the tests of reality. Even though SWS students claim that as freshmen they "were afraid to come up to the fourth floor" because the SWS kids had such bad reputations, an outsider can hardly distinguish SWS students from others unless they are gathered in SWS hangouts. And though they are commonly referred to as "the freaks," conversations with SWS students reveal a great deal of variation in style, goals, and modes of expression. A younger woman who is a senior is neat and preppy looking. After feeling lost and faceless during her freshman year, she applied to SWS because she hated the competitive atmosphere of "the downstairs school," the name used by SWSers to refer to the rest of the school. SWS has been good for her. She reports that competition among students is reduced; there is less concern about grades; and no one is invisible. She plans to apply to a string of elite colleges—Yale, Brown, Swarthmore, Wesleyan—and thinks she now has the self-confidence to thrive in a more highly structured setting.

SWS is a vital community, with a unique ethos and encompassing power. Insiders enjoy and often exaggerate its singular qualities. Says one ebullient student, "In SWS people care about learning. There is a real sense of community." In the weekly SWS Town Meeting that I attended, student and faculty comments often underscored the contrasts between their school and "the downstairs school." The collective body was trying to decide whether to attend the election forum for Town Meeting representatives that would be organized around house structures. There was some curiosity about the big-school process, a slight sense of superiority about their extensive experience as a democratic community, and a wish to maintain their distance and autonomy.

> *First voice:* I don't think we should go. We are not the downstairs school. We're the upstairs school.
> *Second voice:* Yes, we are a community here, but we're also part of Rosemont High School.
> *Third voice:* Maybe someone could go and report back what they saw . . . in·the world outside of Room 401.

There is an ambivalence about how involvement in the life of the larger community and maintenance of boundaries is being faced and negotiated within SWS. The director of SWS refers to it as a "natural process" of identity formation. It is difficult to establish feelings of cohesion and commitment within SWS without some turning away from the outside world. In trying to nurture that "we-feeling" of SWS there is the inevitable rejection of the downstairs school. For some SWS students this rejection sounds exaggerated and defensive; the boundaries are overdrawn. Says one girl who is opposed to following the school-wide rules of detention and suspension, "If you are up here [SWS], you're more responsible than the rest of the school by definition." But other students are searching for a balance between separation from and integration into the larger school structure. SWS is a strong anchor and a comfortable home that makes the entry into the downstairs school less threatening.

Part of the sense of community in SWS comes from its small scale; but part comes from the fact that it is primarily an educational enterprise and is much more homogeneous than the school at large. Additionally, in order to become a member of SWS students must apply at the end of their freshman year. They are interviewed by SWS faculty who decide whether they are likely to become responsible members of the community and thrive in a less structured and open environment. Some applicants seem too immature to tolerate the increased choice or confused about what they want; others are really hoping for a school that will demand nothing from them. These students are turned away in favor of those who appear to have more maturity, energy, and direction.

The students SWS attracts are mostly upper-middle-class white, with only two blacks and one Asian. The director states, matter-of-factly, "It is hard enough being different in this school without also separating yourself off in SWS, with all its negative images." She claims that the black students, in particular, feel that coming to SWS is "like selling out . . . like joining the white forces." After spending some time in SWS meetings, classes, and hangouts, I can also imagine that minority parents would not feel inclined to encourage their adolescents to join what they might perceive to be a loose and permissive atmosphere. The relatively unstructured environment of SWS would be unappealing or threatening to parents who emphasize order and structured authority within their families.

One SWS teacher feels slightly defensive about the homogeneity and says that his concern is more with the social class separations than with the racial sameness. He thinks the community would be more interesting and vital if it were more diverse. Instead, there is a tendency for subcultural, in-group phenomena to be exaggerated. He points to the large proportion of SWS students who come from homes with separated or divorced parents and the assumption of abundance by students. Parents, often guilty about their split families, tend to indulge their offspring with material gifts. With large numbers of students living similar lives, there is less opportunity for witnessing other lifestyles and a tendency to assume that what they know is normal and good.

When pushed to characterize the SWS students, the director at first demures and then says, tentatively, "They are individualistic, risk-takers, nonconformists." Some clearly suffer from emotional and social problems and look to faculty and peers for heavy doses of psychological support. Their pain may be expressed in severe learning disabilities. And many are gifted intellectually, extremely articulate, and unusually creative. The one hundred students display a range of skills, competencies, and intellectual styles, but most agree that SWS has more than its share of "bright kids."

The faculty of SWS also have a schoolwide reputation as competent, caring, and highly committed teachers. One downstairs teacher says, "If I had to choose one spot in this school for my son, where I would know he would get excellent academic attention, I would choose SWS."

The director describes the SWS image as "paradoxical." On the one hand, SWS is resented for "siphoning off" the leaders and skimming the cream of the crop from the downstairs school. This image portrays SWS as an elite academy for the privileged. While on the other hand, there is relief that SWS is an asylum for the wild, uncontrollable types and that the rest of the school can be saved from their negative influences. In this picture, SWS is a place for misfits. To some extent students and faculty must labor under this conflicting imagery and feel the mixed messages sent by outsiders. But mostly they seem to go about the hard work of sustaining a community committed to democratic ideals and developing an academic curriculum that is responsive to student needs.

SWS students take about half their courses in the small community and half in the downstairs school. The five SWS faculty members teach courses in math, social studies, English, psychology, and counseling. The two women faculty, who teach English, share a single job. All of the faculty have been at SWS for more than three years, and there is a strong sense of continuity and stability that is rare in alternative schools. They have a good perspective on pressing, immediate concerns, and also seem realistic about the limits and liabilities of the democratic structure as they try to train students to take more responsible roles. Says one faculty member, who notices some progress in student leadership skills, "We have learned to work very hard behind the scenes before meetings, setting up the agenda, and coaching the kids." Twelve years after its creation, SWS is a sturdy community less threatened by negative perceptions and assaults but still confronted with the persistent struggles of making a difficult process work and still a distance from its idealized goals. Ironically, its survival has a lot to do with the tone and culture of the downstairs school. The director recognizes the fact. "Rosemont High, as a whole, is unusual in its individualistic approach to students." Without that bedrock of agreement in fundamental philosophy between the downstairs and upstairs schools, it is unlikely that SWS would have survived and ultimately thrived.

## Close Strangers

A community can be defined by the characteristics of its members; it can also be defined by those who are excluded from it. At Rosemont

High the group of students that most people identify as "separate," "alienated," "victimized," or "different," are the "METRO kids." The one hundred students in the METRO program are not a monolithic group, but people often refer to them as if they are all alike and as if they all cause trouble and "make waves." I met several METRO students who are thriving at Rosemont, feel comfortable in the setting, and appreciate its abundance; others hate the place. Said one bitter sophomore girl, "There's too much trouble here. It's like a soap opera, and I don't like being part of a soap opera." A middle range of METRO students cope with episodes of exclusion and prejudice but also enjoy moments of accomplishment and friendship. But most people agree that, more than any other identifiable group, the METRO students do not take full advantage of the environment, nor are they treated with the level of respect afforded to other students by their peers and teachers.

At nine in the morning, when I arrive for my appointment with Grace Taylor, the METRO coordinator, she is streaking down the hall responding to an emergency. She sees me and calls, "You can come if you want to. I'm dealing with a very hot situation." Sitting in Taylor's office is Irene, a ninth grade METRO student. Irene is jet black—almost the color of her black knickers. She is carefully dressed in white sneakers and socks, a new-looking, tan down jacket. Her hair is neat and closely cropped. There is a hardness in her face that makes her appear much older than her fourteen years. As I meet her, I think to myself, she would be an attractive person if she only felt good about herself.

Taylor, a slender, attractive woman with red-brown hair and light brown skin is beautifully dressed in a soft-gray pants suit. She is wearing gold chain necklaces, and her wrist jangles with charm bracelets and bangles. She is completely confident. Taylor sits behind her desk piled with papers and introduces me to Irene, who is sitting in the chair closest to her. The small, cramped office is decorated with posters of blacks—jazz musicians, scientists, judges, and sportsmen. There are quotations on the wall designed to encourage pride in blackness and inspire hard work and discipline.

Taylor's face shows a mixture of weariness, pain, and anger as she confronts Irene. The METRO coordinator has heard rumors of a fight planned among METRO girls, and Irene has been targeted as the provocateur. It is to take place after school, off-campus at the streetcar stop. Irene admits to the planned rumble and slowly divulges her part in it. In response to Taylor's tough and persistent questions, Irene confesses that she tends "to talk a lot" about other people and "get into their business." Her talking "gets her in trouble." When Taylor asks how she might change her behavior, the girl's eyes look down to the floor as she whispers, "Well, maybe I'd stop being bad if they would beat me up. . . . If they beat me up maybe I'll stop." "Look at me, Irene. Lift your head up and *look* at me," demands Taylor. "Is this the only solution you can come up with—to get beat up?" After much prodding, Irene thinks of a less violent alternative. "Well, I could just stay away from them." "Well, that's a start," says Taylor, with slight relief.

In the course of the intense exchange, Taylor makes several points that reflect her tough realism, her sensitivity to Irene's pain, and her absolute intolerance of violence and fighting. "It is all right not to like each other. There are lots of people I don't like . . . but it is unacceptable to get into fights in school. Here are the cold, hard facts. There will be no fight this afternoon. If there is a fight, you will be back in Washington High tomorrow. I will not tolerate this!" Irene's shock and sudden grimace indicate that she believes the threat; that she does not want to be sent back to the big city high school, where the dangers are even greater.

Before she sends the girl off to class, Taylor gets the names of all the students involved in the anticipated fight. "Who are they? . . . Whose side are they on? . . . Are they friend or foe?" Irene reveals her allies and enemies. Taylor writes the names down and promises to talk to each one individually and to all of them together, if that becomes necessary. The harsh words seem to have an impact on Irene. She is clearly concerned about the repercussions of fighting and worried about how she can retreat without losing her honor. But her face also shows some relief and perhaps gratitude. Taylor's intervention may save her from self-destruction, and she now knows that she has been noticed and attended to. She is not invisible.

Before she has a chance to take a break, Taylor begins to track down the other accomplices. She calls the houses with which each is affiliated and leaves an urgent message, "Tell her she must come to my office at the beginning of her homeroom period. It is *very* important." These conversations take place within a twenty-minute homeroom slot, before Taylor has to go off and teach her social studies course.

Grace Taylor has been at Rosemont High School for ten years. For the first three years, she was a full-time teacher in the social studies department and then became the full-time coordinator for the METRO program during the next seven years. With the recent cut in tax revenue, METRO funding has been drastically reduced and Taylor now teaches three courses and coordinates the program only part-time. All of the METRO business must be reduced to the two hours between 8:00 A.M. and 10:00 A.M., and the casualties of lost time are great. "I am overwhelmed, overworked, and can't give my kids the attention they need," she complains. In the past, Taylor saw herself as "the protector" of METRO students, in touch with every sphere of their lives. She knew their families, would meet them at the trolley in the morning, have breakfast with them in the school cafeteria, and be available to hear their problems and put out brush fires. Her full-time status gave her the chance to know them intimately and recognize subtle signs of trouble.

Gene Brown, a handsome senior boy, always came to school dressed in snazzy clothes. When he would occasionally arrive in jeans, sweatshirt, and sneakers, Taylor recognized the signal that he was prepared to fight. "You see, he didn't want to get his fancy clothes all messed up." Spotting his casual dress, Taylor would collar him and make him cool off in her office. The fight would be avoided, and Gene did not have to lose face with his peers. "Taylor docked me. She made me sit in her office," he would complain. As Taylor explains, "He was *asking* for someone to stop him because he couldn't stop himself."

With her time severely reduced, Taylor is no longer able to know every METRO student or recognize their cries for help. She complains that she does not even know many of the names of the thirty-six METRO freshmen who arrived in September, and there has been no way to develop the all-important trust and sense of connection with them. Instead of reaching out to her and seeking her support, they are more likely to respond to her approaches with, "Who are you? What right do you have to tell us what to do?"

The coordinator feels very strongly that METRO students need a vigilant advocate in Rosemont High School. She offers examples of the "benign racism" and subtle hostility that they receive from a few of the "pseudo-liberal faculty." This morning, during first period, Taylor looked in the cafeteria and discovered a bunch of METRO students eating breakfast. When she asked why they were not in class, they explained casually, "Oh, you know, we told our teacher that we couldn't concentrate because we didn't have breakfast . . . and she said to go get some." Taylor is floored by the teacher's gullibility, or by her eagerness to get rid of these students. She does not view it as a sympathetic act. "Those kids *all* have breakfast at home. Their *families* see to that. If not, they can get it *before* school." Another example: At the end of last year, a teacher approached a group of METRO students in class and said that they should not have been disruptive in class because that confirms the stereotypes that white kids have of black people. Taylor fumes, "Why didn't that teacher come down hard on those kids at the moment of misbehavior? Why did he wait until the end of the semester? Why did he speak to them as a group rather than individually? Some of them were well-behaved and mannerly students, a few were being terribly disruptive." Taylor feels that the physical education department is most culpable of this subtle racism. The gym is a place where lots of the black guys hang out. "Some of the coaches have come to me and said, 'Taylor, you want to know what *your* kids said' . . . and I say to them, as long as you say *your* and not *our*, the problem's going to be there. . . . If teachers always send kids to me when they have trouble with them, then they are relinquishing some of their power and handing it over to me."

The passion and outrage with which Taylor tells these stories probably reflects her deep commitment to these students and to her role as their protector and advocate. She does not pretend to be dispassionate or objective and is willing to risk the anger and hostility of some of her colleagues in order to do her job. "Sometimes they see me coming and say, 'Oh no, here comes Taylor.' . . . I don't mind them feeling that way about me as long as it helps my kids."

Even those faculty members who are as vigilant as Grace Taylor about assaulting racism in the school do not necessarily share her views of the oppressive environment. Without the encumbrances of the protector role, they see a less discriminatory community than she does. Another black faculty member who is very supportive of Taylor's efforts and admires her courage and aggressiveness says, "Rosemont

High School is not perfect, but it is better than any other school I've seen. White administrators and teachers will not be intimidated by black kids, and that is rare. These are good strong teachers and you will be jammed if you don't do your work. Black kids have to make the grade."

Despite the differences in perception, both agree that the presence of blacks on the faculty is critically important to the tone of the school and essential to their sense of support. There is a "strong cadre" of about ten black faculty (two houseteachers, two English teachers, one librarian, who is new, two math teachers, two social studies teachers, and one physics teacher, who is about to be hired) who refer to themselves as "The Summit." They wanted to avoid the separatist image of listing themselves as "the black faculty" when they announce their meetings in the school bulletins. Besides offering counsel and alliance to one another and serving as important images for black students, they have worked hard to plan specially designed programs for the black students. Last year, they sponsored a weekend retreat in New Hampshire for twenty-five selected students. They worked with them on "some leadership skills and some fun stuff . . . then brought them back and turned them loose on the school, saying, spread the good word." With the recent cut in tax revenues, everyone feels too overwhelmed with work to generate the energy for another retreat. There are tentative plans in the works for a meeting with seniors to do some practice sessions for the SAT's, or maybe a get-together with freshmen to talk about "how one survives for four years in this place."

Black faculty seem balanced between their special affiliations with black youngsters and their general commitments to the school community as a whole. A houseteacher talks about the precariousness of the balance. "You know, some of the black girls that I've been working with on this dance coming up feel that they own me and get angry when other kids come around. They want to claim me as theirs . . . but I am a houseteacher for *all* the kids. Negotiating this thing is sometimes tricky. . . . It *is* possible to feel a special, special commitment to minority kids at the same time as I feel a commitment to the well-being of all kids."

Kennedy recognizes the balancing act. He describes the black faculty as intensely committed and "thoroughly professional." When "enough trust had been built" after Kennedy's arrival last year, the black faculty met with him to talk about the ways they had been misused as faculty members and their needs for administrative support. Because they were black they were often expected to counsel all black students, put out brush fires that erupted among black students, rescue black students from trouble spots, and be authorities on the black psyche and black culture. All of these expectations were loaded on top of their regular teaching chores and committee assignments. Their special status also meant that other teachers were not forced to learn how to deal with black students or even consider them their responsibility. Kennedy claims that, slowly, perceptions have begun to shift. When a black kid gets in trouble, the appropriate housemaster is now called, not a black teacher. If he or she is having emotional problems, the counseling office offers supportive services. But the burdensome expectations still persist to some extent. Observes one youngish, white female teacher, "Rosemont High School has the art of tokenism down to a fine point. . . . The few blacks are expected to sit on all the committees just so the school can say there is equal representation."

Minority faculty are also important in the lives of majority students. I am told a story about Mr. Hall, a thoughtful and caring social studies teacher with an excellent reputation among his colleagues. Last year one of the girls from the Point searched out Mr. Hall and said, "I have a friend who may be pregnant, and, if she is, her parents will kill her." Mr. Hall guessed that the young woman was talking about herself and gave her lots of his own time and directed her to counselors and a social worker. At the end of the year she walked up to him with her girl friend and gave him a gift. The teacher who related the story was there and marvelled, "It was really something to see this Irish Catholic girl from the Point hugging Bob Hall and giving him a poem she had written on a parchment scroll." She shook her head. "See, it's those kids who need minority role models, not just the minority kids. . . . Don't you think it's amazing that a girl from a neighborhood that is basically racist would choose a black teacher to confide in? It is testimony to Bob's understanding and empathetic personality."

## Academic Life: A Broad Curriculum

In recent years, some concern has been expressed about the quality of education at the high school level in Rosemont. Most parents feel fairly confident that their children are receiving a fine education at the elementary school level. The eight elementary schools are small in scale and have distinct identities and affiliations with neighborhoods in Rosemont. Inevitably, there is more sense of connection and accountability between teachers and parent groups in these schools. The high school, on the other hand, is the "great melting pot," receiving students from all over town. Some people link the melting pot image with dilution of excellence, with a lack of purity. This concern about reduced standards created by mixtures is heightened by the recent growth in minority populations and general population shifts. Observers who support the high school claim that the elementary schools are parochial enclaves while the secondary school is a cosmopolitan community. They see what others call dilution as enrichment.

But these perceptions are relative, derived from contrasting the status of elementary and secondary education within Rosemont. If one simply looks at Rosemont High without benefit of contrast or comparison, one is struck by its persistent and unchallenged academic image. The high school population is unusually stable. Ninety percent of the students stay for four years, with only a 2 percent rate of transfers and dropouts. An eleven-year longitudinal survey (1970–1980), done by the guidance department, indicates that an average of 78 percent of the graduates have gone on to higher education—66 percent to four-year colleges and 12 percent to two-year educational institutions. The guidance office also identifies the 19 percent of the students who were accepted at "colleges considered prestigious." It is the latter group that shapes much of the image of Rosemont High, not the 22 percent who do not go on to post high school education but decide instead to work or enter the armed services. Even though the high school's reputation seems fixed on the academic image, the curricula and pedagogy embrace the whole population of students.

The course catalogue for the high school reveals the attempts of faculty to respond to the diverse needs of a broad spectrum of students. There are 300 courses in the formal curriculum (and more than 500 courses listed in the catalogue). These include academic offerings at the "basic, standard, honor, and advanced placement (A.P.) levels," offerings in the arts—fine, performing, physical, visual, and industrial—and in home economics and occupational education.

To an outsider leafing through the catalogue, the choices seem endless and the possibilities overwhelming. For example, twenty-three pages are devoted to career education, with eleven different courses of study (including business/accounting and administration, early childhood education, food service careers, medical careers, technical industrial, and several others). Career education became part of the high school curriculum in 1966, and efforts are made to provide optional part-time work experiences outside of school for those who are interested.

The foreign language department has twenty-one pages in the catalogue, and offers Chinese, English as a second language, French, German, Italian, Russian, Spanish, and Latin. The English department and Individualized Study Program each have seventeen descriptive pages in the catalogue. The English department offers an array of writing courses from composition to journalism; literature courses, including American, British, and minority literature; and supplementary courses in public speaking and grammar and usage. The Individualized Study Program provides alternative ways for students to learn both inside and outside of school. There are volunteer experiences and apprenticeships, college courses throughout the area, independent study with individual teachers, and so on.

The social studies department, with fourteen pages in the course catalogue, offers diverse courses in history, social sciences, and civics. Among the United States history courses are American History for Foreign Students, Black Studies, Afro-American History, and American Constitutional History. The social science courses include World Culture, Women in Society, and American Studies. Civics courses include Law and the Individual, Law and Society, and Introduction to Criminal Justice. The other academic areas of science and math reveal more classical selections, but the same broad array of courses.

It is in the performing and visual arts that one is struck by the eclectic range of courses. It is rare that public schools, even schools for the privileged, are able to provide these rich aesthetic possibilities. The visual arts include drawing, painting, sculpture, printmaking, ceramics, jewelry making, cartooning, photography, and film making, among others. The performing arts department provides experiences in music (with fifteen courses), dance (with six courses), and drama (with five courses).

Faculty express mixed feelings about the great proliferation of courses since the mid-1960s. Some view it as a worthy attempt to respond to the increasingly diverse needs and goals of students. Others are critical because they see it as a retreat from academic excellence. In their view, the broad range of courses reflects a diminished standard; a subtle discrimination against those students who are judged inadequate to make the academic grade. Still others see the thick catalogue as evidence of the school's unclear goals, an unwillingness to decide what is most important in the curriculum. This latter group of teachers sees unanticipated advantages in the recent budget cuts. "We'll finally have to decide what is most important," says one critic.

Perhaps in response to reduced resources, but certainly inspired by new school leadership, a group of faculty developed a statement of philosophy for Rosemont High School. The faculty were also responding to the dictates of the 1980 Ten Year Evaluation, which required the development of a statement of educational philosophy. Working over the summer, four faculty members engaged in deep discussion and prepared increasingly coherent drafts. An ambitious effort, they attempted to create a document that would "guide, confirm, and incite thought about the ways in which this institution seeks to confront a changing and diverse society." Largely the inspiration and language of a faculty member who is described by his colleagues as "deep," "literate," and "philosophical," the words were often labored and cloudy. I was very impressed by how imperfectly the faculty-student relationships and educational exchanges fit the lofty, philosophical language, but many teachers seemed to take the goals it expresses seriously in their work with students. This fall, after several laborious drafts—each becoming clearer and less encumbered by opaque prose—the faculty voted unanimously to approve the five-point Statement of Philosophy.

### I. EDUCATION PRESUMES A CLIMATE OF CARE

The schoolhouse must be a kind of home that offers its inhabitants a sense of belonging, of individuality strengthened by expectation, of security born of respect. As in the home, the student should feel known but revered; the teacher, exposed but esteemed. Reason should prevail, and where reason falls short, tolerance abide. Regard for excellence need not preclude acceptance of human foible; nor should devotion and understanding be devoid of rigor. Care is by nature compensatory, seeking to provide that which would otherwise be lacking.

## II. THOUGHTFULNESS IS THE SOCIAL AS WELL AS THE INTELLECTUAL AIM OF EDUCATION

The habit of reflection is the ideal trait of the educated mind, taking for its concern what others may be satisfied to take for granted. Education should foster this habit, should teach us patience in the understanding and construction of ideas. But it should also teach us to consider feelings, to anticipate the probable effect of our actions and words on others, and to temper these when they augur injury. Education is thus forethought rather than afterthought, abiding thought rather than sporadic thought.

## III. NO STYLE OF LEARNING OR TEACHING IS PRIVILEGED

Learning and teaching are two sides of the same coin. Both rely on a sense of timing, a state of readiness, a heightened sensibility, which enables one to see or say or think something not seen or said or thought before. Readiness is achieved in different ways, depending on what there is to be learned. Sometimes it requires painful and protracted effort—thinking, reading, watching, writing, talking, doing. Other times it is attained effortlessly, almost inadvertently. Either way, timing is critical. Knowing how to learn or how to teach is essentially knowing when to press and when to wait. Styles of learning and teaching are characterized by their mix of pressure and patience. Thorough education will expose teachers and students to a range of styles so that they come to know their own.

## IV. LEARNING IS A MIXTURE OF PLEASURE AND OF PAIN

The love of learning is an acquired taste, an addiction for the tart rather than the sweet. To learn is to change, and to change can be both exhilarating and wrenching. As creatures of habit, we must approach learning with trepidation, not expecting those who learn to experience a smooth trajectory of triumphs, nor those who teach to effect unrelieved excitement about their subject. While it is true that what is most easily learned is usually hardest taught, it is also true that love of learning cannot be taught; it can only be exemplified. As is so often averred, teaching requires patience. Let it also be said that what teaching requires, learning must learn.

## V. EDUCATION EXAMINES NOT THE INDIVIDUAL BUT THE SPECIES

The value of learning lies not so much in its immediate utility as in its generality. Schools are instituted and maintained to serve their communities as havens of learning, not as microcosms of the marketplace. Here students are apprenticed to life in its ideal form, life that is devoted to inquiry, touched by beauty, informed by justice, guided by reason, girded by simplicity, graced by elegance. At the very least, graduates should exhibit competency in the exercise of certain skills—computation, composition—but the aim is to make them literate about the full array of human achievement, so that they will know what it means to do anything well.

In December, the school newspaper, *The Sagamore*, summarized the Statement of Philosophy and compared it to the one developed a decade earlier as part of the school's 1970 evaluation. "The old philosophy stressed individual growth. The new philosophy stresses the idea of the school as a community conducive to all types of learning; where respect for differences encourages caring; and where students can learn from students as well as teachers; where all styles of teaching and learning are valued; and where reason, patience, and tolerance improve the school as well as our understanding of ourselves and others."

The apparent shift of emphasis from individual to community, from competition to caring, from sameness to diversity fits with the current rhetoric and the ideals faculty move toward in practice. The rhetoric and goals seem to express clarity and general consensus. As one would expect, in practice, people reveal their ambivalence, their wishes to hang on to old values, and their difficulties in facing the transition. It appears that, in practice, the community is now precariously balanced between old and new educational and philosophical ideals, poised somewhere between the extremes of separation and integration, individuality and community.

It is only when one contrasts educational practice with philosophical ideals that one feels some sense of discouragement. Mostly, one is impressed with the level of academic engagement in this high school and occasionally disgruntled by imperfections and breaks in the generally good standards. There is visible evidence of educational commitment. When you walk through the halls of the school during class periods and peer through open doors, students tend to be attentive and busy. A typing class is energetically engaged in pounding the keys, working against a stopwatch. In a physics laboratory, small groups of students work collectively on an experiment while the teacher circulates around the room offering encouragement and clarification. It is very quiet, and all eyes face forward in a United States history course where the teacher is lecturing with little attempt at drama. A passing glance finds things going on in the classrooms—minimal chaos and directed attention. Most teachers seem to feel confident enough about order and quiet in their classrooms to leave the doors to the hall open, or exhibit no surprise when an intrusive observer stares through the window of a closed door. Classroom boundaries are not severe. The educational settings seem open and highly penetrable.

Another indication of educational engagement is the absence of school bells, except before and after the homeroom period—a largely procedural event. I am surprised not to hear their harsh sounds indicating the beginning and end of the class periods. The day's rhythms appear to be internalized by both faculty and students. All the classes I visited started easily on time and without much fanfare. It seems to me that a school that was not serious about education could not proceed without bells. They would be a needed enforcer of student and teacher behavior. When I inquire about the lack of bells, one student says in mock alarm, "This isn't a prison, you know! We're not Pavlov's dogs!"

The seriousness attached to schooling is not limited to courses for bright, academic students. It is evident as soon as one enters a classroom. In a reading class for students with major learning disabilities, the room is noiseless as the students work individually at their seats. The teacher insists upon quiet and helps them focus on their assignments. When their attention wanders, she directs them back to the task; when they become discouraged and begin to lose concentration, she supports them and re-engages them in their work. When one begins to be disruptive and distracts his classmates, the teacher reprimands him severely. With only a few minutes left to go in the period, Christopher resists getting another assignment from the teacher. "But it's only four minutes left!" The teacher responds firmly: "I know, but you have to do something in those four minutes. Hurry up or you'll only have three minutes left!" When Randy approaches the teacher for approval because he has a perfect score on an exercise, the teacher pushes him to do more challenging work. "Randy, if you got one hundred percent, it was too easy. Did you feel it was too easy?" This teacher is dedicated, skilled, and committed to teaching students who might be considered unteachable and unreachable in many other schools. The atmosphere is serious, the rules clear, the caring certain, and the methods eclectic. "I will do anything that works," she says with force.

In an advanced ballet class, the teacher has a friendly but no non-sense approach. In a studio well equipped with bars, mirrors, and a shiny wood floor, Ms. Shelley directs students in the formal exercises. With soothing, melodic music, the twenty-five female students go through their practiced movements with silent attention, some with intense involvement showing in their faces, others with glazed eyes and automatic responses. But the teacher's attention is even and focused. She walks around the floor, adjusting movements, occasionally demonstrating, and softly counting the beat. When she presents a new stretching exercise, an anxious student asks, "Will you talk this through when we do it?" and Ms. Shelley responds supportively, "Yes, I'll talk it through." When small groups are practicing a short jazz sequence that is part of a larger piece choreographed by Ms. Shelley, the range of skills is revealed. The more able dancers capture the syncopation and difficult arched back movement by watching and trying it a few times. The less confident dancers break down halfway across the floor and show some embarrassment at their awkwardness. Ms. Shelley continues to prod and direct, and then offers restrained approval. "This is looking so much stronger." These are the best dancers in the school. In order to enter the advanced class you must audition. One expects the level of skill and attention here; and one can imagine that a teacher would feel more committed to these potential protégées. But there is the same expectation that students will work hard when I observe her class of beginning ballet students.

Ms. Shelley is realistic in her assessment of her students' abilities. She knows that, for the most part, she is not training future dancers, but she is committed to teaching the discipline of dance and to offering dance as an important avenue to self-awareness. She sees connections between mind and body. "I've heard so many times from the counselors that dance has had an incredible impact on the girls' self-images. . . . They begin to have a different feeling about their bodies." In giving herself fully to this enterprise, Shelley recognizes her psychological limits. She knows she cannot give indefinitely without the aesthetic highs that all artists need to remain involved in their work. Her teaching is sustained by her own artistic commitments outside school. She says, "I find teaching a pleasure because I also perform. . . . I have rehearsals late afternoon and evenings . . . and that feeds *me*. I need that. It also helps me stay vital in teaching the kids." In order to be a dedicated teacher, Shelley searches for a balance between giving out and taking in and finds renewal beyond the boundaries of school.

Even in courses that tend to attract non-college bound students, there is attention to pedagogy and curriculum, and a commitment to good form. In a food service course, the teacher shows an industrious style, clear goals, and high standards. The students will have futures different from their achieving academic peers, but they are given respect and taken seriously as part of the school community.

The nine students in the food services course are making Italian feather bread. All nine are girls who range from freshmen to seniors. They are working in the large, sun-filled, warm, good-smelling kitchen. There is little discussion among students, who, with the exception of one girl, are working in pairs. I am told that they saw a demonstration of the process in class yesterday, so today they are excited about making their own loaves of bread. They work quietly, familiar with their kitchen work stations. The stations, like the room, are spacious and well equipped.

The only girl working without a partner tells me that her partner isn't in school today. She says, "It would go faster if she was here, but working alone is okay." She is about 5′6″, a heavy-set, large-boned young woman who tells me she washes, sets, and styles her short hair each morning around 6:00 A.M. She has carefully applied blue eye shadow, blue eyeliner and thick mascara. Her lips and fingernails are both glossy and red. The loaf of bread she makes will be served to her father and her boyfriend at dinner. She cooks for them four nights a week because her mother is a cocktail waitress. Her mother has been either a cocktail waitress or bartender all her life. She tells me, "My mother's hours are crazy because of her work. She can never go to bed before four-thirty in the morning. In the summer, I used to try and stay up with her sometimes because she looked so lonely sitting in front of the TV all by herself. But my dad and I need to go to bed by one. We've changed a little for her, though."

She's taking this course along with sewing, a foreign cooking course, English, and typing. "I need English to graduate this year. The other things I'll use. I already do. My boyfriend and me are getting married next October. I want to be able to cook and sew good. I think it's important that a family have good food, you know, good nutrition. They should all be at their dinner together. That's the way I'll be." She tells me how busy she is keeping her hope chest organized. "I want everything in order by October, so we can move into our own place. We're looking for a house now in Pearl River. My brother lives out there and we go out, me and my boyfriend, every weekend. My sister-in-law does a lot of cooking. She even jars jelly and does yeast bread. It's that kind of a place—real country. My boyfriend does construction so he's looking for work there." She explains that she's from a large Greek family, and they're already planning the wedding.

I join another pair who work smoothly, in and out of each other's movements. Both are juniors and both are about 5'7". The young black woman is wearing navy slacks and a red, V-neck terry shirt with RHS in white letters over her left breast. Her navy slacks are dusted white with flour. Her partner is white with shoulder-length brown hair, curled limply around her pale face. The black girl looks directly at me, her shoulders squared, and asks, "What are you doing here?" Her tone is directly curious, straightforward. I smile involuntarily and explain. She interrupts me to ask if I'm working on "that racial study." I tell her I don't know about the racial study. She says, "X.U. has a project here to improve the racial and social climate at RHS." She grimaces. I ask what that face means. She says, "You been hanging out here?" I respond positively. "Well, what do you think about our cliques?" Without waiting for an answer, she says, pointing her head at her partner, "We don't belong to cliques. There's no one we want to impress around here." I look at the other girl who looks down at her bread dough, keeping her eyes averted. Sensing my gaze she looks up, smiling shyly. "We don't want to be in a clique with all the same people. We have lots of different friends. That's better." "Yah," says the black girl, nodding her head. "If you belong to a clique, you do what they do. Wear the clothes they do. Talk like them. Who needs it?"

The teacher is moving among work stations. She is a woman in her fifties with gray hair, plainly and neatly dressed. Throughout the class, she has tended to work with a pair of freshmen who look especially confused. She never approaches the work stations when I'm there. She is teaching constantly. When answering a question that she thinks might help all the girls, she raises her voice. This signal suffices. All of the girls turn to look at her and to listen.

Twenty minutes into class, three girls walk in and approach the teacher. She looks at the clock and then, in a loud voice, says, "This time I'm going to be nice to you and give you dough from the other girls who started on time. That way you can make your own loaf. Girls, I want all of you to weigh your dough. Keep one pound to make your own loaves and give me the rest for these girls."

None of the girls complain, but quietly commence weighing. The teacher collects the dough and gives it to the three newcomers. They are different in appearance from the rest of the students. Their style of dress is preppie. One girl is wearing turquoise pants, a striped shirt, collar worn up, a yellow sweater, Nike running shoes and a yellow ribbon at the end of her long, elaborately-woven blond braid. I watch her throughout the rest of the period and am amazed at her desultory pace. She never touches the bread dough; she never gets her hands wet in the clean-up effort. Instead, she manages to eat three pieces of buttered bread prepared by the last class. She seems to have an easy rapport with the teacher. They exchange frequent smiles and small talk.

The rest of the class continue to work efficiently, watching their time carefully. There is a serious air about the room as pairs murmur to one another, coaching each other. Out of the twelve girls present, there are five blacks, two Asians, and five whites. They are fourteen to eighteen years old. Later the teacher tells me that most have taken several home economics classes, but a couple have taken the class because they "need easy credits for graduation."

As the class nears the end, the out-of-class conversation increases. The teacher announces loudly, "No one can leave until her station is cleaned up and checked out." The clean-up process is purposeful and rushed. At the end of the period, the students are speeding out the door. I stay behind in the now quiet kitchen to help the teacher clean up and to talk. She tells me, "The primary stress in home economics is preparation of food for yourself. In food service it's different. They learn about institutional cooking and clean-up is an integral part of their work. There are different stresses related to the job demands. Since last spring, when they opened the student-run restaurant, we've had to divide Food Service I in half. In the first half they are in classes and in the second half they work in the cafeteria. Some stay in the cafeteria for Food Service II, III, IV, but now students can work in the school restaurant, too. In the restaurant, students cook and serve the food, order supplies, and keep the books with a little supervision from Mr. Kearny, a food services teacher. The restaurant is opened to the general public Tuesdays and Thursdays. Breakfast and lunch are served."

She says, "Up here [second floor] I order, buy, and keep inventory on all the food needed for classes. There's a lot of work involved in teaching cooking, and now, because of the recent cutbacks, the School Committee has got it into its head that we should be teaching more students per class. Can you imagine trying to teach more than twelve kids each class? You've seen this place in action. It would be impossible." She shakes her head, "They've never been in my class. They don't care about quality of teaching at all—just numbers. Churn those students out. Who cares if they learn."

Even though Rosemont's image is an academic one, the school seeks to be responsive to the wide range of people in its student population. Certainly there are lost souls who slip through unnoticed and unchallenged. Certainly not all teaching is at a high level. One hears the typical student complaints about teachers who are uninspired, tedious, and boring. But the general standards for teaching and learning seem to be high and they remain high across the range of academic abilities and choices.

Even more impressive are those "star" teachers who challenge students to even greater heights, who test their limits: the biology teacher who chooses to teach basic-level courses in order to seduce students who normally would not dare to take such a "scary and hard" subject; the Constitutional History teacher who has developed an innovative curriculum using primary sources and original documents and whose pedagogical style incorporates role playing and simulation activities; the English teacher whose course, The Art of the Essay, involves students in writing and critically responding to each other's pieces. Risk taking, passion, discipline, and honesty are encouraged by the teacher who reveals all of those qualities in her own approach to the work.

In a standard-level American literature class, the students are in the midst of reading and discussing *Death of a Salesman*. The desks and chairs are arranged in a circle and the teacher's style is supportive, thoughtful, and responsive to student needs and direction. Many students in this class have been judged to have learning disabilities and their behavior shows that they have difficulties in focussing their attention. At the beginning of class, Ms. Dickerson's comments about their written assignments reveal a beautiful balance of empathy and intellectual challenge. She returns their papers and warns, "Now folks, don't panic. Some of you got low grades . . . but consider this a little grade, the equivalent of a quiz. . . . This is like the core of a paper, beginning ideas. . . . If you have a low grade, it is a sign that there has been a misunderstanding." She clarifies the assignment due the next day. "You will need to develop a thesis statement. . . . A thesis statement means it must be a debatable idea or opinion, not a factual statement. . . . Pitfalls for a debatable statement: it can be too huge and expansive [she offers an example]; it can be so obvious that only a ninny would debate it; . . . Virginia Woolf says a writer is one that sticks his neck out . . . a firm stand with some intellectual risk. . . . Then back it up with evidence." The atmosphere is comfortable and unthreatening, even though Dickerson is urging them to be both disciplined and free, careful and courageous in their writing.

When they turn to the discussion of *Death of a Salesman*, many of the students' comments sound confused and inarticulate, but the teacher pushes for clarity. The discussion centers on Willie's decision to commit suicide, and the teacher encourages students to talk to one another rather than direct all their comments to her. To one girl who is having difficulty with the barrage of comments, Dickerson says quietly, "Assert yourself . . . get in there. . . . You have something to say." When the conversation becomes scattered and directionless, the teacher breaks in, "We have a whole lot of separate ideas on the floor. Let us take a few minutes of silence to sort these out. . . . If you can't remember anyone's ideas except your own, you haven't been listening. . . . I have heard at least fifteen explanations for Willie's suicide. . . . See if you can reconstruct it." The class grows quiet as students begin to write their ideas down. Dickerson walks around the room, encouraging students who seem stuck or discouraged and restating her question for greater clarity. Then she offers a clue to the whole class: "See if you can remember Cynthia's question . . . it was a turning point in the discussion. She didn't give an answer, only a question." After several minutes of silent contemplation the teacher says, "Let's combine our reasoning," and students immediately begin to offer reasons for Willie's suicide: "He wanted to quit a world where nothing was going right for him"; "He felt he had failed terribly and was a disgrace to those who loved him"; "He wanted to have people pay homage to him at the funeral"; "He had only half achieved his dream."

The contributions are energetic and fast-paced. When the exchanges become heated and confused, Dickerson intervenes with a tentative and thoughtful voice. "Let me ask you a very hard question. . . . What happens when a dream you've lived by turns out to be a lie? How do you feel about that. . . . Or are you too young?" The responses are charged and unrestrained. One girl speaks with passion: "People shouldn't circle their lives around one idea." Another disagrees: "But it is not just one idea, it is their whole reason for being." A third: "There is always a danger in being too committed, too closed. . . . You should have one or two goals. You should choose. . . . You don't have to die with one ideal." The discussion becomes argumentative but not hostile. The teacher does not direct them toward a tidy conclusion. They are struggling with unanswerable questions, profound dilemmas, and she wants to encourage them in the struggle. She wants them to recognize Willie's pain. Class is over abruptly and there is no closure.

I am struck by all that has gone on—by the open criticism, hot debate, level of trust, and spirit of inquiry. I am baffled when Dickerson says apologetically to me after class, "It is not merely false modesty . . . but I don't think that went well. . . . *I* was unsure of where I was going in the discussion, uncertain about what I wanted them to get out of it. . . . *They* were wonderful. They tolerated my ambivalence." One of the qualities of a "star" teacher seems to be tough self-criticism; never accepting oneself as a star.

## A Committed and Serious Faculty

The perceptions of the faculty at Rosemont High School range from good to extraordinary. The most critical voice I heard said that there are three categories of teachers: a small group of "stars," a large group of "slightly above average" teachers, and a few "duds." To one who has visited numerous schools, Rosemont seems to be rich with talented and committed teachers. A department chairperson describes her peers as "gifted and highly professional. . . . I always think of them as people who could do whatever they chose to do." A houseteacher is even more enthusiastic about his colleagues. A relatively recent arrival to the faculty, he exclaims, "If I had my choice of all the high schools, I would send my kids here. I think this is the best school I've ever been in. They have the discipline . . . and tough academics. . . . You can't slip through. If you can't make it here, you can't make it anywhere. Faculty will always be sensitive to students' needs."

Teachers not only seem to be admiring of one another, they also express satisfaction with the tone of professionalism, resourcefulness, and good will that the school culture seems to generate. "Almost everyone loves coming to work," says a ten-year veteran of the school. Along with appreciative smiles there are persistent complaints. "Rosemont teachers tend to complain. In fact, they *enjoy* complaining. This should *not* be misread as dissatisfaction with the school. . . . Perhaps their standards are too high and they are struggling to meet those unrealistic goals."

Throughout my stay at Rosemont, I was struck by the competence and dedication of the faculty. Occasionally I heard teachers talking about ideas, pedagogy, and styles of learning. More often I saw teachers conferring together about how to help a difficult student; how to support and comfort a girl whose mother had suddenly died; how to ease the racial tensions that had erupted at a recent football game. They seemed to be joining together as student advocates, pooling information, perspectives, and skills. Although I heard many conversations about students, I heard very few careless, derogatory statements about them.

In class sessions, most teaching seemed to be at a high level. I was impressed by the careful preparation of those classes I observed, the respect teachers showed for student opinion, and the focus on curricular matters rather than on discipline. Although I heard rumors about mischievous behavior, discipline did not seem to be a problem in the classrooms I visited. Teachers appeared not to be threatened by the possibility of disruption and students did not seem to want to provoke disorder or create chaos merely for the purpose of undermining the teacher. When I asked a fifteen-year veteran teacher about disciplinary battles in the classroom, she looked slightly puzzled. "That has not been a problem for me. Nor does it seem to be a problem in this school. Teachers offer kids respect and it comes back to us full circle."

One does not sense the tensions and sharp divisions of power that often accompany teacher-pupil relationships in secondary schools. The tone of the school is relaxed, with teachers admonishing students who get out of line or encouraging them "to focus" their attention. Teachers seem to be free of the policing function; both in and out of class, teachers and students seem to mix well, relationships appear comfortable, and there is minimal adult dominance. During a fire drill, for example, with crowds of people streaming out of the school, I was impressed with the general calm of everyone, the minor supervisory role teachers took, and with some of the informal, friendly conversation between students and teachers as we gathered outside the school.

Another teacher offered a different view of why disciplinary problems are minimal. "Rosemont is unusual in its individualistic approach to students. . . . Teachers know students well and are concerned about the whole person. They work toward communicating at many levels." Violence often accompanies anonymity. Faces lost in a crowd are more likely to act irresponsibly and be moved toward anarchy. Rosemont teachers seem to see individual faces and students respond to the focused attention.

Many students spoke of appreciating the unstrained, nonthreatening setting. When a teacher asked her class to tell me what was special about Rosemont High School, many recent arrivals from other high schools testified about "feeling safe for the very first time." A pretty blond-haired girl from New Jersey said, "This is the first school I have been in where you can walk in the hall without being supervised." A girl from Connecticut said, "In my school, there was graffiti all over the bathrooms and kids used to torch lockers." After several statements about the threats of violence in other schools and the feelings of asylum in this one, a thoughtful boy summed up the tone of his peers' remarks. "This is a sort of a *free* school. . . . Teachers are not abusive."

The feelings of circular respect and good will must sustain teachers in their work. But one also has a sense that teachers are supported in their individuality as well; that there is little pressure to conform to prescribed patterns or styles from administrators or colleagues. A social worker is admired for his unorthodox methods and his unending, limitless commitment to the lives of students. Two history teachers, with greatly contrasting pedagogies and philosophies, are both perceived as extraordinary. Their differences are valued. Claims one observer, "There is lots of variety in the faculty. Kids can plug in where they want to. . . . There is an adult for every student."

A few teachers I talked with did not share this view. They spoke of the difficulties of innovation and change in a faculty overly committed to conservative academics and traditions. One member of the biology department has designed a course entitled Body/Mind Research. Proclaimed as "great and fantastic" by many students, the course has slowly gained a mixed reputation among faculty as "esoteric," "different," "controversial," and "fascinating." Inspired by student responses to the course, a few faculty and administrators have enrolled in a summer session course and become converts and enthusiasts. Julie Wilson has been teaching at Rosemont High for almost a decade. For several years she taught conventional biology courses and "for free" experimented with other forms of scientific exploration using "paradigms and frameworks" that caused suspicion among many of her departmental colleagues. Three years ago she introduced her new course for the first time. Ten students, all from the School Within a School, dared to take it. "They were considered on the fringe of life here," explains Wilson, "and that is the way I was perceived as well." Much of her energy was spent fighting the traditions and conservatism of her department. Her style, pedagogy, and the course content were thought to be too unconventional, and people suspected her missionary zeal. Whenever the department's budget required trimming, Wilson's course would be immediately threatened. She blames some of her colleagues for lack of courage, not malice.

The course has not only survived, it has thrived and grown. This year, one hundred students applied, and there was space for only fifty in two sessions. Wilson could choose who she wanted and she selected very carefully. Juniors and seniors only; students who had parental support and interest; and students who were school leaders. "Now I have the college-prep, all-American kids. . . . They are great and I love them," she exults. The large numbers and "chosen ones" have increased the visibility and status of the course in Rosemont High. Clearly, Wilson is the inspiration and drive behind the course. To her it is more than a course. It represents the potential for a different world view, a transformed image of self, a chance for increasing human capacity and potential among students.

Body/Mind Research meets in the basement of the new gym, in a huge padded room usually used for wrestling. "You can tell when it's wrestling season," Wilson smiles. "It begins to stink in here." When students walk in the room, they take off their shoes. The temptation in this large space is to whirl around and do cartwheels, and, upon entering, students do begin to tussle with each other, or slowly turn in absent-minded motion, or charge across the room at high speed. They seem freer, unencumbered, and glad to be there. Wilson, an attractive woman with dark curly hair, alive eyes, and a dramatic style, directs all of us to sit in a circle on the floor. She is not willing for me to observe, but wants me to "experience the process." Perhaps she is concerned that an observer might distract others from being involved. "In the beginning of the year, there are spaces in the circle. By the spring, the circle is closed. The feeling is wonderful. In the fall, I have to drive them and be the taskmaster. Later on, I can let go and let it happen."

The class is active and physical, with students and teacher exploring physiological questions through direct experience. We all do a series of experiments on muscle strength. With a chosen partner, Wilson demonstrates the exercise, but leaves questions unanswered. Her demonstrations are lively and theatrical, compelling attention. Students then choose partners and try out the experiments themselves. Data are gathered from each pair of students and compared with the "results" of more conventional, carefully controlled experiments found in the scientific literature. Wilson explains to students her motivation for leading this journey of discovery. It is an explanation that points to different ways of knowing, the nature of evidence, and the problems of bias. "Some of you have been worried about the unscientific nature of what we are doing here. It makes you feel uncomfortable. . . . How can we grow increasingly critical and systematic while we still remain sensitive and open?" She warns students that even scientists who claim to be doing the most careful experiments are guided by unconscious assumptions of what they expect to find. It is important to become increasingly self-critical about those hidden assumptions and to recognize that more of our senses can be involved in exploring scientific terrain. Wilson's explanations are not defensive. They reflect the open-mindedness she is encouraging in her students.

Even though Wilson recounts the subtle exclusion, skepticism, and misunderstandings inflicted upon her by some reticent colleagues, the tale of her course and its great success also points to the eclecticism and diversity that this institution is able to tolerate and absorb. Many remain unconvinced, but they seem willing to "let her do her thing" without interference.

Strong alliances among teachers may support this openness to diversity. Faculty seem to create friendships and gather support within their departments. There are some generalized stereotypes about the character of departments that seem at least half true. The biology and math departments, for example, are described as more conservative than the English and social studies departments. Wilson's philosophies and pedagogy may not have made waves in another department with more sympathetic colleagues. A member of the social studies department claims that they have earned a good academic reputation among their colleagues but that they are considered "a little left of center" in their ideological stance. They no longer wear the 1960s garb, but underneath their more conventional, "grown-up" clothing is the spirit of those who wear "jeans and sweatshirts."

Faculty in the English department also seem to be admired for their commitment and skill. Many are described as gifted, even "poetic" teachers. But they also are resented by members of other departments because they are given a lighter teaching load. Historically, it was expected that English teachers would spend a great deal of their time counseling students, since writing and reading, the essential skills of all academic work, were the province of the English department. In order to support that special responsibility, English teachers were required to teach only four courses, rather than the normal load of five. That policy is still in effect. In this period of diminished resources, however, many faculty resent what they consider to be the privileged position of the English department. One English teacher admits, "I understand why others are indignant. After all, faculty in other departments now do as much individual work as we do. The historical distinction no longer makes sense."

These generalized characterizations of the departments do not appear to be firmly entrenched or markedly divisive. Departments are less expressions of territoriality and image than they are environments of support and exchange. Some teachers speak of departments as if they were extended families, with the positive qualities of loyalty and connection and the strains of competition and closeness. One teacher complains that her productivity and happiness at work are diminished by her complicated, adversarial relationship with her department chairman. In the same breath, she appreciates the enduring friendship and nurturance she gets from a few close colleagues in the department. These friendships sustain her through tough personal and professional times, and allow for the kind of mutual criticism that is only possible when there is high trust.

One chairperson I spoke with describes her department as "very close." It is not that everyone feels trust and intimacy, but that they share common goals and care for each other's well-being. "If you are out sick, you can expect a call from someone in the department who is concerned about you." There are two or three people she perceives as being "on the fringe" and hopes to "bring them into the fold," but she does not believe that they feel excluded and ultimately respects their decision to remain aloof.

A young woman, Janine Jones, recently succeeded an older man, who had a benign, fatherly image within the department, as chairperson. He expressed his caring by being protective and taking younger colleagues under his wing. When Jones entered the job, she was determined to see administration as a "task to be done" rather than play a superior, maternal role; and she wanted to increase the sense of responsibility and leadership from within the ranks. Since September she has seen subtle but very moving changes. Some of the younger faculty who had been fathered by the former chairman have "been able to grow up" since his leave-taking. They have begun to assume leadership roles in departmental committees and act more responsibly in relation to colleagues. One departmental member had anticipated how the change in leadership would affect her behavior. She admitted to Jones, "I wanted you to be chairman but I was worried when you got it because I knew that I would have to work hard." Departmental chairs have clout and status at Rosemont. Their style and temperament seem to have an imprint on faculty life. Because the high school's image still rests securely on an academic reputation and because teachers primarily view themselves as thinkers and pedagogues, the traditional departmental arrangements of academic life appear to have force here.

## Diminished Resources and More Demands

This year, faculty enthusiasm has been dampened by the budget cuts that have devastated many of the state's public services. Hospital staffs have been depleted, firemen have been laid off, and policemen with long years of experience are suddenly without jobs. Public parks suffer from lack of upkeep; municipal pools have been closed because there is no money to pay the salaries of lifeguards; and publicly funded child-care centers have had to drastically reduce staff and supplies. But public attention has been focused primarily on the ravage done to schools.

In the city school system, more than 1,000 teachers were laid off in September, many with more than a decade of teaching experience. The "extras" of art, music, gym, and field trips have all been eliminated as teachers and students face a bleak future without abundance and resources. Increasingly, those parents who can afford other alternatives have decided to take their children out of public schools. The waiting lists for private schools have grown impossibly long. Many families, once committed to the convenience and style of city life, have decided to move to the relatively affluent suburbs. And parochial schools are being oversubscribed by desperate applicants. As one public official said recently, "The public schools in the city are becoming the prisons of the poor." Without alternatives and clout, the poor are left to inhabit a rapidly deteriorating system.

In comparison to the gloomy picture of the city, the Rosemont schools appear relatively untouched. They still seem to enjoy the resources and privileges that have been denied to the city. Last year,

Rosemont's superintendent was a visible and powerful spokesman for the opposition to the tax cut referendum and parents and community people rallied to save their schools from the destructive cuts. When it was rumored that the proposed cuts would lead to a double-session kindergarten, the community was up in arms and ready for battle. Says one slightly cynical observer, "Parents were outraged. They were convinced that their kids' lives would be unalterably damaged!" The parents of high school students tended to be less threatened by the repercussions of the tax losses than the vocal and protective elementary school parents. There is always a tendency for the parents of secondary students to be less involved with the schools than they were a few years earlier. But some citizens claimed that, in this case, high school parents showed extreme irresponsibility toward the schools and their children and did not fully recognize the potential damage of diminished resources. An angry parent of a high school student, who felt she was fighting the battle "all alone," claimed, "No one said anything in opposition to a proposal that the first year of language at the high school be eliminated. . . . If the faculty had not gotten enraged, that proposal would have gone through. . . . Why don't parents scream when the number of guidance counselors is cut. There are now two hundred and fifty students to every counselor. It is impossible!"

Despite the comparative view that Rosemont has suffered little in relation to its big-city neighbor, school people in Rosemont feel a sense of loss and discouragement. From the superintendent, who was used to winning and wielding power effortlessly, to the individual teacher, who feels less supported and rewarded, the sense of loss in this town is palpable. Because Superintendent Turner's fight against the referendum had been so dramatic and visible, its passage was a personal defeat for him—a defeat with high political and professional costs. Said a budding administrator, who has always admired Turner's inspired leadership and deft style, "I always thought he was invulnerable and suddenly I recognized he was a mortal and could lose."

Beyond the personal defeats, faculty in particular speak of the harmful repercussions. Many paragraphs begin, "Well, before the referendum we could . . ." and end, "Now we are not able to . . ." An invisible line seems to divide the time of abundance from the period of retrenchment. Some faculty speak of being "discouraged and frustrated," others, more dramatically, talk about the assaults of a "conservative reign of terror." But most seem to be seeking a resourceful and responsible approach to the losses. A housemaster captures the mood eloquently. "My sense is that morale is down . . . the spirit is being tested. Before, faculty would go to unbelievable lengths on behalf of kids. Now their efforts have to be more realistic, more circumscribed." The chairperson of a department is slightly more buoyant in her perception of faculty responses to the budget cuts. "Last year, there was a lot of fear and anguish. Everyone worried about losing his or her job. Over the summer, people seemed to rally and returned feeling renewed. . . . Faculty are now doing a much more difficult and consuming job but they have somehow discovered inner resources." As a department chair she has had to meet the harsh realities, protect her department, and stimulate her colleagues' morale. A relatively new appointee, she is eager to be seen as competent, but finds her energy and ambitions can sometimes become liabilities. "Everyone says you're doing a great job and I say I'm in a double bind. ᵇ want to do a good job because I am ambitious and want this to lead to other good jobs. . . . But if I prove I can be a superwoman, under impossible conditions, that is not right either. The structure is still all wrong."

To conform to the requirements of the law, Rosemont had to decrease its budget by 18.5 percent this year and will have to cut back 15 percent in 1982-83. Part of the anxiety among faculty stems not so much from present conditions but from anticipation about a more difficult future. This year, the high school managed to keep most of its faculty despite the large budgetary cuts. Administrators and teachers agreed that monies should be taken from other corners. Middle level, system-wide administrators were let go rather than deplete the core teaching faculty. For example, the curriculum coordinator for social studies, who is responsible for orchestrating efforts across grades and among schools, was fired; and there is no longer anyone who can serve as a resource for teachers and department heads. Some of the recently hired guidance counselors had to leave, and the custodial staff was substantially cut. One teacher, picking up trash as she walks through the quadrangle, says, "For the first time in my fourteen years here, this building is not being kept absolutely clean. Some of the custodians have been fired and their buddies are protesting with a work slowdown, in defiance."

Mostly, the high school has tried to cut non-human resources. Money for books, paper, and other supplies is very scarce. The chairperson of social studies has only $1,000 this year to buy all the books for her department. In parts of the school building, the roof is leaking badly, but it was decided that no repair should be made for at least another year. The brass sign on one of the housemaster's doors still bears the name of his predecessor. "No money for new signs," he explains with a smile.

Some of the attempts to save money seem fairly trivial, until people begin to point to the subtle and unexpected repercussions. Several teachers told me about the impact of budget cuts on food service. The lunches have become almost inedible and faculty no longer have a separate food service for their exclusive use. They still gather in the faculty dining room, but they have to wait on student lines to get their food. Rather than endure the crowds, the hassles, and the bad meals, most faculty have begun to bring their lunches from home and to gather in their department offices. On a given day, the faculty dining room is likely to be almost empty as teachers, with their brown bags, gather at desks or around conference tables. "No one really leaves work. They talk shop or they don't talk at all," complains one teacher who misses the camaraderie and humor of the old cafeteria days. A more compelling complaint made by many more teachers focuses on the unanticipated divisions among faculty that have arisen. It is a large school and the lunch room was one of the few places where teachers from different disciplines and departments could gather informally. Now, they are forced to retreat to more confined areas that diminish their sense of community.

Clearly the impact of the tax cut referendum is central in the minds of adults at Rosemont High School. Kennedy speaks proudly of their efforts "to hold the line" on those things most central to the process of education, and he admires the resourcefulness and resilience of his teachers. But he worries out loud about how much they can endure and he does not want to test the limits of their good will and energy.

Beyond the press of the budget, faculty and administrators are facing another major intrusion. This is the time of the Ten Year Evaluation of the New England Association for Secondary Schools

(NEASS), and a great deal of energy is being channeled into this self-evaluative effort. In response to the demands on their energy and time, teachers speak with a collective voice. They feel harassed, resentful, and frustrated by a process that seems largely superficial and predetermined. Evaluation committee meetings are held every Tuesday and Thursday afternoon from 2:30 to 4:30, and most faculty members are assigned to two committees.

The only time I heard angry and accusing exchanges among teachers was in connection with committee assignments for the evaluation. A chairperson of one of the large committees was trying to track down a reticent faculty member whom she had never met by sending notes and leaving telephone messages with his department head. He was enraged by her pursuit and felt she had gone over his head to his superior in order to get him in trouble. The accusations exploded on both sides. As I listened to the heated exchange I sensed that they were both overwhelmed by the demands of their work and furious at the intrusions. Quite by accident, they became each others' targets. Once their anger was released, they became the reasonable and dedicated people I had met before.

The committee meeting I observed reflected none of the hostility but all of the boredom and weariness that often accompany unwanted chores. The School and Community Relations Committee is trying to decide how to portray their school: what should be the level and depth of their response to the questionnaires provided by NEASS? The struggle to define their task and set their goals is combined with the tough issues of work load, methods for gathering needed information, and ethical considerations. The questions on the evaluation forms seem inappropriate and superficial to the committee members: "This assumes that each area of the school is monolithic. . . . If you begin to even touch on the complexities, it makes our tasks even more difficult." The chair of the committee, a housemaster known to be politically wise and knowledgeable about community forces, tries to shift the discouraging tone. "I think we have to grapple with attempting to describe the complexity of the school. It helps to respond in the most honest way possible." Eleven faculty members, weary from a long school day, rally in response to her urgings. They try to figure out how to design appropriate responses as well as how to gather information that might be useful to them. Their spirits are slightly enlivened by the thought that this exercise could be ultimately beneficial to their knowledge of the community and their interactions with parents. An enthusiastic participant feels that the form does not reflect the concerns of Rosemont's diverse population. "One question that is not on the form concerns that growing population of kids who are deciding not to go on to college. Don't we want to ask their parents if they think the curriculum is adequate for persons who do *not* plan to go to college?" Another worries about the tone of the question, a tone she feels encourages bias and negativism. "In sympathy with the striking Philadelphia teachers, I'm feeling a little paranoid and threatened by these questions that ask for subjective judgments. . . . Can't we include some clear, objective questions, like how many times they have come to parent-teacher conferences and how they decide when to let their kids drop a course? . . . Some parents let their kids drop a major that they haven't attended for five weeks!"

Although some good suggestions emerge from time to time, the discussion seems labored and inefficient. The mandatory instrument for gathering data gets in the way of progress, inhibits their exchanges, and depletes their initiating energies. By the time the chairperson begins to assign tasks to people at the end of the meeting, everyone is worn down. "Will you do an announcement about the Back-to-School night, Rose?" the chair asks one of her more resilient members. "Do I have to?" pleads a childish voice. And then Rose says, with a smile, "Gee whiz, I suddenly felt like a kid being given an assignment by the teacher." Rose's plaintive voice and her immediate recognition of "quick regression" captures part of the experience of this process. For teachers, who mostly enjoy autonomy and confident feelings of adulthood, this task seems almost degrading. Its infliction seems unwarranted. Despite their complaints, however, one has a sense that these teachers will produce a more than adequate evaluation report. They are too wise and too realistic to pretend this hurdle is trivial.

One should not overemphasize the recent experiences of deprivation and loss. Rosemont High is a brave and resilient school that is facing important challenges. Unlike many schools, it does not seek to ignore the world around it but tries to confront the hypocrisies, endure the uncertainties, and rally against the assaults. In its responses to the persistent challenges, there are imperfections. It is a school that seems divided. It is a school where class, race, and ethnicity are vivid markers of status. It is a school where bright, academic, and efficient students continue to form the public image and get more than their fair share of admiring attention. But these imperfections are not being ignored by faculty, students, or administrators. The struggle is palpable. It is a school searching for a clearer moral code and standards of behavior. It is a school testing the limits of diversity. It is a school experimenting with new and unconventional arrangements of power and responsibility. It is a school in visible transition.

One senses that the risk taking, the unusual openness to change, and the responsiveness to community are possible only because of a long history of security. The contemporary bravery follows generations of stability and certainty. That self-confidence is a bedrock for responding to the uncertainties and threats that will shape the future. It will require the patience and endurance of a long-distance runner, and also some of the quick, intuitive responses of a sprinter.

# 5

# SEQUOIA HIGH SCHOOL

## MARLENE MCCRACKEN AND
## ROBERT A. MCCRACKEN

$S$everal contextual factors related to Sequoia High School seem significant. There has been a major decline in funding; there has been a major drop in the school district's population (approximately 10,000 fewer students); there has been deterioration of the building and grounds; there has been a rif (reduction in force), mostly of teachers with less than ten to twelve years of district tenure; there has been a reduction, severe in some departments, of class offerings. In contrast, there has been little shift over the past twenty years in the ethnic or socioeconomic background of the students, except for some recent Southeast Asian refugees who are students in a segregated class for English as a Second Language (ESL).

For many years, schools in this state were funded by a combination of state and local revenues. In the mid-1970s the state legislature decided that funding for basic education should come solely from the state and that a single salary schedule for teachers should be implemented. The legislation was to be implemented in 1982; however, revenues in the state were so high in 1978–79 that the state decided to undertake 100 percent funding immediately. Until this time, there was considerable variation in per pupil costs within the state. Some districts, Sequoia being one, consistently passed high local taxes for school support in yearly levies, experiencing only one levy defeat since the opening of Sequoia High School in 1957. In the early days, Sequoia schoolteachers had been paid the top salaries in the state (this has not been true in the past few years) and there had always been funding for special programs. Coupled with this was the fairly consistent growth in housing and population in the district, so that for most of the 1960s and early 1970s elementary schools were built and additional teachers were hired. A serious industrial recession in the early seventies created a problem for several years, and the loss of school-age population in the mid to late seventies has changed the school climate.

Since state funding is based on per pupil cost, the loss of pupils has meant a loss of funds. The state's effort is devoted to providing equal funding regardless of geographic location. Inasmuch as Sequoia was well above the average in expenditures per pupil, the new state funding program has forced Sequoia to reduce its expenditures to the state average. This has meant a kind of double loss of revenue. The state commits itself for all basic education and then declares, in effect, that Sequoia had been paid too much, so that full funding from the state is now less than the district had been used to spending. There were only three ways to meet the financial crisis: rif faculty, close some schools, and increase class size. All of these were carried out.

In the fall of 1981, as this study was being made, the governor declared a financial emergency and asked all schools to prepare for a 10.1 percent cut in funds for 1982–83 (the second year of the budget period). The legislature was in special session the entire time we were working in the school.

While most of the Sequoia High School faculty are fairly safe in their jobs, since they have so many years' tenure, the specter of additional faculty cuts and the loss of even more funds has left many feeling uncertain and a bit disgruntled. There had been a dramatic increase in class size already, and the prospect of even larger classes was troubling. Most of the faculty were surprisingly philosophical about their personal situations, but they did express concern about the effect of larger classes on the students. Four or five faculty members felt strongly that any additional cuts should be made in the central office staff, which had actually increased in recent years in spite of the significant decline in the school population.

There had been a move about four years earlier to close Sequoia High School because the students could have been accommodated in one of the other high schools in the district. Parents, either led or abetted by faculty, protested so vigorously that the school remained open. The faculty recalled this period as extremely difficult but felt the display of parent support was gratifying and that the overall effect was salubrious. This year it was necessary to shift from a grade ten to twelve structure to a nine to twelve structure in order to have sufficient population and avoid more pressure to close the school.

This shift to a nine to twelve structure was accepted by the high school staff, but having ninth graders was viewed as a loss of stature since all the other high schools continued to have a ten to twelve organization. There was no fall orientation or welcoming for the former junior high teachers who were transferred to Sequoia. There was no assigned teacher-buddy system, no explanation of where the supplies were kept, what the lunch procedures were, and the like. The new teachers were all experienced teachers, but they did not feel any kind of personal or professional welcome.

A tracking system was instituted this year without any apparent discussion or consent of the faculty; however, class content seemingly has not been modified in any way for either the more able or the less able. The faculty seems to feel that tracking merely puts most of the hard-working kids together so that the less serious students do not interfere with their learning. One group of students we interviewed reported that being in an honors section meant they were "three chapters ahead of the regular sections."

There was noticeably less faculty complaint about the ninth-grade students as the school year progressed to late November and into December. Faculty had by then accepted their presence. There was, however, some student concern about the "immature ninth graders," expressed most frequently in such statements as "the ninth graders were the only ones silly enough to smoke regularly and to deal in drugs on campus." The upper classmen insisted that one did not bring drugs on campus because the vice principal always got her man; apparently she had "busted" the drug scene so regularly and severely that students had pretty much. agreed to keep drugs off campus. Dealing took place just off the school grounds, however. And even though the campus was officially closed, it was no problem for kids to leave legally, or otherwise, if they chose. "Misbehaving students," we were told often, were transferred to other high schools. One student reported that he was sent to another high school for half the year because he had kissed his girl friend.

Our first visit to the campus was just after the heaviest three-day rainfall ever recorded in this area. The open corridors connecting the campus facilities were flooded. The corridor roofs leaked; blacktop walkways were without drainage and so uneven that water settled up to three inches deep. The classroom and office buildings leaked so terribly that several classrooms were flooded, and the library carpet and many of the junior high books that had been stored on the floor were soaked. Fall continued to be abnormally rainy. Added to the dampness was lack of heat. The campus was not a pleasant place to be.

The grounds were littered with paper of various sorts. No one seemed to accept any personal responsibility for the litter, merely citing the loss of custodial staff because of budget cuts.

As we walked across campus, one faculty member commented on the disarray and the deterioration of the buildings. He said, "They're not going to fix it because they [central office] want to close this campus, and they aren't going to fix it unless somebody raises hell. I've asked the principal, and he just isn't going to protest because the central office doesn't like principals who fight them."

We asked students about the litter, and their response was that picking up was the custodian's job. There was little sense that someone had caused the litter. However, they would like a nicer school, one that was painted and kept up. While they indicated a willingness to work with clean-up, there was no leadership and considerable acceptance that nothing much could be done over the long run.

## Students

Initially, we tried written interviews with some students. We asked a series of questions and the students were given time to write their responses. This was satisfactory, but it seemed evident that we needed to probe the responses in depth. For example, one student wrote: "In school there is really no way to find out the things that are really important, and that we want to know . . . nobody is teaching the things that I want to study."

We wanted to know what the "things that are really important" were, but we had no way of asking at that time and in that format.

We later shifted to oral interviews with groups of four or five students from the same class. The teachers and administrators asked us what kind of kids we wanted. It was only after we understood what they meant by "kind" that we got a representative sample of students. Each group was anonymous; we recorded only grade levels and sex. We asked the groups to answer for themselves and then to tell us what they thought most of their peers would have answered, and to indicate agreement or disagreement with what any single speaker was saying. Throughout, the students were courteous to us and to each other, and seemed to answer with candor. Most seemed to know when their opinion of something was commonly accepted and when they were expressing a minority opinion.

The class we "interviewed" through writing was a tenth-grade basic English class. It had one or two nonsophomores in it, and seemed fairly representative of the school as a whole, in that 70 percent seemed to be thinking of college and most liked school fairly well. There was one ESL student. Two students just slept and didn't participate; a few clearly didn't like school very much and would rather have been elsewhere. We were a bit surprised to receive several written responses that used a four-letter word in the vernacular to describe some aspects of life in the school. In the oral discussions there was no swearing, but there was an equal proportion of dislike. Perhaps being able to express dislike orally allayed the need to swear, or perhaps it was just social convention. However, in the oral interviews the students who didn't like school were polite. The responses in the written interviews supported, for the most part, the oral responses.

Most classes, with the exception of the ESL class, which began two years ago, have no students who are identifiably not caucasian. Most of the students in the ESL program are thought of as identifiably not caucasian; they are thought of as Vietnamese by the faculty and students although several are from non-Asian countries. The Vietnamese custom of males holding hands and embracing when saying "hello" was mentioned by several faculty and students as a bit disturbing on what they described as "the macho campus." There seemed to be little thought by either faculty or students of ignoring or tolerating these customs. "If they are going to live here, they should behave as we do," said one student.

The Vietnamese students we talked to said that in math, science, and mechanical drawing classes they were treated like everyone else, and felt reasonably well accepted, although no one went out of the way to be helpful or friendly. On the campus and in other classes they were treated as persons to be stared at, as curiosity pieces, and no one would make a serious effort to talk with them. A Vietnamese student who enrolled three years ago, when there was no special program, was cited by several students as an example of how the rest should behave: "They should all learn English and mix in." No one seemed to realize that mixing in was quite difficult with the imposition of ESL, which segregated kids for much of the day in order to teach them English.

All the Asian students agreed that the teachers here were much nicer than any they had ever known: "They are friendly and let you talk. Back home you had to be absolutely silent." They also agreed that there was too much talking in classes and that the native Sequoia students did not show teachers enough respect.

Most students at Sequoia are white and come from middle- and upper-middle-class socioeconomic backgrounds. One notices an occasional oriental countenance, but otherwise the students reflect a sameness in appearance. The students recognize this about themselves. Eighty percent or more say going on to college or university is their goal, whether they are enrolled in the college preparatory track or not. (Official records indicate about 60 percent actually do.) Many who say that they want to but don't expect to go to college think they should go or, at least, should get some additional technical or community college training.

More than half of the students in grades eleven to twelve work after school, and most of the younger students say that they hope to work. Of the working students, about half do so to have a car or pocket money, the other half are working to have enough money to go to college. They agreed that there were jobs for anyone who was willing to work and who was dependable.

Drugs and alcohol are not visible on campus. However, ninety percent or more of the students interviewed said that they are used heavily after school and on weekends by the high school-age group. There seemed to be no attempt to hide usage, although this could be misjudged. The consensus was that to use drugs and alcohol was a personal decision, that no morality was involved, and that, so long as you bothered no one, you could do what you wanted without censure. The users did not feel that the nonusers were imposing any moral censure; users and nonusers could be friends on campus or off. On almost all moral issues, it was felt that individuals should make their own decisions. Few wished to impose their own standards on anyone else. Hypocrisy was almost universally damned.

Getting pregnant was thought by many of the students to be "pretty bad" or wrong. We did not determine if this reflected a belief that contraceptives should be used or that some degree of continent behavior was expected.

The faculty commented that there are more one-parent or divorced parent homes than there used to be. The students acknowledged this, but didn't believe that it was a school-related issue. There was a consensus that coming from a divorced-parent or a one-parent home was "no big deal," and that it had no effect on a student's personal or social standing with peers. They agreed that home break-ups were difficult, but the peer role was to be friendly and helpful, not to find fault. Those who had gone through this said that it was rough, but just "one of those things," and that it really was not affecting their school life socially or academically.

There is a small group of "born again" Christians in the school. Most of the nonreborn students view them as hypocritical because the born-again don't behave any differently than anyone else. It is not the Christianity that bothers the students, but the hypocrisy. We asked several teachers about the group. Most said that they were unaware of them or that they were a meaningless minority. A counselor, on the other hand, said they were an effective moral force on the campus and were the school leaders. (The class leaders we interviewed said the born-again were ineffective. They tended to agree with those students who labelled the born-again as hypocrites.)

As a group, Sequoia students seemed uninterested in politics, religion, or moral values as subjects to study or discuss. They seemed to feel that these were personal issues.

There was, however, a great deal of concern that education was not sufficiently funded. Undoubtedly, students heard this expressed by teachers and, possibly, by their parents. Common personal worries were getting into a good school and affording an education.

Students for whom English is a second language, and those who are hearing-impaired and educationally handicapped, are found on the Sequoia campus. There are some mainstreaming activities for these students, but there is little of substance. "They can be here, but we have no obligation to them," is a fairly typical student response. We pushed students about their sense of personal obligation and the possibility of learning through real association with students in these programs. There was agreement that this would be desirable; that the boys likely would not cooperate, although most of the girls would; and that there was no leadership, faculty or student, interested in trying to do anything. Hostility was expressed by several boys who said that these kids didn't belong and had no right or business being in the school and "messing us up."

There is pressure to be an enthusiastic supporter of Sequoia High School, particularly off campus, when you are identifiable as an SHS student. It is good to be from Sequoia High as opposed to any of the other four high schools in the district. Everyone agreed that the other four high schools were undesirable. This feeling seemed to be much stronger than the normal love of one's school.

There are several in-groups. By consensus, the most important is the athletic group. Students agreed that within any one group there was tremendous pressure to conform, and that some of the groups ran counter to each other, so that belonging to one made it impossible to be in another. Although the pressure to be in an in-group came from both students and many of the faculty, 40 to 50 percent of the students described themselves as not "in." Some said that they weren't really wanted and wouldn't be accepted even if they tried to belong; others clearly did not want to be "in." We sensed considerable pressure from faculty for students to be enthusiastic supporters of all athletic contests, and, while attending, to behave in an exemplary way. We had a sense that the exemplary behavior was to demonstrate superiority, particularly over some of the lower-class schools, not because good behavior was itself important. (Many of the seniors at a pep rally we observed rejected this ambience by not cheering or applauding much and were chided for not doing so.)

We had been told that the senior class was peculiar. It did not have as many participants as it should in athletic and social programs. Its members didn't demonstrate as much enthusiasm for the school as they should. We asked some seniors about this observation. They said, in essence, "We've been an academically bright group right from elementary school. We've always been somewhat individualistic and not much impressed by the usual rah-rah things. We want a good education from school, not a bunch of social trappings and time wasted on school busy-work projects. This has bothered the faculty, but so what!" This sounds a bit arrogant, but the students who felt this way did not impress us as arrogant; they seemed to be trying to explain something they obviously were aware of, their supposedly not behaving as seniors in this school should behave. They did not seem to like the label of nonconformists or nonparticipants, but they saw no personal gain by participating; they wanted, as several said, "to be graduated without hassle."

Grades were obviously of great importance to Sequoia students. They all seemed to know their own grade-point average and the grade-point averages of several others besides. We were unprepared for this litany of averages (to two decimal places) and the knowledge of class ranking that many of the students displayed. Grades were important for one reason: to get into a good college. Despite this apparent obsession, it was repeatedly stated that getting grades was a personal thing, and that you were neither respected nor disliked because you got good grades. However, individual bright students (in calculus, which enrolls only fifteen select math students) were obviously admired by the lesser members of the select group.

There was a good deal of agreement that there were no real demands to do homework outside school, and that even within school there was not a great deal of work. Those who did homework always spoke of their math assignments as predictable (a page of problems); and there was agreement that just before the end of the term there was a spate of homework from every academic class. The students acknowledged that they would do more work if such demands were made, and that they wished that there was a demand for real work, not just busy work, as homework. They also agreed that they would like more challenging and harder work, but that they would resist it, unless the teachers firmly demanded it, because it was just natural to resist and there would be peer pressure to complain and resist.

Similarly, they wished that the teachers would teach more in most classes, and that greater intellectual challenge existed. Students seemed unable to explain what they meant by this, but they seemed to feel that the state demands for minimal competencies as part of graduation had made many of the basic subjects (math and English, primarily) a waste of time because they were taught little they hadn't already been taught in junior high school. They made no claim that they had all of the basic competencies, but said their time was wasted in being taught all the same things again.

There was a consensus that the buildings needed repair. In the aftermath of all the rain, students joked about, but resented, the leaking corridors and classrooms, and the pools of water they had to wade through to get to their lockers.

Most students agreed that Sequoia had good teachers. Some administrators, however, drew criticism. While a majority of the students felt the vice principal in charge of attendance was personally "doing a good job," almost all felt the office, overall, was nasty, abrasive, and mean in its every-day dealings with students. "Violate a rule and you go to detention, regardless of the reason. To appeal is foolish because no one ever listens and you serve your sentence anyway."

The vice principal in charge of student affairs was not known to all students. Those who knew him thought he was pleasant, but that he always wanted to tell the students what to do and how to do it. "We do things here because they are traditional. The calendar is set a year in advance so we have to conform to tradition," students noted. The students liked many of their traditions, particularly their homecoming weekend, but they felt they had no say in most decisions, whether significant or insignificant.

The three guidance counselors were known only for their help with schedules and were not viewed as an important part of the school. One was mentioned favorably because he spoke to individual students in the halls, something the others obviously did not do.

The principal was virtually unknown to the students. They knew his name, knew him by sight, and knew that he rode a motorcycle to school, but they said they never saw him in classrooms or around the campus.

Several commented, in contrast, that their superintendent of schools was occasionally on campus and in their classes. They liked this interest on his part.

## Class Leaders

We interviewed the Associated Student Body president, secretary, and vice president, and the senior and junior class presidents. One of these officers was also the school's outstanding athlete. We interviewed them near the end of our study, enabling us to pursue particular interests in greater detail. Overall, we were surprised by their candor and perspicacity. They clearly like their school and seemed to hope that their interviews with us might alter some of the school's operations, although they seemed not really to expect that our discussions would change things.

While they had individual perspectives, and occasionally disagreed with each other, there was considerable agreement. We present here some of their thoughts.

The school's purpose is to give us a basic education. They want us to get the basic requirements. The basic isn't much. We now have four English classes. There used to be seventeen. The teaching is toward the average. There is some independent study if you can get a sponsor. . . . Most of the classes make single assignments with single texts. The honors classes are new this year.

Homework is not much. . . . Less than an hour a night. We would like more challenging work. Nothing this year makes me proud to have finished. We have too much lecture and then tests. Not much discussion. We need more open discussion rather than just lectures.

We don't change things here. We are just told, "That is the way we do things here." We get little faculty support. Students develop a lethargic attitude.

There is not much real concern between students and faculty. The relationship is Boss to Peon. Go to class, sit, behave. There is no inspiration. We'd like some independence, but the teachers aren't strict enough.

I had the same content three times under three different titles [referring to social studies].

The younger teachers get riffed; we need their energy. We work when the teacher loves his subject.

Everything is so military-like; there is nothing that is not prescribed.

The class leaders are burned out. We are tired of being class leaders. Our senior class is the least spirited. We don't stand up and cheer. We've shifted from male to mostly all female. There seems less respect for girls.

The administration and faculty don't listen, aren't involved with student requests or beliefs. The rules they are writing down for standard classroom behavior are insulting to your intelligence. There is no inspiration or motivation.

In this school we have really good teachers or really bad teachers; there is no in-between.

Athletes and student leaders are treated a lot better than other kids. I'm an athlete and I'm treated better. There is little recognition for kids who aren't jocks. We are a basic jock school. Athletes party and drink, about eighty percent, but they don't get kicked off the team. Rules aren't enforced.

The whole world here is impressing your peers. There is very little value placed on honesty. There is so much cheating on tests and in class that a lot of teachers just turn their backs so they don't have to deal with it.

We are known as a partying school. They can never really cover it up. There is very little use of drugs or alcohol in school, but lots out of school.

I can put off all my homework and still get a B in my classes.

I'm disappointed in the administration and teachers. There is no real concern. I've gotten my basics. I am not pushed to work. [This from the one leader-student who had been pointed out to us with great pride by two teachers and the principal as one of the finest students ever to be in the school because she was such an all-around person and so concerned about school and her peers in all classes.]

Despite all we have said, we'd rather be here than at any other high school. Compared to other schools, we're still the best, but, compared to what we used to be, we're not good. The educational value we are getting is zilch. I would have liked to have had a challenge.

We share below a number of statements from *other*, nonleader students. There is a representative quality that provides a fuller view of the school.

This school is better for those who conform. If you do what you are asked to do, you are okay.

A great place for kids. It's always different. Like a big family. This is one of the best schools around. Not much hazing or vandalism.

I don't like class competition. We should have pride, but not compete with each other.

There are too many rules. We get the rules without explanation.

We need tougher classes. Our BAC's [Basic Academic Competencies] are ruinous. We need tougher discipline.

Teachers go by the book, chapter by chapter. The questions are no challenge. We read and do a work sheet and take a multiple-choice test. Facts are emphasized. We would like to be challenged, but we get a lot of busy work.

The advanced classes and the business classes are good.

We need English, but basic English is boring. I fall asleep. We have to take the skills class. It is nothing but tests. This makes it easier because there is nothing to study and no homework, and we talk a lot in class, but we don't learn much.

If I know the teacher doesn't check the work sheets, I don't do them.

It is the "in" thing to study, but you are "out" if you are a brain and argue with the teacher.

The popular kids are rich, really smart, and athletic. Sports has a lot to do with popularity. A lot of kids are into religion. Some of them think being religious is the thing to do. They are telling us they have quit using drugs, but you know they haven't quit.

The ski club is *the* club, but you have to be rich to be in it. They all went to Sun Valley.

The athletic program is geared to the outstanding. There is nothing for the ordinary student.

We'd like a longer day and time to take another class.

The short class days don't permit us to take as many classes as we'd like.

We'd like more honors classes. . . . [We] resent having to listen to so much elementary stuff.

The district controls what is going on, not the school. In my other school, things had to do with school, not the district.

Teachers are basically fair, but the discipline is not as tough as it should be. The teachers seem unwilling to confront the students. A lot of parents would probably object. Parents don't understand that their kids are not disciplined.

Most teachers here are great. A few could be more understanding of your needs. I don't mind strict, but some are too strict. If you are two minutes late, they won't accept your work.

A good teacher teaches you a lot, makes you think, makes it fun to learn, is fair, is understanding . . . gives all an equal opportunity.

The football coach won't talk to me because I broke my arm last year and couldn't play. All the coaches shoot for the championship. They don't care about anything else.

A lot of teachers here enjoy their subject, but they don't care as much about kids as they should.

## Goals

We asked all teachers and students about the goals of the school. There was almost a consensus in the immediate response: "To graduate everyone." This was followed closely by: "To pass the basic tests." Another common response was: "To get into college." There were many other responses, some of which seemed to reflect embarrassment about the pragmatic nature of the first response. The faculty was aware that there are stated goals for the district and that the faculty had helped to state them, but there seemed to be no attempt to implement them or to determine if they were being implemented. They were prepared for some external purpose. The faculty also was aware of stated departmental goals, but, again, these were not central to the current discourse of teachers. Overall, goals have not been explored in any systematic way for a long time. As a result, there are no common expectations about such things as teaching and learning, curriculum, and standards.

## Climate

Sequoia is a pleasant campus in many ways. The staff are pleased to be teaching here; the students are happier being here than in any of the district's other high schools or in whatever high school they transferred from. Student after student said this.

There were, however, other factors that detracted from the euphoria. There was general agreement, for example, that the campus needed repair, particularly the roofing. There was also agreement that the heating plant was a problem and that some days temperatures of fifty-eight to sixty degrees were endured because there was no way to adjust the temperature. Coats and sweaters and outerwear were common in the classrooms.

We were told often that Sequoia High at one time was considered to be one the state's few outstanding high schools and perhaps one of the best in the nation. While teachers still see it as a good school, few believe it is as good as it was. Students, while believing the school could be better, still thought it was probably the best high school in the state. There was almost unanimous belief that teachers were doing as well as they could, given the financial and basic education restraints imposed by the state. We could not determine the source of these feelings.

Financial restraints within the state are drastic, and there is a legislated basic education and objectives program. It seemed strange that the students were so consistently apologetic about their school's shortcomings "because the state was taking away local control" when they professed so much disinterest in social and political concerns of any other nature.

Physically, the campus is open. Access to the campus is from 360 degrees, except for an occasional tree or sign. But once students are on campus in the morning they are not able to leave without a permit. Several persons, commonly referred to by the students as "narcs," check students leaving or returning to campus. The students feel that the system is foolish for two reasons: first, they feel old enough to attend class responsibly; and, second, they all said they could cheat and leave without being caught or could get permission to leave legally any time they wanted. They felt the attendance office was so miserable about excuses and the enforcement so demeaning that only those who wanted to behave responsibly were penalized by the closure.

Related to the closed campus issue was the ban on smoking. None of the students interviewed indicated that they wanted to smoke on campus, although some were smokers. But they thought the total ban was foolish because kids then used the toilets for smoking and the narcs apprehended everyone in the toilet if they detected smoke in the area. They felt there was no such thing as using the toilet normally because of the chance of being caught there during an inspection. No one, they said, would believe them innocent if they were apprehended.

This feeling was expressed by almost all the students interviewed. Several said that the only ones who would be believed if they were questioned about smoking would be "jocks," and that they would probably be among the smokers. After we became aware of this toilet/smoking problem we asked twenty or more students directly about the situation. Almost all of them supported the opinions cited above, but many commented that they had never had any personal experience because they just never used the toilet at school. Two freshmen stated that they had never been to the school toilet because they were afraid that if they were there when someone smoked they would be caught and blamed. There was a strong feeling that students were always judged to be guilty in the eyes of the attendance-discipline office. In spite of such feelings, these same students said that they liked their school and enjoyed being there.

Most of the teachers expressed satisfaction with teaching at SHS and said that their main satisfaction was working with such marvelous students. Most students said the same things about the teachers. They felt that most teachers were trying their best to prepare them for college or the job market. Perhaps students want more than care and love. They frequently spoke of not being listened to, not being asked to work up to their abilities, not being required to produce their best.

## Curriculum

This was one of the hardest areas in which to engage teachers and students. Their answers tended to be nebulous, or seemingly evasive, without anyone wanting to be evasive. Course content is set at the district level by a committee in each of the departments. Many of the committee chairmen are teaching at SHS, so they all feel that they have had input. Very few new courses have been added in the past five years, however. Those that have been added are in vocational areas such as firefighting and practical nursing. The faculty says there have been serious deletions, and, even where there have been no deletions, the elective courses are not offered as frequently because there have been severe staff cutbacks. It would appear that there has been at least a 25 percent reduction of staff during the past five years. Class sizes are now large, many classes that had previously had fifteen to thirty students now have thirty-five to forty. English is probably hardest hit. Offerings in that department have dropped from seventeen to four. These four offerings are required basic courses, so there no longer seems much opportunity for teachers to teach in their favorite areas. Faculty response is to teach what has been taught before. Little time is spent reflecting on the total curriculum.

Art and music were not considered particularly important. We had to ask for permission to visit both these areas and needed to make a second request to visit the art class. Both music teachers seemed to be doing excellent work and to have the training and spirit to do well. They sensed, however, that there was no support for trying to implement their programs. The one art class we visited was disheartening. Students spent most of their time visiting with each other; the teacher made no attempt to get students working on anything.

Drama seems to be gone from the curriculum, no longer of any importance. We attempted to discuss curriculum with the principal, and only heard that the teachers were all "exceptionally good and knew what to teach." There is no leadership in curriculum from the administration. The administration is concerned with orderliness and friendliness—orderliness coming first. The school appears to be overorganized, in the sense that there are rules and regulations covering all routine and all conceivable emergencies. While the principal expressed an open and honest interest in the results of our interviews and a desire to know how "we at SHS are doing," he stated that he plans to put in two more years and then retire. His concern is that the final two years pass without incident.

Faculty are split in their view of the principal as a leader. Without qualification, they like him as a person, as a social companion. Twenty percent say that he is the best principal they ever worked for or could hope to work for. Half say that he is completely unqualified or inept in regard to curriculum and instruction. Most, but not all, of his leadership support came from the nonacademic areas.

Students saw the curriculum as geared to state requirements for graduation; they saw the teachers as concerned that all students meet the requirements. Students believed that the abler students were bored by the slow pace of presentation and the level of expectation, but they defended their teachers: classes were too large to individualize instruction or to differentiate between instruction and requirements. One teacher, however, reported that his proposals to individualize instruction and to develop honors projects were turned down summarily by the department's chairman because to implement them would create dissension. Students might expect the same of other teachers, and those who didn't want to change their curriculum "would be resentful of those who did." The same teacher reported that he had 120 students signed up for a special course in photography (with the understanding that he could teach it if students would enroll), only to be told, "There is no way to select those who can take it, so you can't teach it."

We felt that curriculum had no real place in the thinking of the faculty, except for the administrative concern that state regulations be met.

## Teachers

All of the teachers were asked if they wished to be interviewed, and almost all wanted to be. Notably, five of the six teachers transferred from the junior high level in the shift from the ten to twelve to the nine to twelve configuration felt that they did not yet know enough about the school to have much of value to say. Overall, we interviewed twenty-seven teachers (almost two-thirds of the full-time teachers), three guidance counselors, and three administrators.

We sensed a consistent willingness of teachers to respond candidly and openly. Teachers and administrators seemed to want to talk, and they wanted us to listen to their opinions, hoping, it seemed, that we might be able to ameliorate some of their frustrations.

We also sensed a high degree of dedication to teaching as a profession. Teachers felt well rewarded by the behavior of the students, and proud and successful as teachers. Most gave concrete examples, without hesitation, when asked how they knew they were successful. Most referred to the achievement of students after graduation—in jobs, or college, or just as good citizens. They mentioned that students returned to school to visit and talk, and cited significant state and national awards. Some admitted to short-term frustration and burnout, related in large measure to the difficulties of this particular year, but most teachers expressed continuing enjoyment in teaching.

The teachers at Sequoia are an older group. Their average age is in the upper forties. Only two teachers were below thirty. Most of the teachers had taught at Sequoia for at least ten years; some had begun teaching there, and this was their only high school. A few had been teaching there since the school opened in 1957. They liked this school. There was agreement that the school had been better, both physically and educationally, in the past, but the financial dilemma of the state had to be endured for the moment since there was nothing that could be done. Almost all supported their local teachers' union, although it was not particularly important or effective now "because the state had taken over funding and was setting salary at the state level." All agreed that they missed the energy and stimulation that they used to get from younger, new faculty members, but the practice of riffing on the basis of seniority seemed to be accepted.

All teachers felt free to teach. No one expressed concern about being constrained by an externally developed syllabus or felt pressured to teach in a particular way. A few, however, were concerned about not being able to offer some courses, and expressed considerable unhappiness over the demise of many of the senior electives because of the financial crunch and the back-to-the-basics movement.

Teacher evaluation is required in the district twice a year. Much of this is done by the principal, although each vice principal has six to eight faculty members to evaluate. The administration's only contact with the classroom seemed to be related to this evaluation activity. Currently a very structured observation checklist developed by a nearby university is being used for teacher evaluation. Reaction to it is mixed. Those in areas where the goals are overly performance-oriented believe the system is excellent; those who are concerned with integrative thinking beyond recall of information are less favorable. Nonetheless, the process has tended to produce positive evaluations for almost everyone.

The teachers seem to be well prepared academically. With the exception of one foreign-language teacher, all were teaching in the area in which they had their major training. All were teaching what they wanted to teach, although a few were unhappy about being assigned classes for students not bound for college. One teacher, however, wished that he had more noncollege-bound students assigned to him.

About 40 percent of the teachers interviewed actively keep abreast of their fields. However, few participate in organized discipline-oriented groups or attend college classes. The amount of in-service training available through the district is reduced from what it was several years ago.

With few exceptions, teachers felt that their student load was too great and that it interfered with their teaching. The exceptions were the few teachers who, by some fluke of scheduling, had small classes. All teachers involved with courses related to basic requirements felt oppressed by state-mandated competency standards. Those who taught basic English and mathematics said they found these the least desirable classes to teach. They seemed to agree that the basic achievement tests were not serving any useful educational purpose, that, in fact, they might be deleterious, but that there was no purpose in fighting "city hall." There was, nonetheless, a feeling that basic competency skills could be acquired *only* by direct teaching. So the skills had to be taught before they could be used in learning. There seemed to be little consideration of the possibility that writing skills might be developed through content learning and not just through specific courses on writing sentences and paragraphs.

The teachers enjoyed working with the students. Many said they found it invigorating and stimulating, an antidote against old age. Most felt that they had excellent rapport with their students. At least half were obviously enthusiastic about teaching.

Most teachers saw their goals as teaching skills (typing, spelling, sentence writing, for example) or imparting correct information. Grades were based on the accumulation of correct information or skills, and completing requirements. Sometimes, requirements were graded, but much of the time they seemed merely to be counted, so that anyone who chose to do the work got a good grade on the non-test part of the requirements. There were numerous work sheets and some workbooks. Those we saw were not particularly instructive and seemed to involve busy work. (This may reflect a lack of knowledge of current practice on our part, but we were unprepared for the complete dominance of workbooks and textbooks, with everyone on the same page at the same time, or everyone going through the same material at slightly different times.) The major teaching techniques involved lectures and work sheets. We did not detect independent or group work on any sort of study project where information was later to be pooled, nor did we sense any substantial differentiation of assignments.

In interviewing individual teachers, we tried to take their comments verbatim. Below are comments we judged to be representative of particular groups of teachers.

### ABOUT FRUSTRATIONS

We have so many forms to fill out that we lose out teaching.

I am having a hard time with the people I work with. They don't understand the problems I have in teaching music and band; they don't understand that music is important. And they don't seem to want to understand.

There is not enough professional sharing about teaching. My only contact with other faculty members is during lunch time.

## ABOUT TEACHING

I spend lots of nights grading papers. I teach all the time during class. [This teacher's students affirmed that he did teach all the time during class; most said he was the only one of their teachers who did, and they like him for that.] I don't push my kids as much as I should or could. It would mean using essay exams, and I have too many kids. [He taught 200 students each day.]

The kids seem to be getting lazier. They seem to want me to do all their thinking and to tell them exactly what to do. They won't take initiative and go on individually. Maybe it is just that the classes are so big now that I don't get around to the kids as much as I should. [This was a shop teacher whose students worked individually on projects.]

The district gives the principal so many teachers and the principal assigns you your courses. You really have no say. The student scheduling is done by the office and the tracking is done by the computer.

I wouldn't teach in any other school in this district.

We have a very professional faculty. We demand that the staff live up to high professional standards.

## ABOUT STUDENTS

This year's seniors won't give of themselves. They are intelligent, but they don't work.

One of my goals would be to get more respectful behavior.

There isn't an emphasis on that here.

The seventies were a revolting time. The kids are now open and friendly.

[A counselor reports that] the suicide club no longer meets. This is not the problem it was in previous years.

Students now seem less willing to work. I am still demanding and expect high caliber work. The students aren't bothered by failing. TV is the biggest bane. It discourages creativity, and it takes so much of the kids time; it puts their minds to sleep.

For ten years in a row, my students have represented our state in national competition. I've had two second- and third-place winners against forty-two states. [Vocational teacher.]

We're out of the seventies. Drugs are not apparent now. More than half the students work after school. None did twenty years ago.

I am trying to prepare students to take their place in society and to increase their achievement in their course of study.

I demand of students. I want their best and I want them to think.

I don't know what the goal of the school is; the kids just have the goal of getting out.

We don't require as much of them now as we used to. The good are as good, the middle are the same, but the worst are only worse because they didn't used to come.

## ABOUT "ENGLISH AS A SECOND LANGUAGE" STUDENTS

They are mostly ignored by other students. The culture shock is so great that they just stay together. They have to be pushed into contact with the other students. There are no discipline problems among the beginners. Some of the ones who have been in school for a while create problems. They are great TV watchers, and it seems to help them learn English.

## ABOUT CURRICULUM

I wrote the curriculum for this course. It was new. Of course, I had to follow the state guidelines and have it approved by my advisory board and the curriculum committee. [This was a new vocational teacher in practical nursing.]

I've been teaching for eighteen years and I am the youngest in the department. We are all so old that we are stagnant to some degree.

I sense that there is no teacher input into the curriculum, the scheduling, the goals, or the rules for the school. I am allowed to make suggestions, but I don't think anyone ever pays any attention to the suggestions. Even if they were implemented I don't think it would be because I suggested them.

I wanted to teach a course called World Geography. I discovered that I had to present this to the consultant and to the committee and then pilot it for a year. I just didn't get it done.

It is very difficult to teach the same course to three different levels of students. I forget what I did with each group. There is no time between classes to write down what I did or what I planned. Plus, I am supposed to keep track of the absentees and give them special make-up work. With the big classes it becomes impossible.

Kids now run the school.

School boards have lost their commitment to quality.

Counselors shunt all the misfits into vocational classes.

The budget goes down and down and down, and the class sizes go up and up and up. We seem to be developing an adversary relationship with the public. Our school board seems to have become less sensible over a period of time. They seem more concerned with meeting state law than with the best education for children.

I have five distinct preparations plus twenty-eight kids in middle school. I just don't have time. I provide band for all the athletic contests plus at least one concert a month.

The budget cuts have made the classes too large. My largest class this year has sixty students in it. We went eighteen years without a levy failure, and now we have had two recent ones. We have had to rif faculty, and five years ago we lost all our vibrant young faculty members; it broke up an excellent faculty.

[A science teacher]: For equipment, we are not too badly off, but I need cabinets and shelves. Our closed junior high has cabinets, but I can't have them. I was told that someone else might want them if they ever used the junior high room. My faucets drip and I report it; no one ever comes to fix them. My faucets have an anti-siphon device on them. It is unneccessary and useless. It sprays water all over so that we really can't use the faucets. But I've been told that they can't be taken off, at least not officially. We are always behind the neighboring districts when it comes to spending money for equipment.

The paperwork is unbelievable. If you even have to discipline a student it has to be fully recorded, dated, and submitted. You just ignore lots of things.

I enjoy working with the kids. The frustrations are from the top side.

The size of the classes is a great concern. A lot of students get lost in a large class and the good students aren't challenged.

## ABOUT BURNOUT

If you had asked me five years ago what I would like to be doing in five years I would have said teaching, just what I am doing now. I am no longer sure. I might go back to farming. I like teaching, but I've started to think there are other things I want to do. Teaching used to be enough. I won't leave, but I may have to do some other things to get my rewards.

"Burned out equals boredom," we were told at a preschool lecture, but I think tiredness is always a factor. All my colleagues like teaching, but with my big classes—thirty-nine to forty-nine this year—I feel frustrated and tired at the end of the day.

I seem to burn out temporarily just before vacations. With me it is more physical. I don't think you burn out if you are happy and successful in your work.

I'm not burned out. I have the easiest job in the world. The kids are neat. I love this work.

I experienced burnout. It was much greater in special ed than any regular classes. There are so many individual needs that we aren't meeting. You can pass the buck, but you know you aren't doing a good job.

I am new to this building. I think I could get pretty burned out quickly if I continued to work here. I have a hundred and eighty-six pupils a day in English. I haven't yet been able to find a ditto machine that works or where I am supposed to get ditto paper. My room was built to hold thirty chairs. I have forty-one, and usually they are filled. I don't think I can continue at this pace. I come in between 6:15 A.M. and 6:30 A.M. and teach four straight periods before lunch.

I am burned out just sometimes. It's a frustration. Sports come first. Half of my musicians are in sports. No one considers the music performance schedule. I wish the coaches would come to the concerts.

Burnout comes from discipline problems. We don't have any discipline problems in this school. The pupils haven't changed over the past twenty years.

## ABOUT PARENTS

I don't perceive that the public really cares about what goes on here. Twenty percent of the parents come to open house. We send home progress reports, and a low percentage of parents is obviously concerned about the children learning, even when they are failing.

We don't have a great deal of parent involvement at the high school level.

The curriculum council has to approve new courses. Texts are prescribed by the district. There is no flexibility among the five high schools. We need flexibility in choosing texts.

We are mainstreaming our special ed kids now. We didn't do that when I was a regular classroom teacher.

Latin was the most fun to teach because it wasn't necessary to learn any particular things, so there was no pressure. English matters, so I have to be concerned with the basics, and it's not as much fun.

We used to have seven periods a day. It was better for students and teachers. They had more choices and so did we. Some of my classes are now terribly big; I have fifty-three pupils at all levels in beginning German this year.

We can't be integrated in our teaching. We are required to meet the basic skills. We are expected to have high standards but to teach tasks that have little meaning.

We need longer hours and a longer year with a less hectic pace. We start at 7:30 A.M. and then just work toward getting out at 2:00 P.M. The students, the administration, and half the faculty just want to get out. I'd like to make sure that students ask questions, become curious, and get interested in many things. The students seem to just want a good job without caring what it is. Good means good paying.

[Shop teacher]: My classes used to have thirteen to sixteen students. Now I have thirty or more. With thirty they seem lazier.

In honors classes, we go into greater depth, use harder books, and more materials.

I want students to be able to handle life after graduation, and to have the skills to work.

We have a tremendous amount of freedom here in this building. I am constantly learning myself.

## The Administration

Sequoia has one principal and two vice principals. One vice principal is assigned to discipline, which includes attendance, and the other is assigned to supervising the social activities of the school. Discipline is handled in a suite adjoining the principal's office. The office of the vice principal for social activities is in another building—as part of the "Tub," a large social center that more or less joins the cafeteria to the gymnasium. As far as could be determined, the two vice principals function autonomously.

The vice principal in charge of social activities has been in the district sixteen years as an administrator. His doctorate was in curriculum, but he has never worked in that area, and has made no attempt to keep up with or to work in that area. He plans to stay in the district until retirement. His satisfactions and frustrations come from a single source—holding back and allowing kids to organize and do things. When students succeed, he feels satisfied; when they fail, he is frustrated to a degree. Most of his work is with the highly motivated students who want to lead and to work for the school.

During the past twenty years he has seen the shift from "uptight students of the late sixties and seventies" whose main concern was "fighting for their rights" to the students of today, who "attend school games and work on school functions." Students now have the "rah-rah" spirit, and attendance at all school activities is on the rise. However, only a minority of students participate actively in the planning and the work. The majority seem willing to let someone else do the work while they enjoy the function.

As a staff member, he feels that "we all, self included, are becoming tired professionals. We no longer want to give the extra time and effort to extracurricular activities and to attend. The students sense this lack of interest and reflect it in their own lack of interest."

The vice principal in charge of discipline has been in education for eleven years; she has been in her present job three years. She took over when, according to most of the faculty, discipline was at an all-time low, and, within a year, she won the admiration and respect of the staff. She is completing her doctorate this year, if all goes well. She sees her role as helping kids grow and be responsible. First offenders are handled within the school; parents come in after that. She would like to have a shift so that all her work is not disciplinary. She functions autonomously within the job. Her previous two years were gratifying, but the added enrollment of 400 students this year (the ninth graders) and the budget cuts that make classes so large and seem to increase the discipline problems make this year's work seem too much. The time demands of the job are physically tiring. She is in at 6:30 A.M. and is expected to attend all evening functions. This means at least two late nights a week. She seemed genuinely to like the students and did not seem to be aware of the students' negative feelings toward the attendance office.

The principal was cooperative and helpful in arranging for our visits. His arrangements reflected his preference for having things strictly planned and organized. Our days were always fully scheduled, with a dittoed format of people, classes, times, and rooms. We never felt, however, that there was an effort to hide or to keep us from observing and inquiring freely, which we did.

The principal, a twenty-nine-year veteran in the position, has been in the district more than twenty years. He has been at Sequoia High School for six years and likes the district policy of switching principals after they have been in a school for seven to ten years. He expects to finish two more years and then retire. He isn't anxious to leave, but figures it will be time to get out, and he does not look forward to having to change schools if he were to stay on.

He spoke of the troubles at the beginning of the school year. The addition of the ninth-grade students had caused great problems. "This year has been an absolute bear and I haven't been able to get on top of it. We miscalculated our number of kids, and shifting kids from class to class has been hard to do. For a while this fall, I thought I might bail out. However, I do like making decisions."

"Our goal," he said, "is to provide successes for kids, to develop their self-image. If we make the kids feel good about themselves, this is important to their achievement. We teach them the facts of a subject, but attitudes and beliefs are more important. We do a far better job of teaching content than we do attitudes. Most of my staff has this same strong feeling for kids and about kids feeling good about themselves."

His recent faculty meeting was concerned with standards of conduct. It focused particularly on the need for ninth-grade students to get to know the school-wide standards. This had been the only major concern in the shift to a nine through twelve school.

The principal was displeased about the heavy rains that were causing more than usual leaking, but he seemed to accept the fact that the buildings were not well maintained, and that there was not enough money to maintain them. He also was dismayed about classes being so large, but, again, he seemed to feel that there was nothing that he could do. He said that there was no point in worrying about those things you couldn't change; that everyone needed to put their efforts into those things that could be changed.

I asked about curriculum, and he replied that he had initiated very little. "I've made some efforts, and I've supported others. I've been stumping for a reading teacher, but right now we don't have one. Each high school used to have a remedial teacher. We need to focus on helping classroom teachers teach reading in content areas." (No teachers mentioned wanting a remedial teacher, nor did anyone mention reading as a problem for students.)

He professes to be democratic because he felt "the process pays dividends." He has little direct dealings with the union. The union negotiates with the central office, and he follows the agreement to the letter.

He finds evaluation hard to do because there is insufficient time. He has to do two formal evaluations of each teacher twice a year. The visit must be fifteen to fifty-five minutes long and be filed in writing within three working days. "This year I have forty-four and I am finding it hard to find the time to do it properly. Most get only the minimum time. However, I feel very positive about our evaluation system."

At no time during our interview with the principal was there mention of the subjects or areas in which he had taught. He did say that he had never been academically inclined and, indeed, would never have finished his education except for the service. As soon as he began teaching in junior high, he thought becoming a principal would be the best kind of job ever.

## Guidance Counselors

All three guidance counselors were interviewed. Each one has the responsibility for one entire class—the seniors, the juniors, or the sophomores. The counselor serves the class for a three-year period. With the addition of the freshman class, each counselor took one-third of the students from the ninth grade.

The counselors carry three main responsibilities. They provide advice for careers—this means mostly college prep advisement and course scheduling. They work with discipline problems and truancy. They do individual counseling with students. Scheduling and college prep advisement take the larger portion of their time, particularly at the beginning of any semester.

They are involved in PSAT and SAT-ACT testing, in which about half of the students participate. They are also involved with the district's basic achievement tests: math in grade eleven, English in grade ten, reading in grade nine, and retesting those who fail. The district is considering dropping the basic tests because the cost is so great. It takes a minimum of eight class periods to administer a test. No one commented on whether the tests were either useful or useless, and this did not seem to be a consideration in their being continued.

As did many of the teachers, the counselors saw keeping kids in school as one of their goals. One counselor responded that he sometimes worked to "devise an alternative program within the building to meet the needs of those kids who can't handle the tight rules and regulations. I'd far rather keep the kids here than send them on to a school where there is an alternative program." He seemed to be reflecting SHS policy (unstated, except by the students) that behavior problems were shipped out rather than dealt with. Students told us, "You either behave or they send you to another high school for a semester." He did not think that it was his job to worry about the "tight regulations," and seemed to accept them as inevitable.

This same counselor felt that there was a general apathy within the school, on the part of both students and staff, in trying to impart knowledge. Students merely work to meet graduation and grade requirements, with emphasis on whatever minimum is acceptable. Seniors who have met all the graduation requirements by their senior year opt for short schedules and early dismissal from school. He believes school is of secondary importance to the kids. Most of them work, and they prefer working to coming to school, even if they are going on to college. He said he would like to be moved to another school. This was unusual in that he was the only staff member we interviewed who said he wanted to move; most said they wouldn't want to teach in any other school in the district.

One counselor spoke of the prejudice within the school against the foreign students, the pre-vocational tracked students (the SHS label for the discipline cases and the slow learners), and the special education students (mostly the hearing-impaired in Sequoia). He wishes there were some way of getting the other students to accept these kids. He felt there should be greater integration of these students into the regular classes, but felt there was little if anything that he could do.

All three said that they really liked the students with whom they worked, and seemed genuinely concerned about them. They all wished they had more time, particularly this year, to counsel students who need help and to contact parents to work out programs.

## The Library

Physically, the library is somewhat central to the campus. It houses both print and nonprint materials, and all of the audio-visual equipment. It has a number of study carrels, which are equipped with individual headsets. The librarian's training, and his main concern, is in the audio-visual area, as opposed to books. The equipment is old and needs repair. He said it is not used heavily because it is old.

During the past year, more than 400 books were lost, so he is in the process of installing a detection system so that books cannot be removed. Students are supposed to enter the library through only one of the three access doors, and to pass through a turnstile system coming in and going out so that they can be checked for books. Students seemed to accept this without question. There are four conference rooms within the library, and we used them regularly when we interviewed students. Only once did we observe anyone else using the rooms.

We were told that teachers did bring their classes to the library for assignments, but observed only one class during the time we were on campus. The teacher brought the class to the library to use the carrels while taking a test so that students could be suitably separated to prevent any cheating. Use of the library seemed minimal, and it was not a place that students used in lieu of going to study hall, although apparently this was permitted.

## Class Visits

We made several class visits that lasted an entire period, and a number of shorter visits. In only two classes was there quiet discipline and attention to subject matter throughout the entire period. All the other classes seemed to reflect a noisy, talkative, visiting, gossiping atmosphere for the first ten to twenty minutes and the final five to ten minutes. In some classes, students carried on quiet, whispery conversations throughout the hour. In most classes, there were some students who appeared to ignore the teachers. The teachers tended also to ignore them.

Students told us that some classes were very good, and that the teachers wasted no time and taught the whole period and demanded student attention. They said they liked these classes and these teachers. They indicated that there were others, and we observed several, who didn't demand much or teach much, who never started class on time. They did not particularly like this kind of class. Students did not think it was their responsibility to be quiet unless the teacher demanded it; even though they preferred the disciplined class, they said it would not be likely that they would behave well unless they were made to.

We sensed that teachers did not view the noise and talking as we did. They all felt that their classes were well disciplined, except for those kids who really didn't belong at SHS. There seemed to be an unstated feeling that it was better not to rock the boat or to make an issue of moderately quiet misbehavior. In one class, four students listened to a transistor radio, playing softly, while a fifth student staggered in and slept the whole period. This did not seem to be of concern to the teacher.

## Teaching and Learning

Teaching in SHS appears not to have changed much in the past twenty years. No one was touting new methodology or defending methodology. Only one teacher referred to ITIP training; he had taken the course and felt he learned a great deal about how to teach. This was one of the few younger teachers. We both observed him teaching, and would not judge him to be particularly effective.

Preparing students for college seems to be the goal for most of the teachers, and there seems to be concern with form rather than substance. The emphasis seems to be on how to write and present a term paper rather than on the intellectual inquiry involved in producing the paper. Students affirmed this, and seemed content that this was the teacher's proper role: to get them ready so that they would be able to handle the demands of college when someone finally taught them something.

We asked students about teacher demand for independent thinking, for creative endeavor. Some seemed not to understand the question, or indicated that in most classes you were not supposed to think. Two teachers stated that their goal with kids was to develop thinking, and both teachers were mentioned by students as being different. Independent study and thinking were not recognizable goals for most of the teachers, and most of the students did not sense that these might be expected of them.

The school leaders we interviewed sensed that the school was concerned that everyone succeed and graduate, and that students shouldn't be pressed too much. They were all open in saying that they liked their school and their teachers, but that they were unchallenged throughout school, even though they got top grades and were considered to be marvelously successful. Further, they felt that, since they had met all their graduation requirements, except for the total number of credits, by the end of their junior year, the final year in school was really a pleasant waste of time.

The science areas and one English teacher's classes were consistently rated as demanding and intellectually active. Math was viewed by students as hard, or confusing, but not intellectually demanding, even in the advanced courses. Otherwise, the teaching was viewed as aimed at the average student, with the less able failing or getting low passing grades and the brighter student being bored.

## Education Beyond the School

Education beyond the school is of little concern to most individuals at Sequoia. In this regard, the four vocational teachers are an exception. They do maintain contact with businesses and social service agencies; but there are no more than 100 students involved. The newly begun vocational programs of firefighting and practical nursing entails practical work in the community, based on community needs. As far as we could determine, these two programs served about fifty students a year. They seemed to have support mainly because special funding was available for them. The business vocational program for consumer education had a total of twenty-three students; there was a small component that involved some interaction with local businesses. The drafting class in house design had some community involvement, although most of that was through another high school that did the actual building.

## Media and Technology

There is no computer study on campus. Computer use is confined to putting students into classes.

Television is not used as a vehicle for instruction. Teachers seem annoyed by the television watching of the students, although most of the students say that they watch very little and are not influenced by TV. We couldn't help remembering the book title, *Seduction of the Innocent*, and wondered if the students were victims without knowing it. We wondered whether what the teachers called "a lot" of TV watching and what the children of TV referred to as "not much" didn't equal about the same number of hours per week. There is talk everywhere of a media revolution but it hasn't yet reached Sequoia High School.

## Summary

Sequoia High School is in the doldrums in many respects. Teachers feel they are in the best school in the area, yet they seem dispirited. So many of the conditions that would make life in the school better appear to them to be beyond their control. There is little real leadership in the school in regard to curriculum or the establishment of clear educational purposes. Given the overall ability of the students and their interest in a more academic setting, the school could likely be much better than it is. Yet, there seems no impetus for everyone in the school community to make the necessary efforts.

PART III

RURAL HIGH SCHOOLS

# 6

# RIDGEFIELD HIGH SCHOOL

## MARILYN COHN AND ANNA D. STEFANO

The road to Ridgefield traces a path well worn by many former city inhabitants who left an urban environment and its conflicts for the wider horizons of a more peaceful, rural America. The super-highway entrance closest to our large midwestern city home marks the beginning of a route that covers quickly some 45 miles of suburbia and the two-lane county road that will wind its way to the center of Ridgefield. No need to linger in the shopping malls or huge factories along the highway; once on the county road, the aesthetic pleasure grows: large green spaces, some farms, a few animals, trees colored with autumn tones, rolling hills, small roadside businesses.

*First Impressions*

As the panoramic beauty increases, so do the initial questions. What are adolescents like who grow up here today, removed from suburban sophistication and urban resources? Who are the teachers and administrators in Ridgefield—city folk who traveled the distance in search of needed jobs or long-time community residents who might be uncomfortable elsewhere? Will curriculum and instruction be different from what we ordinarily observe in more densely populated areas? Do drugs, alcohol, and alienation abound—in town, in the school? Where do high school graduates go—to state universities, to city jobs, to the family farm? How will the inhabitants of Ridgefield High School react to strangers from the city who come to observe? With hostility or hospitality?

Our curiosity shifts to anticipation as Hamilton Community College, a Ridgefield city limit sign, and the home of the annual Ridgefield

Horse Show come into view on the right. A little farther down on the left appears a complex of buildings that represents Ridgefield's educational history: buildings that have become too crowded and were converted and joined by new buildings. So, the current junior high school (grades seven and eight) is the old high school, and the old junior high is the middle school (grades four, five, and six), and so on. Behind these buildings and the intervening athletic stadium is Ridgefield High School—"Home of the Eagles," as the lettering above the brick and glass façade tells us.

The front foyer of the building leads off in three directions. To the right, at an angle, there is a large cafeteria with the traditional rows of long, narrow tables and chairs. The predominant color is blue. Straight ahead is a long hallway lined with brightly colored lockers and leading to a set of back doors. To the left is a wider, main corridor that leads to the rest of the building. Almost immediately on your left is the main office with a front wall of glass. On the brick wall across from it is a Weekly Activities board that announces sporting events, assemblies, and other events. On this day, it also wishes Melissa Landkowski a "Happy Birthday." The corridor opens up into a wider area with three sets of doors to the gymnasium on the right and special education and guidance offices in clusters on the left. The area is dominated by trophy cases that are very full. An Armed Services display stand is located directly across from the gym. On the way down this corridor, there is yet another set of outside doors on the left. On the right, there are two more long, locker-lined hallways, where most of the classrooms and the library are located, and a wall covered with huge, composite senior class portraits dating back to 1975. The interior partitions are all dry-wall. There are no windows anywhere. Behind the building is a small unpaved smoking area, an athletic field, and an annex of additional home economics and industrial arts classrooms. In both buildings, the classrooms are carpeted and furnished with standard, modern desks.

Everything is on one level. Little more than some rather clichéd posters and several handwritten announcements of Teenage Christian Fellowship meetings decorate any of the walls. No graffiti. Fairly clean. Except for an occasional hole or dent in the wall, there is no apparent vandalism.

The busses that cover the far-flung geographical area that comprises

Rural C-3 district have come and gone, depositing a thousand or so students at the front door. Those students who have put together the money to buy and maintain cars park them on a gravel lot beyond the teachers' paved parking area. Some of the student drivers are probably still lingering at a quick-stop on the highway, eating and/or getting high.

Once in the building, students mill about, visiting with friends, stuffing possessions into lockers, and smooching with boyfriends and girlfriends.

*A Typical Day*   A tardy bell warns students not to be late for "first-hour" class. Although there is no dress code as such, there are trends in style of dress that speak to adolescent conformity and a mutual understanding between students and adults about propriety. Jeans and running shoes abound, especially on the boys, but they are not predominantly designer labels or famous brand names. T-shirts, especially football and rock group shirts, seem most popular. The girls may wear the more feminine versions of this "uniform." Some girls are in dresses, either conservative and plain or clinging and dressy. The two "looks" are supplemented by straight, long hair and no make-up, or spike heels and plentiful make-up. The narrow halls are crowded, but not unmanageable. On occasion, an activity like voting for Homecoming Queen may take up the first ten or fifteen minutes of the first period. It is at the beginning of second hour that Carol, the main office secretary, makes announcements over the schoolwide public address system. Her tone is informal as she runs down the schedule for yearbook pictures, or she promises that "to-morrow's assembly will be good, so don't forget your twenty-five cents admission." (It turns out to be an elderly couple who do ESP demonstrations.) Sometimes there are "special days," Hat Day, for example, when most people, including teachers, wear distinctive hats all day.

The main office has a pleasant atmosphere: popular music on the radio; students and teachers wandering in and out looking for specific forms or a ladder; lunch tickets being sold. Occasionally, a student will come in and use the phone, although this clearly is not a standard procedure. We saw a boy come in and ask one of the two secretaries where he could find another student; while he was there, he regaled her with a story about seventeen busboys being fired at a nearby country club restaurant "for getting into the beer." A teacher or two came in and struck up a conversation. Most often, physical education faculty members hung around the office.

There are four rooms off the large, main office area. One is a storage room, one is the assistant principal's office, another the principal's office. The fourth room holds the coffee machine and sweets or pastries for the latest fund-raising sale. Its walls are decorated with plaques that keep student council presidents from total obscurity.

The principal's office is not spacious. A desk, several chairs, and filing cabinets fill it almost completely. The walls contain posters of teachers' assignments, schedules of school events, and the like. As one faces the principal, Greg Owens, one sees on the wall to his right a Nike shoes' poster of marathon runners after the race. On the wall behind him is a poster which reads:

> Bitter are the tears of the child—sweeten them.
> Deep are the thoughts of the child—question them.
> Heavy is the grief of the child—lighten it.
> Soft is the heart of the child—embrace it.

Greg Owens is accessible. Several sophomore girls walked in and asked Carol if they could see him; they did, almost immediately. These four sophomore cheerleaders were upset about the conflict between their sponsor, Ms. Taylor, and the volleyball coach, Ms. Carpenter. The fifth member of their squad is a member of both groups, and they practice at the same time. An apparent compromise solution, splitting the time had been ignored by Ms. Taylor and she had benched the girl the previous night during cheerleading practice.

Mr. Owens had already discussed the issue with the superintendent, the cheerleader's stepfather (who is an RHS teacher), and Ms. Taylor. He spent forty minutes trying to answer one of the girl's question: "Why are the adults acting like kids—even younger than us?" One explanation he offered was that they were just "two stubborn women," but neither he nor the students believed that to be the whole answer. He assured them he would speak to all the parties concerned again. It was obvious that Mr. Owens thinks any attempt a student makes to be involved in school activities should be accommodated. The communication between the girls and Owens was direct and caring.

Out in the main office, a prospective student came in with a social services worker and inquired about the enrollment procedure. She was directed to the guidance office, where things were pretty quiet. The student was warmly greeted by Mrs. Black, who, given the transience of the RHS community, knows the procedure very well. She explained that students are sometimes shuttled between divorced parents, or that families move to seek seasonal or other employment, or that people move to Ridgefield to be closer to county social service programs for a while. She finds it frustrating to work laboriously on a schedule for a new student only to see the student move away in a few weeks.

As long as students remain at RHS for a reasonable length of time, they find it comparatively easy to find individuals or a group with whom to make friends. Students will tell you that RHS has all kinds of kids—some good, some bad, some active, some withdrawn, some academically serious, some coasting through. So, it is usually possible to find another like oneself with whom to spend time.

The other guidance counselors were conducting "credit checks," that is, reviewing student records to determine if students are "where they should be" at this point in high school. A list of students to be taken out of class was given to Carol, who checked the schedule, called each classroom on the public address system (a lot of communication of this sort goes on between the main office and classrooms), and asked that the students be sent to the guidance office.

By now, the day's activities were in full swing. Physical education classes, which are a favorite of many students, were going on in the gym or in back of the school. This hour's study hall was held in the cafeteria. There, students were quiet—either sleeping or studying. Owens says the football coach walks in and out and has everything very much under control. In the library, one class of students was learning how to find things. Other students sat quietly and, if they were doing anything, it was probably reading a magazine from the library's large and diverse collection (*Outdoor Life*, *Guitar Player*, *Family Circle*, *American History*, *Scribe*, etc.) Some students were working in the library this hour (during the day, many students work in various offices for credit) and their interaction with library supervisors was easy and warm. Down the hall, in the teachers' lounge, four or five people were drinking coffee, eating snacks purchased from a machine, and shooting the breeze. They seemed to know the other "regulars" at this particular hour. The young, male guidance counselor has made it a point to cover different periods on different days, as a way of trying to break down the "mystery" that has grown up between the teachers and the counselors.

At lunchtime, groups of students shuttled in and out of the cafeteria. They complained often of the quality of the food and of the meager choices available to those on the last shift. Some ate hurriedly, and made their way out the back door to the smoking area. There, students either visited with one another (exchanging school pictures, for example) or smoked cigarettes or dope. One student estimated that 40 percent of the school's population gets high during the day, and that over 90 percent gets high at some point during the week. A security guard monitors this area during lunch. His problem, however, is similar to that of other adults who might be upset about the drug problem. A student explained: "Teachers don't like it, but what are they going to do about it. When we see them coming, we flip the joint away and that's that." The kids in this area are thought of as "burnouts," in contrast to the "jocks" and the "socies": "All you have to do to be considered a burnout at RHS is smoke cigarettes!"

RHS's drug problem pains Greg Owens. The burnouts aren't the only students who get into this and other kinds of trouble. He has a drawer in his desk with confiscated material: knives, pornographic playing cards, joints, drug "tabs." Owens doesn't think the juvenile justice workers are very committed; in any case, they don't seem to him to be very effective.

Owens also has a tape of a conference he had with two boys who were fighting in the bathroom. He tapes all such conferences so the affected students and parents hear the same story he did the first time around. For the first part of the conference, the two boys spent most of the time arguing about who won the fight. Each seemed to need badly to win. When the boys were talked with individually, Kevin started crying because the expected suspension meant he wouldn't be able to play football. Both Kevin and Owens agreed it was fortunate that Kevin didn't have on his football jersey (even though it was Friday, when the team members all wear their jerseys to lunch). The coach was in on the conference and assured Kevin that dealing maturely with the punishment might well mean he'd be allowed to rejoin the team.

The athletic teams are not only important to the student body but also to the community's residents. They provide the teams' total budget through gate receipts and fund raisers. An example of the community's devotion to sports was Homecoming, when, in the chilling, pouring rain, they watched Ridgefield beat Sparta 6-0.

After lunch, the afternoon bus to HAMCO (Hamilton Community College) was about to leave. HAMCO runs a vocational program that serves not only Ridgefield but also surrounding school districts. Students spend either all morning or all afternoon in one of ten specialty areas. Because many of the programs are two years long, students are often able to use this experience as their "first year of college." Both jocks and burnouts are represented in HAMCO's enrollment. Some people at RHS have the impression that HAMCO students are next to dropouts and, therefore, low in academic skills, but the college counselor and teachers explain that the written materials require good reading and study skills.

Near the end of the day, those students who are on athletic teams were scheduled for study hall last hour, so they could head for practice early. After school, there are not only sports but also the standard fare of high school activities: National Honor Society, Spanish Club, Speech and Debate, Student Council.

Every so often, student council representatives are given time during the school day to meet with their "constituency groups." At the beginning of the year, each student is given a student council card. Any student who gathers the support of twenty-five or more other students, who donate their student council cards, becomes a representative.

On weekends, there may be a dance. The attendance at these activities is primarily made up of socies and jocks; the burnouts make it a point not to go.

In the library after school, "eighth hour" keeps in detention students who have broken one rule or another. Usually, they're there because they have been tardy to class (a pet peeve of Owens).

Some students work after school, either at paid employment or, more often, doing chores for their families. They complain about too much homework, but claim that one can get away without doing it.

Another day at Ridgefield High will probably be a lot like this one. As one student said, "Nothing much happens here."

*In the Classroom*   The student perception that "nothing much happens here" may stem, in part, from the general lack of incident, drama, or change in the daily social environment at Ridgefield High School. It may, however, also spring from the students' experience within the classrooms. Although there is considerable choice in some departments and a deliberate effort to vary instruction according to student interest and ability, there is an overwhelming sameness for students, from classroom to classroom, from department to department.

In the English department, for example, students taking college prep English work independently on term paper topics or chat quietly with one another. The topics have been selected by the teacher and seem far removed from student interest and experience. The teacher is available to answer questions. Students in both Practical English and Composition II work independently as well, but on grammar exercises from their textbooks. Here again, the teachers are available for help. In Achievement in English, yet another level, the students listen or sleep while the teacher reads aloud, for the entire period, portions of a paperback book on motorcycle gangs.

In the history department, students listen to lectures, copy notes from an outline on the overhead projector, do work sheets, and, on occasion, orally answer factual questions with brief answers. In World History, for example, during one period we observed, students went over a work sheet on the Dark and Middle Ages they had completed earlier and then heard a lecture that spanned the Vikings, the reasons why Constantinople was a good location for a capital, the differences between the Greek Orthodox religion and those of the Western world, and the characteristics of Gothic church architecture. Key ideas and terms were put on the overhead for students to copy.

In World Religions, students listened to a lecture on the Chinese. On the overhead the teacher outlined information on the Gentry, Confucius, Lau, and Daoism.

In the mathematics department, we saw trigonometry students work independently and seriously on problems from the text while the teacher circulated to give individual assistance. Functional Math students worked individually as well, but not seriously and not with a text. They had been given packets with catchy titles—"Prime Time," "Wit Kit," "Math Path," "Skill Drill," and "Game Frame"—that included manipulative equipment such as headphones, tapes, and projectors. The students, however, were not "caught up" in the material. They talked or walked around the room while the teacher worked with one student at her desk.

Pre-algebra students were watching and listening or talking to one another as the teacher, using the overhead projector, worked a sample of each kind of problem that would appear on an upcoming test. As she worked out each problem she asked, "What do I do and what do I do next?" Students shouted almost unintelligible answers. The pace was fast because she wanted to cover all problems. There was not time to pause for questions from the students.

In the science department, we saw Biology II students listen to a lecture on the coloration of fall leaves. The presentation was complete with flash cards on the different types of pigments: a reddish orange card was labeled carotene, a green card was labeled chlorophyll, a yellow card was labeled xantophyll, and a purple card was labeled anthocyanin. Students listened but did not take notes. Later, they were given a quick review and a work sheet that involved the same facts and key terms of the lecture. Students still, however, needed individual assistance and the teacher walked around and helped those who raised their hands to complete the work sheet.

In Section A of Biology I (the most advanced group) students listened to a twenty-minute lecture on information needed in preparation for the next day's lab. The teacher outlined her presentation on energy on the overhead and the students copied it. There was an occasional factual question, which students answered with one word. Students asked two questions: "When are our study guides due?" "Aren't there two kinds of respiration?" At the end of the presentation, students were given time to work on their study guides.

Chemistry students also listened, but only for about ten minutes, to an explanation of how to go from moles to molecules and from grams to molecules. The teacher put the formulas on the overhead and then assigned five problems in the text, saying, "I'll come around to help you, but you should have no trouble if you use these." They did, however, have trouble, and he spent the rest of the time helping some while others helped their fellow students.

The student experience was essentially the same in classrooms outside these four major academic departments. In reading class, students worked independently on work sheets while the teacher worked individually with one of the foreign exchange students.

In Spanish, students watched slides of the teacher's stay in Peru.

In home economics, students worked on a seek-and-find work sheet on sewing terms, other homework, or nothing, while the teacher helped one student with a sewing pattern at her desk.

In Introduction to Business, students listened and followed directions as the teacher gave step-by-step instructions, in a very loud, clear, and precise voice, related to the use of a new instructional packet.

> First, put your name and "seventh-period" on the outside of the packet. After your name is on the packet, then take out every item in the packet and put your name on each of the items [she waits]. After your names are put on all materials, put all of them back except for the booklet entitled *Instructions*. Now, look at me please. I will go slowly, and you can put what I say into your own words, but these statements are to be written inside of your instructional manual. One: These packets may not leave the classroom. Two: If absent from school, you need to come before school, during study or after school, to make up for time that you've missed in class. Three: Pay attention. If you don't pay attention, you may get so lost and since we are going to be working on this for three weeks, you'll be lost for all three weeks. . . . Now, let's go back to page one of the instruction booklet. Pages one, two, and three are introductions to the packet. On pages four and five is the actual beginning of the packet and page nine is where you actually start working on your packet.

Thus, even though students moved through their seven-period day by changing classrooms and curricula every forty-five minutes, their role was essentially the same—passive and non-thinking. For the first half of every period, they mostly sat and listened. Note taking, when it occurred, was merely a matter of copying from the overhead outline in which the teacher had already selected, reduced, and sequenced the key ideas or facts. During the last portion of the period, students filled out work sheets and study guides that asked them only to remember the prepackaged information, while their teacher circulated to give further individualized assistance. They were not asked to identify, comprehend, analyze, evaluate, or apply ideas. They were, in short, not expected to think or, in any way, actively participate in the learning process.

## Context and Characters

It is not readily apparent how the social and intellectual climate of Ridgefield High evolved. Closer examination reveals community involvement as well as internal constituencies that play different roles in creating and maintaining the current environment. And there are multiple perspectives on how productive and satisfying this whole educational venture is and can be expected to be.

*Community as Context* A tour of Ridgefield, the Hamilton County seat, takes just a few minutes by car. There is no main street—only the courthouse and adjoining county offices, three eating establishments, a bank, a drugstore, and several small two-story buildings that house the local legal and medical professionals in a three-block radius. Beyond this "center" of town lie a number of relatively new subdivisions dotted with moderately priced homes, several churches, a few large farms, one small grocery store, and an area of low-income housing in bad repair. Before long, the city limits of the neighboring town of Balboa come into view and Mason City is just a few miles farther away.

Until the late fifties, Ridgefield was a stable rural community with farms and dairies. Four or five wealthy farmers, who considered themselves "founding fathers," became the backbone of Ridgefield by actively participating in community and school affairs. The school population was homogeneous and small. In 1953, for example, there was a total of 147 students in the high school and 18 in the graduating class. A long-time resident and teacher recalled the "good ole days":

> We couldn't have had a more supportive community. We never had a bond issue that was voted down. Anything the school wanted we would get. [But] they were a little shortsighted in terms of inviting business in. They wanted to keep it the little ole Ridgefield. Anything new was taboo—including supermarkets. Discipline problems were nil. All you had to do was talk to a parent and everything was taken care of. The few who drove back

and forth to the city were old Hamilton Countians. If we did get newcomers from the city, they would fall in line with our students.

The sixties and the seventies, however, brought dramatic and far-reaching population changes. As the cost and complexities of urban living increased, many middle- and lower-middle-class whites left their city dwellings and headed for Ridgefield in search of a less integrated and less expensive lifestyle. Gradually, acres and acres of farmland were tilled and prepared for new homesites rather than for crops. The new landowners were mostly blue-collar workers with jobs in automotive plants and factories in the city. During the week, the adult population drove eastward to the city; on the weekend their adolescents drove west to Balboa for its skating rink, bowling alley, and movie theater, or to Mason City where their friends were "cruisin' the main." In effect, Ridgefield had become a bedroom community.

With the change in population and the times came some major changes in family life. The divorce rate grew enormously, and both children and adults moved in and out and back into the community as separations and remarriages forced changes in address. Drugs became common and statistics revealed the existence of more child-abuse cases in Ridgefield than in any area of the state; almost 50 percent of the elementary school population was referred to family services. Teen-age pregnancy increased and children were generally difficult to handle for parents and teachers. Despite, or perhaps because of, these family and social difficulties, the new population established strong ties with their churches. Strong Baptist groups existed alongside the Mormon and Pentecostal churchgoers. More recently, a Christian Missionary Center has also established a small but highly vocal presence in the community.

Accompanying the shift and increase in population was a corresponding decrease in school-community relations. As the school population became more scattered, children with Balboa addresses and Mason City telephone exchanges were bused long distances to Ridgefield schools. With student allegiance to these neighboring towns and parent allegiance to the city, the one-time cohesive quality of the Ridgefield school district became a relic of the past.

Parent-teacher communication practically disappeared. A P.T.A. organization functioned only at the elementary school level. Formal contact at the high school occurred once every four years—at freshman orientation. Informal contact was possible only at athletic events. School board meetings, which featured reports on budget, building, and maintenance issues, attracted no community interest. In the absence of a Ridgefield newspaper, school events were communicated only by word of mouth.

Ridgefield today is much the same as it was late in the seventies. The blue-collar worker predominates, but there are lower-class welfare recipients as well as a small local élite. The last group is comprised of the few remaining large farm owners, the sheriff, the superintendent of schools, the president of Hamilton Community College, and the several lawyers and doctors in the area. Since many of these men meet on a regular basis at Rotary Club lunches, there appears to be some semblance of cohesiveness within this segment of the community.

Religion still plays a large part in the lives of most Ridgefield residents. Teachers' meetings are scheduled around church. At football games, the superintendent gives an invocation wherein he thanks God "for the good men on the field" and prays that "all will be safe, no one will be hurt" and "sportsmanship will reign." Even the Christian Missionary Center makes its presence felt at the high school by pressing for the removal of certain films, books, and magazines.

In fact, the only difference that can be observed in the Ridgefield of the eighties is the end—perhaps just temporarily—of the home-building boom, with its resulting decline in general and school population. As a district that is solely dependent on state funds for its survival, Ridgefield is watching, with some anxiety, state revenues decrease with the population and with the overall state budget cuts. School staff reductions are imminent and feared. No one wants to lose his/her teaching position, and no one wants to leave Ridgefield. As one teacher put it, "It's an ideal spot to raise a family. You have the rural-type environment to hunt and fish and do what you want to do, and yet, if you want the big city, you are only forty minutes away."

*The Students*　While the adults in Ridgefield High talk in general terms about how today's adolescents are happier, more compliant, and more cooperative than those of the past two decades, it is impossible to find the "average" adolescent. In spite of the push toward conformity, there is so much diversity in chronological maturation and environmental influences, that any composite is never wholly accurate in its depiction of an individual boy or girl. Moreover, adolescents often see themselves in ways that are significantly at variance with others' perceptions of them. How would the students of Ridgefield High describe themselves? Males and females have different perspectives.

The "typical" boy enters ninth grade at RHS caring about the concrete realities of high school—that is, the quality of lunches, the crowded hallways, insufficient locker space. He may develop good relationships with teachers, or see them as "unfair" or "stuck-up." He's also concerned that some of his classmates are troublemakers (fighting, doing drugs) or that they think they're "better" than other people. *If* he likes his classes (which is doubtful), it's most likely he feels best about math and physical education.

He'd rather be outdoors playing sports or hunting and fishing. Or, he could be watching TV, doing odd jobs around his family's farm, body building, or collecting something.

In thinking about the man he'd like to become, he looks to models such as Burt Reynolds, John Wayne, his family, or Jesus. He talks about eventually being a lawyer, doctor, engineer, *or* a carpenter, electrician, truck driver. He may still dream of becoming a pro athlete. Yet, he is not immune to the fear that "the way it looks, we might have a world war and all of us might end up dead before I graduate."

By tenth grade, his academic preferences have expanded to include history, and his writing skills have improved a bit. He still has a rather negative attitude toward high school, generally, complaining that there's "too much work" and characterizing people as "trudging through the hallways." His peers continue to be divided into the "nice guys" and the "bad guys." Teachers have grown in his estimation; some of them even seem to be "more friends than teachers." But "high school is [still] just a place where people pressure each other, and nothing comes out good from it and nothing ever will."

After-school interests may now additionally include paid employment or motorcycle riding. Also, his Christianity may have assumed greater importance. He admires the people (especially family) who persevere. One said, "I admire my father the most. He was a farm boy and grew up to be a successful lawyer." Another told us, "I admire my mom and dad for never giving up in hard times."

His career interests haven't changed much, except for the addition of such possibilities as mortician or Navy cook. When he lets himself think about it, he is upset that so many students seem to have planned their lives "with a max of working at Chrysler," and that they'll be "happy to leave and end up digging ditches."

Eleventh grade brings several changes in the typical Ridgefield young man. Cars are now important; he often gets a job to help pay car expenses; in any case, he enjoys working on his or others' cars. He persists in his first loves: hunting, fishing, and sports, sports, sports.

There may be signs, though, of increased maturity and thoughts of the future. For the first time, he mentions marriage among his goals. He dreams: "My life will be one with complete success, it has become a vital and mandatory part of survival," and, "I believe life after high school will be a challenge, but if you really put your mind to do something you can do it if you try hard enough." He considers joining the service, or becoming a skilled craftsman, a professional, or a musician. In any case, he's possibly "a 16-year-old man who is looking forward to putting as many miles between me and Ridgefield as possible." While his intellectual side may have begun to be tapped ("I like to study how man developed"), his overall appraisal of RHS remains negative. He doesn't find it objectionable enough to be worthy of protest and he blames no one: "The people aren't bad or evil in their own right but are blind to the situation we are all in. It's been a prison since junior high to me and I'm glad as hell to get out next year."

Yet he has found at RHS people whom he admires—for example, his coaches, his teachers, or "the athletes and smart people who have it all together." Musicians round out his models: Eddie Van Halen, Willie Nelson, Ozzy Osbourn, and Waylon Jennings.

Those men remain his idols as he enters his last year in RHS. They are joined by the diverse trio of Clint Eastwood, Carl Sagan, and Bill Murray (and rejoined by his ninth-grade hero, John Wayne). He admires those "who stand up for what they believe in," "who do things for all of mankind," and "who succeed through hard work." His career interests reflect those values, although he seems surprisingly uninformed about how to prepare for his occupational goals. He may still want to be a skilled craftsman, but he also considers conservation work or firefighting or coming back to RHS as an industrial arts teacher.

The last choice isn't too surprising because shop is one of his favorite classes during twelfth grade. History, math, and P.E. were favorite subjects throughout all four years. His senior academic tastes have also gone to the sciences and he bemoans the lack of variety and availability of classes in this and other areas. He continues to complain about the food and the boring routine. However, he begins to view things in balance. There are good student-teacher relationships at RHS, he observes, and people do care about him. He wishes there weren't so much rivalry among the cliques (the burnouts and socies and jocks) and he, too, worries that drugs may be too plentiful. He will probably graduate carrying two seemingly contradictory feelings with him: "It [RHS] sucks" and "I'm a better person for being at RHS."

High school is the context within which the typical ninth-grade girl gets to spend time with her friends. She likes RHS's friendly atmosphere and abundance of clubs and sports that keep people busy and involved.

Like her male counterpart, she thinks the food is terrible and that one day is too much like another, but she is more concerned about the prevalence of drugs and the limited course choices. She, too, likes math and P.E., but her favorite class is history. She may even have developed a sense of herself as an intellectual. One said: "I greatly admire people with developed minds, people such as Albert Einstein. I myself am making a 3.9 average. I am very proud of myself." In any case, she characterizes herself as a caring person, which is a valuable trait at RHS, where, "if you are nice to everyone, everyone will be nice to you." She's aware of the different social groups, and, although they concern her, they do not get in the way of a typical day's activities: make out, fight, argue, laugh, and just plain have fun.

In her spare time, she plays at sports, draws, helps out at home, and watches T.V. She admires characters in the books she reads, her teachers, her parents, and, of course, John Wayne. As one girl said, she admires "people who try against all odds and make something of themself [sic]."

Her career interests are both extraordinarily stereotypic and amazingly unusual. She wants to be a nurse, a secretary, a teacher, or a stewardess; *and* she wants to be an astronaut, a neurosurgeon, a trucker, or a mechanic.

In tenth grade, the paradox continues. She contemplates a future as a cosmetologist or stewardess or oceanographer or bartender. Moreover, she seems aware of a wide range of occupational choices (a much wider range than RHS's tenth-grade male), although she, too, seems unaware of how to get "from here to there" regarding her career goals. Although she includes marriage among her future plans, she does not plan to marry "until I achieve my own personal goals first."

Her academic favorites are many: music, math, history, biology, English, and the ever-present P.E. She writes fairly well and talks of her "love [of] writing for newspapers," or of her interest "in the way living bodies function and how they go through their life stages."

At the same time, she is preoccupied with her physical appearance. When asked to tell a little about herself, she may describe herself literally and physically. She is concerned about the boys in her world and about establishing good relationships with them. She's pleased to go to a school of manageable numbers which, in spite of the cliques, has an aura of warmth.

Her nonschool time is used to ride horses or motorcycles, do a little babysitting, and work, either at home or for a nearby store. Church is an important part of her life, and Jesus is someone she admires.

Her heroes and heroines are a varied group. They include parents, relatives, teachers, and a classmate or two. Media personalities, like Cheryl Tiegs, Barbara Mandrell, and Nancy Reagan, are also models. And professional roles such as "physician" or "veterinarian" get a positive mention.

By the eleventh grade, her positive feelings about RHS are accompanied by dissatisfaction with its academic preparation. "I'm just another student who would like to learn more"; "I think this school could be better if more people cared about going and making better grades for a more promising future." In sum, her "home away from home" is a friendly place that could be more educational as well as entertaining.

Her spare time is dominated by sports, school activities (like Student

Council), and part-time jobs (usually waitressing). She may already be married. In any case, marriage is very much in her future plans, although she, like her younger classmates, plans a career in engineering or trucking as well as cosmetology or nursing. For models, she looks to Robert Redford (for his conservation work), Alan Alda, or her preachers, or "anyone that sticks to something no matter how hard it may be to accomplish."

In her senior year, that sentiment is expanded to include those "who face up to their mistakes but live through them." She now sees that life "and the world are very tough," and "life is ruff [*sic*] and *not always fair*."

She wishes RHS had offered her a wider choice of classes and that the counseling available to her had been more timely and useful. Yet, everyone has been so friendly and she's enjoyed classes in math, science, business, and music, and, especially, a course in "Senior Survival." She's been active as a cheerleader, in Pom Poms, the National Honor Society, and debate. She has also begun working: in one of the courthouse offices, as a nurse's aide, or in a purse factory.

She more firmly intends to marry in the future. But she has not given up her individual version of the dream career: a photographer; the police academy; a travel agent; a gift shop owner; an accountant; a dental assistant; a minister; or "a self-made millionairess."

*The Administration*   Students at Ridgefield High School come into varying degrees of contact with administrators, counselors, and teachers who shape and share their world. Their points of view are interestingly different and remarkably similar.

The highest ranking administrator—the superintendent of Ridgefield school district—is a local, congenial, soft-spoken gentleman who serves as an accessible resource for his four district principals. Hardly a day goes by that he doesn't informally chat with each of them. They, in turn, do not hesitate to call him to discuss matters as mundane as a teacher who is consistently tardy or an unpleasant encounter with the fire marshall during a school fire drill.

High school students, however, rarely come in contact with the superintendent, although the administration building is situated just a short block from the end of the student parking lot. For a small group—the students who are consistently tardy, absent, or in trouble—the administrator in their life is Danny Restemeyer, the assistant principal. While Danny's duties include building maintenance, his major responsibility is discipline and attendance. Teachers send their troublemakers directly to Mr. Restemeyer, and, for much of his day, he is closeted behind the doors of his small office, conferring with some nonconforming student. As a former P.E. teacher and basketball coach at the junior high, he knows well many of the students who are sent to him, and he responds to them in a friendly but firm manner.

For the student body as a whole, as well as for the faculty and parents, the man in charge is Mr. Owens. He, more than anyone else, give shape and substance to Ridgefield High School spirit, policy, and procedure.

Greg Owens is young, attractive, "sharp with figures" and personable—a "child prodigy" in the eyes of Danny Restemeyer. Like almost everyone else in the school district, his roots, his schooling, his professional training, and his job experience are local. What separates him from the rest is the speed and ease with which he has successfully climbed the academic and career ladder. Graduating from high school (in the town next to Ridgefield) at the age of sixteen, he completed his undergraduate study at Hamilton Community College and the nearby state university. Greg then received a graduate assistantship, but chose instead to accept an offer for a part math, part P.E. teaching position at his former high school and to work on his master's degree at night. Two years later, when asked to teach math full-time, he decided to make a change. He "didn't enjoy being cooped up in the classroom." He informally sought and immediately found a junior high P.E. and coaching position in Ridgefield. Shortly thereafter, he was tapped to be assistant principal at the high school, and, after four years as second in command, he is, today, at the age of thirty, serving in his first year as principal.

In Greg's view, the man he replaced was a "great salesman," a "good speaker," a "PR person who could say unpleasant things in a way that would make people leave his office smiling." As his assistant, Greg was the nuts-and-bolts person, the disciplinarian, and the resulting team was a strong one. Feeling that he shaped a good portion of the administrative policy as assistant—particularly in the area of discipline—Greg did not enter the principalship with a laundry list of immediate changes. That does not mean, however, that he would not like to make changes; it simply means that, as a newcomer, he is not in a hurry. As he puts it:

> This year has been kind of sit back and look at the things from this side and let's see where we can make some changes. I'd like to do that rather than come and say we're going to do it this way, and have it backfire right in your face. . . . That's what the books say. Never go in and make all these changes right off the bat.

This "sit back and look at things from this side" philosophy may, in part, explain the fact that Greg always appears so relaxed, unhurried, and accessible. It may also partially explain why he permits most of each day to be consumed by immediate and what sometimes appear to be rather mundane matters. He spends time, for example, on locating homebound teachers for students who have to be home because of pregnancy complications; or he responds to a school board member who wants him to find a white plastic eagle for the front of the building. He also spends two to three hours out of the building in order to make football game arrangements when Ridgefield unexpectedly finds itself in a play-off or when he wants to argue before the Hamilton County Community Association that the association-sponsored trophy for a debate tournament should only be won by association members.

Because he does not come into the building each day with a heavy agenda of items to be accomplished, he is available for the more serious matters that arise. For example, when a student became violent over a trivial incident one morning, Greg was there to talk with the student for about thirty minutes, to call in the nurse for an examination, to arrange for the boy to go home, and for the mother to come to school. He then held a joint conference with the mother, the counselor, and the boy's special education teacher, listening carefully for over an hour and ultimately coming up with a reasonable set of next steps that were agreeable to all.

While being new is clearly an important factor in Greg's low-key approach, one gets the impression that there is a personality variable as well. Greg, for example, appears to be a basically modest and humble person who would feel uncomfortable presenting his views as the voice of authority:

I still think of myself as being just out of college, young and not knowing a lot and very naïve. People call me "Mr." and I have a hard time accepting that because I am dealing with people who have been teaching for thirty years . . . sometimes I'm very surprised by the superintendent—this man's fifty years old and has been in the business for thirty years and you make a suggestion and he says, "Good idea!" And other people are always asking for my opinion—I'm just not used to that. I'm still used to being a peon.

Moreover, he appears rather conservative in nature, and it would be difficult to imagine him having any radical changes in mind.

Finally, his recent past experience as an assistant principal is yet another factor in his approach to his job.

You know I sit back and look at two different principals we had in this school. I saw one that didn't do a whole heck of a lot. He drank coffee all day. I saw another who was always running around—looked busy all the time. And the school kept going, and I don't know if the quality of education has changed as far as what goes on in the classroom. I don't see a big change there. But I do see change in the order, other things, and attitudes. But, here, two people approach the job two different ways, and probably get the same results.

In light of these factors it is not surprising that the leadership style that has emerged thus far is, as one teacher labeled it, "laissez faire." Greg clearly prefers to have teachers govern their own curriculum and behavior and to intervene only when necessary. Most often, interventions seem necessary to Greg when an issue of fairness is at stake, and, on those occasions, he does not hesitate to act promptly and firmly. For example, although teachers are supposed to attend assemblies, scatter themselves, and monitor student behavior, Greg deliberately refrained from assigning seats in the hope that teachers could use their own judgment. At the first assembly, all were in attendance. At the second, a few skipped. At the third, many skipped. Greg maintains that "they're just like the kids." The next day, a teachers' seating chart was issued. Similarly, when he noticed one day that several of the teachers were not in their rooms at 7:30 A.M., he wandered down to the lounge and just said, "Hey folks, get going." As he explained it:

I think for the most part, they appreciate it; in fact, some of them admitted it to me individually but not in front of the group. But it's only fair.

The biggest gripe I get from the teachers is, "Hey, I see another teacher doing something that they shouldn't be doing and nothing is said to them."

The fact that Greg is inclined to give teachers considerable freedom in governance and curriculum does not mean, however, that he does not have some confidence in his own judgment and that he does not have some definite personal directions he would like to pursue. He recognizes, and quite correctly so, that although he doesn't have the knowledge and experience that some of his faculty have in their areas, he does have an intuitive sense of good judgment and a broader perspective:

When I first came into the high school from the junior high, I really felt bad because the people seemed so intelligent. I guess it was the level that they were teaching on compared to the simple things that we did in junior high. But, at the same time, I think my biggest asset was the fact that I feel like I can look at things halfway objectively in a common-sense way. And you say to yourself, "Hey, this person is very intelligent but he's not getting it done in this area. He's not looking at the whole picture." I think we have some very narrow-minded people here who think their department or their class is the only class in the school.

His major aim for the future is a more organized and systematic approach to curriculum.

I am an organizer. I'd like to have things more cut and dried. I'd like to know what to expect and where we're going. I don't see that right now. I see too many people going in different directions. I'd love to be able to sit down and work out objectives for every class. And I'd like to have [the teachers] say, "These are our objectives in these classes, Mr. Owens," and know that. I'd like to see some semblance of progression in the curriculum, which I don't think we have a whole lot of now. Well, in math classes, sure, it's just automatic. Some other classes, there's so much overlap that I wonder if you could tell what class you're sitting in unless you knew in advance. I think that's my biggest goal. I don't know if I'll ever achieve it or not.

A second aim is to continue to have "good discipline." He is very proud of the policies he initiated as assistant principal.

We're probably the only school in the area, where there is detention after school, where the assistant principal and the principal are the ones teaching it. We're the only school in the county that doesn't pay somebody to teach it. We do it not because we don't want to give them the extra money but because we wanted to. Some of the schools have it as a duty to teachers. I don't like that. Mr. Smith is in here today, Mr. Jones is in there tomorrow. And the kid doesn't know what to expect or how to act.

A third major goal is to have more student participation in activities. This goal, however, may be almost as difficult to achieve as the first because of transportation problems. Nonetheless, for Greg, participation in school activities is a serious goal, a deep value, and, perhaps, even a strong bias. He sometimes seems to unconsciously favor the small active segment of the student body, finding it difficult to understand those students and, for that matter, those teachers who are not interested in extracurricular activities.

In short, Greg Owens would like his school to be "Number One" in the county. He told us, "I'd like to make Ridgefield the type of school that, when people spoke of it or talked about going to school, they'd pick ours as the one they'd want to go to." And Greg doesn't see any real administrative constraints in terms of actively pursuing his aims of being "Number One." He claims, in fact, "Whatever I want to do down here I can do." Nevertheless, he is at times frustrated and overwhelmed by the enormity and complexity of the task:

> I guess the biggest frustration is that I've got so many different—it seems like thousands—of areas to be accountable for. And there's no way possible. . . . You know you've got to have the people to do the job. You're ultimately responsible for everything. And I feel like—it's almost like an "I'd rather do it myself" situation. You don't feel like you can walk through with somebody and hold their hand. And we're talking about . . . trying to be on top of that and knowing exactly what's going on, knowing all [the teachers'] needs and what they're doing and how they're doing it. And you've got art, business, science, math, history, the whole works. . . . You get Title 4 in time to start working on finding computers, and you don't know a thing about computers. I feel like I [should] go back to school just to learn about what I want to put into the school. [And there's] the guidance department. I go to the superintendent's office and all I get are complaints about the guidance people because they don't do anything. And these are the people who have master's degrees, and I'm supposed to know how to do their jobs. I guess the biggest frustration is that I don't know how to do everybody else's job. . . . And I [must] rely on them. But then I catch the criticism because they're not doing the job. Who knows what their job is or how well it's being done? All the testing that goes on, and interpretation of tests. And which tests to offer and which not to offer. And just dealing

with things that come in the mail every day. . . . So much to do . . . being so spread out and not having expertise in every area.

Still, there are rewards enough to compensate for the responsibility. Greg, for example, prizes the freedom:

> You're not tied down to a classroom—you don't have to be in class by the bell. That was probably the biggest change I noticed when I [came here]—the bell rang and I wasn't hopping to be someplace or to do something.

The fringe benefits are pleasant too:

> Like I told Danny . . . there [will] be a lot of days when you're going to wonder if I still work here. I'm going to be gone. And I'm going to be doing some neat things, like going to Ridgefield Mountain Lodge for three or four days for meetings and playing a little golf when I'm down there. Or going to dinner here and going to dinner there. Or getting my picture in the paper here and there. And you're going to be sitting back thinking, "I'm doing all the dirty work." And, I said, you will be.

But in the final analysis, it is the students that make the job worthwhile for Greg. He experiences, on a daily basis, pain and concern for those who are troubled or in trouble, and joy for those he feels are leading wholesome and productive lives.

Given these satisfactions, what rungs remain on Greg Owens' career ladder? Like so many in his position, he talks of some job in teacher training at the nearby state university. The superintendency is always a possibility, and, in Greg's case, it seems more than a reasonable bet. Given his skill and interest in figures, "company" loyalty, congenial manner, clean-cut appearance, and organized approach, he seems a natural for the Ridgefield community. And if, as principal, Greg Owens has been a "child prodigy," as superintendent he would surely become Ridgefield's "boy wonder."

*Guidance*   Greg Owens isn't the only one to hear complaints about the guidance counselors not doing anything. Are the complaints valid? Are they based on information and experience? What is the role of the guidance staff? Who are the counselors? What do they do during a typical day? What are their relationships like with students and with teachers? Are they doing what they'd like to be doing?

There are three full-time guidance counselors, two males and one female. The head of the department is Bob Street, who began the guidance program at RHS in 1956. Ann Marie Black joined the staff about ten years ago. She was hired, she says, "to *be* with students, [to be] a listener, a *true* counselor." Newest on the staff is Rufus Marion. He's been a counselor here for three years. Before that, he taught social studies and science and did some coaching. He has also worked as a salesman and as a welder.

They divide up the duties according to areas of "expertise." The expertise is of two sorts. One has to do with the needs of a particular clientele; so, Bob works with seniors, Ann Marie with juniors, and Rufus with sophomores. Everyone is supposed to deal with freshmen, although it seems that no one really gives them full attention ("We hope for the best"). Rufus tries to attend to them because doing so grows more naturally out of the work he does with the junior high counselor. He spends three days or so in the junior high answering questions and providing information. The junior high counselor, along with the junior high teachers and Rufus, in effect make the course selections for students coming into the high school. The guidance staff also sponsors an orientation night for new students and parents.

The other type of "expertise" has to do with administrative responsibilities. Bob Street functions as a kind of self-appointed registrar; he computes the grade-point averages for all students. He also helps to prepare the master schedule of classes. Ann Marie Black has administered the special education program for the past two years, and she finds its extensive bureaucracy "a bitter pill." Rufus Marion is in charge of the sophomore vocational testing program, which includes alphabetizing the results sheets and filing them properly with student records. He has also taken it upon himself to monitor the list of excessive student absentees in an effort to "filter out those students who may have legitimate problems they're trying to deal with." When asked to estimate how much of their time is spent doing administrative work, the counselors guessed conservatively at 20 percent and more likely 33 percent of their time. Their feeling is that guidance has had "a little bit of everyone else's [administrative] work . . . thrown on it."

One area of responsibility that belongs exclusively to guidance is standardized testing. Incoming ninth graders are given an achievement test that is used to screen students who might be in need of special educational services and to determine eligibility for the special vocational program offered in conjunction with HAMCO. Tenth graders take a vocational interest inventory, whose only purpose is to better inform students making occupational decisions. Eleventh graders are given the state SCAT, the results of which no one seems to use. During the latter half of high school, perhaps one-third of the juniors take the PSAT's, SAT's or ACT's. Most often, they take the last option because HAMCO is a testing center. When asked about median scores, Street hunted up some data and estimated the median composite score (on the ACT) at about 20.0.

When they're not filling out forms, filing papers, or averaging numbers, the three counselors try to meet with students. They see the average student once (*maybe* twice) a year, usually to do a "credit check," that is, to make sure the student has sufficient credits at this point in high school. Each counselor also has students whom they feel they know better than others. Rufus spends time with the "less affluent students and students who are thinking of dropping out, or students struggling with identity issues." Besides the special education students, Ann Marie works with the sort of students who want to join a communication group or with girls dealing with teen-age pregnancy. Bob finds he notices those students who somehow "stand out," either because of intellectual skills, physical attributes, or problem behavior.

The guidance office sometimes seems like a revolving door. Because the Ridgefield district is characterized by a good deal of transience, the counselors find themselves doing intake with new students who may very well be gone before too long. Street says that the average class (for example, 1981) will have 400 members at various points in its four-year history, even though it starts and ends with about 225 students. Thus, counselors, as well as teachers and administrators, are dealing with a student body in flux. Scheduling students into classes becomes an exercise in finesse and frustration.

The individual department heads establish course offerings and course prerequisites. Course frequency and sequencing can determine de facto which students will and will not be able to enroll. Therefore, freshmen for whom certain choices have been made, or new students who enter the process in midstream, may find themselves out of luck with regard to curricular choices. Even "non-mobile" students may suffer later if they don't make the right selections early on. Most of this decision-making is handled informally, that is, the counselors' role in the process is usually minimal.

Another area of little involvement for guidance is that of discipline. Counselors are pleased to leave that function to administrators. Street says that has been his philosophy for as long as he has been in Ridgefield. Counselors also do not interfere in student-teacher conflicts unless a student wants to talk about the problem to sort out issues and options. If a student wants to *do* anything about a complaint, he or she must take it to the administration. In any case, the counselors are not aware of many such conflicts; most student dissatisfaction with teachers seems to be caused by "having favorites" or "not caring."

For the student who wants to come in and talk, the office doors are almost always open. When it comes to personal issues, students go to that counselor with whom they feel comfortable, not necessarily the person who handles their class. Students who do not have free periods (study halls, for example) must get permission from their teachers to go to the guidance office. Sometimes that is a problem. The teacher may not see any benefit in the student's missing class or may ask: "What's wrong with you [that you want to talk to a counselor]?" Ann Marie Black thinks this may be a carryover from the strong influence of sports on the school's climate. "I wonder about the athletic influence of 'be strong.' " Or it may be the "mystery" that Rufus says exists between teachers and counselors. He wonders if maybe teachers do not get enough information about what the counselors are doing. He tries to spend a different hour every day in the teachers' lounge just to keep in touch. He also spends time in the halls between classes and in the cafeteria at lunchtime to maximize informal contact with students. Ann Marie wishes she had more time to do that, too.

All three of the counselors entered the profession hoping to "touch lives more closely," yet they find their professional training largely irrelevant to the activities in which they are involved. They want to help produce "good citizens" and "people who carry their weight," but they are under-resourced. They could use a computer terminal to help with occupational counseling and full-time clerical support to keep track of the required forms and necessary filing.

Rufus also thinks they could use a new, "positive attitude" that would encourage them "to take risks" and "get out of ruts" and start doing "what [they] like to do." As it is, they aren't very involved in the students' transition to life after high school. Street "doesn't have time" to develop contacts with potential employers. Somewhere around a third of RHS's graduates go immediately into the work force; most of them go into semi- or unskilled jobs. Another third or so go to college, but 75 percent of those students enter HAMCO, usually in one of the technical programs, and often they don't complete the programs. Under 10 percent of the graduates go on to some other form of postsecondary training (for example, cosmetology school), and at least 10 percent are unemployed and looking for work. The smallest percentage (about 5 percent) join the armed forces. Clearly, Ridgefield's students don't usually achieve the occupational goals they may envision for themselves.

Ridgefield High's guidance department may try to help students find their way through high school to those goals, but it seems hampered by the way it spends its time and energy. Rufus was talking about students but he might as well have been talking about counselors: "[They] see themselves in a trap—working but getting nowhere."

## The Teachers

The teachers of Ridgefield High work within constraints much like those of the counselors. They deal with those realities in ways that reflect who they are and how they would like to live.

Despite their different subject matter specialties, the faculty of Ridgefield High is, in a number of ways, a remarkably homogeneous group. Most were raised in small, rural towns—not unlike or far from Ridgefield—by conservative, middle- or lower-middle-class parents who were farmers, factory workers, house painters, and grocery-store owners. Successful as students in high school, and admirers of their favorite teachers, they went on to become the first generation of college graduates in their families. While supporting themselves with part-time employment, most, because of location and finances, attended the small state university near Ridgefield for both undergraduate and graduate studies during the late sixties and early seventies. Given the nature of their higher education institution and the tenor of the time, a career in teaching was perceived by most to be a rather natural choice—a multi-faceted opportunity to live out one's idealism, do something personally rewarding, and move a step upward economically and socially. Armed with youthful enthusiasm and a desire to make school a positive experience for others, they sought and found jobs in familiar settings like Ridgefield. While a few did embark upon their teaching careers in other rural towns, most went directly from college campus to Ridgefield High School. Although a bustling suburb lay only forty minutes away, all chose to live either within the Ridgefield city limits or in neighboring rural communities. Being close in terms of age, experience, interests, and neighborhood, many soon became social friends as well as colleagues. Feeling relatively well prepared in their subject area, but almost completely unprepared in terms of classroom practice, each learned the skills of management and instruction on the job from his or her own experiences and those of others.

Several describe their initial encounters at Ridgefield High School as somewhat "shocking." For one, the shock was simply "that students didn't like literature as I did—for its own sake." For another, it was that "they couldn't read and they wouldn't do homework." And for still another, who had attended a parochial high school, the shock was two-fold: "The student was exposed to so many philosophies at one time—it seemed so confusing and unstabilizing"; and "The difference between what's appropriate privately and what's appropriate publicly didn't exist here. You could tell that from walking down the hall."

The passage of time, however, has had quite a mellowing effect, and conversations with teachers reveal a consistent history of accommodation and compromise. The teacher who loved literature for its own sake, for example, "learned to use content to teach them something, but not to expect them to enjoy it in and of itself." A history teacher claims:

> We all have compromised on our values. Inside the classroom they will work for me or they will not stay there, but I don't give them nearly as much homework as I would like. . . . I have been beaten down because they will not do it.

Perhaps, however, the experience of a science teacher most clearly captures and typifies the process of shifting expectations at Ridgefield High School.

You'd give them assignments and they would come in and say, "I don't have to do this," or, "I didn't do this," or, "I couldn't do it." My biology teacher was so hard, but anybody can be a good teacher if you have good students. You don't have all this discipline and you have highly motivated kids. When you don't have highly motivated kids, you teach for about twenty minutes and then the rest of the time you spend hearing this kid cry about this or that. I just changed with it. Mostly they work in class. We have an "A" section and a "B" section. "A" section is highly motivated freshmen— "B" 's are freshmen, sophomores, and juniors. The "A" 's will do it, but the "B" 's—we just do class work or I get nothing. That's pretty much what I learned. Tests basically come from the study guide and I go over everything with them. Last year, I had a student teacher from the city come in and teach over their heads. I guess that's what I did my first year.

While everyone expresses some degree of discomfort over the lowering of standards, most also contend that the situation is essentially out of their control. Parents are generally held to be the culprits:

The system reflects the community. What the parents want, they get— darn near down the line. And they want a system where Johnny can pass. They want a system that doesn't demand a lot of time at home from the typical student.

Some teachers, however, also take personal responsibility:

In world history classes, I used to give more essays and more things where they had to write out their ideas. But, in terms of time, I've reduced [the work] to multiple choice and matching. And so I am partly to blame. When I first married, there was tremendous pressure the first year. On Thanksgiving I was grading papers no matter where I went. Christmas, I was preparing . . . at that time our semester carried over to January, which was horrible, and [we had] to grade things or prepare . . . so it just became a matter of time. I didn't want to spend all that extra time away from my family.

We are a conscientious faculty, even though we mourn our lost idealism. The trade-off is that we are settled here. We're in our mid-thirties. People choose security over challenge—sort of like the kids. The faculty sort of mirrors the kids. People get in the habit of doing the same thing in the same way, time after time, be it good or bad. We're all pretty static, people who are no longer real flexible or real innovative. We've all found the way we like to do things and do them. We've settled into a rather practical routine; there are few idealists on the staff.

While everyone admits to succumbing to lower expectations, as a practical measure, a few still argue that students are being seriously underestimated and underchallenged. One of the speech teachers put it this way:

> I just don't go along with that negative feeling that they can't learn. I also try to fight this old bug-a-boo that debate is only for the intellectual brain of the school. Many of my students are of average ability.

Essentially the same sentiment was expressed by another teacher as he spoke of the selection of a holiday movie for the entire student body.

> Try to pick a movie. It should be a good, educational show—a good show that is interesting. I suggested a show like *To Kill a Mockingbird*. I think the kids would have watched and enjoyed it, but another teacher who teaches a film class says, "You have to entertain them. They won't watch that kind of thing." I don't agree with that. . . . They thought unless it's a *Smokey and the Bandit* type of thing, forget it. We've shown a number of movies here that weren't *Smokey and the Bandit*. I just can't see taking one thousand kids for two hours out of educational classrooms and putting them into seeing junk like that. If you continually tell kids they are not on the ball and they can't do this and can't do that, then by gosh, they'll believe it.

Just exactly what to expect of students at Ridgefield High is, of course, a highly individual matter. In the absence of strong district, building, or departmental leadership in curriculum, teachers experience a high level of autonomy that they have grown to expect and prize. Without exception, Ridgefield teachers express appreciation for the fact that there is no pressure or interference from their principal regarding their classroom practice.

> I think Greg respects the faculty as professionals. He is not that authoritative. He doesn't say, "Do what I say because I am the boss." That's what I rebel against. They don't know how to tell us to teach, and I don't think they should. It's not part of an administrator's job to know more about what I'm teaching than I do. I'm in the classroom because I want to be. I expect him to respect me professionally. I'm not going to go in and tell him how to do his job. I may make a suggestion, and he will do the same for me, and that's fair.

In addition to feeling that they have control over their curriculum, Ridgefield High teachers are generally satisfied with the amount of input they have regarding overall school policy and procedure. In expressing his personal sentiments, one teacher also effectively conveys the prevailing attitude regarding faculty participation in decision-making:

> To me, personally, in the past there's been too many committees. This committee meeting to do this and this committee meeting to do that. Sometimes you have to just go ahead and do something rather than talk, talk, talk, meet, meet, meet on it. There are times now I feel that things are done that I would like to have some input, but maybe that's an egotistical or selfish viewpoint. Who says my view is that important compared to others—I'm not sure my views are the same as [those of] the other forty or fifty faculty, is what I'm saying. I'm one [who], if there's a problem, will go to the source.

Another teacher echoed the notion of individual access to the administrative system: "I can even go to the superintendent and say . . . what I think!"

In addition to valuing their control over curriculum and access to decision-making, when desired, most Ridgefield High teachers are quite content with district benefits. Almost to a person, teachers believe that working conditions are better in Ridgefield than most other places. An active and proud Ridgefield Education Association (REA) member recounts some of the recent organizational gains:

> In the elementary we almost have a duty-free lunch. We have life insurance, dental insurance—all kinds of fringe benefits. We had a decent salary schedule until we ran out of money. All kinds of rights and protections. They can't change the school calendar without our OK. Workdays every quarter. Part of our problem is [that] people are basically satisfied.

While there is clear agreement on the positive features of these benefits, there is some rather strong disagreement as to the appropriate organizational approach to securing them. In fact, the only substantive issue that seems to divide the teachers is that of organization membership. District-wide, two organizations—the REA and the Ridgefield State Teachers' Association (RSTA)—compete for membership and involvement. The philosophical differences and the mildly negative feelings about affiliation come through in these statements by advocates of each organization:

> RSTA considers teaching to be a profession. I don't think it will remain that way unless there are some major changes. REA considers it a job and,

of course, AFT is labor oriented. You know you are getting paid for every moment you're doing something. I don't think teaching can be handled that way. I feel RSTA can meet my needs because they are a state organization. They have influence with the local legislature. I see things going in the wrong direction because of teacher apathy. They don't have an activist approach.

RSTA are supposedly the nice guys who get along, but we get along with administrators better than they do and make changes. When we say something, they listen because they know we mean what we say. When the other organization says something, they ignore them. We butt heads, we negotiate, while the other group twiddles their thumbs, in effect. We have a reputation of being radical and making demands—but we only ask for what we know is there. The whole country is saying people my age went into teaching with the idea of being good teachers but not with the idea [of sacrificing] the rest of [their lives] to a poverty wage. Why can't I have this, this, and this? My friends who went to school with me have it, and I have more education than they do!

Despite this fundamental difference in perspectives on the profession, the entire faculty favors preserving the existing occupational structure. All, for example, see tenure as a necessary protective measure that must be maintained even though it sometimes protects incompetent people. Similarly, all like the ideas behind merit pay and teacher competency exams, but believe, nevertheless, that they are too impractical and unworkable to be implemented.

I wouldn't mind having a merit system because I think I could compete very well. But the problem is that people doing the evaluating are not that qualified. We all give lip service to the idea of professional educators but Greg and Danny—bless their hearts, they are [among] my best friends— but they can't evaluate my teaching. Greg is a baseball coach.

Merit pay wouldn't work here because there is an in-group that does extracurricular activities and they would get the rewards.

Finally, and perhaps most importantly, teachers generally feel good about their own level of performance. When asked to describe the greatest strength of Ridgefield High School, most talked about their own strength as a faculty in one sense or another. Teachers characterized themselves as part of a "dynamic and energetic faculty," "stable," "caring about the kids and willing to develop a curriculum that meets the needs of individuals."

It would, however, be misleading to suggest that, because a surprisingly large number of teachers share so many ideas, each and every teacher fits into a pattern. To the contrary, there are a few who are relative beginners, a few who are approaching retirement, and a few who have taught and taken educational coursework outside the immediate area. One, in fact, has taught, studied, and traveled abroad. Their differing and broader perspectives clearly add a subtle flavor of diversity to the basic homogeneity of the vast majority.

It would be equally misleading to suggest that because teachers express a high level of satisfaction with the status quo, there are not also some deeply felt frustrations. For example, while most of the faculty plan to stay in teaching, the reason is not always given in the most positive of terms:

> I can't do anything else. I was part of the graduate school explosion in the early seventies. I was a whiz at going to school. I can't perceive of myself as being able to do anything else. There are several of us who are not satisfied with teaching but, as we perceive it, there are no alternatives. Besides, we are in our mid-thirties—it's awfully old to begin a new career.

Secondly, every teacher talks about some form of "burnout" at one or more junctures in his or her career. Some relate burnout to their own personal need for periodic change; others relate it to the absence of motivated students in a particular year. One teacher spoke of both factors:

> Four and five years ago, I was willing to sell shoes at a department store. I wanted out. I signed up with Employment Security. Very badly, I wanted out. It didn't matter where. There were lots of reasons—the money was better than it is now—what it was, I'm not really sure. The only thing I could pinpoint was that I didn't have any students who were interested. Now, it's just the opposite because I have students who are interested—somebody to work with and for. One thing you can't do is take schoolwork home with you—if you do you are doing schoolwork at home and on weekends, and you are never away from school. I was mentally depleted for a while. I stopped smoking, started running, lost thirty pounds. Now I lift weights. A lot of stress is reduced by physical exhaustion, and, in summer, I try to find a lake or some mountains, if I can. Collect those negative ions and recharge.

A third area of frustration that is widely shared revolves around the public's lack of esteem for the teaching profession. Three of the most reflective and skilled practitioners at Ridgefield High made these rather poignant comments regarding their image in the community:

> I work as a meat cutter at one of the nearby butcher shops in the summer, and I don't usually tell them I am a teacher. One butcher found out that I was a full-time teacher and he said to me, "Man, that is a dead-end job. You must be a real dummy." Right now my salary and the meat cutter's are about the same for a nine-month period, but in three years, with the current contract, if I were a regular meat cutter I'd be making $32,000. Of course, that's for twelve months.

> I go places collecting items for my various courses and I'm almost embarrassed to say I am a teacher. It's just the people's view of teachers as goof-offs—getting a fourth of the year off to do nothing—that really hurts.

> I think other professions look down upon us. It's the "There must be something wrong with you because you are a classroom teacher!"

A fourth general frustration is the lack of positive feedback. As one teacher put it:

> You rarely get any thank you. You sometimes do from students. It is a rarity that you get any kind of thank you from community, superintendent, school board administrators. There is no positive reinforcement for anything you do. There are no pats on the back. There's no reward system; there are no bonuses. You know, it makes me very ill sometimes when you look at somebody who's given thirty-five years of service to a school district and they leave and they are not even recognized for any contribution.

Of course, feeling "locked in," "burned out," and "unappreciated" are frustrations that Ridgefield teachers share with their counterparts in districts big and little, rich and poor, urban, suburban, and rural, in every section of this country. There were, however, also a number of expressed frustrations that appear to be somewhat more indigenous to Ridgefield High School. One of these is the lack of parental stability, concern, and support—particularly from those whose children were having difficulties. Over and over, teachers complain about lack of communication:

> Students won't do homework because there is parental apathy toward learning. They won't support teachers in homework. In one year one hundred and forty out of two hundred and forty failed, and one parent called.

> You send home grade cards . . . and out of fifty you send home, you might get one response.

Another is the perceived priorities of the school board. One teacher expressed the problem with considerable passion:

> We are tremendously frustrated with pay. We are college graduates; we are professionals; we receive such a low salary in comparison. It's coming from all levels. Reaganomics, the state level, the governor is not very sympathetic, the school board has different priorities. The [construction] of the administration building came at a time when the teachers' fund was depleted. It's rather plush—money went there instead of into the teachers' fund. I joke that I have a piece of the wood floor because we pay more for that building than others in the community. The Board of Education meeting room is especially a thorn in our side because they meet once a month. The cafeteria here is well lit, clean, spacious, and could have been used just as easily. If you get down to people really involved, that is a really sore spot. There is a feeling that the priority is not classroom teaching but buildings. . . . There is a feeling that people elected to the board are not really concerned about what goes on in the classroom. They are more concerned [about whether] we come here at 7:30 A.M. For a long time, we fought the issue of whether you could wear a beard. They are more concerned with what it looks like to the public versus what we are teaching the children. This creates an immense feeling of frustration. Most share this view, but few will talk openly about it.

Related to the general frustration with the board is a highly specific complaint regarding the board's new evaluation form. Two active members of REA explain the issue:

> Of all the thorns that are here now, the new evaluation form would be the one which would most upset teachers. Most of us feel we had very little input into the form and that it is not a very accurate barometer of how well you teach. We feel that it is connected with rifs and that it is an instrument designed to criticize teachers instead of helping them do a better job.
>
> Fourteen out of twenty-four items have nothing to do with inside the classroom. How can a principal who comes into your room for forty minutes interpret your public relations in the community, that you support school board policy? It mainly has to do with outside activities. Do you come to ball games? This form simply labels you, whether you are willing to go along with what everybody wants or whether you are not going along.

Thus, after talking to teachers at some length, one can clearly find at Ridgefield High School the same kinds of frustrations that inevitably exist among caring teachers who have the awareness and insight to uncover the flaws in the system and the desire to make it better. But, after observing Ridgefield teachers at length, both inside the classroom and out, one can also see that they can live with these frustrations with more comfort than most. Be it a lack of pressure from without, a lack of passion within, or a lack of vision for what might be, the faculty moves through the halls in a pleasant, relaxed, and untroubled manner. Stopping by the office on brief business inevitably involves light-hearted banter with the principal and assistant (who are their contemporaries and former colleagues) as well as with the two congenial women who comprise the office staff. In the classroom, they present familiar material either through lecture or film for perhaps half of the period, consciously or unconsciously avoiding questions or teaching strategies that might arouse disagreement or disorder or take additional planning. Written work is then assigned to be done in class while they circulate at a leisurely pace to help individuals in a patient and affable manner. As students leave or enter their classroom, they joke with the most verbal, or they move into the halls to talk for just a few moments with the teacher next door. On those rare occasions when an incident occurs in the halls, they take the time later in the day to follow up on what happened to students when they were taken to the office.

On their "prep" period, they rarely feel the need or desire to do any preparation. Instead, they usually wander down to the lounge, purchase a snack or drink from the two vending machines, and speculate as to whether the machines will choose to devour their money and give them nothing in return, as they have been known to do in the past. They chat with whoever is present, mostly about nonschool and nonintellectual issues. Occasionally, when they are asked by Mr. Owens to spend their prep period "subbing" for someone who had to leave because of illness or an activity, they give up their chance to relax with surprising good humor.

At lunchtime, they crowd into the lounge, which is a relatively small room, long but narrow. Most probably feel the same as the students do about the cafeteria food, for large numbers bring brown bags from home. Those who are finished eating courteously give up their seats to newcomers even though they might prefer to linger. Conversations are often dominated by the men, who talk of local and national football scores, how many miles they ran over the weekend, and whether or not they will participate in an upcoming race. The women join in when they feel it's appropriate, and are not offended by sexist wise-cracks and laughter generated when attractive female students knock on the door and ask to speak to male teachers. While no one appears highly energetic or intellectually stimulated, no one appears harassed, overworked, or hostile. There is, instead, a calm and casual demeanor born of a work style that is at once pleasant and predictable. Although some of the close social relationships of the past have been somewhat diminished by a growth of individual family responsibilities, one still feels a strong underlying sense of kinship in the group. While the school district itself clearly does not serve as the center of the Ridge-field community, the impression is that the school district is, in effect, at the very core of this faculty's lifestyle.

Family ties abound within the high school and the district at large. Currently, there are five married couples on the high school faculty as well as a father-and-son coaching team. Moreover, the spouses of many faculty members teach at the junior high, middle, or elementary school, and one faculty member's wife drives a school bus.

Thus, for most, it appears that living within the Ridgefield High School setting is not unlike living within one's own smaller family unit —a process wherein you attempt to cope with day-to-day events with a minimum of hassle and a maximum of acceptance because of a long-term commitment to the institution and a concern for the individuals who inhabit it. Almost to a person, they share the sentiments of a history teacher who maintains that "While there are day-to-day frus-trations, when I reflect overall, I think I basically do a good job and as a system we do a good job."

## Curriculum Formulation and Implementation

When either educators or lay persons speak of a school system or of individual teachers as doing "a good job," they are usually referring to the curriculum and the overall teaching-learning process. And when most evaluate the scope and sequence of any major curricular effort, they are generally asking: Do the formally arranged courses and class-room experiences achieve the established and written goals and ob-jectives of the district, the school, and the teachers? At Ridgefield High School, however, no one ever talks or thinks systematically about goals or objectives—let alone writes them down. A few of the more cynical faculty members speak of implicit goals in this tone:

> The goal, I guess, is to keep things quiet, have kids come to school and get their ADA [Average Daily Attendance], have a good team, whatever sport we're doing, and to get through the year.

> Our goal is to get our students so that they can function adequately in blue-collar society. You wouldn't write that down, and it would be real embarrassing if someone from the university saw it written, but our goal is to get these kids to be like their parents. We're not real satisfied with their aspirations, but that's our goal.

Most, however, speak in a more conventional and acceptable educational vernacular: "It's what any school tries to do" . . . "the best environment for students" . . . "to help students at all levels." One said:

> We try to meet the needs of the average student. We're doing some things for the gifted, but our concern is mainly with the average students, with the college-bound student still being able to get the background he needs.

Most of the faculty think of goals and objectives as something "to be written in teacher education courses and then forgotten." Their absence, therefore, is not lamented. As one teacher put it, "If we had them, we wouldn't follow them anyway."

A few, however, view the lack of goals as a critical problem in terms of curricular coherence and expectations for students.

> We have no overall goals and I think that's where we're in trouble. I've talked to Greg about it. I'd like to see some curriculum coordination K through twelve. There is no thread or sequence. We have no formal speech instruction until ninth grade, and I think that's a disaster. No image of the kind of student we're aiming to produce.

> If you bring up curriculum, it is a big bugaboo. Professionally, this school is not where it should be. Every time someone mentions a North Central evaluation, everybody says, "Oh, that's too much work, too much money for the superintendent's office. Too much work here and there." How in the world are you going to know where you're going or if what you are doing is right, if you don't have a plan? Things just sort of happen around here. There's no real organization; it's just random happenings.

> I think you have to set some goals out there you want students to reach. You can't always make everything so easy that they're all going to perform.

The explanation for the absence of an overarching set of curricular goals, curriculum guides, or any kind of curriculum leadership can be clearly traced to a well-rationalized system of "buck passing" down the administrative chain of command. The superintendent does not have an assistant who might be given curriculum responsibilities, nor is he comfortable with the notion of a district curriculum specialist. Past experience in Ridgefield and other districts has led him to believe that curriculum responsibility should rest with the building principals.

> Each principal is pretty well responsible for his building. And coordination and articulation is between principals, and I feel that principals work together pretty well. Now, I've been other places where there were particular individuals who were responsible for curriculum development, and the people were always mad. The principals were mad at this person because he overstepped his boundaries.

Although the curriculum ball has been thrust into his hands, Greg Owens, as principal, does not feel capable of handling it, and he quickly passes it along to the department heads and their teachers:

> Sometimes I find myself in a position where I am working with someone who almost has a doctor's degree in English and I am trying to tell him how to teach and what to teach. . . . I don't feel confident enough to walk into an art class and say what they should be doing. I see myself as organizing and facilitating so they can do what they want. They're OK. I really think that they know what to do, and they feel that they are in a better position to know what should be done.

The department heads, however, view their responsibility rather negatively. According to one:

> It is basically a short straw situation . . . a pain in the rear. In fact, I told them I didn't want to do it after this year, somebody else could put up with it.

Departmental meetings are rarely called, and one reason given has been the lack of financial remuneration for the department head:

> You're paid twenty dollars per department member and that doesn't encourage you to take on a lot of added responsibility.

When it comes right down to it, then, each teacher develops his/her own curriculum in relative isolation. Individuals rarely know what others are doing within their own departments, within their school, or within their district. As one history teacher summarized it:

> There's not any coordination between kindergarten, elementary, middle school, junior high, high school. There's none. Everybody is basically their little autonomous area. There's duplication, there's gaps. I would like to see some leadership tying us together.

Moreover, the basis for much of the individual curriculum decision-making is, "What do I want to teach?" rather than, "What do students need to learn?" Thus, when the English department considers a request from the counseling office to offer a course in creative writing, a major portion of the discussion revolves around who is willing to teach such a course. And when a teacher gets tired of teaching Ancient Civilization or Society and Ideas, it disappears from the social studies curriculum. If the general scope of curricular choices is, in large part, a matter of faculty interest and preference, the interior and thrust of specific courses is, of course, largely shaped by the personal goals and values of individual faculty members. These personal goals and values vary considerably among faculty members but also fall into a few broad categories.

The aim of some is simply to make school more enjoyable for students. A history teacher, for example, states that his overarching personal goal is "to get them through American History and World History, making it as enjoyable and good as I can, using a variety of methods." The Spanish teacher tries "to put a little more enjoyment into teaching Spanish by incorporating a lot of fun-type activities, cultural projects," his personal slides, and by taking a group to Mexico. Other faculty members aim primarily at character development. A history teacher, for example, tries to impart self-discipline and self-pride: "Look, it's important to learn how to learn and make yourself learn—to have a little pride." One of the coaches talks of pride in this way: "We have pride in our appearance, and I'm speaking of haircuts, uniforms, and cleanliness. We definitely have sportsmanship. Above all, we want to win within the rules and good sportsmanship." A few faculty members aim primarily at awareness: "Awareness of what is going on around them, of things they can't see"; "Awareness that all there is in the world is not Ridgefield"; or, "Awareness of what it means to be an informed and educated citizen." The only one who speaks of skills is a speech teacher who strives for "improved articulation and increased vocabulary."

Of course, the teachers' basic control of the curriculum development process is necessarily constrained by the formal requirements of the three different diplomas that Ridgefield High School offers, but only slightly so. Because the requirements are relatively minimal, the teachers' freedom to choose what to teach is considerable. If anything, the requirements merely create a broad framework within which to choose. Currently, to obtain the regular diploma, 20 units are required, but for the class of 1983 the figure will be changed to 21 and in 1984 it will be 22. To obtain a comprehensive diploma, 21 units are presently required, but the figure will be 22 in 1983 and 23 in 1984. For the college preparatory diploma, 22 units are required, with the figure moving to 23 in 1983 and 24 in 1984. Approximately 10 percent receive the college preparatory diploma, while approximately 45 percent receive each of the other two.

The move to require more units for graduation in the coming years reflects a belief that standards generally need to be higher. It does not reflect, however, the rather widespread concern among both high school faculty and administrators that there also needs to be more required courses. Table 1 provides an overview of the current set of required units and courses.

TABLE 1
1981 GRADUATION REQUIREMENTS, RIDGEFIELD HIGH SCHOOL

|  | Regular Diploma | Comprehensive Diploma | College Preparatory |
|---|---|---|---|
|  | 20 units required | 21 units required (A cumulative grade average of 2.0 is required) | 22 units required (A cumulative grade average of 3.0 is required. No semester failing grades are permitted in any course.) |
| COMMUNICATION SKILLS | 3 units required ½ written, ½ oral | 3 units required 1 written, 1 oral | 4 units required 1 written, ½ oral; 2 courses for grades 11-12 |
| MATHEMATICS | 1 unit required | 1 unit required 1 beginning | 3 units required 1 beginning |

TABLE 1. (continued)

| | | algebra or both courses in algebra and basic algebra | algebra, 1 geometry, 1 advanced algebra |
|---|---|---|---|
| SCIENCE | 1 unit required | 1 unit required Must be other than general or physical science | 3 units required 1 general biology, 1 chemistry, 1 other than general or physical science |
| SOCIAL STUDIES | 2 units required 1 American History, 1 World History | 3 units required 1 American History, 1 World History | 4 units required 1 American History, 1 World History |
| FINE ARTS | 1 unit required | 1 unit required | 1 unit required |
| PRACTICAL ARTS | 1½ units required, ½ typing | 1½ units required, ½ typing | 1½ units required, ½ typing |
| P.E. & HEALTH | 2 units required | 2 units required | 2 units required |
| OTHER | 8½ units required | 8½ units required | 2½ units required |

| COMMUNICATIONS ENGLISH | | COMMUNICATIONS DRAMA & SPEECH | | FOREIGN LANGUAGE SPANISH | |
|---|---|---|---|---|---|
| Achievement in English | 1 | Creative Communications I | ½ | Beginning Spanish | 1 |
| Practical English | 1 | Creative Communications II | ½ | Intermediate Spanish | 1 |
| English Survey | 1 | Speech Composition | ½ | Advanced Spanish | 1 |
| Composition II | ½ | Novice Debate | 1 | | |
| Composition III | ½ | Advanced Debate | 1 | | |
| Films | ½ | | | | |
| Poetry | ½ | | | | |
| Short Story | ½ | | | | |
| Journalism | ½ | | | | |
| American Novel | ½ | | | | |
| English Novel | ½ | | | | |
| Mythology | ½ | | | | |
| School Publications | ½ | | | | |
| College Preparatory English | ½ | | | | |
| College Preparatory Literature | ½ | | | | |

The concerns most often expressed are that there is only one math and one science unit required for the regular and comprehensive diplomas and the fact that students consistently choose the easiest courses for their electives:

> I think it is a real shame students can graduate with one unit in math, which is very minimal, and they are not very well prepared. . . . They can get out without knowing how to divide, but they have a math credit. They can probably earn a credit if they multiply. The one credit can be in functional math and that is very minimal.

> We offer kids too many choices. The ones who are not achievers because they choose not to be are never forced to achieve. They can get into a semi-easy, "just show you're alive" class that slow kids come into and make the C or D or whatever they need to keep Mom off their backs and to get a diploma. I believe in tracks and that you have to find something that the slow kids can do, but the only thing wrong with that theory is that we're not successful in separating the really slow kids who can't achieve from those who just won't. But that's what the parents want. . . . Homework is not a viable alternative for the typical student at Ridgefield. They just won't do it.

> I don't think we push them enough; we allow them to glide a lot. There are enough courses here that someone can graduate with a high school diploma without being challenged a whole lot. We don't encourage them in foreign language, and I think that's a mistake.

In explaining why there has been a declining interest in Spanish, the only foreign language offered, the Spanish teacher also explained how a lack of curriculum requirements can encourage students to "glide":

> It doesn't fulfill any requirement; it is an elective but doesn't count for the fine arts requirement. Some of the college-bound will take it, but many don't because it's not required and they know the school they are going to doesn't require it. . . . Last year was the first year in five years that we didn't go on a trip to Mexico. Maybe that contributed to disappointment with the program. That created a lot of animosity with kids. I got after some of them and that drove some of them out. We had a lot drop out after second [semester] last year. One reason is that most need to take something to satisfy a fine arts requirement. I give homework Monday through Thursday, and I find myself competing for numbers with other electives like art and guitar, where there is no homework.

The combination of multiple electives, minimal requirements, relatively unmotivated students, and a lack of parental pressure appears to make it possible for students to leave Ridgefield High School without what many would call the basics. A few are pained by this situation. In the words of one history teacher: "Students graduate who can't read, write, think, or talk."

Another was even more dramatic:

> I've only been to two graduations. I'm not interested in them. I see some of the kids who are getting diplomas and I think, "My god, if I had to put my name on that diploma!" They don't know a darn thing; they don't even know who their state senator is; they literally don't.

Most, however, are relatively satisfied:

> Our kids don't get too bad an education here. They don't have great expectations, and no one has great expectations of them, but they can almost all sort of write a sentence by the time they graduate. They can almost all do simple math. They have adequate skills to perform blue-collar tasks. . . . I don't think we do any worse job here than any of the schools around us. We are typical of Hamilton County schools and Hamilton County schools are typical of any fringe suburban school.

In the final analysis, however, the judgment of whether a school district is not doing "any worse job" than any other does not rest on any external set of requirements or electives. It depends, instead, on the nature and quality of teaching-learning experience within the classroom setting. The conceptions of teaching and knowledge, the attitudes and the skills that the teachers bring to their individual courses will, in fact, give the curriculum its shape and substance.

At Ridgefield High School, with only a few exceptions, faculty members firmly cling to the notion that "teaching is telling" and that "knowledge is given," something to be presented and digested rather than something to be examined, questioned, applied, or discovered. In advanced classes, as well as those aimed at the average or below average student, teachers are invariably doing almost all of the talking. They present the information; they pose the questions; and, in most instances, they answer their own questions. The chemistry teacher, for example, who has some of the school's ablest students in this particular class, conducts questioning in this way:

TEACHER (working from an overhead projector): Anyone have an idea of how to go on from moles to molecules?

STUDENTS: Multiply.

TEACHER: OK, multiply. (The teacher then writes out a formula on the overhead projector.) Now, how would you change from grams to molecules? (He writes on overhead: *G Molecules*.)

STUDENT: We haven't done this.

TEACHER: If you look at step one [a previously given formula], it will tell you how to go from grams to moles; then, if you put moles to molecules, you can get the answer, or, if you want, you can go the reverse.

This lack of opportunity for students to figure out for themselves what to multiply, or what formulas might be combined to go from grams to molecules, or to, in any way, actively participate in class is typical throughout the academic curriculum. As one student put it: "All we do all day is sit and listen to teachers talk. I know they're supposed to know more than we do—but it's boring to listen to teachers talk all day."

The faculty's general convictions about the nature of knowledge and teaching appear to be closely, and perhaps causally, related to two more specific and situational factors—namely, their attitudes toward students and their lack of teaching skills. The widespread conclusion among most teachers is that large portions of the student body cannot, or will not, learn or work in school, and that, under such circumstances, teachers must be both realistic and practical. This means reducing complex ideas to one- or two-word answers, giving the answers to students, asking students to copy them down and transfer them to work sheets and study guides, and reviewing them thoroughly before a test. Since all students, however, cannot be counted upon to succeed—even with this much assistance—many teachers have developed the "accommodating" practice of giving credit or points for simply turning in one's notes or homework, finding out what newsworthy event is occurring in Cancun, or bringing in yeast, grape juice, and nuts for a lab on fermentation. One teacher said:

> Teachers are very accommodating in this school, although I do not know if students perceive it that way. I know that sometimes in my lower-level classes I give credit or points just for turning in assignments, knowing if I did grade them all, or had my aide grade them, all of their grades would be dropping and dropping, and, Lord knows, their grades are low enough as it is.

Interestingly, a rather significant number of students perceive teachers to be "boring" and "easy," as opposed to "accommodating." In their words: "You go to classes and get bored"; "Not much happens during the day"; "You sleep half the day"; "It's easy to pass the classes"; "I usually get [my homework] done before other people, which leaves me sitting there doing nothing"; "Ridgefield is all right if you are an average or below average student. However, if you are above average, it is hard to find classes that are challenging. Many of the classes are designed for an inferior student. Some classes could be challenging, but they are slowed so much as to be simple and consequently boring."

The most incisive student comment, however, was: It is an easy school to learn in, but it is a hard school to get motivated to learn in.

A second factor that appears to be closely linked to the faculty's attitude toward student capacity and motivation to learn is an absence of alternative teaching strategies that might enable teachers to stimulate student interest and facilitate understanding. Experiential activities (except for science labs), discussion, group projects, student reports, role playing, simulations, application, and problem-solving activities are practically nonexistent. Practically, but not totally. There are, in fact, a few striking exceptions to the dominant teaching-learning patterns. The most unusual of these falls outside the academic departments. It is the opportunity that students have to attend Hamilton Community College, located just down and across the highway.

HAMCO runs two parallel tracks of programs. One is a traditional liberal arts sequence that culminates in an associate's degree and enables its graduates to pursue a bachelor's degree at a four-year institution, if they so choose. The other track involves technical training in ten areas such as welding, hotel/motel management, or auto mechanics. This second track is also available to a select group of high school seniors from neighboring school districts. Each district is allotted a certain number of spaces based upon its total student population.

Students in the program spend half a school day at HAMCO and half in their home schools (some Ridgefield students spend the other half day in work release). While they are at HAMCO, they are treated like regular junior college students with all attendant rights and responsibilities. Many of RHS's students mention how much they enjoy being treated like adults. They are delighted that their last year of high school is also their "first year of college—and Ridgefield pays for it!"

The programs themselves combine classroom work with hands-on experience. The classroom activities are unimaginatively structured. For example, students read their prepared answers to twenty-four homework questions at the end of a textbook chapter. Yet, the students work hard on these tasks and remain attentive throughout class sessions. They really come alive, though, when they enter work areas and watch the instructor's demonstrations.

The students' enthusiasm is shared in varying degrees by Ridgefield's administration and teachers. The program is a relatively small one, fifty students per year, and thus many interested students are turned away. Also, the Ridgefield industrial arts staff seems ambivalent about the rationale for a program that describes industrial arts as aimed at personal pleasure, while the HAMCO program strives to develop vocational skills. Nevertheless, for a few, the HAMCO experience serves as a major source of innovation and the primary focus of their postsecondary planning.

Some variation in the teaching-learning process can be found within and among the academic departments as well. According to Greg Owens, "Social studies is the strongest department" and "English leaves something to be desired." A more in-depth look at each of these academic departments sheds additional light on the variations in scope and quality of the teaching-learning process at Ridgefield High School.

At one end of the spectrum stands the English department. According to the student curriculum handbook:

> The Communications Curriculum has been revised to offer more nearly an individualized instructional basis. Students of varying ability levels are tracked into certain courses, which allow them to reach an established goal at a time when they are ready and able to achieve success.

Reading further, one finds that there are four entry-level possibilities: Achievement in English (for freshmen who failed reading or language courses, or who made no better than a I in the eighth grade and who score low on achievement tests); Practical English (for freshmen who score below 75 percent on a grammar test at the end of the eighth grade and sophomores who have successfully completed Achievement in English); English Survey (for freshmen who have done well in eighth grade and students who have completed Practical English); and Composition II (for honors freshmen and those who have completed English Survey). All courses thereafter, starting with Composition II, are one semester courses and have prerequisites to keep the tracks clear and functioning. In the first two entry-level courses, students do no writing—they focus strictly on grammar, picking out parts of speech. In the third, in addition to an emphasis on grammar, students are asked to write some sentences and, in the fourth, students are asked to write some paragraphs. Thus, students who receive either "regular" or "comprehensive" diplomas can and do graduate without ever having to write a sentence.

Moreover, since there is no systematic course work in reading (the two reading classes have a total of ten students), students can and do graduate from Ridgefield High School unable to read any literature and many textbooks. Observations of Achievement in English, for example, reveal that the teacher reads to the students for the entire period. She explains her practice in this way:

> These students cannot read, and I think the best I can do for these kids is to show them someone who enjoys reading and is enthusiastic. I am teaching this course for the first time and last year's teacher gave me a whole collection of books with audiotapes. Now, I have never heard them, but one of the kids listened to one and said it wasn't very good. . . . So I just started reading to them, and I'm holding them with my voice.

Observations of English Survey, the third entry-level course, also revealed a reading problem. The teacher showed a filmstrip of Bret Harte's "Outcasts of Poker Flat" because "It's too hard for them to read and we do not have enough copies." After the filmstrip, the teacher explained:

> Before we do a work sheet I want to tell you that Bret Harte invented the Western. His characters are stereotypes. John Oakhurst is The Gambler. Bret Harte is also noted for local color. There is Tom, The Innocent, The Mother/Prostitute is the Duchess, and there is Uncle Billy. We have not read anything with four conflicts, but this one has four. Man against nature; man against man; society versus man (the people in town took it upon themselves to judge them); and man against himself.

Finally he passes out a two-page work sheet. The first page asks for most of the information he has just given, and the second page asks students to define a long list of vocabulary words from the story—words like "sententiously" and "vociferation." There are two student questions: "When is this all due?" and "Do we have to do all of this?" The period ends with the students trying to answer the questions and struggling to define the words while the teacher walks around giving help.

The lack of instruction in reading skills is defended by one of the counselors: "These kids have had remedial reading year after year in elementary and junior high school. They just don't want it any more."

The emphasis on grammar as opposed to writing in the lower-level classes is strongly defended by the entire English faculty. The ex-department head explains:

> We found that everybody would fail if we tried to teach everybody how to write in composition class, so obviously that was the wrong thing to do. The administration didn't like that; parents didn't like that; and kids didn't like that. . . . That wasn't what we were supposed to be doing, apparently, so we decided that maybe we could give them something that they could do, which turned out to be grammar. They already had a little bit of it, and they can also see some success. Most of them can pick out all the verbs so they feel like they've accomplished something. Again, I question the value. I don't think there's much correlation between writing and learning verbs . . . on that level at least. So, in one respect, we're doing something good in there. I think we're making students feel like they're accomplishing something. The value of what they're accomplishing? I don't know about that.

English teachers also contend that although a goodly number of students leave there without being able to write a sentence, there is little they could do to change that:

> You can't force a kid to do something. And I don't care who he is, you cannot make him write a sentence if he doesn't have any interest in doing it, and won't do it. And you can't make him learn to write a paragraph. You can try to. You can go through the motions. You can make him stay in English forever, until he is thirty-eight if you want to, but he's still not going to do it unless he takes a notion to. So that's the problem you run into.

> They can't write. They won't write. There's absolutely no way. It was just hopeless until we all went to the grammar Mickey Mouse and somebody could finally pass.

Moreover, there is the belief that it won't matter much anyway:

> They are not going to be good writers, but I don't think very many of them are going to write anything. I'll bet you that in this county, that eighty percent of the adults don't write anything. They never write a letter. They probably sign their name to a check. I doubt if they draw up their income tax. I think they plan on becoming factory workers, where they don't have to write. They can survive in that field. That's what most of their parents do, I think.

The relationship between the English department's attitude and approach and the students' lack of knowledge or skill seems clear. The instructional decisions to read to students or show a filmstrip rather than to work on reading skills, to develop vocabulary by giving lists of isolated words rather than by helping students use context clues, to focus on picking out parts of speech rather than on the ability to express one's ideas on paper, are obviously born of frustration, failure, and a lack of ability or enthusiasm to do anything else. The unfortunate result is that large numbers graduate with passing or even good grades in English but without the ability to read or write.

At the other end of the spectrum is the social studies department, where students are not generally tracked, although an honors American History has recently been instituted. All electives are open to those who have passed the two departmental requirements: American History and World History. The department is characterized by a number of teachers who display a high degree of enthusiasm for what they are doing, a deep knowledge base in their subject area, and a wider array of teaching strategies than can be found in other departments.

The lecture format predominates, as it does elsewhere, but the presentations are typically longer, richer in detail, and more dynamically delivered. Teachers generally come across as highly knowledgeable people who focus on interesting and important historical events and aim at stimulating student thinking. One history teacher, for example, supplements a well-prepared lecture with relevant charts, colored slides, pictures, and periodic injections of humor. Another, focusing on the Indian struggle, shows a dramatic filmstrip on Wounded Knee, poses some thought-provoking open-ended questions (which, unfortunately, go nowhere), and concludes with some disturbing current statistics on suicide, infant mortality, life expectancy, and median income among the Indians.

In addition to well-executed lecture presentations, other teaching strategies are employed. One teacher uses simulation games to get across complex concepts. Another, who aims at developing informed and involved citizens, requires students to attend one public meeting in the community. Still another conducts a stimulating discussion on war and survival in which he presses students to think and take a position. He begins with the question of whether women should be drafted, moves to the issue of combat and noncombat choices for men and women, and ends with the questions of whether Americans do and should have the right to go against the government by declaring where they will and will not fight. In this particular class, students are actively expressing their own views. In several of the other history courses, students are involved, but more in the sense of being attentive. In most, there appears to be content worth knowing and a process aimed at provoking student thought.

The fact that a few teachers can and do get student involvement and thinking immediately raises the issue of in-service training for the others, either at the university or district level. Over half of the faculty have masters' degrees from the nearby state university, but most speak disparagingly of the graduate courses in education. District-wide, there is no in-service education, except for occasional voluntary workshops sponsored by the REA. These workshops, however, are not strongly supported; neither is there any expressed desire to have a more systematic program. One teacher explained both the problem with the district and university in-service education in these terms:

> Most teachers think workshops are a waste of time. There is a mentality among teachers that "I can't be taught anything else. Going back and taking education courses is a waste of time. Any kind of course in transactional analysis is a waste of time. I know what I'm doing. I'm satisfied. I can function." The actual intellectual curiosity of learning is gone out of so many people. It's partially because they have gone to so many workshops that are so useless. Plus, teachers tend to think they do know everything. They often take education courses at the nearby state university where the instructors are ex-principals and superintendents who are not such good teachers and haven't done much research. I took a course in supervision

last year at the nearby state university taught by an ex-principal. He taught literally out of the textbook. He stood in front of the classroom and read the textbook with us.

In light of the faculty's past experience and current attitude toward in-service education, it is unlikely that new efforts in that direction could significantly alter the dominant teaching-learning patterns in the future. In light of the existing educational experience for students, it seems reasonable to ask: Is the faculty at Ridgefield High School justified in its belief that they and the system are, in fact, doing a "good job"?

## Some Personal Reflections

The preceding pages represent an attempt to answer in descriptive terms the question of how good a job Ridgefield High School is doing as well as other relevant questions posed by the architects of the Carnegie study. The adequacy of these descriptions is mitigated, of course, by the relatively limited time available for observation and analysis. Also intervening are the very persons of the researchers. We are two white, middle-aged, middle-class women, who serve on the faculty of a major research-oriented university. What we saw and thought important in Ridgefield surely differs, at least in part, from what others, unlike us, might have seen and heard.

In the end, both the questions and answers of this study will prove most worthwhile if they are of use to the interested reader, to the thoughtful policy maker, and, we hope, to the people of Ridgefield. Such usefulness implies, however, further examination of the data. If evaluations are to be made, they will be based on interpretations of what we have described. Such an analysis depends on theoretical and practical frames of reference. That is, what conceptual lens is used to frame the data, and who is holding the camera, and at what angle?

The two of us see education as an interactive enterprise. We believe in the power of individuals to affect their circumstances and in the power of systems to influence the individuals within them. Regarding Ridgefield, we were, and are, "outsiders" committed to painting a fair and accurate picture, but, in the end, able to walk out of the resulting scene. Before commenting on the meaning or implications of our work, a summary that tentatively begins the process of interpretation may be helpful.

From our particular vantage point we see the Ridgefield community as a fragmented residential locale wherein a transient, white working-class population mixes with the rural roots of the few remaining farming families. Escaping from the integration of their urban environments, this fluctuating and perhaps implicitly racist populace has attempted to create a haven of their own design, one characterized by deep religious commitments and simpler and earlier notions of morality, patriotism, and justice. Having little or no faith in education as a force for liberation or upward mobility, they view the high school experience in practical terms: the opportunity to obtain a diploma, a necessary credential for entrance into the world of work.

For most, Ridgefield High School itself appears to be a pleasant, friendly, and warm environment to live in for the four years it takes to receive the desired piece of parchment. There is a genuine spirit of congeniality and caring that exists within and among the administrative circle, the faculty, and the students. For a minority of students and faculty, however, the experience at RHS is characterized by frustration and failure.

As an intellectual environment, Ridgefield High School appears relatively barren; it is a place where ideas are rarely discussed, where significant and controversial questions are rarely posed, and where knowledge is rarely applied. For the most part, teachers and students go through the sometimes painful and often meaningless process of giving, receiving, and giving back factual information.

Ridgefield administrators are indigenous to the area. Further, since their training has been at nearby institutions, professional inbreeding has occurred. Holding few, if any, imaginative or lofty aspirations for their students, they see themselves primarily as managers rather than as educational leaders. The counselors are well meaning, but are themselves "misguided." They recognize their lack of effectiveness but feel victimized rather than responsible. The teachers feel victimized as well by a parent community that doesn't reinforce their educational efforts and by students who are consequently unmotivated to learn. Their response is to lower expectations for themselves and for their students. In effect, they seem to have made an implicit contract with students that promises a light work load and a heavy dose of teacher assistance in exchange for student compliance. They are bright, reasonably knowledgeable in their content areas, and caring individuals, but they are also weak and lacking in skills in the craft of teaching.

Ridgefield High School students are basically nice, polite, passive, and unsophisticated individuals. The drug problem notwithstanding, they are rarely in trouble, and when they are, it is for relatively minor infractions. They have highly unrealistic expectations for their future. Their troubles may first begin when they discover that the curriculum has not prepared them to think through their options or to compete in the marketplace.

What implications do these summary interpretations have for those concerned directly or indirectly with the many schools like Ridgefield High? Paradoxically, our answers take the form of further questions.

First: What is the essential function of schooling? Our experience reveals that there is no single, definitive answer in Ridgefield. Students, faculty, and administration acknowledge the social purposes fulfilled by the high school. As Owens said, "I think that the most important thing the kids can learn in school is just how to get along with people. I really believe that. If they can do that, then those other things will come."

Besides providing an arena for interpersonal relationships, Ridgefield High also prepares its students for their roles as perpetuators of community values. No one, it seems, is arguing that schools should develop the kind of intellectual inquiry that would result in the careful examination of those values. Consequently, neither individuals nor institutions are stretched to anything approaching their potential. If, however, the function of schooling is primarily cultural reproduction, then RHS's teachers are, indeed, justified in feeling that they and the system are doing "a good job." Does this de facto definition of the function of schooling reflect a consensus among Ridgefield's constituencies? Have these decisions been made consciously or unconsciously? By whom?

These concerns lead to a second major question: Who's in charge? Central administration sees itself as a resource for the individual building principals. The individual principals see themselves as resources for the teachers. The teachers see themselves as pawns of parental disinterest and adolescent apathy. The counselors see themselves as ignored as they fall through the cracks of administrative bureaucracy. Ironically, if any group sees itself as responsible and in charge of learning at RHS, it is the students, "The smart people and the people who want to learn." We were told, "It all depends on the kids, what they want, and how much they want to learn." This acceptance of responsibility reflects not a sense of empowerment but, rather, a willingness to accept blame for the failures of the system. Moreover, there is a pervasive atmosphere throughout Ridgefield that seems to have a life of its own: it exalts athletics; it minimizes cultural expressions such as drama and art; it espouses morality in the form of simple imperatives, such as the Student Handbook's exhortation: "DO WHAT IS RIGHT."

Determining how this atmosphere developed and is maintained is critical to our third and final question: Can and should this system be changed? And if so, by whom and how? These multifaceted questions provide a powerful example of the kind of dilemma that confronts education as it attempts to meet the needs of individuals, communities, and the larger society. For it is the interrelatedness of the conflicts and their solutions that makes simple answers impossible as well as undesirable. Ridgefield, as a community and as a collection of individuals, may offer answers to that question that differ substantively from either ours or the answers of a larger society. Further, there may be significant differences within the community itself. What is troubling, however, is that it appears that alternatives to the status quo have neither been identified nor systematically explored. Given the encapsulated quality of RHS's educational life (for example, teacher training and background, administrative roots), there are few opportunities for the additional, outside perspectives to be shared meaningfully. This insularity suggests that narrowly focused and externally defined interventions (such as merit pay or teacher examinations) have little hope of significantly altering Ridgefield High School. Effective interventions must deal with the system as a whole and within its community context.

Perhaps the best way to begin is to provide a forum where these complex questions posed by outsiders can be systematically examined by all segments of the insiders. In our view, each of the Ridgefield constituencies is only partially aware of the implicit decisions they have made and totally unaware of the full implications of and alternatives to the way in which they have chosen to school their adolescents. Until they have been empowered to ask and answer these questions for themselves, these questions will remain purely academic and largely irrelevant.

# 7

# ARCHER HIGH SCHOOL

## ROBERT ANDERSON AND ARTHUR DUNNING, JR.

Uniontown, the community in which Archer High School is located, is an incorporated city of approximately 2,000 people. Its Main Street, reminiscent of years past, is the center of activities. Most of the town's stores are located along its two blocks. City Hall is just off Main Street while some of the churches and a few businesses are in other parts of town.

## Setting

Archer High School is about half a mile "across the highway" from Main Street. The location in relation to the business section of town is not unusual. Its position "across the highway" may reflect, however, the basic relationship between the school and the community. It is a point of pride for some and an object of scorn for others. To the black community, it represents a high level of achievement and a promise for the future. To the white community, it is a reminder of other days when there were two high schools in town and life was simple and "good."

Archer was formerly Perry County Training School, an all-black school, and only within the past three years, when two high schools in Uniontown were consolidated, has it had white teachers and students. The consolidation of the two schools has been more in word than in fact. Of the approximately 400 students enrolled this year, only 3 percent are white and the faculty of twenty-three has three white members. The other white children of the community attend a private school in another town about twenty miles away.

General community support for the school is essentially non-existent. Although the mayor and most city council members are black citizens, the wealth and power in Uniontown are largely controlled by white citizens. Parents in positions of influence send their children to the private school. The financial support businesses had once provided for school activities has been greatly reduced and, in many instances, has been discontinued.

In addition to retail sales, the primary business of the Uniontown area is farming, with soy beans, wheat, and cattle as the main products. There are two small manufacturing concerns in town, but they employ only a small number of people. Many residents commute to one of the slightly larger communities approximately 30 miles away in order to find employment. For the youth attending Archer High School, the most prestigious and promising occupation, if they are to stay at home, is in education.

The economy of the school community is directly related to the level of program funding to aid low-income families. A pronounced majority of the parents of Archer students receive some type of financial aid. Almost all the students receive free breakfast and lunch, or pay reduced prices when they choose to eat at school. At the time of our visits to Archer, federal budget cuts were being discussed but had not been felt in the homes of the students. Teachers, students, and parents expressed concern, however, about the future and the difficulty they all expected to have when the proposed reductions were implemented.

Archer High School is a source of pride for its teachers, only two of whom live outside the community. The pride they express is similar in many ways to that of ownership. More than 90 percent of the faculty grew up in or near Uniontown. They graduated from Archer, and now they live within five miles of the school. They remember their high school years as great ones filled with happy memories dominated by basketball games and championships. Many of the teachers became educators because other Archer teachers encouraged them and sometimes helped them go to college.

Faculty pride in the school is highly commendable at a time when professional educators at many schools seem to be experiencing negative feelings. The basis for this pride, however, may need further study. All members of the faculty have baccalaureate degrees, but only one was from an institution outside the state. More than 70 percent have master's degrees, almost half of which were received at the same relatively small institution. The faculty is stable with the average age approximately forty-two and an annual turnover rate of 4 percent (one teacher). The pattern seems clear: students respect the school, and many look upon teaching there as an important life goal. It is less than ideal, however, when the faculty becomes almost entirely composed of former students whose educational and life experiences are very much the same. The result is likely to limit teachers' objectivity about the school and support the continuation of existing patterns and programs with little consideration for alternatives.

The population of Uniontown has been relatively stable for many years. Although six industries that were major sources of employment closed in recent years, and the number of available jobs was decreased dramatically, few families have moved away. In addition, there has been only limited movement into the area.

Students at Archer have few opportunities to travel away from home. Basketball trips, other school-related trips, and shopping in nearby communities constitute most of their experiences outside the hometown area. Television and radio have probably had more effect on their lives than it would be possible to document. These media provide a limited view of the world to this group of teen-agers, but, nonetheless, it is a view that has expanded the concept of life beyond their hometown. As would be expected, the effect has been both positive and negative. Students have lived, vicariously, the lives of those represented in the television plays and serials they chose to view. They have seen and heard something about how people live in other parts of the country and the world, and they have had their sights broadened to the possibilities available to them in education and in work. On the other hand, the nature of the programs selected has also tended to give them a distorted view of life and life styles, one that is somewhat unrealistic in relation to their lives in Uniontown.

The day at Archer High School moves rather smoothly from beginning to end, even though its movement may seem sluggish at times. There are the usual teen-age jokes and teases, but seldom is the relative calm broken by scuffles or other students initiated disturbances. Although students seem to be in the halls for an eternity between classes, the teachers are in charge in the classrooms. It is much more likely that the teacher will be interrupted by an announcement over the intercom than by an act of overt disrespect or misconduct by a student.

Students at Archer High School do not appear noticeably different from students at other schools. The style of their clothes is similar to that of other teen-agers and they are clean and neat.

Teachers generally feel that the students have changed during the past few years. They suggest that many students want to make good grades and receive other rewards without putting forth the effort required. They believe that their students are more oriented to the "now" and are less concerned about their future than they were as high school students.

Teachers are convinced that the difficulty and number of their tasks have increased while rewards for teaching have decreased. They have little interaction with parents about much that matters to them. Few parents, they report, ever ask about curriculum matters or teaching practices. Teachers complain about parents who do not understand the need for students to be in school *all* day *every* day; parents who are unable to offer much assistance to their children with homework and other school-related projects; parents who offer little, through example, to encourage students to set high-level goals for themselves; and parents who seem to expect the school to take increased responsibilities for their children's basic needs. Many of those Archer parents who are employed work in another small city approximately 35 miles away. As a consequence, many of them leave for employment early and arrive home late. These circumstances often discourage active participation in school activities. One teacher noted, "We have students who can be absent from school for several days because parents leave home before it is time for the children to attend school and arrive home after children are scheduled to return home. About the only thing we can get parents out at night for, or during the day, is a basketball game."

Not having productive contacts with the parents is discouraging. In addition, the teachers comment almost universally about the increased paperwork they are required to complete and the financial strains of trying to meet their family responsibilities on salaries that have not kept pace with the cost of living.

## Students

For students, Archer High School is a congenial place to be. It offers an opportunity to be with friends, and it represents the "right thing to do." It is a place where teachers genuinely want them to feel successful and where the pressures of a complex life are eased by the orderliness and calm of the school day.

Many of the homes students come from lack stability and even moderate levels of basic needs. Although some students come from small families, it is not at all uncommon for Archer students to have six to twelve brothers, sisters, and cousins at home with one parent or grandparent. More than 97 percent of the families receive welfare benefits. The adults in a significant number of the homes either do not have jobs or are semi-skilled or unskilled workers. Only slightly more than 25 percent of the parents of Archer students have completed high school.

Although there is an economic need for students to work, there are few jobs available, and very few students are employed. A small number of students live on farms and assist their families with planting and other farm chores. Others have after-school and weekend jobs in local stores or do housework. Many of the students have chores to do at home after school. They may have inside cleaning or gardening to do, or they may be responsible for attending to younger children. A larger number are involved in athletic or band practice, while still others are free of adult supervision and play with friends, watch television, or do whatever else they choose. Free time on weekends is likely to be spent in similar activities, with some visiting in nearby towns. On Sundays, a majority of the students attend church activities.

Alcohol and drugs are used by Archer students, but probably not to the extent common in most high schools of America. Occasionally, a student has to be taken home because of alcohol or drug use, but it happens so infrequently that it is not seen as a problem. Students and faculty members believe that since wine was made available in the grocery stores about two years ago, there has been an increase in the use of alcohol, most of it wine. Marijuana and a variety of pills seem to constitute the drugs occasionally used by students. Harder, more expensive drugs appear not to be available to them.

Crime and vandalism are not much of a problem among students.

While the school building and some of its contents give evidence of lack of care and/o· misuse, this seems to be more a product of inattention, and a growing belief that nothing can be done about the facilities, than of outright vandalism.

Contrary to what might be expected, the dropout rate at Archer is very low—considerably lower than it was ten years ago. Perhaps it is because opportunities for work are more limited. Whatever the reasons, most students expect to stay in school and graduate. Of the sixty-six students in the senior class, teachers and administrators expect that no more than two will fail to graduate at the end of the year.

Students at Archer place a high value on completing high school. Although faculty members feel students are less academically oriented than in past years, students comment, "Everyone should want to get an education and become something." One student said, "Once you get it [an education] they can't take it from you."

The primacy of the individual is important to students at Archer. They feel that everyone should have their own "beliefs" and should live by them. They generally agree that "no one should force you to do things."

Students believe in equality of the sexes, and think that boys (men) should not be treated differently from girls (women). They see it as a simple problem with simple solutions. Except for some concern about voting rights, few mention anything about racial equality. It is almost as if it does not deserve attention. While teachers are discouraged about Uniontown's white students going off to a private school, the students don't talk about it much. Civil rights issues are generally not discussed by them.

Students, for the most part, are not interested in politics. Although two members of the faculty are on the city council, and social studies courses are required for all students, most of the students express a lack of understanding of politics. One student said, "It doesn't do much good to think about things like that." Another remarked, "I don't like to watch the news on TV. I don't know too much about what is going on." Politics seems to be viewed as a necessary evil that must be endured and cannot be understood or changed.

Students accept the fact that authority is needed, but have some concern about people who misuse positions of authority. One student commented, "There always has to be a leader. We need someone in control." Another said, "People shouldn't be rebellious toward the leader," while another said, "Some people have it and don't know what to do with it. They just throw it around."

Religion is a natural part of the lives of most students at Archer. They come from "religious" families and religion "makes you feel good." Many agree that Bible reading and prayer shouldn't be a part of school activities but think that "everybody should have their own say about themselves."

Marriage and child-bearing are almost unrelated in the minds of the students. Most of them are positive about marriage but they don't feel they should get married until they have had time "to build something." Others think it is too easy to get out of a marriage.

Teen-age pregnancy and child-bearing are not viewed as unusual. There appear to be few negative attitudes about this. One student expressed the feeling that, "If God wanted you to have a baby, you would." The main concern of students is that the mother return to school as soon as possible after the child is born and that she not allow the pregnancy and birth to cause her to miss a year away from school.

In informal discussions with us, most students said they intended to go to a four-year college or university after graduation and to enter a profession or skilled occupation. In a recent survey of seniors carried out by the counselor, however, more than 50 percent indicated that they expected to become skilled workers or to enter the military. A follow-up study of graduates of two years ago found 29 percent attending a postsecondary technical school, 27 percent in semi-skilled occupations, 23 percent in four-year colleges or universities, and 16 percent unemployed.

Students at Archer High School may be fairly typical of rural America. They have little stimulation to broaden their interests and involvement. Their thoughts and actions are largely confined to their immediate geographic area. They express little interest in government or politics. Therefore, the interpersonal relationships of the present place and time largely consume them. When, on occasion, they think about the future, they are likely to be idealistic. Yet, when a major change in their lives occurs, graduation from high school, for example, a surprisingly large percentage of them make the change successfully, even though they may experience severe difficulties in the process.

## Goals

The goals of Archer High School are relatively simple yet idealistic. Teachers, administrators, and students agree that the primary goal of the school is to improve the quality of life for students by helping them to prepare for a vocation or to enter the college of their choice. Additional goals include such things as "to allow students to develop according to their abilities," "to develop 'well-rounded,' self-supporting citizens," and "to broaden the horizons of students."

There is little discussion of these goals at Archer, except during preparation for a school accreditation visit. School goals are largely taken for granted. It is accepted that the school exists to help students "learn," that the school is important, that everyone understands the goals of the school, and that there is no real reason for discussion.

The administrators and teachers would like to see the school have a strong academic as well as vocational orientation. They attempt to offer all the courses necessary for college or university admission, and they long for facilities and personnel necessary for additional vocational offerings.

Several conditions make the academic goals difficult for all but a few students. The experiential background of students and the nature of the schooling provided for them have given them minimal preparation for advanced academic work in the high school. In most of the academic classes, the lack of adequate and appropriate materials and equipment, coupled with low expectancy levels, result in an overemphasis on textbooks and tests with little real drive for academic excellence. In these settings, objectives seem to be aimed at achieving the minimum necessary for moving to the next step. A few teachers have academic expectations that are exceptionally high, and they do try to challenge their students in an effort to counter their limiting environment, but there aren't enough to noticeably alter the overall climate.

Facilities and personnel restrict vocational offerings to home economics and vocational agriculture. Although the teachers in these two areas have practical class activities and assignments, materials and equipment are extremely scarce, and the content is narrow and basic. The home economics facility includes the necessary space and equipment for cooking and sewing and a limited, but adequate, space for home economics instruction. The vocational agriculture facility, on the other hand, consists of an old building on another campus approximately a mile and a half from the school. The condition of the building and the equipment supports, at best, only minimal learning experiences.

There are practically no jobs available for high school graduates in the community. Few of the graduates appear to want to leave the area to work, and few can afford to leave to enter higher education. Such factors make the achievement of the school's primary goals problematic.

Despite the grim economic conditions that exist in the community, Archer High School has undergone a major transformation in the last three years. The principal, a native of the area, has been the catalyst of change.

Discipline, authority, and responsibility have been the focus of his plan for change. His commitment to the school is sincere and strong. He suggests that the school is effective in its efforts to prepare black children for productive roles in society. He believes that the school, for many students, provides the discipline, nutrition, and other resources that are lacking at home. He said, "We try to improve the quality of life for our students. We also seem to be preparing them well for future careers."

The principal believes that, "A disciplined and orderly environment is essential for the growth of our kind of student." As a result of this belief, emphasis is placed on rules, regulations, and standards of conduct. The vice-principal monitors the halls and campus to handle between-class stragglers and to maintain order. Adherence to rules and regulations is apparent in the behavior of most students.

In fact, the temper and behavior on campus is disciplined and polite. There is not the preoccupation with safety that pervades the daily life of many large urban high schools. Foyer areas, halls, and bathroom walls are free of drawings and graffiti. Hallways are swept, and students have regular assignments to remove debris and paper from the school grounds.

The students are friendly, and they seem clearly excited when there are visitors in their classes. They are anxious to learn the reasons for the visits, and, when interviewed, they are enthusiastic in discussing career goals. All of the students we talked with expressed hopes of improving their economic well-being. However, for some students, their stated career goals appear to be somewhat exaggerated in light of the opportunities that exist.

In response to questions concerning their lives at school, the students interviewed appeared forthright and sincere. However, a few comments from students regarding rules and regulations can best be described as a bit strident. One student leader who described herself as an "easy-going person," expressed particularly intense feelings about the "excessive and unreasonably burdensome rules at school." She said, "All of these rules are unnecessary because most students behave." Even though several students were harsh and vocal about rules and regulations at school, the majority were untroubled by them.

A majority of students felt that life at school is pleasant, and they feel comfortable when attending school. Most students obey rules and regulations without difficulty. The quality of relationships among students is satisfying and productive. There are few conflicts between students that are not resolved quickly and satisfactorily.

Part of the attempt to provide quality education for students requires that administrators and teachers cooperate and work together on educational matters. In some schools, the principal's straightforward focus on leadership and educational responsibilities is often perceived by teachers as an excessive use of power and decision-making authority. The school climate at Archer encourages the principal to have a direct hand in educational matters. In curriculum areas, he relies on subject-matter committees and self-study committees to utilize the leadership talents of teachers. In this structure, leadership is associated with tasks to be performed rather than power or privileges associated with the principal's position. A fundamental belief of the principal is that a major part of his responsibility is to provide the resources and proper environment for leadership.

Of the nineteen teachers, a majority seems to feel that the school environment is pleasant and open. However, several are concerned about excessive paperwork. One teacher commented, "We don't see the sense of all the paperwork we have to complete." Another commented, "I have worked in rigid and constricting environments before, and to work here is a welcome relief! I believe our principal's way of running this school is the reason that most teachers like to work here."

Several teachers also noted that it is the behavior of the principal that largely sets the tone for interaction between groups at the school. They respect his propensity for hard work, warm human relations, and consideration for the needs of others. His leadership style is characterized as a mixture of autocratic and democratic. Structure, authority, assigned rules and vertical communications are strongly emphasized, but he is perceived by teachers as warm, cooperative, open, and friendly.

Communication, a problem in many schools, is reasonably good at Archer High. "Don't get me wrong, we have our grapevines and gossip like everywhere else, but we can get the information we need without difficulty," one teacher commented. "Weekly faculty meetings are held for information dissemination and to receive questions from us." Because the school is located in a small rural community, one gets the feeling that communication within the school and to the community is relatively free of distortion. There is generally enough information available about problems in the school to ensure that a correct identification of the difficulties can be made. "We have the information we need to do our jobs, and usually we get it without any problems," one teacher noted.

One frequent criticism voiced by teachers is that goals for student academic performance are not clearly defined by administrators or teachers. The basis for this concern is the low scores students make on the standardized achievement tests. Faculty members who express this concern believe that too many teachers have low expectations of students. They do not accept the fact that nothing can be done about low student performance because parents are no longer interested in school activities.

The effective utilization and overall coordination of resources are such that teachers are neither overloaded nor idle. There seems to be minimal strain regarding their duties and work assignments. The teachers feel that they work very hard and that they are not working against themselves or against the organization. The role expectancies of the environment are suitable for their temperament. One possible reason for this is that many of the teachers are graduates of the school.

In summary, most teachers feel that the school's goals and priorities are reasonably clear and reasonably well accepted by the staff. However, those who differ note that clarity and acceptance do not mean necessarily that the school is functioning as it should. They believe that the present goals are not achievable with existing or available resources nor are they congruent with the needs of the environment.

## Curriculum

The curriculum at Archer High School has been limited to that required by the state department of education for high school graduation. This year, however, it was decided that no student in this school would have an assigned study hall. Therefore, since the schedule includes six periods, each student has six rather than five classes, as was customary.

The state department of education requirements are traditional. They consist of 4 units of English, 3 units of social studies, 1 unit of science, 2 units of math, 3 units of physical education, ½ unit of health, 6 units of electives, and ½ unit of driver education.

Electives provide the only flexibility in the curriculum. Previously, students took six electives during their four years in high school. Now, with the elimination of study halls, they must take an additional elective each year, which gives them ten during high school. As students are not permitted to take less than a full load of subjects, they may have as many as twenty-four units when they graduate. The electives available to them include: algebra, band, biology, chemistry, geometry, junior ROTC, shorthand, Spanish, trigonometry, typewriting, vocational agribusiness, vocational home economics, and world history.

ROTC was added to the program this year and promises to be very popular and valuable. Most of the student leaders are enthusiastic about ROTC and the instructors are qualified, experienced men who are liked by everyone on campus. In addition to the stated objectives, ROTC opens a new area for students. It provides them with challenges as well as recognition. Faculty members feel that it will have a significant, positive effect on the entire school.

Although a majority of the students score below the national norm on standardized tests, there are no remedial courses on the schedule and no teachers are available to provide remedial assistance. One special education teacher works as a resource teacher with approximately fifty educably mentally retarded students. She is the only "special" teacher in the school. Teachers indicate considerable concern about students' inability to read, but there is little evidence that reading help is being given in the "regular" classes.

The counselor meets with groups of students each year to review course offerings and to assist with course selections for the next year. Home room teachers provide additional help in the course selection process. Although the school does not identify any tracks, students and teachers acknowledge that some graduates will go to postsecondary institutions, others will go to work, and others will be unemployed.

The selection of elective courses is intended to support the aspirations of individual students. Students indicate that this is the basis of most of their selections, but the reputations of particular teachers contribute to their choices. Taking a course to be with a friend is of some importance. However, because the school is small, and friends are likely to be together in other classes, this does not seem to keep students from taking courses they want or need.

One day each year is devoted to careers. During the entire day, representatives from various career fields and postsecondary institutions are in the school. They make brief presentations at an assembly program and have sessions with all the seniors to help them learn more about the career and/or institution they represent. A large number of careers and institutions are represented each year, and students look forward to the day. Frequently, graduates of the school return as a career-day "consultant."

A state minimum competency examination is required in the ninth grade and a state graduation examination is to be initiated next year for all students in the eleventh grade. It will be necessary for students to pass the three sections of the graduation exam—reading, language, and mathematics—before they can receive a high school diploma.

Teachers and students express concern about the competency examination and the graduation examination. Students in this school have had low scores on the competency tests, and teachers feel that they will have difficulty with the graduation test also. Except for a few teachers who have been working on their own, there does not appear to be any follow-up on the results of the competency examinations, either to use them as diagnostic tools or to provide additional instruction in areas where need is shown. It seems as if teachers and students expect trouble but do not know how to prevent it.

Curriculum materials used at Archer are largely limited to adopted textbooks provided by the state. Aside from a small amount of money for instructional materials, which comes from the legislative appropriation, few funds exist for instructional support. Those available are used for duplication supplies and the barest essentials. A few pieces of audiovisual equipment are available, as are some materials to use with them, but when equipment is broken or a bulb burns out, it is likely to be out of service for the remainder of the school year—or beyond. Science classrooms are not much different from other rooms. The furniture is appropriate for laboratory activities but the required equipment and materials are not likely to be available. A mixture of electric and manual typewriters is in the typing room, and most of them are operable. The home economics rooms seem to be adequately equipped. There is no piano or other musical instruments in the room where the school choir meets.

Teachers want more instructional materials. On the other hand, it appears that they have not worked together to secure the materials that might be available through some pooling of resources. Only a few indicate much awareness about materials that might greatly enhance their teaching. There is little evidence that teachers improvise or secure free and inexpensive materials from local sources. Most teachers seem resigned to using the textbooks supplemented by occasional use of materials from the library.

## Teachers

Teachers at Archer High School can be best described as interested in the school and the continuing development of their students. Because most of them are natives of the area and were students in this school, they can easily identify with the students and the local community. Generally, their values, beliefs, and mores are the same as those of the school and community.

Several teachers feel that it is important for the school to hire teachers with similar value systems who have "an understanding of what it is like to live in our town." A few teachers disagree. One teacher noted that some of the problems at the school can be attributed to the fact that too many teachers are graduates of Archer and the same state university. She believes that the school will not grow and prosper until more teachers are employed with varied value systems, or until something is done to lessen the provincial outlook of many of the teachers.

Of the eighteen teachers, thirteen hold advanced degrees, all from colleges and universities within the state. To promote the continuing professional development of its teachers, the school district has a very active and ambitious in-service program conducted largely by faculty members from a nearby university. A few teachers continue to enroll in courses at state universities during the summer and in off-campus courses during the academic year.

As a group, the teachers are very active in community and governmental affairs. The following organizations were identified as those in which teachers lend active support: (1) the Civic League, (2) city government, (3) the district education association, (4) the public library, (5) Boy Scouts of America, (6) Girl Scouts of America, and (7) boards of local churches.

With one exception, all members of the faculty were the first in their families to receive a college degree. Yet, one of the strongest influences to enter teaching came from their parents, who expressed a desire to "make a better life for their children." A number of the teachers were among the earliest supporters of Archer during the early years of "integration," and they take considerable pride in being teachers in the school.

Most of the planning for in-service activities is done by central office staff and school administrators. The teachers are somewhat divided regarding the usefulness of the in-service program. Many express the need for assistance in getting parents of students involved in and supportive of school activities. Many express a desire for help in motivating low achievers. As it is presently structured, teachers do not believe the in-service program addresses these primary needs.

The teachers' feelings regarding tenure range from "very necessary" to "good." One teacher noted that tenure is "essential for good teachers, but often protects the very poor teachers." None of them would like to see it abolished. Tenure was viewed by some as a needed benefit for persons in a low-paying profession.

Teachers' strongest feelings are centered around competency exams. Several feel that competency exams for teachers would help improve the "image" of the teaching profession. In contrast, one teacher feels that "teacher competency exams are not needed. There already are enough hurdles for one to cross to enter the teaching profession." Their reactions to this issue indicate that teachers are concerned with their work and with their public image.

## Teaching and Learning

Because of the size and stability of the school and the community, the teachers know all of the students and their families. They know that although there are some strong academic students, only a few of them can read the textbooks with ease. Most of the students struggle with the language and must work hard to get through reading assignments. There are some students who find reading so difficult that an assignment in the textbook will not be read.

Perhaps because of student learning difficulties, the experiential background of teachers, the minimal level of instructional involvement of administrators, and the limited participation of parents, teaching is largely traditional in nature. In the classroom the teacher is "in charge." The learning process is directed by the teacher with very little initiative taken by students. Some "project" assignments are made, but almost every day an assignment is made in the textbook. In class, students are asked frequently to read a portion of the lesson from the text and teachers then ask questions about the content, or add further personal explanations from their own knowledge and experience.

Tests are very important at Archer. Teachers frequently remind students that a certain bit of information is important to remember for the next test. In most classes, a "big" test is given every six weeks, or at the completion of a unit of work. Prior to these tests, a class session is usually devoted to review. It is not uncommon for teachers to prepare a series of questions and ask students to look up the answers outside class. These questions and answers are then used as a basis for the review.

Teachers are concerned that their grading is "fair." Almost all of them keep detailed information in their grade books and include as many different kinds of sources as possible. In addition to scores on tests, they are likely to give "credit" for the completion of outside assignments with as much or more value given for completeness and proper use of form as for correctness.

Classes are generally routine, with the only sign of enthusiasm coming from the teacher's interest in the subject being covered. There are a few exceptions. A few teachers, because of the nature of the subjects they teach, work with students in small groups or individually. This usually occurs in classes where life skills are to be learned. Even here, the teacher directs the activity and students follow instructions with little or no creativity.

A typical class period is scheduled for fifty minutes with five minutes between periods. However, there does not seem to be enough time. It is frequently five to eight minutes after the "tardy" bell rings before any class activity is likely to begin. The teacher usually calls the complete roll and then directs the class to an assignment that has been written on the board. Most frequently this is a section they are to read in their textbook. Alternatively, the teacher may call on a student to begin reading to the class from a section previously assigned in the text.

The class proceeds in about the same manner from beginning to end on most days. Exceptions may occur when there is a review for a test, a test, or a review of the test when the papers are returned.

It is not uncommon for classes to be interrupted by assembly programs, students on errands, announcements, and other events. There is no regular activity schedule. Therefore, when there is an assembly program, a club meeting, or any other type of special event, classes must be cancelled. There are times when these events seem to be relatively unplanned and unexpected by the teachers. On these occasions, classes are omitted and plans are not made to compensate for the time missed. When classes are meeting, interruptions are not infrequent. Students may be allowed to enter classrooms and to talk with other students for various purposes with little or no apparent thought about the disturbance of the teaching-learning process. When students, teachers, or adminstrators are needed in the office, they are called over the intercom. The call goes out to every room in the building that is connected to the system. There may be some periods when no one is called, but, usually, there are several calls during each class period.

At the conclusion of a class, if the teacher has covered the material intended for the day, students may be allowed to find something they want to do until the bell rings. On the other hand, a teacher may detain the students for a few minutes to cover material in the day's lesson plan.

In most classrooms, control is not a problem. New teachers quickly learn that students are not to be given a chance to misbehave. During the time when the teacher is "in charge," students are expected to be quiet whether they are actively involved in the lesson or not. It appears that more emphasis is placed on having students refrain from disturbing others than it is for them to participate in the class. When the teacher gives the students time on their own, however, student behavior does not seem to be a major concern of the teacher, who may not even indicate an awareness of the noise level.

When there are behavior problems in classrooms, teachers usually send the offenders to the guidance counselor or the assistant principal. The problem is then handled outside the class with the understanding that disruptions are not to take place during a class.

Teachers are relatively autonomous. They have textbooks that are adopted for use in the school, but they are free to vary the content according to their knowledge and desires. Most of them choose to follow the text almost from beginning to end and with relatively little expansion.

Teachers are expected to meet after school every Wednesday for a faculty meeting. Approximately two of these meetings each month are devoted to staff development activities. At these times, a committee or a member of the faculty is assigned to lead the group. Sometimes, members of the faculty bring reports from meetings or readings and sometimes a consultant is secured to speak to the group. There are no recognized objectives for the meetings, nor is there evidence that changes occur as a result of them.

Three or four days each year are devoted to staff development meetings that are planned by members of the school district's central office staff. On these days, students are not in school, and educators meet in a central location with all others in the district. These meetings are planned with little or no assistance from faculty members. Teachers attend sessions that are planned for them with no preparation prior to the meetings and no follow-up after the meetings. Although those who plan these meetings may have objectives or themes in mind, teachers usually see them as sometimes interesting one-day meetings with little relationship to their practice.

## Education Beyond the School

Although there is considerable evidence that teachers at Archer High School are active in community and governmental affairs, there is little evidence that the school has established partnerships with outside agencies. Work-study, internships, and volunteer-service experiences are not available for students through any formalized agreement with any external agencies.

## Media and Technology

Television, the most powerful medium of communication in the lives of students at Archer High School, has caused changes in the way many perceive and act upon their public and private world. Before the advent of television, a child growing up in Uniontown built his or her model of reality from images received from a tiny handful of sources—the teacher, or minister, and above all, the family, usually an extended family. There were only a few radios in town to give a child the chance to learn something about people who lived in other regions of the country and who had life styles different from their own. The few people that students met from other places were relatives who had moved away and returned "home" for visits. The result was that students had only a small number of people to imitate or to use as models. Their choices were even more limited by the fact that their role models were themselves of limited experience.

The older teachers agree with this description of life in the community before television. One teacher noted that children heard the same "thou shall not"s in church and in school. There was little interaction with people from outside the community. Strong pressures to conform from school, home, and church acted on children from birth to narrow still further the range of acceptable behaviors.

In recent years, most families have television, and some have moved from one set and one channel to two sets receiving several channels. Students now receive the same images that flow to all parts of the country and the world. They are faced with new models and new life styles. However, for the most part, the church, the school, and a number of the families continue to agree with and to support the values of earlier years. The resulting conflict between the media and the community makes it increasingly more complicated for students as they begin to make life decisions.

The school library subscribes to two daily newspapers and several national magazines. The librarian indicates that few students read the newspapers or magazines because of lack of interest, lack of time, or low reading ability. To encourage reading of books, magazines, and newspapers, she stated, "I will let them keep materials as long as they want them or until someone else needs them and I will allow them to take as much as they can carry in their arms."

Student estimates of the amount of television they view range from two to six hours nightly and from twelve to fifteen hours each weekend. Athletic events, situation comedies, and crime drama are the most popular.

Little of what they see relates to what they do in school. Many students are members of families that receive public assistance. The "good life" image portrayed by television is far removed from their daily realities.

So many hours of television explain, for many teachers, why opinions on everything from authority to drugs and alcohol have become less uniform among their students. Consensus, in many areas, has been shattered. One teacher commented that "since our students spend so much time watching television, they are bombarded with messages that are often contradictory or unrelated. This really shakes up any old-fashioned ideas that are being taught."

Many of the teachers, yearning for the accepted moral and cultural certainties of the past, are irritated by the changes television has caused in the teaching and learning process. They say that the respect for authority and the desire to learn have decreased. They feel that students want immediate gratification in most areas of their lives. One teacher attributed this change to the way most students receive information from television—the thirty-second commercial, a ninety-second news update. Huge amounts of information are provided in short periods of time and major problems are solved in a one-hour show. She commented that "this placed an enormous burden on persons responsible for teaching demanding and rigorous subject matter. The idea of any exhaustive study of diverse concepts is unlikely."

Many students encounter difficulty with academic subjects because of serious deficiencies in reading. Almost without exception, teachers identified this problem as the most critical one for students. One teacher commented, "I don't mean to equate illiteracy with stupidity. We have students who have highly developed skills in farming, music, sports, and hunting."

For teachers, literacy is far more than a job skill. Along with skills needed for academic subjects, they are concerned with helping students prepare for an environment in which machines and appliances are programmed to talk. The role of literacy in the lives of Archer students will be different than of earlier generations.

Students do not have the opportunity to use computers in school and it is doubtful that any are available in homes. With present economic conditions and competing needs, it is not likely that the school will purchase a computer in the near future.

# 8

# PRAIRIE VIEW HIGH SCHOOL

CECELIA E. TRAUGH

$\mathbb{G}$eographic isolation and small size are important aspects of a rural school in this state. For the school's structure, being rural means that a central administration, consisting of a superintendent and his secretary, are housed in the high school building.

For the teachers, it means that they are a homogeneous group—all but one are white and all but three were educated in the state. Those teachers who stay are from rural communities and most often from the area. It also means that they have broad teaching responsibilities and that there are no reading or special education specialists to assist with classes that include students whose abilities differ. Two teachers have five different subjects to teach during the six-hour day; six teachers have four; eight have three. The school has never been able to fill the state-mandated positions in special education, speech therapy, or reading.

For students, being rural means that they must travel long distances for sports competitions, that very few out-of-school or family work opportunities are available, that the curriculum is limited in its variety or specialization.* Prairie High students participate in a social life that is not accessible elsewhere, and they are known by name by all adults in the school. In this particular school, rural does not mean a homogeneous student body for one-half of the student population is Indian.

* Examples of available courses in English include English I, II, American Literature, and Indian Literature; in science there are Physical Science, Biology (general or regular), Ecology (1 semester), Human Physiology (1 semester), and Chemistry; in math, Vocational Math, Algebra I and II, Geometry and Trigonometry are offered; in business, there are Bookkeeping, Typing I and II, General Business (1 semester), Business Law (1 semester), Office Filing (1 semester), and Business Machines courses.

## Teachers' School Life: Attempts to Communicate Purpose

No goals of education are presented in the various handbooks available to faculty, students, and parents. A "Statement of Philosophy" is provided instead. It affirms the school's close connection to the community: "The Prairie View Public School is vitally aware that the school of today is the school of the people it serves." It encourages students to "attain academic excellence and social well being. . . ." It describes the faculty as "educators who are knowledgeable in their subject matter and who are dedicated to serving all students and their needs," and the "physical facilities," as "comfortable, aesthetically pleasant, and conducive to learning."

One teacher was "scared" to respond to questions about goals; another said to look at the teachers' manual, and one didn't know "if they've been coherently thought out." Even so, most teachers and both administrators were able to delineate their personal goals for the school. Many of the faculty prefaced their remarks about goals with, "Well, I don't really know. Perhaps . . ." However, their descriptions are congruent with the intents of the "Statement of Philosophy" in that they relate to what they want students to become and what they want the school to become. In regard to students, teachers believe they are "attempting to develop functional adults," "providing a public service by making kids better citizens," "helping develop self-discipline so these young people can contribute to society," "preparing them for participating in the 'adult world'—for dealing with society and other people," and "helping them develop pride." In sum, "We should put out a *product* [the administrator using this word later said it probably wasn't the most appropriate one he could have chosen] that has the ability to learn, that is emotionally mature and not the victim of life, and that feels good about having been at Prairie View High."

In regard to the high school itself, teachers and administrators want it to be a place where students can "have some fun" and "select an occupation." It should also provide opportunities for "the better students to get a well-rounded education," or for "each student to have a broad education." Related to these goals for the school, teachers believe some curricular changes are needed: make all classes more interesting; drastically change science and social studies courses; hire at least one more teacher in every area so class sizes can be reduced;

add a first aid course; provide more science and language; develop remedial reading and math programs; stress exposure, not specialization; develop a tracking system. The principal was the only person whose goals included the acquisition of physical objects. He wants to "get more computers and to build a lounge with offices in it for teachers."

In regard to the community, goals were stated two ways: "Encourage more community support"; and "Develop harmony between school and community." Internally, the school's need to develop "better interaction between Indians and whites" was frequently mentioned.

Two goals, both stated by teachers, defy categorization, yet they are critical to understanding the teachers' views of this school. The first was mentioned in discussions of both goals and of current expectations. "Our most important goal is to get attendance and graduation numbers up." The second was stated in connection with what the teachers want the school *not* to become. "Teachers here don't want a White Hills." White Hills is an all-Indian high school on the nearby reservation. The teacher turnover rate is high; student attendance is reputed to be sporadic; horror stories abound. As the number of Indian students grows, both goals seem increasingly to be voiced.

With a few exceptions, teachers were very general in their discussion of school goals. They were not the ones to offer plans for new programs or for changes in the school building. Discussions of overall goals, long or short term, are not at all regular and, perhaps, do not occur among teachers.

While not offered in direct response to our discussions on goals, some of the assessments of the school's program add to an understanding of teachers' views of the school's purposes. "The academically bright are not being challenged [and] the curriculum is watered down." "The present image of the school is one of getting Indian students through—actually all students—but what are we doing for them? We have no reading program, and we can't get Indian students to stay in college. It does seem as if we are just cranking them out." "I know something is wrong, but I can't change it"—a reference to student behavior and discipline learned from parents. "Schools everywhere are not accomplishing what they should." In relation to the program, the principal acknowledges that "we don't reach everybody. Some are not prepared to live in society." But, he also believes "there are opportunities to get involved and to have fun. We provide a good 'basic' education. Students can learn to interact here."

The school has changed over time, and, for teachers, student attendance has become a greater problem. "This is not just an Indian problem; it needs to be 'cracked down' on." Student attitudes and behavior also appear different. "There is more apathy among students. This year, my geometry class can't get to where I want it. It is a little more difficult to stress 'hard core education,' the basics." "I don't see much difference in the area of respect in my classes. However, students are able to get away with things more easily; they are less willing to accept consequences. Teachers fear handing out a consequence; they don't want their car to get egged."

"When I first came here," a teacher said, "ten percent of the students were Indian. They were quiet and looked down at their desks. They are not that way now. They can express themselves. This is a sign of growth. I don't know if the cause is the change in the ratio or a change in the students." For a number of teachers, the question raised in this last statement is an unspoken theme running through their conversations about the school.

One teacher mentioned other changes. "Teachers are better trained now. If students cooperated more, we would be even better. It takes a stronger teacher to be successful now." Another, whose pupils include the children of former students, said, "We did well in hiring new teachers this year. They are friendly and enthusiastic. We have had only four superintendents in thirty years."

While teachers are not firmly convinced that they are universally successful in achieving school-wide goals, they talk easily about the purposes of their particular classes. "Getting the job done" most often focuses on presenting content. This might be "introducing English to all students and providing a broad base [in English] so they can handle anything else they get." It might be "exposing students to a wider variety of music than the radio," or, "preparing for higher math [or science]." "Getting kids to write coherently," "to know literary terms," or "to learn about the prairie biome," are other examples of ways content-oriented purpose is specifically described.

Somehow connecting content with life is another dream of teachers. Statements of this goal often pertain to students' future lives. For example, one teacher sought to "develop a sense of communication, as it is basic to success in life." Another said, "I am training future secretaries." Still another asserted that "knowledge of government is really important because it's material they will use." In a similar vein, we were told, "Indians should learn English because they need to broaden their horizons; they can't 'live off the land'; they gotta be prepared to live in the white world; they can't live in their own world." Teachers also have hopes of helping students now. They talk about assisting students to "enjoy reading," "know themselves," "write to express themselves," "develop listening skills," "become aware that what happens now is history." They say they want to "keep them [students] going and not be quitters," to "challenge" them, or help them "learn to take notes."

A third, very small category of teachers expressed interest in "teaching students to think." A mathematics teacher reported the emphasis has changed over the years from "stressing the picky little things" (memorization of theorems, for example), to emphasizing "figuring things out." In the physical sciences, the goal is described as "critical thinking and problem solving." In art, attempts to teach techniques through "step-by-step planning processes" are no longer made because students appear to have found them too difficult. Instead, more direct teacher guidance is given to each student.

Connections between those goals that are related to learning content and what the teachers do and require in the classroom are the most easily made. In fact, it appears that the remaining two groups of goals are infrequently approached directly but are instead hoped-for side effects of the study of subject matters.

## Teachers' School Life: Environments They Construct

Situated one block north of Main Street, the school building is easily found and identified. It is a one-story building on a large open space, with a flag pole, buses, and a few cars in a surprisingly small parking lot.

At the door, visitors are told to check in at the office. In the entryway, the smell of lunch and a big picture of the 1980 state Class B basketball champions greet all who enter. There are five doors to the building, but, unless one has a key, one enters through the front door—and through that only after 8:30 A.M.

There are only four distinctive pieces in the classroom puzzle of Prairie View High School. The art room is somewhat special, with its clean-up sink at the front and individual work and storage benches instead of desks. The science rooms can be identified largely because they include lab facilities. The chemistry/physical science room is divided between classroom space and lab benches. The biology room is equipped with immovable lab tables that double as desk space. In the home economics room, desks and tables are crowded among the cooking lab stations. All other classrooms are nearly identical, each filled with rows of desks, some with tell-tale sinks and closets that recall their previous use as elementary classrooms.

If it were not for special occasions, it appears that classrooms would by and large show no signs of the activities they house. Students' work is not displayed as regular practice. There are few signs of ongoing teacher or student projects. Empty animal cages are stored in the biology room. The teachers and students do not impose themselves on their environment. The rooms are places to be for an hour at a time; few expect anything more of them.

There is a typical pattern of events in a class hour at Prairie View, although variations occur many times each day in most subject areas. Some teachers move from room to room, pushing their portable "desks" in front of them; others use the interval between classes to dart into the lounge for a smoke or a quick cup of coffee. A teacher often comes into the classroom with the students, just before the bell rings. The first task of the hour is taking attendance. This is the teacher's responsibility; no class monitors are used. After the absence list is posted by the door, the day's "lecture" begins. The teacher is the principal actor, listing points while students take notes. Usually, few questions are asked either by the teacher or by the students. After ten to fifteen minutes of the lecture, the teacher gives an assignment for students to work on quietly at their desks. Then, the teacher sits at his or her desk reading or waiting for student questions. Less frequently, a teacher will walk among the desks for the remaining twenty to thirty minutes.

Variations on the lecture format are found in classes that help students solve problems, such as math and chemistry, lab sessions in sciences, classes in which media are frequently used, or in classes that are oriented to practicing manual skills.

One variation on the lecture is solving problems on the board. While this, too, is the teacher's activity, students are invited to participate. Lab sessions occur in chemistry and biology once every six to ten days. In these sessions, students complete the experiments outlined in the text's lab manuals. In courses for which text materials are few, media, most frequently videotapes and movies, serve as partial substitutes.

Art classes and the vocational-technical courses are structured differently than the "academics" in that they focus on individual student projects. The teacher's role is one of observing, helping at critical points, prodding into action, and waiting for questions to arise. Each student spends the entire class period on his own work.

In many ways, the teacher makes it clear to students what they need to know to pass the course: "I'll write on the board what you need to know"; ". . . helium we won't worry about"; "Don't worry, we won't have problems that hard [on the test]." On the overhead, a list of terms that serves as the basis for a lecture is as clear as a direct statement. In all cases, the lectures are a primary means of providing information to students.

Often, teachers use notetaking phrases: "Only a couple of things I want to throw at you today . . . isolationism—using a natural barrier for protection." In another class, we heard, "Segregate—to keep races apart. Integrate—to mix races." Lectures closely follow the texts. Little or no elaboration, expansion of ideas, or inquiry-type discussion is included. The teacher's assumption appears to be either that students have not read the text, which contains most, if not all, of the information in the lecture, or that if they read it, they did not understand it.

Most teachers provide class time for students to complete their assignments or their "homework." "I want to go home at four, and so do the students." Students' use of the time varies. Teachers intend, however, to give them opportunities to complete their daily work comprised of end-of-the-chapter questions, work sheets on the chapter of the novel or story they are reading, problems from the text, vocabulary sentences, preparation for chapter tests, or completion of semester or nine-week assignments such as four- to six-page research papers for a history class, one to five book reports for English, Contemporary History, or Indian Literature classes, or the poems, legends, or four-paragraph essay required in Indian Literature.

The mainstay of regular class activity is the textbook. Texts are the bases for lectures; they provide questions and problems for assignments; the teachers' guides supply tests and work sheets. "The materials textbook companies supply save me a lot of time," one teacher told us. Teachers of the new courses for which there are no texts express consternation, at least at first. However, in most cases, this uncomfortable situation results in the use of a wide variety of materials that reflect more of the Prairie View setting and that are generally more interesting to teach and learn from. For Indian Literature, Indian Language, and locally oriented ecology courses, teachers have collected a range of print materials. For Contemporary History, the teachers use videotaped materials they glean from cable TV; trade books, such as *Coming of Age in Mississippi*, *Helter Skelter*, and *Nam*; and their own collections of primary sources on the Vietnam War.

Some curriculum project materials and State Department of Public Instruction materials are used, particularly in the vocational areas such as electronics, business, and home economics. While their appearance is less formal than a text, their properties are much the same.

Classroom life does not go on without interruptions, which teachers accommodate, often with very little advance notice. In fact, some weeks appear to teachers to be nothing but shortened schedules and cancelled classes. Seniors are often out of class for visits to career day displays or conversations with university and college recruiters. Classes are cancelled for the Iowa Tests of Basic Skills. Students take off the first day of the hunting season. Athletes leave in the afternoon to travel to competitions at schools some distance from Prairie View. Periods are shortened to provide time for events such as parent-teacher conferences and Indian Day. Students provide interruptions when they are tardy, visit with their friends at the wrong time, or doze off. Teachers usually react to these variations in the flow of events quickly and easily, but they are at least momentarily sidetracked. Teachers themselves regularly vary the routine by letting classes "go to the library." Except for math, art, and vocational classes, students in every class spend an hour in the library about once a week. The absence of study-hall time in the students' schedules is the basic rationale for this activity, but most teachers do not impose any requirements on how library time is spent other than in reading the magazines, newspapers, and books that are available. Exceptions to this practice are the Contemporary History, Physical Science and Chemistry courses. Teachers in these classes have structured research, journal critique, or book review assignments that are supposed to be accomplished during the time spent in the library.

The teachers at Prairie View High School do not believe expectations for students are what they once were. The superintendent holds that the school's expectations are not particularly high, explaining, "We have a very large disadvantaged population." Some teachers describe pressures to continue to adapt; others describe the inevitable and almost daily conflicts resulting from different expectations held by teachers and students. While acknowledging different times and students, the changes are generally believed to be evidence of decline. That is the implication of statements such as: "In English I, no speech is required because the Indian students are shy." "Having levels of classes shows how we have made a diploma easy to get; we put it on a silver platter." "Students have trouble reading and understanding. The teacher needs to introduce material so that students understand." "I expect students to be on time, to do work when given time in class. I believe that because I am training secretaries, punctuality and attendance are important. Students say, 'When I start working for money, my attitude will change.' "

In part, teachers define their expectations and their standards in terms of their grading systems. Again, teachers seem to be seeing themselves as making accommodations and, in so doing, lowering standards. A teacher of six years speaks: "Because about five out of seventy freshmen can't read at all, I try to make English survivable, so I grade by points. One-half of the grade is based on a journal in which quantity is most important [they are to write three pages each week]. Students earn points by doing it and can pass with a D by doing the journal and work sheets. In English I, one-third should have failed; sixteen [23 percent] did. Thirteen earned an A. I believe teachers on the whole have lowered standards. My personal standards are lower than when I went to school. My first year, I had too high standards. A score of 95 percent was an A, now it's 90 percent; 70 percent was a pass; now it's 60 percent. If I held to 70 percent almost half of the students would be lost." A teacher of twenty years: "Standards have slipped. In my advanced classes I still use 93 percent for an A, 86 percent for a B, 70 percent for a pass; in other classes I use 90 percent for an A and 60 percent to pass." A teacher of thirty years: "I can't help think that standards have slipped. Athletes are better, but in classes, I can't cover the material the way I once did."

Teachers base their grades on a variety of types of work or of personal characteristics: "Contemporary History is not difficult. I try to make it possible for all to do OK. Grades are based on a 90, 80, 70 scale. One-third is based on book reports. Participation is taken into account. No one failed in the first nine weeks. There were five A's and a few D's. There were three no credits."* The music teacher said: "In band, I use a point system to grade. Students earn points by attending class and rehearsals, and playing at athletic contests. They can earn extra points by taking lessons." "Grades in physical science," a teacher said, "are based on daily work, quizzes, tests, and an estimation of whether or not the student is working to capacity. The span of grades for the first nine weeks was A, 25 percent; B, 25 percent; C, 35 percent; and D, 15 percent." A mathematics teacher told us, "I try to determine their potential. I reward personal qualities. Ninety percent is an A. No one earned less than a C in geometry. I seldom give less than a C, unless the students don't work."

What do teachers think about their teaching and their effectiveness? A small number of teachers said that they asked students for information about their teaching, but only one continues that direct interaction. Currently, the teachers' own evaluations of themselves as teachers are based mainly on informally gathered information, and instinct. Some typical comments were:

> I've tried everything. I know my strengths and weaknesses. I've learned over time through trial and error. I measure myself chiefly by what progress students make. Principals have played a small role.

> I measure success by receptivity and this varies from year to year.

> I use the response I get from kids.

> My assessment of my teaching results from what I feel, what I sense.

> I expect a lot from English students and feel successful when students learn it. I feel successful when teachers say next year that students are doing well.

* A "no credit" is given when a student is absent from a class ten or more days.

## Teachers' School Life: Professionalism

The teachers at Prairie View entered the profession for many different reasons. For some, it was "a long-term desire." "I don't remember deciding," one teacher said, "I was just always going to do it. I wouldn't want to do anything else, except maybe be a librarian." The principal, too, "always wanted to be a teacher, and I enjoyed [my teaching] immensely. I coached, directed plays." Others were specifically looking for a way to serve. "Why did I become a teacher?" one began. "A good question. I wanted to make things better and to work with people. I had a secretarial job that had only limited contact with people. And I always looked up to teachers." Another teacher said, "I thought I would enjoy working with teachers. I am a liberal type and wanted to accomplish something with my life. I thought I could get kids interested in grammar, literature. I thought I could make a difference in the lives of kids. Money was not important."

Some knew that teaching would provide a way for them to do what they really wanted to do. "I wanted to coach basketball. When I began, I didn't think of myself as a teacher, but as a coach." Others saw teaching as a means of continued connection with a subject, music for example. Circumstance was the compelling factor for a few:

> I started out in wildlife management. After two years of military service, I ended up in a town with a teacher's college, so I ended up a teacher. I have two great loves, biology and woodworking. Being a game warden required more training.
>
> I lived near a teacher's college and wanted to go there to school. So, I was trained to teach. Since then, I have found myself over- and under-qualified for other jobs. Why did I return to teaching after being a principal . . . for five years? I was tired of taking on everyone's problems as my own. I had less unrestricted time.

Still others wanted to do something else, but decided instead to teach in high school. One, for example, "wanted to do something with kids while waiting to go to medical school." Another started in college wanting to be an accountant, but, in the beginning, he thought he could set an example for kids. While working as a restaurant cook, a teacher who had wanted to teach on the college level "got some experience helping kids and found it fun. I went back to school to earn certification."

Seventeen faculty members teach one or more courses in grades nine through twelve. All but one of them are native to the state, coming from towns similar in size to Prairie View. Three teachers were educated outside the state. Of those educated in the state, two graduated from the universities, and twelve from three small teachers' colleges in the state. Of this latter group, nine grew up and were educated in this part of the state.

All of the content-area teachers at Prairie View teach in their major or minor fields. In science, the current chemistry teacher majored in chemistry, and the biology teacher majored in biology; in math, both teachers majored in their field. Of the English teachers, two have majors in English, one took English as a minor, with a major in physical education. All of the social studies teachers are coaches of major sports; two majored in physical education with minors in social studies; one has a major in history. Teachers in the vocational areas and computer science are not regularly certified teachers. They have specialized expertise and teach on a provisional basis.

Teachers and administrators have a considerable range of experience. Of the teachers working with students in grades seven through twelve, five are new to the district and four are new to teaching. Two of these new people teach physical education in grades nine through twelve; one of the new arrivals is the music teacher; two teach primarily in the junior high, with one teaching one ninth-grade math class. Coming to Prairie View with two years of teaching experience, the principal has had no prior administrative positions, but is close to completing a master's degree in administration. The superintendent has been in Prairie View two years, having had two years of teaching and eight years of central office administrative experience in one of the state's larger school districts. He has a master's degree in administration. The counselor is also new to the district but came with some experience in a rural district in the eastern half of the state.

Of the teachers who are not new to the school, four have been teaching there for four to seven years, seven for ten to fifteen years, two for twenty, and one for over thirty years. Nine of these teachers have had all of their experience in Prairie View. The teacher with over thirty years' experience began his career in a school that was flooded when Prairie View was built, so he has been a teacher and coach at Prairie View since its beginning. When the four new teachers are included with the group that has taught only in Prairie View (or who virtually have done so) four teachers remain who have taught in schools other than Prairie View High School. Considerable stability exists, but the number of new teachers required in the district this year and the difficulty of recruiting teachers to schools on or near Indian reservations are sources of some concern.

The characteristics of the best in their profession, according to teachers at Prairie View, can be found in their personal traits, teaching skills, and intellectual abilities. Of the three, personal traits are most frequently mentioned. For example:

> Rapport is needed to get the job done. The best way to go is to get along instead of hammering kids into the ground. You may not always cover the ground you otherwise would, but . . .

> Who are the right people to teach? People who care, who are creative, who have the desire to be real teachers.

Additional qualities that supplement this primary one are: "willingness to spend time beyond the classroom," "willingness to be present at student events," "sense of humor," "ability to 'B.S.,'" and "enthusiasm," "patience," "ability to provide a positive role model," "cooperative attitude."

Ability to manage or discipline a classroom was mentioned only once by a teacher.

Ability to motivate was described in several ways. "An excellent teacher has the ability to motivate, to direct students into useful ideas." "An excellent teacher can keep kids interested." A good teacher "knows how far you can push a kid and when to back off."

Flexibility plays a part. An excellent teacher has a "teaching style that can adapt to students." An excellent teacher is "someone who keeps trying different strategies or materials when what was tried first doesn't work." An ability to "handle all levels in a class" is important to the principal.

Other skills, some very specific and some very general, figure into the definition of a good teacher. Among them are "question-posing skills," and "ability to counsel, to help students work out their problems."

A good teacher also is "someone who can get material across," who "can help students learn."

With little variation, intellectual abilities are defined by those who include them in their overall picture of a good teacher as "knowing the material." The administrators of the school broaden this idea a bit with statements such as "love for the subject matter," and "an interest in the teaching field and in a lot of other areas." Two of the teachers who mention this category temper their support. One said, "A good knowledge of the subject is possibly not as important as other points such as the ability to understand students, be cooperative, and like people and children." But a good teacher "can't act as if you know everything; you have to be a bit human." Good teachers also "speak and write clearly," and "demand a lot."

When teachers and administrators describe conditions that support good teaching at Prairie View High School, students figure importantly. Good teaching is fostered, they say, when students "are active," students "accept you," and students "cooperate with you." They did not say, however, that they always had such acceptance or cooperation.

Independence is also important, and the teachers' views on this are found in such statements as "a teacher has to have his own 'inner drive,' " and "If you're innovative, you can do a lot."

Supportive colleagues were also cited. "What keeps me going," one teacher said, "is my roommate, who knows about the situation and who is supportive of the struggle." Another said, "The staff [here] is helpful. If you are having a rotten day, you can talk about it. You can ask almost anything."

The sports interests of the students are considered generally to provide positive support. One hears, for example, comments such as "Sports help with discipline," and "Athletic activities are a help to teachers." And lastly, school size is seen as a support. We were told, "We have a small faculty that gets involved out of class," and, "The school's size allows faculty to get to know students' backgrounds and families."

In the opinion of Prairie View teachers and administrators, there are many constraints that hinder the attainment of school and teaching excellence. Most of these constraints, they believe, are beyond their personal control. Some exist within the school, others outside.

> You can't do a good job, even in a small school, with the number of classes each teacher has each day, with the number of students in each class, and with the general psychological stress.

You can get to know students too well here; you categorize families.

We offer a limited number of classes and thus have a broad range of ability [within each class].

Teachers here [generally] don't demand a lot; this makes it hard on those who do.

Students are indifferent.

Being the only Indian teacher in this school speaks for itself.

We can't keep experienced teachers; we lost many in the last three to four years.

The location of vocational education keeps teachers from crossing paths. Teachers are not aware of what goes on down there. There is a lack of knowledge and communication.

Home Ec. gets students from other classes students can't hack. This means their experiences and interests are low.

At least one teacher had doubts about the capacity of schools to cope, saying schools generally "have too great a burden: children who are carelessly created, not really wanted. There are too many kids who don't want to learn, who are indifferent, uncaring. In my eighth grade class, 70 percent are burdens." At another time, this same teacher said, "The problems of a school on an Indian reservation are too great. We are going to leave. I can't take the daily hammering." The special problems of an ethnically divided student body were of concern to a teacher who said, "We try to serve two cultures. Indian and white bias when they exist are a problem. However, students who have these feelings are eliminated or eliminate themselves."

Another teacher reported that "the Johnson-O'Malley cutbacks are a problem. Now these funds will only pay half of the Home Ec. supplies. I approve of the cutback, but it does hinder students from getting fabric."

The one exception to this outward look was the teacher who described himself as blocking student achievement of a goal he had mentioned. "It is easier to do things myself than to help students develop responsibility."

Prairie View teachers believe the quality of their teaching is affected a great deal by the types of community and parental support they and the school receive. The fact that the community is "not college educated generally" is regarded as a handicap. Descriptions of this support vary considerably. "I feel the support of parents who like to see the band at games." "The community is interested in student welfare. But this interest is hard to express because of cultural differences." "The community basically supports the school. However, parents will often look out for themselves and their kids. One cause for the change in kids is parents' backing of kids. This is not a race issue." One teacher explained, "I think there are three groups of parents. Half of them support you because you are a teacher. A small group (10 percent) always supports their kids. The third group (40 percent) says to the school. 'Handle it all and don't bother me.' " The secretary of the school, a seven-year veteran and long-time resident, believes parental support is decreasing and considers this decline to be a recent phenomenon. She is concerned about its effect on teachers, and observed that "young, inexperienced teachers need support from parents or we will lose them." Further, she noted that such comments as, "I wouldn't be a teacher for all the money in the world," are fairly common from parents. In the fall, 60 percent of the parents came to teacher-parent conferences. I was told that the attendance probably was down from 80 percent because of an error in the advertisement the school placed in the local paper.

Discussions of improving school life for teachers focused on actions "someone" needs to take. The teachers wanted students to take more interest in their own education, for example. They expressed the need for improved attendance, and stricter discipline. One teacher said, "This school needs severe, lay-it-on-the-line rules. For example, if a kid doesn't want to do anything, he ruins education for others. Students should have to go to the school board and explain why they deserve to stay in classes or in school." Another teacher, who believed this issue was beyond his background, stated that, "The backing the administration gives teachers on discipline is the issue that comes up most."

To improve the curriculum, teachers suggest the school should "go back to the basics—for example: term papers, basic algebra, and social skills, meaning socially acceptable behavior in groups. Classes need specific curricula, material to be covered." One teacher complained about "stuff-em in, hodgepodge classes." An effort to track students is supported by several teachers directly, and by many indirectly. One advocate of tracking claimed, "I can't do what needs to be done with good students. I want to use contacts with poorer students. When I first came, we had a Title I reading class; it made teaching easier."

Teachers in Prairie View try to keep up with the profession and to keep interested in teaching in several ways. The most formal effort involves taking graduate courses and workshops. This requires a special effort because there are no graduate schools within close driving distance and the nearest undergraduate college is 75 miles away. Still, a teacher told me, "Most summers I take workshops at the university. I have family there and I go for a week each summer." Another teacher goes to one or more coaching clinics a year. He said, "I take classes when possible, but I'm a little lax on this. I have twenty-seven hours beyond the degree. Fewer courses seem to be offered in nearby towns." Graduate courses approved by the administration improve teachers' pay. However, one teacher with an M.A. does not receive a salary increase because his degree is in administration. The courses teachers at Prairie View have taken include both work in their teaching fields and in subjects related to specific teaching issues, such as Indian Studies, Exceptional Children, Classroom Management, Lab Safety, and Science for Teachers of American Indians.

Teachers described the state teachers' convention as useful, at least in the past. A teacher who used to go to the teachers' conventions says that lately "I've been disappointed. They are more political now." Several teachers say they still attend every year: "I take three to six hours of credit each year. I'm taking a course now on discipline on T.V. I read and I visit with faculty." Two teachers mentioned attending conferences of their professional organizations. One told me, "I always attend the Vocational Educators Conference in August. I wonder how I could kick off the year without it. I also attend the in-service session of the FHA convention." The other said, "I will attend the National Science Teachers Association national convention in Chicago this year. I will pay my own expenses."

Reading professional literature and talking with colleagues were mentioned by only three teachers.

The district's in-service program was not mentioned as an important part of any teacher's continued education. Teachers see the activity as administrative. One complained: "The district doesn't do much. I've suggested several ideas, first aid, IEP's for all teachers, detecting learning problems, classroom management (not discipline), teacher-student communications, CPR training for all faculty, developing human resources lists for Prairie View teachers. None of them have been used." The fall's in-service program was focused on Project SAVE and issues related to working with Indian students.

One teacher viewed this issue quite differently than his colleagues: "I feel I've been successful. Teaching has been rewarding and easy. Discipline and respect come easy. The money is getting better. Summer and Christmas vacations allow time for business and things that interest me."

The principal's in-service opportunities parallel those of the teachers in many ways. However, his administrative colleagues in Prairie View appear to be more important to him than teacher colleagues are to teachers. "I went to sessions for new administrators at the state capitol. We went over forms, and the like. I have gone to Project Equal [a Title IX] in-service. I attend regional and statewide meetings of the National Association of Secondary School Principals. I go to school-masters meetings. We have visits from officials of the state department. The administrative team here is also supportive and helpful."

No teacher organization appears to play a strong part in the Prairie View teachers' professional lives. The local teachers association has thirty members (out of a total of forty elementary and secondary teachers); eighteen attend the meetings. Long-term teachers can point out areas of growth: "I have been a member since 1953. The Prairie View organization wasn't strong in policy making until negotiations came in. In early years, the Christmas party was the main item of business." One teacher, who has belonged to the association for twenty years, said that "negotiations have helped bring the standard of things in the district up. The uniqueness of the community demands good teachers. We need to pay good people well." Others, however, point to a current decline in the association: "Now, only about half of the teachers belong. When I came seven years ago, all did. Now there may be no need to be in a group. Insurance is paid by the district. We are having trouble getting a president and other officers this year." Another teacher felt that the local organization "is a sore spot. Lots of people are dropping. The administration discourages participation. The superintendent and elementary principal say if anything happens to you, the school will take care of you."

No issue divides members of the teachers association from non-members. The insurance issue, concerns about political stands, and the effects and conduct of negotiations are discussed by both groups. But members of the organization express a belief in the need for a professional organization, while teachers who are no longer members do not. One nonmember "quit this year because of the cost." Another said:

I'm a scab. I never belonged in the previous state I taught in. I joined here for four years, but I left this year. NEA supporting Carter was bad. Teachers pick the most abrasive, hard-headed people to negotiate. School boards are equally muddle-headed. I know. I have served on a school board.

Members speak:

I belong to the State Education Association. At first, it was for insurance. Now, I belong so I can have a say about policy. Critical policies are being discussed now, tuition tax credits, binding arbitration. Local issues are parent-teacher conference day being considered a school day and a parents' rights policy. The board supports it and it appears to remove teachers' rights.

I belong, but I'm not active. I belong because of insurance. And, professionally, I think I should. They help with grievances. If we are going to help ourselves, we must do it through this organization.

We don't have too many grievances now. Last year, the industrial arts teacher's load was cut.

I belong mainly for insurance and in case the administration pulls a strong one.

I'm not excited about teachers' organizations. The trouble with labor unions is they promote laziness and poorer quality work. They hinder firing people. I have trouble with NEA's backing of political candidates, pushing federal aid and bussing. The State Education Association provides workshops and protection from abuse, lobbies for state aid, provides publications. Locally, it has been helpful in raising salaries. It does give a bit of security. Some teachers have nothing to do for a job but teach. Teachers do end up pushing for things [higher salaries, improved schooling] parents should be doing.

I have been president and chief negotiator. I found negotiations emotionally difficult because the former superintendent held a grudge. He didn't like pushy women.

Negotiations have the potential for petty bickering. Long-term residents and teachers don't support negotiations. So they [the board] will tell them [the teachers] they are worthless and will invest in a new gym floor but not in teachers' salaries.*

I benefit from the publications and conferences of AHEA and AVA. Some things have resulted from a stronger education association, but I'm not too aware of what they are. I don't think the local organization has much influence. Asking for too much antagonizes.

Within the administration at this time, the superintendent is the active force in relation to the teachers' organization. His views are strong: "I don't like unions at all. I only deal with it when forced to, when a grievance is raised. With a strong administration with a reasoned base, teachers have no need for a union. If the administration is credible in the community, the union has no base. In negotiations here, the superintendent is close to being the chief spokesman of the board. Last year, they [negotiations] were not petty or personality-based, but were reasonably professional. We met six to eight times. Teachers should maintain the organization for when I leave."

The principal, new to Prairie View, has not been involved with the local system. His comment was: "In comparison to the district I came from, an organization doesn't exist."

Overall, the teachers at Prairie View High School are positive in their attitudes toward their profession. Their positivism is tempered, however, by what they view as the frustrations of their work. It appears that their expectations and the reality of teaching are not much different for most of these teachers, with the exception of students' attitudes and behavior. The following statements bear this impression out:

Teaching is usually fun. I do not like fighting [students to get them] to learn. I knew there would be discipline problems, but I resent it when kids take their problems and frustrations out on teachers.

It is about what I expected. I'm bugged that kids don't like to learn, never look things up, pursue an idea, etc.

I have to teach to coach. But I enjoy kids, so I enjoy coming to school. Teaching is only moderately hard. I have to do lots of reading, but I can do it in school. I don't have time after school because of coaching.

* Reference here is to a new Tartan floor installed in the gym in the fall of 1981.

Overall, I like teaching more than I don't. What makes it reasonably good is the security it provides.

It turns out that money has become a problem, that students in the eighties don't want to read and write, that things I consider important, students consider worthless.

The rewards of teaching come from the students. Again, some typical comments:

My rewards are seeing kids succeed, finally understanding something, or reading a book for the first time; being the play director and getting close to kids; having kids ask questions.

Coaching and changing people. I see the changes in athletes. Rowdy kids calm down.

It depends on what you want out of life. When you accept the role of being a teacher, your satisfaction comes when you know you've helped . . . served. Satisfaction in teaching is having students come back saying, "I learned something." Being around young people is a reward. Rewards have not been monetary. I do not own my own home, and I drive a 1966 car. I have been trying to make the best of it. The rewards of coaching are easier to determine. Life as a coach was enjoyable. Winning made people feel good and gave me a reputation. Coaching kept me in teaching.

I feel I have been successful, I've taught good students who have been successful as doctors, etc.

The frustrations of teaching come from students. Here are some more observations by teachers:

Kids disrespect teachers, anybody. They think they have the right to talk when they wish. You see it in the horsing around in the halls and the vandalism.

My major misgiving is how to motivate students who don't care about themselves. Few students come back to say thanks.

My biggest frustration is students not caring . . . their "what's the difference" attitude. Achievement-oriented students are fewer. Another frustration is a lowered trust level. Personal instances of theft this year have not helped my attitude.

The two or three hours of homework cut into my family life and there is a lack of communication among teachers and between teachers and administration. However, I feel agony and grief when I can't get through to kids, when I am trying to stop kids from ruining their lives.

"Burnout" is not a word that teachers at Prairie View generally believe applies to them, but while one teacher did not use the term in reference to herself, she did use it in speaking of others: "There does appear to be a burnout rate on caring. Half of the staff here view teaching as a job and put in a set number of hours. A few don't care. Their tires have been slashed too many times. They don't leave because their job flexibility is limited. They don't feel good about themselves as teachers anymore."

As these teachers assess their profession, they define its major changes, rewards, and frustrations in terms of the students they teach and not in terms of the changes they have felt in economic support, or new knowledge about learning, schools, and teaching, or in the support their organization now gives them.

A final aspect of the Prairie View teachers' definition of themselves as professionals is their relationship to the community. They have mixed opinions about parental support for their in-school efforts. Other aspects of this issue include their interactions with parents; their beliefs about what the community expects of them; and their connections to other levels of schools, for example, the junior high school and colleges. Keys to understanding Prairie View teachers' professional relationship to other members of the community are the size of the town (about 1,400 people) and the teachers' generally high level of participation in community affairs. The principal described the teachers as being very active "socially, economically, politically. They work in the scouts, the volunteer fire unit, the ambulance service." This assessment was born out in conversations with the teachers themselves. Some teachers' lists of community activities appeared to give them a role in almost everything people in Prairie View were attempting to do. So, for most teachers, at least some of their major contact with parents comes in their nonschool activities.

Teachers' formal contact with parents occurs in parent-teacher conferences. There is no parent-teacher organization, even though many of the teachers believe one would help. Such an organization disbanded twelve years ago. The teachers clearly expect parents to come to the school to see them about any problem or question. Twice a year, three hours of the late afternoon and early evening are set aside for these conversations.

The conferences are advertised in the paper, and students are encouraged to urge their parents to come. Additional inducement is provided by having report cards available at the conference. Students cannot pick them up prior to the conference. This year about 60 percent of the junior and senior high parents came. Among them were many Indian parents. Some parents or relatives came only to receive the report cards and left after signing them and shaking hands with the principal. Most stayed for thirty minutes to an hour, going from desk to desk in the gym, talking to all their children's teachers, standing in lines waiting for their time with some teachers, and standing by the refreshment table talking to friends. Many parents wore a school jacket that announced the fact that Prairie View had been Class B basketball champs in 1980. Most appeared to enjoy their experience and to get the information they wanted—usually information about how their child was behaving in class.

The teachers were ready for the occasion. Most had dressed up for it. They all understood and appreciated the purpose of the conferences, but they also accepted as fact that they would not see the parents they wanted to see.* Teachers sat at student desks placed around the gym. There were signs with their names and the names of the students in their Project SAVE groups. The teachers were prepared to show their grade books, but they did not have class work papers to show parents or to talk about. Not being in the classrooms made this type of sharing difficult, and parents did not appear to expect it. The general press of parents created by their having to line up in front of teachers gave teachers little opportunity to go beyond each student's immediate situation and talk about what happens in classes or the purposes of their classes.

A different and special effort to contact parents is being made by the administration, including the principal, secretary, Title IV director, and attendance monitor. Their goal is to improve the school's attendance. After the first period's attendance has been recorded each morning, this group divides up the names of the students reported absent. Each person then contacts the parents of the absent students assigned to him. This is done by phone to the parent's home or work, or by driving to the home and visiting with the parent or guardian

* Several weeks after the conferences one teacher reported that she had been surprised by the number of visits (4 or 5) from parents of failing students.

personally. The Title IV director is the person who usually makes the home visits.

Another effort to contact parents and the community at large is made by the superintendent. His "Superintendent's Column" is a regular feature in the Prairie View *News*; the Superintendent's goal is to have a column in every issue of the paper. The topics discussed in these columns vary greatly. He hops from point to point, devoting a few lines or many to each. One column included casual descriptions of his infant son's precocious enjoyment of Vikings football, and invitations to parents to come to school to participate in parent conferences or in Spirit Week activities. Another included outlines of his goals and discipline tenets, descriptions of unsportsmanlike behavior exhibited by Prairie View students, introductions of new faculty and staff members, encouragement to participate in community activities, and explanations of aspects of school finance. A few quotes will help capture the flavor of the columns:

> We have an open noon hour, but that is the only time when students can or should be away from school. Consequently, if you see students in public at other times [during the school day] it is unauthorized. I invite you to call us and to use your personal acts of persuasion to let the students know that you know they are wrong. It is all part of caring. The consistent treatment of youth in developing a sense of right and wrong is another component of a community on the move. It is most gratifying to see many positive changes, from painting-reroofing of the Catholic Church to the residing of Exxon, from the painted theater sign to the berm remodeling. It is also good to see the street sweeper working so frequently. But, most gratifying is the variety and number of people involved in the community upswing. If you are not involved, beware, it is contagious.

> Elementary Parent-Teacher Conferences are coming up October 1. More information will be coming directly from the elementary school. The doors to the school are open to parents every day. Come in and visit any class, program or office. The school belongs to the people.

> The school district is financially stable at this point. Our future is severely threatened by the possible loss of 874 funds. 874 is a federal program to transfer funds from the federal treasurer to local school districts which are impacted by tax exempt property like air force bases, Indian reservations, etc. We could be caught in a dilemma of not receiving funds and not being able to tax the land. I hope reason will temper Reagan's sword but we must be prepared.

In addition to the superintendent's efforts to inform and encourage, the school gets fairly regular newspaper coverage of its activities generally. The school band is shown marching down Main Street; Title IV elections are described; new teachers are pictured. And very complete coverage of all athletic activities, male and female, is provided.

The school's people clearly have hopes and expectations for the community. They hope for parental involvement and expect parental support, and, usually, they expect this support and involvement to come on their terms. The community also has expectations for the school and its staff. There are only hints—inferences from school board policies, beliefs teachers hold—of what some of these expectations are. The rules and regulations concerning attendance, for example, are evidence of at least one community expectation. However, even in an area as basic and seemingly clear-cut as this—students attending school—there are complications. It is not at all clear that the entire community is represented on the board making the policy; there is only one Indian on the school board. School people implementing the policy find that many parents, white and Indian, are ambivalent about its enforcement. At a meeting of the administrators' group, a fellow described as representing "Main Street interests" expressed some frustration when he said that, "In some ways parents want a more relaxed attendance policy. They take their sons hunting, go to football games, let kids take time off when life gets tough, as adults do." The principal, too, was amazed by a mother who, at a parent-teacher conference, described the family's plans to take their son out of school for a few days to go to a professional football game. These absences would put the boy over the ten-day limit, and he would receive no credit in several classes. The mother's response to this information was that her son could graduate late. One month before the end of the fall semester, there were thirty students, all but two Indian, who, because of absences, and according to the attendance policy, were to be suspended. After much discussion of their alternatives, the administrative group in the end decided to "bluff it." The parents of the thirty students would be sent a letter which described a required conference with the principal. At the conference, the parents would be told about their child's attendance problem and about the possibility of suspension. The administration felt it could not go to the board and ask for the suspension of thirty students. They believed the board would not be able to support the school in the administration of the board's own rule.

Teachers believe they have a special position in town. They generally feel they are respected and are leaders. They also feel they are watched. This issue is particularly important to the young teachers new to teaching and to the community. "If you are not a townsperson, a person born and raised in the area, you are expected to be careful. Next to a minister's wife, the teacher is expected to know everything and behave well. It is pretty good here, though. We can go to the bars in town—unlike other places." When a teacher or group of teachers steps outside the fairly broad boundaries drawn for him, the school learns of it. Several people reported the incident of the new teachers who, one evening in a local bar, began to talk negatively about some of their Indian students. They were reprimanded by the superintendent and principal.

There are some long-standing differences of opinion between the school and the Indian community. Indians have felt that the high school is not doing enough and is not concerned enough about Indian students. Indian parents have not felt comfortable about the school or their presence in the school. The school officials, particularly the superintendent, principal, Title IV coordinator and the Project SAVE director, are working actively to change this relationship. However, the history of contrary action is long, and the current tribal council is not very interested in the Prairie View school.

## Teachers' School Life: Inside Connections

The lounge is the center of faculty in-school interactions. Housing a soda machine, a sofa, a phone, a long work table, and, importantly, a coffee pot and the Xerox machine, this half-a-classroom provides a place where teachers go between classes, during their preparation periods, and during lunch if they are "brown baggers." It is one place in the school into which students cannot go without knocking and in which smoking is allowed. Teachers go to the lounge to relax, to rest, and to visit with whomever is there. More typically, they photocopy work sheets. The tone of conversation is bantering; the topics are casual, usually incidents of the day—students letting air out of a teacher's tires, teachers' general states of mind and body, or the football pool. Several teachers describe their relationships with colleagues as lounge-based. One said, "My relations with other teachers largely depend on who has break at the same time; I have coffee friends among the faculty." But, apparently, there are limits to such relationships. A teacher told me, "We are friendly at school in the lounge, but we do not have a social relationship. I always associated with colleagues of my former profession, but I find teachers trivial."

Some teachers clearly have relationships that go beyond the school. The single new teachers form a natural and fairly compatible group; they "party" together in their homes and in local bars. Several pairs of teachers share apartments. One long-term teacher reported a change in his socializing: "When I first started teaching there was more. We bowled, hunted, and fished together. We were age-mates. Now, the replacements are younger, single. Many of my friends are in the community. Teachers my age are not such a clique."

While the general description of faculty rapport was positive, two teachers expressed reservations. The first reported, "It is difficult to communicate with teachers when I see a teacher give up on a class." The second explained feelings of isolation: "I am in a shell which is hard to get through. I learned it from my experience as one of two Indians in college."

Teachers' in-school contact with administrators is limited and largely informal. However, Prairie View is a small town, which means you know everyone. The newness of the principal made it difficult for teachers to assess their relationship with him or to even develop a substantive connection. One teacher "still has doubts about the 'backing' the administration will give on discipline issues." Another said, "The administration has not laid out what to expect from them. It is easy for a teacher to expect more than they will put out."

The issue that connects principal to teacher most frequently is discipline. For example, a teacher observed that, "We talk chiefly about discipline. . . . He came in, for example, to check up on a student who may have been drinking. I feel a bit isolated because I can't call the principal's office from my room. Of course, some teachers don't use this issue to interact with the principal. They choose to handle their own problems."

Needing something is another point of formal contact. Orders for equipment and texts come to the principal. The superintendent interacts with all the head coaches and also appears to get requests for maintenance, leading a teacher to observe, "With the superintendent, my contact is limited to things like plugged drains."

A few teachers appear to have a broader content for interaction. One claims that "We talk two or three times a day about students, discipline, ideas for classes, or books to read." A former principal reports that "At the beginning, I helped [the new principal] with class schedules, with 'getting the door open.' I helped him get off to a good start. I have very little contact now."

The principal wants to develop more openness with teachers. He believes in shared decision-making. However, at this early point, his formal implementation of these ideas is his plan for evaluating teachers—a three-step model for new teachers involving visiting classes and conferences, and a two-visit plan for remaining teachers—and his faculty meetings. These latter sessions are usually called with little warning, sometimes with no advertised agenda. At their core, they appear to be information-giving meetings. At a meeting held soon after some major items were stolen from the school, the principal reported that he had received "feedback" from community people about teachers talking about the kids involved in the "Halloween escapade." "I ask that you maintain a professional silence," he said. "It is up to the police to solve the mystery." On another occasion, the principal had to let the teachers know that in less than a week an Indian Day would occur—a day set aside to celebrate aspects of Indian history and culture—and that there would be a shortened day and a program. However, at each meeting I attended there were some minor decisions made in concert. For example, the exact schedule for the Indian Day was decided in a faculty meeting the day before. The principal suggested that school end at 2:30; there would be no shortened periods, but sixth hour would be dropped. The teachers responded, "Why can't we do what we have always done, have shortened periods?" Quickly, the principal agreed to this plan. One teacher, in an aside to the principal, asked if this were what he meant by shared decision-making.

Prairie View has no department structure in the traditional sense. Little work is done as an English faculty: "It is an informal relationship." The social studies faculty meets a couple of times a year: "Last year we worked on three new courses." The science teachers work semi-independently, but, "We consult every nine weeks about how things are going. We are going to work on working together." The head of the science department handles the ordering for life sciences and setting up labs. He says, "I am a 'go-between' for the science teachers and the administration. I'm not involved in curriculum development or teacher evaluation."

The guidance counselor is new to the district, and the way teachers describe their relationships with him reflects it:

> I have very little contact with the guidance counselor. Lack of time is part of my problem.

> My contact with the counselor is due to his being my assistant football coach.

> I have not worked a lot with him. There is no good way to refer students, no clear understanding of what to expect or what he does.

One teacher reported discussing "problem students" with him.

Project SAVE is attempting to incorporate important aspects of the counselor's role into each teacher's work with students, but the counselor does not play any special part in that program. He was not involved in the training that teachers received in the fall, and he is not now a member of the faculty coordinating committee. These responsibilities are those of the Project SAVE director.

Decision-making processes also define relationships. On one hand they are diffuse. As has already been described, communication between teachers is informal, appears to be focused on the immediate, and is not typically focused on long-term problem-solving efforts.

Curriculum planning is an independent process. The superintendent has started a summer-by-summer plan for district-wide faculty curriculum development, and one project—a K through 12 English curriculum guide—has been completed. Teachers, however, still view themselves as independently responsible for the curriculum and define it as what goes on in their classrooms.

The social studies teachers agreed on three new courses, but, when two were approved by the administration for implementation, the teachers responsible for the courses had to define the content and find and select materials. All that the faculty group had decided was that United States history would end at World War II, and contemporary history would begin there.

Teachers describe themselves as independent decision-makers as far as their classrooms are concerned. "Our administration lets us do what we want; it is up to the individual to do it." Another teacher described the teacher's role in curriculum decision-making a bit differently, but she still describes a basic independence. "We have a lot of say, as long as it fits in the schedule, doesn't cost a lot, and doesn't conflict with a required class."

Only the home economics teacher described any prescription. In her case, the state department of vocational education outlines the curriculum.

Outside the classroom, decisions result from a centralized process. The superintendent states that "nothing gets decided" without going through his administrative team.* "The principals are my faculty; I rely on them. They should rely on their teachers. When they lose touch with their teachers, they must quit." The team meets every week and discusses and decides on issues of major and minor importance to the school. For example, should the board be asked to suspend the thirty students who have "no-credited" courses and no longer carry a full course load? What should be done about in-service plans and Indian Day? The superintendent makes budget decisions; the principals implement them.

Teachers agree that decisions are centralized. In regard to scheduling: "If a teacher is around in the summer when it is done, he can participate, but the principal is in charge." I was told that "the principal decides on scheduling and grouping. The principal and school board decide on the rules and regulations." Teachers believe they have little input on goals and priorities. Only one teacher expressed any specific ideas for in-service for the faculty. She did not believe, however, that any of her ideas would be implemented.

Communication is necessary and expected; however, it is most regularly directed from administration to faculty. Faculty communication to the administration is casual and diffuse.

* This group includes the elementary school principal, who, while white, is characterized by the superintendent as representing the Indian point of view; the vocational education director, who has a "Main Street point of view"; the Title IV director, who is an Indian woman; and the high school principal, who is new.

## Students' School Life: Attempts to Communicate Purpose

One route to understanding students' school lives is to define their reasons for going to school. These reasons are also expressions, albeit indirect, of parents' expectations. The 160 reasons given by approximately 100 ninth-, eleventh-, and twelfth-grade students are of three basic groups. Students' various plans for the future are contained in half of the comments. The attractions school has for students are described in one-third of the comments. The agents who force them to school are portrayed in one-sixth of students' reasons. Almost all of the students have more than one reason for going to school.

As they discuss why they go to school in terms of their future, students include plans to attend college, desires to get jobs, hopes to "be something." Desires to "get an education" might reasonably be included in the description of the school's attractions, but this goal is almost always paired with college and job plans. The statements that follow, and those that are included in each section of this essay, appear as the students wrote them in class sessions or as they were recorded in interviews.

It isn't really that interesting to me, but I know that it can be if I just try a little. I know that in order to be anything or succeed in life, an education is very important, and it is preparing me for college.

To get an education because I do want to better myself and also go to college.

To prepare for college and to learn as much as I can about everything so that I can express, write, and understand intelligently.

Because it prepares me to go to college. You learn basic subjects you have to know in order to live in this world. It is good for me. Gives me some challenge. I think it is necessary.

I want to get a good education for college, so I can do well in life. I don't want to waste my life sitting around, when I am capable of much more.

To get a diploma and go to college and then get a good stable job and make some frog skins [money]. To get educated.

Because that's the only way I can go to college. So I can have a good future.

I would like to go to college, and I don't want to be known as a high school drop out.

Because I want to graduate and go to a vocational school.

So that I can get an education and go into the Army.

Most of the attractions of the school are positive—friends, fun, athletics, something to do. One attraction is comparative—it's better than staying home.

To get an education for college. I see all my friends there. I'd hate to just bum around.

Prepare myself for the future and participate in school activities.

Good education, seeing my friends, knowing about different things. Sports, learning things of importance.

I would have to go to work, if I didn't. There are friends there.

Sports, and you have to so you can get through life.

Nothing better to do. I might go to college.

Because it's no fun staying home with no one around to talk to. I have to. My boyfriend's here. It's fun, most of the time.

There's nothing else to do at home.

Because I want to learn as much as I can. Because I need it to become something. It gives me a chance to be in athletics. It lets me see my friends a lot.

To learn and . . . go on to a good university. To be around people. It isn't so good in the country.

Parents and the law are the critical forces mentioned by students who cite an outside agent as a force getting them to school. The law figures most importantly for the ninth graders who are not yet sixteen.

Because they make you. [It's] the law.

Have to. It's the law until you're 16.

Parents are frequently mentioned as a source of support or push.

My mom makes me and I plan to go to a trade school.

Parents make me. Friends, something to do.

Because it would hurt my parents if I quit, and maybe someday I'll be glad I did even if I'm not now.

It used to be I wanted to learn, but now it's because my parents make me.

A slightly different perspective on these issues is given in students' explanations for the existence of the school. Almost all groups of students said, "To give kids an education"; "To make something out of the people"; or, "To help us in jobs" and "provide for our future." Some of these same groups also included some additional reasons for the school: "Keep kids out of trouble"; "Jobs for teachers"; "If there wasn't a school there probably wouldn't be a town. People would have to move near a town with a school"; "[So] students can get an education"; "Keep us busy so we can't steal or vandalize"; "So we can be in sports"; "To get kids away from the Circle A and Bowling Alley"; "[To] teach responsibility."

Going on to school or getting jobs are the reasons most students have for going to high school, so it is not surprising that these same objectives are among personal goals or plans. Almost half of the students interviewed had specific plans:

I'm thinking about going to a vocational school to learn auto body. Then later I'll farm with my dad.

[I have] agricultural interests. I want to further the production of animals. I live on a farm. I will go to college.

I'm thinking about going to a junior college to study forestry, then go to college in Colorado for forestry. I'll get married and have kids someday, but not for a long time.

I'll go to college. I want to go into engineering, then get a job and get rich! Ha! Maybe have a family.

I'm going to college and have a teaching career. Be happy.

I want to go to college and major in P.E., to be a P.E. teacher. I'll get married, but I'll wait awhile.

I'm going to a community college; then get a job as a secretary so I can move away from here. I'll get married when I'm older—twenty-seven maybe.

To become an architect—to go to college.

I'm going into the service, then nursing after the service. I want to travel and I'm not really interested in marriage.

The remaining half were less certain about what they were going to do. Some had several different specific plans:

I'd like to work with computers or numbers, or work with older people, or be a beautician. I would prefer to go to college instead of vocational training. I'll wait a long time before marriage.

I don't think I'll go to college. I'll never make it in math. I'm thinking about the Air Force; otherwise, I'll be a secretary here.

I'll just keep working at a nursing home. Maybe I'll be a vocational agriculture teacher. I may end up getting married at the end of high school.

I don't know—computer programming maybe. I want to go into architecture or engineering.

Others were general in their thinking:

I will attend college, then get married and have a family. I want to be happy.

I'll go to college. I don't know what to go into yet. I want to be happy, to see the world.

I'm going to college and whatever that leads to. I don't know if I'd get married right away.

I haven't thought about it yet. After high school, I'll go to college.

I'm not really sure; probably work on the family farm. I'm not sure about college.

I plan to go to college, then look for a good job. Some day I want to have a boy—I like kids.

Go to college and get a master's degree in whatever I want to do. I may go into computer programming. I don't think that far ahead. I want to be single for a while.

The dropout rate for Prairie View High School is difficult to determine. One of the major reasons for this difficulty is the itinerancy of many in the student population. Children of oil workers move frequently. Many Indian families move from reservation to reservation in the region. While it is expected that many will return to school after a move, students report to the school when they leave that they are not certain. The official drop-out figures for the first three months of the fall term were three seniors, five juniors, five sophomores, and four freshmen.

Indian students frequently cite laziness and family and personal problems as explanations of why fellow students drop out of school. Pregnancy is one clear-cut reason for girls to leave school, "but a lot of them come back." Absenteeism is another reason. "They screw up on the limits [for being absent] so they just quit." Not liking school or teachers and not getting along with other students are other explanations. Lack of interest is also mentioned, expressed in such comments as, "They don't care"; "There's not enough to keep them interested"; "Because they don't know what they want out of life." Fighting and "being afraid to come back," "rebelling against something," "drinking too much," "following a friend," and "getting behind" are still other reasons students believe their colleagues drop out.

Explanations may vary, but opinions about the wisdom of dropping out do not. The most supportive comments came in the recognition that "it's their life," or, "it's their business," or, that, "they feel they had no choice—she was pregnant." Overall, when a friend or acquaintance drops out, students "think it's a mistake. They will kick themselves in the ass later." Comments in a similar vein were: "It's kind of stupid if they want to go to college later"; "They're not going to make much out of their lives"; "I think they're just wasting time. They won't get good jobs"; "I'm disappointed"; "It's stupid. They could just finish"; "It's hard to say why they dropped out. It's hard to understand why."

### Students' School Lives: Outside the Classroom

The principal attests to a great deal of interest in school activities. "Sixty percent of the students are involved in varsity athletics—also there is considerable involvement in school clubs, drama, etc." Of 106 students visited in classes, all but 11 claimed they were part of at least one team or club. Most—boys and girls alike—listed an athletic activity. Students, in groups or individually, agree that "athletics," "sports," or "basketball" are the aspects of the school of which they are most proud. In 1980, the Prairie View team won the state Class B Basketball Championship. All the male teachers, the counselor, and the two female P.E. teachers coach a sport—wrestling, football, basketball (boys and girls), power volleyball (girls), cross country (boys and girls), or golf.

There is a range of clubs in which students list membership: Eagle Feather Club, an Indian organization; Future Farmers of America; Future Homemakers of America; Science Club; and Medical Explorers. Faculty advisors describe the activities of these groups variously. The Eagle Feather Club is growing, and members have their own jackets, and plan many events. "The Science Club does very little." An advisor said, "I am willing to give students ideas, people for speakers, and the like, but I am leaving the responsibility up to the students." The F.H.A. membership is declining and is small—about ten students. Drama productions receive enthusiastic support from the cast of students and the faculty director. Two other activities students list are the band—jazz band and just plain band—and the cheerleading squad. The cheerleaders and the band are part of the athletic activities.

Overall, students have little to do with the operation of the school. Student government consists of class officers—a separate group for each class. Their responsibilities are few. Students credit their officers with planning a dance now and then. There are no student office monitors, library aides, or other such student positions.

Compared with athletic activities that draw "a lot of kids," partly because "there's nothing else to do around here," dances are less attractive. Students have many explanations for the low attendance: "About half of the students go. Some don't have a way to town—if they don't have a car"; "Mostly more white students go than Indian"; "Those who drink go"; "I don't care for them. There's lots of liquor there"; "I went to Homecoming, but not many others. At the last dance, there was a fight"; "Guys who have steady girls go."

As in all schools, there are students who go it alone. But many have friends who share their classes and their extracurricular activities. "I know everybody. I have no enemies," one student said. Other typical comments included: "I have a few very good friends—quality not quantity"; "Most of my friends are in my classes. We signed up together."

As observers of student relationships, teachers note that status appears to be based on athletic success. "If students are not athletes, they have problems. The honor roll means little."

The "shame out," primarily observed among Indian students, is used to keep classmates, even athletes, from standing out too far from the group. A student who stands out too much is labeled "son" or "daughter" of the teacher or coach involved in that student's activity.

Relationships among white and Indian students also receive attention. I learned that "elementary school is the place where Indians and whites are closest. They are less close in high school but are closer than they'll be in the community." The principal states that "there is limited racial conflict." The Title IV director believes, "There is increasingly better mixing among the races. There used to be a major separation by race at grade seven. This is no longer the case."

Students, both Indian and white, pick up on this theme when assessing their school. White students speak:

> It comes from back in grade school. There are two different races. That happens to cause problems. Some kids don't give a damn, and they ruin it for everyone. I'm looking forward to getting away. A lot of kids don't try in school. They don't think it's cool. The prejudice stems from the parents, both Indian and white.

> Sometimes Indians and whites get into it over prejudice.

> It's a pretty good school if you let yourself learn, if you're not prejudiced.

Indian students speak:

> It's all right. Prejudice is not too bad.

> Mostly it's jealousy among students over how good they are at sports. Fighting.

Other insights came from students' descriptions of what makes their friends and fellow students proud of them. Different students usually had different points to make. The prime ones are "doing something really good" and "being a good friend." Others suggest:

> Do good work, get along with other students and other teachers, have a nice personality. Attend school activities.

> Be loyal; be good in sports.

> Stick up for them in a fight or argument.

> Don't tell their secrets; don't spread rumors about them; be their friend when they need one.

> Be good in some kind of sport.

Be a one-in-a-million nice guy or person; be a sport jock.

Be their friend and don't cut them down behind their backs.

Dress nice. Keep myself looking nice.

Be nice to them, by giving answers if they need them.

Doing what the group wants is mentioned by some as a special aspect of making students proud or being a friend:

Do what they do. Do daring things.

Do what they want to do—peer pressure.

Join their group and do what they want you to do. Stand up for them if they get in trouble.

Demonstrating some kind of independence is mentioned by a few.

[Do] not let anyone [teachers, friends, etc.] push you around.

Become the best you can be in what you try. Be nice to them. Show them you can be independent.

Win the basketball game by [scoring] the last point. Stand up to the teachers.

Guys like it when you say something witty to a teacher.

When you ace a test; stick up for your rights.

As a formalization of relationships between groups of persons and of relationships between students and the school, rules are important. Written regulations comprise the bulk of the *Prairie View High School Student and Parent Handbook*. There are requirements and policies to govern admissions, bus riding, church nights, dances, student conduct, who controls students, due process, suspensions (both in- and out-of-school), expulsion, corporal punishment, detention, dress, early graduation, athletic eligibility, grades, graduation, gum, candy and pop, illegal substances, contact with junior high students, lavatories, out-of-town events, passes, class schedule changes, sportsmanship, telephone use, and student rights and responsibilities—including freedom of expression and search by school personnel.

Students learned or reviewed the school's regulations in two ways this year. At the opening of the school year, the principal and superintendent met with small groups of students to discuss the rules. The small advising groups, key groups, spent their first sessions going over the handbook.

This school does not, however, seem burdened with rules. Neither faculty nor students complained of over-regulation. One set of policies, however, stands out as particularly important to both faculty and students. The administrative focus for this year will be on improving attendance. One expectation is that students will "be present and punctual for all classes, lyceum programs, and other official functions of the school throughout the year." Another is that all students must be enrolled in six classes in order to attend school. "There is no differentiation in the way excused and unexcused absences are treated. No admit slips are required."

Some specific rules:

A non-credit may be issued for the semester for each class in which you have missed ten (10) days. Your continued attendance in that class may be required for the balance of the semester. Administrative and professional intervention counseling will be available for chronic attendance problems.

Make-up work will be required for all absences.

All participants in extracurricular activities must be in attendance the day of the activity in order to be eligible to participate.

Students who are absent two days or less do not have to take semester finals, three days if they have A and B grades.

When asked about which rules are most important, students say things like:

I think the attendance rule is most important because it's important that we're here mostly every day in order to understand what's going on in our classes and for them to be beneficial.

Attendance—because this year we have really a strict attendance rule that people have to follow and it seems to be working pretty good. I know it's working good for me.

Attendance. People have to be in class to learn anything. In this school, it is a problem. They had no choice but to set some kind of limit.

The attendance rule. Because otherwise the school would be half empty half of the time.

Overall, they believe the policies are enforced fairly:

> Everybody gets treated the same, but it really hurts the better students because they get A's but still can't miss more than 3 days.

> Yes. I think it is [enforced fairly]. You just don't not go to school when you don't want to. I think it is very fair. If I can follow it, anybody else can.

Those who don't believe it is enforced fairly have specific concerns.

> Some students have already gotten out of it by making up lies for excuses and they keep getting more chances to stay in school.

> Some people have legitimate reasons for missing school.

> You could be flunking and you wouldn't have to take the test. And what if you had to go see the dentist on days you would have to take tests?

Student suggestions for alleviating the problems the rules raise are two: increase the number of days to fifteen and reinstate study halls so students have a place to go other than back to class when it is clear they will not receive credit for the class.

When assessing aspects of student life, some teachers and students believe that drugs and alcohol are a problem. A teacher said, "There is a lot of drinking here. Kids coming in drunk is not infrequent. Monday they are 'shot'; Friday, they are talking about the party of the weekend." An Indian student said, "Students drink too much, smoke too much grass. Too many people leave school because of pregnancies." A coach: "I know my athletes drink, but I can't stop it. I tell them not to get caught." The "Superintendent's Column" contains a description of square dancing as an activity that doesn't require drinking for a good time. On the other hand, the community accepts drinking. Young teachers use the bars as one arena for their social lives.

## Students' School Lives: Inside the Classroom

Students follow classroom routines established by the teachers. They alter those routines by talking when they aren't supposed to, daydreaming, reading their own materials, or asking if the class can go to the library. Students know what they are expected to do: take notes, complete assignments of questions at the end of a chapter, study for an upcoming test. Even when they are not attending to the task, they are usually quiet. Some observations:

In a sophomore class students are to read a chapter in their text. The teacher interrupts their work to give them five minutes to talk. This is expected, and students settle back into their work reasonably quickly.

In a junior-senior foods class—75 percent Indian and largely male—the students are not attentive while the teacher is giving the class notes. Several students appear to be sleeping and the teacher does not wake them up. The twenty minutes given for studying are used for visiting instead. The teacher tries to get students started, frequently mentioning the test scheduled for the next day, but she has little success.

In a freshman social studies class, the students sit at the desks at the back of the room. While notes are being given on the overhead, most students are reading other materials. They are quiet, however. A question is asked, and students appear surprised; two can't answer it, a third student finally does. Students do not initiate questions or discussion. When points are elaborated, students drift and don't take notes.

The teacher comes in late to chemistry. She teaches a junior high class in the preceding period, and the schedules don't mesh precisely. While they wait for class to begin, students sit in seats and visit or work on problems. Most of the chairs are full, and are crowded together in the half of the long room devoted to desks. Four boys go to the teacher's front table and visit while she takes roll. There are several tasks for the day, to which everyone attends. First, the homework problems are corrected. The teacher does them on the board. Most of the questions students have relate to whether or not they need to know a point for the test. "Helium we won't worry about. . . . Number three we won't do; it's too difficult . . . don't worry, we won't have ones that hard." Then there is a quiz consisting of two problems. One student, who does not complete the quiz, goes to the library to complete it while the class exchanges papers and corrects the problems. The teacher asks for the number of points earned and records them. Some students file the quiz in their notebooks; some toss them in the trash. As the bell rings, the next assignment of problems is given.

In Algebra I, the teacher begins class quickly after the bell rings and, because class has not met for three days while students took the Iowa Tests of Basic Skills, he conducts a review. The review and the presentation of new material is a mixture of demonstration and asking questions. Students are attentive; at least, they are looking at the teacher. One girl is reading a book for English but volunteers an answer to a question. Two girls at the side of the room whisper one time. One of these same girls plays with her hair. Another is called down for playing with a Rubik's Cube. When the assignment is given, the teacher goes from student to student helping each one with difficulties.

Teachers believe that students find their course work difficult or unpleasant in some way. No teacher described a class as eagerly engaging in difficult assignments or motivated to take the initiative in learning.

> Most students find English I difficult. It is on the high school level, and even if they are good students, they see the course as drudgery.

> In art, students want good things to come out of their class, but they also don't want to be challenged too much. They appear to be afraid to be original. They want and are allowed to copy others' designs. Students appear to expect instant success; they want perfection. Their frustration level is high. They have trouble gauging their abilities. [The students this teacher is describing are Indian males. There are two or three non-Indian males and just a few Indian females in art.]

> Over half of the students in physical science [ninth grade] believe it is too hard. This is a matter of their willingness to work, not the abstractness of the concepts.

> Students [in home economics] now feel they need to be entertained. They are more worldly-wise. They have unrealistic attitudes about money and marriage. They live in a fantasy about life. They get bored sooner because they have learned more earlier. They are willing to absorb but not work to learn.

Students are neither sophisticated nor detailed in their descriptions and assessments of critical aspects of their classroom life—the teachers they have, the subjects they study, the homework assigned to them. They are not strongly negative either. The tone is generally one of acceptance.

A class of college-bound juniors and seniors listed the characteristics of good and poor teachers, asserting that they had had some of both at Prairie View. The number of good teachers reported ranged from 3 to 10; the mode was 5. The number of poor teachers ranged from 0 to 7; the mode was 3. In order to capture the nature and tone of the opinions, the complete list is provided below.

| A GOOD TEACHER | A POOR TEACHER |
|---|---|
| Is a friend | Is a slave driver |
| Is understanding | Is narrow-minded |
| Is cooperative | Is prejudiced |
| Is patient | Is grumpy, crabby |
| Is open-minded | Is short-tempered |
| Is able to relate to kids | Doesn't care (is unconcerned) |
| Is respectable | Doesn't cover subject well |
| Is a communicator | Won't listen |
| Is thorough (covers subject well) | Has favorites |
| Listens to new ideas | Picks on you |
| Is concerned for students | Ignores you |
| Works individually | Goes through things too fast |
| Does fun things, not just lecture | Lectures all the time |
| Pays special attention and helps slow students | Is very strict |
| Doesn't have pets; doesn't have favorites | Doesn't give any time to do school work |
| Understands kids and their problems | Is hard to understand |
| Is humorous | Has a short temper |
| Helps out | Is a diehard |
| Doesn't repeat over and over again | Always makes you work hard |
| Is a fair grader | |
| Is not grouchy | |

Indian and white students expressed the same generally positive, accepting viewpoints of their teachers. The few accusations that were made had to do largely with grouchiness. One or two times, teachers were described as sometimes not being fair or being boring. One student said; "A few are real special. Some I don't respect because of what I know about them out of school."

Students' beliefs about what makes teachers proud of them cluster around being a good student and being good. Over half of the descriptions of ways to make teachers proud are related to being a good student. Within those bounds, getting good grades, working hard, and doing assignments account for the majority. A few students also include trying their best and participating. A very few mention taking notes, graduating, or showing enthusiasm for and taking interest in schoolwork. No one mentions asking questions in class. Students' definitions of being good vary widely: behave, don't talk, don't act smart or mouth off, cooperate, obey, listen, don't goof off, use good manners, come to class, be on time, pay attention. It is clear that students know the basic code of how to get along.

A small group of students count on doing well in sports to please teachers; an extremely small number of students mentioned participation in an activity, such as a science fair or band contest as helping. Another small group described certain personal characteristics as important—for example: showing common sense, being honest, trustworthy, mature, responsible, having the ability to get along with other students and be nice. A very few students mentioned special efforts to relate to the teacher: "Treating them like human beings"; "being cool with them"; "having and showing knowledge of things they're interested in."

Most students say that plans for college or other future activity determine the courses they take. A second, but smaller, determining factor is interest in the subject matter. School requirements are the third factor. Students also take courses because they relate to particular skills: "I took auto mechanics because I wanted to learn how to fix my car if I got into trouble and home ec. 'cause I wanted to know about those things for my home." Finding an easy or a challenging class, or doing what friends do were mentioned frequently. The limited number of courses available and the sequential nature of some courses ("I had geometry last year so algebra comes after that") makes it easy for students to advise themselves.

In fact, most students report that no one advises them about courses. Teachers and parents are consulted with about equal frequency, but teachers are the chief source of information about school requirements. Course selection does not appear to require meaningful or extensive student-teacher interaction.

The criteria students use to define their favorite courses and subjects are wide ranging. A course in health careers, social studies, and shorthand may be selected because "It's interesting. I find out new things I didn't know before." Math may be selected because "I like to work with numbers," or because "I'm confused at first, then I get the hang of it." Enjoyment is mentioned frequently. "I get to judge at livestock shows. It's fun. I get to go on trips and meet lots of people." Liking the teacher and finding out that studying a subject will help achieve goals for the future are additional criteria.

The criterion students use to identify their easiest courses is the amount of preparation required. Physical education is easy because "all you have to do is dress and participate." Other "easy" courses: "Band, all you do is play"; "Vo Ag, because you don't do much in there and you don't have to work very hard if you do."

In identifying their most difficult classes, students talk not only about the amount of work required, but also about the content, the teaching method, or their own characteristics and behavior. Hard classes are:

Civics: Too much work and tests.

Contemporary History: A lot of reading, more than any other one of my classes.

Physical Science: Too many formulas.

Office Filing: Because you have to cross reference.

Algebra II: Because you have to listen . . . if you don't you'll get all mixed up and not understand what you're doing.

U.S. History: I can't understand the teacher, and it is so ancient it doesn't seem worth it to learn it.

German II: It's just getting hard to figure out, it's moving so fast.

Math: It is hard to understand the teacher.

History: We have to take notes.

Civics: I don't understand it, but it's because I don't listen, I guess.

Problems of Democracy (Social Studies): I don't work hard enough at it, and I have a hard time catching on to things, understanding how and why.

From observations in classrooms, one would conclude that homework is regularly assigned in some classes. It consists of a variety of assignments, but usually there are questions or problems in the textbook, book reports, or study for tests. But "homework" is a misnomer because part of class time is typically devoted to the completion of assignments. Students say they are assigned homework in from one to three classes a day. While practice varies, of course, from student to student, much of the homework is done in school. One student confessed: "I do my homework five minutes before it's due, usually. Sometimes at home, but seldom." Studying for tests appears to be a major homework task.

What happens to daily homework, students say, varies with the teacher. Overall, they believe it counts, but they say they usually grade it themselves. They say that teachers don't usually check the homework: "Most of the time they just want the scores." Major projects such as book reports, term papers, and other writing assignments are graded by the teachers and make up major portions of grades.

Students do not report that they go directly home after school to complete their school assignments. A few students have paying jobs; more say they wish they did. Some go home to complete their farm and home chores. Many more, however, stay at school for a sport, go to the Circle A to play electronic games, or go home to watch TV or be with friends.

> I go to football and wrestling. I go home and work. I milk cows, do odd jobs.

> I go to play practice, or to Circle A, or to a friend's home. I like to go bowling, but it's hard to get lanes 'cause of leagues.

> I work at Ben Franklin. I'm in the swing choir and the jazz band and I go to play practice.

> I go home or play basketball in the neighborhood or drive around.

> I go to open gym, go home and watch TV. Sometimes I read (not schoolwork) or play basketball. I play video games at the Circle A.

> Sometimes I do homework, then I go downtown and sit around the Circle A with friends. On weekends I go to dances.

Students' overall assessments of their school are positive. Indian and white students alike say they believe it is a good place to go to school.

> I think it's a good learning experience. P.V. is a unique experience, with oil development and Indians.

> It's a pretty good place to grow up. But it's a pretty rowdy town.

> It's getting more strict. I'm glad it's my last year.

> It's a good school and it's worth it to go.

> I don't think it's average; it's better.

> It's been nice. I like it here. They have a good athletic program.

> It's an exciting place to go to school.

> It has helped out a lot. It teaches you about yourself.

## Teachers' and Students' Lives: Connections

In many ways the lives of the teachers and the lives of the students, while being played out in the same spot, are quite separate. Many aspects of their school lives do not genuinely intersect. Even so, the size of the school and the size of the town contribute to a sense of intimacy. The principal, superintendent, secretary, and teachers know all students by name. All the parents who came to the parent-teacher conferences were recognized and called by name. One wonders if teachers and students are able to develop their relationships much further than this.

Genuine, meaningful interaction between students and teachers can come about when, for example, teachers serve as advisors or as coaches for an extracurricular activity. Such activity gives them the informal setting they need to get beyond the formal relationships they have defined for themselves and for their students in their classrooms. It is clear that the teachers involved in these activities take them seriously and enjoy the opportunities they provide to be with young people. A few teachers clearly prefer these activities, particularly coaching, to classroom teaching.

A second point of connection is Project SAVE and the key groups that are part of it. This is a new enterprise, one conceived by the superintendent and strongly supported by the principal. The people involved in the project are struggling to make it work and to establish its goals and methods firmly in the structure of the school.

When they describe their interactions and contacts with students, teachers talk about a lack of information, myths, settings, a sense of loss. Typical comments include:

> I keep students at a certain distance. You can't be too friendly and get work done.

> I get along with everyone until I walk into the classroom. Getting to know students—it's a myth. I know everybody a little, some a little bit more. Unless a teacher is involved in extracurricular activities, he doesn't and can't get to know kids.

> It takes a while to establish good contacts with students. New teachers don't understand why kids don't do their homework, etc.

> I get to know some students fairly well, some not at all. It depends on

students' reactions how I react to them or others and on my going out of my way to ask about them. Teachers don't get enough information about students. We are not informed about major problems—for example, epilepsy, stuttering, pregnancy. We get no information on basic skills. We should know family history. It is important to know about relationships.

I like relationships with students formed in FHA and labs. It's informal. My chief sources of information about students are my questionnaires I give at the beginning of the school year. These ask about magazines, hobbies, and the school grapevine. Also, parent/teacher conferences.

In art you get close to students.

Somehow teachers have lost rapport with students. Students don't confide in teachers as they once did.

I have come to know students pretty well over the years. I know the parents. Also, because I have them in class several years, I know what they know.

There are some clues to how students view their relationships with teachers in their statements about how much they believe teachers care about them. Students are tentative about the willingness of teachers to spend time with them outside of class. Typical comments were: "I don't know if they have time or not. They have helped after school," or, "If you ask them, probably." When they are sure teachers will take time, they describe limits or conditions: "If you can't finish a test during class, they'll let you finish after school," or, "If you ask during class about it."

Teachers have demonstrated to students that they care, at least where completing class work is involved. Students report that "They tell you about make-up work," or, "If you miss too many days, they'll tell you and they help with the work," or, "If you're sick, they'll send another student to help you. If you're having trouble, they'll help."

Key groups were mentioned as a vehicle for teachers to show they care about students: "They're accessible. You can go to any of them. Like with key groups. For example, they figure out why you're doing poorly"; "Lately, since the key program started."

The principal finds it difficult to balance the expectations of his position with his own sense of what his connections to students should be:

My contacts with students are chiefly discipline referrals that come from teachers and my being in the hall. I have an open-door policy. Discipline is hard to do combined with staying in touch with kids. When kids come in for discipline, the temptation is to talk to them about "things"—girl friends, sports. I find it hard to get tough.

For their part, students believe the principal knows who they are, and they report having some regular contact with him. Some of the interaction is casual. "He says, 'Hi,' in the halls, and he talks to everybody in the gym." Some of the contact results from the principal's role as advisor to student government. And, of course, some interactions are initiated by him or the student. One student reported, for example, "I went to him over some problems I was having with some other students."

The tone of the principal's interactions with teachers and other staff is pleasant and light. He is calm, quiet, and relaxed. His interactions with students appear to be similar. Students certainly approve of him and describe him as "fair," "terrific," "nice," and "helpful." One student said: "He's better than anyone we've had. Instead of being the big boss, he understands us." Another reported, "He doesn't holler or get mad. He's pretty fair to students."

The counselor has not yet established a pattern of interaction with students or a reputation among them. However, as with so many aspects of school life, students are willing to give him the benefit of the doubt with remarks such as: "He's a good football coach," or, "I haven't seen him much . . . he seems to help kids."

In his grant proposal for Title IV-C funds the superintendent states: "The present high school schedule does not have any homeroom-type program. Students come directly to their first-period class. During the second period staff members read a daily list of announcements. There is no scheduled interaction between adults and students other than academic assignments." Thus, the primary focus of Project SAVE is on the organization of a "cross-grade advisor-advisee program in which the activities are bi-culturally sensitive." Additional problems of the school—for example, drug and alcohol abuse, drop-outs, and poor attendance,—lead to the second priority of the project: the employment of a part-time home-school specialist to encourage better attendance by all students.*

* In a survey of student use of drugs and alcohol, only 27.6 percent of Prairie View students indicated they didn't use alcohol. In the first three months of the fall 1980 term, 3 seniors, 3 juniors, 5 sophomores, and 5 freshmen had dropped out of the high school. The overall district attendance rate was 89 percent for 1979–80. The statewide average is 95 percent. The high school's average is lower than the district's.

The superintendent originated this project, perhaps basing it on an idea he had seen implemented in his former school district. A community task force was created to put together an "action plan for adult and youth development." The school board agreed to continue the program after the third year of federal funding. Teachers do not appear to have been actively included in the program's development.

Teachers are, however, critical to Project SAVE's operation, and the degree to which their support is successfully enlisted for the key group activities will determine its success or failure. Observations of the project's implementation reveal a struggling enterprise, a good idea fighting the weight of old forms. Two teachers, the project coordinator (an Indian man from the area with a master's degree in education), and the principal meet each month to plan the schedule of key group activities for the upcoming month. These are usually a mix of value clarification discussions and sustained silent reading. The key groups are also supposed to be placed where issues important to the school and to students can be discussed, as in the conversations the key groups had of some thefts of school property. Several leads for investigation resulted from these group sessions.

At the planning group's meeting in November, the heart of the program—teacher as counselor—and the problems of successfully implementing it were revealed in the discussion of how to get teachers to take time to talk to their key group members (15 students) about their report cards. It became clear that not all the teachers would do it, and the final decision was to suggest that these conversations be held, that those teachers who want to have them be permitted to do so, and that word-of-mouth advertising do the rest. Teachers vary in the amount of energy they are willing to devote to make this kind of connection with students. One teacher, who is taking the activity seriously and who believes her group is going well, in spite of the long time it took to get to know its student members, feared an outsider to the group would inhibit student discussion of values related to behavior. In another teacher's group, the steps of the activity were followed, but no efforts were made to engage students in the subject. Students were left with fifteen minutes to talk. On a more general level, some students report they don't need to see the school counselor because of their key group activities. Others say that most of their time is spent reading silently.

The second aspect of the program (better attendance), or at least part of it, is enthusiastically supported by teachers. They clearly view the project coordinator as being able to deal with discipline and attendance problems of Indian students in ways they believe they can't.

## Teachers' and Students' Lives: A School for Everyone

"Prairie View is a unique experience, with oil development and Indians." School people agree with this senior's statement. The issue of race is raised in almost every conversation about the school and life within it. The questions contained within these discussions are whether the uniqueness of the place created by the meeting of two cultures is a source of creative energy, whether it is a source of problems, or whether it is something that is best ignored. There is, within the school, evidence that the point of view defined by each question has supporters who are attempting to shape the school's future to conform with the educational implications of each position.

Efforts to make creative educative use of the cultural diversity of the school and community have been largely in establishing special and separate courses and activities. Indian Literature and Hidatsa language courses are the two special classes that reflect the Indian culture of the area. Enrollment in these classes is mainly Indian. There are usually three or four white students in the Indian Literature class, but this fall there was only one; no white students enroll in the Hidatsa class. There are also some efforts to incorporate Indian culture and history into "mainstream" courses. A novel dealing with an Indian theme is read in English I; Indian motifs are encouraged in Art 1 and 2; Indian uses of native plants are briefly studied in Ecology. Teachers do not incorporate relevant content about Indians into U.S. History and American Literature. In history, the reasons given are lack of knowledge and the limitations of the text. In English, the reason is that students in Indian Literature are also students in American Literature and the teacher does not want to repeat herself.

Indian Day represents another effort to incorporate Indian culture into the life of Prairie View High. The event originated in the elementary school, but, for the first time this year, it was celebrated in high school. On Indian Day, half a day of school was devoted to demonstrations of various Indian crafts, Indian speakers, and Indian dancing.

Project SAVE is, as has already been described, another effort to recognize various cultural values and to find a place for them in the school's activities. The in-service program for teachers held prior to the start of school focused on cultural issues. The degree to which cultural issues and values are incorporated into key group meetings at this stage in the project's development is questionable.

Some of the fundamental concerns of people in the high school seem to be the result of basic cultural differences or of the mere existence of a sizable proportion of Indians in the student body. Such concerns include the students' academic performances, attendance, discipline, and their parents' involvement and interest in the school. These problems were discussed broadly earlier. Aspects that make them appear to have a strong racial component are highlighted here.

While there is some disagreement between those who see activities such as Indian Day as necessary and those who do not, there is no disagreement that Indian students have greater academic difficulties than their white colleagues. The classes labeled as "slow" or "difficult" by teachers are made up of Indian students, by and large. Where *de facto* tracking exists in the form of a special class, such as Practical Mathematics, the majority of students in the lower track is Indian. The number of Indian students in classes such as chemistry and advanced mathematics is less than half the proportion predicted by the number of Indian students in the school. Of the total, according to the Title IV coordinator, there is "not enough support of Indian students. They need special assistance with reading, writing, etc. We need special teachers and tutoring services." The superintendent indicates that "while Indian students are going to college in increasing numbers, their success rate is not high. Most return to the reservation during their first year."

Teachers think of Prairie View as an "abnormal" school, and when they describe it this way they are thinking of absenteeism. While teachers and administrators do not readily label attendance issues as an "Indian problem" and, in fact, go out of their way to say it is not, the lists of students who have major attendance problems or who have non-credited classes because of absences include only a few non-Indian students. Of the fifty-four students listed as having major attendance problems in the fall semester, six were white students.

The discipline problem that some Prairie View teachers consider so pervasive has a special definition. High school classrooms appear orderly and quiet. School-type misbehavior—talking out of turn, restlessness, throwing papers—is most frequently found in the junior high classes and does not appear to be the heart of the issue. What teachers define as a decreased motivation to learn and a decreased interest in school—attitude changes in students described in more detail elsewhere—form the core of the problem. The degree to which Prairie View teachers ascribe this problem to the increased Indian enrollment cannot be definitively stated. Most teachers leave the impression that these difficulties have become greater in the last few years—there has been a significant proportion of Indian students only in the last few years—but some doubt they would find a different situation in another school. Only one teacher expressed views in this regard that were clearly antagonistic to Indian students.

Parental involvement is another issue that appears to be directly related to the number of Indian students attending the school. The decline of parental support is traced by some teachers to the increased number of Indian students.

In spite of the sense that non-Indian parents and some teachers question the attention being paid to Indian students, several efforts are made to give Indian students special support and help. The Title IV coordinator is hired to give support to Indian students through counseling and tutoring, curriculum development, and contact with Indian parents. "Two to three times a year, I bring all of the Indian students together. This is a means of supporting the separate identity of the students. It is important to know they are different in order to involve themselves well with non-Indian students in the school." The Eagle Feather Club, advised by the Title IV coordinator, is open only to Indian students and, as has been seen in previous descriptions, is a growing and active group. The director of Project SAVE provides additional support by aiding faculty development, making home visits, and helping teachers work more effectively with difficult students. Several teachers have studied aspects of Indian culture through graduate course work. The superintendent affirms a desire to redress the balance, which tilts in favor of white students. "Success is built in for white kids," he said. "We want to favor our Indian students, but it is not easy. The administration must take the view the school is for everyone."

Whether in response to the rich cultural diversity of the community or in response to the educational problems and needs generated by cultural difference and long-term racial prejudice, school people in Prairie View are making efforts to develop a unique place. However tentative, these efforts generate the tension revealed in the superintendent's statement. The wish to be "normal," or at least wondering what it would be like; the beliefs that schools should be impartial in their efforts, and that cultural differences do not justify variations in schooling; and the support for the goal of helping students become members of society all lead to efforts to keep the school like all others— or at least to try to make it conform to a concept of all other high schools. The attempts to provide special support and curricular offerings, while of good quality, do not, in the final analysis, have the potential of pushing the school far from the traditional mold of a high school. In creating a "school for everyone," a search is not being made for alternative formats for a high school education. The uniqueness of the place will continue for some time to be the nature of the student body, not the nature of the program.

PART IV

ALTERNATIVE HIGH
SCHOOL

# 9

## NEILL HOUSE

### WAYNE B. JENNINGS
### AND RUTH ANN OLSON

Neill House, a product of the radical sixties, began in 1971. Its roots lie in the generalized social unrest and the specific demands for political, social, and educational reform that characterized the era. Throughout the nation, educators such as Silberman, Holt, and Featherstone were advocating substantive educational change, and demands for students' rights were loud. Throughout this city, private storefront schools rejected the public system. In several neighborhoods, groups agitated for reform, and a local college hosted a multistate meeting for people interested in defining and demanding public school change.

Early in 1971, district administrators decided to learn from this ferment of ideas and to tap into the energy of the people involved. They concluded that a pluralistic society should offer its students and parents a choice of several forms of educational programs. One section of the city would serve as a pilot project wherein teachers, parents, and students would decide how to structure excellent education within the labels of traditional, continuous progress, open, and free schools. Parents and students would choose the schools best for them. Not so incidentally, the district hoped that the goals of desegregation and integration would also be served. No one was certain just what the labels should mean, but, with the help of federal funding, the school staffs and communities were given a summer to get the schools started and several years to work out the bugs before the system would be expanded to other parts of the city.

An historical report describes the initial developers of Neill House:

As was expected, [Neill House] people came from the ranks of left-liberal dissent. Many were reform-movement activists for such causes as civil rights, ending the war, and feminism. Some were radically doubtful that "Amerika" was reformable at all by any normal political process. They might harbor hopes for revolution, or by lifestyle and associates rest their faith in the growth of a counter-culture within.

What brought [Neill House] founders together in education was their own experience of it. As parents, teachers, and high school students, they had all found that public schools were places that contradicted the values which they themselves considered important. The contradiction was more than a matter of distasteful pedagogy, though certainly it included that. It was crucially a matter of ethos and expectation. The emblems of school—compulsory attendance, prescribed texts, the threat of failure, administrative hierarchies, social workers, patriotic exercises, dress codes—were badges of belonging to "the system." Public schools were part of the establishment [Neill House] people were dissenting from. That was why free schools were needed.

Yet, now the suspect system itself had invited those who despaired of it to get organized, draw from the public purse, and do their thing within the system.

For its first year, seventy students in grades K through twelve were chosen by lottery from a larger list of applicants. They were virtually all (95 percent) white and were heavily from families of high educational background. These students and their parents were given the right to interview and select staff, and also the right to pool the money budgeted for three teachers and a coordinator and divide it equally among six staff people—thus increasing the expected staff and furthering their cause of equality. Five of the six teachers chosen were under twenty-five years old, five were male, all were white, and none had ever worked in a public school. One person was selected to be head teacher and to serve as the administrative link with the larger school district. The original home for Neill House was space rented from a local church. Before its doors opened for the first day of school, virtually no curricular planning was accomplished. The need to ready the space had consumed all the available preparation time. The absence of curriculum was generally acceptable to people because the intent was to "create the program with the kids."

During the first year at Neill House, staff and students informally sorted themselves out by age groups (for example, big kids, little kids) by the people who most enjoyed working with each group, and by interests such as gym, art, and current affairs. Extended field trips and campouts were seen as important activities. Debate about the meaning of "freedom" was constantly present as problems of schedules, choices, and responsibility began to get in people's way. Eventually, a governing board of staff, parents, and students was formed to ponder problems both large and small. Confusion, chaos, individualism, and unfocused idealism dominated the school.

Over the years, Neill House has changed in many ways. The student body has expanded to 181 students (114 in grades K through eight and 67 in grades nine through twelve). Participants worked with local street academies and so-called survival schools in order to expand their appeal and to change the white, middle-class nature of their student body. The current student body is 37 percent minority, including 7 percent black students and 30 percent Indian students.

The school now has a principal assigned by the school district central administration; an allocation of 7.2 staff positions, divided among state-certificated full- and part-time teachers; civil-service hired aides; and part-time social worker, nurse, counselor, special education and other support positions typical of the allocated assignments of other schools in the same district. Staff salaries are determined by standard district union-negotiated salary schedules.

The school is now located in a public school building, and the governing board has effectively become an advisory council. The curriculum meets rough district guidelines, though teachers assume a high level of autonomy in determining the specific content of their classes. Students continue to take regular field trips, including a secondary students' trip to Mexico or other distant site each year. Graduation from Neill House depends upon completion of a comprehensive set of competency-based graduation requirements—a system unique to this school within the district. The chaos and confusion has been replaced by a sense of organization and calm and an intense pride in an atmosphere of personalized caring.

In an urban district faced with typical conditions of declining enrollment, increasing costs, and aging staff, decisions are on the drawing boards for closing schools and merging programs. Even so, staff at Neill House feel relatively confident of their place in the system. They talk of the possibilities of moving to another building, of sharing space with another school, and of joining political forces with other alternative schools within the district in order to press for survival. They have weathered great changes in the past ten years. They continue to feel confident of the importance of their original reasons for the existance of Neill House and of what that existence means to students.

## Students

Some quick and easy observations can be made during a visit to the halls and classrooms of Neill House. The students are relaxed and friendly. They are at ease talking to a visitor. In general, they are open and courteous to each other and to adults.

The presence of elementary school children in and about the building seems to give teen-agers a sense of responsibility. Young children have more freedom than those in most schools, and high school students exercise a gentle form of supervision. The younger children respond well to this attention, and the older students sense their value as custodians of an orderly society. Both ages benefit from each other's presence. A sort of kindness pervades the school.

As students got off the school busses one morning, a snowball fight started up in the fresh moist snow. Two camps, one of older the other of younger students, formed. For the most part, they kept their distance, only occasionally raiding each other's supply of people or snowballs. The interaction had an easy naturalness about it, without the aggressiveness that sometimes occurs in such a setting. When the principal came out and said it was time for school, the students dropped their snowballs and, with lots of laughter and chatter, went inside. One senses that students are regarded as important in their own right by staff and by each other. This works well for all.

There doesn't appear to be a smoking problem within the school. The telltale signs of a drug problem in or about the building are also absent. The student minority population is 37 percent, but no racial problems are observed or spoken about.

As with students everywhere, the peer group is important. Yet peer groups are not entrenched. It seems as though students can endure being alone in this school. There is an absence of labelling by students and teachers. There are few cliques, but there appears to be some separation between the more recent enrollees and students who have been at the school longer. The long-termers are less tolerant of peer group behavior that smacks of fronting or showing off. This is considered immature and unnecessary at Neill House. Recent enrollees say it takes time to break into the crowd and make friends. However, if anything is in vogue it is individuality of dress, personal style, and goals. Conformity in these matters is absent.

In grades nine to twelve there are 67 students at Neill House. Balance by gender and race is representative of the school district as a whole, except that there are fewer black students and substantially more Indian students. A previous principal, who was Indian, was thought to be the primary reason for a large influx of Native American students, who found the school more compatible and who continue to enroll at Neill House as a citywide alternative school.

The student population is diverse in academic ability. Among long-term enrollees are students who handle school work easily and those who have difficulty. Among recent enrollees are students who did well in their former school and those who experienced much trouble with academics or school rules. Some students can be described as in the fugitive class—that is, those who fled in desperation from their previous school.

As the day begins, groups of students socialize all about the building—talking of the previous evening's activities, wondering about the new student, making the rounds of the halls, as if to see whether anything has changed, saying hello to friends and teachers. In a few cases, they prepare a lesson or project, or have a smoke near the back steps.

Teachers feel there are two main groups of students. One group of academically talented students had been bored and constrained by regular schools. They rebelled in their former schools and, for the most part, are doing well at Neill House. The other group has personal and emotional problems that are not automatically solved by transfer to Neill House. In fact, this group is very difficult to help, and there is discussion of the need for more careful screening of applicants in order to avoid becoming a dumping ground for other schools.

One student has attended Neill House since it opened. He likes the school and describes himself as one who reads a lot. Questioned about reading tastes, he lists several areas of science and music. A number of students fit the constellation of bright and independent. They enjoy the school and its freedom. They use the school as a broker or facilitator to arrange a wide range of learning experiences in and out of the building.

One student describes himself as gay and interested in acting. He says he would have been persecuted in his former school if these things had been known. He expresses considerable appreciation that he can be himself and is respected for it at Neill House. He speaks of a friend who is interested in tailoring and who also would have been subject to negative peer pressures at his former school.

Some students who are academically able are making poor progress with their studies because of attendance and personal problems. These and a number of other students exhibit serious problems characteristic of high school students in any large city. Some are emancipated and alienated from parents. Some are chemically dependent. Some seem unable to focus on school because of problems that range from neglect or abuse to physical ailments. When absences become prolonged, students are dropped from the rolls after several warnings. Some of these students remain at home doing very little; others work full-time.

Teachers report that fewer students than in the past claim emancipation and job problems. This may reflect a changed school population, though teachers feel this relates to societal changes. Confrontations over student rights are diminishing, and this may mean fewer conflicts within families. The number of student dropouts is increasing in both percentages and in absolute numbers. Some may drop out rather than struggle with the challenges of school.

For students experiencing problems, the openness of the school tends to surface such problems more readily than would be the case in regular schools. Trying to hold a conversation with a counselor during school hours is impossible because of the constant parade of students wanting to discuss a problem. Students signal this in ways ranging from the obvious: "Can I talk to you about a problem?" to "I'm feeling depressed. I think I'll go home," in the hope of an invitation to come in and talk it over. This may mean that youth have more problems growing up and adjusting than school people are generally aware of. It is not until one is close to youth that such matters surface. The staff of Neill House is accessible, and their interest in students as persons is an important factor in the willingness of students to disclose their problems. Staff estimates of the proportion of students who would not have completed high school if Neill House did not exist range from one-third to one-half.

Neill House uses a weak advisor/advisee program. That is, each student is assigned to a staff member as advisor. The advisor's responsibilities include knowing the student well, helping him/her develop a suitable program, helping with problems, and maintaining contact with the home. Some advisors interpret this as being available to students if the students seek them out. Other advisors give a high priority to their role as advisors and check with their advisees frequently.

Students are quick to express their positive feelings about Neill House. They like the informal and personal relationships with peers and staff. Teachers are called by their first names. Students report they feel trusted and respected. They feel free to express their feelings. They say the school is fair and reasonable in its rules. There is little evidence of hostility or resentment, and virtually no vandalism or damage to the building. No one is threatening to get even. Many students like the small size of the school and the fact that one can know everyone. The most frequent comment by students is that they feel liked by their teachers and that the staff really cares about them.

Students were asked about their previous schools. Almost all say they like Neill House better. In some cases the feelings are very strong: "————High School sucks"; "My old school is all petty rules, and they treat you like a baby." A few students have reservations about Neill House and are planning to leave for another school. One said, "I don't feel like I'm learning enough here." Another said, "My parents want me to go to a parochial school." This student, when questioned further, disclosed that she wanted to remain at Neill House.

Some students are concerned about the limited curriculum offerings. For others, this problem is solved by taking courses in other high schools or at the state university a few blocks away. Students also like the individualized programs built around their needs. They feel a great freedom to develop their own course of studies, and they speak fondly of some of the long field trips.

Students at Neill House are idealistic about such values as justice, the environment, and peace. One told us, "There are too many people who don't get a fair shake." Several feel there is too much violence on television and that there is not enough love in the world. When asked about watching television, the typical response was they don't have time and there isn't much good on anyway—"Television rots the mind." They like radio. As background, it relaxes them. They don't report much time spent reading the newspaper.

In contrast to teachers' views, a perennial area of teen-age concern is jobs. Jobs are hard to find and sometimes school hours interfere with getting one.

A staff member who had been at the school for many years and is well liked by students made a number of interesting observations.

> The kids have changed a lot since I first came to this school. Ten years ago, the kids were pretty well informed about lots of things. They were not necessarily smart, but they liked to read, to discuss issues, and to analyze their opinions. The kids now have a very limited general knowledge. They know a lot about their favorite topic, whatever that may be. But otherwise their opinions are terribly shallow. They don't read books or newspapers, but rely on the opinions of friends for their own opinions. Most of these kids know they are against Reagan and for whales. But they can't give you a single reason why.
>
> Kids are attracted to each other by good times, not by common interests. It's pretty eerie to walk into a party and find kids drinking with other kids they don't even like. Being friends isn't what matters. Having fun is what it's all about. In all, I think kids are more self-destructive, less self-honest than they used to be. They've been through more; they care about things less.

Students at Neill House span the spectrum of youth. But, for the most part, it seems Neill House students are more alike than different from students in other high schools. The setting of the school—informal and caring—seems to help them examine themselves, help them deal with their problems, help them feel better about themselves.

## Goals

There are four sets of goals at Neill House that will be examined: student outcome goals, operational or process goals, stated goals, and implicit goals.

The Neill House student outcome goals are:

1. Learning the basic skills of communication, mathematics, science, social criticism, and personal maintenance.

2. Understanding the inner and the outer forces that influence individuals and society so that the student can use those forces to increase freedom rather than diminish it.
3. Recognizing that racism, sexism, and social and economic stratification are major societal forces working against freedom.
4. Recognizing that one of the major societal problems of today and of the future is the preservation of a healthy world ecosystem.

Except for the first goal, these are not the standard goals of most schools. A classic free school model that was popular in the late 1960s and early 1970s is based on freedom from political, social class, and economic domination. Neill House fits this model. The school's first staff complement wrote these goals and parents ratified them. They have been reviewed and ratified several times since. A walk around the school reveals posters that support the political posture of these goals.

The observers recall a far more vivid stance by Neill House in its earlier years. The posters and slogans then created a climate of instant readiness to march on City Hall or to vigorously argue the cause of justice. Feelings were worn on the sleeve and visitors could feel the zeal for a more just society.

Today's observer doesn't pick this up nearly as quickly. There are fewer posters and slogans. A mellower mood prevails. Staff and student views are much less in agreement, though the issues are not spoken or argued about as much. There seems to be a tacit agreement not to fight or create unpleasantness about such matters. Still, goals are the same. It is apparent that the original ideals issues are important to the most powerful people in the school, though they are less universally felt.

The concentration on traditional basic skills is more obvious now than in previous years. Earlier, it was more readily assumed that basic skills would develop as a matter of course while working on larger projects; that is, the learning would be more integrated and correlated with large-scale learning activities. However, school district authorities were determined to demonstrate that students in all schools were learning the basics. When the district decided to test Neill House students, using standardized tests, it was confronted with considerable opposition.

Most alternative schools question standardized tests as a measure of achievement. Except for some aspects of goal one, the usual annual standardized tests do not touch on most of the goals Neill House has selected. After some acrimonious debate, Neill House consented to district testing if it was enhanced with criterion-referenced testing. All tests indicated little statistical difference in the attainment of Neill House students and students of similar ability in other schools. In more recent years, the staff (including administration) has become more traditional, and the testing issue lies largely dormant as a public controversy.

The operational goals of the school, listed below, were recently revised in response to a need for a clear statement for new staff and parents.

1. Children learn by imitation and observation. Adults should make their activities open to children. Use the skills of parents and community to enlarge children's experiences.
2. Create a learning environment full of manipulatives and games and objects to play with and that lead to exploration.
3. Provide inter-age experiences. Use the resources of the whole school. Give children opportunities to be with other teachers and children of all ages to provide continuity and stability through the years.
4. Give children responsibility for their own learning. Give children choices. Involve children in problem solving. Use goals set and agreed on by children. Children should keep their own records with periodic review by parents and teachers.
5. Use flexibility in teaching. If children have no interest in one subject, try another. Let children's interests come up.
6. Be aware of the needs of the whole child. Children need physical activity. Teach social skills in groups. Talk about feelings.
7. Avoid competition as motivation for learning. Competition can only satisfy a few and discourage many.
8. Use child-centered values, not teacher-centered ones.
9. Avoid comparisons between children.
10. Children should be encouraged toward excellence.
11. Use encouragement, not praise.
12. Do not use food, prizes, or behavior mod for motivation.
13. For children who are out of control, give positive attention and responsibility.
14. Avoid power struggles. Be consistent and avoid long harangues after the rules are set.
15. Teach children to use words and to express feeling, not physical reactions.

16. Provide natural and logical consequences.
17. Separate the doer from the deed.
18. Work cooperatively with other staff with open communications, using other's suggestions, taking criticism, being flexible, and encouraging others.
19. Be willing to work with other age groups.
20. Avoid value judgments in relation to lifestyles, language style, and clothing.
21. Be receptive to parents and use their skills and ideas.
22. Free school works only toward the graduation requirements and there are no grades, credits, or pressure to perform on standardized tests.

For the most part, these operational goals are part of the tenets of the progressive education movement. In fact, many of these statements can be found in most methods textbooks for traditional education.

The implicit daily operational or process goals appear to the observers to be:

1. Attend school regularly.
2. Care for each person. Exercise humaneness.
3. Provide an appropriate educational program tailored to each individual.
4. Get students through the graduation process. Provide a rescue mission in some cases.
5. In earlier years: question authority.

If these appear to be the daily operational guides, there remain deeper core values. These seem, after observation and talking with Neill House parents, staff, and students, to fall into the following categories:

1. Students are to become autonomous. They are to think for themselves and be self-directed.
2. Students are to have integrity. Their behavior is to be consistent with their beliefs and values. They are to be open and nonmanipulative.
3. Students are to be life-long learners. They are to be open to ideas and experiences and to seek new ways of thinking and new information.
4. Students learn from experiences. Therefore, the more experiences, the more learning. Knowledge is not planted by others. Knowledge develops as a result of many experiences tempered by previous learnings.

Neill House appears to operate on the assumption that the fixed courses of a base curriculum are not appropriate for all secondary-age students because the world is moving too fast, and fixed bodies of learning become obsolete and outmoded. Traditional subjects as the base curriculum are dull and artificial. Academic goals are left to fend for themselves as ancillary to the graduation competency requirements. Few school people would be comfortable with these approaches, yet there appears to be no evidence that Neill House students are not doing as well as their counterparts in traditional schools.

Aside from planning for meeting the graduation standards, students do not appear to be involved in goal setting. The school has an existential feel about it. Students could be true architects of their own education, yet this opportunity is partially lost with staff arriving daily to teach in their subject specialties. This is not always the case, but, as in most schools, it seems teachers often assume traditional roles as the easiest course of action. It is not easy to plan with students and to involve them in the design of their own education. The difficulties diminish, however, when the school becomes excited over some project such as social action or long-distance field trips. Such activities are powerful learning experiences for youth.

The goals indicate that Neill House is a school devoted to a fairer society and to seeing its students assume social responsibility in that direction.

## Climate

Neill House is in an old inner-city school building. It is well maintained but lacks any particular look of welcome to the stranger. The visitor's first impression of the interior is a long expanse of hallway broken only with an occasional college recruitment poster or out-of-date calendar.

Only slowly does one begin to notice signs that people are relaxed and welcomed here. Big adolescents and little kindergarteners move through the halls together with an easy matter-of-factness, largely ignoring one another, but with an occasional exchange of greeting or inquiry. In the front hallway, there is a rack of small coats and boots, apparently unmolested by the hourly passage of big and little bodies. Nearby, several drawings are taped to the wall with an appeal:

Dear Friends,

The kinders would like to display their good work here. Please help it be a positive experience by refraining from tearing our work.

Thank you,
Shirley and the Kinders

None of the drawings is torn.

The area for most secondary classes is upstairs. Passing through a cluster of secondary students at the bottom of the stairway requires some maneuverability; they neither help nor purposely hinder the passing stranger. The stairway landings display more artwork—graphics painted on the wall, posters advertising art exhibits and theater productions throughout the city, and an announcement of an upcoming Indian pow-wow. In the upstairs hall, is a hexagonal dome greenhouse and two teachers' desks complete with books, papers, staplers, and plants. Though the area is often unattended by any adult presence, it is intact. The objects suffer from neither vandalism nor theft. Individual classrooms are a jumble of small tables, bookcases, sofas, books, posters, and display cases.

As students pass between classes (no bells—people just watch the clocks), there is much conversation. People know each other's names and use them. A teacher is greeted, "Hi, Joyce," and the stranger, too, "Hi, Joyce's friend." Students call to teachers to check out a detail about an assignment or a special project, or to give a verbal explanation for absence from class. At one point, a group of six or eight students cluster together, their conversation spattered with tough talk and profanity. A teacher steps into the hallway and says sharply, "Phil!" The students move quickly into classrooms, unwilling to push their rebellion to a point of hassling with the teacher.

In the school office, a teen-ager, who has injured his knee in gym class, tries to phone his parent to arrange a ride home. No one at home has access to a car; he will have to take a city bus. The counselor overhears the conversation and calls to him, "John, you need a ride home? The bus will be kind of hard; I'll give you a ride." They disappear down the hall toward the parking lot, the counselor inquiring, "You still live on the north side?"

The students and most of the staff are at Neill House because they've made a clear choice to be here. When asked why they've made that choice, answers from students and staff alike are generously sprinkled with words like "attachment," "belong," "safety," and "a real home." Students like having teachers who know who they are, teachers who will take the time to talk with them and listen to them.

One result of the commitment to fill the need for personalized caring is a lack of attention to some administrative details. In November, the calendars in the hallways appear not to have been updated since September. The school graduation requirements, written in 1973, still refer to all students as "he." Parents complain that without advance information about course offerings, they are unable to participate in their children's schedule decisions. Non-sexist language and good communication are clearly issues in which Neill House staff are interested. Caring about kids, however, is an all-consuming task for them. The paperwork of administrative detail receives much lower priority.

Some teachers have been here for as long as nine years; others are new this year. One person is assigned as a long-term substitute to be replaced by another teacher in November. They all have reasons for liking to be where they are—the easy interaction with students, the curricular autonomy, the sense of belonging.

But, as in any community, there are differences and tensions. Among the seven secondary staff members, there is a social and philosophical division, largely, but not entirely, between the old-timers and the newcomers. For the old-timers, Neill House is part of their family. Their friends are here, their sense of vocation is here. They talk about the attachment they have to the school, the difficulty they would have in leaving it. They have known some of the students for a long time. In a very real sense, the old-time students and the old-time staff have grown up together.

The teachers who have come to the school more recently like the school, but it is not the center of their lives. Their friends are elsewhere and, though they have come here by choice, they are confident that they could do much of what is important to them in other jobs or at other schools.

Opinions differ on issues of curriculum, academic expectations for students, and appropriateness of social relationships between students and staff. Some of the relative newcomers believe that the "in group–out group" feeling within the staff also carries over to some of the students, with old-time staff giving preferential attention to certain students while others are excluded.

The tensions are real, but they do not consume the feelings of people toward one another. Conversation is generally easy, and staff members find pleasure in socializing with each other at an occasional staff party.

To some degree the feeling of community at Neill House is based on a sense of providing protection from the outside world. A frequent answer of students, when asked why they chose to come to the school, centers on the presumed evils of the larger public high schools in their neighborhoods. Students report not liking what they perceive to be the rules of those schools—dress codes, having to take certain classes, having to sit alphabetically—and the mean kids who beat up other kids. Though these perceptions are of debatable validity, they have been a factor in those students' choice of schools.

The most immediate community within which Neill House exists is its community of parents. Some families have had children at this school since its beginning ten years ago. Many of those people worked hard giving birth to the school and nursing it through its early traumas. Though they still believe deeply in the school, their lives have largely turned to other activities, and they are often not able to help in any regular fashion.

For a few years this left a vacuum. Recently, though, another group of parents has stepped forward. They are new to the school; they are, for the most part, parents of elementary-age students; and they are anxious to learn and to contribute. They volunteer in classrooms, they plan all-school events for students' families, and they intervene with the central district administration when they think their school has gotten a bum rap. There are many opportunities for those parents who want such a relationship to become deeply immersed in the workings of the school.

Staff members all report a strong sense of support from parents. One teacher explains, "At one time we had lots of philosophical support from parents. Now, there are more people involved and we get more overall support." Several teachers talk about the advantages of working in a school where parents keep track of kids' progress. "Parents show up. They volunteer. And they have something to say about school policy."

The larger community of Neill House extends far beyond its immediate neighborhood, for it is a citywide alternative and draws students from the entire school district. As a result, it has few ties with the neighborhood. It successfully solicits contributions for fund-raising activities from nearby merchants, but otherwise has little contact with them. To the extent that they do interact, Neill House people report a sense of acceptance by those around them.

Neill House exists solidly within the context of the community of alternative programs in the district. As the only public free school, it has not been involved with the support groups that have developed around some of the other alternative schools. Nevertheless, it depends on and receives generalized support by being part of the larger alternative system.

As budgets are cut and buildings face closure, Neill House looks more seriously at the possibility of sharing a building, and possibly staff, with other programs. The district's board of education is well aware of the high administrative costs of Neill House. At least two board members have expressed strong support for it as a free school alternative, but both say that ways must be found to reduce costs.

In the ten years since its birth, Neill House has undergone many major organizational changes. Its supporters are relatively confident that they can retain the flexibility necessary for its survival.

## Curriculum

In 1971, Neill House started with a staff that had never taught in public schools and whose feelings about curriculum were, "We'll work it out as we go." Historically, curriculum has been a point of frequent disagreement at the school. There have always been those who have argued that the curriculum must be flexible enough to do whatever is necessary to keep students in school and to help them graduate. Others take the position that such endless flexibility results in a curriculum without standards, one which is watered down to the extent of doing students a disservice.

*Graduation Requirements*  In 1973, it was decided that a way out of the dilemma was to establish a set of graduation requirements. Staff and students could have almost unlimited flexibility in how to meet the requirements, but a certain agreed-upon set of competencies would serve as the final standard by which to judge a student's readiness to leave the school. This detailed document, entitled simply "Graduation Requirements," is still the basis for the curriculum at Neill House.

The basic requirement states:

> [Neill House] defines its graduation requirements in four very broad areas of basic skills and responsibility: (1) communication and language; (2) mathematics and science; (3) social perspective and humanities; and (4) personal achievement and independence. In each of these areas, every student will show a minimum level of achievement. In at least two of these areas, each student will show proficiency beyond the minimum.
>
> The heart of this system is that each student shares in making each decision about his own graduation from [Neill House]—when he thinks he can be "ready," what special expectations are appropriate for him, how to evaluate whether, in fact, he should graduate, and what should be the final entry in his public school records. A student may be certified for the diploma any time after his 16th birthday.

The twenty-page document includes detailed definitions of "minimum achievement" and "additional proficiency," samples of study contracts, procedures, and checklists. The process for each student requires a committee consisting of the student, the student's advisor, two staff members, a parent or other significant adult, and a non-Neill House adult, such as a job supervisor.

Throughout the process, "proficiency" is defined as "demonstrated skill or knowledge." Examples of ways to demonstrate proficiency include:

1. Teach someone else the skill or knowledge.
2. Publish one's own writing or artwork.
3. Participate in area of proficiency—i.e., school governance.
4. Demonstrate skill on a musical instrument.
5. Write a log or analysis of a travel experience.
6. Make or produce something.

Because fulfillment of these requirements depends on "demonstrated skill," it is often difficult for the outside observer to know or to see just what that means. Teachers talk of filmstrips made by students, participation by students in leadership activities, logs of trips, and other demonstrations that are logically not available for someone to look at in a file.

Some teachers express skepticism about the actual implementation of the requirements. An English teacher questions the legitimacy of a student being able to complete the language requirements without ever having taken an English class. Another teacher is curious about how some students, who had never accomplished anything during several years at Neill House, can suddenly complete all the requirements in one year when they are seventeen years old and ready to leave.

Other teachers vehemently defend the system, saying that the whole purpose of the school is to accept students where they are and to individualize the curriculum and the graduation requirements accordingly. They argue that the standards are high—for each individual.

The most carefully defined and standardized requirements exist in the area of mathematics, where students are required to complete a series of work sheets, ten tests covering particular areas of mathematics, and a general graduation test. The math teacher is new this year, so she has never worked with this system before. When asked what would happen if a student did not finish all the math sheets and tests, she replied that the student simply would not be able to graduate. She hastily added that she can't imagine that such is a real possibility, however. She says that the point is to work closely enough with each student nearing graduation to make sure that everyone is on schedule and to give whatever help is needed to make sure that completion is possible.

*Course Offerings*　Course offerings at Neill House fall within the major areas of staff assignments—math, science, social studies, English, physical education, and industrial arts. Within these general departmental headings, individual teachers are responsible for naming their own courses and for defining their own content. Courses offered to the sixty-seven secondary students during the first grading period of 1981–82 included:

World Geography—Africa and East Asia
Western Civilization—ancient and European history

Political Science—how governments work
English Vocabulary—spelling, writing, using new vocabulary words
*Man and Superman*—reading the play by George Bernard Shaw
Paperback Reading—reading your choice of paperback books and writing a book report or project on one of the books you read
Industrial Arts—learn the use of tools and machines. Design and complete an individual woodworking project
Algebra—learn to solve equations and apply to practical problems
Consumer Math—geometry, advanced algebra, trigonometry
Kung Fu—learn to discipline your mind and body
Holistic Health—study functions of the mind and body, how they relate separately and together
Body Shop—weight training, running, aerobic conditioning, yoga, and meditation
Secondary Science—scientific method, health, drug use, the human body, planet earth, and current events in science

An additional course offering each year is the extended field trip—to Mexico, Jamaica, or to Washington, D.C. The bulk of the students who choose to participate are seventh and eighth graders, with only fifteen of the sixty-seven high school students choosing to participate this year. The field trip is variously seen as both a contribution to and a distraction from the Neill House curriculum. It contributes to students' learning through participation in preparatory classes on geography, language, and history of the area to be visited. Further, students are not allowed to participate unless they are doing well in and regularly attending their other classes. As one might expect at Neill House, major curricular goals of the trip include learning to plan to get along with one another and personal problem solving.

Some staff, however, see the extended field trip as a distraction and an annoyance. Students are called from their regular classes to prepare for the trip and, as the departure date draws near, the importance of routine classwork pales beside the flurry of trip activities. Further, the monetary demands of the trip dominate virtually all fund-raising activities of the school.

Curriculum is a major concern for many people at the school. The staff is very small and all the teachers and many parents express frustration over the courses that they cannot offer. They are keenly aware of the weakness in the science curriculum—no physics, no chemistry, no advanced science of any kind. Within some subject areas, there is disagreement about the strength of the offerings. Some people argue, for example, that the English curriculum needs to be made more demanding. There is, however, a strong commitment to the autonomy of the individual teacher to make curricular decisions. People are aware of the uneasy balance between individual and institutional needs—between, on the one hand, the interest of a teacher in teaching a certain subject and of a student in learning that subject and, on the other hand, the interest of the school in providing a balanced curriculum. As one person explained, "Any negotiating among the staff about curriculum must be done *very* diplomatically, and no leadership person has the right to assign anything to a teacher."

The school has developed two basic ways of enriching its curriculum. One is through use of volunteers to teach certain subjects. At any given time, three to five volunteers will likely be teaching classes for which students receive transcript credit. These tend, however, not to be the hard academic classes, about which people are concerned because they are absent. More likely, they are courses such as conflict resolution and career exploration. The other common means of enriching the curriculum is by encouraging Neill House students to take particular courses at a nearby high school or community college. Though they have rarely been willing to use these resources in the past, about ten students are enrolled in such institutions this year.

Extracurricular activities are virtually nonexistent at Neill House. Debate, intramural or interscholastic athletics, chess, drama, and other organized activities typically offered to high school students outside the defined school day play no part in this school, except to the extent that they are part of a particular course activity. Students may take part in the athletic teams of their home attendance area school. One student does so.

*Students' Curriculum* Neill House schedules are organized around three twelve-week trimesters. At the beginning of each trimester, students work out their class schedules with some help from a faculty advisor. Since graduation depends on demonstrated abilities rather than on completion of credits in predefined areas, enrollment in courses is a matter of negotiated choice rather than requirement. Examination of twenty-six cumulative records, 40 percent of the current secondary students in the school, shows that students have been enrolled in anywhere from one to nine courses during single trimesters from grades nine through eleven, with an average of 4.5 courses at any given time. The table below shows a breakdown of time spent by students in curricular areas. The normal state requirements listed for curricular areas are approximate since the state requirements are for grades nine through twelve, whereas these students have only completed eleventh grade.

AVERAGE NUMBER OF TRIMESTER CREDITS EARNED BY 26 STUDENTS

| Subject Area | Grade 9 | Grade 10 | Grade 11 | Total Credits | Approximate State Requirements (in Trimesters) |
|---|---|---|---|---|---|
| Math | 2.6 | 2.3 | 1.9 | 6.8 | 2.0 |
| English | 1.8 | 2.9 | 1.4 | 6.1 | 12.0 |
| Social Studies | 1.0 | 1.7 | 2.0 | 4.7 | 9.0 |
| Science | 0.8 | 1.2 | 1.5 | 3.5 | 1.0 |
| Shop | 2.3 | 1.4 | 1.4 | 5.1 | 2.0 |
| Art/Dance | 2.0 | 2.0 | 0.6 | 4.6 | 1.0 |
| Health | 0.3 | 0.3 | 0.5 | 1.1 | 2.0 |
| Gym | 1.3 | 1.5 | 0.6 | 3.4 | 3.0 |
| Work Program | 0.0 | 0.5 | 0.7 | 1.2 | 0.0 |
| Field Trip | 1.0 | 0.5 | 0.4 | 1.9 | 0.0 |
| Graduate Seminar | 0.0 | 0.5 | 0.6 | 1.1 | 0.0 |
| Foreign Language | 0.2 | 0.0 | 0.0 | 0.2 | 0.0 |
| Miscellaneous | 0.1 | 0.1 | 0.0 | 0.2 | 0.0 |

## Teachers

Ten years ago, when Neill House was created, its seventy K through twelve students had six staff people to work with them. Though they were legally hired by the school district, their selection depended on recommendations by an interviewing committee of students and parents. Five of the six staff were under age twenty-five, five were male, all were white, none had ever worked in a public school, and all were ideologically and practically supportive of the decision to divide four salaries among six people.

None of those original six people are still teaching at the school.

The student body has grown to 181 students, 67 of whom are in grades nine through twelve. Eight people have pieces of time assigned to teaching classes to these 67 students. It is still largely (six of the eight) a male group and, though not as young as they used to be, their average age of less than thirty-five makes them younger than other high school staffs throughout the city. They now include two people of minority backgrounds. All but one are fully licensed teachers. The one exception has been at Neill House for nine years and, though classified as a teacher aide, he functions in the school as one of the teachers. Other staff people who interact with secondary students as well as with all other students in the school include a community resource coordinator, a principal, and part-time people including a social worker, counselor, special education teacher, and a Title I teacher.

Though it is generally accurate to say that staff members at Neill House are there by choice, the choice is of a different quality than that faced by the original staff. Ten years ago, teachers had to seek out Neill House. They had to apply for the position, face a series of interviews, and pass muster by Neill House standards. Parents and students no longer have any role in the selection of teachers and administrators. Now, the central office assigns someone to the school. In the case of the principal, it is a firm assignment. In the case of most other staff members, they can say "no," but the consequences of such a decision depends upon what other positions are open to that person in the district.

Students, parents, and staff all speak of the vulnerability of the school in regard to staffing. The school is in its eleventh year of existence and has had five administrators during that time. Though some teachers have been there for many years, it is not uncommon for people to leave after one year, or even in the middle of a school year.

Though it cannot be clear just how much the current staff would defend the official Neill House philosophy, all of these people share a clearly visible characteristic—they like kids. They like to be with them; they like to teach them; they want them to succeed; and they worry about them. The doors to their classrooms are always open, and conversations between adults and young people flow easily. The quality of their caring, however, has changed over the years, and the four staff people who have been with the school for many years talk freely about it. The change is apparent in the attitude of the staff in terms of their role as adults—the awareness of the difference between caring about kids and trying to be one of them. The chatter, the ease, the laughter is present, but both teachers and students appear to know who is in charge.

Conversation in the teachers' lounge often centers on what kids are doing or problems one teacher thinks should be shared with another. The teachers do not always agree on where to draw the line when it comes to appropriate interaction with students in and out of school. But they all bring to their jobs a strong conviction that people need to care.

The primary motivation for becoming a teacher varies among the Neill House staff. One person reports that he decided when very young that he wanted to be a teacher, his image being one of maps, chalk boards, and being in command. Several people went into education because influential adults in their lives were teachers who liked what they were doing and convinced them as well as others that it was a joyful profession. A major motivating factor for two of the Neill House women teachers was that teaching was a profession that was accessible to them. One woman explained with a smile, "My mother always said, 'Be a teacher. Then wherever your husband goes, you'll be able to find a job.'" Two other people became teachers because it was a way to use the skills—coaching and woodworking—that are important to them.

Generally, these people are very critical of the preservice training they received. They describe method courses as being dry, irrelevant, and far away from the actual demands of teaching. Several people, however, have high praise for some of their preservice training. In those cases, where memories called up a sense of excitement and enthusiasm, the teachers were in situations that demanded a great deal of direct work with schools and students in the classroom. For one person, it was a single university class that made the difference— an introductory class that put him in an exciting public school classroom and demanded, early in his training, that he know the realities of schools. Two other people were in experimental university programs that combined a demand for large amounts of time to be spent in schools and classrooms with structured times for the participants

to meet with each other and with classroom teachers. Neither experimental program required them to take any of the standard education
methods courses; in both cases, the theoretical and the practical were
blended together from the very beginning of their training.

In-service training activities get mixed reviews from people at Neill
House. They are generally regarded as being too theoretical and too
short-lived to be very influential. As with preservice, what makes a
difference for people is the hands-on approach—theoretical ideas
combined with practical materials. Studied by itself, people regard
theory as a waste of time and it is fast forgotten.

Adults at Neill House appear to think a lot about what they are
doing and how they might do it differently. They talk readily about
curriculum and the place of their own subject area within the larger
framework of the student's total experience at school. The industrial
arts teacher, for example, talks about his discipline as a medium for
getting kids to think. In teaching woodworking skills, he expects that
students will plan their projects; make some hard decisions about cost,
process, and use; stick to it until they are done; and evaluate what
they have done to see the relationships between the decisions they
made and the completed projects. The science teacher ponders the
meaning of individualization in his class, wondering how one can
group kids for projects yet simultaneously individualize. He has
largely restructured one of his classes this year and he wonders aloud
whether those changes are for the better.

These people also talk readily about the support they need as teachers. Some of them get it from each other; they are each other's best
friends, and their lives, both in and out of school, blend together into
one. Others never turn to people inside this school for friendship but
talk about the other pieces of their lives—the activities and people
that satisfyingly fill their time and give them support.

The teachers' union gets quick praise from some people. They see
it as the primary vehicle for survival as a teacher, especially in the
current economic environment, where the central administration
seems so powerful. Others, clearly a majority, are more hesitant. They
wonder whether the union cares too much about teachers and not
enough about kids. They wonder whether such an organization is
doing any real good for the system in the long run. The union is not
a big thing to these people, one way or another. They accept it as a

presence, but one which they have not, personally, put to any kind of test.

In some ways, Neill House may well be vulnerable to union charges against it inasmuch as several of the curricular offerings are taught entirely by uncontracted people, including aides and volunteers. Fortunately, as most of the teachers agree, the union has not chosen to make this a major issue. The state licensure of these noncontract, often noncertified people is not an issue because the regional accreditation agency allows up to 25 percent of the staff of alternative schools to be unlicensed.

Most of the staff do not have strong feelings about merit pay or tenure. Some say merit pay would be nice, "but how in the world would you do it?" In general, they seem to regard these issues as beyond their influence; as not particularly important to them as teachers because other issues involving classrooms and kids place a more immediate demand on their attention.

Most everyone reports being content for the moment with where they are at Neill House. They are confident in their ability to do other things—to teach in other kinds of alternative programs, to go into sales, to begin a business—but for now, Neill House is where they want to be. As one person said, "I still look forward to coming here. I'm happy with that."

## Teaching and Learning

Textbooks have become a big topic of discussion. Neill House made little use of them in the past, yet teachers, students, and parents have recently concluded they need them now. This decision is reported with a bit of embarrassment. As one person said, "Whoever would have thought five years ago that I, of *all* people, would think that kids need textbooks. But I do."

The creators of Neill House, and many of their supporters, talked of "the real world"—a place quite different from their view of education ten years ago. Then, the real world was action, experience, and people relating to people. They saw the schools at that time as sterile, theoretical, book oriented, and far from providing what they felt children and young people needed to know as they grew up and established their own place in the world. It was the mission of Neill

House to create a school that merged the reality of the world with the activities of the schoolhouse. Students and staff of Neill House wanted to deal with the issues of their day, most of which would be far more immediate than any that found their way into the timeliness of textbook publishing. Those early Neill House people also believed that the issues needing attention would be too controversial for the staid bureaucracy of publishing to be willing to deal with. Nonetheless, eleven years later, Neill House participants are planning to buy textbooks.

The interest in textbooks appears to reflect the changing cultural climate, one in which social and political causes are not so intense. But it also stems from at least three other factors. One is the need for continuity. Staff turnover is high. In a small staff where only one person teaches math, one person teaches English, etc., there is no one to maintain curricular continuity in a subject when the staff changes. As a result, many people at the school look to textbooks as a vehicle for telling new staff what the classes have studied before and what things they are looking forward to doing next.

A second factor is the need for a few people to be able to teach many things. When a group of students at Neill House expresses interest in learning about a particular period in history, several teachers of the social studies department do not sit down and decide who has the best background to teach the course. A social studies department does not exist at Neill House. The one social studies teacher must be those "several teachers" all rolled into one. As one teacher said, "It is not unusual for me to be teaching something that I know very little about. I just don't have the time to dig thoroughly into so many things. A textbook would at least give me the general parameters, the basic outline of what that subject is about. Then I could build on that with other research and study on my own."

A third dimension of the new interest in textbooks is the methodological narrowness of teaching at Neill House. The school began out of a criticism of the usual modes of teaching and learning. Though people were fairly clear about what they objected to, they did not know a great deal about what they wanted to work toward. Very quickly, the methodological mode of the school became the offering of a variety of discrete and separate classes, taught by individual teachers, during six fifty-minute periods each day. Throughout the ten years of the school's history, the staff has found it difficult to develop a working sense of a holistic curriculum. There are English courses, math courses, industrial arts courses, physical education courses, and so on. On a consistent basis, there are no large blocks of time within which subjects can easily be integrated or during which a student can become deeply involved in the task at hand—at least not in the school. There is very little systematically organized connection between courses. The strong value placed on individualism—a major political tenet of the school, upheld by teachers as well as students—provides an environment in which one teacher has no real obligation to press for cooperative planning with any other teacher.

Within particular classes, individualized instruction is clearly the order of the day. In the paperback reading class, for example, each student chooses a paperback book, reads it, and reports on it. Students do not read the same books; they do not discuss what they have read, except in an informal exchange. In math, students work in small groups according to their progress toward completion of the graduation requirements. Students in the math room in any given period may be working on topics ranging from general math, algebra, geometry, through trigonometry. The teacher's task is to move from group to group, individual to individual, and to make sure that each student is making progress toward the next step ahead. In areas such as social studies and English, however, the instruction is much more interactive and group oriented.

The entire system depends on each teacher's knowledge of individual students. The math teacher, new to the school this year, described her confusion during the first few days of school. "I came in here with ideas about what to have kids work on, but they let me know that they just weren't going to get involved in the kinds of things I had planned. I spent a lot of time at first just talking with kids. Slowly but surely, I was able to understand where each kid was, what helped each of them learn. Then I could begin to put together ideas for each one. Then I could know which kids could be working together and what kind of activities to bring in for whom."

Another teacher described the process a little differently. "I look at a kid that's not involved in what I'm teaching—someone who's sitting in a class, but is not involved. And I tell myself, 'I want that kid to be attracted to me.' If that happens, if I can get the kid to notice me, then I can put my skills at his disposal. Then I can be a teacher to him."

One topic that is discussed a great deal at Neill House is instructional activity. Is the outcome of such activity to be principally the information that can be derived, or such critical skills of learning as problem solving, analysis, and synthesis? The current interest in textbooks suggests that subject matter is becoming more important.

While Neill House teachers do individualize content to a large degree and display considerable interest in their students, they tend to work with a fairly narrow pedogogical repertoire. This was not always the case. There is little use of simulations or of small groups, committees, or task forces; little indication of efforts to find better ways to involve students in the design of content and methods of their courses; little use of cameras, tape recorders, overhead projectors, computers, or the copying of fugitive materials.

One traditional educational method Neill House rejects is homework. Most teachers explain that they never assign homework—that some students may do such work by choice, but never by teacher assignment. It is likely, however, that students do some work on projects outside of school. They do not, however, label it "homework." Another traditional trapping that Neill House rejects is letter grades. Grades recently became an issue for several of the school's parents. Arguing a case of individualization, they asked that students who wanted to receive grades should be allowed to do so. Discussion by staff and by the governing board finally resulted in the decision that an option to be graded would not be available at Neill House. They decided that such a practice was too far from the philosophical intent of the school, and that if grades were important to a student, then that person would simply have to attend one of the other alternative schools in the district.

An important aspect of the teaching and learning environment visible to the observer is the fact that the teachers at Neill House like the subjects they are teaching. The physical education teacher coaches at a community college, the industrial arts teacher has a woodworking business of his own. The English teacher enjoys the theater and talks with students about plays she has seen and books she has read. In almost every case, these are not just subjects that people teach, they are interests that teachers hold, and this fact is communicated to students in big and little ways, possibly replacing the necessity for what appears to be the traditional trappings of public school instruction.

## Education Beyond the School

Neill House began with a clear expectation of being involved in social issues. The community was to be a part of the school and its curriculum. The outside doors of Neill House were to swing both ways with resources from the community coming into the school and students going into the community for part of their learning. The community was to be more than the local city; it was, in fact, to be the entire world. The Neill House founders felt too many high school graduates were illiterate in political and economic matters. There was hope that Neill House students would have less need to fight or rebel against the educational system and therefore would have more energy to focus on learning about the world.

To support the expectation of student involvement beyond the school walls, Neill House has waivers from state requirements for clock hours of subject matter coverage and waivers from Carnegie unit requirements for graduation. This provides the school with breathing space for modifying the curriculum. The results are, nonetheless, mixed.

Neill House publishes a monthly newsletter for parents. Special needs, such as volunteers, are listed so that parents and others may respond. Activities of the school are described with the expectation that parents will be interested and participate to enhance the program. The observers attended an evening meeting of the governing board and witnessed the request for help and the subsequent volunteering of several parents as tutors and teachers of activities.

Neill House works with nearby colleges and universities in providing a site for student teachers and interim interns. Neill House students are encouraged to serve as apprentices, workers, or interns with community resource people. A student is required to arrange for a community adult to serve on his or her graduation committee. Independent study in the community, at an agency, business, or governmental office is possible. A student with a special talent can link with a mentor. One student we interviewed is interested in radio and television. Another wants to build a recording studio. A third wants more work in photography. These students have outgrown the school's limited resources in these areas. Nothing prevents them from making arrangements outside the school and being released to pursue their interests. It should be noted, however, that not very many make these arrangements. More such programs might be developed if there was a staff person available to assist students with such interests in making the necessary arrangements.

Overall, five students are taking courses at a nearby high school. Another student is participating on his home attendance school's extracurricular athletic team. Three students are taking courses at the state university; two are at a nearby community college for part of the day. Two students are in Upward Bound, one has a course at a music school, another participates in a half-day program at the children's theater. Students regularly participate in the district's urban arts program.

A major use of the community at Neill House is the Friday field trip. Each week, students help plan and sign up for a field trip. This might be a visit to a museum, a school picnic, a bowling outing. At least once a year there is a three- to five-week trip to somewhere in the United States, Canada, or Mexico. When we visited, students and staff were busy planning a three-week trip to Washington, D.C. Among the many details to attend to was the problem of raising the funds to finance the trip. Most staff and students consider these trips to be loaded with learning. Students have to calculate a budget, time, and food supplies, for example. If a foreign trip is being contemplated, students have to learn the country's culture, customs, language, history, and money conversions. They need to cooperate in all manner of activities. They learn health and sanitation standards. They keep journals, take photographs, and interview people. They prepare by following events in the news. This activity is an excellent example of community-based learning.

The school lacks the resources to have a regular and integrated work-experience program. Students do work, of course, after school, and in some cases are allowed to work during part of the school day. Some students also participate in the district's vocational learning centers. But there is little formal linkage with business and industrial settings in the city.

Teachers believe the potential is far greater than what exists but suggest that to do more would demand more resources or a way of using existing resources differently. They note that the school district's formula allocations for staff and field trips, for example, are stated as budget line items that are virtually unchangeable at the school level. The school's small size means a relatively small allocation. The formula provides only seven teaching positions to cover the entire program. Efforts to alter the formula, to provide a single block of money for decision-making at the school level, have been made but with few positive results. School site management is an idea whose time has not yet come to Neill House.

## Media and Technology

In statements of purpose or operation, little mention is made at Neill House of media and technology. Computer literacy, for example, is not a requirement for graduation. While, in the past, there was considerable support for a simpler lifestyle as encompassed in *Small Is Beautiful*, the "appropriate technology" movement, and naturalism in health and nutrition, that support has declined. Sophisticated technology is not now viewed necessarily as a problem. There is more openness about machines and high technology.

Interest in computers has grown considerably, possibly as a result of the tremendous exposure by media and advertising. Students are particularly interested and want to learn more about computers. One says, "I need to learn to type so I can run a computer." Another feels computers should be as common as books. Teachers also talk increasingly about the potential of the computer to reduce much of the drudgery and drill and practice on skills. Nonetheless, the school has only one terminal.

Beyond the single computer, there are other resources. The school possesses simple audio-visual hardware (overhead projectors, tape recorders, film projectors, video equipment, and the like). It draws easily upon the audio-visual library of the district, the science media center, and other resources. Student interests in photography, for example, are partially accommodated by a simple darkroom. The student interested in a recording studio for music is encouraged to build it at home and is released to utilize any available resources that can be found in the rich community of this large urban center. The school possesses a primitive copying machine and has electric typewriters.

School size is a factor. If Neill House were to install $100,000 worth of technology capitalized over five to seven years, it would cost one staff position unless additional outside resources were made available. Spending the salary of one teacher out of a staff of seven is impossible. Not only would it be unacceptable, but the school is not given authority over those types of budget decisions.

In closing this discussion of Neill House, we provide a full statement of graduation requirements. Clearly, Neill House is not a typical school. It represents, however, part of the diversity of America's secondary schools.

## Neill House Graduation Requirements and Procedures

Neill House defines its graduation requirements in four very broad areas of basic skills and responsibility: (1) communication and language; (2) mathematics and science; (3) social perspective and the humanities; (4) personal achievement and independence. In each of these areas every student will show a minimum level of achievement. In at least two of these areas each student will show proficiency beyond the minimum.

The first section gives brief statements of "minimum achievement" plus examples of "proficiency" for the four areas. Section II outlines how Neill House students may request and be awarded their high school diplomas.

*I. Requirements*    COMMUNICATION AND LANGUAGE Minimum achievement in this area means:

1. You can use the mass media (newspapers, magazines, TV, movies) with a critical sense of their points of view, and an awareness of their viewpoints, too. This means knowing where the media are coming from, as news or information sources, opinion formers, entertainers, advisors.
2. You can read adult-reading-level books and clearly retell or summarize what they are about—both by speaking and by writing.
3. You can tell about yourself—what's happened to you, what you have done, how you think and feel—in two or more of the following ways: essay, song, art, film, lecture, tape, drama, journal, poem, letter, job application, etc.

4. You can respond in speaking or writing to opinions you disagree with, stating your own ideas and feelings and the reasons for them. For instance: you can defend your opinion in talking with other people; you can write a well-thought-out letter to the editor.
5. In group situations, you can get across what you want to say, and hear what other people are saying—even when they are different from you in age, sex, race, class, customs, vocabulary, values, etc.

Additional proficiency in this area may be shown by such activities as:

- Learning a foreign language.
- Helping other people learn what you know and care about.
- Getting across your ideas in some way other than speaking; for instance, dance, music, mime, graphic arts, film or video reporting, etc.
- Carrying out a project in imaginative or creative writing for publication.
- Researching, organizing, and writing up a report or essay on a topic important to you, which you want to be important to other people, too.

MATHEMATICS AND SCIENCE   Minimum achievement in this area means:

1. You are thoroughly familiar with what the following things mean, as well as how to do them: measurement, number, ratio, percent, proportion, addition, subtraction, multiplication, division of whole numbers, fractions, and decimals.
2. You can show that you know the basics of geometry, and how to use these basics in problems of perimeter, area, volume, angles, symmetry, and similar triangles.
3. You can figure out the steps in solving a mathematical or scientific problem.
4. You understand and can practice activities meant by "scientific method" and "inductive inference."
5. You can observe things in your natural environment and note differences and similarities, ask questions, collect, record, and organize information, draw conclusions and test them to see if you are correct, and write down what you saw and did.
6. You can read an article or see a program on a current scientific topic, such as ecosystems, or an energy crisis, or sickle-cell anemia, or holography, and can understand it well enough to explain it to someone else.
7. You know enough about your body to know basically how it works, how heredity works, how different types of diseases enter and work on the body, such as V.D., sickle-cell anemia, etc., and how to stay healthy (food, rest, etc.).

8. You know enough about your natural environment to tell the difference between living and non-living things, understand basic relationships (plant to plant, and animal to animal) in terms of such things as parasitism, predators, herbivores, etc., know what is meant by "survival of the fittest," and have begun to think about "crisis survival" (over-population, intense air, water, land pollution, or nuclear warfare).
9. You know the names and groupings, uses and effects of America's most popular drugs.

Additional proficiency in this area might be demonstrated by such activities as:

- Carrying out an independent scientific study or research project of your own.
- Learning how computers work, what they are being used for, and how to write simple programs.
- Studying the theory behind and what has been done with one major scientific discovery (e.g., the transistor, penicillin, DNA, general relativity), and know something about the discoverers.
- In-depth study of mathematics beyond arithmetic: algebra, geometry, trigonometry, calculus.

SOCIAL PERSPECTIVE AND HUMANITIES Minimum competence in this area means:

1. You have a basic grasp of world geography (physical, political, economic) and human population groups (culture, values, lifestyles).
2. You have a basic background in United States history, including the Constitution and Bill of Rights, viewpoints and problems of minority groups, and ways this country is feared or respected elsewhere in the world.
3. You know your own cultural roots and values, can talk about influences shaping your life, and can identify your own "place in history"—starting with your city today.
4. You have information and ideas about the emerging world you will live in, major conflicts and opportunities before you, and how you choose to deal with them.
5. You are familiar with the "isms" of today (communism, capitalism, racism, sexism, socialism, classism, imperialism, etc.) and can define them and identify where and how they operate.
6. You are exploring and thinking about at least one alien, foreign, or different culture from your own.
7. You can come up with what you need to know in order to do something

about a practical political or cultural problem (e.g., financing Mexico trips for Neill House students).

Additional proficiency in this area might be shown by such activities as:

- Working with a local community organization to achieve some particular political or social reform.
- Travelling to another place, learning your way around, and doing an analysis of how it is different from our place.
- Becoming an expert on some particular person or period of history (e.g., the Chinese revolution), some particular author or artist (e.g., Langston Hughes, Bertol Brecht), some particular social controversy (e.g., women's liberation).
- Preparing and leading a project on How to Be Happy in 1984.

PERSONAL INDEPENDENCE AND INITIATIVE Minimum competence in this area means:

1. You have found and held a job (paid or volunteer) where your performance was evaluated by someone not connected with Neill House.
2. You can tell about your plans for six months from now, or at least be able to offer some realistic alternatives.
3. You have developed a particular skill or interest of your own, which you enjoy, are proud of, and are glad to be asked about.
4. You have enough self-discipline to take on responsibilities, which other people can count on, and also to let people know when you *cannot* accept a responsibility.
5. You are learning how to "come across" to different sorts of other people, and how they affect you.
6. You can suggest people for your own Graduation Review Committee and help design your own "final exam."

Additional proficiency in this area might be demonstrated by such activities as:

- Almost any venture or project the student defines and the advisor agrees with.

## II. Procedure

The heart of this system is that each student shares in making each decision about his own graduation from Neill House—when he thinks he can be "ready," what special expectations are appropriate for him, how to meet those expectations, who should evaluate his performance, how to evaluate, whether in fact he should graduate, and what should be the final entry in his school system records. A student may be certified for his diploma any time after his sixteenth birthday. The procedure is as follows:

1. Student and advisor agree, at least six months in advance, on a target date for graduation.
2. Student and advisor, working with other staff, agree on a written *contract* for the final several months' work.
3. Contract covers minimum competence requirements not yet met, plus additional proficiency areas agreed to be appropriate for the student.
4. Student and advisor agree on student's Graduation Review Committee, to include:
   two staff (other than advisor)
   one Neill House parent (chosen from governing board)
   one secondary student
   one adult not formally related to Neill House. Advisor serves as student's advocate before this committee.
5. Committee meets monthly with student and advisor to monitor progress on the learning contract.
6. At completion of contract period Committee meets with student and advisor for final graduation interview—one to one-and-a-half hours in an informal setting. Advisor summarizes his own and other teachers' records of student's accomplishments. Committee and student discuss these, if necessary, and any other areas or topics considered relevant within graduation requirements.
7. On basis of interview, previous meetings, and School records, Committee responds for or against graduation. Positive recommendation goes (in writing with comments, if desired) to Governing Board for ratification. Negative recommendation goes to the student and the advisor, with reasons, and with suggestions for additional work to be completed.
8. Governing Board ratifies Committee recommendations and certifies the student has completed Neill House graduation requirements. [The] Official diploma is awarded by the school system. [An] Unofficial and *real* diploma is conferred by Neill House Governing Board.

PART V

VOCATIONAL SCHOOLS

# 10

# THE SAGE AREA
# VOCATIONAL SCHOOL

MAJA APELMAN

If it weren't for this class, I would have dropped
out of school. I like to study things I can use. Out
there they apply the stuff you learn in school. If I
have a reason to use it, I want to learn it.
                        —STUDENT IN AGRICULTURE PROGRAM

School is not enough of what life is about.
                        —AREA VOCATIONAL SCHOOL DIRECTOR

From the standpoint of the child, the great waste in
school comes from his inability to utilize the experience he gets outside . . . while on the other hand,
he is unable to apply in daily life what he is learning in school. That is the isolation of the school—its
isolation from life.
            —JOHN DEWEY, *The School and Society*, 1915

"This Area Vocational School is not a school but a concept."
That is what I was told by one administrator on my first visit in late
September 1981. I already knew that the vocational classes were held
at several different sites, but I was completely unprepared for the fact
that students from twelve different high schools and six different
school districts attended classes at nine separate locations spread all
over the southern section of the city's metropolitan area.

The Sage Area Vocational School (AVS) was organized in 1975 by

Warren Bruce, a school district vocational director, who got his and three other districts to pool resources and cooperate in the administration of one new area school. Soon after, an adjoining county outside the metropolitan area joined the AVS. That district's high school is located some 30 miles south of the nearest vocational program. A few years later, another large metropolitan district started to use the AVS's agriculture program for the students of its three largest high schools.

The districts involved in Sage are spread over a fairly large area—there are 25 miles between the most eastern and most western participating high school and 30 miles between the most northern and the most southern. The districts also vary economically and demographically. They include one of the poorest of the city's districts as well as the wealthiest district in the state. One district is losing students as its younger population declines; others have been growing significantly over recent years. By making the existing vocational programs of the original four districts available to all the students in the six cooperating districts, overcrowded schools could take advantage of underused facilities in other districts, poorer districts could avail themselves of programs they would not otherwise be able to afford, and all the districts could benefit from a larger selection of vocational programs without having to build an expensive new central facility. I was told that the districts saved more than $16 million by using and renovating existing structures.

"Satellite Concept" was the phrase mentioned most frequently when I asked teachers and administrators to explain how the school functioned. "It's like a separate high school with classrooms at different sites," one person said. "The only difference from a regular high school structure is that classrooms are not under one roof."

Apparently, there were many early organizational problems. "The way it was on paper," one person said, "the superintendents didn't see how it was going to work. But it worked and it's serving a good purpose." Another area director talked about "the utter chaos, especially in transportation" during the first year. Yet, apparently, there was enough good will and cooperation among the staff to overcome many of the initial difficulties. "The spirit was there," one administrator said, "and our attitude has been: let's take it and use it and make it as effective as we can."

There are twenty-two other vocational centers in the state and, though many may be serving more than one school district, none is spread over several sites. The structure of the Sage AVS is unique not only in the state but probably in the whole country. "In many situations," an area director said, "this kind of satellite program would not work, but the people in the districts work well together. There has been a good cooperative effort."

## Structure

Apart from the overall director of the Sage AVS, who is accountable to the executive director of the Board of Cooperative Services, important roles in the overall functioning of Sage are carried out by persons designated as area directors and liaison counselors. In addition, there is a job placement specialist.

The *area directors*, who were compared to department heads by one person I talked to, supervise the AVS programs located in their particular districts. They are also the directors of all other local—non-AVS—vocational education activities in their respective school districts and thus carry many responsibilities beyond administering the AVS. The area director of one district told me that he spends 30 to 35 percent of his time on Sage Area Vocational School matters.

For the first five years of its existence, the AVS had an assistant director whose main responsibility was to supervise the programs at the various sites. It must have been a frustrating position because two assistant directors resigned. After the second resignation, it was decided to eliminate this job and to restructure the organization. The area directors were given greater responsibility for running and supervising programs at their sites. While there seems to have been some initial resistance to this change by superintendents who did not want to burden their vocational directors with this added responsibility, the change was instituted and resulted in smoother functioning.

The four area directors, the director of vocational education at the community college, and the director of the AVS make up the Director's Council. This council meets every other week to discuss matters of common concern.

I attended two such meetings—efficiently run by Bernard Corwin, the new AVS director—and gained a good understanding of some of the problems of administering such a widespread program. The agendas of the meetings covered many subjects: reports on current AVS enrollment by program, school, and district; discussion of various financial matters; allotment of extra money available from the state board; attendance policy; vocational credentialing; new staff evaluation forms; planning upcoming open-house programs at the various sites; and a proposed informational bulletin on AVS activities to be produced by the commercial art class. The main topic was a proposal of a major scheduling change, and the discussion of this proposal made me realize how complicated the administration of the AVS could be.

At present, almost all AVS classes meet for one hour and fifty minutes. Exceptions are the food service program and advanced construction, which meet for two hours and fifty minutes, and cosmetology, which runs in four-hour blocks. Many instructors would prefer a longer time period. As they noted, with occasional late busses and clean-up of equipment, the actual teaching time is probably only one hour and thirty-five minutes. But there are problems. One person mentioned that some principals don't want their students away from the home high school for such a long time; another wondered if the AVS would lose students by requiring three-hour attendance. The low attendance in the second year of several two-year programs was mentioned, and there was speculation about whether a change to a one-year, three-hour program might not be preferable. "Would that meet state requirements," someone asked. It was finally suggested that two or three programs be chosen for three-hour classes on a trial basis. The discussion then turned to the logistics of bus transportation.

Bernard Corwin had made up a large timetable showing the current AVS schedule, the starting and ending times of classes in the twelve participating high schools, and the times of the heaviest junior and senior enrollment at the various schools. Starting times ranged from 7:00 A.M. to 8:15 A.M. and ending times ranged from 2:00 P.M. to 3:00 P.M. Bussing students to and from their home high schools to the AVS classes is already quite complicated. These complications would increase considerably if the AVS classes were to be of different durations.

If the Director's Council could work out a satisfactory system, it would then need the approval of the instructors of the programs that were to be changed, the principals of the schools where the programs were to be held, the superintendents of the districts affected by the change, the Board of Cooperative Services, and, finally, the executive director. Listening to this discussion, I was reminded of the earlier quoted remark: "The way it was on paper, [they] didn't see how it was going to work." But somehow, these dedicated and creative people seem to find ways to overcome most obstacles.

Finally, the conversation turned to the bus drivers. "Can you make them cooperate?" one area director asked the BCS executive director who attended this meeting. A great deal, obviously, depended on the bus drivers' willingness to be flexible and cooperative!

In each of the twelve high schools, one of the regular student counselors is appointed as *liaison counselor* to the AVS. In the larger schools, counselors are assigned approximately 300 students each, and have additional responsibilities, such as advising students going to college or into the military, being in charge of part-time employment, and so on. Being a liaison counselor to the AVS is one of these additional duties.

Liaison counselors are supposed to be familiar with the vocational courses so they can give information to students interested in enrolling. They are taken on tours of the various programs, can ask for slide-show presentations, and are given attractive pamphlets describing each program. Since each school is allotted a certain number of slots for each program, the liaison counselors are also responsible for screening and selecting students if there is more demand for a program than there are available slots.

According to one liaison counselor, most of his AVS time is spent on "information processing, bus schedules, attendance problems, enrollment and withdrawal, and program consultation." In addition to his 300 assigned students, and his AVS responsibility, he is also in charge of part-time job placement for the students of his school. His busy schedule does not allow him enough time to visit and really get to know the AVS programs and the approximately 150 students from his school who are enrolled in AVS classes. This counselor felt that it might be a good idea to have strictly vocational counselors who would be in charge of placements and have more time to visit the various programs and counsel AVS students when problems arise.

The AVS position of *job development and placement specialist* currently is held by a very able, efficient, and creative young woman, Noreen Crawford. Her primary responsibility is job placement. She looks for job opportunities in the community, passes the information on to participating high schools, and tries to find full-time employment for graduating students. Employers familiar with the AVS frequently call when they have job openings and Noreen processes their requests. She also helps with new student orientation at the beginning of the school year and talks to students about job opportunities, both individually and in classes. "It's a big public relations job," she said to me. "I like my job because I'm left to my own resources and creativity." She also provides the state board with follow-up information on the work status of AVS students who have graduated.

In addition to the administrators and information-counseling personnel, there are thirty full- and part-time instructors teaching twenty-one different vocational classes.

## Problems and Strengths

A common complaint of Sage-related teachers and administrators was that counselors use the AVS as a "dumping ground." "They are sending us kids who are not really interested, and are failing in school; they put them in the vocational classes to give them the needed credits," said one administrator. Another one said, "We have a problem with some of the counselors. They all have an M.A. and about three years of teaching experience, but they don't have any knowledge of the real world so it's difficult for them to orient the kids to the vocational programs."

One outspoken teacher said, "How do you get to be a high school counselor in the vocational education area and not know anything about this trade? Counselors should sit in classes and observe the problems students have. Students need a lot of eye/hand coordination to do this work, but counselors bring in students who can't chew gum and walk a straight line!"

Although there are real problems when uninterested students with poor reading and math skills are sent to vocational classes, counselors may also hope that such students will have their interest sparked by a vocational class and will then make an effort to improve their reading or math skills because they see the need for greater proficiency. In some cases, students' grades in academic subjects improve when they are successful in the vocational class.

Though I suspect that these problems are not unique to the AVS, they are probably aggravated by the structure of the area school, which makes communication more difficult. It would certainly help if counselors had more time to visit programs and get to know the teachers to whose classes they refer students.

In spite of the many complaints about the quality of some of the students sent to the AVS by counselors, it was also clear that most of the students who *chose* to go to the vocational programs attended regularly and learned well. As one student said to me, "It takes a lot of commitment to take an AVS class that meets two hours every day of the year."

When I first began to visit the program, I thought it must be hard for teachers to work in such an isolated way. Having spent a good deal of time working with elementary school teachers who often complained of feeling isolated and not getting sufficient feedback, even though they were working with many others in a school, I wondered how the AVS teachers managed. One teacher said, "Teaching in the AVS is really different. It gives you a lot of independence, but it is lacking a support system. I don't know as much as I would like to about other programs and other people. Because of the way the school is structured, and because of my schedule, I can't get around." Another person remarked, "It would help if there could be more in-school communication, if teachers would know what other members of the staff were doing." One teacher said that he received no help or guidance when he was first hired to teach. "Nobody showed me what a teacher does." He would have appreciated supervision and feedback, but "the only time I see my principal is when he needs something from me."

Some of the teachers in the AVS miss a support system more than others, but all of them, it seems, would benefit from more interaction with their colleagues and with vocational teachers in other schools.

Administrative tasks in the area school require constant coordination. "Logistics are difficult, paperwork and communication are difficult; it is more time-consuming to administer this program," said one area director. A good example of cumbersome procedures was given to me by another area administrator: "Say a student in welding has a problem. He talks to his school counselor, who will phone the home school area vocational director. He, in turn, will phone the area director in charge of the welding program, who will talk to the welding teacher." In practice, of course, shortcuts can be taken. The liaison counselor may call the instructor directly, especially if he knows him well, but the official line of communication is time-consuming.

The biggest problem of the AVS is transportation. It was mentioned by all the administrators and by many instructors. "An exorbitant amount of money was spent on transportation during the first year," one administrator said. Though many efforts have been made over the years to reduce riding and waiting time for the students by changing bus routes, and to cut down on gasoline costs by using smaller vehicles, traveling time is still an obstacle. For some students, the ride may take only fifteen minutes, for others it can take as long as an hour each way, especially for students in the large districts, who may first have to go from their home school to another school in the district to catch the AVS bus.

I talked with a senior girl in the food services program: she comes to her home school by bus for the first-period class at 7:30 A.M. She takes a required English class in her second period, at 8:30, but has permission to leave the class early in order to catch a 9:00 A.M. bus that takes her to another school in the district. There she has to wait half an hour for the AVS bus. She arrives at the restaurant program in time for the 10:00-to-1:00 session, after which she returns to her home high school in the same way, arriving just before the end of the school day. She spends about one and one-half hours at her school and five hours traveling to and from and attending the AVS class. When I asked her what she did in her free time after school, she said, "I talk with my friends to see what I missed at school."

One area director thought that traveling limits enrollment. Not all students are willing, or can afford, to make such a major time commitment. The students who do enroll, however, don't seem to mind the travel—in fact, they appear to enjoy the time away from school and the social aspects of riding the bus together. (There are also quite a few students who drive their own cars to AVS classes.)

The logistics of transportation are complicated, and the fact that starting and ending times in the different districts are not standardized doesn't help. But transportation will always present some problems in a school as spread out as the AVS.

In addition to its problems, the area school also has great strengths. Although the prime consideration in organizing the AVS was a financial one, an important benefit is the resulting mix of students from different schools and districts. In one of my early interviews, an area director told me that students going to AVS classes lead a double life. He thought that it was not easy for students faced with considerable peer pressure to break away from their friends and enroll in a class that met for two hours each day at another location. "That requires a fair amount of maturity," he said.

I also thought that it would be hard for students to be absent from their school for two and one-half to three hours each day, traveling back and forth between their home schools and AVS classes. I therefore asked almost all the students I interviewed how they felt about leaving their home school. Much to my surprise, the answers were almost unanimously positive. Although some students admitted to initial feelings of apprehension, they all talked about the rapport that quickly developed in each class between the students from different schools—even if these schools were in intense rivalry in their athletic programs. The students said that they enjoyed meeting kids from other schools and districts and spending time on a different campus. Seniors, especially, liked to get away from their own school. Except for a few minor disadvantages, such as not being able to attend after-school athletic events if their AVS classes were scheduled in the afternoon, and occasionally having to attend AVS classes when their home schools were on holiday, the students were most enthusiastic. Neither the daily bus rides nor leaving the home schools, nor the fact that they would be in class with people they did not know, were ever mentioned as serious problems.

From what I observed, the mixing that occurs in the AVS classes is an important strength of the program: it helps students overcome prejudices and revise stereotyped views of other districts. It also teaches them to work and communicate with a much wider range of peers than they would meet in their own schools. One student in the health occupations class, who goes to a middle-class school with a high proportion of college-bound students, told me that lots of people at their school think vocational education is easy and for dumb kids. I asked her how she felt about being in a vocational program. "I wondered whether I would be the only one of my type," she said, "and whether there would be only dumb people. Once I got there I met other kids from my school and also kids from other schools. There are totally different kinds of people with totally different backgrounds in this class and they learn to get on."

## Goals

The State Board for Community Colleges and Occupational Education, which supervises all vocational programs, has clearly stated goals for its high school vocational classes. According to the law, the primary purpose of vocational education is to prepare students for entry-level jobs. A counselor told me: "The goal of the AVS is to give students employable skills at no cost. Many AVS students might otherwise drop out or have to pay for learning these skills after they get their diplomas." The state expects students who graduate and have attended vocational classes to be employed in a field related to their training.

Vocational education can be very expensive. Class size in many courses is limited to fifteen students because of the cost of equipment and the need for extensive work space—stalls for repairing or painting cars, darkrooms, computers, welding stations, for example. Since the state contributes approximately 30 percent of the funding for vocational education, it is understandable that it wants a return on its investment.

There are annual as well as five-year follow-up studies of randomly selected vocational students. Job placement in a related field is one of the state's criteria for a recently established cost-effectiveness formula that determines the amount of state funding for the program. Sex equity, racial integration, completion of vocational courses, and, of course, cost, are the other criteria. One vocational director expressed concern about the formula: "If money is spent for a first-rate program that duplicates the equipment of the real world, you are in a Catch 22 situation; this makes it an expensive program, and therefore it will be ranked lower."

One area director said that the really motivated students continue their education "and then they can't be counted. The state board considers only kids placed in jobs, not kids who go on to school, as fulfilling the purpose of vocational education." Another area director felt that vocational training can benefit all students, even those going to college. "Wouldn't it be better if you could work your way through college as a welder than fry hamburgers?" he asked.

Noreen Crawford, the job placement specialist who is responsible for filling out the state's accountability forms, told me what kind of information the state asks for. Are the graduates working? Are they working in a field related or unrelated to their training? Are they in the military or are they going to school continuing their education? She added, "I use my own philosophy to interpret what the state wants. If a student completes the program, works in the field and goes to school, I count him or her. I list students working full-time and those working part-time while continuing their studies. I wouldn't like to think that vocational training is limiting. I see it more as a catalyst. Lots of training areas lend themselves to further study."

The liaison counselor of an upper-middle-class school with a high percentage of college-bound students felt that vocational courses were not a bad idea even if one did go to college. She added, however, that many of the parents at her school had high professional expectations for their children and did not like their children "to dirty their hands" in vocational classes. Only 119 students out of a total of over 3,000 at this school are enrolled in vocational classes, and the highest enrollments are in subjects such as photography, commercial art, and data processing. Just a small sprinkling of students go into the trade programs. At a middle- to upper-middle-class school in another district, the liaison counselor reported that the 10 percent of the student body taking vocational classes were mostly students who were not planning to go on to college. He was pleased that the school offered this option and gave these students an opportunity for skills training.

In addition to administrators and counselors, several teachers commented on the state goals. One of the data processing teachers told me that the state evaluates the program according to how many jobs students have in the field. "They see the AVS as offering a terminal program." He thought this attitude was foolish since his field changes constantly; new computers come on the market every day. He would like to see students in his program take jobs *and* continue studying in the field. Another teacher mentioned that many of his best students want to go on to trade school after graduation and that those students who attended the class specifically for job-entry skills were at the lowest end of the spectrum of student abilities.

It seems ironic that the state policy, if strictly adhered to, would penalize the AVS for producing graduates who became so interested in their particular field that they wanted to continue to study it. Dialogue between state representatives and AVS staff might help to clarify this situation and possibly lead to amending the state policy. Compared to state policy, the area school's interpretation seems more realistic and more supportive of learning and growth.

Teachers' personal goals for their students reflect their understanding of today's teen-agers. Though most teachers obviously hoped that students would obtain adequate entry-level job skills that would make it easier to find employment, they also felt that vocational training was useful even if it did not lead to a job in the field. A trade teacher said that he didn't expect sixteen-year-olds to make up their minds about what they want to be doing for the rest of their lives; another teacher commented that he didn't care if the students in his class changed their minds and didn't make a career out of what they were learning since they always would have a useful skill to fall back on. Another teacher, after saying that even students going into engineering could benefit from some practical experience in this highly technical field, stated that his personal goal was for his students to become productive members of society and contributing members of a family unit. "*How* they achieve this is not that important," he added.

Some teachers felt that vocational classes give students an opportunity to learn more about a field before making a career decision. I felt that three programs—child development assistant, health occupation, and restaurant arts, were particularly useful in this respect. These programs put the students into "real world" work situations: the child development program runs a preschool; the restaurant arts program operates a restaurant; and, in their second semester, health occupations' students are placed in health jobs in the community. Several students from these classes said to me that the vocational class had helped them make up their minds about future possibilities. "I'm almost positive I'll go on working with children. Before I took this class I wasn't positive, but now I am. The class helped me make that decision." Some students were less positive, but, in a way, it is just as important to find out what you don't like to do as what you do like to do.

The students' reasons for taking AVS classes and their goals after graduation varied enormously. Some students were in the vocational classes "to get away from school" or to learn skills for personal reasons. "The machine class is helping me build my jeep." Others were very clear about their goals. A machine shop student was set for a career as a machinist and hoped to get a job in the company where his father worked; a restaurant arts student had been admitted to a prestigious culinary school in the East and wanted to open a small restaurant in a city "with strong social class and culture, where I can do what I want to do and people would appreciate it"; a child development student planned to get a degree in elementary education and eventually open her own preschool; and a health occupation student wanted to become a physical therapist. Two students I talked with in data processing and printing planned to continue their studies, whereas several students in trades classes were set to work in their fields if jobs were available.

In addition, the students on the farm—the only vocational program of the AVS that can be attended for three years—own their own animals and are responsible for them all year round. This requires a serious commitment, as does enrollment in the cosmetology program in which students spend four hours each day in a beauty school and also work during school vacations. I would guess that these two programs rank high in graduates working in the field of their training.

Speaking to a liaison counselor, I wondered if there was a way of screening students so that those who just wanted to get away from school or who hoped to learn skills for personal reasons would not take away class space from others with more serious career interests. "You've got to take the student's word," he answered. From one point of view, it would be nice if all students who were really interested could take vocational classes even if they did not intend to make careers out of their training. On the other hand, I can see how, with limited funds, this would be difficult for funding agencies to justify.

In my interviews with students, teachers, and administrators, there were several references to parents. One came from an administrator who felt that the vocational enrollment in working-class districts should be higher than it was. "But," he added, "it doesn't always work out that way. Parents often don't want their kids to do what they are doing." Another comment came from a student in child development who told me that her mother wished that she could have had a similar chance when she went to high school.

With massive cuts in educational funding all over the country, vocational education is likely to be carefully scrutinized. One administrator told me that his district will soon have to take a position: "It will depend on the philosophy of the superintendents and the board of education how vocational education is going to fare. Our district is committed to alternatives for its students."

## The Programs

In the 1981–82 school year, the Area Vocational School offered twenty different programs to the students of the participating high schools. These programs are described in a special section of the schools' catalogues and, as mentioned before, liaison counselors have additional information for students who are interested in enrolling.

Students may read about the vocational classes or they may be told about them by their counselors or, quite often, by their friends. One girl mentioned that she read about the restaurant program in the city's newspaper.

In the 1981–82 school year, the following programs were offered by the various school districts:

*School District A*
Child Development Assistant
Health Occupations
Restaurant Arts (food service and baking)
Machine Trades
Printing/Graphics

*School District B*
Carpentry
Masonry
Auto Mechanics

*School District C*
Major Appliance Service Technology
Air Conditioning, Heating, and Refrigeration
Marine Service/Sporting Vehicle Technology (small-engine repair)
Cooperative Career Development (a work-study program)
Coop G (same as above but for students with special needs)

*School District D*
Photography
Commercial Art
Data Processing
Agriculture

*At the Community College*
Auto Body Repair
Welding

*Contracted Out to Private Businesses*
Cosmetology (offered at three different sites)

When I began my observations of the Area Vocational School, I was not planning to visit every program. After a while, however, it became clear that it would be difficult to omit any classes if I wanted to have an understanding of the school. Each site has its own flavor, each teacher's background and experience are different, and each program makes a unique contribution. There was just no way to select a few representative programs.*

*District A Programs*    District A was described to me by a person who is well acquainted with the city as a "ninety-nine and one-half percent Anglo middle-class area." It is a suburb of the city, but functions as a separate small town. An older community with pleasant neighborhoods, this district has a strong conservative city government and is almost 100 percent Republican. Many of the people who live there work in the downtown area of the city. Because of its geographic location, the community cannot expand, and many of the younger people have been moving out. As a result, there has been a steady decline in the school population. The high school was built for 1,500 students but now has an enrollment of only 1,100.

The AVS classes in District A are housed in a two-story former elementary school next door to the high school. All the AVS programs are on the ground floor; the second floor is occupied by the high school's mathematics department. A teachers' lounge on the ground floor is used by everyone who works in this building.

The printing/graphics program is located at one end of a long

* Although the original essay prepared by Maja Apelman describes all of the AVS programs, this version will omit many, focusing only on programs in two of the districts, because of space limitations as well as the similarities that exist across a number of the programs.—ED

corridor in a double-level room that used to be the school's auditorium. At the opposite end of the corridor, which runs the length of the building, is the AVS restaurant, complete with kitchen, bakery, and small office. It was remodeled from the old gymnasium and opened to the public in January 1981. Two other programs are located in the building: the child development assistant and the health occupations programs use five classrooms and two offices. A sixth classroom is available to all the AVS staff for a variety of purposes—meetings, film showings, and the like. The machine shop is in a separate building that also houses the high school's auto mechanics shop and other industrial arts classes.

Thomas Brown, the district's area vocational director, has been working at the high school for seventeen years. He was hired as an industrial arts teacher, later became a vocational teacher, and is in his second year as area director. In addition to his administrative responsibilities—he supervises all the AVS programs at this site as well as the high school's industrial arts classes—he also teaches the AVS machine trades class and an introductory metal trades class for the students of District A's high school.

When Brown first applied for the job as machine shop teacher some seventeen years ago, he had just graduated with a B.S. in industrial arts. He hadn't really planned on a teaching career, but the job was available and he was interested in working in the machine shop. "If I had known then what I know now," he told me, "I probably wouldn't have gone into teaching. But when you have a family, you just stay year after year." Brown has four children between the ages of three and ten. Both his parents were teachers. He owns a printing shop and hopes to retire, when he has twenty years' service, to work full-time in his business.

He is a friendly, easy-going man with a good sense of humor. As administrator, he relates informally to the teachers, who seem to like and trust him and who freely come to him with questions and complaints. He told me that he finds being an administrator frustrating—"I'm tired of not having answers for my people"—but he also said that he was ready for a change after teaching for seventeen years.

Brown does not hold regularly scheduled meetings with his staff. He sees his teachers when he needs to talk to them or when they come to him. He has many opportunities for informal contacts with the

AVS staff in District A since the teachers often eat lunch at the AVS restaurant. The restaurant is open to the public from 11:00 A.M. to 1:00 P.M., but the coffee pot is always on, and teachers and administrators are welcome there any time between nine and three. Brown thinks that the AVS teachers at his site are a more closely knit group than teachers at other sites. The personalities of the individual teachers, the availability of the restaurant as a meeting place, and his informal style of administration probably account for that.

THE MACHINE TRADES. As a teacher, Brown operates in a low-keyed fashion. First- and second-year students are mixed. He has no problem with that because most of the instruction is individualized. He gives his first-year students some group instruction at the beginning of the year, but after that students work on different projects and progress at their own rate.

I was a little nervous on my first visit to the machine shop, not having any idea of what to expect. I mentioned this to Mr. Brown, who said that most of the students who sign up for the class don't know what to expect either, unless they have taken a beginning metals course at their home high school or have visited the class on their ninth-grade tour of the AVS. "They don't even bother to find out," he said, "but once they're in here, it's the easiest class to get them interested in."

I asked for a brief tour of the shop on my first visit. Mr. Brown was pleased by my interest and showed me a lathe—"the only machine which can reproduce itself"—and the other machines in the shop. "Whatever you're making, tools and dies are needed, and they're made in a machine shop." He told me that manual dexterity was important for a machinist since he works within small fractions of an inch. Over the years, only a few of his students have come to class with a sense of precision, "but if they have the dexterity, they can be taught."

Mr. Brown is totally task-oriented with his students, who clearly respect his knowledge and skill. The most striking thing in this class was the students' involvement with their work. They were serious and purposeful, each working alone at a machine. Occasionally, someone would stop to talk to a friend or to ask another student for help. When students needed further direction, they went to Brown, who sometimes sat at his desk trying to get some administrative work done.

Whenever I was in the room, the class seemed to run by itself in a relaxed, yet serious, atmosphere.

Mr. Brown does not really know his students well. "It's partly my fault for not engaging in social conversation," he said. Though he may not know much about the students' lives outside school, he knows them well as far as their work in machine shop is concerned. He will share his knowledge freely and work with students who ask for help, but he is probably a better teacher for the motivated students than for those who need a lot of direction.

I interviewed three students from this class: a senior from District A, whom Brown described as an outstanding student, and two juniors from an upper-middle-class school in District C.

Ralph, from District A, described himself as a B student with straight A's in the two-year machine trades program. He likes school, especially math, is good at drawing, loves to work with his hands, but is "a poor reader." He thinks a lot of students in the machine shop "goof around." Ralph has very clear career goals: he wants to be a machinist at a large local manufacturing plant where his father has been working as a machinist for twenty years. He is also quite busy outside school. He works from 5:30 to 9:00 P.M. four days a week and all day Saturday, helping an uncle and a cousin who have a sign company, and is, in addition, presently managing his father's customized sign business. Ralph was obviously talented and creative, and the machine shop offered him an excellent opportunity to train for a vocation. I felt, however, that given his broad interests and enjoyment of school, Ralph could have benefited from a richer academic curriculum. I also wondered about his poor reading skills, which obviously bothered him. Will he find ways to improve them after graduation or will he always be a poor reader?

The other two students came from upper-middle-class families. The fathers of both boys worked for the same manufacturing firm as Ralph's father—one as an electronics engineer, the other as a computer programmer. The two boys are friends who decided together to sign up for the AVS class. They said, "The machine shop is a lot better than sitting in classes that don't interest you. . . . There is not so much book learning, you get to learn by doing." They described Thomas Brown as a good teacher: "You can learn on your own; he doesn't get mad when you make a mistake, and you don't have to do required projects as long as your own projects aren't all easy." Both boys said the machine shop was their best class. When I asked them whether there were other classes at their school they liked, one said he never did like school and the other said he liked life-saving.

These two students signed up for the AVS class partly because they wanted to get away from school and from classes they didn't like. Since both are tinkering with cars—one is building a jeep, the other is rebuilding a Volkswagen—they are using the class to make parts for their vehicles, probably the best motivation they could have. I doubt that either of them will go into this trade, but they are acquiring useful skills and are serious about learning in this class, while they seem quite turned off by their regular high school courses.

PRINTING AND GRAPHICS. The printing program occupies a large two-level room. The printing equipment is on the lower level; desks, chairs, blackboards, and bulletin boards are on the smaller upper level. The teacher, Mel Smith, is a friendly, energetic young man. His style is informal. When I entered the room, a radio was blaring. "Turn that down or off," he called over to a group of students, "I don't want to hear that obnoxious song."

Two out of the five classes Mel Smith teaches are part of the AVS program—a beginning and an advanced printing and graphics class. The other three are industrial arts classes at District A's high school. Mr. Smith finds that the AVS students are more serious about their work; some of his industrial arts students, he feels, come to class for easy credit.

When I visited, students were working independently on individual projects, going over to Smith whenever they needed help. A few kids were fooling around—it was near the end of the class period—but others were working very well indeed. As in the machine class, students were able to work on personal projects—printing their own drawings, making Christmas cards, and the like.

Mr. Smith told me that he became "hooked on graphics" in the eighth grade in his New Jersey junior high school. His father, a twenty-five-year employee of the Bell Company, was transferred to this state, where Mel got his B.S. in industrial arts. This is his first year teaching. He is giving himself five years to see if he likes teaching. He hopes he will; but, "If I find that teaching is not for me, I plan to go into

sales of graphic arts products or start my own silkscreening company."
To get his vocational credentials, he must have the equivalent of two
more years of work experience, which he plans to get during summers.

My visit to the printing/graphics program was relatively brief, and
I talked to students only casually, while they were working. They were
seniors, one from District A's high school, the other two from District
C. One student told me that he planned to go to the local community
college to continue his study of printing; another is joining the Air
Force after he graduates; the third, Brent, with whom I talked a little
longer—he was waiting for the AVS bus at the end of class—is working
after school to save money so he can attend a trade school to study
commercial art. Brent was a serious student who felt that some of his
classmates from District A were "lazy." "If I can make every class," he
said (he is bussed in from another district), "they can too."

I asked Brent whether the AVS class was different from his other
classes. "You have more freedom," he replied. "You do things. You
don't have to sit down while they talk and you listen. You don't get
bored in this class." I was interested by the similarity of his answer to
that of the two machine shop students.

CHILD DEVELOPMENT ASSISTANT. The child development
assistant program operates a state licensed preschool for two and one-
half- to five-year-old neighborhood children. The same two teachers
have been in charge of the program for the past five years. The
program occupies three classrooms—two for the preschool and one
for the academic work. There also is an office, manned by Louise, a
graduate of last year's AVS program, who takes care of the children's
records and tuition, is available to talk to parents, and helps wherever
help is needed. Louise is continuing her studies in early childhood
education at a local community college.

There are seventeen high school students currently registered for
each two-hour session. Students spend three days a week in academic
classes and one day in the preschool. On Fridays, the preschool is
closed and students use the time to review, evaluate, and plan for the
next week.

Five different high school students are assigned to work in the
preschool every day. They are supervised by one of the instructors,
who observes them and fills out daily rating sheets. The other instruc-

tor teaches the academic curriculum. The instructors switch responsibilities every two weeks.

The program is extremely well organized and seems to work well for both students and children. Although it is more highly structured than the other vocational programs, I'm not sure how one could handle three daily sessions in any other way. On their planning day, students are given the preschool schedule for the following week and are asked to prepare the activities they have been assigned to. They are responsible for their time with the children and are evaluated both on their planning and their performance.

Denise King and Joan Martin, the two teachers, try to maintain contact with the home economics teachers of the participating high schools, and they go to the high schools in the spring of each year to interview the students who have applied for their program. This selection process seems to pay off extremely well. It would be good, I believe, if all AVS teachers were given time and were encouraged to interview interested students. Better screening and greater teacher involvement in the selection process might help to reduce teachers' complaints about the caliber of some of the students sent to them by liaison counselors.

Both teachers have degrees in home economics and both have masters' degrees—Denise King in early childhood education, and Jean Martin in supervision and administration. Jean is a lively, very poised woman with many years of experience in a variety of jobs ranging from directing a child care center and teaching adult nutrition classes to supervisory work in a state health department. She has worked in many parts of the country, following her husband who is a hospital administrator. Denise is young, vivacious, self-assured, and appears to be doing an excellent job in her first teaching assignment.

The teachers regret that their schedule doesn't allow much time for involvement in professional organizations or for visiting other preschools and neighborhood kindergartens. They feel that the administration doesn't quite understand their double responsibility—teaching children as well as high school students—and they sorely miss having some time for planning and for communicating with each other.

This child development assistant program is staffed by warm, outgoing and caring teachers who are offering a well-planned year's course in child development and early childhood education with concurrent supervised lab/school experience. The teachers' philosophy, their way of relating to students, the care given to the children, and the friendliness toward parents, all combine to make this a high-quality program. Two local colleges waive their requirements for the introductory early childhood education course for graduates of this AVS program.

I talked to four students in this program. Two are currently enrolled. Two—Louise, who works in the office, and Doris, who attended the class as a junior and now comes one day a week on a work-study program—are graduates of last year's program.

Claryce, a senior from District D said, "I don't consider this a class. It's a school within a school, and it gives me a chance to get away from my school. I took it partly because I heard it was an easy class, but I like it a lot now and I'm learning a lot."

Judy, a senior from District C is a quiet, somewhat shy girl who told me that the class "turned out better than I expected. I didn't think it would be so friendly. I expected to be lonely. In regular classes you don't meet people. . . . AVS is a good program. The teachers are more caring than at the high school. Other teachers don't know much about us. We can go and talk to them if we need to, but students don't particularly want to talk to teachers."

Doris, who took the program as a junior, was equally enthusiastic. Like most of the students I interviewed, she finds regular "lecture/test, lecture/test" high school classes boring and enjoyed the friendliness and informality of her AVS classes. She also enjoyed meeting students from other schools and getting away from her own high school. She is all set to go to a state university and major in elementary education.

Louise hopes to transfer to a four-year college after completing her early childhood course. She wants to major in child psychology and eventually have a preschool of her own.

I talked to some highly motivated students. They may not be a representative sample of the class, but it appears that a fairly large number of students from this program continue their studies in the field of education.

HEALTH OCCUPATIONS. This is the second year for the health occupation program in its expanded form. Previously, there was a one-semester nurses' aide program taught by the same instructor, Mary Brunson, in a hospital located a few blocks from the high school. A few years ago, the state department of education wanted to broaden this program and asked Mary Brunson to do a community survey to assess needs for aides in twenty-five health-related occupations. As a result of this survey, Ms. Brunson expanded her nurses' aide program and added training for physical therapy, ophthalmology, and veterinary aides. Other occupations will be added gradually as time allows.

Health occupations is now a full-year program. All students receive the same instruction during the first semester: a comprehensive overview of the health care field, a survey of human physiology, classes on first aid, CPR, and nutrition, as well as on job-seeking skills, leadership, ethics, and law. Speakers from various health care fields come to class and students take trips into the community to learn about job opportunities in the different fields. During the second semester, students spend four days a week in a field placement of their choice. Nurses' aide students work at the hospital under the direction of Linda Oring, Ms. Brunson's assistant; Ms. Brunson supervises all the other students and teaches them on the day each week that they attend class at school.

I asked Mary Brunson how she handles the class when her students are working in so many different areas. "Last year," she said, "I tried to teach them all together, but that didn't work. I can't teach physical therapy students about arthritis and how to give whirlpool baths, and veterinarian kids how to give shots to dogs, and ophthalmology aides about eye anatomy, and nurses' aides about enemas, all at the same time." She is spending part of each day writing up curriculum for the new areas, hoping that when that task is completed, and when she can get additional materials for her students, they will be able to work fairly independently in the classroom, using her mainly as a resource. In addition to her new responsibilities, Ms. Brunson continues to be very active in the Health Occupations Student Association (HOSA)— the vocational club of health occupations students. She believes that the leadership and parliamentary training that students receive when they compete at district and state meetings is extremely valuable. Her students are also involved in community projects such as health fairs and they do volunteer work in nursing homes and hospitals.

Ms. Brunson tries to interview all the students who apply to her program. "I don't just accept the top students," she told me. "I take some D students. They may get D's in tests, but many of them are very good clinically."

Ms. Brunson's classroom reflects her interests and her involvement. Posters and charts cover the walls, clippings from AVS and HOSA activities are on the bulletin boards, books and magazines on health occupations as well as scrapbooks made by former students are scattered around the room. The classroom clearly invites students to become interested in a field that Brunson herself loves.

I watched one academic class in which the metric system was being taught in a rather unimaginative rote fashion and I volunteered to be a patient in a clinic class (taught in a second room with six hospital beds) during a review lesson on TPR (temperature, pulse, and respiration). Relationships between students and teachers were easy and informal—as in the child development program, teachers are called by first names—and Mary Brunson obviously knows her students well. "We're like a big family," she told me. A student confirmed this: "Mary and Linda care about us," she said. "If someone is absent, they ask a friend to find out what's the matter." In the often impersonal atmosphere of large high schools, these students valued their teachers' interest in their lives.

Mary Brunson has a graduation ceremony for her students at the end of the school year. She also organizes an employer/employee banquet. Parents are invited to class on a special "parents switch day," and they are also asked to sign a training agreement that Ms. Brunson has prepared for students when they go into the field. Parent and community support are obviously important to Ms. Brunson, who, in addition to her activities at school, is raising three young children, cares for three horses, and sells Amway products in her spare time!

I talked to two students in this program who came from different school districts. I asked them how students at their respective schools felt about vocational programs—was vocational education looked down on? Debbie, who attends a middle-class school, said, "Yes, to some extent. It's quite common for kids at my school to think this way. All my friends are going to college and many of them are rather snobby about the AVS." "Not at my school," said Barbara, who goes to a school in a working-class district. "When kids find out about the AVS program they want to go. At our school, if you have a chance at something, you take it."

Both girls are planning to continue their studies at two-year colleges, one in physical therapy, the other as a veterinarian's aide.

RESTAURANT ARTS. Restaurant arts, the newest program of the AVS, is in its first full year of operation. The program currently enrolls twenty-seven students who come for three-hour shifts—from 10:00 A.M. to 1:00 P.M. or from 11:00 A.M. to 2:00 P.M. The restaurant is open to the public from 11:00 A.M. to 1:00 P.M. The early group sets up for lunch and then works during the lunch period from 11:00 A.M. to 1:00 P.M. The second group also works during the lunch hour and cleans up afterward. There are three different areas in which students work. In the "front of the house," as the dining area of the restaurant is called in the trade, students wait on tables, bus dishes, and run the cash register. The "back of the house" includes food preparation in the "galley" and the set-up for salads and desserts in the pantry. The third is the bakery. Three different instructors are responsible for these areas, and students rotate from area to area every two weeks.

Restaurant arts is a two-year program enrolling both juniors and seniors. According to the teachers, the career objectives of students in the program are to own, manage, or work in restaurants.

The three teachers make an interesting team. George used to own a local franchise restaurant where Warren Bruce, the former AVS director, often ate lunch. Bruce asked George if he would be interested in the job. "What made you accept?" I asked him. "I was tired of the long hours and of being short of help. I was burnt out. I had my fill after seven years." This is George's first official teaching job, though he said, "When you own a restaurant, you're teaching all the time."

Frank, the part-time baking instructor, is Swiss-born and has worked as a baker or cook most of his life. He served in the Swiss army and spent twenty years in the U.S. Air Force. He was working as a plant supervisor for a dry cleaning firm when a former Air Force friend who taught in the AVS asked him if he would be interested in the restaurant job.

Carolyn, who is in charge of the "front of the house," is the only one of the team with an academic background. She has a B.S. in occupational home economics and taught home economics at the high school level for four years before joining the AVS. She has 3,000 hours' experience in food service work and plans to work summers to complete the requirements for her vocational license.

I enjoyed going into the restaurant both to eat and to watch the students. The restaurant always functioned smoothly. Students—including a couple of retarded youngsters who were helped by specially assigned aides—were obviously well trained and supervised.

Some of the students I talked to thought that George tried to give the restaurant too much of a real-life atmosphere. "He keeps getting on our backs," they complained. "George and Frank expect too much; they could be a little more understanding if you make a mistake." It sounded as if in their effort to create a working atmosphere, George and Frank forgot that they were still dealing with high school students. Carolyn, who came to the job from teaching, seemed more sensitive to the students' needs. The three restaurant teachers make a fine team, but it might help the program if they could talk about their differences and arrive at a more unified approach.

All three teachers liked the autonomy they have in running their program. Frank especially enjoys not having a boss and being able to organize his own program. "In the outside world," he said, "someone is always telling you what to do." The teachers feel that it's good for the students to experience some pressure, since that is what they will have to cope with when they look for jobs. Ninety percent of the restaurant students are not planning to go on to college. Working in the AVS restaurant offers students a good opportunity to find out if they want to continue working in this field.

I talked to six students. Four were chosen at random: their bus arrived before ten and they were just sitting around. The other two were chosen by the teachers.

Three of the first group of four students were in the program last year, and all three said they liked it better the previous year. "Last year was a lot better; there were only nine students and we worked hard. This year there are more kids, and the teachers are stricter and more picky."

Two students from the relatively small high school in District B found leaving their home school difficult. "At first I wanted to drop the class," one of them told me. "I was too nervous. But once you start working together, it's fine and you get to know everyone." The other student said, "Leaving school was a weird feeling. Now I don't mind saying that I go to two different high schools. Once you start working, you meet everyone. We've grown into a family."

Joan, an average academic student, travels a great distance to attend the restaurant program. She is enjoying it, learning a lot, and has decided to make food services her career. After graduation, she hopes to get a job in a restaurant and go to a two-year college to study cooking, baking, and catering.

Kent was the star pupil of the class. Highly motivated and unusually mature, he performed in the dining room with style and assurance. He seemed thoroughly professional. He feels that most of the students regard the program as just another class. "It's considered an easy class," he said. "You leave after three hours and are done." He thinks that only three or four students in the class are serious about a career in the restaurant business. The others do just what they have to do. Kent feels that students are not adequately screened and that some of them can't handle the pressure of working in a restaurant that is open to the public. He also thinks that as a two-year program there is not enough challenge—"It's repetitious; you could learn it all in one year if the class were smaller."

At Kent's home high school, 90 percent of the students go to college. He is an A student both at his home school and in the AVS. A hard worker, he attends classes from 7:30 to 10:30 A.M. in his home school, goes to the AVS from 11:00 A.M. to 2:00 P.M., and works in a restaurant from 3:00 to 10:00 P.M. He has been accepted at the Culinary Institute in Hyde Park, N.Y., one of the top training schools for chefs in the country. After completing his two-year course there, he hopes to open his own restaurant.

Kent feels that restaurant arts is a good program, though he is personally a little disappointed. "I thought when I enrolled the limits would be boundless," he told me. "That is not so." He was a bit discouraged by many of his classmates and the pacing of the program.

## The Trades Programs

In addition to the programs already described, the Sage Area Vocational School offers the following trades programs: Major Appliance, Service and Technology, Air Conditioning, Heating, and Refrigeration, and Marine Service/Sporting Vehicle Technology at District C;

Carpentry, Masonry, and Auto Mechanics at District B; and Auto Body Repair and Welding at the community college. The programs in Districts B and C will be discussed here.

*District C Programs* District C is fairly large. Its three high schools have a combined enrollment of about 4,500 students. It includes a small town that used to be the independent county seat and many new developments south and east of that town. The average income level is high, and there is a large professional population. "We serve very few blue-collar families," the area director said. The town has an active human relations council, and although there is a section of the population that is quite conservative—mostly personnel of two large industrial firms—there are also many liberals. There have been clashes on the school board between these two groups.

Hubie Ryan, the area director, has been with the district for nearly nine years. This was the first district I visited when I began my observations, and Hubie Ryan was most cordial, patient, and helpful. His background is academic—he is the only area director with a doctorate—and his vocational area of specialization is business education. Like the other area directors, he not only supervises the four AVS programs at his site and the District C students enrolled at other AVS sites, he also is in charge of all other vocational and career education programs in his district. His administrative style is somewhat more formal than that of District A's director. Hubie Ryan likes to have regular staff meetings and has recently asked his teachers to submit lesson plans.

The AVS site of District C is located in a converted warehouse close to the downtown section of the town. Small-engine repair—officially called Marine Service/Sporting Vehicle Technology—and Major Appliance Service Technology, which also includes Air Conditioning, Heating, and Refrigeration, are located in two large adjoining rooms on one side of the building. Two regular classrooms serve the other two programs taught at this site. One is called Cooperative Career Development, a work-study program in which students spend a minimum of fifteen hours a week in a paid job and attend class one hour every day learning about various aspects of the world of work—anything from how to dress for a job interview to how to fill out income tax forms. The other program (Co-op G) is also a work-study program but it is geared to younger students with special needs.

In addition to classrooms and offices for the teachers, this site houses the main administrative offices of the Sage Area Vocational School. The AVS director, the area director, the job placement officer, and secretarial support staff work at this site. The atmosphere is congenial. Teachers come out for a cup of coffee at break time, chat with secretaries, or confer with administrators.

Hubie Ryan told me that elementary-secondary enrollment in this district was declining, but enrollment in vocational programs has been increasing "in the last several years."

MAJOR APPLIANCE SERVICE TECHNOLOGY AND AIR CON-DITIONING, HEATING, AND REFRIGERATION. Ron Long, a new teacher at the AVS, taught both of these programs at the same time. His teaching approach is quite different from that of his predecessor, who apparently spent much of the time lecturing. He is trying to get more equipment into the room to give his students more opportunities for practical work. Some old refrigerators and ranges were being delivered when I visited the class. Long not only teaches both programs at the same time, but beginning and advanced students together with students from the nearby community college attend his classes. He starts wherever students are in their knowledge and does not have any difficulty mixing college and high school students.

I made two visits to his class: the first on my first day of observation. Mr. Ryan introduced me to the teachers at his site and I spent a short time in Ron Long's class. I was left with a strong impression, which I recorded in my notes.

The first thing that struck me was the informality of the setup, the small class size, and the fact that the students were involved in what they were doing. I watched the end of the practical work—students were pretty much on their own—and then I sat in on a brief discussion of how to repair a broken refrigeration unit. One boy came up to Ron Long at the end of the discussion. He had some questions and felt quite free to approach his teacher with them. Long talked with the boy until his problem was solved. Long's style of teaching and interacting with his students, the general informal atmosphere, the mixed grouping, the individualized instruction, and the students' interest reminded me of some of the really good primary classrooms I had seen. It didn't feel like school and I saw none of the tuned-out, turned-off high school students you hear so much about.

My second visit was later in the school year, and I spent most of my time talking with Long. He is a large man, easy-going and sure of himself. He knows and understands his students. "I don't mind if the kids spend the first ten minutes talking about their cars," he told me. "They'll make it up in class." I commented on his informal, individualized teaching approach. He admitted that some of his high school students had to learn to handle so much freedom; they were not used to it in their regular classes. But, he added, "This way I don't have to hassle with them. They don't pay attention to lectures anyway. They're more interested in their pickups and their girl friends at school. But they know it's not a free-for-all here. Some days we don't get much done, but other days we work hard. You've got to be realistic."

It's important to Mr. Long that his students learn to work independently. "In this kind of work," he said, "you work alone most of the time. You see your boss perhaps once a week." He would like to send his advanced students out on service calls by themselves so they could get used to working on their own.

In addition to teaching mornings at the AVS, he teaches evenings at a community college. He also has a partnership in an air conditioning business and does some consulting work. "This is a good trade for summer work," he told me. "I make as much money in the summer as in my two winter jobs combined." He has fifteen years of experience in the trade, three years of full-time teaching at another vocational high school, and additional part-time teaching experience at an adult education center.

SMALL-ENGINE REPAIR. This is the fourth year at the AVS for Dan Morgan, the other trade teacher at District C. Before coming to the AVS he taught for eleven years at a community college. Prior to that, he was head of a repair shop for a large trucking company.

Dan Morgan grew up in Mississippi and told me about the "opportunity classes" in his elementary school, where you could advance at your own pace. In his junior high school, there was a program in which students worked part-time and went to school part-time. He worked as a mechanic and feels that this program helped him stay in school. Morgan is not a young man, and I was interested in these experimental aspects of his Mississippi schooling. He was currently working toward his A.A. degree and told me how much he was enjoying his physics class.

Not quite as free as Mr. Long in his teaching style, Dan Morgan nevertheless individualized his instruction. He was irritated when his director asked for lesson plans. "Lesson plans don't make sense in vocational education," he said to me. "You can't keep everyone in a particular spot. Students in the advanced class work at their own pace at a specific job. If they have a problem, we discuss it." In their practical teaching, the trades teachers had strong convictions that instruction had to be geared to the individual student's knowledge and ability. In their academic teaching, most of them seemed to accept existing curricula without much questioning.

Special arrangements are sometimes made for individual students. Morgan mentioned a girl who spends one hour in class and then works four hours in a motorcycle shop, for which she gets another hour's credit. If she has any problems, the manager of the shop calls to let him know where she needs extra help. "Last week I showed her how to set points," Morgan said. "You learn more in one hour working in a shop than in three hours in school. It teaches you self-confidence. You learn how to think."

Morgan likes teaching, and understands the problems of some of today's high school students. He talked with feeling and compassion about "a little girl" who had just started to improve in his class when her home high school expelled her because of other problems she was having. He also expressed concern about a gifted student with attendance problems. "In my own school," he said, "I was always bored. I hated lock-step and rebelled against it. I see this now in so many kids."

There is no lock-step approach to teaching in Morgan's classes. On a visit to his shop, I talked to two students while they were working on a motorcycle engine. "How is the AVS different from your other classes?" I asked them. "At AVS teachers help you more," one of them said. "They are sharing their interest, they give you a few hints on what works for them, what might work for you." They went on working on the motorcycle but they continued to think and talk about my questions: "[AVS teachers] don't teach from the book . . . they're not always going by the book. . . . It's not repetitious . . . not like clockwork . . . not exactly like the book says. . . . It's not exactly what the English teacher says . . . not like diagramming a sentence . . . you don't have to do it just one way . . . you don't have to put the spark plugs in first and then the carburetor." They were both seniors in the advanced class and they obviously appreciated the opportunity to work independently and learn to think for themselves.

*District B Programs*　District B is the poorest of the six participating school districts. It has a predominantly working-class population and is the only one of the AVS districts with a sizable minority group. A large percentage of the population, many of Hispanic origin, qualified for federal aid and, until recently, the district had many federally funded programs.

There is only one high school in District B, built for approximately 500 students. It is the smallest high school of the AVS and one of only two schools that does not have an open campus. Dick Williams, the AVS area director, told me that discipline was tight at his school. There is a dress code, and smoking is not allowed anywhere. Students caught smoking are suspended for five days, and students caught smoking pot are expelled. He said that the school board made these rules but he personally believes in strong discipline and enforces the rules. District B students are not allowed to drive their own cars to AVS classes—they must ride the school bus. No other school enforced such a policy.

Williams lives in the district and has been employed there for twenty-six years. Supervising his AVS teachers is only one of his duties. He is also in charge of the school's career and industrial arts program and supervises business and home economics classes.

The high school is a gray, somewhat forbidding-looking concrete-block building that sits in a landscaped grassy area close to a major traffic artery on the southwestern periphery of the city. It is the farthest west of all participating high schools, and transportation for the students is sometimes a big problem. About 25 percent of District B's juniors and seniors are currently enrolled in AVS classes. Fewer than 10 percent of the school's graduates go on to four-year colleges.

Dick Williams seems to function somewhat like a liaison counselor.

He interviews and screens AVS applicants, takes pride in knowing about all the AVS offerings, and visits his students once they are attending classes. "Some of my best students come from that district," Larry Jamrich, the data processing teacher told me. "Dick Williams screens them well and sends us good kids."

Williams' own vocational background is in carpentry and he strongly identifies with students going into the trades, trying wherever he can to help them succeed. He may be a little paternalistic, but, at the same time, he is extremely caring and concerned. He thinks the AVS concept is great. "As a small high school," he said, "we could never have had all these programs for our kids."

I have little sense of his administrative style but suspect it is rather informal, with only four AVS teachers involved—two in the construction trades and two in auto mechanics. He feels that students in the construction trades shouldn't spend too much time on academics. "It's not their thing," he said. "It should be eighty to ninety percent hands on and ten to twenty percent classwork." Then he added, "School is not enough of what life is about." This remark probably reflects the feelings of most of the teachers in AVS.

CONSTRUCTION TRADES: CARPENTRY AND MASONRY. Both the carpentry and the masonry programs are housed in the basement of the school. A large work area is accessible directly from the outside. There are also several smaller classrooms, and an office shared by the two teachers. This is the second year in the masonry program for Curt Phillips, who came to the school from a job as a foreman in a masonry firm. He had no prior teaching experience and has worked all his life in the trade. Charles Wiley, the carpentry teacher, was in his first year at the AVS, but he had taught carpentry for ten years in a boys' reform school.

Beginning students in both programs worked mostly in the shop— masonry students learning the basics of bricklaying and carpentry students practicing the beginning skills of their trade. Later in the year, the carpentry students build houses scaled down to one-third size. Charles Wiley told me that other vocational schools buy lots so their students can build full-size houses, which are then sold, but District B could not afford to tie up such a large sum of money. Both teachers liked to take their students out to work on real-life projects.

Advanced carpentry students were building a spook house for a Jaycee-sponsored Halloween party, and advanced masonry students were making tuck-and-point repairs on a nearby Masonic lodge. Wiley felt that the carpentry program should be changed to one year; second-year students should be placed with private contractors and come to class one day a week. "If students are advanced enough in job responsibility and work skills, being in class one day a week would be enough," he said. "If they have problems on their job, they could always come in for fifteen or twenty minutes and get help from me."

Curt Phillips, a warm, outgoing man, has a fatherly relationship with some of his students. "They come in here with this 'I'm tough' attitude," he told me. "They had trouble in their academic classes and they think, 'I'm not smart, so I'm tough.' But their personalities change after they're in class for a while." I saw him trying to talk a rather disheveled-looking student into getting a haircut. I also observed him after class sitting and chatting with a group of students who obviously enjoyed the camaraderie with their teacher. Phillips had told me that he took a large cut in salary when he accepted his teaching job. I think he gains a good deal of satisfaction from the interaction with his students and this may partly compensate for his financial loss.

AUTO MECHANICS. The auto mechanics program is located in a small building next to the now empty old high school, a few blocks away from the new school. It is taught by one full-time instructor, Fred Weltzin, and a half-time assistant who works mostly with students who need extra help with academic skills. My visit to the shop was brief—I came almost at the end of the afternoon class. Although I got only a glimpse of the students, I had a nice long talk with Weltzin. He has spent most of his life in the trade; his last job was service manager of a large garage. He had some previous teaching experience as instructor in a Chrysler school for mechanics. He regards his present assignment as a retirement job: he likes teaching, he likes the students, and he likes his free summers.

Weltzin tries to screen the students who apply to his program. He goes to the three high schools in District C (Districts A and D have their own auto mechanics program that is not part of the AVS) and talks to prospective students about his expectations. He wants his students to be at least interested in the field, even if they haven't decided to make auto mechanics a career. "I tell them that it's not a hobby shop," he added. Since many students have their own cars, often older models in need of repairs, it would obviously be a temptation to students to enroll in this class and learn to work on their own cars. As in the auto body shop, only second-year students are allowed to work on their own cars.

Mr. Weltzin feels that his talks to students at the home high schools pay off—the majority of the students in his classes are there because they are interested in the program. He seems to have a good feeling for his students. Seventy-five percent of them used to be placed in jobs, but at the time of the interview business was slow so jobs were harder to find. In his seven years as an AVS teacher, he had only two students who went on to college. "Most of the kids I get here don't fit into the academic high school program," he said. Relatively few girls sign up for the program. There was one girl in his advanced class, the only one ever to go into the second-year class.

Weltzin is one of the few teachers in the AVS who mentioned that he got insufficient feedback on his teaching. He regretted that I didn't have time to talk to his students—he had hoped to learn from me how they felt about his class. "No one ever told me anything about teaching high school students when I started," he said. As the teacher of the only program on his site, he has little chance for communication with others.

*The Community College*   Two AVS programs—auto body repair and welding—are located at the community college in District C. Since these are subjects that also are taught at the community college, there are large, well-equipped shops on the ground floor of the college building. Glen Tait, the auto body teacher, and Allan Strand, the welding teacher, are the only instructors at this site who teach high school students. Their supervisor is employed by the college, and his major responsibilities are to the college's vocational courses. For that reason it is hardly possible to speak of the climate of this AVS site. The teachers share their classroom space with college instructors and work pretty much on their own.

Both programs have two daily morning sessions and one evening session that meets twice a week for four hours. The teachers don't like this split schedule, but evening classes seem to be fairly popular with the students, partly, perhaps, because they can earn a lot of credits with just two classes a week. The teachers feel that their morning students are more serious. "Kids just like to get out of the house in the evening," they said. "We are just baby-sitting them." However, administrators feel that evening classes give students who work in the afternoons a chance to take more courses.

WELDING. When I went to the welding class, all the students were working at their stations, wearing helmets and eye protectors. This was one class where I could not just walk up to students and casually engage them in conversation. Allan Strand took me to his little office in a glass-enclosed cubicle at one end of the classroom.

He regretted that about three-fourths of his students were seniors. He told me that if they started the course as juniors, they would have enough time to learn all the different welding techniques and could leave the AVS as certified welders, having passed the American Welding Society's certification test. He also mentioned that three unions—the pipefitters, boilermakers, and ironworkers—give some credit to AVS graduates entering the unions' apprenticeship programs.

Strand started work as a shipyard laborer, then got into the apprenticeship program of the boilermakers' union. He has been a welder for fifteen years and he had done some teaching for the union before accepting his AVS job. He feels that many students are counseled into trades programs with promises of good wages in the skilled trades and are not prepared for hard work and for starting at the bottom when they graduate from school. Still, about 50 percent of his one-year-program students and seven out of his eight presently enrolled advanced students are seriously training to be welders.

Like most of the trades teachers, Strand works at more than one job: he has his own welding and fabrication business and also teaches some courses for the community college.

AUTO BODY REPAIR. Glen Tait, the teacher for this program, is a man in his late fifties. He has worked in the trade all his life. Tait grew up on a farm in Kansas, where his grandparents homesteaded. He is one of eight children and has five children of his own. He graduated from high school in 1940 and joined the Army Air Force the following year. During World War II, he rebuilt wrecked planes.

Tait has always liked custom body work, but he said, "When my family came along, I went into production work." When his family was raised, he wanted to get out of production. That's when he went into teaching.

He told me that he liked teaching and found it to be challenging. About 90 percent of the students who enroll in his classes finish at least one year of training. Students who complete the two-year program start in the trade as knowledgeable apprentices. "I trust my students at the end of one year more than ninety percent of the body men in the field. They know all the basics they need to know."

He is a proud craftsman and a strict teacher. He holds his trade in high regard and wants his students to be proficient, with all the varied skills they will need. Welding is the first of the skills the students have to learn. He showed me a lot of little metal pieces welded together with different types of welds. Students had to master these techniques before they were allowed to weld directly on a car. When I talked to the students, some of them complained that too much time was spent on welding: "We have to do it till we pass, and then wait for everyone else to get done." Other students, however, while admitting that learning to weld was boring, felt that it was important. "We need to know welding and he wants us to do it right."

Tait explained to me that in many body shops work is specialized— some people weld, others paint, and so on—but his job was to train the students in *all* aspects of body work. He really wanted me to understand which knowledge and skills were required, and I appreciated his desire to educate me in his field.

He had strong feelings about permissive parents. "It has done a lot of harm to young people," he said. "There can be no freedom without rules or limits. . . . I've always wanted to know where I stand. Why should kids go to school and not know where they stand? Today's kids don't respect authority—they are an unhappy generation."

He also expressed concern about the poor academic skills of many of his students—a theme that came up in almost every interview with trades teachers. "When I went to high school, a diploma meant I was ready to go to college. Schools today should concentrate more on reading and math and upgrade vocational education so that the students we get would be achievers."

Glen Tait said he didn't miss contact with other teachers; he has many plans and projects apart from his teaching job. He wants to start his own auto body school, he wants to write a book on how to start one's own body business on a shoestring, and he wants to build a custom car that working men can afford. He has already designed it and wants to see how it can be marketed. "I've got a hundred years of work planned, so I haven't got time for small talk and socializing."

A craftsman at heart, he didn't like the time pressures of production work. He told me that the tension between quality and time gives you ulcers. Perhaps teaching at this stage in his life will give Tait another chance to work for quality. Some students may not like his emphasis on perfect craftsmanship, but others appreciate it very much.

## The Students

I had a brief talk with a junior from District A who attended the carpentry class. He had just moved to this state from Illinois and liked this class better than his other classes. "It's easier to get to know the kids in this class and we do more here," he said. A senior from District B, who was in the masonry class, told me that he had been in trouble for "ditching" and smoking. "But since I've been in the masonry class I haven't been in trouble." This was the boy whom Curt Phillips encouraged to get a haircut. I suspect that the instructor's caring relationship contributed to his changed attitude.

The two students from small-engine repair, whose comments on their AVS class were cited earlier, came from two different schools in District C. They had decided on their own to enroll in this class. One student thought he would like it, but found out that he is interested only when he works on his own vehicle. The other student may continue his studies in a trade school. They liked the AVS class but were quite critical of their other high school classes. "English is a bunch of baloney," said one boy. "We've been talking for fifteen years and don't have to learn how to do it. Up to ninth-grade English is enough if you don't go to college." The other student added, "What do you need history for? High schools should teach more toward fields of life."

When I first visited the evening auto body class, the welding equipment wasn't working and I had a good opportunity to talk to the students while the instructor was trying to get help. It was an interesting experience. When I entered the classroom, about a dozen students were sitting on chairs looking rather bored. Glen Tait handed out work sheets from the auto body curriculum and asked the students to study them while he went to see if he could repair the welding equipment. I asked if I could talk with the group and he was glad to let me be with his class. As usual, I started out by asking the students how they liked their AVS class. Many of the students said they didn't like it. They had started with work sheets in the fall and thought it would have been better if they had started with taking a car apart. They complained that they spent too much time on welding and that there was only one car to work on. While one student worked on this car, the others had to watch. They thought there should be one car for every two people. One boy said they hadn't accomplished anything in three months. "What's good about this class?" I asked, slightly overwhelmed by all the criticism. "It's small and you get a lot of credits."

I realized that some of the students were unhappy with the negative answers I was getting, although no one spoke up to present another point of view. When Tait returned to announce that it was time for a break, a couple of students stayed behind to talk some more. One was a junior from District A, a quiet, rather young-looking boy who told me that he liked school, but that he was taking this class mostly for the credit. He thought, however, that he was learning some useful skills. "You can do it to make extra money, or it might be the only work you can find."

The other student was the only girl I talked with in the trades classes (I saw one other female student in the advanced auto mechanics class).* Good-looking, self-assured, and rather fancily dressed for this type of work, Teresa worked after school in a local department store and hoped to become a buyer. I asked her why she was taking this course. She likes cars, she told me, and spends all her weekends with her boyfriend working on them. She is good in art, likes to paint, and thinks it would be fun to paint cars. That is what she is most interested

* I asked five out of the eight trades teachers how they felt about girls in their classes. All but one were positive: "Appliance repair is a good field for women. . . . Women do outstanding machine work . . . girls are very good welders." One teacher said he likes to have girls in his class because "they make the guys work harder." Only one teacher felt that girls created problems "because they sign up when they have boyfriends in the program." His was a minority opinion.

in. She clearly does not plan to make auto body work a career, but, "When you take your car to a body shop, you'll know what's needed and you can look at your car afterward and see if it's been done right." She also thought that the class was boring, especially practicing all the different welds. I compared the little metal pieces to sewing samplers. "Yes," she said, "if you could do the whole garment, it would be more interesting." On the whole, she felt that the class was valuable. "Even if you don't want to become an auto body worker you can learn something useful here rather than sit in some other dumb class."

A little later, two students from District D came over to me. They had sat apart from the rest of the class during the group interview and had not participated. One of them said, "This is a good class if you want to learn how to do it and plan to take it for two years. Most kids are here just for the credit. It's boring only because it's so long. Most of the guys here just want to work on their own cars and then ditch the class." "It's a good class," added the other student, "the teacher is real good."

I was sorry that my allotted time did not allow me to visit some of the participating high schools and observe a typical "book learning" class. Over and over again in my talks with different students, AVS classes got higher ratings than the academic classes because "you learned something concrete and useful from teachers who knew their trade and were eager to share their knowledge."

## Summary

A number of themes or topics emerged from my inquiries into these programs. They are summarized below.*

*The Real World vs. the School World*   As I noted in relation to my interviews with the restaurant teachers, I became aware of a theme that I call "the real world vs. the school world." This theme ran through my talks with trades teachers and students almost like a *leitmotif*. Most of the trades teachers have had many years' experience in the real world; they feel that their values are somewhat different

* Much of Maja Apelman's summary statement regarding the trades programs is included. She prepared similar summaries for all of the programs but these are not included.—ED.

from those of academics teachers and administrators. One teacher said: "Teachers of academic subjects and teachers who have worked in the trades come from two different worlds. They have completely different backgrounds. [The academics teachers] don't understand where we come from and what we are trying to achieve. They teach to satisfy the school's requirements rather than to satisfy the needs of the students."

Trades teachers know that in their world, skills and knowledge are more important than academic degrees, and they are sensitive about any hints of lack of recognition. One teacher, a self-educated man who did not finish high school but advanced to a position of considerable responsibility in his trade before joining the AVS, had strong feelings about the attitudes of some of his academically trained colleagues. He resented administrators who, he believed, thought that because trades teachers didn't have academic degrees they weren't capable of making decisions for their programs. "In industry," he said, "you can go as far as you want without formal education." Another teacher commented that educators have no business ability. "There is a lot of money wasted with our present purchasing policy," he said. "The district needs a purchasing agent. I could save them three times my salary if I could buy where I wanted to buy."

Many of the trades teachers talked about their independence. They had other jobs or businesses of their own; they had marketable skills; and they did not depend on teaching as their only source of income. "Academics teachers are so bound by regulations, they've always got to protect themselves—that's all they have. They don't understand how we can be so independent," one teacher said. Another stated, "Trade experience is the most important thing in teaching. I have friends who went into teaching after being in the trade. After they got their B.A.'s their programs went down. Everything had to be set up in a nice little schedule after they'd been to school."

I can understand these teachers' impatience with administrative red tape and academic hierarchies. Teachers are always on the lowest rung of the ladder, and vocational teachers seem to be at the very bottom. That is unfortunate. There is a lot of talent and know-how, a lot of spirit and dedication among the trades teachers, some of whom could make valuable educational contributions beyond their own area of expertise. I know, of course, only half of the story. I am not quite sure which teachers are being criticized: teachers in the high schools, or academically trained teachers at the AVS, or both. It would be interesting to talk to some of these academics teachers and find out how *they* perceive their vocational colleagues.

There is no doubt in my mind that both groups could learn from each other. AVS students clearly state what they like in their classes, and academics teachers might take note. On the other hand, there were a few trades teachers who admitted that knowing a trade is not quite the same as being a good trade teacher. One of them told me, "It took me three years to learn to slow down. I assumed too much at first. I was used to being in industry and thought everybody else knew what I knew." Experienced teachers could help new trades teachers to make this transition.

*The Programs Could Be Better*   Whenever you encourage teachers to talk freely, there will be complaints. The AVS trades teachers are no exception. They complained, like most teachers, about their administrators. Here are some of their remarks.

> Administrators don't ask, "Can you teach thirty kids?" They say, "You have to teach thirty kids."

> We need money. We can't get capital items. The administration doesn't understand that this equipment is more expensive than pencils and paper and textbooks. We're offering good programs and have outstanding teachers, but we're top heavy in administration.

> He wants me to start classes with five or six more students than there are working stations for because only about seventy-five percent of the students who start the program finish the year. They push the numbers game.

> When they quit playing their silly little numbers game on how many students graduate and get back to educating students, things will be better.

The teachers want small classes and good equipment, but they have little sympathy for administrators' concerns. They accuse the administration of playing "the numbers game," but how would vocational education be financed if you couldn't use numbers to justify needs?

> Many counselors see vocational education as a dumping ground. They send us dummies.

Counselors sometimes phone teachers and demand that certain students get a passing grade so they can graduate.

Many of the counselors are very young and not very worldly. They've never been exposed to the work world.

Counselors don't understand what is involved in learning the trades.* They think we can take any kid and teach him. What do you do with kids who can't read or do math? It's a pacifier type thing: "Let's put them into welding or auto body or machine shop with the understanding that they go to their home high schools." It's a trade-off.

Seventy percent of the students sent by counselors are the dumb kids, too dumb for any other class. Why do we have to have the castoffs? They take it for the credit because they can't get it somewhere else. It's like closing the gate after the horse is gone. It's a useless effort. We have to re-educate the counselors as well as the kids.

Complaints about counselors came from administrators as well as from teachers. Although several counselors were highly praised, I suspect that some of the complaints were probably justified.

There were complaints by all but one of the trades teachers about the students' poor reading and math skills. One teacher told me that over 90 percent of his students needed help with math. "I have only two students who understand math at the level needed—eighth grade." Another teacher said, "Most of my students have a fourth-grade math level. To the question: 'How many sixteenths are there in an inch?' I get every answer from 'three' to 'seventy-one.' We're fighting math all along." Another teacher told me that only two of his evening students passed the eighth-grade math test. He added, "These kids need a lot more at high school than they are getting. [Teachers are] doing them a great disservice when they pass from fifth to sixth grade a kid who can't read or do math." Another teacher added, "Students have gotten through school without basic skills and without any rationale for learning." Most of these teachers are older men who could not have succeeded in their trades without math and reading skills. They were concerned and disturbed by the low achievement level of so many of their students.

Although administrators told me that the AVS was less of a dumping

* Some counselors obviously have a different point of view. One counselor said about a trade teacher: "He treats the kids as if they were forty-year-old men coming back for a refresher course."

ground now than in former days, the vocational classes still have a large percentage of poor students. Few academically gifted students take vocational classes. But that is not the problem—vocational education is meant to offer other options. The trades teachers know from their own experience that college is not for everyone, and that one can make a good living in a skilled trade. But they have worked hard to be successful in their fields and they are upset about the poor skills of some of their students, wondering rightly how counselors expect students to learn a trade when they barely read or do the simplest mathematical calculations. Some students become motivated to learn math when they see the need for it, but other students aren't motivated to learn anything and are sent to the trades programs as a last resort. These are the "castoffs" teachers complain about, and teachers resent the fact that they end up in their classes. It is, after all, a real put-down when counselors send such students to the AVS. "If a counselor thinks you can learn carpentry or welding or engine repair without knowing how to read or do math, then they must think that we, the teachers, don't know very much either." I am not saying that this is what counselors actually think, but I believe this is the message the trades teachers get when these students appear in their classes. Vocational teachers suffer for the failure of a system that allows students to progress to twelfth grade with elementary school levels in the basic skills.

Some of the trades teachers expressed concern about the relatively small enrollment in the second-year classes of their program. Many students don't start a program until their senior year. That could be because the program is not really a career choice—students might have been sent by a counselor, or they might have enrolled on their own to pick up credits, or to learn skills for personal use. But it could also mean that students find out about the programs too late, or that the benefits of the advanced classes are not sufficiently publicized. It would be helpful to give this problem some further thought. Teachers, I believe, would get more satisfaction from their jobs if they had a greater number of advanced students. As one teacher said to me, "You want to get *some* top students, otherwise it's just baby-sitting." Several trades teachers mentioned that they would like to "co-op" more students in their second year of training; that is, have them placed in jobs and come to class either one day a week or whenever they need some help. The auto mechanics teacher thinks that his program would be more economical if it were restructured. He would like to screen the students more carefully and have only a one-year high school program. After students graduated, they would be placed in jobs and could then use postsecondary facilities for further training. "In the two-year program as it stands now," he said, "kids may have forgotten what they learned the first year by the time they get a job." For some students, co-oping might be a useful second-year option.

*Why Become a Teacher?*   Since almost all the trades teachers had told me that they took a large cut in pay when they left their trade job to get into teaching, I wondered what attracted them to this new profession. I therefore asked many of the teachers what made them want to teach. Some had health reasons—back injuries or "arthritis and working outside in the winter." Most of them were tired of the pressures in their work—"there were too many hassles," "I got tired of fighting the warranty situation." Others, as previously stated, had done part-time teaching, found they liked it, and gradually switched over to a full-time teaching job. Some were told of openings in the AVS by friends and decided to give it a try. Several of the teachers have evening teaching jobs, some have additional income from their own businesses, and others work summers in the trades to make up for their smaller winter earnings.

Most of the teachers told me that they enjoyed teaching. They liked young people and derived satisfaction from seeing their students change and learn and sometimes become sufficiently motivated in the trade class to improve even in their academic work.

I think there are still other reasons why teaching at a lower salary is acceptable to these men. The trades classes are quite small and teaching three two-hour sessions is probably easier physically than working an eight-hour day in a shop or on a building site. There is relative job security, there are good fringe benefits, especially long summer vacations, and you can work on your own. No one tells you how to run your classes. I think also that at least some of the teachers enjoy the higher status that goes with a teaching appointment. They have become experts whose knowledge and skills are sought and appreciated by most of the students in their classes.

## Comments

I would like, briefly, to comment on a number of issues referred to in various sections of this report.

*Goals*   The state policy for vocational education—to give students skills that will ready them for employment in a variety of fields upon graduation from high school—causes some problems for AVS teachers and administrators. The state apparently considers only those students who are placed in jobs as fulfilling the official goals of vocational education. Students who are continuing their education full-time cannot be counted even though they are advancing their skills in the field they studied at the AVS. Several teachers and administrators felt that this was a rather narrow view of vocational goals, especially with the demand for advanced technical skills in today's employment market.

It would appear wise for vocational teachers and administrators to enter into a dialogue with members of the state board about the present goals and about possible revisions in the future.

*Selection of Students*   There does not seem to be a consistent selection policy for students going into AVS classes. Students in the participating high schools can take an optional tour of AVS sites in the ninth grade, but, since they cannot sign up for the classes until they are in the eleventh grade, these tours should probably be supplemented by other, later visits to the particular program in which the student wishes to register.

A number of teachers have close ties with liaison counselors in the home high schools, and they talk to groups of interested students during registration time. A few teachers make an effort to interview all the students who have applied for their programs in order to screen them and to tell them about their expectations for the class. These teachers did not complain about the quality of their students as did many of the trades teachers. Perhaps *all* teachers should be encouraged to talk to or to interview prospective students. Time for this lengthier, though more thorough, selection process would have to be built into the structure of the programs. In addition, I think students should be encouraged, even required, to visit the programs before they register in order to have a better idea of what to expect. Finally, if liaison counselors could be given more time for their AVS duties so that they could keep in touch with their students and pay regular visits to the programs, many of the existing problems might be ameliorated. More and better communication between AVS teachers, prospective students, and liaison counselors is a real need.

*Isolation of Teachers* Isolation of teachers is created, in part, by the structure of the AVS. Although most teachers liked the independence and autonomy this structure gave them and did not complain about isolation, a few did talk about feeling cut off from both the other teachers in the program and from professional colleagues in other settings.

The AVS is trying to address this problem by instituting a tour of all the programs for all teachers prior to the opening of the school year. The administration is also trying to raise funds for the publication of a newsletter to help keep teachers informed about events and activities in the various programs.

A few of the trades teachers mentioned that they did not know enough about teaching high school students when they started to work at the AVS. The few complaints I heard from students about AVS teachers were mostly about teachers' unrealistic expectations. Opportunities for new teachers to talk to more experienced colleagues in related fields would improve this situation.

Although teachers did not make a big issue of feeling isolated, I believe that *all* teachers can benefit from more interaction with colleagues and from more feedback on the style and content of their teaching. Vocational teachers are required to have advisory committees made up of people from industry or the professions as well as from the schools—mostly administrators and counselors. These committees must meet at least twice a year. This is obviously an attempt to put teachers in touch with what is going on in their fields and to give them input from people in the schools who may have a wider perspective because of their greater opportunity to get around. Some of the teachers use their committees well; others could use help in taking advantage of the expertise of their committee members. I think that in addition to the advisory committees and to school-arranged in-service days, teachers would be given a certain number of professional days each year to use at their own discretion. Some possible options might be: visiting other classes, talking to teachers or administrators, visiting places of work in their respective fields, or doing whatever *they* feel would benefit their teaching.

*Field Experience*   Several of the AVS programs (data processing, agriculture, health occupations) arrange for students to have related field experiences during the second year or the second semester of their courses.

In three programs—restaurant arts, child development assistant and cosmetology—students get experience in working with the public during their class time in the AVS.

Field experience is generally valued by both faculty and students, and several trades teachers mentioned that they would like to make changes in the second year of their programs, incorporating more out-of-school work for their students. The teacher of appliance repair would like to send his advanced students out on service calls to give them experience working on their own; the carpentry teacher would like to place his second-year students with private contractors for four days a week and have them attend class for the fifth day. The auto mechanics teacher thought about changing his program to a one-year course for seniors who, after being placed in jobs, could use postsecondary facilities for further training. Apprenticing students while they are still in school and have easy access to the knowledge and support of their teachers could be a valuable experience for AVS students as well as a good transition toward working on their own. Occasionally, teachers made such arrangements for individual students—a girl enrolled in the small-engine repair class was working in a shop, coming to class only when she needed help—but I don't know how common such arrangements are. I hope that the administration will listen to these and other suggestions from teachers and try some of them on a pilot basis.

*Teaching and Learning*   I have quoted impressions from my diary notes as well as numerous comments from teachers and students that illustrate the teaching style prevalent in most of the vocational classes. Instruction tends to be individualized, class size is relatively small, the atmosphere mostly informal. The content of the class is learned through direct experience. A few instructors mentioned that the relatively loose structure of their courses causes some initial difficulties for a number of students, yet almost all the students I interviewed liked the teaching style as well as the content of the AVS classes and contrasted the instruction favorably with that in their regular academic high school classes. The following comments (previously quoted) are fairly representative of the students' opinions:

> The machine shop is a lot better than sitting in classes that don't interest you. . . . There is not so much book learning here, you get to learn by doing.

> You do things. You don't have to sit down while they talk and you listen. You don't get bored in the class.

> Lecture/test classes are really boring. I like the AVS class much better than classes where you just sit and listen all the time.

Students also liked the small class size. "In regular classes you don't get to meet people. . . . We're like a big family here. . . . It's easier to get to know the kids in this class." And they appreciated the concrete knowledge of the teachers: "AVS teachers help you more. . . . They are sharing their interest." The men and women teaching in the AVS love their fields and they communicate their enthusiasm to the students.

In most cases, the practical teaching in the AVS is excellent. Instructors know about that aspect of teaching from their own work experience, and they are able to use their knowledge in the classroom. The academic part of the program is much more conventional, especially in the trades programs where teachers tend to use standard curriculum guides. It is the concrete learning in an informal but businesslike setting that accounts for the success of the vocational classes. This struck me in the first class I visited and every class thereafter. In contrast to students in "lecture/test, they talk—you listen" academic classes, AVS students are involved in active learning of useful and interesting subjects. Their enthusiasm for this kind of teaching indicates that changes in this direction in the regular academic high school curriculum would be welcomed by many students. When vocational students complain that "English is a bunch of baloney, we've been talking for fifteen years and don't have to learn how to do it," or ask, "Who needs history? I hate Western Civilization, it's all lecture," they more than likely speak for a good percentage of all high school students. Students get turned off by the way these subjects are taught and then come to dislike the subject itself.

When an obviously bright student in a career development class said to me, "I've been working in my uncle's jewelry shop for seven years. Why do I have to take history? It isn't going to make me a better jeweler," I wondered how this student could be helped toward a greater appreciation of history. I asked him if he had ever thought about how jewelry was made in past times, and whether he ever saw an exhibit of ancient jewelry in a museum, and whether he knew anything about the role of jewelry in other cultures. "Might you be interested in the history of jewelry-making?" I asked him. He looked at me with obvious surprise and then said, "Maybe."

I am sure there are many opportunities to relate the practical learning of the AVS classes to some of the required high school courses. This kind of teaching would demand a great deal of cooperation between AVS and regular high school teachers and would present innumerable logistical problems, quite apart from the fact that teachers might not be interested in trying. There is no question in my mind, however, that the students would benefit enormously.

In mathematics, especially, cooperation between AVS and academics teachers should be strongly encouraged. Although there are special tutoring services in math and reading for AVS juniors and seniors whose skills in these subjects are below the eighth-grade level, it would help if the math instruction in the home school could be more related to the math needed in the trades.

I watched one tutoring session for some masonry and carpentry students. It left a strong impression with me. Here are excerpts from my diary notes:

> When I visited the construction programs I was surprised that there were so few students in the class. I was told that it was tutoring day. The great majority of the students were working with their tutors. Mostly they work in small groups, but occasionally tutoring is done on a one-to-one basis, probably when a student's reading or math skills are so poor that even a small group situation becomes embarrassing. I am glad there are funds to help these students but I was shocked by their poor math skills. When I expressed my surprise to the tutors, they started to criticize the schools.

"You can get through high school just on attendance," one of them said. Another one added, "The only way you can flunk out of school if you are attending classes is if you beat up your teacher. Teachers will pass the kids if they show up and make some effort."

The students clearly disliked their tutorial sessions. When they were called in from their shop class, I overheard one boy say, "Why do we have to go? We're not stupid!" Even though seven out of nine students in the masonry class were being tutored, they still felt singled out. The tutors were well meaning, but the students were hostile. They felt humiliated by the whole experience.

Picture a group of seventeen and eighteen year old boys all lined up in front of a blackboard, trying to work out the problem 7½ divided by ¾. They had learned to change 7½ into a fraction—though multiplying 7 × 2 caused a problem for one student—and they had also learned the "invert and multiply" rule. One boy worked the problem pretty fast, a couple of others remembered the rule and labored their way through the fractions. Someone said the answer was 18⅔. "You're wrong, it's 10" said another. "No, it ain't," "It's 10." "No, it's 18⅔." Then the boy who was wrong was told that 10 was the right answer and to copy the calculations from the boy who had done it right. I did not see the tutor asking him what he did to get 18⅔. It reminded me of first graders getting a wrong answer in their workbook, finding out it's wrong, and then guessing until they get the right answer, without really understanding the problem. After division, students had to practice multiplication: 3598 × 63.

It is hard for me to put into words how I felt during this class. I was embarrassed for the students. I empathized with their humiliation. I tried to figure out how else they could be helped. I also wondered how kids could get to the twelfth grade with such poor skills. And then I wondered whether their skills really were that poor or whether this tutoring situation made it worse. I don't have a solution to propose, but I feel that there must be a better way to help these kids, and to prevent them from having to take such remedial classes at the end of their high school careers.

What will be the future of vocational education in these times of renewed attention to the problems of our nation's schools? *Newsweek* magazine, March 7, 1983, reported a spectacular growth of community colleges in the last 10 years, with two-thirds of the students enrolled in vocational courses. Private technical and trades schools are also doing a booming business, often training students to meet the needs of local industries. With such a growth in postsecondary vocational education, what will be the role of vocational education at the high school level?

I believe there *is* a place for vocational education in high schools, but it should not cut the students off from learning in other fields. Since subjects like history and literature, as they are presently taught in many schools, seem not to interest a large percentage of students, practical and immediately usable skills have a stronger appeal. Yet a broad liberal arts education can greatly enrich and broaden one's appreciation of life, and many of the currently less popular subjects can be exciting and rewarding if taught in more imaginative ways. All students should be exposed to areas outside their specialization so that in later life they can make informed choices about their vocations and their leisure-time activities.

# 11

# CARVER HIGH SCHOOL

## B. DELL FELDER AND
## W. ROBERT HOUSTON

You reach Carver Senior High School for Careers traveling about seven miles north of the central city on the freeway. The freeway passes through a number of relatively poor neighborhoods and small industrial installations. As you round the bend that leads toward the school, you see the six-foot chain-link fence that encloses the school grounds.

There is no grass. The area surrounding the school is paved and lined for parking. A small, attractively designed, raised planting area fronts the entrance to the building. On nice days, small groups of students sit on the low concrete walls that contain small plants and saplings.

The school is a very modern two-story building built in the shape of a triangle. On the first level, small narrow windows curved at the top and bottom give the appearance of elongated portholes. On the second story, an expanse of glass spans the entire front of the school. On the upper level, narrow porthole windows ditto those on the ground floor. The exterior is composed of green, gray, and blue metal panels. Across the front are the words: Carver High School for Careers.

The windows are treated to reflect the sun. Viewed from outside, they have a bronzed-mirror quality. You cannot see through them into the building. As you approach the front entrance, the glass distorts your image in a way that reminds you of the mirrors in a fun house at a carnival.

You enter through large glass doors. The foyer is huge, with a two-story-high ceiling. There is a staircase slightly to the left and near the center of the area. It leads to a second-floor bridge that spans the foyer and connects the north and east wings of the building. Directly across from the front doors is a glass wall through which you can see into an inner courtyard, where concrete planter boxes in interesting geometric shapes play host to plants struggling to survive. No one is in the courtyard. The doors leading back into the building are kept locked most of the time. Once outside, you are, in a sense, trapped, unable to see in through the reflective glass.

Dominating the right wall of the foyer as you enter is a huge collage of pictures and newspaper headlines of George Washington Carver, for whom the school is named.

On the left of the foyer, display windows invite you into a small general store and dress shop. Here, students in distributive education programs practice merchandising during certain periods of the day. Students and teachers purchase cold sandwiches here at noon. Goods made at the school, greeting cards, notebooks, pencils, and other school supplies are also sold here.

In the center of the foyer there are several small wrought-iron-and-wood benches grouped among attractive plants. During lunch break, students and faculty come here to eat and visit. When students are in class, maintenance staff or security guards occasionally sit on the benches for a moment or two of rest.

The principal's office is down the corridor to the left. As you walk in, you find a large open room virtually devoid of furniture. Teachers' mailboxes are built into the wall to the left. A small low table and two chairs are pushed against the wall to the right. A 15- to 20-foot-long counter separates the office area from the public area. On the office side of the counter, an area about 20 by 30 feet, a couple of desks along the wall seem to be slightly in the corner.

Teachers and guests sign in and out on several clipboards on the counter. Everyone is expected to register when they enter and leave the building. Should you forget, you will be graciously reminded.

The principal's private office is down a narrow corridor off to the left of the large open area. Offices of two assistant principals are adjacent to it. The school registrar also occupies an office in the area and her door opens into the public part of the office, making her accessible to students and faculty alike.

Across the hall from the principal's office, three academic and two vocational counselors have offices. On the wall outside, the bulletin boards are filled with notices of scholarship opportunities, college recruitment posters, and testing dates. One or two student workers sit at a front desk to greet visitors and assist the counselors in their work.

Down the hallway, biology and chemistry labs are filled with equipment and supplies. Fish swim in salt-water aquariums with a filtering system made by a teacher in a school shop. Specimens of snakes, frogs, and mice occupy glass containers. The teacher hopes that this year funds will be available for a "constant ocean" in his classroom. The teachers' lounge is at the end of the wing.

Down the corridor in the opposite direction from the science and administration wing are located areas for distributive education and commercial cooking. Three days each week, during lunch period, the commercial cooking class offers students and faculty an alternative to cafeteria food. A small, attractive restaurant with cafeteria-style service is operated by students in this program.

Classrooms for academic subjects, commercial art, drafting and business education are upstairs. There also is an attractive but rather small library.

On the ground floor and much of the second floor, various shops house the equipment and supplies for vocational programs. Auto mechanics shops extend across the back of the building. Diesel mechanics and heavy-equipment repair shops are close by. Welding, small-engine repair, marine-engine repair, and machine shops occupy space directly behind the courtyard area. A print shop and small-appliance repair area are nearby. The "cafetorium" is in the center of the building and serves as an auditorium as occasions demand.

Carver Senior High School for Careers was originally located downtown in the central city, where it occupied one of the oldest senior high school buildings in the city. As the city's population sprawled, the old Central High School, once the elite academic school, became City Technical Institute, serving principally a growing black and Mexican-American central city population. The building soon became inadequate for the programs it housed, and the present facility was built far north of the central city. Renamed the Carver High School for Careers, it was first occupied in January 1980. A teacher who lived through its transition wrote:

In the summer of 1970, the Board of Education announced the creation of City Technical Institute to be located at 1100 Holt Street in the near downtown area of the city. This signaled the closing of one of the city's oldest and finest schools, Central Senior High School. Central had first opened its doors in 1914. In 1941, Central became a community night school. From 1941 until 1970, it [also] served . . . as a citywide adult evening school and adult vocational training school. It coordinated all of the vocational programs in the city.

In 1947, the first classes in the city for the orthopedically handicapped were started at Central High School. Classes for the mentally retarded, the brain damaged, the deaf and hard of hearing and the blind and partially sighted were added to the program. In 1956, Central became the first four-year high school in the city. In 1960, the vocational classes at the Taylor Vocational Center were closed and moved to Central. They were housed in two wings that had been added to the building. In the spring of 1970, when Central closed its doors for the last time, it had a student enrollment of 4,300. Twenty-eight hundred students attended day classes and fifteen hundred students attended night classes.

When the Board of Education created City Technical Institute, it stated that the school was designed to fill the needs of the people of Howard County and the expanding industry of the state. It also stated that in teaching the curricula, "the changing needs of a dynamic industrial city and state require constant interaction between the business and industrial communities and the teaching staff." The board specified that City Technical Institute offer courses only in the vocational and technical areas, including health occupations and academically related courses fulfilling the need either for graduation and/or occupational competency. The board stated that the purpose of the school was to provide areas of training in fields that cannot feasibly be provided in the regular high school.

When City Technical Institute opened in 1970, it had an enrollment of 1,500. This happened to be the maximum capacity for the school. Under state law, a technical and vocational school must have a certain amount of space and equipment for each student enrolled. The capacity remained at 1,500 until the school was moved to a new, larger facility in January 1980.

One of the most interesting characteristics of the student population of City Technical Institute is the fact that for the entire ten-year period between 1970 and 1980, the student body was not only desegregated but truly integrated. And in the middle to late sixties, before the school district was under pressure from the courts to desegregate, the school population of Central High School was desegregated. Perhaps one factor contributing to successful integration at the school is the fact that many of the students (not all of them) came to the school with a real interest in a certain technical or vocational area, and they spent at least half of the school day with other students who shared the same interests.

In 1976, shortly after a successful bond election, the Board of Education appropriated $10,000,000 for a new facility to house City Technical Institute. The enthusiasm that was generated by the announcement of the new facility was overshadowed by anger, resentment, and disappointment felt by much of the technical high school community when it was learned that the new facility would be relocated. During the year that followed the announcement that the school was being moved, rumors had the new facility placed in at least five different locations. Finally, the Board of Education announced that the new school would be located at 5800 Eastern Freeway. News that the new school would be located in the northern part of the Fifth Ward, in a black neighborhood called Cashen Gardens, infuriated the Mexican-Americans and Anglos attending the school. But the ultimate blow came when, in the spring of 1979, the Board of Education announced that the new facility was going to be named after a black man, George Washington Carver. The real impact of this situation is reflected in present enrollment figures.

When the move was made, enrollment in the school dropped by 30 percent—from 1,439 to 1,013 students. The downtown location was much easier for students to get to. A significant number of students now have a transportation problem. They must either come by private car or take a school bus that picks them up at their neighborhood elementary schools. Some spend an hour and a half on the bus each way; fifty minutes is typical. Seniors who work half days catch a city bus to jobs downtown and often have difficulty getting home in the evening. Many students at the school, when it was at its original location, apparently decided that transportation would be too great a problem, so they stayed in their more immediate neighborhoods.

The enrollment of Hispanics and whites declined dramatically when the school moved to its new site. People at the school say that Mexican-American parents are reluctant to let their daughters attend a school in an all-black neighborhood. The racial make-up of the school in 1980–81 was: whites, 5 percent; blacks, 71 percent; Hispanics, 23 percent; and Asians, less than 1 percent. The table below summarizes enrollment figures for whites, blacks, and Hispanics during the past five years. Asians and others accounted for less than 1 percent each year.

## PERCENTAGE OF ENROLLMENT BY RACE, 1976–1981

|          | 1976–77 | 1977–78 | 1978–79 | 1979–80 | 1980–81 |
|----------|---------|---------|---------|---------|---------|
| White    | 18      | 15      | 13      | 8       | 5       |
| Black    | 34      | 39      | 44      | 62      | 71      |
| Hispanic | 48      | 45      | 42      | 30      | 23      |

The sharp increase in black students occurred when the new school was occupied in 1979–80. The neighborhood in which the school is located is described as "rough." One of the security guards told us that he frequently hears of somebody being shot or stabbed in the area. "But we close the gates and only leave one unlocked. People do not like to come on campus if they are looking for trouble because there is just one way out."

The school has experienced little vandalism. There has been only one break-in since it opened. The principal believes that vandalism is low either because people in the area have a healthy respect for the school or because "they can't see in. They don't know if somebody is looking out at them." The security guards believe that security is tight and discipline is firm in the school. It is the only school in the school district with two security guards. Most have only one or perhaps none at all.

As you walk through the building you are startled by the incredible cleanliness and orderliness of the school. There is no clutter. Not a scrap of litter can be found on the floors. Shops are immaculate. It looks as if there is a place for everything and everything is in its place.

Nowhere in the building can you find graffiti. There are no pen marks or scratches on toilet stalls and none of the students' lockers appear defaced or damaged. The school gives the impression of a clean, well-lighted, and orderly place.

## The Students

Carver High School for Careers is a magnet school. It offers programs for students who are interested in vocational studies. Students from throughout the school district are eligible to apply for admission. Students come to the school because they want to, because they believe the school offers a program that is right for them, because they are interested in learning a skill or trade that is taught there.

Your first impression is that students are especially friendly. As visitors enter the building, students will greet them and offer assistance. It is easy to strike up a conversation in the hallways or foyer; they appear genuinely interested in talking. They are quick to tell you that they are proud of their school.

A majority of the students are from lower-class and welfare families with limited experience with college. Many of the parents have not completed high school. Most of the parents of Carver students work with their hands; they hold blue-collar jobs in and around the city. Many of the families are pinched economically. A surprisingly large number of students have older brothers and sisters who attended Carver or City Tech, its name in the former location.

The students behave at school. There are very few conflicts, few disruptive incidents in the classrooms or shops. There is little racial tension. Students are not troublemakers. They are not into heavy drugs, although some marijuana is smoked. They drink some, but generally do not abuse alcohol. Students report that discipline in the school is strict. They know the rules and the consequences for breaking them.

Students may not bring guests, radios or record players, skateboards, or anything else that might disturb classes onto the campus. Once their cars are parked, they are not to go near them until they are ready to go home. Students are not permitted to leave the campus for lunch.

The principal does not hesitate to call a student's parents, or suspend a student for misconduct or violation of the myriad rules. If the offense is serious, the principal will call the police and offenders will find themselves taking a trip downtown to the jail. If a student misbehaves too often, he is sent back to his home school.

Students treat teachers with respect. One student said, "One of the best things about this school is the way teachers treat you. The teachers here treat you with respect. If you have something to say, they are not going to say 'no, no,' just because you are a student and they are teachers. They listen to you, will compromise, and I think they understand students."

The students are not professionally oriented; they look forward to being mechanics, welders, construction workers, office workers, and salespeople. Few plan to become doctors, lawyers, or teachers. Within their vocations, they are motivated to do well. Basically, what they see themselves doing when they graduate from school and get jobs is what they see themselves doing at age fifty-five. They have little upward career-path orientation. There is little in the school that encourages such thought.

Few students in Carver High School aspire to go to college; they want to go to work. They have needs right now for cars and clothes— needs that only money can satisfy. Parents cannot provide those luxuries. So, students do it for themselves.

A lot of the students have jobs after school and on weekends. Some teachers complain: "These students can't see the future in terms of preparation in the present. If something they are doing doesn't pay off right now, they don't want any part of it. Adults in the school think some of the students are mad at the world. . . . Some will go off on an 'I don't care' kick. Their parents are separated or divorced or maybe have a lot of domestic problems. Our students tend to have more difficulties. They have money problems. They have problems with the father going out drinking because he can't take care of the family as he wants to. You know, there are a lot of family difficulties that develop because of not having money; when your utility bill is costing you as much as your house note or rent. Some of them are mad at society and at their parents because there is nothing they can do about it."

One teacher, suggesting that it is harder now to get to know students than it used to be, described a guidance lesson she had conducted with her homeroom students.

In this guidance lesson, we were discussing people's personalities. One of the reasons [given for shyness] was "frozen anger." And so the students were supposed to list what they thought the reason was for a person exhibiting shy behavior. And a large percentage of them responded with frozen anger. That gave me an insight. They are angry. I don't know why they are angry and I don't know what they are angry at, but whatever it is, they exhibit behaviors that I assess as negative.

When asked why they chose to attend Carver, students responded in a variety of ways:

- The local comprehensive school is not a good school. Students don't want to learn. So I came here.
- I wanted a vocational school, and this seemed the best.
- Here they tell you that you *have* to learn, not that you want to learn.
- I can work one-half day in my senior year.
- I'm a good commercial artist—that's my work hanging there on the wall. I'm better than lots of people now, and I want to do better. When I graduate I'll go to a commercial art college or wherever I can get a scholarship. I don't want to be wealthy, but I do want to be famous.
- In zoned schools, you can mess around and still make an A or B. You don't have to work hard. Here you do.
- I don't want to have to go to a school that would lower my potential.

Despite their family circumstances, the students in this school are exceedingly well dressed and very well groomed. The girls wear skirts, smartly tailored blouses, high-heel shoes and hose. Jeans, when they are worn, tend to be designer jeans worn with a crisply pressed blouse, sometimes with a smart tie or bow at the neckline, and blue or white running shoes. Particularly on Tuesdays, several wear R.O.T.C. uniforms. The boys are in jeans or slacks, with shirts neatly tucked into their trousers, and running shoes. Clothes are not trendy or high fashion. There is an impression of a "business uniform," of dressing for the world of work.

Teachers support this. A business education teacher told us that her seniors worked in the afternoon and therefore dressed for work. She does not hesitate to tell them when their dress is not acceptable in the business world, and she reminds them that they represent Carver High School. Sophomores and juniors not currently working through school programs are required to dress the part on Tuesdays, Wednesdays, and Thursdays.

The school has a dress code. One girl explained that this means no tight pants, no knees showing, no halter tops, no see-through blouses, and no rollers. The official dress code is more formal, spelling out in detail the requirements and explaining why such requirements exist at Carver. Shoes are to be worn; hats or sunglasses are not to be worn in the building; and "no rakes are allowed according to school district policy."

More than a hundred students in the school have been placed in a special vocational program for handicapped students. These young men and women are usually emotionally disturbed or learning disabled and have applied for admission to Carver. After reviewing each case, an Admissions, Review and Dismissal (ARD) committee of the school's area administrative office places such students in appropriate programs in the school.

The handicapped/learning disabled students have a program that parallels the program for regular students. They have their own wing of the building, where they are taught academic subjects such as math, English, science, and social studies. They also have their own vocational programs with teachers assigned to work just with them. Vocational programs are tailored to the students' abilities and potential employment opportunities. They include office duplication, building maintenance, health care, home and community service, general construction, and general mechanical repair.

According to security personnel and assistant principals, these special students tend to have more discipline problems than regular students have. But the school appears to have a genuine concern for the welfare of these students. An assistant principal reported:

> . . . A number of these kids are low-level and need a smaller concentration of students in the classroom so that the teacher will have time to deal with their problems. We mainstream some of the kids. It is a special thrill to me to be able to tell a kid that I believe and the committee believes he has improved his achievement so much that he is ready to be merged into a regular class. It will nearly make you cry to see that kid shine and light up because somebody has noticed. My goal, if I stay here long enough, is to see that every one of these kids is properly placed and achieving. I spend quite a bit of time with that program, but much of the time I spend is with discipline.

## The Teachers

None of the eighty-seven teachers live in the immediate neighborhood of the school. Some drive as far as thirty-five miles to school, and two van pools have been organized. Teachers leave at 3:15 P.M. and tend not to socialize with each other outside school. They maintain two relatively independent lifestyles—one as Carver teachers, the other as neighbors, parents, and community members. Evening school-related activities by students and/or teachers are not just discouraged; they typically are forbidden. One reason is that community college classes use the building in the evening. But potential problems in the neighborhood combined with the dispersed locations of students' homes are others. The result is that teachers are not expected to be at Carver after school is out.

About 35 percent of the teachers in the school have a master's degree. Teachers fall into two categories: academic and vocational. There are about thirty teachers of academic subjects and nearly twice that many vocational teachers. Special education teachers work with Carver handicapped students.

Like the students, teachers are well dressed and immaculately groomed. Women are not often seen in slacks; they wear tailored business suits or dresses, skirts with blazers, or white nursing or restaurant uniforms. Men who teach vocational subjects take off their coveralls when they leave their shops to go into other parts of the building. Administrators are usually seen in coats and ties.

Teachers get along well with the students and are concerned about their welfare. They want their students to achieve and to get good jobs. They worry about the low aspirations of many students and wish they would reach for more out of life. They are troubled by students who cannot read well or who have not mastered the basics. They want their students to enjoy their classes, and they work hard to bring this about. One teacher described his effort this way:

> I like to teach. I come from a family of teachers. They inspired me to teach well. I make work interesting for my students. Even if I don't like the topic myself, I teach it with so much enthusiasm and charisma that I make my students like it anyway.

Some of the teachers think that parents are not pushing their children hard enough or are not supporting what the school is trying to do to educate the students. "When a parent lets a teen-ager work half the night and every weekend, then that parent isn't very concerned about how much education his child is getting." Some parents, one staff member observed, "are very apologetic about what their child does if he gets into trouble, but some come in with the attitude that says, 'Why are you picking on my child?' A lot of times, right off the bat, we can see what the student's problem is and a lot of times it is the parent."

The vocational teachers come from industry and either already have teaching certificates or are working on their certification. There tends to be more turnover among the vocational teachers than among teachers of academic subjects because they can often earn more money in industry.

Most of the academics teachers have had experience in other teaching positions. They received their teacher training from several different universities and are generally lukewarm regarding the effectiveness of their preparation programs.

Teachers of academic subjects are taught much the same way that teachers have taught them for years. They lecture, lead class discussions, have students answer questions on work sheets or in the textbook, assign small group work or individual projects. Teachers are fairly free to plan and present instruction the way they choose.

Teachers of academic subjects rely heavily on materials sent to them by the district office. They evaluate student progress by considering attendance, performance in daily work in class and homework assignments, and test grades. Teachers use tests for both diagnosis and evaluation. They give teacher-made tests primarily, although the district office requires that standardized tests be administered periodically to assess student achievement.

Many teachers of academic subjects believe that students resent homework and do not work hard enough at achievement in their courses. Teachers also complain that the outside work responsibilities of students make it difficult for them to maintain high standards of achievement. Referring to the administration, one said:

> They tell us to "back up." We can only fail a certain percent. This new program they have to test students before they go on may help. But for a number of years, teachers have had to back up and lower their standards, cut down on the amount of work. You can watch the kids get on the bus in the afternoon, and a lot of them won't have one book in their hands.

There is a tendency among academic subject teachers to give small amounts of homework because so many students have jobs. Many assignments come from textbooks and most teachers feel compelled to grade every assignment they give.

There is a big difference in the approach to teaching used by vocational and academic subject teachers. Vocational teachers tend to teach by having students actually *do* things rather than study *about* things. Auto mechanics students learn to repair cars by working on cars. Students dismantle air-conditioning equipment or refrigerators. They construct small buildings or build bookcases. They design the artwork for a newspaper advertisement or cook and serve food to students and faculty in the school. Vocational teachers rely on "learn by doing" strategies. Teachers of academic subjects rely on textbooks and other vicarious, secondhand learning experiences.

Some of the academics subject teachers in the school seem to feel like "second class citizens." One of them said:

> It is very evident that vocational education comes before education in the academic areas in this school. This is evident by the attitude of the principal toward the vocational programs because they get more money for equipment and supplies. Frequently, requests from the academic teachers for money for materials or field trips are denied because of lack of funds.

Some academics teachers believe they receive little positive feedback regarding their efforts. They complain that when accolades are issued, they are usually offered to vocational teachers after students have won contests relating to their various construction projects.

Every vocational teacher in the school is expected to sponsor a club. "When I interview teachers," the principal says, "I tell them it is a requirement that they sponsor a club in their field. That makes a better teacher and a better student. I am the only principal in town who insists that they do that."

Each week, teachers must submit lesson plans for the coming week to the principal. They also must keep elaborate student attendance records because there is a district policy that students who are absent without permission more than six times during a semester may not receive credit for a course.

Most teachers resent the amount of paperwork they are required to complete. As one teacher explained:

> There is a lot of paperwork. That is one of the things that competes for my time. You have to check roll in homeroom and then you have to see if anyone is tardy. You have to fill out a report for that. In second period, you have to fill out an attendance report that is audited for average daily attendance. You have to keep those records in your grade book. Then, if a student is absent three times you have to list him on a special form that

goes to the principal with your lesson plans. And you have to call the student. On the fourth day, you have to send a letter to the student's parents and send another form into the office when the student is absent the sixth time. I think that is a lot of time that surely could come from some other source, like from the attendance office. It is an every-period activity.

Another teacher estimated he spends three to four hours each week on administrative paperwork, not counting grading papers. This was verified later in a small group discussion with other teachers. "But at least there are few extra duties, such as cafeteria or schoolyard, as in other schools," one said.

There is very little emphasis on staff development. Some in-service programs are offered through the area administrative or district central office, but ongoing programs for improvement of staff performance apparently have not been implemented. Also, there is little supervision of the instructional staff other than what is implied by the weekly lesson-plan review. Administrators do not visit classrooms either formally or informally, yet they do evaluate faculty once each year in a process considered perfunctory by almost everyone. After her yearly conference with the principal, one teacher reported she received all threes on a five-point scale. "He told me he had to write a defense if he gave me a one, two, four, or five, and that it was not worth the effort."

The same teacher who complained about the paperwork on student attendance told us that she would like to see in-service programs directed to helping teachers "troubleshoot problem areas," but usually these areas were not the focus of in-service sessions. "I need in-service on several areas of confusion, like attendance reporting, for example. I think it would be worthwhile to find out where the breakdown is and what we are going to do about it. We need to try to eliminate some of these recurring annoyances."

There is little interaction among teachers. The size of the building and the variety of teaching assignments segregates teachers into small departmental groups. Some could not even name teachers from another area (particularly in academic areas if they were in vocational areas, or vice versa).

Although it is not apparent among students, there is a strong undercurrent of racial tension among teachers and administrators. Race was mentioned by almost every teacher and administrator we interviewed; references were made to the "black" assistant principal or the "white" assistant principal; counselors were characterized by the color of their skin; staff was referred to as that "Dago" or that "mouthy Mexican." Seemingly spoken in lightness and jest, the frequency of such references suggested a racially oriented overtone. The teachers' lounge reflects racial segregation in seating and personal interaction. The racial make-up of the teaching-administrative staff is: whites, 51 percent; blacks, 46 percent; Hispanics, 3 percent.

One event appears to have precipitated a great deal of unrest and division along racial lines. According to many of those we interviewed, a young black teacher, who had moved from the old school to the new site, changed his behavior dramatically. "He suddenly became much more aggressive and assertive, and began to show his 'black bias.' " This teacher wanted to have many special activities for black students that the school's administration opposed. The principal told of parties the teacher would give for students and complained that "this was not good for the young ladies and young men." He said:

> I would describe him as a man who had a giant ego, and the only way he could fulfill his ego was to be in front of the students acting. He wanted activities for them, and he didn't care whether they were school-blessed or not. Young people need parental supervision even though they are in high school. So he was angry because I wouldn't let them have these things. He had them wear red on two occasions as a protest. I ignored this, because I felt that if I fought it I would be playing into their hands. The senior class officers followed him one hundred percent. It was a miserable year.

Other teachers told of the black teacher's insistence on moving the school's senior prom from an inexpensive but nice facility that had been used for years to an expensive downtown hotel. He viewed the past setting as contributing to class separation. "Because of the cost we couldn't have had some of the niceties, like hors d'oeuvres, that we usually have." When the black teacher mobilized students to wear red in protest, the white teachers thought the principal did not take a firm enough stand. "He should have stopped it before it got out of hand. Students were difficult to handle and everything got out of whack."

The principal spoke of going to his area administrative officer and being told to "ride it out—to try to work it out with the man." So the principal said he waited until the end of the year when a drop in enrollment made it possible for him to transfer the teacher out of the school.

The incident left deep impressions of racial conflict in the minds of some teachers. They see the affair as dividing the school, as pitting blacks against whites. They tell about a faculty meeting when black history week was being discussed and a white teacher blurted out, "When in God's name are we going to have white history?"

Burnout symptoms were apparent among some of the staff. The principal freely admits the past two years have been difficult and is looking forward to his retirement next summer. In fact, he had intended to retire a year ago and was disappointed when circumstances prevented him from doing so.

Teachers really feel the pinch economically. They talk about how a vocational teacher took a summer job and was offered a continuing position with the firm at a much better salary. "He really wanted to stay in teaching, but just couldn't afford to do it."

It is especially hard for single teachers who depend on their salary as their sole source of income. One told us:

> Utility bills, house notes, and car notes eat up a teacher's paycheck and you haven't even talked about putting any clothes on your back or about doing your grocery shopping or paying doctor bills. It is really tough on a single teacher. So a lot of them are disenchanted with the teaching profession because they can't live on what they take home. I mean, how can you like what you are doing when it is not taking care of you?"

Burnout symptoms are evident in other ways. Teachers, most notably the teachers of academic subjects, reported feeling less effective in the classroom than they used to feel.

> I'm not receiving the positive response from my students using the same kinds of methods that I have used in the past. In the past, I felt more like a coach to my students, helping them achieve the highest level of skills they were capable of. But I've felt more in an adversary position recently, and I don't know why. It is almost as if they say, "I defy you to teach me." I had one class of students last year with a dozen chronic behavior problems. I dreaded dealing with that class every day. It affected my whole life.

Several teachers we talked with are looking toward changes in their careers. One, a commercial foods teacher, is hoping to start her own catering business. An English teacher wants to continue work as an educator, but hopes to establish her own business. One young man, after recounting the financial difficulties his family was having trying to live on a teacher's salary said, "God only knows what I will be doing five years from now."

Teachers complain of the administration's lack of support. They are expected to be in the hall between periods, but they seldom see the principal or assistant principals. After repeated complaints, administrators are becoming somewhat more visible. A faculty advisory committee generally is ignored, and concerns it expresses on behalf of the faculty are not dealt with. The central administration of the school district and even the area superintendent's office are considered remote. Teachers believe those offices respond politically and have little real positive impact on teachers.

Teachers also feel frustrated by the way they perceive society views their profession, by the low status accorded teachers by people in their community. One teacher of English, who worked in a sandwich shop during the summer, did not tell her summer co-workers she was a teacher because "I did not want them to know I worked for the school district." She encountered a lot of negative attitudes.

> They talked a lot about the school district and really expressed some negative attitudes toward the schools. It made me feel real small. All of their comments were negative; and being part of the district, I felt it was a personal attack. I especially felt bad when they said that teachers did not know what they were doing and that all of the schools are bad. They could not support what they said, but I could not really refute what they said, either.

## The School Program

There is no question or confusion about the goal of Carver High School for Careers. It is to prepare students to get a job and to earn a living. Students know that, and that is the reason they choose to come to the school. Teachers understand that goal, and reflect it in what they choose to teach and how they teach it. The administrators, principals, and counselors stress the importance of this goal, and make decisions consistent with it. And parents see the school as a place where their sons and daughters can be trained in the skills they need for gainful employment.

The clear aim of the school is to socialize students for the world of work. This socialization process manifests itself in numerous ways. You see it in the way students and teachers are dressed. You are reminded of an office atmosphere when you see the small bud vases filled with flowers and the paper clip and pencil holders on each neat desk in the business education classroom. You experience it when you encounter students assuming "official" public relations roles as they usher you into their classrooms or shops and discuss, with a Madison Avenue manner, the programs in which they are involved.

The emphasis in the school is on developing work skills. There is, however, notably little emphasis on acquiring advanced academic skills, particularly in the liberal arts tradition. The idea that students might make a living primarily by using their minds is not prevalent. The students are not aspiring to become lawyers or teachers or managers or owners of businesses. Thirty-eight percent of graduates this past year indicated in questionnaires they were planning to attend college, but the breakdown by academic grades shows that only 42 percent in the top 5 percent, 26 percent of the next 10 percent, and 39 percent of the remaining 85 percent of the class plan to attend college. Informal discussions with students and teachers suggested that this latter estimate may be high. Up-to-date college catalogs, including those for nearby colleges, are difficult to find, even in counselors' offices. Most students intend to work primarily with their hands. One teacher, who did a survey to find out what her students wanted to do some years after their graduation from high school, reported:

> I only had one student who wanted to go into business for himself. If you look at the courses the students are taking, they are courses that will help them be skilled laborers. But at the same time you would think there would be someone here who might want to own his own business, have his own welding shop or his own body repair shop.

There is a strong esprit de corps in the school. Everyone seems to be aiming in the same direction. There is not much interference from people with different values or goals. There is little conflict over what should be offered in the school's program, other than the feeling that some academics teachers have regarding the need for a few advanced courses.

Students are quick to tell you they like the school and are proud of it. They show that pride in the way they keep their building and the way they conduct themselves. The teachers, especially those teaching in the vocational areas, are proud of their programs and of what they are accomplishing with students. There is a lot of respect among the people in the school. Despite some racial tensions, teachers are respectful of each other and especially warm and caring for their students. Students return respect to their teachers and get along well with each other.

Two separate plans, developed by the school's administration and teachers in collaboration with the area district administrative office, guide development of the program at Carver High School for Careers. One is the Magnet School Campus Action Plan, required by the school district of all magnet schools. This plan identifies specific objectives the school hopes to accomplish in its magnet program during an academic year and details procedures the school staff will follow. For example, for 1981–82, the Magnet School Campus Action Plan for CHS called for increasing student achievement scores, increasing enrollment in the school, improving certain aspects of the vocational programs, and improving the ethnic mix of the student population.

The other major planning document is the State Education Agency Accreditation Campus Action Plan, required of all schools by the district. This plan sets forth specific objectives the school will strive to accomplish in relation to certain district priorities. For 1981–82, Carver High School identified three major objectives: that student achievement would be maintained at the same level as the previous year, that attendance would equal average attendance in the district, and that there would be fewer incidents requiring disciplinary action.

These plans serve as the basis for a district administrative audit of the school's program and are carefully monitored by an assistant principal. That assistant principal told us:

> I look on the Campus Action Plan as a statement to the area office that we are going to teach certain things. The other assistant principal and I have worked closely with the area action plan. We have just been audited and we have finally been able to get the Campus Action Plan and the Magnet Action Plan coordinated.

The Magnet Action Plan has to do mainly with those areas that make us a magnet—our vocational program. I coordinate the development of the action plans. We are audited by the state agency and by our area superintendent to make sure we are doing what we say we are doing. The superintendent audits us twice a year.

Before we start building our action plan, we get a printout from the area office containing the things the area office says they are going to do in instruction. We take a good part of our plan from the area plan and then add some on our own.

Our plans are made by going through the department chairpersons. It is not just a matter of my sitting down and deciding what we are going to do. We have several meetings with department people and they go to teachers and get input into the plan because they are the ones who have to implement it.

The curriculum grows out of the school district's requirements for graduation and the vocational thrust of the school. Every student in the school is enrolled in a vocational program but must also take the academic subjects necessary for graduation.

The district requires a minimum of 21 credits for graduation. Students must complete 11 required academic credits, 2½ credits of physical education, or an approved substitute, ½ credit of health, and 7 elective credits. Required academic subjects include English, world history or world geography, American history, American government, economics, mathematics, and science.

To be eligible for admission to Carver High School for Careers, a student must have completed ninth grade and make an acceptable score on the General Aptitude Test Battery. The student may take these tests at any one of several school district test centers. After completing the tests, the student is interviewed by a vocational counselor at the school, who reviews the student's transcript of previous schoolwork and discusses the pattern of interests and aptitudes the student's tests reveal. The vocational counselors, along with the student and his parents, are responsible for making the decision about what vocational program the student will enter.

The student is then assigned to an academic counselor. There are three in the school, each of whom works with a class of students from the time they enter as sophomores until they graduate three years later. The principal wants it that way:

The academic counselors stay with those children all the time they are in the school. They move up through grades ten, eleven, and twelve. They will know that child by the time he leaves here. They have to write the program with the kid in front of them, because I want them to sit down and talk to that kid and let the kid know what he has to have to graduate. The kids often come here without having passed Algebra I or English I. Sometimes the kid says he will make it up in summer school, but doesn't. I want the counselor to call the parent and tell him, because I want the parent to know why the kid may not graduate. If the kid doesn't take care of the problem, I'll call the parent and get them in here and say, "Now look, the kid is not going to graduate because we don't offer that subject. He has got to go to summer school. That was our agreement. Or he has got to go back to his home school." Usually, that gets them. There is no excuse for that kid not graduating.

The school day for students begins at 7:50 A.M. and is out at 2:50 P.M. During the two 45-minute lunch periods, students may not leave the campus. The day is divided into a 15-minute homeroom period and six 55-minute periods. Teachers are expected to be in the school from 7:45 A.M. to 3:15 P.M.

The school offers courses in the required academic subjects for grades ten, eleven, and twelve. There is some attempt, however, to modify the academic program for the vocational orientations of the students the school attracts and for the basic skills levels that many of them possess. Several teachers reported that the academics tend to be "watered down." One teacher described the opportunity for study in advanced level courses as follows:

> I think we lack something in the academics. As a vocational school, I think we are tops. We have turned out some good welders, good draftsmen, good chefs—and there is need for all of this. Not many of our students want to go to college, but for those who want to go, I think the school should have more advanced courses. For example, we don't have trig or foreign languages or chemistry.

Indeed, only eighteen students (less than 2 percent of the student body) are registered in second-year algebra, and ninety-one (9 percent) in geometry.

Academics teachers are pressured to cover the content of minimum competencies required by the district and the state. The Test of Achievement and Proficiency (TAP) is administered in March to all high school students in the city. The purpose of the test is:

To measure achievement in the areas of reading, mathematics, written expression, work-study skills, social studies, and science, so that teachers, counselors, and students may be made aware of the student's progress and relative standing in these important skills areas.

Tenth graders in all city schools take the Differential Aptitude Test (DAT) in November. Its purpose is:

To give the student, parents, and staff information about eight of the student's abilities, important in school and work, to assist the student to make informed occupational and educational choices.

The citywide Minimum Competency Test and the state Assessment of Basic Skills are also administered.

Academic courses are one hour long. Vocational courses typically are two hours and may be three hours long. Co-op programs for seniors provide half-day work experiences.

Whatever the academic program may lack, the vocational program is strong and comprehensive. The list of vocational areas in which a student may study would pale the Yellow Pages of the telephone directory. A recruitment brochure used by the school includes the following programs:

| | |
|---|---|
| Academic and Related Areas | Drafting |
| Air Conditioning–Refrigeration | Heavy-Equipment Repair |
| Appliance Repair | Home Economics Co-op Training |
| Auto Body Repair | Home Furnishings |
| Auto Mechanics | Industrial Co-op Training |
| Auto Painting | Machine Shop |
| Business Education | Marine Engine |
| Commercial Art | Pre-School Child Care |
| Commercial Foods | Printing Trades |
| Commercial Photography | Small-Engine Repair |
| CVAE Co-op Training | Vocational Electronics |
| CVAE Office Duplication | Vocational Education for the |
| Diesel Mechanics | Handicapped |
| Distributive Education | Welding |

That same brochure describes each of the vocational programs in some detail. Very little space, however, is devoted to the academic areas. Students are told about career options. After they learn how to repair automobiles, for example, the brochure suggests they can expect to progress to positions as foremen or estimators. They are informed that the program stresses "using the tools of the industry" and that they can expect to be working on the same machines they will find in the shops and offices where they will ultimately get jobs. If they want to become chefs, they will have lots of practice planning, preparing, and presenting food. They will be ready for a job when they graduate. At a minimum, the program will train them for entry-level skills. Their options are extensive. Their vocational teachers are skilled craftsmen who have worked in the areas they teach.

To understand these vocational possibilities better, consider six classrooms. The home economics cooperative education program is housed in a large area with industrial sewing machines, irons, and presses. Nearby, a dozen long tables are piled with draperies being made for city residents, six to eight pairs of slacks waiting to have the seams in their legs sewed, blankets for baby beds, Christmas stockings, pillows embroidered with football emblems, sweetheart pillows for sale on February 14, and five hundred aprons to be sold throughout the school district. Students will use the proceeds from the sale of these goods to travel to Atlanta, Georgia, where they will visit factories and see people in the industry for which they are training.

Students are learning to be seamstresses by doing alterations in local department stores and working in the garment and home furnishings industry. Since the program is only two and one-half years old, there are not yet graduates, so no employment pattern has been established.

Next door is a child care program for pre-schoolers (licensed by the state for two- to five-year-olds). Three- to five-year-olds come four hours per day on Tuesdays, Wednesdays, and Thursdays at a cost of $8 per semester. This pays for a light but wholesome lunch (on the day we visited it included ground beef, corn, bread, and milk).

Two classes of Carver students work with the pre-school children. They wear smocks and hairnets ("We want them to feel comfortable doing what business requires," says the teacher). Nine students are in their first year and twelve in their second year. They rotate duties— music, science, and mathematics, naptime, free play, and cooking— but all assist each other in completing the tasks. Mondays and Fridays are devoted to planning and cleaning up. These students do all the work in the day care center and are supervised by the teacher. They plan to work in day care centers after graduation.

In a Co-op Office Education class, students learn office practices such as transcription of audiotapes, use of calculators, human relations, typing, shorthand, composition of letters, drafting memos, and parliamentary procedure. In one lesson we observed, tenth graders alphabetized 3- by 5-inch cards as part of an exercise to apply rules they had learned earlier. Each student sat behind a clerical desk for this activity, with the teacher monitoring their progress. During tenth and eleventh grades, students are engaged in two-hour secretarial skills courses. Twelfth graders leave school at 11:10 A.M. for work.

The students in commercial art participate in weekly contests in architectural rendering and airbrush techniques. In addition to aptitude tests administered to all students, commercial art students take a drawing test to enter. They are tested for closeness to a commercial pattern in their work. In the tenth grade their curriculum includes drawing, technique, design, and lettering. As eleventh graders, they study poster drawing, architectural rendering, screen printing, and fashion artwork. In the twelfth grade, students work with furniture drawings, airbrush photograph retouching, and production (camera-ready art). The curriculum is determined by needs specified by commercial artists who are members of an advisory committee.

The building maintenance program is for VEH (Vocational Education for the Handicapped) students. Their shop includes a band saw, table saw, drill press, pipe-threading machine, and other equipment that would typically be available to maintenance crews. The curriculum has been defined by the instructor, formerly the head custodian at City Technical Institute (the former location of Carver).

The curriculum in this two-hour course includes learning how to lay flooring, make minor repairs, replace air-conditioning filters, replace window glass, sweep and clean buildings, and do outside grounds work. Graduates will be able to do more than just sweep floors and clean rest rooms, the instructor tells us. He stresses safety. Students are painting yellow lines on the floor to establish "safe zones" around equipment in their classroom. There were three students in this class and eight in another. Of the fifteen students who began the year, two were mainstreamed and two returned to their zoned school.

The health care class for VEH students is divided into several areas.

Three hospital beds with mannequins are in one part of the open room, a formal classroom setting is in another, kitchen facilities are in a third, and a hospital-like bathroom is in a closed room. Students learn to make beds, take vital signs, and transport patients to surgery or from the scene of an accident. They study the four basic food groups and how to cook them; they learn about the digestive system from a plastic model of the human body with removable parts. A basic nursing assistant's book and the experience of the instructor, a registered nurse, are used to determine the program's curriculum. Thirteen advanced students attend class from 8:10 to 11:10 each morning, while twelve beginning students are in the health care class from 11:50 A.M. to 2:50 P.M. All belong to the Health Occupations Students of America (HOSA), a club stressing leadership and skills competition. The area HOSA schedules annual competition and a conference in Aldine (about fifteen miles away). The state meet and conference is held in Dalton, some two hundred miles away, during the spring. Class members always attend the state competition, according to the teacher, and their expenses are covered by local companies.

Each day, school begins with a fifteen-minute homeroom period used to check roll, hear announcements, and complete records required by various governmental bodies. Students often are late; they may be in the building but visiting with others. Teachers generally believe that this is wasted time and have recommended the homeroom period be eliminated. On Wednesdays, homeroom is extended to thirty minutes for a guidance lesson selected by the school district and led by the homeroom teacher. Only academics teachers have homeroom; vocational teachers have that time free to prepare for the day's activities.

There is no athletic program. When Carver High became a magnet school, an agreement was made with the Interscholastic League that students could retain eligibility to participate in athletic programs in their zone schools if Carver High School for Careers did not offer an athletic program. Some teachers see this as a problem, and some students would prefer it otherwise. More students might select Carver if there were athletic programs. One adult said:

> I would like to see this school have a basketball team. The students are always hyper. They don't have athletics. Students are limited to certain

functions. You need to have some type of recreation for them to let off energy. A lot of them don't eat lunch. You can go outside and see them hanging around. It may be they can't afford it and are too proud to get a lunch card. If they had something to do during lunch to work off some of that energy, it would help.

There are a number of special days and events, including Oh Yeah Day, Christmas Dance, Valentine Dance, Faculty Follies, Student Talent Show, Dress as in the 50s, and Western Day. In September, there was a special week, including School Color Day, Wacky Tie Day, Different Colored Socks Day, and Frontier Day. These are organized by the Student Council but require the principal's approval.

Every vocational class has a club activity that promotes the purposes of that vocation and is supposed to teach leadership. Most are affiliated with a national organization (for example, Vocational Industrial Clubs of America, Future Business Leaders of America, Office Education Association, and Distributive Education Clubs of America), and most students pay dues (typically about $6.00 per year). Every vocational teacher sponsors a club.

The clubs are enormously important. They sponsor contests and, according to the assistant principal, "those contests are like football to these students." But contests cost money, and the school district does not provide financial support for the clubs, so each club has to make its own money to support its activities. "They need transportation, registration fees, things like that. So club members make and sell things." As we learned, they also solicit funds from local businesses and trade groups.

Each day at noon, students will be in the front foyer of the building selling things. One day they may sell tortillas; another day hot dogs, po' boy sandwiches, or pizza. Some clubs operate small eating establishments in the school for profit. For example, the commercial cooking class prepares a fine meal that you can enjoy in a pleasant café environment. Food is especially good there on Friday, when seafood is featured. A VEH class for handicapped students operates a restaurant called The Barrister. Students prepare simple, wholesome foods that are served cafeteria style. In the woodworking shop, students make nameplates and commercial art students paint stylized names on them. The plates are sold for $2.00 each. Woodworking students also plan to sell the 8- by 8-foot building they are making, and will roof houses that are nearby. With the home ec students selling pillows, and other clubs offering their services for a fee, school, clubs, and money-making activities soon are tied together.

Clubs have officers and are organized to get a job done. Conformity and organization are stressed. An assistant principal monitors the fund-raising activities of clubs and hopes to establish a president's council to coordinate club activities. He says:

> The major purpose of clubs is theoretically to teach leadership and character building and things of that nature. The first Monday of every month we have a club meeting during class time. We do that because half of our student population lives so far from campus. Nearly all our students belong to clubs.

The school has a large, active R.O.T.C. (one hundred eight members and still growing). Sixty-five percent of the members are female. Members wear their uniforms on Tuesdays (for formation) and sometimes on other days. Last year, they were the honor company in the city and have a flag to carry in parades that proclaims this fact. Within R.O.T.C., there is a girls' drill team, a boys' drill team, a rifle team, an all-girls' color guard, an all-boys' color guard, and a mixed color guard. A rifle range provides an opportunity to earn marksmanship medals, and participation in events earns ribbons to add to the uniform.

The R.O.T.C. program emphasizes leadership, courtesy to one another, and the need to achieve, according to a student who is an R.O.T.C. sergeant. "Our motto is 'Honor and Courage,'" she explained. "We currently are preparing for a district inspection on November 16 by getting files in order, painting the firing range, and drilling. We serve at visitation days, area football games, and at official school events. People respect the uniform."

There is a National Honor Society, a school newspaper called *NOW* (News of Worth), and a high school yearbook, the *Jaguar*.

*The underlying theme pervading everything the school does is to socialize students for their vocation in life.* The school recruits students from junior high school who already see vocations in their futures. Then, through its programs, the school reinforces those expectations.

Equipment used for training in the shops is industrial equipment. The shop teachers do not assume traditional teaching roles; they assume the roles of supervisors or foremen. When vocational teachers and students complain that the academic subjects are not taught in ways relevant to the acquisition of vocational skills, the academics teachers feel the pressure intensely, and grudgingly respond.

In industry, when a worker does not fit in, you get rid of him. Similarly, Carver does not tolerate much variation from the norm. Excessive deviation in behavior or attitude is dealt with by sending the offender back to his home school. There are no "jocks" because there are no athletics. There are no freaks or drug abusers, because they get sent away. And there are not those few outstandingly exceptional scholars setting a pace impossible for the rest of the students to maintain and aiming for admission to Harvard or Yale. The school is almost completely egalitarian.

When we asked vocational teachers how they knew what to teach, they never told us their curriculum came from a district curriculum guide or textbook. They would always say, "It comes from my experience. I know how to do the work myself, so I know what to teach. I have an advisory group that helps me keep current and I get into business and industry as much as I can so I can keep up with what is needed out there."

The craftsman/apprentice model is used extensively in vocational training. Quality is emphasized. Skill in using machines is stressed. And every scrap of material is turned into something useful. The woodworking teacher was proud because he had no scraps:

> People come in here and want scrap wood and we don't have it. We use everything. See that scrap over there? We will take that down to the commercial art teacher and he will have a student trace a name on it and we'll make a nameplate out of that scrap.

Classes tend to be fairly small. In the academic subjects, class size is usually between twenty and twenty-five. In the vocational subjects, the numbers are always below twenty.

Every Friday each teacher turns in lesson plans for the next week to the assistant principal. These are completed on standard forms provided by the district administrative office. One assistant principal checks the plans of academics teachers; the other, those of the vocational teachers. One of these men said:

Basically, [the lesson plan] serves as a medium for preparation for class. On the form, they list their Essential Learner Outcomes and Desired Learner Outcomes and lay out the activities through which they [will] meet [their goals]. I have been known to read the English text . . . before I go to visit a teacher's class. The lesson plans tell me what the teachers are going to be doing, and so, when I visit, I can be sure of what he or she is planning to teach at a certain time. I realize that there has to be some flexibility in the lesson plan, but, basically, if a teacher is not teaching to the Essential Learner Outcomes or Desired Learner Outcomes, then I go to the teacher and find out why.

I check one hundred and fifty lesson plans every Friday. I read a number of them just to see that they are pretty much following the right line. I think it is a good requirement. Sometimes, though, I get a little frustrated, when it's 4:00 P.M. and I'm not yet finished with them.

## The School and the Community

Because the school is a magnet school, Carver High does not serve an identifiable neighborhood. There are no boundaries that define its area in the community. For this reason, it has unusual status in the community with regard to parent involvement and support.

Most of the teachers believe that parents are involved very little in school activities. One teacher told us, "It is too far for parents to come. That is the reason some students don't come."

Teachers also believe that there is a general tapering off of parental interest in their children these days. Teachers talk about the lack of parent involvement. A common complaint is that the parents of students who need help do not seek a conference with teachers. It is the parents of good students who come. We were told:

As a teacher, there is only so much we can do. I can talk to them [students], stand on my head, cut my wrists, and bleed for them, and still, if they don't get the push at home there is nothing I can do. I think parents have messed up their priorities. One of my students was falling asleep a couple of weeks ago. She works until ten or eleven at night. She has no reason to work, but her parents let her. When does this girl do her homework? She falls asleep in class. What is she learning? Her parents let her work so she can buy herself designer jeans! You know, parents like that have got their priorities mixed up.

The administration presses teachers to contact parents but provides no telephone for private conversations. The school district "Fail-Safe" programs, an attempt to get parents directly involved in their children's education, resulted in very few parent visits to Carver despite special days and intense publicity.

Teachers believe some parents are guilty of just "brushing their children off." They complain of a parental attitude of "If you want to do something, go on. Just leave me alone." The teachers insist: "That is not good. High school should be the first thing, especially these days, when everything is so technical. You either have to have technical training or a college degree to get a job."

The feelings toward the school in the community at large appear to be mixed. When we mentioned we were going to study the school, some people said, "Oh, I wish another school had been selected for you to investigate. They have a lot of problems at that school." The blacks in the city have considerable pride in the school. They associate the school with the person, George Washington Carver, and will quickly tell you that it stands for something great.

When students are asked if they would recommend the school to another student, they invariably say "yes." Usually, they found out about the school from other students, often an older brother or sister, and the grapevine appears to convey a positive image. When asked whether they would send their child to the school, vocational teachers will generally say they would, "if the school has a program that would be interesting to my child." There is a bit more ambivalence from the academics teachers.

Each of the vocational areas has an advisory board made up of members from the community. For example, in the health occupations program, the advisory board has a parent, lawyer, minister, person from the Exxon Corporation, and a person from a local hospital. This group was responsible for helping finance field trips to contests. The commercial art advisory group suggested a curriculum that would be useful to students. But many teachers reported that the advisory boards did not function well. The involvement of board members was limited, and sometimes the role of the groups did not appear well defined. One advisory committee was to provide five consultants from banks to lecture to classes. On the day of the visit they called to say they had only two persons and would not be able to come.

But parents apparently do put some pressure on teachers when it comes to programs for their children:

There are some parents who want their child to have a better job while they are in the school. In some of the programs, they place students in a variety of jobs, like in restaurants or fast food places, or hotels. And parents have come to school and said, "Hey, if I wanted my child to work at McDonald's I wouldn't be sending him here. He is not going to this school to work at McDonald's." And I can understand that. I wouldn't want my child to be in a vocational training program for an occupation and end up working at McDonald's.

The assistant principal gets "fantastic support" from parents, in his opinion:

When you call a parent on the job, and really that is about the only time I can get them, because it is during the day and usually both parents work, it gets their attention right away. But they do appreciate knowing about their kids. For example, right now I am going to call about a student who has fourteen absences. And I don't believe that his parents know. His mother is going to tell me how much she appreciates my call. Most parents will try at home to support us. But there are some kids here that you just wonder how they make it, because it is apparent that they have not had a lot of support at home.

## Conclusion

Desegregation as a legal/societal trend has affected high schools in America during the past decade. The magnet school concept was spawned by the need to integrate racially by providing specialized high schools that would attract (act as a magnet) students from all parts of the school district because of the quality of its programs. The magnet school was viewed as complementing the comprehensive high school.

The comprehensive high school was based on *breadth*—a wide range of student abilities, interests, and needs, and a broad-based curriculum to meet those needs. The student population was drawn from a specific geographical region. Programs ranged from third-year physics to basketball to woodworking to remedial reading—it was as its name implied, comprehensive.

The magnet high school was based on a narrow, *focused* curriculum to serve a particular student need. Magnet schools were organized for students preparing to enter the health professions, the engineering professions, the performing arts, and vocational careers. Some concentrate on the sciences, others on the academically talented. Their students come from all areas of the school district and from other districts in a few cases.

A number of observations can be made about the change in secondary schools resulting from this urban school movement.

By draining off students who had already identified a life vocation or specialized interest, magnet schools changed the student body composition of zoned comprehensive high schools.

Comprehensive high schools became the dumping ground for students with problems because of compulsory attendance laws.

As magnet schools grew in strength and number, comprehensive neighborhood high schools declined in strength, power, and scope.

Magnet schools may have had little long-range effect on segregation, the original rationale for their organization.

The students in magnet schools are more homogeneous in their abilities, achievements, vocational values, and lifestyles than the student body in comprehensive high schools.

Such homogeneity may limit the future potential of students in magnet schools to their vision of the immediate future (for example, Carver students who could complete college and enter an engineering profession become auto mechanics because this is what high school prepared them for).

The academic curriculum of the magnet school is shifted from broad knowledge of the "well-educated person" to vocationally oriented content.

Teachers, at least in Carver, segregated themselves by vocational or academic areas and by race.

PART VI

# SELECTIVE ACADEMIC HIGH SCHOOLS

# 12

# BRETTE HIGH SCHOOL

KATHLEEN DEVANEY AND
AMITY BUXTON

In picking Brette High School as one of the best public high schools in the nation last fall, a national magazine certified the continuing success of the school in preparing able students for admission to prestigious colleges. College admission—not just to any college but to an academically rigorous college—is the single, simple goal of this 125-year-old jewel in the crown of the Far West Unified School District. Continuing success in meeting this goal is the result of the talent and determination of the students themselves, the pressure of their parents—exerted upon the students and upon the school district— and the wealth of the Brette tradition as it is husbanded by the school faculty. Although future success in meeting its goal seems jeopardized by the budget-cutting attendant to the district's loss of revenue and the resentment elsewhere in the school district of Brette's selective admissions policy, the school's best protection appears to be its record of placing more than one-third of its graduates in prestigious Ivy League colleges and western institutions like the University of California at Berkeley, Cal Tech, and Stanford University. Ninety-nine percent of Brette's graduates enter some college.

Although Brette is frequently labeled an elite public high school, this should not be construed as dilletantish. At Brette, erudition is not its own reward or sufficient pleasure. Brette's goal is as utilitarian as that of a trade school, and its students and teachers, in the main, uphold and practice the traditional American belief that society should bestow rewards on the basis of talent and diligence in equal portions.

That said, true Bretteites also understand that all work and no play makes dull students—not just dull in the sense of uninteresting but in the sense of not quite bright. So Brette cherishes and strives to nourish the whole person through participation in the arts, physical sport, and self-government, for purposes of self-expression, recreation, friendship, and community. This mission of broad personal and community development is as pragmatic as that of intellectual development. It is seen as not only enjoyable but necessary for the production of superior college material and for the maintenance of the institution.

## Contextual Changes

Even foreknowledge that the student body of this historic public prep school is now 45 percent Chinese, with additional Asian cohorts of Filipinos, Japanese, and Koreans, does not prepare a visitor entering the school for the first time for seeing only Asian faces during the first few minutes' walk down the second-floor corridor—the science wing. The scene soon becomes a mingle of youthful Asians and whites, with occasional black and Latino students. In the principal's office, Alan Feiman points out that the majority Asian population actually conforms to the Brette tradition of serving the able children of the city's most recent immigrants along with children of the affluent. Jewish students once formed a greater proportion of Brette's student body than they did of the whole school district population, because talented Catholic students went to parochial schools and affluent Protestants went to private schools. Now, the Chinese, from a demographic standpoint, are over-represented. They might be even more numerous at Brette, Feiman says, if standardized test scores were not recently added to the requirement for high grades in junior high school. The test scores tend to disqualify many middle school graduates who have earned good grades on the basis of orderly behavior but who have inadequate mastery of English.

The use of grade-point totals is a change in Brette admission procedures, which were less precise thirty years ago, when students were admitted simply on the recommendation of their junior high school principals. The more objective procedures have merged over twenty years in response to heavy increases in applications for admission and sensitivity about supposed favoring of the children of privilege. While the reputation for elitism still lingers, Brette's population now contains, in fact, substantially more children of working-class and poor families than it did before. As many as one-third of the students are eligible for federal lunch subsidy.

Some Brette insiders worry about what the demographic changes portend for the political support from parents and prestigious alumni, almost all of whom are white. Such support has been needed frequently in the past to preserve Brette's special academic status. Alan Feiman, the principal, noted:

> Brette in the sixties was primarily a Caucasian school with a few Asians. There were a lot of Jewish students. By the late seventies it had become predominantly a minority school with a large population of Chinese. There is a racial element in declining community support now, I think. For instance, it is getting harder to sell ads for the student newspaper. Brette is a minority school, and it didn't used to be a minority school. People make the conclusion that it is less good. "Oh! You have so many minority kids!" What is implied is, "Well, it couldn't be as good as it used to be. I wouldn't want my kids going there with so many Chinese kids." It's discouraging.

The persistent demands for equity in the student body over the past two decades also has produced a student body in which more than 60 percent are girls. The court ruled out what earlier had been a preference for boys that balanced the student body sexually.

The magnetism of the school's safe climate has contributed to crowding. Although its building, first occupied in the early sixties, was designed to be a spacious campus for 1,800 students, the pressures for admission to its preeminent academic program have inflated the population to nearly 3,000. The school district's recent "re-design," in which middle schools replaced junior high schools, and ninth graders were assigned to high schools, also contributed to overcrowding.

The reorganization has affected more than enrollment. Brette's curriculum, designed for tenth through twelfth graders, has been extended down to ninth grade. The school has long considered itself a liberal arts college, junior grade, requiring its students to be unusually responsible for their ages. Now, 750 fourteen-year-olds join the student body each year. Many of them have to strain to grow up and keep the fast pace of Brette. The addition of the ninth grade has necessitated the addition of another classroom building, located a twenty-minute walk away, where ninth graders attend morning classes. This physical separation hampers the integration of the young newcomers into the Brette community.

The changes in ethnic mix, numbers, age, and family background of students have coincided with drastic reductions in school district expenditures, which, in turn, have brought in a strict, budget-minded central administration. The generous amounts of time, thought, and dollars idealistic educators might wish to use to experiment and to accommodate Brette's tradition to its changed student body have simply not been available. We were told by a counselor:

> The big change since the seventies is that the personal problems students are faced with at home are now tremendous. We can work out the problems a student has in math or science class, get him tutoring or a teacher's help. But we can't work out problems with their families. In this school kids feel a lot of pressures. Kids are eligible, but the college of their choice may not take them. I came away from the meeting at the university feeling very down. What are they doing to these kids? Each year we see the requirements go up a little higher.

The pressures to cut back and make do that might be accepted as a challenge to their creativity by a confident, energetic, and resilient staff have, instead, fallen on a faculty that is aging because of layoffs and was embittered by a prolonged and crippling teachers' strike two years ago—a faculty that also perceives itself as resented by staff in high schools that are plagued by the typical urban school problems of underachievement and occasional violence. Thus, the genial face of a youthful faculty that relished its expertise, dedication, and companionship with students very much like themselves, has grown gray and sometimes cranky with overwork, underappreciation, and responsibilities to serve students they do not so easily understand. One of the teachers said:

> Twelve years ago, students were more dazzling, and I was a brilliant teacher. I had to be much more on my toes. Now students are more ambitious. They *have* to succeed. They're materialistic. Before, they read more. They knew literature. They had more experience of and with the language. Now, they have no sheer love of reading. . . . In my basic composition class half of the students have problems with the language.

Nevertheless, if wealth is measured in educational terms—the heft of the curriculum, the variety of the student activities program, the reputation of the faculty, and the productivity of the students—Brette is a uniquely wealthy school. It is especially rich in comparison with the high school norm today. Brette has maintained its singular goal of college preparation by retaining its choice to enroll only those students who value and manifest their talent for academic achievement. That learning at Brette is valued less for its own sake than for its future marketability seems inevitable. As the arts and letters seem to be of declining value in the society at large, and youth's fully living and enjoying the high school years is no longer sufficient rationale for a public school, Brette's survival as a special academic school increasingly must depend on the personal and societal benefits to be gained almost exclusively from academic achievement, especially in science and mathematics.

## Students

Brette sends 99 percent of its students on to college. The largest percentage—28 percent in 1980—go to campuses of the state university. At the most academically prestigious campus in the university system, Brette is the top feeder school. In the fall of 1980, 103 freshmen at the university were Brette graduates. The next highest feeder school sent 78. Twenty-three percent of Brette's 1980 graduating class went to the next tier of colleges in the state's public higher education complex. Ten percent of the graduates went to private colleges. Thirty-eight percent went to City Community College, a few miles away from Brette. Most of this group plan to transfer to a four-year college later. These figures bespeak the wide range in the levels of scholarly and economic privilege among Brette's students.

The state university is by all odds the institution of choice for most Brette students. It is 14 miles away, but each year it becomes more distant in terms of accessibility, as its requirements for entry go up and its costs in fees and housing also rise. The rising imperative for a college education and the narrowing chances of being able to afford or being admitted to a prestige college put very great pressures on Brette's students and strongly shape the character of its student body. The de facto commitment for every student at Brette is to take four solid subjects every semester and do at least two hours of homework every day.

George Hsu, assistant principal for counseling (who is himself a Chinese immigrant), says that the Chinese parents' press for success, not just obeyed but endorsed by their children, accounts for the near majority (45.5 percent) of Chinese among Brette students. With Filipinos, Japanese, and Koreans, the Chinese comprise a student body that is more than one half Asian. Less than one quarter is white. Forty percent of the Chinese are the children of recent immigrants, and some of them are, by American standards, very poor. (Like all other city public schools, Brette also enrolls recent arrivals from Latin America, Southeast Asia, the Middle East, and all parts of Europe.) Some counselors and teachers worry about what they judge to be the extreme pressure Asian parents exert on these students, some of whom also work after school to contribute to family income. And students— Chinese-Americans included—decry the grade-grubbing tendency of many of the Chinese students and their isolation from the social life of the school.

Still, the orchestra and band, dramatic productions, student newspaper, athletic teams, social functions, and student government all draw increasing participation from Chinese and other Asian students. The short-term visitor thus gains a reassuring impression that Brette is a strong Americanizing influence. Conversations with Chinese students and observations of their free-period socializing in the schoolyards and corridors leave an impression that friendship is as strong a value for Chinese students as academic success. It is probably the antidote to the parental pressure they feel. Certainly the school recognizes and legitimizes the values of friendship to students. One teacher suggested, in this regard:

> The student population has changed, but the type of student is very much the same: upward-bound students from every neighborhood in the city. The math and English scores [on the standardized tests] do predict success here well. Some kids are workaholics, [but] school dances, plays, athletics get a huge response here. This place goes from 7 A.M. to 6 P.M. You have to kick the kids out. It's a place where kids adjust and are able to do things the way they want to individually. You can really honestly be your own person.

Blacks (7 percent of the student body) and Hispanics (6.5 percent) are under-represented at Brette in comparison with their numbers in the whole district. Hsu explains the small numbers of black and Hispanic students as the result of either low-income parents not, upholding achievement goals for their children or the students not endorsing those goals. Without these objectives, kids choose the immediate rewards of part-time jobs over the delayed rewards of doing homework. A special admissions policy attempts to attract blacks and Hispanics by admitting students whose scores fall slightly below the GPA test-score cutoff. In practice, though, this provision admits no students with an average lower than B in middle schools. In spite of this policy, many black and Hispanic students, with realism it is hard to fault, may prefer other public high schools. Brette may prepare them better for the SAT's, but if they want to go to the university, which admits half of its freshman class on the basis of GPA alone, they could be wiser to attend a less competitive high school, where they can get higher grades. A math teacher told us:

> Noncompetitive kids have problems here. A competitive kid is one who within his own mind has said, "I want a stake in society that's the *best!*" A kid has to have a drive and a goal. Parents' drives and goals aren't enough to sustain kids here.

Brette is a citywide high school, so it takes unusual independence for black and Hispanic fourteen-year-olds to choose it, particularly if they know their old friends will be elsewhere. They can expect to find relatively few students like themselves. Brette students seem unusually open to acquaintanceship with kids from other races, but the need of adolescents to have close friends who understand them intuitively produces social groups of students from homes projecting similar values. Although some black students mix easily with students of other races, black counselors express concern for the social self-separation of those black students whose families have not given them experience with white people. Filipinos, who are not under-represented at Brette, and Hispanics also seem to hold themselves separate. The following student's perspective is not, however, uncommon:

> I go all over the school from one group to another and another. I'm not just with blacks. I came to Brette because I felt it was a chance for me to learn. I really enjoy learning. I want to experience everything here because when I'm older I don't want to say, "I wonder, if I'd have tried that, would I have liked it?"

Among all racial groups one finds students who have chosen Brette because it is seen as the way to avoid fights and drugs and disrupted or lackadaisical classes. It is not uncommon to hear white students say they do not want Brette's academic prestige as much as they want the safety guaranteed by its selective admissions policy. In fact, some see the school's academic competitiveness as a price they have to pay to get through high school without what they, or their parents, perceive to be violence or lax standards at other high schools. One student explained:

> This school makes me feel stupid at times. Lots of the kids are really smart. They don't have to try. The courses I'm taking are hard for me. Now that I know Lincoln [another high school in the city] kids, I wish I'd gone there. They're real easygoing. They don't worry about grades as much.

These are not the students who give Brette its special quality. The school's reputation has been made and its contemporary tone is set by a critical mass of students who project a panache that is more than competitiveness with others. It is also a drive to find their own limits. A student told us:

> Brette is what you make it. You have to put a lot of yourself into it. My friends at private school seem to me as if they are on the people-mover at the airport. The adults cradle them.

For this group of students, Brette is the school of their dreams. To a surprising degree, their dreams are realized on Brette's big, colorful, complicated but youth-sized and youth-styled stage. This quality continues to attract students whose families could send them to private prep schools but who prefer Brette for its sense of the big time: rigorous curriculum, highly reputed faculty, democratic but challenging mix of students, and its rich "co-curriculum" of arts, drama, journalism, student organizations, and government. Thus Brette students convey a kindly and unexpected reassurance to adults possessing the conventional liberal values. They are neither hostile and alienated nor supercilious and smug. In a setting where they have broad scope to be themselves and to express their own values, they endorse adult middle values and reach out to join adult middle-class society. A veteran Brette teacher provided the following perspective:

Students are very interested, apt, hardworking. Students in class are at least as good if not better than they were ten to fifteen years ago.

In the early sixties the paper was very social and gossipy, with a lot of emphasis on school activities. Students now are sophisticated. They are much more concentrated on their future after high school. "Where are we going? What's happening to our country? What can I do about it?" They are more into studying: "I've got to make it in high school or else there's no chance." Many of them have brothers or sisters who have put the fear of Brette into them. There is none of the dances and parties and clothes and cars talk now, as in the sixties. And we don't have the unrest of the seventies. Kids are saying, "I want to get an education. I won't carry a picket sign." But nuclear weapons are what they are concerned about. They are very opposed to the draft. The kids I have now are doing a much better job than the kids I had in the sixties. They are more perceptive and caring.

The criticism that Brette creams off the best students from other high schools has been a source of recurrent attempts to end Brette's selective admissions. One response to the criticism is simply to stonewall it and to organize politically powerful parents and alumni to fight attempts to disperse the school's wealth of student talent. Another response is to accept the possibility of dispersion but to ask whether the gains in equity would balance the probable losses—loss of Brette's clear focus on its single goal of preparing students for college (an especially cogent question in these times of growing concern that comprehensive high schools must try to meet too many goals), and loss of Brette's climate of self-discipline. As it is now, Brette is a privilege that must be earned in advance by students themselves. A third possible loss must be considered—the loss of students who would not enroll in other public schools in the city but would attend private schools instead. So far, the district administration has been either unable to resist Brette supporters' political clout or unwilling to risk the loss of still more white students to private and parochial schools. Thus the district's answer to criticisms that Brette is elitist has not been to distribute Brette's student wealth, but to reaffirm its special admissions policy and start other specialized high schools that can try to motivate students as Brette does. Schools cannot build tradition with the magnetic attraction of Brette in a few years' time, so no other public high school has been able to compete with Brette for superior students.

A still different response to whether it is acceptable in a democracy to reserve a community's best students within a specialized academic school is to pose another question: Is it bad policy to pass on to demonstrably talented and highly motivated young people an academic and social environment charged with a challenge from previous generations of students that they excel?

## Climate

Brette is a charged environment, although it does not feel that way to the first-time visitor. It feels friendly and calm, even serene—especially when its reality is contrasted with the popular image of high school as a teen-age ghetto where alienated kids doze, dawdle, or fight to break out. The Brette visitor enters scenes that alternate in mood from concentration to relaxation and observes students at turns purposeful and playful. In schools as big as Brette one expects that students may feel only a marginal relation to other students outside the classroom. This can be the result of apathy, turbulence, or coldness in the climate, chilling all but a select and closed inner circle. But here, while there is an inner circle, students cast themselves as citizens rather than socialites, and they seem genuinely open and heartily welcoming. While there are students who seem to stay on the periphery, they seem to be there by choice—withholding their energies for studying or for friendship with their own kind. For instance, the Filipinos are observed to separate themselves into Junior R.O.T.C., the Black Students' Union tends to relate to blacks in other schools rather than to other races at Brette, and everyone acknowledges that there are friendship cliques. A white student described her experience as follows:

> Here there's lots of cliques. In classes it's good that we get to know a lot of minority people. But who I go to parties with and hang out with during free mods—that's pretty much segregated.

Overall, one observes a strong sense of community and school spirit, participation of all racial groups in school events, and a sense that all feel proud of the school and enjoy wide circles of acquaintances.

Brette is fight-free, drug-free, cigarette-free. Youths who are not Brette students are not allowed in the building without special permission. The two corridor guards are employed to keep outsiders out, not to restrain the insiders who enforce the school's norms of order by unspoken peer pressure. Actually, there is little need for enforcement because there is no rage that must burst out and no repression of expression. Students meet the school's expectation that they do not have to be coerced or managed, that they are ready for responsibility. What this means is described by a senior student.

> Here you walk into a classroom and everybody there is ready to study. At other schools you go in there and you intend to mess around and the teacher has to put you in control. That's what's made this school good. If I went to Mission High I would have more friends, but friends will get you in trouble. These four years are the most important years of your life. They tell you where you'll go.

After the freshman year, students select their own courses and make their own class schedules, with guidance from counselors. The school is also largely graffiti-free, and again one speculates that this is due to a combination of peer pressure and experience that has proved adults in the school willing to listen to responsible student expression. Thus students have use of the public address system and corridor and stairwell walls in the school, where they post handmade signs ranging from "Happy 16th Birthday, Lisa," to ads for the winter ball, or to pitches for something a student club is selling—usually ethnic munchies. The occasional visitor does not see political messages here. Perhaps this is because there is no current political campaigning in the state or the nation, or perhaps because, as the principal notes, the sixties mood of student protest has disappeared from Brette. This does not mean students are less concerned than were students of the sixties. Some teachers believe that, if anything, they are more serious about the state of the nation and the world.

The greatest faults that teachers and students find with the order of the school are litter and noise. Because of the school's flexible scheduling of classes, students congregate freely in the corridors at all times of the school day—studying, chatting, playing cards, and eating, while seated on the floor in front of their lockers. The school's overcrowding, combined with the lamentable quality of the cafeteria food, result in kids eating all over the school. The resulting litter seems to be accepted as inevitable by everyone except the principal, who steadfastly but cheerfully patrols the corridors picking up orange peels and milk cartons and remonstrating with students to do the same. They comply just as cheerfully, but with a suggestion that they regard him, on this issue, as some sort of fanatic—fringey but harmless.

While the students' spontaneous posters and their careless litter strike visiting (and perhaps resident) adults as a rather playful counterpoint to the earnestness on the other side of the classroom doors, the noise is another matter. Teachers are irritable about the constant buzz of chatter that invades the classroom quiet, and the principal silences radio players. Youth music seems important to students. They sort themselves according to preference for rock or soul and attend school dances on the basis of the kind of music to be played.

One sees pairings of boys and girls, but dating seems to be the exception rather than the rule, owing to the priority students place on their schoolwork and to the shortage of boys.

Outside the low two-block-long building, kids study or talk or play games like touch football on lawns that are grassy and tree-studded like a college campus. A big inside patio is another relaxation space.

The gym is inadequate and cramped on rainy days when the outdoor ball courts behind the school cannot be used. The auditorium is of sufficient size and quality to support Brette's excellent dramatic productions with community patronage and income. The outside of the twenty-year-old building was recently repainted for the first time so it would not discredit its impeccably groomed middle-class neighbors—the single-family homes of the city's Sunview district. Because of budget restrictions, this could only be done by foregoing needed interior painting. Classrooms are institutionally bland, their main attraction being cleanliness, natural light from windows, and carefully mounted maps, posters, and reproductions of paintings in rooms used for language and humanities instruction.

Beyond Brette's back yard and football field is the campus of a university and a large regional shopping center catering to the middle class. Although the campus is not closed, a recent survey of the shopping center's merchants turned up no awareness of students even hanging out there, much less creating a problem. Brette's natural setting is so fair—especially on a winter day of brilliant blue sky and golden sunshine—that the visitor is convinced it must be a significantly beneficent influence on the psychic climate of students.

In that other sense of the word *fair*, meaning just, Brette is also favored. One hears general agreement that grading is fair and that students' rights to due process, individual respect, and participation in decision-making are wholeheartedly acknowledged by administrators and teachers. Since 1969, Brette students have possessed a student charter, granted by the principal. It was modified in 1972 and revised again in 1981. The charter guarantees such rights as "to understand the rationale of a professional decision; to seek redress of a grievance against a teacher, counselor, administrator or another student, and . . . appeal from any decision, according to procedures . . . ; to circulate petitions and handbills, to use bulletin boards to post materials, to wear insignia, to form societies . . . and to have reasonable use of the public address system; to determine their own standards of dress and appearance; to discuss, inquire and to express opinions with impunity inside and outside the classroom."

With all that, Brette is still an unpleasantly intense environment for some of its students. One parent observes that students dare not miss school even if they are sick. Besides the physical crowding, there are shortages of books, supplies, and, most critically, of teachers, so that sometimes students cannot enroll in courses they need, and electives they came to Brette to enjoy cannot be offered. Additionally, some students find the intellectual pressures—heavy homework, frequent instructional-style lectures by teachers and book work by students, the relentless feeling that their present is being sacrificed for the future (which will be more lectures and books)—painful. English and history teachers observe that Brette students in the eighties are not so interested in learning for its own sake as were previous generations. They do not read as much, are not as creative, not as interesting to teach. They are more concerned with good jobs and good money. Some students retort that the school is not meeting their ideals of what a liberal arts education should be. They say that teachers contribute to the competitiveness and complain about anxiety and the priority for rote learning and grades. They complain, too, that overambitious students use school activities not for friendship and self-development but for bonus points for college admission, and thus narrow the experience of school to grade grubbing. One particularly vocal student argued in this regard:

The major thing I have found that is unpleasant is superficialness: emphasis on grades, what's going to look good on your transcript. [For instance], some people don't join the French club to experience French but because Yale will look at it and say, "This kid has extracurricular activities." I wish appearances were less important and really gaining knowledge were more important.

However, the prototypical Brette student thrives on an intensity that is not so anxiety-laden. A senior student who is taking advanced placement English, analytic geometry, advanced placement biology, and physics, is also playing in the concert band and leading the student government. Another with a comparable course load is editing the student newspaper and working as a teaching assistant in physics. Another is running cross country—winning the city championship—and heading the boys' honor and service society. These are not rare examples, although they are not average either. Between both extremes there is a large cohort that seems to resist intensity of either type. Their school life seems relaxed and measured: go to class, study, hang out with friends, take part in some intramural sports or student clubs without striving for leadership, do homework, watch a little TV, go to parties on weekends. The predominant impression of Brette is one of order, relaxed courtesy, friendliness, earnestness, task and future orientation, respect for individuals, and fun. High school the way "it spozed to be."

With a student climate like that, Brette is reputed to be a haven for teachers. The staff does not endorse that impression, although none of them would willingly teach in any other high school either. Most Brette teachers have passed the age of easy tolerance of teen-age messiness and noisiness, which are magnified by Brette's overcrowding and liberal student policies. Many seem harried, railing against what they perceive as a vendetta by the downtown administration against the school. Whether it is a vendetta or simply that the district's cupboard is bare, or that its bureaucracy is typically deaf to need and blind to reason, teachers keenly feel shortages of textbooks, supplies, and loss of staff. These shortages cause closure of some of the learning resource rooms, cuts of AP classes, overenrollment of classes, and elimination of electives. The cafeteria food is unappetizing, the faculty lounge is small, windowless, and nearly airless (say non-smokers). Teachers have no private work space in which to prepare for classes or tutor students. Such complaints are dismissed as cranky by teachers who have come more recently from other schools and who say that the veteran Brette teachers do not appreciate the enormous advantage of the school's talented and motivated students. It is perhaps more fair to say that the Brette veterans do appreciate the students, feel an intense identification with the school, and accept responsibility to maintain its standards. Because they have inadequate collegiality with each other, however, they are burning out in the effort. A new social studies teacher provides his view of the climate for teachers:

> Almost everyone has been here twenty years or more. It is a very big, impersonal place. It is very, very hard to get to know people. I know only four or five people, and them only in passing. I worked before with a faculty where everyone knew everyone and supported each other. That was a very, very tough school, and we had to work together and help each other in order to keep the lid on. It is not necessary here, so it doesn't happen. This situation has been going on for years. . . . Because so many teachers have been here so long, they are very provincial. Their whole world revolves around Brette. There is no faculty leadership here. It is disjointed. Nothing works as a whole; sometimes nothing works at all. There is no one person whom everyone says they respect. Feiman has had to do fence mending. There is never one single faculty meeting. The school is too big. The south campus for freshmen is a real shame. The whole first year they are not part of the school. It is difficult on everyone.

All of these indignities are merely exacerbations of the deep wound to faculty morale inflicted by a teachers' strike in the fall of 1979. Actually, it is not the strike itself that still festers but the fact that it split the staff between those who stayed out and those who came in and kept the school open. These factions are represented by the AFT-affiliated union members, who called the strike, and the Teachers' Association (NEA-affiliated) members who came in. A strong contingent of Brette's leading teachers have been leaders of the Federation citywide, and their bitterness against the strike-breakers has been reciprocated by the Teachers' Association teachers' outrage at strike-line hostilities. Last spring, the Teachers' Association defeated the Federation in the election to determine the teachers' bargaining agent. Some members of these two factions still do not speak to each other.

Almost all teachers speak of the absence of community among faculty as a wound to their professional morale. The school is a bit like a large, once-affluent household full of bright, spirited, independent, affectionate kids, presided over by glum workhorse parents who stay together only for the sake of the children.

The principal, who was assigned to the school shortly after the end of the strike, has not been able to bring the faculty together. A variety of reasons are cited: He is still comparatively new to the school, whose academic program has long been run by the department chairmen (and "men" is the right word—there is no woman chair). Some of these have been chairmen for more than twenty years (twenty years each, not twenty years all together). Another reason cited for the principal's inability to mold the faculty together is the school scheduling, which provides no period in the day when all teachers are free to be together for lunch or for a meeting. Also, the principal is perceived by many teachers as the superintendent's man, appointed to replace a popular principal who was removed for unseemly independence.

The principal says that the most effective unifying element in a faculty is perception of a common enemy—often the students. Since Brette students are gratefully, protectively, and affectionately regarded by all teachers, faculty members do not seek collaboration with each other, he says. The Brette faculty does, however, perceive the downtown administration as a common enemy, so one of the principal's main strategies for gaining the confidence of the faculty appears to be his reports of battles with downtown. Given the hard-nosed and hard-pressed condition of the central administration, these battles cannot all be won, so faculty regard for the principal remains guarded.

The principal also defines his role in terms of preserving the school's reputation and tradition, and appears to bank on this solidifying his position with the faculty. He was planning to host a national conference of principals of several leading high schools, and obviously hoped it would be a major public relations stroke that would protect Brette against further depredations by the school board or administration.

The principal also personally monitors the scholarly environment and strongly supports the unique student culture of Brette. He has begun to confront the problem of weak teachers, but has not yet been able to make enough new appointments to make a substantial improvement.

The opinion is widespread, on the part of the most talented and dedicated staff as well as on the part of parents and students, that the school has too many teachers who do not serve students adequately and who tarnish the faculty's reputation for brilliance. With no way to remove poor teachers, the principal has attempted to improve them by informal and formal teaching evaluations and by convening departmental meetings that focus on curriculum as a way of shoring up the failing instruction. None of these efforts, however, has been sufficient to cast the principal in the role of the faculty's reconciling and invigorating leader. (One quality that distinguishes leadership from management is the existence of followership. Leadership might be gained by eliciting teachers' thoughtful, sustained, mutually respecting partnership in reviewing and renewing the intellectual foundations of the school.)

The principal, other administrators, department heads, and teachers (with a couple of exceptions) all speak of the lack of community among teachers solely in terms of social interactions and events—having lunch together, seeing each other socially (there is a lunchtime bridge club and a circle of amateur winemakers), having department or all-faculty parties. Although the principal has considered plans for all-faculty meetings to heal the wounds of the strike, there is no talk about cross-faculty communication about teaching and learning—issues involving the whole school's instruction and curriculum, as distinguished from departmental planning. In the context of community among teachers, no one speaks of the need for teachers to work together to confront the school's present weaknesses and future uncertainties, or to examine their own need for professional renewal. Brette teachers consider themselves professionals, but they do not speak of the need for a professional community in which to measure themselves and find stimulation and support.

When some teachers recommended (as part of the faculty self-evaluation for the accreditation process) revival of the Faculty Council, union leaders protested that this body had been useless in the past and would tend to dilute the school's bargaining unit. An inference to be made is that union members can see no subject for cross-faculty communication aside from issues of wages and working conditions. The ailing state of faculty health—advancing age, isolation, overwork, and tedium; the malnourished state of staffing, curriculum, and supplies; the changed and changing ethnic population of the school; the strong possibility of lessening parental political support in the future—all strongly suggest an overwhelming priority for Brette teachers. With the leadership of the principal, they need to get together as colleagues and face the issues of their own professional adequacy and choices for a changing population of students in a changed society.

## Curriculum

Brette's course of study has a breadth and depth that would be envied by many small colleges, but the genius of the curriculum is the inclusion of a strong arts program and the concept that student activities are a "co-curriculum." These exist in parallel strength to the "solids" curriculum by virtue of the structuring of the school day so that activities such as the newspaper, orchestra and band, forensics and drama, and student government can be carried on during the school day rather than after school, when they would compete with the need to study or with athletics. The flexible schedule is composed of fifteen-to twenty-minute modules throughout the school day, which begins at 7:40 A.M. and runs until 3:19 P.M. This allows teachers to design courses for varying lengths of time. It also permits any student above the ninth grade to design a personal class schedule that satisfies the school's requirement for four solid courses a semester and still allows time for electives, labs, field work, and participation in activities. Because students come to Brette from all over the city, modular scheduling also assures that the more distant students are not closed out from activities.

The co-curriculum and modular scheduling were introduced by Barton Snow, Brette principal during the late sixties and early seventies. Remainders of the progressivism of that era, they glow like well-used antiques whose fashion has not faded, and they give students a sense of real-life experience that is absent in a strictly college prep curriculum. They also impart relaxation and self-expression that are needed to balance uptight lessons. The co-curriculum works because of the mods, and the mods work here—in contrast to their failure at many other high schools—because students want the flexibility, not to give them time off from school but to intensify their time in school. Activities like the student newspaper at Brette, which is consistently rated first-class in national judging, attract twice as many students as can be accepted. Like participation in drama, it carries English credit. The journalism advisor described the value of work on the newspaper.

> The paper gives students a chance to get out of the classroom, get into the school community, work on their own, and learn how to collect information, sift it, mull it over, and put it into clear, concise, accurate language. High school students have a hard time doing this. They overwrite, generalize. Journalism is one way you can show students how to write concisely, to the point, and have it read by everybody in the school. The kids learn the hard way. They've got to do it better, got to make it clearer. It's so real is what I like. It makes them see the real world out there. It teaches them to meet people, how to listen and how to be careful. In an English class, whether what they write is correct or not I have no way of knowing. Only in public speaking and drama—also first-quality here—do students also get up and show what they do. I let them write whatever they want, and they take the criticism when it comes. I tell them they must become conscious of how other people perceive things, and just learn how to develop sensitivity to other people and still get their point across. I will not censor, although there is a real risk of libel. I will talk with them about libel and the lesser infractions of embarrassing or hurting people, but students must censor themselves.

The experiences the co-curriculum provides are not just hands-on, which is possible in a laboratory, but real, for they take place not just with students' participation but according to their choices. Thus they provide the special kind of learning that comes from choice and consequence. When the district office forwards the state's ruling that all vending machines of "non-nutritional" food must be removed from the school, the principal does not order the machines removed but explains the notice to the student government, which operates the vending machines to support athletics. Student leaders contact the area superintendent, the downtown office, and vow to take on the state superintendent himself, if necessary. The visitor observing the Brette Executive Council (BEC) in its efficient twice-a-week business meetings, has no impression that its determination is a fantasy or a bluff.

The BEC perceives not only that litter in the corridors detracts from the school's quality of life and reputation but also that it results from some students' insufficient identity with the school. They decide to attack litter by trying to increase student friendliness and participation. A student member of the council noted:

> We want to reach the invisible students—the ones who just go to class and study. We want to make the Brette experience good for them. High school years are special. There is no other time like it. We want to make it so that when you look back on Brette you think, "Those really were the best years of my life."

Nearly forty student clubs, school spirit and social activities, which are managed by elected student boards, and a potpourri of minicourses and workshops designed by students for students, are the engines that will have to be revved up to generate more warmth.

Student drama productions are valued as much for their power to create this warmth among students as for their reputation of grooming and spotlighting performing talent in productions that in some years are of near-professional quality. Colleges that recruit for dramatic and musical talent are as high on Brette as is the Ivy League, and the music and drama programs at Brette make it a magnet school for talented performers. However, the administration and other faculty consider the arts program to be a priority not as career preparation but as relaxation and enrichment, and the visitor with a bias for experiential learning is likely to regard it and the co-curriculum as the essential ingredients in the school's uniqueness. A student described her entry into the co-curriculum in the following manner:

> I went out for the musical show [*Destry Rides Again*] because I had to do something around here to keep me going. Studying gets monotonous. In an arts activity, your mind is broadened. I like the two different types of learning. Understanding *why* things are is the whole basis of learning for me. School work is easier for me when I can take something apart and know *why* this is. Having a dramatic part, you have to take it apart and build it up to know why this person is this way. *Destry* was wonderful. I truly loved every single moment. It was a lot of work. We built an imaginary world and made it real. I felt something give in me yesterday when I walked on the stage and it was all removed. It was made out of love, time, passions, hollering. I really do enjoy being close with people. That's the way the cast was brought up to be. When you walk in you get a big hug. It opened a lot of people's eyes. So many people knew only one race, one type of personality. There are a lot of open aspects now. I say, "Oh, I won't knock anything until I've experienced it for myself."

There is another reason the arts and co-curriculum can be seen as indispensable, and that is that without them Brette's curriculum would be substantially tracked. In science and math, English and foreign languages, there is a regular course of study and an honors/advanced placement track to which superior students are recruited and which is counted on to draw the "gifted" students from the city's middle schools. The social studies department also offers honors and AP history, but its required civics courses are not tracked.

The school's most veteran and highly reputed faculty contend that the uniqueness of Brette derives in large measure from its AP courses. This may only be a defensive reaction: the AP classes, which require an attached preparation period for the teacher to do the extra work of a college-level course, are the most expensive (the *only* expensive item) and thus the most vulnerable aspect of Brette's curriculum. Threats to AP last year mobilized parent/student/faculty marches on the school board and the principal's most dead-earnest confrontation with the superintendent. Probably, if the arts program and the modular scheduling that makes the co-curriculum possible were comparably threatened, they would receive equally fervent support. There is no question that the school's prestige is boosted by its seniors who consistently rank as the prima donnas among AP performers in the nation. And it is understandable that in today's materialist educational climate the key to Brette's survival as a special academic high school is seen as the maintenance of the AP courses that seem to guarantee entrance to the prestige colleges. But the uninitiated outsider wonders whether the colleges do, in fact, still set such store by AP exams, and even whether it is still considered an advantage to take college freshman courses in high school, thus shortening one's stay in college.

The case seems to rest on the students' monetary savings and the big universities' low reputation in lower division teaching, but in view of the enormous influence the AP program has on all of the students at Brette, one would like to see evidence from recent AP graduates and their college professors that these courses are, in fact, of such importance that they deserve to continue to be the hallmark of a superior academic high school. From a purely educational standpoint, is something accomplished in the AP course that could not be accomplished in an honors course without the AP test? This is an issue beyond the scope of this study. But from brief observation it does appear that the rigor that results from AP courses and their examinations may not be entirely healthy, may actually be somewhat deadening sometimes for AP students.

The effects of the AP curriculum on the other students in the school arise because of the stringency of the school's budget resources. In some departments, keeping AP preparatory periods means raising class sizes in other courses. A more subtle effect is that, as long as the AP course is seen as the heart of the curriculum, teachers are unable to perceive or to repair weaknesses elsewhere.

Two changes with radical consequences occurred at Brette in the past decade: the addition of the ninth-grade and the increased enrollment of students who come to Brette for its academic calm but are disadvantaged by its competitive chill. In the face of the need to invest more resources in the ninth grade curriculum in order to prepare these students to take advantage of Brette's riches in later grades, the faculty maintains and the administration supports the absolute priority of preservation of the AP courses. It seems as if the major resources of the faculty are going to the students who need help least.

It is, of course, pragmatic to take the position that the greatest educational benefit a marginal student can receive is to be in a school with a peer culture like Brette's. Thus, the most practical action to take on behalf of marginal students is to keep the prestige curriculum beefed up to retain the highest-achieving students. Even if this point is granted, the question remains whether the high-achieving students are satisfied with a curriculum that is so inexorably controlled by the tests—AP exams and SAT's.

The evidence of the faculty's creativity in curriculum still abounds in the civics courses, with their options for learning first-hand about economics, law, careers; in English department electives; in the foreign language department's annual all-school ethnic fairs, the Kermesse—to cite a few examples only. But when you ask whether there is any concern for new curriculum development, you are told that the only development anyone has in mind is the restoration, apparently hopeless, of the electives that have been cut. It seems that people are thralls to higher education and that their creativity is not challenged by, but held captive to, the grim necessity to maintain Brette students' scores on the college admission tests. This is a counterpoint, in a rather wistful minor key, to the tune being called by American colleges and universities—that high schools must conform more strictly to college prerequisites.

## II

This *is* a special school. But, beneath the overall sense of excellence, there are students who struggle, teachers whose interest in high-quality teaching has declined, conditions that threaten the continuing superiority of the school. In this section of the report, we examine a number of themes developed earlier in greater detail, especially in relation to instruction, curriculum development, and staffing.

### The Instructional Program

"Brette is the stepping stone to the big university," we are told over and over. University admission requirements, it turns out, are the real basis of the curriculum, even though the less demanding requirements of the district form the minimum requirements for graduation. Although there are complaints about the increasingly difficult standards being set for university admission, the Brette community, nonetheless, accepts the meeting of such standards as the school's purpose.

In spite of the university-driven purpose, however, many students—honors and general alike—complain about the lack of nonacademic classes such as "shops," which would provide more diversity of learning. But they know such courses won't be offered.

Despite the cutback in honors and advanced placement courses—an action faculty cite as an example of the diminished academic level of the school—there remains a tremendous variety of course offerings. In English alone, as an example, there are twenty courses in literature; fourteen in media, including cinematography, drama, journalism, linguistics, mass media, public speaking, communications, reading, and speed reading; five in composition; eight in sophomore-junior honors, including The Adolescent in Literature, From Beowulf to Virginia Woolf, The Knight in Not So Shining Armor, and Continental Literature; and eight in senior advanced placement, including, Heroes, Shakespeare and Shaw, and Comparative Themes.

Individual Study remains available, although it is no longer given much encouragement because of the considerable demand it makes on teacher time. It is intended to proceed under the guidance of a faculty advisor and to involve "freer access to and use of school facilities and materials, constructive use of individual study time, and adherence to self-imposed deadlines and objectives."

Although current ninth-grade students were pre-enrolled in basic required subjects, students in the upper three grades had 427 courses from which to select: 78 in English, 63 in social science, 70 in science, 61 in math, 80 in foreign language, 44 in creative arts, 31 in physical education. Of the 427 courses, 34 are honors classes, which exist in all academic subject areas except social science, 22 are advanced placement classes in all academic subject areas.

For all the arguments expressed against the advanced placement program in terms of expense, discrimination, and elitism, the program furnishes considerable substance and psychic energy to the academic climate. We were told often: "The AP curriculum adds a sense of professionalism for teachers and provides a place for students to shine."

The high caliber of teaching and learning in these courses and the eventual economic savings they make possible for college-bound students and their families contribute to the importance the program enjoys. A counselor expressed the relationship as follows: "A single passed AP exam earns a student ten quarter units at the university— a savings to students and taxpayers." The high record of AP success is always cited in defining Brette's primacy. The counselor kept close track of this success.

Last May, 326 students took 489 examinations to rank the program among the nation's largest. A remarkable 90 percent of the examinees earned 3, 4, or 5 [top] grades to qualify for college credit and/or advanced standing—a success unmatched by any other secondary school of comparable size.

An AP class represents college-level teaching, an opportunity many of the teachers value. Because of the need for adequate preparation, AP teachers have historically been given a "prep" period—until the recent cutbacks, which eliminated prep periods. While this loss has lessened the attractiveness of the AP courses for teachers, the courses continue to help define the school.

The Teacher Assistant (TA) "class" offers a unique learning opportunity for students. The following statement comes from the formal description:

Ideally, your duties should range from routine clerical matters to occasional classroom instruction. The total experience may include service to students needing help, aid to the teacher to improve his instruction, and experiences that will contribute to your own educational and personal growth. . . . Five credits can be earned for a semester's service although no letter grade will be given. A total of ten credits may be earned as a TA while at Brette. To qualify, a prospective TA must have completed successfully the course in which he will assist. Since personal service and commitment to helping others may be of interest to employers and colleges, evidence of your TA experience will be noted on your permanent record.

Although athletics hold a secondary place to the academic subjects in the minds of staff and students alike, they nonetheless play a large part in the school program and motivate more parental involvement than the Parent-Teacher-Students Association (PTSA). Boys' and girls' teams have, in recent years, placed first or second in citywide competition in basketball, golf, fencing, soccer, volleyball, swimming, tennis, gymnastics, and track.

Rich as it is, the curriculum is viewed by many of the teachers and students as impoverished because of the budget cutbacks of the past decade. They note the elimination of twenty-four courses such as Hebrew, Russian, genetics, advanced electronics, and computer science. They also suggest that students have fewer opportunities to pursue subject areas as thoroughly as they may wish. In addition, the reduced budgets have resulted in smaller district expenditures for paraprofessionals, counselor time, library books, laboratory equipment, and instructional materials. At Brette, these reductions have affected laboratory equipment for the math, science, and foreign language departments.

The class-size limitation established by the teacher contract is another major constraint to enabling students to take all the courses they desire. There can be "no more than 25 students in an English class and 30 in other subject classes." Up to two more students may be added, but only if the principal asks the teacher to do so in writing and the teacher agrees to add the extra students. Teachers cannot be assigned to courses until students select the classes, and students who want certain classes cannot start them until teachers are assigned. Some strong union members who feel they won the class-size issue by losing wages while on strike, will not admit one "extra" student, regardless of the effect on a student. Thus, although the need for exceptions to the class-size limitation rule seems to be recognized by everyone, there is little voluntary give-and-take to allow them.

A major gap in equipment is computers. Thirty-four students now go to a commercial high school in a distant part of the city to use computers since a neighboring college, which once provided access, began to charge for the use of theirs.

In spite of rich community resources that are available to Brette, the school makes only limited use of them. Social science classes typically include outside speakers and community field trips. Creative arts classes and "free mod" activities utilize museum tours, creative arts performances on campus, and attendance at ballet and opera performances with tickets donated by a local organization. Foreign language activities include campus performances and occasional media presentations by French educators and celebrities.

In addition to these formal activities, however, many students are active on their own in community organizations—community recreational leagues, Junior Statesmen, and the League for Handicapped are examples. Students are also involved in the community service activities of the forty or so clubs that are part of the co-curriculum. However, none of these projects guarantees continued collaboration with the community or makes an explicit connection with the school's academic curriculum.

## Curriculum Development

Even though courses listed on the district computer cannot be changed nor can courses be added, several teachers, with the support of department heads, have made internal changes in their courses. For example, it was necessary to introduce creative thinking and projects into the drafting course so that students could produce portfolios necessary for college interviews.

The department heads seldom initiate changes, perhaps because they have held their positions for so long, or because of a pragmatic response to cuts in their pay, or because of the high priority they place on preserving what remains of teacher and school autonomy. Mainly, the lack of curriculum revision and development seems to stem from the lack of discretionary or categorical funding to supplement the basic budget and the resulting sense of "lack of control." As the chair of the science department noted:

> There are no funds to develop new curriculum. We can't buy equipment even to replace broken and stolen things. We can't start new programs without new money. We cannot do lab-oriented programs like ChemStudy and BSCS because we have no money for supplies, so we switch back to text-based curricula. We used to have thirty microscopes in every science room. Then we expanded to the ninth grade and added two new classrooms, but we got no extra microscopes and no money for equipment repair. So kids have to share.
>
> We can do absolutely nothing creative, such as team teaching or special demonstrations. We lost our science and math resource center, where students could be assigned to do special projects and special readings, because they cut the technician. I can't do it all myself.
>
> If the university said, "Come and help us develop a new curriculum," what good would it do us? This district wouldn't even pay you to have the curriculum pages copied, much less give you any time off for the necessary study.

Constraints to curriculum development stem not only from teacher energy levels, which seem now to be a bit low, but also from the emphasis on text and test content. Students are succeeding in their quest to get into higher education settings; tampering too much with success seems risky to some.

In some ways, the same institutional conditions that sustain what excellence exists in the Brette curriculum keep it from being further developed. There is no felt need to change. One senses that the instructional program is stagnating, neglected by tired teachers who have been there for years, protected by a sense of "the Brette tradition," and crippled by the lack of adequate resources and equipment.

Even as Brette continues to be a potent school, those within feel threatened by the growing power of the central office. In response, staff members direct their physical and emotional energies toward defense of the Brette image, "making do with less." Some fan the embers of the unresolved personal conflicts of the 1979 strike and cry out against the "downtown enemy."

Writing a self-study report for a recent accreditation visit could have been an opportunity for the departments to take a fresh look at curriculum, staff, and materials, and to propose creative strategies to reconstruct their battered program and demoralized climate. But this did not happen. Although the central office of the school district could legislate away much of Brette's excellence, it is also possible for those within Brette to redirect their intellectual and emotional energies to examining seriously the instructional program and parent-community involvement for the purposes of expanding the curriculum, incorporating the scholastic and global advances of the eighties, as well as reinstating the best of the past courses.

## Administrative and Teaching Staff

Since the arrival of the new superintendent in 1976, principals no longer control teacher selection or relocation—another example of the increase of central control and of the collective bargaining contract. In the past, principals selected their teachers from the several names submitted by the personnel office after appropriate screening. Now, teachers—and principals—are assigned with little input from the schools.

Although the principal of Brette now has only minimal authority in selecting teachers, he has nonetheless clear criteria for the kinds of persons he wants: competency in subject matter and willingness to participate in co-curriculum activities. In practice, within the teacher transfer procedures outlined in the teacher contract, the principal does not hold the power to seek the relocation of teachers judged to be ineffective. His first attempt to do so failed, apparently because of central office mishandling of the evaluation. Furthermore, given the tenuous nature of yearly assignments, there seems to be a very narrow arena in which any principal can exert leadership in the district.

The assistant principal for instruction and curriculum appears to be the central organizer of the instructional program. He conducts the weekly Administrative Council meeting, which includes department chairpersons, supervises the development of the master schedules, controls input to the curriculum computer downtown, acts as liaison to the district curriculum office, and coordinates necessary accreditation activities.

Another assistant principal oversees counseling. Counselors handle discipline problems (mainly class cuts) and advise students academically. The reduction of counselor positions has increased the work load of those who remain. Writing college recommendations and advising students in academic matters take most of their time. There is almost no time for personal counseling. From 7.2 counselors (including two head counselors) in 1977, the staff now has shrunk to 5.8 counselors (including one at the south campus, which serves ninth graders). The counseling load is now 630 to 1. To relieve the burden, some group counseling is done in "registries" (homerooms). Each week, the counselor responsible for alumni affairs prepares and distributes a "Senior Bulletin," which lists college admission visits and information about testing, college applications, scholarships, and colleges and universities. Along with the newsletter, there is a college information office staffed mainly by parent volunteers.

The department heads are credited with "running the school." In important ways, they control the instructional programs that are the heart of the school. Because of the number of students, department heads organize the master schedule of classes for their departments. They assign teachers and students within the class-size limitations with varying degrees of shared decision-making. They meet weekly with the principal, assistant principals, and teacher organization representatives (in an organization called the Administrative Council) to handle practical matters (for example, textbooks, budgets, student teachers) and to address particular school issues.

Some department heads are less involved with the co-curriculum currently than they were in earlier years, partially because of the psychological and practical effects resulting from a reduction in their stipends and partially because of their age and length of teaching experience. Some are simply tired. Others supplement their salaries by "moonlighting" and just have less time to devote to nonacademic activities.

Among the teaching staff, there is a range of skills, teaching strategies and backgrounds. Sixty-three percent are men. A majority (61 percent) have their master's degree, 38 percent have thirty hours beyond their master's, and 7 percent possess a doctorate. Racially, the staff does not match the composition of the student population or district staff: White 77 percent (67 percent district staff); Hispanic 10 percent (7 percent district); Asian 8 percent (12 percent district); American Indian 3 percent (2 percent district); and Filipino 0 percent (3 percent district). The average salary is $21,373, $858 more than the district average, due to the length of service and educational backgrounds of the staff.

It is an aging faculty; the average teacher is forty-nine. There are several reasons. Teachers often come to Brette as the capstone of a teaching career in this city. Many then stay beyond possible retirement age because of the need of a salary to maintain the lifestyle they have chosen for themselves and their families. The lack of younger teachers, however, relates mostly to the budget problems of the past decade that caused the riffing of teachers hired after 1969–70—in most cases these were the youngest and most energetic teachers. There is a good deal of conversation at Brette about the lack of young teachers. Many suggested to us that "it is very bad for the faculty to age. We need young teachers who have more contact with student culture. Young teachers bring a freshness, new ideas and energy to the staff."

A majority of the teachers are lauded as outstanding by colleagues and administrators, but a few are described as ineffective by students, administrators, and parents. The comments suggest that these "ineffective" teachers are "burned out," unresponsive, dispassionate, or aloof.

While it is "a dream to be transferred to Brette," teachers find out that teaching at Brette is hard work. *All* of the students come to class and do their homework. There is no relief from constant forty- to sixty-minute teaching and nightly reading or grading of papers. A few teachers leave because of this kind of pressure.

At the same time, almost all of the teachers consider themselves to be professionals in their subjects, deserving and privileged to be at Brette, where they can interact with young minds as "sharp" as theirs. They can teach content and abstract concepts and assume they will be understood by their students. Student response, generally cooperative and positive, is probably a major source of the teachers' sense of professional reward because there is limited time and space for professional teacher-to-teacher interactions even within departments. Isolation is a problem. As one teacher explains:

> Faculty meetings occur in mods so you're not seeing everyone together at any time. The way things are going, there's not that closeness, which a lot of people miss. Everyone is so snowed under they spend the time in the office trying to keep up, keeping office hours, tutoring. A good part of the faculty does a good job. I've seen them work through lunch, take stacks of

papers home. Correcting papers . . . is a big, big job. I commute with one of the math teachers. He said to me, "There's no way I would teach calculus next semester—not with the load I've got." He was a good calculus teacher in the past. So you lose people who would like to teach advanced classes but can't carry the extra load.

The sense of the faculty as a "community of professional colleagues" no longer exists, according to long-timers, as it apparently did in the past. Many professional activities in which teachers used to participate on a regular basis, such as committees for adopting texts or meetings about articulation between grades and subject areas, no longer take place. One newer teacher suggested:

> I find my own intellectual and professional stimulation coming from association with people in my professional organization. The meetings are interesting, worthwhile, stimulating, offer new ideas, news of what's going on elsewhere. I find it surprising others don't participate. Older teachers begin to view things that come and go as fads. I'm always curious because I'm afraid I might be missing something.

When teachers rally their energies collectively, it is around a common enemy or threat, such as the recent proposal to abolish modular scheduling and return to a seven-period day. This threat catalyzed a student-teacher-parent squadron which launched a successful "Save the College Preparatory Program at Brette" campaign at the school board.

## Teaching and Learning

In 1969, the modular system of twenty-minute time blocks was instituted so that "instruction could determine the length of the period," not vice versa. Each department selects from among five possible time patterns—one, two, or three "mods" or an alternating pattern of two and three mods each week. Science courses usually last three mods (sixty minutes) and other "solids" two mods (forty minutes).

Several mods of free time are planned for the middle of the day in most students' schedules to allow time not only for co-curricular activities but also for the informal student socializing the school values. There is a real fear that "downtown" might reinstate the traditional seven-period day. In the view of students, parents, and faculty, such a move would sound the death knell of the far-ranging curriculum and co-curriculum opportunities and the student freedom to pursue academic excellence.

The effect of the modular plan on academic achievement depends on the students' ability to handle their own free time responsibly. One student told us:

> Modules make it convenient. You don't have to go to class after class after class. If you want extra time to study or for a break you can take it. It is more like a college: not easy but not too hard. I study at night and during my free mods.

Looking at the entire student body, however, one staff member noted,

> Perhaps 25 percent to 30 percent of the students account for the high public rating. A great many students don't know how to use time wisely. It's easy to overlook students who aren't competent. Ninth graders, for example, don't know how to use the library, even those who are intelligent and motivated.

Each Brette student is expected to take at least four "solids," although many take six. Prior to the staff cutbacks, the maximum number of courses a student could take was seven and in some cases, eight. Now, because there are fewer teachers and class options, some seniors are encouraged to take fewer than the four solids. The reduction of the course maximum to six poses a significant difficulty for talented students who wish to combine academic and elective courses such as the creative arts.

Student enrollment figures show social science, humanities, English, mathematics, science, and physical education to be the most popular courses, in that order, reflecting the university requirements for admission, student interest and ability, and the reduced number of classes students can presently take. A "tracking" system exists, though it is likely a misnomer inasmuch as the three available "tracks" are flexible and voluntary. Students are recommended to enter the honors courses from the regular program and they can choose advanced placement. They can opt out of either, however, and do all of their work, as the majority of students do, in the regular program.

The shared premise and motivation for attending Brette and choosing classes—which we encountered in almost every conversation—is simple: "This class is going to help me get into college." This expectation affects the overall teaching/learning environment. "Everyone studies for the exam and 90 percent are achievers." No one seems to be overly concerned about the 10 percent who lack drive, background, or individual support to achieve. One teacher said it this way:

> One is lucky to be at Brette, although the older teachers may have forgotten this. We have students and no money but no cutting. You can teach from the book and teach well and the students learn well. They turn their homework in. . . . The reason for the existence of Brette is that you can teach courses for high achievers economically.

Much of the teaching is directed to the learning of facts and formulae, with a minimum of time spent on inquiry, critical thinking, analytical problem solving, or conceptualization. In part, this is related to the pressures of the testing required in the AP program and the SAT.

Several courses in media are offered jointly by the English and Creative Arts departments; Film as Literature is an example. There is also a film club for movie buffs. The journalism courses and student newspaper, *The Brette*, afford the only opportunity for the study and practice of a medium that influences the public mind and values. *The Brette* issues are of high quality and demonstrate that the journalism students are well trained to manage media tools.

The library is used more as a study place than as a reference or resource room to supplement classroom teaching. The social science teachers use it more than other teachers for assignments and research, perhaps because it was once their resource room.

Homework is universal and incessant, including vacation assignments to which some students object, according to parent testimony. Testing occurs constantly, even on the last day before vacations. At the same time, the general tone of the teaching is supportive: "Teachers are nice—not harsh or strict or wanting to make you suffer."

There is an observable imbalance, however, in the quality of teaching across the staff. "Teachers could and should be doing more," commented one teacher,

> [They] are knowledgeable but in some cases [they] sit and relax. They are not doing the things they should be doing with this caliber of student. There should be more lab work, more quantification, more math rigor. The advanced biology classes are not that much advanced.

Students describe the differences more tersely: "Half of my teachers have been really good and half say, 'Go to the library and find out for yourself.'"

From the students' perspective, the "good teachers" are the ones who explain, help them learn, challenge them, make subjects understandable and interesting, trust the students, and communicate enthusiasm, interest, and knowledge.

> He is so interested in what he's talking about . . . for example, he had the students read a small booklet on a minute aspect of American history, such as carpetbaggers, take notes, and write an essay—all within the forty-minute period.

Students say the poor teachers—and almost all students say they have some poor teachers—attempt problems they cannot do, act confused, "talk the whole hour while the class flunks," point out what is wrong with a paper without suggesting how to improve it, lecture on learning rather than on the subject, grade hard and seem mean, or "don't know how to relate to kids and help them understand."

The overall impression from random observations of classrooms is of serious intent on the part of both students and teachers. In the classrooms, one sees little evidence of the frustrations and dilemmas of the administration, the faculty divisions, or the curriculum gaps. In most of the classes, maximum "time on task" is strikingly evident. In general, the teachers start to teach the minute the class time begins, sometimes as the students are walking into the room. The students stay quiet until the last minute. There are no bells, but everyone knows when the mods begin and end. During work periods within a class, most of the students work while their teachers give them individualized attention. Whatever occurs, it moves on with almost a mechanical regularity.

The advanced placement classes are the most evident examples of "teaching to a test"—much like New York State Regents classes. The AP exams, unlike the multiple choice California Test of Basic Skills (CTBS) exams that determine which students can enter Brette, include problem-solving and essay-test questions—even in science.

The AP and honors classes are rigorous. They move at a fast pace by virtue of the teachers' tightly planned lessons. The typical dialogue and interaction between teacher and student is convergent. The teacher seeks responses that fit the text or test the concept or theorem being taught. The style is pungent, the pace is brisk, the tone is friendly but provocative. Many AP classes are like a delightful dramatic production out of which one cannot tune for a minute without being lost or behind an idea or two.

An honors class in French looks like this to a student:

> He takes you into an environment. From the minute you walk in, you must speak in French . . . be fluent . . . must catch on immediately. There's a test every day, a constant bombardment. There's an atmosphere of total stress and pressure. It really shows that one can do one's best. But he really doesn't know that the students go back to English once they leave the room. It works for that hour.

Honors English teachers, from a student's perspective, have a similar expectation.

> . . . demanding . . . [they] expect students to catch on the first minute and not let go till the class ends . . . to follow the work level and load . . . [to] absorb what they say . . . to write essays to show you comprehend the materials.

An honors class calculus teacher exhibited the same quality to another student. "His lectures are clear. He drills well. He pushes . . . puts you on the spot . . . motivates."

Whereas the honors and AP classes are fairly uniform in terms of quality, the regular classes are more uneven, ranging from the exciting and innovative to the dispassionate and rigid. Many teachers experiment with and vary their teaching strategies; others "deliver" the content and appear inattentive to students' individual problems, interests, or styles of learning.

The range of teaching styles provide the students with a rich day's experience as they go from class to class. Although there are complaints, the students appear to be able to adjust to the varying styles. In general, despite the variations in classes, there is a pervasive sense of caring and expectation that the students can and will learn.

The sheer number of courses offered helps somewhat to account for the uneven picture of teaching. Given the large number of courses that have to be taught, it is difficult to locate enough teachers who can teach all of those courses effectively in a system that eliminated the youngest and newest teachers with the 1979 budget cutback. How many teachers who have taught twenty or more years can sustain energy, drive, sensitivity to adolescents, and an active interest in their subject areas in the negative climate of budget cuts and downtown-versus-school battles, with the slow-healing strike wounds, and within the impacted pace of each school day?

The picture of uneven teaching, regardless of the conditions, raises questions, however, about the renewal of qualification credentials, about tenure, about evaluation, about staff development, and about relocation. From the principal's perspective, "The people who have worked intensively with the student body are the ones that are jewels for me. They're the ones who can call it their school."

As defined by the teachers' contract and supervised by the personnel office, administrators are responsible for a three-year cycle of teacher evaluations. One-third of the teachers are evaluated each year by the principal and the assistant principals. The principal has specified his criteria for effective teachers: "I have expectations that they will behave in a humane manner." In particular, he expects that they will create a business-like atmosphere, establish a pleasant classroom tone, plan for a learning process that will challenge students and encourage achievement, participate in the life of the school, encourage and be a model of good attendance, be scholarly, be professional, be analytical and self-critical. Active participation in the co-curriculum is a major concern for him.

There is no formal staff development program to help teachers increase their professional skills. The principal attempts to guide teachers toward professional development on a one-on-one basis through conferences and group work in departments. But this appears inadequate.

Most students have chosen Brette as the best public high school in the city, a view shared by their parents and often an older brother or sister who attended the school. Several students agreed with one who said, "It's something you've worked toward. Everyone in our family has been talking about Brette since elementary school."

Many students have been in "gifted" classes since elementary school and have "aimed" for Brette. For them, the poor teachers are "deadly" and many of their classes are boring, especially in ninth grade, where little choice exists. The "special admissions" students and those who are not gifted or have modest academic aspirations—that is, the good B students—take the variety of teaching in stride and struggle to perform well according to their teachers' standards.

While the demands on the students to achieve differ between the regular and honors or AP classes, the grading does not. The A's and B's earned in the latter classes may not make a difference to the university admissions officers even though it is more difficult to earn high grades in these classes. This undifferentiated grading poses a dilemma for the students: "Do I take a high-level course and possibly earn a low grade or take a regular course and earn high grades?"

Many students elect to be in the honors and AP classes and struggle to stay in them for the challenge and learning they offer. But some find the pressure too great, with too few satisfying results, and return to regular classes. Some students never enter honors classes and do just enough to "get by." The large majority elect to take regular courses and strive to gain a high enough grade-point average to enter the university.

> I've gotten a lot out of Brette this year though it's not been as challenging academically as it could have been. The only way to get really challenging education is to take AP's and even those aren't as rigorous as they could be. Friends in private schools have to do more reading.

Grades are even more important than self-esteem in many cases. Final achievement counts more than temporary failure.

> I flunked algebra last year because I didn't get along with the teacher who threatened to give the whole class D's and then at the last minute said he would pass certain people. I took it over again and got a B. Now I'm taking Algebra 2 and getting an A . . . I'm doing pretty well in this school. I do what's assigned . . . If you do that and listen in class you can do okay.

The students seem to learn best in total class or individualized instruction situations. Seminars and small-group work within classes are not very successful. "We forget that youngsters aren't yet responsible adults," stated one administrator. Responsibility for learning and self-direction are perhaps different from the responsibility for community affairs and political actions the students assume and execute so well. Perhaps, too, the structure of the co-curriculum clubs provides the direction a teacher or student, alone, cannot.

The students' learning is affected by their personal style, cultural background, and academic preparation. Most students are self-directed within the course structure and modular schedule. The reason for students doing poorly is most often a matter of their not organizing their time well rather than, for example, their watching too much television. Television-watching during the weekdays and even weekends seems to be curtailed by the demands of the co-curriculum, homework, hobbies, and community and church activities.

One result of the demographic shift to a majority of Asian students is a subtle mismatch between their cultural background and the Western European background of the curriculum, especially the humanities. The Asian respect for education, scholarship, intellectual activity, and artistic skills does not include experience with the Western literary heritage or language. Thus, student sensitivity to literature and language is less frequently observed than it was fifteen years ago when the student population was primarily Caucasian with both a shared Jewish and Caucasian knowledge of Western culture.

Despite the predominant respect for education, a large number of the students do not engage in reading for pleasure. Exceptions include members of the Sci-Fi Club and readers of the science fiction books stocked in the school's Book-to-Book store. An English teacher suggested:

> They're heading toward the Brave New World. When I read Hopkins' "Dear Margaret" to the students twelve years ago, it would strike a chord with half of the class. Now one or two will sit up, realizing it is "their poem." They're skilled in math and computers instead.

The products or observable results of the students' learning present a varied picture. All are not excellent, suggesting that the image of excellence rests upon the work of a minority of students, particularly those who enroll in honors and AP courses. It also suggests that the preservation or extension of academic excellence will have to come from a different interaction between the teachers and the students who are not in the honors and AP classes.

A variety of factors help to explain why more of the 3,000 students are not doing outstanding work. Some students have not had appropriate preparation in junior high; for example, not enough laboratory science or writing experience. Some, because of a different language background, cannot use English sufficiently well to grasp ideas in English literature classes. Half of the students in one basic composition class we observed had problems with the use of English.

Despite the emphasis on achievement, or perhaps because of it, there is generally no stigma attached to students seeking tutoring help. Students seek help from teachers or, more often, other students in order to understand concepts better or to work through specific assignments. Teachers will ask students to come for help before or after school or during their free mods, which coincide with the teachers' lunch or preparation periods.

There once was a formal tutoring system, but it has "broken down" with the loss of aides for the resource centers. Now, formalized tutoring is available as part of a program involving university students and student teaching assistants.

Resource centers and hallways are always crowded with students studying and helping one another. The space problem was exacerbated when the math and science resource center was closed because of the staff cuts and its materials were moved to the social science center, thereby taking up room formerly used for tutoring. A student pleaded in an editorial in *The Brette* to "replace the light bulbs [in the halls] as soon as they are burned out so that hall studiers can see well enough to read."

In the same issue, an article on the recent Brette elections referred to the tutoring situation.

> . . . academic help is available whenever Bretteites need it, which is good, because . . . students have to constantly keep up their studies in order to pass those surprise quizzes that teachers frequently give.

Of concern to some students and to the outside observer is the apparent emphasis on grades, even though co-curriculum and free-mod socialization seem to keep the students from being "egg-heads." The emphasis on grades is clearly realistic, inasmuch as the university of choice for Brette students now requires a 3.8 GPA for admission while the other public college campuses require minimums of 3.0 to 3.2.

The grading issue brings other problems. Each department computes its grade averages on the curve, including honors, AP, and regular classes. This means that students in honors and AP classes may often receive C's. When Brette students' grades are reviewed by the universities and colleges, the same criteria are applied to them as to the grades of students from less academic comprehensive high schools.

Parents are particularly anxious about grades and a number complain about the math grades—an "unrealistic" complaint according to the department. Two years ago, a parent protest succeeded in changing a teacher's manner of grading. "In the mathematics department, 50 percent would be expected to get A's and B's and 20 percent D's and F's"—leaving 30 percent at C level." One wonders if this is because of the Bell curve or actual low performance. If the students entered with high GPA's and high math scores, parents and others wondered why they should be earning low grades.

The mathematics department has the lowest GPA of all the departments. The staff tried to raise the students' mastery level recently by extending the time spent on algebra, but the attempt did not work. The staff say the parents who complain do not understand about learning math. The students say some teachers don't teach, or "don't care." "They trick you; they are burned out."

A student analyzed the learning-versus-grading problem in a recent issue of *The Brette*, claiming that the causes of the emphasis on grading include conditioning by the grading system itself, the clichés of "preparing one for getting out in the world" or "the learning experience," and the fact that "quite a few teachers have stopped teaching . . . and are instructing the students to memorize."

The emphasis on students' pursuit of grades rather than learning for its own sake, helps explain why the library is used primarily to study, why an occasional student has been tempted to bribe a TA to be guaranteed a good grade, why locker thefts rise during mid-terms and finals, why articles are cut out of reference books, why some students cheat on tests, why library books often were stolen until an electronic monitor was installed, and why the best sellers in the Book-to-Book store are study guides and SAT-related materials.

Pragmatic economic and cultural factors contribute to the emphasis on grades since many students come from families who cannot afford the cost of private or out-of-state public college education and view the grade-point average as the key to the inexpensive state system of higher education.

## Summary

The force the Brette image exerts comes from the shared goals of staff, parents, and students; the climate of safety, cooperation, and concentration; and the totality of life experienced by the students during their Brette hours. It is both an interactive and intensive intellectual oasis.

"Brette is a dream life for students," affording them a human environment in which to grow and a democratic forum in which to practice rational decision-making. Students are encouraged to run their own lives and to give service to the community.

The label of "elitism" is not accurate in the traditional sense inasmuch as one-third of the students come from lower socio-economic strata and non-Western backgrounds and a number of these students are in honors and AP classes. The issues of tracking and of homogeneous-versus-heterogeneous grouping, however, do apply to the honors and AP classes; but the groupings are not fixed nor wholly decided by teachers, and students can elect to return to regular classes. Strict tracking exists for the less able students who are not recommended for honors classes and who struggle in regular classes. These students do not seem to receive as much attention or help as the "achievers," who seek challenges. For the latter, "the sky's the limit" within Brette's current program.

Excellent as Brette's program appears to be, there are obvious gaps in computer literacy, career development, interdisciplinary humanities, and global perspectives. Scant evidence of such programs raise several questions. What preparation should the students have in order to cope with national and global issues of human survival and betterment? What critical thinking skills and conceptual understandings should they have learned when they graduate? Does the co-curriculum alone provide sufficient opportunities to develop those skills? Do all students participate fully in the co-curriculum?

Viewing the Brette program alongside its image of excellence, one begins to discern larger issues about education, learning, the organizational structure of public school systems, and the roles and responsibilities of public school staffs. Four issues emerging from the case study revolve around the external forces that are eroding school autonomy and staff capability and the internal conditions that are weakening professionalism and shared excitement about learning. They are:

- Downtown control of personnel and curriculum
- Minimal professional responsibility (or energy) for continual curriculum review and revision, and revitalization
- A pervasive emphasis on grading rather than on learning
- Minimal attention given to individual student differences (cultural, linguistic, cognitive)

Opportunities and resources to address these issues are available: community outreach, computer assisted instruction, interdisciplinary courses, team teaching, and collegial support groups among the staff. These resources can effect utilization of staff involvement in curriculum review and revitalization, a re-emphasis on learning, attention to individual student differences, and increased staff development opportunities and resources.

Offsetting the implementation of programs that could provide a positive response to these issues are real deterrents in the budget situation and the growing power of the central office. At the same time, resources lie in the staff members themselves, but greater leadership is needed to rechannel their energies toward working with the curriculum and the students to maintain the excellence for which Brette is respected and sought by students, staff, and parents.

# 13

# JENNER HIGH SCHOOL

## MARIANNE AMAREL, ANN COOK, AND HERB MACK

Jenner High is a public school that is prospering when high schools are believed to be troubled institutions. It offers a rigorous academic program with an emphasis on science and mathematics at a time when these subjects are losing ground in high school curricula. It honors diversity in a society skeptical of integration. It maintains a safe environment at a time when urban schools are often perceived as disorderly. More surprising still, the pressures of competitive entry, the exacting program, and the diversity of students has not affected the essential civility that characterizes the relations among members of the school community; there is courtesy and respect among faculty, students, administrators, and the staff who keep the enterprise going. Teachers, students, and parents share a common set of expectations. Jenner students are expected to gain admission to good colleges, and they do.

Jenner's principal helps to set the tone. While reassuring nervous freshmen that they "can make it" in the tough academic environment, he resists the more commonly heard, "You are the best and the brightest" accolades. This emphasis ultimately results in a self-confident rather than an arrogant student body. A product of the city's schools, he believes that Jenner's excellence should serve a wide range of the city's students and has initiated an Outreach Program to make less advantaged junior high school students across the city aware of the school and its course offerings. While encouraging students to achieve, he is both firm and humane, handling situations with the sort of good humor, ease, and straightforwardness that comes perhaps with the knowledge that one's school is nationally recognized and greatly admired.

## An Overview

Jenner is one of the city's three public academic high schools with selective admission. Of the 20,000 students taking the entrance exam each year, about one-third, drawn by the school's academic reputation, record of safety, free tuition, and location, designate Jenner as their first choice. Approximately 900 gain entry.

Regarded by many as elite, Jenner might be more accurately described as selective. While it does serve a bright college-oriented student body, its population is mixed ethnically, economically, and culturally. The school recruits and caters to students with specific academic aptitudes; it does not attempt to serve all who are talented, such as those gifted artistically, athletically, or mechanically. Once students are admitted, such talents as these, while admired, are not the focus of the school curriculum.

The school first opened its doors in the fall of 1938 to 300 ninth and tenth graders in an old building not far from its present site. It came into being under a mandate of the Board of Superintendents that called for the establishment of a specialized high school for academically gifted students who "shall be selected by entrance examination and survey of record based upon ability and interest in science and mathematics." The first cohort of students was all male, all white, largely Jewish, and drawn from the upwardly mobile middle-class neighborhoods surrounding the school.

Jenner counts scores of eminent scientists and mathematicians, as well as labor leaders, lawyers, and politicians among its graduates. The ultimate in recognition, the Nobel Prize, was awarded to three former students, and a Jenner math whiz became the first winner of "The $64,000 Question" TV quiz show. Such winning traditions are maintained by the present student body: Jennerites dominate the list of Westinghouse Science Prize finalists and winners; they win National Merit scholarships with predictable regularity; student publications gain special recognition frequently; the debating team captures trophies in such numbers as to create a minor storage crisis in the school.

News articles or magazine features regularly single out the school as one of the best, and single out its prize winners. Sometimes, students wistfully comment that they should have attended an academically less rigorous school so they would stand a better chance in the selection process for college admission.

Jenner enjoys a measure of continuity and stability rare among urban secondary schools. At the same time, significant changes have taken place as it has responded to, adapted to, or given in to forces impinging on it. The student body now numbers upward of 3,000; girls were first admitted in 1945 and now make up 43 percent of the student population. Today the school is 9 percent Hispanic, 13 percent Oriental, and 18 percent black. The remaining 60 percent includes sizable Jewish, Greek, Irish, and Italian contingents. About one-third of the student body qualifies for school lunch subsidies, which means the family annual income is below $11,000.

Though students living around Jenner may regard it as a neighborhood school, many others submit to arduous commutes, taking buses and subways for journeys of up to three hours a day.

There are approximately 160 faculty members. With an annual turnover of 3 percent, they contribute to the stability of the school. Once here, teachers tend to stay—having secured one of the choice placements in the city, few leave for greener pastures. No teacher in recent history has requested a transfer. The average age of the faculty is forty-two. Ninety-nine percent of the teachers hold masters' degrees; seven have Ph.D.'s.

Continuity in administrative leadership is another stabilizing influence. In its forty-four-year existence, Jenner has had three principals, all rising from the school's teaching ranks. The present head of the school first came to Jenner more than thirty years ago and chaired the biology department for a number of years.

## Students: Diversity and Quality

Reflecting on the essential ingredients of the school, the principal unhesitatingly begins with "the kids." He freely acknowledges the contributions of the students to the quality and character of Jenner. Attracting students of high caliber is, in fact, first on the list of priorities drawn up by the school, in compliance with school board requirements. Most attention focuses on Jenner's academic achievements, on the awards students win, and the colleges they will attend. Parents may send their children to Jenner because of its academic reputation and its safe environment. The children, however, leave applauding the school's ethnic and social mix. Said a Harvard freshman on a return visit:

> When I think of Jenner, more than anything I miss the diversity. . . . We had black students, Hispanics, Italians, Chinese, Koreans, Jews, Greeks, Catholics, rich, poor. . . . With the exception of one group, Jenner seemed more diverse than Harvard. At Jenner, we had no Midwesterners.

Another student commented:

> For me, what really stands out . . . has been the people. All my life I was sheltered. Up until I went to Jenner, I only knew people like myself. Here I met people I wouldn't have been friendly with, and I am glad I did. It's nice to talk to people who are from other backgrounds and see things in a totally different way.

Overall there is the impression of authentic intermingling among students.

One would not deny, however, the tendency of various groups at Jenner to hang out in ethnic or neighborhood clusters. During a visit to the cafeteria at lunchtime, one can see all-black, all-Korean, and certainly all-white tables. It's clear, too, that subgroups from particular areas of the city often hang out together because of travel patterns. In addition, students with cultural allegiances have formed clubs that meet regularly to screen films, hold discussions, or participate in planned activities. Within Jenner's pluralistic walls, however, there is virtually no evidence of overt hostility or expressions of disrespect between groups or individuals. The appreciation of differences is genuine, and individual friendships across ethnic or social class lines are not uncommon.

Significantly, the absence of visible barriers between groups extends to the academic life of the school. The assumption is that all students, by virtue of their presence, are capable of succeeding if sufficiently interested and industrious. Consequently, there is no formal tracking system at Jenner and no particular group of students is considered especially gifted or otherwise favored. A student said:

In one English class there were lots of books assigned to read. The teacher would sit in the back of the class and every now and then would ask a question. The teacher allowed the kids to talk to each other . . . let us have a free rein to learn from one another. . . . We all come from such different backgrounds that you really do learn a lot from discussions. Other kids see things so differently.

Honors and advanced placement courses exist, but not an honors group. Some students have special gifts in math, science, English, or history, yet no course or selection of courses is dominated by any special body of students. This differs dramatically from the effect honors classes have in most high schools.

The mix that exists in classrooms also dramatically affects student friendships. Noted one student with amazement:

I remember being told at freshman orientation: "You won't be friends with the people you are best friends with now." I thought that was the most absurd thing I had ever heard. I was *loyal*. I was going to be friends with the same kids I was then, until I died. Here I am a senior, and I'm not friends with the same kids at all. My friends have completely changed.

The diversity fosters a tolerance of individualism.

At Jenner . . . people can act a little odd and no one will make fun of them. . . . You can be different and be respected.

Jenner's principal shares—indeed, actively supports—that view. Calling the observer's attention to individual students on a walk through the halls, he seems to take pleasure in the students' individuality and their vitality.

One is impressed with how nice a group Jenner students are, how tolerant of eccentricity and how admiring of many members of the faculty. Said one thoughtful student, who suddenly paused while naming teachers with a good reputation, "There are just so many, it's hard to name them all."

Students seem equally supportive of one another, groaning good-naturedly when a fellow student responds incorrectly to a question and applauding when the student recovers.

Teachers, too, see Jenner students as special. Said one teacher:

I've been teaching here for twenty-seven years. There is such a richness of student background. Once I had Ring Lardner's son, and when he sent a note about the boy's absence, I kept it.

*Kevin: One Student's Story*  Kevin is one of the individuals who make Jenner distinctive. He is the only child of working-class Catholic parents. He belies the traditional expectations of a Jenner student by doing outstandingly well in English, history, and Spanish, but poorly, if not dismally, in the physical sciences and math. In the course of his four years, he never got turned on by trigonometry, physics, or chemistry, but speaks eloquently, almost reverently about the benefits of a Jenner education and of the students who go there. While he is atypical, his thoughts accurately reflect many aspects of Jenner and illustrate the effect the school has on its students.

Kevin credits the school with giving him the framework in which to grow and allowing him—indeed, expecting him—to cope with academic pressure and the impersonality of a large school. For him, the experience was "refreshing and challenging."

In turn, Kevin is a refreshing human being. Well known and well liked through the school, he is a rare combination of wit, warmth, and intelligence—a student who takes learning seriously and has a clear sense of himself and his future. Although he has always taken religion quite seriously, he never considered parochial school a serious alternative to the mixture and academic challenge he found in the public schools of his neighborhood. For him, attending Jenner was the fulfillment of a young boy's dream—not to mention that of his parents:

> I can remember from the time I could walk, my mother telling me she wanted me to go to Jenner. All my friends went there. It was expected. Of course, my mother and father were overjoyed when I was accepted.

His mother is a housewife; his father a fruit and vegetable wholesaler with a seventh-grade education.

> I can talk to my parents about anything. They have always been completely supportive of me. But when I want to talk about something academic, I go to my uncle, who is a counselor, or to my priest. He has his own library and is an extremely intelligent man.

Kevin credits Jenner with sharpening his ideas about the future.

> I thought I wanted to be a lawyer and that Jenner was the best school to challenge me intellectually. People don't just go there for science. They go there because it's a good school and because it's a safe environment.

As Kevin reflects on his four years at Jenner, he emphasizes the diversity of the student body. He believes it is the most important and single best aspect of the school.

> If I had gone to parochial school, it would have been very, very dull. Jenner is so very, very interesting . . . it's very mixed. A majority of my friends are not from my religion. They are different colors and cultures. Of my closest friends, one is a Chinese boy, who is very familiar with the punk rock clubs around the city, and a black student, who has wanted to be a doctor since seventh grade. I don't doubt that he will be.

Kevin also describes the importance of the bonding that takes place between students.

> I met my friends through classes and because of homework and tests. . . . There is a huge workload—three or four hours of homework a night— and students are very cooperative. Kids study together for tests and call each other to get help on homework. There is a great sense of camaraderie.
>
> They say we are very competitive, which is certainly true. But, it is very rare for a Jenner student not to help another student. There is a great deal of cooperation.

Kevin's comments clarify what at first appears to be a contradiction: a high degree of support and cooperation within an intensely competitive environment. He points out that while students often ask each other what they got on this or that exam, such curiosity does not imply competition between students. Rather, he insists, students compete for a grade or a score, arguing occasionally about a point or two (especially if it is a question of failing or passing), but not with one another.

> You're happy when a person gets a good mark. It's not like I got a ninety and I want everyone else to fail. I don't know anyone like that. Most people shoot for a ninety and feel happy when people do well.

For him, the basic objective of the school is clear: "The goal is for everyone to do well and go to a good college."

Like most of his classmates, Kevin had a difficult time adjusting in his freshman year. Coming from a smallish, protective junior high school, he was regarded as something special. Here, he was one of some 800 entering students, all of whom were exceptional and special. It was hard to feel at home.

> No one advised me at all at the school in terms of what to take. You're on your own, by yourself. You are left alone—sink or swim. That first year I cried sometimes.

This initial insecurity eventually gave way to confidence.

> Perhaps if the school gave too much help to the kids it might take away from the learning experience. You learn to adjust . . . to take control of the situation. Because of the size of the school and the fact that they didn't protect me, I had to use my personality combined with my skills and learn to get along.

His experience in failing trigonometry underscores this. "If you don't do well, no one is going to call you into the office. No one will make a fuss. You could fail quietly. I failed, then made the course up in summer school."

Kevin's courses over the four years emphasized the liberal arts as much as the school's program would allow:

| 1st Year | 2nd Year | 3rd Year | 4th Year |
|----------|----------|----------|----------|
| English | Honors English | Honors English | AP English |
| Introductory Science | Biology | Chemistry | Physics |
| History | History | AP History | AP History |
| Algebra | Geometry | Trigonometry | Animal Psychology |
| Spanish | Spanish | Conversational Spanish | Advanced General Art |
| Art | Mechanical Drawing | Woodshop | Gym |
| Gym | Gym | Music/Chorus | |
| | | Health | |

In addition to his academic schedule, Kevin played an active role in school activities during his four years—serving as an elected student representative and participating for one year on the school speech team ("Debating would have given me an ulcer; in speech you have to listen, not argue"). His main activity is socializing with his classmates every chance he gets.

His school day during his senior year consists of a heavy academic program (including advanced placement English and history) punctuated by free periods, when he consciously socializes with individuals from the various school cliques: the Greeks (which he describes as including Italian and Jewish students), blacks, Orientals, and the debate team.

Once the regularly scheduled school day is over, he leaves immediately for his neighborhood, where he spends several hours at his parish church. One afternoon a week he does volunteer work at the local nursing home, visiting with an 84-year-old Hungarian. ("He and I have long talks; he's very knowledgeable.")

Kevin is deeply religious and extremely active in church affairs. He is a lector—he reads the scripture to the congregation at Mass—and is the youngest member on the spiritual development committee and the liturgical committee at the church. His entire neighborhood belongs to the church and he feels very much part of his community. In the last four years, he has taught himself Latin and, through outside reading, has become versed in canon law and church history.

> I plan to attend [a particular Catholic college] because I want to stay in my diocese. After that I will go to Columbia to study philosophy and then enter the seminary.

This commitment to religion extends to his schoolwork. "I always bring everything on to my home ground," he says, pointing out that his senior English term paper compares the Gospel of St. Matthew in terms of structure and spirituality to the Gospel of St. John.

Predictably, his closest relationships with faculty tie in with his commitment to religious philosophy. He is particularly friendly with his homeroom teacher—an Orthodox rabbi with whom he discusses the Talmud and the Torah ("I give him stuff to read")—and his Spanish teacher, a devout Greek Orthodox woman with whom he discusses church liturgy and ritual. Over all, he has had several very good teachers, a few that are outstanding, and two that were terrible. "They came to class unprepared."

The school, he concludes, "prepared me for life."

## The Intellectual Challenge: The Course of Study

*Jenner is education. It is synonymous with excellence.*
—A Senior

The experience of attending Jenner does, as one would expect, have a significant intellectual effect on students. For three or four years they are part of an environment in which expectations are high and pressure intense. They are offered courses as diverse as Russian, constitutional law, probability and statistics, college level biology, forensics, and women's literature. They can join an award-winning debate team or a laser club, contribute to a holocaust center and a biology journal, tutor high school students in marine biology, build a telescope, and play on a winning tennis team. They can study with teachers who went to the school themselves, taught Nobel laureates, and qualify as Orthodox rabbis. They take courses with teachers who make such comments as, "Most important is the challenge of teaching students who are as bright or brighter than I am." For the most part, the students are aware of the heady atmosphere and are affected by it. Some see it as having already had a real impact on their lives.

> A lot of things were opened up for me that I wouldn't have known about at the local high school. Math, biology, English, and constitutional law were great. I'm certainly a much different person than I was three years ago.

> In AP biology we really delve into the subject . . . because we're interested in it. The teacher doesn't teach to get the course material done; he'll teach something that we don't have to know because it's interesting. He'll bring up questions that will make you stop and think. . . . It's exciting.

Of course, the reverse is also true: the fact that everyone in Jenner had to qualify on a written exam leads to a great deal of anxiety on the part of entering students. Said one senior, "When I first got to Jenner I was so worried. . . . I was sure the other kids were all going to be geniuses. I was going to sit in class and they were going to have to institutionalize me because I was so dumb." Another commented, "I was so scared my freshman year. . . . I expected the kids to have computers and pencils behind their ears, to whip them out and take down notes." Jenner's principal is well aware of the school's reputation and its effect on students. Each year he spends the first semester making the rounds of the freshman homeroom classes. In each class he tells the students, "You got into Jenner because you're bright. You wouldn't be here if you weren't. You can make it and you will."

Students may not initially believe this, but over the years the message seems to sink in. Almost all entering students graduate and enter college. For a variety of reasons, the central one being physical relocation of families, approximately 150 students each year leave the school without graduating. These students transfer to other schools and continue their education.

Now, as in the past, students come to Jenner expecting a rigorous curriculum. The formal course requirements have hardly changed at all in the school's forty-four-year history. Now, as before, students are required to take five major subjects each semester. Many take more. The curriculum consists of four years of science, English, and social studies, and three years of mathematics and a foreign language. In addition, one year of mechanical drawing and one-half year of science techniques lab, as well as courses in music, art, health, and physical education must be taken.

An array of elective courses deepen and broaden the core curriculum. Students are required to choose two additional courses from the science and math electives: offerings that range from traditional fourth-year calculus and advanced general physics to newer courses in the faculty repertoire, such as field biology, urban ecology and laser optics. There has been a dramatic increase in the number of advanced placement (AP) exams taken. In 1961, students took 179 AP exams in five subject areas. Today that number has swelled to 700 exams in thirteen subject areas.

All in all, 124 different courses are offered for the current school year. Seniors alone have 25 electives to choose from. A little less than half of all courses offered in the school are in the sciences (biology, physics, chemistry) and mathematics, confirming the continuing emphasis on the subjects that are integral to the school's identity.

The pace at Jenner is intense. A routine school day, subdivided into nine periods, begins at 8:40 and ends at 3:15 P.M. Optional courses, including some of the honors courses, are offered during an unofficial tenth period. A typical class is forty minutes long, a unit of time that appears rather short to an observer impressed by the potential of the students for sustained and probing inquiry.

A lesson often unfolds in the following way: the teacher comes to class prepared with a rather specific aim or theme, which my be written on the board or identified by the teacher as required by the central board. Frequently, a textbook chapter or some other reading serves to focus the theme and provides the base of information for class discussion. After briefly introducing the topic, a teacher-guided discussion ensues, usually with active student participation.

Teachers skilled in orchestrating the forty-minute period conduct the class discussions to focus on two or three major points and move to closure in time for a brief recapitulation before the bell signals the end of the period. The four-minute allotment for getting from one class to the next does not encourage lingering or even completing thoughts in progress; many classes thus end abruptly.

There are exceptions to the single period class, mostly in science labs where double and, occasionally, even triple periods are scheduled to accommodate an experiment. While the laboratory period differed markedly from a class discussion, there were elements common to both. In each case, students were guided through a well-structured experience in which active participation was fostered not so much to explore alternative interpretations or solutions but more in the belief that active engagement on the part of students facilitates learning.

As at any school, the quality of teaching at Jenner varies considerably from classroom to classroom. One student described the variation this way:

> I had one history class in which the teacher relied completely on mimeographed sheets that students had to go over every class period. They were certainly a lot of work, but also quite boring. On the other hand, I took honors biology in which the teacher challenged us to think through problems and approaches to solving problems.

In addition to honors biology, this student mentioned honors chemistry, history (economics), and calculus, particularly, as challenging courses that made her think. Over her four years, she took several "special" courses because: "For the most part, I think I did have the better teachers in the honors courses."

If the honors courses *were* better for reasons cited by the student, this would appear to seriously undercut the principal's stated intention to expose Jenner's youngest students to the most inspiring faculty. It could even be regarded by some as a violation of the union contract, which provides for a rotation system for particular teaching assignments. Something else appears to be at work, for, in general, when one looks at the curriculum, sits in classes, and talks to students, teachers, and administrators about Jenner's courses, what emerges is the realization that the "best" and "most exciting" courses offered are those that benefit from some sort of *specialness*, where new ideas, materials or teachers' interests and abilities figure heavily in the development of the course curriculum.

For examples: the English elective that is taught with a forensic emphasis. In this course the required Shakespeare play was analyzed as student debate teams argued the question, Resolved That John Would Be a Better Heir Apparent Than Hal; the constitutional law class, where American jurisprudence came alive in a mock trial courtroom session focusing on constitutional guarantees and the rights of the individual; the honors biology course, where students discussed recent discoveries; the statistics and logic course, where students dealt with philosophy and mathematics. These were courses where a faculty member's interest in a topic allowed for, indeed fostered, breadth and excitement.

Conversely, courses that came in for the heaviest criticism appeared to be those at the introductory or beginning level, to which teachers are assigned and are required by the board to teach a more narrowly prescribed curriculum. Teachers don't relish such courses; students find them tedious and uninspired.

Some students draw a distinction between courses that are hard work and those that are challenging. Many students spend an average of three or four hours a night preparing for classes and studying for tests.

The heavy workload seems to serve an important function, underscoring the school's mission to outsiders: in this school, kids don't play around, they work. They work hard. In some significant way, the homework, the tests, and the grades uphold the tradition of the school as a place for the serious college-bound student.

Over time, the students seem to learn how to study, how to marshall their time, and how to cope with teachers whose style and demands vary enormously. A student's testimony:

> I found I wanted to do the work for a lot of the courses I had. This semester is my last, and I thought I could relax, but here I am, after midterms, still staying up late and studying. You know, if the teachers really care and want you to learn, you just want to do it.

One major complaint expressed by students concerned the emphasis on tests and grades, rather than on discussion and writing. For example:

> My main criticism of Jenner is that there isn't enough free exchange in classes. Everything is oriented toward grades and tests and not toward learning, which is what you should go to school for. Probably I'm in the minority on this. For most kids, grades are all they know. That's how they got into the school; they worked and worked. The more they work, the better grades they get. I'd like to see more emphasis on writing.

This criticism is echoed by many students as well as by parents and faculty. Teachers think students do not write as well as they should; old-timers deplore what they regard as a decline in writing skills and say it's possible to graduate without ever having done a "proper research paper." Students hold the faculty responsible; faculty blame the elementary schools and television for the decline in standards. Many suggest that the number of students per class and the class load of each English and social studies teacher often precludes the assignment of a sufficient number of papers because so much time is required to properly mark and comment on each one. Others complain that an overreliance on source materials makes it difficult for faculty to be as critical as they feel is necessary.

Some English teachers feel that when colleagues do assign papers they aren't tough enough markers. They say they often find themselves having to explain to a student why they consistently give marks in the 80s while another teacher, just as consistently, grades the same student's paper in the 90s. Some faculty use new techniques to improve writing skills. One individual teaches students specific criteria for literary criticism, then has students exchange papers with classmates for comments and suggestions. In this class, students are graded on their ability to raise appropriate questions and provide helpful criticism to their peers as well as on their skill in writing their own papers.

Whether students get practice in writing a careful research paper appears to depend on the particular faculty member to whom a student is assigned.

*Electives*  A number of students also raised the issue of electives. Many would agree that ". . . there are too many required courses at Jenner and not enough time to take electives. . . . Students here need more opportunities to try things out."

While there appears to be a wide range of subject choices, they are perhaps more accurately viewed as subject area alternatives, offering, as they do, a choice *within* required subject disciplines. Thus, students taking the required senior social studies course can, in their last semester, pursue some of the following topics in depth:

The Holocaust in History
Contemporary America
Sociology
The Legacy of the Ancient World
Psychology and History
Introduction to Constitutional Law
Asian Studies

In deference to its science reputation, most students at Jenner take their additional major in either science or math, where most of the truly "elective courses" are offered. These include:

Microbiology
Physiology
Field Biology
Marine Biology
Nutritional Science
Animal Behavior and Human Psychology
Advanced Placement Biology
History and Development of Science
Astronomy-Astrophysics
Geology, Meteorology, and Geography
Urban Ecology

Plant Physiology and Horticulture
Human Genetics and Evolution
Energy Sources and the Environment
Logic, Probability and Theory of Equation
Probability and Statistical Inferences

The traditional course structure is extended by special programs such as the Model Program for Developing Creativity in Science, which originated in the biology department and now includes the physical and social sciences as well. A program of independent study, it offers honors courses and research opportunities for eighty students selected from the incoming pool of 700 ninth graders. The students are selected on the basis of grades and teacher judgment, and are committed to an additional three hours of class time a week.

The program has high visibility. Projects developed by students in this program regularly capture prizes that keep the school in the limelight.

Another program, begun in the biology department when the present principal was chairperson, is the Outreach Program. It is designed to increase the number of applicants from disadvantaged junior high schools. The program began in 1976, when a link was made with a particular school in the city's most impoverished neighborhood.

Groups of thirty students from this district visited Jenner once a week for a seven-week cycle, and worked with ten seniors in the school's laboratory. The program has expanded considerably both in size and scope—five districts within the city now participate, with 800 students attending. Each of the districts is required to provide funds for a Jenner teacher, who serves as a trainer to teachers in the local districts and works with the students who come to Jenner.

The number of students from disadvantaged schools who have taken the entrance exam has increased, and the participating teachers report positively on their joint experiences. Although the program is likely to continue, its funding base is unstable, depending, as it does, on the resources of the participating districts.

Questions arise about the weight and value Jenner gives to science and mathematics. The school's commitment to the sciences is clear; nearly half of the course offerings are devoted to these subjects. Yet a goodly portion of students have no special interest or aptitude for the sciences, having been drawn to the school for its general academic

excellence. The chair of natural sciences estimates that about 40 percent of the students enter with a stated interest in the sciences, and
about as many of the graduating class intend to pursue a career in
science.

For the school as a whole, the curriculum is largely guided by college
requirements; program planning for individual students anticipates
that prospective environment. The transition from high school to
university, particularly for the top layer of students, is regarded more
as a gradual process than as a break with Jenner. The transition is
eased, or hastened, by the large number of AP courses. (Even though
students are restricted to taking only two at a time, the stricture is not
enforced.) The independent study program permits students to take
courses in nearby colleges or participate in research projects at some
of the city's institutes and universities.

In a similar vein, an item in the program planning guide for juniors
anticipates the students' college careers:

> To prepare students to meet college language requirements and cope ad-
> equately with college language placement tests, language study is recom-
> mended through the junior year. This means that students completing
> Level 3 of language at the end of the sophomore year will automatically
> be programmed to Level 4 of language unless they make other arrange-
> ments with their grade advisor. A signed letter from your parents with a
> list of 3 possible electives to replace the language course must be submitted.

## Student Activities

Central as it is, the formal curriculum does not fully describe life at
Jenner. Student activities add much to the character of the program.
By one count, there are some sixty-four clubs, squads, teams, and
student organizations. There is an astronomy club, an Asian society,
a Latin cultural society, a West Indian club, and an Irish society. There
are debate, math, swimming, gymnastics, handball, track and field
teams. Students can join a frisbee team, photo squad, Arista (honors
society) and elementary physics prep. They edit twelve publications
including the newspaper, biology journal, feminist publication (*Free
to Be She*) a social studies journal, and a math journal. Some students
belong to five or more groups.

Since the central board first eliminated then restored funds for activities at absurdly low pre-inflation levels, much energy is spent on fund raising. Advertisements fill the school bulletin boards and fund-raising drives to benefit one or another activity seem to be constantly underway. According to students and faculty sponsors alike, without the money raised from the sales of food, T-shirts, and popcorn jars, there would be no school newspaper, debate team, or Outreach Program by the video club to name a few.

As one member of the student newspaper staff, giving us a lesson in elementary economics, pointed out:

> A bagel sale is worth fifty dollars. You need twelve bagel sales for one issue of the paper. If you put out an "Extra" you need an additional bagel sale. You know, we'd do better if we sold donuts, instead of bagels.

Yet, with all this, students say the school lacks spirit: "At Jenner there is no school spirit. . . . Zero"; "I miss a football team [the school fields a team in every major sport except football], cheerleaders, and Saturday games. I may find out in college that I really dislike all that rah-rah stuff, but it is something I've missed at Jenner." Other students offer a different analysis. For example: "People say the school is apathetic, but the school spirit at Jenner is in the camaraderie."

To some extent, the enthusiasm associated with "school spirit" is dampened by the location of the school. Some students must leave their homes at 6:15 A.M. to make the first class at 8:30 A.M. It is not only difficult to schedule activities before school, security curtails the day at the other end; many parents are concerned about their children getting home after dark. And students who use chartered buses are locked into their schedules, effectively eliminating after-school activities.

Even so, there are students who do stay late and who find time during the day (many giving up their lunch periods) to join activities and service squads throughout the school. According to the principal, the library could not function as well as it does without its 200 student volunteers, nor could the student tutoring service, in which students help one another in course work.

Still, the lack of focus on a key activity, on a team, dramatic production, or musical event does raise some perplexing questions. Why do students join so many activities and yet feel unfulfilled? The answer may have something to do with why students join in the first place.

There seems to be general acceptance of the idea that the more activities you join, the better it looks on your college application. A student said: "You hear a lot about colleges looking for good students who are well rounded. Here you get the idea that it's important to join activities in order to show colleges that you're interested in something besides grades." One Korean student described how more experienced Korean students exerted a powerful influence on their younger cousins, advising them which activities to become involved in: "Don't join the basketball squad if you want to get into Harvard. Sign up for some extracurricular activities—take honors math. . . ." This student worried about his decision to join the soccer club, fearing that, although he enjoys the game, it will take too much time away from his studies and won't be helpful when he applies for college.

## Counseling

Counseling at Jenner is seriously affected by the central board's personnel allotment. The systemwide distribution formula does little to recognize differences among the various city schools. The department is strained to serve the large numbers of college-bound students, to deal with admissions, and to handle the routine emergencies that inevitably arise. Although advising students about their programs and supporting those who are encountering pressures either in or outside school are viewed as important, these areas do suffer. The counselors are unable to fully support all the activities they, themselves, recognize as important. Students reported difficulty in such areas as getting letters of recommendation for special programs from faculty already overburdened with such requests from seniors applying to college.

In a school that stresses academics and uses personnel units to do so, that has almost all of its students applying for college; that has a high daily attendance rate, and is faced with an admissions policy that requires considerable expenditure of time, there are severe coverage problems.

The board has recognized the problem by granting some additional personnel units. Nevertheless, in the face of tight budgets, there have been compromises, and counseling has been one of the areas affected. Often the principal is used as an appeals court. Students and parents come to him if their direct efforts with the counseling staff founder.

He is accessible, his advice sensible, and he is generally able to suggest a useful alternative course of action for the student to pursue.

There are also examples of students relying on each other. More than 300 students at Jenner are tutored by their classmates. This service is organized on a department-by-department basis. The counseling department is not involved. Students also draw support and helpful advice from parents of fellow students who seem particularly informed and caring.

Though Jenner is free of the most oppressive problems afflicting urban schools, in one area it is not fully immune to contemporary ills. A drug support center with a full-time staff member funded by state substance-abuse funds, exists. At a meeting at the center we observed several troubled youngsters who are struggling with drug-related problems. For some of these students, the school is an anchor in an otherwise unstable existence; for others, the school seems to have precipitated varying degrees of difficulties, even crises. The center offers a supportive nonteaching atmosphere in which group sessions allow students to air their feelings.

Some departments discuss the primacy of science at Jenner but accept its encroachment on scheduling and resources philosophically. The chairman of industrial arts (a department which contains music, art, mechanical drawing, science techniques lab, and architectural drawing) sees a slow, but steady growth in the strength of his department through the introduction of one of the few nonscience electives (telescope making) into the curriculum of the school.

Members of the physical education department often feel they receive little recognition from either faculty or administration. As one student pointed out: "The fact that our tennis team won the citywide high school championship last year seems to have gone largely unnoticed; that's never the case with the debaters."

With the exception of a few schoolwide committees, faculty at Jenner have little opportunity to work interdepartmentally. Only in the physics department, where the chairman encouraged the staff to use the sophisticated computer equipment for all subject areas, and in video-English, where the students and their teacher made a videotape advertising the electives available to seniors, were any attempts being made to initiate exchange between departments.

## Safety

Interviews with students and parents (as well as reports from the administration regarding recruitment meetings) indicate that safety is one of the most critical factors influencing school selection.

Ensuring the students' safe arrival requires effort and expense. Some parents pay up to $5.00 a day for chartered buses to transport their children to and from school. The school administrators are in frequent communication with the local police precinct—to report disturbances or to negotiate for a mobile unit to patrol the area adjacent to the school. Every attempt is made to keep the students inside the school once they arrive. An advisory committee composed of students, faculty, parents, and administration endorsed, then lobbied for, the installation of an innovative lunch program so that students would not leave the building for the neighborhood candy store and food-vending vans parked on the street.

Inside the school, a security force of eight uniformed guards patrol the halls with walkie-talkies. Another guard is always on duty at the main entrance to the school.

As recently as last year there was frequent friction between the officers and the students. The hiring of an entirely new security staff seems to have eliminated the problem. Efforts by the principal to convince the new guards that the students are "nice, decent kids— people like you," have paid off. From all accounts, most problems come from outsiders who occasionally try to enter the building.

## Free Tuition

Another factor in the choice of a school is cost. The fact that Jenner is free, and is seen as outstanding academically and safe, as well, allows it to attract significant numbers of students from private schools into the public sector. This year 30 percent of the school's entering class was drawn from private schools; 20 percent of the entering class came from parochial schools in the city.

## The Faculty

The career path of the Jenner faculty is determined by the structural constraints of their profession. There are no formalized distinctions among teachers; the salary scale and advancement on that ladder are negotiated through collective bargaining. In large part, major and optional assignments are procedurally determined by contract. Moon- or day-lighting is common among the faculty; as many as half may be supplementing their income with additional work. Some of the jobs are related to teaching; others are not.

Teachers do have the opportunity, if not the likelihood, of moving into administrative responsibilities; department chairs rise from the ranks and balance teaching with administrative responsibilities. They assume the title of Assistant Principal and hold the post with tenure.

The faculty with a long history at Jenner will occasionally lament the passing of a golden era and comment on the generally lower level of preparation among students today. Said one, "The kids are just as smart as they were when I started teaching here years ago; they just haven't read as much." Significantly, no faculty member ever suggested that expectations had been lowered to meet the altered composition of the student body. Rather, what some perceived as a shift in literary sophistication or ability to articulate opinions was attributed to a broader pattern—a sign of the times.

If some veteran teachers indulge in nostalgia, the younger teachers' impressions are still fresh; they detail the many ways Jenner is unique among city high schools. Overall, the faculty look on the students with fondness and respect. A teacher, who is regarded as "tough, but good" by students, said: "Teaching at Jenner is a humbling experience." Most faculty will say it is the students who make Jenner what it is— their ability, industry, and interests distinguish the school from its counterparts. Accordingly, the faculty expects a high standard of work.

Though there is a good deal of informal discussion and sharing of anecdotes over coffee in the teachers' lunchroom, such relationships are largely personal. There appears to be little collaboration between departments. To some extent, this distancing is a result of size and time. Departments at Jenner have enough difficulty finding time to meet and plan as units, without attempting to engage in interdepartmental exchange. However, there may be more to the problem than such surface explanations would indicate.

Nonscience departments recognize, though not happily, the school's emphasis on the sciences. The chair of English describes his situation as "the tail that does not wag the dog," and contends that the resource distribution in the school favors the sciences, by both the smaller number of students and the flexibility of the multiple laboratory periods. The comparative similarity with secondary-school science scheduling across the country notwithstanding, he argues that a much higher density prevails in the advanced English class, which must be contained within the daily single period, and he regards these classes as analogous in educational significance to the lab classes.

As to their own contributions to the educational life of the school, the faculty emphasize their command of their disciplines. For some, expertise in subject matter may eclipse teaching skills in perceived importance.

While almost all the faculty seem invested in teaching, and some teachers are clearly esteemed for the quality of their craft, regularly evoking their colleagues' recognition as "great teacher," few can point to any particular experience, available or desired, that would enhance the quality of their teaching. They talk of keeping up with the field by reading. A few talk about the importance of personal renewal through something other than teaching. Few profess to have benefited from more institutionalized forms of in-service experience. Overall, one gets the impression that Jenner faculty do not regard the enterprise of teaching as an ongoing concern; the craft of teaching is secondary to knowledge of the subject area. This becomes a problem when changes in the patterns of instruction are proposed.

## The Question of Change

The quality of instruction at Jenner and the pedagogical values that guide teaching practices are of paramount concern to the principal. A man who spent twenty-five years in the classroom, he has not shed his primary identity as a teacher and brings strong convictions about teaching to his administrative role. At the first meeting with the study team he stated:

> I have a dream for the school and for what goes on in the classroom. I'd like every teacher to focus on problem solving, to make the process of learning, not factual recall, the center of instruction. I'd like us to challenge our students to think.

| | YEARS |
|---|---|
| *Average length of service in the school* | 10 |
| *Age groups* | |
| 21–30 | 11 |
| 31–40 | 25 |
| 41–50 | 82 |
| 51–60 | 33 |
| 61 and over | 9 |
| *Distribution by subject* | |
| Biology | 18 |
| English | 22 |
| Foreign language | 15 |
| Health education | 11 |
| Industrial arts | 8 |
| Fine arts | 3 |
| Mathematics | 22 |
| Music | 3 |
| Physical science | 20 |
| Social studies | 23 |
| Drug specialist | 1 |
| *Number residing in the city* | 90 |

His approach pivots on the belief that the active involvement of students in their own learning and the cultivation of an inquiring posture are the primary aims of teaching.

Implicit in his approach to education are an emphasis on the capacity to formulate problems as well as to work through and resolve them and an appreciation that there are a variety of ways to solve a problem or reach a solution. The principal regards the independent studies courses in biology as prototypical problem-solving classes. In these courses, students either work on independent projects within the school building, utilizing labs, woodworking shops, and the library, or find an outside placement in a hospital research laboratory, scientific institution, or university setting. The school assists in helping students find an appropriate setting. The school's high percentage of science award winners are drawn from this group of project students.

In classrooms, however, problem solving is both a controversial and difficult goal to attain. It requires commitment to process—an emphasis with which most faculty are often unfamiliar. Said one student:

> Jenner has a big emphasis on taking tests and in-class examinations. You can have three exams in one week. . . . There are too many tests.
>
> Some teachers will put stuff on the board and, five minutes before the bell, they'll say, "Copy this stuff down and memorize it." That's not teaching or explaining it.

Students say that the tests force students to overemphasize rote learning: "People at Jenner are just so conditioned to sit down and memorize . . . that's what's so bad about all the tests. You're not doing it because you know you're going to get something out of it." Having faced objective exams at every step of their own education, the teachers frequently question the value of a slower-moving problem-solving approach, where depth sometimes replaces breadth and handling ambiguity causes anxiety. Said one teacher: "In preparing the midterms, only ten percent of the questions require a problem-solving approach. This gives the kids a feeling those skills aren't so important." On one level, there seems to be a conflict between achievement and learning, between test-taking, teaching to the test, and reasoning. As one student explained: "There's such an emphasis on learning for tests. I would prefer to learn to know something."

While teachers who concentrate on factual recall can usually anticipate conclusions students will reach, students who are required to identify problems, research the literature, frame hypotheses, and draw supportable conclusions may not produce such predictable results.

As the principal has attempted to expose teachers to inquiry-learning, he has respected the formal channels available to him. "I work through my chairmen," he says. "They are the educational leaders and they work with their staffs as colleagues."

The principal also uses cabinet meetings and teacher observations to achieve change. He encourages chairpersons to utilize departmental meetings, their own supervisory observations, and the daily give and take in the departmental offices to support his effort. This approach encounters many obstacles.

Cabinet meetings, consisting of the principal, two assistant principals, and the eight department chairpersons, are held every two or three weeks. In one meeting we observed, chairpersons were requested to ask for volunteers willing to videotape their classes with a view to improving instruction. This approach is being pursued, but has been met with limited response.

In addition to the cabinet meetings, departmental meetings are held on a monthly basis. However, a central office directive regarding the uses of instructional time has resulted in the curtailment of any activities interfering with instruction, including meetings. Since Jenner operates on a nine-period day, some teachers are scheduled periods one through eight and others, two through nine. There is no forty-five-minute period during which all teachers are available at the same time *without* disrupting instructional time. Some of the teachers in a given department attend the meeting ninth period, the others attend tenth. This poses a serious problem to department chairpersons as they attempt to work with members of their departments to achieve educational change.

Having noted this external weakness, the departmental meeting format still seems limited as a vehicle for instituting significant change. The meetings occur once a month, and by contract, are very brief. They occur when teachers are tired, having spent the day teaching.

But even with these shortcomings, the departmental meetings observed at Jenner were substantive, dealing for the most part with curricular problems. In fact, several centered upon the attempt to broaden the problem-solving emphasis in the school. It was unclear, however, whether this focus would have the desired impact.

At one departmental meeting, the chairperson described a model problem-solving classroom session. Practical teaching devices to raise questions and encourage students to think and to speculate were placed in a theoretical (Piagetian) framework. There was confusion: was problem solving a teaching device or a learning process? Some regarded it as a classroom technique designed to increase student participation. Viewed as such, some insisted that using the technique slowed down progress because, in class recitation, five or six alternatives have to be listed on the board in advance, and, as one teacher said, "You give the students a hint which is the one you want." Many teachers did not see inquiry as being open-ended. For example, one said,

> You have a direction you want to go. You act neutral, and then with your questions you get the answer you want from the students. The student who gets the right answer gets extra gratification and the others have participated. It gets the kids to respond who wouldn't otherwise.

This understanding bears little resemblance to the process articulated by the principal. It appears as if the essence of what the principal means gets distorted as it moves from level to level within the school.

In addition to the monthly departmental meetings, curricular change is consciously fostered through formal supervisory observations and informal discussions between supervisory staff and teachers. Classroom observations are conducted according to a formula suggested by the central board. The numbers of observations recommended are related to the experience of the teacher. Teachers are observed by either the principal or department chairperson as many as six separate times during a single school year. Observations are followed by teacher-supervisor conferences in which a discussion of the lesson takes place. The written report is based upon a post-observation conference. The teacher is given a copy of the report and the report is filed in the teacher's permanent folder.

In practice, formal observations do not seem the most fertile ground for training. Teachers observed were nervous both during class observations and follow-up sessions. When asked why the students didn't participate more fully, one teacher told her supervisor, "You were there. I wanted things to move faster. I didn't want to get bogged down. Usually, there is more give and take."

Specific questions in the post-observation sessions tended to be probing:

> Why did you start the lesson where you did?
> What would you have changed?
> In terms of efficiency, how do you feel you did?
> How can you get the students to step back and spot a pattern to the work they are doing?
> How did you know the class understood what you were doing?

The supervisor's comments often attempted to push the teacher to involve students in the thinking process:

> You don't need to be the font of knowledge; the students can understand that you're learning together.
> When a kid asks you a question you don't have to answer. You can say, "That's a good question, what's the answer?" and others can help out.
> If the students summarize at various points it may take longer but they understand better.

In the follow-up session with the supervisor, there was considerable hesitation to engage in self-criticism. There was little response to standard opening questions: "How did you feel about the class?" "How did you like it?" Teachers seemed to feel that admitting weaknesses to a supervisor in a formal conference was not the same as considering a problem with someone in an advisory role. A discussion of weaknesses or problems might lead to critical comments being placed in a permanent folder with no recourse for appeal. There wasn't the give-and-take one would expect to be part of an effective training process, where a master teacher develops the resources of a less-experienced colleague.

What is also true, however, is that there are exceptions, that in some cases, a supervisor can prove an effective catalyst for prodding an individual to make changes over time. It is equally true that few people, in any field, can alter their working style easily. It is unrealistic to expect teachers to successfully restructure their approach over-night, although the slowness of the process often proves frustrating to those encouraging it.

Further, in a school that recognizes the importance of high college-board scores and has many students whose sights are set on National Merit scholarships, the move to problem solving is especially difficult. The factual nature of the various examinations makes this so.

Teachers did mention support they had received from other teachers or from administrators. Supervisors seem to agree that the two most effective ways to contact teachers are by responding to specific problems brought to them by teachers and by unscheduled exchanges in the corridors or in departmental offices.

In general, one gets the impression that Jenner teachers regard themselves as experienced and competent. They are not, for the most part, anxious to make major changes. Despite all the difficulties in bringing about instructional change, the principal seems quite determined to move ahead with inquiry-teaching, conducting exemplary demonstration lessons for various audiences.

As biology chairperson, he helped to establish the three-year sequence to develop creativity in science. As principal, he has supported the establishment of similar courses in the physical sciences, and at present he is helping the social science department initiate a project-style class. There are now upwards of 300 students involved in these classes. And the fact that the staff is aware of his position means that problem solving (inquiry-learning) has been granted a legitimacy that allows, even encourages, some teachers to move in that direction.

In some classes, teachers encourage students to think, even if only within a narrowly defined task. Some faculty tried to encourage an open-ended discussion but allowed for little complexity to develop. Others, who stressed their support for a problem-solving approach, voiced concern about the time taken from "covering the curriculum." One observed, "There are issues the students must face, and you have a lot of ground to cover, but . . . the process is important." A few teachers went further, encouraging students to use primary source material, to compare, make judgments about and offer evidence to support the conclusions they reach. While in one setting the students' efforts seemed strained and awkward, the teachers argued that, over time, the students would meet the challenge: "There's not so much pressure to rush with our kids. We've got four full years to get through to them. A nice thing is that they appreciate the effort a teacher makes."

It seems clear that although many teachers say they accept, even use, a problem-solving approach to teaching, their understanding and technique vary considerably. While theoretical support for the principal's position is evident throughout the school, its practical application requires continued dialogue and direction. The principal appears to realize this; he seems prepared for a long-term effort.

### External Influences: Central Control vs. Local Autonomy

That there has been any movement toward pedagogical change comes as something of a surprise to the observer of this immense urban bureaucracy. There are enormous systemic constraints to overcome. An enveloping bureaucracy is the iron fist in the paper glove; memoranda are its hallmark. Daily, the school and its administration face a massive volume of generally unimaginative, arguably unnecessary, and often barely literate directives issued from central board headquarters. In addition, there is a union contract, which frequently seems to severely limit thoughtful planning and support options.

Unlike the city's primary schools, which are organized within a number of decentralized districts, the secondary schools are centrally governed by the Division of High Schools of the Board of Education.

There are actually five separate administrative layers above the building principal, each a source of directives. In the course of one school year, an estimated forty-five pounds of documents came into the school. A count of the concerns addressed in the memoranda from just one source during a one-month period added up to thirty-seven different topics.

Typically, the policies and regulations emanating from the central administration are designed to apply across all of the city's high schools. Given the diversity within the system, the application of this governance principle proves problematic to a school that so sharply deviates from the modal city high school. Even policies that are intended to provide room for local decisions appear, on closer look, to be highly constraining. A telling illustration is the budgeting process. Budgets for each school are arrived at by a complex formula based on tax levies, and are provided in the form of staff units rather than funds. The units are converted by the principal into specific positions, with each classification having a certain unit value, permitting a degree of discretion in the pattern of faculty and staff allocations. This leeway, however, proves to be circumscribed by such contractual obligations as limits on class size, hours of instructional time per teacher, and state and board mandates. Nevertheless, the circumstances of individual schools are sufficiently different to result in differentiated staffing patterns. At Jenner, for example, about 80 percent of the budgeted units—the second highest in the city—are allocated to instructional positions. The average for the city high schools is 73 percent with a low of 63 percent.

Uniform policies for all schools can be inappropriate, and, occasionally, have paradoxical effects. The formula budgeting, the principal claims, works to the disadvantage of schools like Jenner, where attendance is high, library and other facilities are intensely used, and the load on counseling services is heavy because of a wholly college-bound graduating class. The school is ineligible for Title I or other compensatory funds, with the result that allocations per student are smaller than in schools where these conditions do not hold. In an effort to respond to the need for funds beyond those allocated in the board's budget, Jenner's principal recently created a tax-exempt educational foundation, tapping many of the school's illustrious and well-connected alumni. Although in its infancy, supporters hope that the effort will provide a valuable source of funding for selected school needs. Specifically, the foundation seeks to raise money for the debate and speech program (involving over 100 students in after-school forensics activities and budgeted at $50,000), the Holocaust Studies Center, a resource center open to the public and tied to the Holocaust elective in social studies, the upgrading of the school library facilities (normally funded by the board at $2.69 per student and serving some 1,000 students per day), and the continuation of the independent research programs, through which more than 200 juniors at the school work on independent research projects in biology, chemistry, physics, and mathematics.

The effort and time spent on the development of this foundation underscore the concern with which the school's administration regards the school budget formulas, which make no special allowances available to the school. To some extent, the foundation also speaks to the changing role of parents in school affairs. In the past, parents visited, organized, and ran fund-raising events during school hours. Today, there are more single-parent families and more working mothers, meaning fewer participants in volunteer activities. In general, today's parents tend to be more distant from the school, which adds additional burdens to the principal's responsibilities. At times, these externally determined burdens are relatively manageable. Some of the mandated procedures have no serious consequences beyond their nuisance value. The elaborate attendance reports, and the requested plans for reducing absenteeism, for example, are simply irrelevant to a school where attendance is consistently high. Other edicts, however, have more deleterious effects. The directive to maximize instruction time, a reasonable policy on the face of it, has interfered with the longstanding practice at Jenner to administer uniform exams, for it does not categorize time used for examinations as instruction time. Faculty, however, consider the tests, designed by the various departments, as instructionally valuable. They provide an occasion for monitoring the curriculum by members of departments, and are regarded necessary for maintaining the school's high standards. The directive thus effectively usurps the faculty's judgment on those issues. The policy was fought and ultimately defeated, but not without cost.

The directive, in fact, has a ripple effect on local administrative discretion to run the school. Many other activities besides direct instruction are involved, and the best judgment about educational value of such activities is unlikely to be made by administrators quite distant from the particular circumstances of each school. Planning and implementing staff development, informing students of special programs, communal activities, and more may be inhibited by the literal enforcement of such an edict.

A more recent example of a demand that, despite the considerable effort it required, brought minimal benefits to the faculty or the students was the preparation of minutely detailed course descriptions. It was yet another exercise that may be selectively productive for faculty who need to think through their purposes and directions. For the vast majority of the faculty, it was a time-consuming and ultimately wasteful activity.

Perhaps predictably, the faculty hold little regard for the central bureaucracy, which is seen as dictating rather than discussing educational policy. Since most teachers and supervisors believe teaching to be a profession, they resent what they see as bureaucratic attempts to mandate change in teaching practice such as was done by the central board in the case of a mandated course on global history. Teachers complained that although they were expected to have classroom skills, others had the power to insist that they undertake procedures they saw as counterproductive. Many attributed the low morale among teachers in general to such control. Just how much improvement can, in principle, be mandated from the top in an educational system, where the significant events occur at the lowest administrative level, is in itself an open question.

The administrative staff at Jenner appear to have adjusted to the more routine outside pressures, and will resist or go to battle only when something they consider essential to the school is at risk. The principal relates that when he first came into the job, he felt overwhelmed by the paper flow, but learned, in time, to discriminate between requests that needed serious attention and those that called for perfunctory responses, or could be ignored altogether.

Unlike the board's efforts to dictate methodology and pedagogical planning, the most fundamental changes have come as a result of political and societal influences. Lasting transformations came in the 1960s, a period of turbulence and dissension in the school, when the school's raison d'être—education for the academically talented—came under attack. The board of education devised a plan whereby all secondary schools were to be converted into comprehensive schools, equipped to offer the full range of academic and vocational programs then provided by the functionally differentiated schools. The specialized high schools were to be no exception: the selective admission procedures would be scrapped and the distinct programs eliminated. Supporters of the specialized schools rose to the challenge by organizing the Council for Specialized High Schools. Bypassing the city board and exerting influence directly on the state legislature, the council succeeded in preserving the school's status by a legislative mandate. This legislation, however, also deflected the attack on the school from yet another source, the Office of Civil Rights. An arm of HEW, it called for an investigation of possible bias in the entrance exam. The state bill institutionalized the Discovery Program by stipulating that approximately one hundred places be reserved for disadvantaged students who come recommended by their junior high schools but fall somewhat below the cutoff point on the admissions test. These students are admitted on condition that they attend a summer school program ostensibly designed to upgrade their skills and ease their passage into the school.

## Daniel: A Discovery Program Student

Daniel, now a sophomore, was admitted as part of the Discovery Program. A quiet, thoughtful boy, he attended atypical public schools. His first school, an alternative elementary program, provided a great deal of personal attention. In junior high, he was part of a special group within the school. Both programs were small, with close faculty-student relationships. They provided little preparation for the kind of impersonal experience he had his first year at Jenner.

> The teachers at Jenner are always stressing *what* you have to do in this course or that, but they don't tell you *how* to do it. . . . There's not a lot of *explaining* of what teachers expect you to do.

The year Daniel applied, he missed normal admission by five points, attended summer school (described by him as "punishment") and entered Jenner in the fall. It is apparent that this was a tremendous boost to his ego. He knows he passed a test that many others fail. "If I had taken the test one year later," he points out, "the cutoff score was lower, and I would have made it without the summer course." There appears to be no student or faculty awareness of his special status.

Once he was admitted, there was never a doubt about acceptance. A good math student, he wanted a school that focused on science and math, a school that would prepare him for a career in engineering. Daniel is trilingual—he speaks Spanish in his home and neighborhood, French when he visits his paternal grandparents, and English with his teachers and school friends. His mother works for a community organization; his father teaches French in a public junior high school. He is the eldest of four children. His program so far includes these courses:

| *1st Year* | *2nd Year* | *3rd Year* |
|---|---|---|
| History | History | History |
| English | English | English |
| Algebra | Geometry | Trigonometry |
| Introductory | Biology | Physics |
| Science | Spanish | French |
| Spanish | Mechanical | Music |
| Gym | Drawing | |

Having come from schools where the teachers were attentive and supportive, he is particularly sensitive to the way Jenner teachers handle their jobs: "Not all of them seem to be into teaching. Sometimes I think they are more interested in the grades we get than in students really learning something." Speaking to a group of graduating junior high school students, however, he told them to aim for Jenner.

> It's a good place to go. . . . They have lots of courses . . . there are no fights . . . the kids are smart.
> Some students excel in particular subjects; few excel in everything. I might be better than other kids in Spanish, they might be better than I am in math.
> It works out.

## Epilogue

As stated earlier, Jenner is a school that works. Faculty, administration, parents, and students share a set of common expectations. All assume that the work will be hard, but the students will do it; that the standards will be maintained and Regents passes will follow; that colleges will get good students and students, of course, will get into good colleges.

The students, for their part, accept the challenge, meet it, and, in the process interact with one another in ways that fundamentally affect their school experience and, perhaps, their lives.

While the school is imperfect, these imperfections have been examined here only because so much does work well. We have had the opportunity to speculate, for once, not about how to right a malfunctioning school, but, rather, about how to proceed in a school where basic educational tasks are being fulfilled.

After a month of observation, no simple image emerges. The diversity of Jenner's student population and its important effect on the school's academic and emotional well-being is a critical aspect of the school. The quality of the students' instructional experiences varies enormously: just as some courses are uninspired, even poorly taught, others are outstanding for their intellectual stimulation and challenge. Some classes are test-oriented and emphasize memorization, while others concentrate on critical thinking and substance. Most students experience a mixture of the memorable and the tedious.

The importance of Jenner's principal to the school's continuing success cannot be overemphasized. He is an effective educational leader within the school and articulate as a spokesperson outside.

Significantly, there is a fundamental understanding among his constituency that provides the critical mesh between what he can offer the school and what the faculty and students require in order to function well. We would want to underscore the importance of such a match in looking for "replicable" lessons from Jenner.

What aspects of this particular configuration are integral to the overall success of the school? What if any are replicable? While there are important implications for schools across the country, they must be understood in context and translated appropriately to suit each unique situation.

Would transferring the Jenner student body en masse, two blocks up the street, to the instructional care of the faculty there, erode student achievement? Could the Jenner faculty increase the number of college-bound students in another setting? Would the principal's administrative style prove effective elsewhere?

Short of certain predictions, the key to these questions resides in the interplay of forces impinging on the school that we attempt to portray in this essay.

# OBSERVATIONS ON THE CARNEGIE THEMES

VITO PERRONE

In the introductory reflections, I provided an overview of the schools that were observed, highlighting issues that emerged without attempting to be altogether comprehensive. A number of observations related directly to the themes outlined by The Carnegie Foundation for the Advancement of Teaching also are possible. I originally presented the following discussion as a way of assisting the Carnegie Foundation staff. In doing so, I tried to remain close to the information making up the school observations.

## Contextual Changes

Secondary schools appear to be in transition. Challenged heavily in the sixties and early seventies by demographic changes in relation to student numbers and the composition of student bodies by equity and student rights issues, altered economic conditions, changes in social values and lifestyles, and a significant decline in public confidence, as well as fiscal support, schools struggled—surviving but in most cases not thriving. In the face of these challenges, many schools tended to appear indecisive, to shift between extremes, become defensive and more insular, as well as somewhat ambivalent about academic and behavioral standards.

Virtually all the schools we visited are different today in relation to the foregoing issues than they were a decade ago. Equity issues, in particular, have become more muted. The schools tend, for example, to view seriously their responsibilities for accommodating a wider range of students from many different racial, ethnic, and social backgrounds, even though the difficulties in meeting the responsibilities remain large. Standards are being reaffirmed. Declining resources have forced several of the schools to reconsider the number of course offerings, to make decisions about what is important. In addition, schools no longer bear the bulk of the responsibility for developing programs to serve particularly troubled young people. Other agencies, such as mental health centers, churches, Y's, hospitals, and juvenile courts, have become more involved.

While not as beleaguered as they might have been a decade ago, the schools still face a number of persistently difficult issues. Growth was, for a long time, the norm. Now, however, people in the schools fear decline, and do not see prospects for fewer students as an opportunity, a constructive challenge. In part, this is related to the corollary of declining enrollment, namely reduced fiscal resources. All of the schools, for example, have fewer counselors; new teachers fresh out of the colleges and universities are becoming rarer; many teachers who brought new energy to some of the schools five to eight years ago are now gone, victims of falling resources and entrenched seniority systems.

There is a good deal of understanding among teachers, counselors, and administrators of the fact that one-parent families are increasing dramatically and working parents are becoming the norm. This understanding, however, has yet to translate into very many different mechanisms for interacting with parents. There is, it seems, a tacit acknowledgment, if not acceptance, that parent interaction with the schools is likely to continue to decline; in addition, there is a growing belief among teachers and administrators in the schools we observed that parents don't really support their interest in fostering higher academic standards, homework, and the like.

It should be noted that the societal shift toward greater conservatism—the call for slimmer programs, fewer options, more attention to skills narrowly defined, more concern about order—has in a number of ways taken pressure off the schools, providing them good reasons to reject some of the philosophical and pedagogical progressivism of the 1960s and early 1970s that challenged their thinking about curriculum, teaching, and learning. The highly utilitarian view of education that is now embraced in most of the schools we observed has, after all, a long tradition that is supported by a majority of teachers and school administrators who tend, themselves, to be fairly conservative.

*Students* We learned a great deal about students as a result of our school-site observations. They were enormously open, eager to share their views of what life is like in the schools. Along with the society at large, they, too, have become much more conservative. They are certainly more accepting of institutional authority than they were a decade ago, even though we heard a litany of complaints about school rules they viewed as unnecessary or unduly restrictive. Less optimistic about the future, they view their high school programs from a more vocational perspective as vehicles for further schooling or job skills rather than as opportunities for personal exploration, intellectual challenge, or speculation. More materialistic—not surprising in American society today—large numbers of them work. In the urban and suburban settings, it is not unusual to find that 70 percent of the students hold part-time—some even full-time—jobs. For many of these students, the schools tend not to be a central focus of their lives, and that creates a number of frustrations for teachers and administrators. In commenting that "school spirit isn't what it used to be," teachers and administrators acknowledge this shift. In the rural communities, part-time jobs are less available; students in these settings are more involved in school activities than are students in the urban-suburban settings.

While drug use—marijuana and alcohol in particular—remains fairly common, students and teachers alike indicate that the associated problems have declined. From all accounts, there is considerably less drug use on the high school campuses, greater awareness of potential difficulties, and more willingness among students to accept assistance.

Television, once an important force in the lives of these students, is not as potent for them now. Outside of the rural settings, where watching television remains something to do, high school students view much less television than junior high and elementary school students. Large numbers just do not have time to watch television. While it is impossible, on the basis of our interactions with students, to comment on the real effects of television, teachers, even in the selective academic schools, note that students appear to have less basic knowledge than students in the sixties, a condition they attribute to a history of too much television viewing and too little reading.

Without question, increasing numbers of students in the public high schools experience difficulties with reading, writing, and mathematics. There was a time when these kinds of students, in too large a measure members of poor minorities, did not remain in the schools. More recently, certainly in the 1970s, the response of schools to many of these students was to devise special, generally not very challenging, programs that provided a high school diploma. Unfortunately, many of these special programs gave too little attention to skill deficiencies. Now, under considerable public pressure, there is an acknowledgment by those within the schools that these students need to be attended to more constructively, but the schools seem ill-prepared for the task. They don't have resources for the special teachers they believe they need, and most of the regular subject-matter-related teachers don't feel they know how to provide significant help or where to go to receive the special training. The pressures on many of these struggling students tend to be large. They are urged to stay in school because the diploma is so critical, yet they often feel incompetent in the school setting.

What stood out in the school observations, and in this there is room for optimism, is that most students in the high schools appear responsible, express a desire to become competent individuals, are generally caring of other students, and are fairly open to learning. Teachers generally acknowledged the validity of such observations, especially as they thought about student behavior outside class; they noted, however, that the students were not always interested in what they had to offer in formal courses. Higher-quality teaching, more energy and imagination, better curriculum work might close the gap between the teachers' in-class and out-of-class perceptions. Students, as we learned, perceive in most settings that teacher expectations are not generally very high. They told our observers they could and would do more if the demands were made understandable and were followed up consistently by teachers. Overall, students had fairly positive feelings about teachers, seeing most as persons who cared about them.

Students desire a larger adult role in the schools and in their communities. Providing them with constructive experience is a challenge for the schools that might become easier to address as overall enrollments continue to decline.

*Goals*  The high schools we observed had a number of implicit, if not explicit, goals ranging from preparing students for work to preparing students for competitive colleges and universities. In general, however, the schools struggle for a consensus about purposes. Seldom, for example, do teachers and administrators—let alone teachers, administrators, students, and parents—come together to discuss seriously their purposes in relation to the particular groups of young people served by a school. Few of the teachers and administrators we met were particularly articulate about purposes. Although in almost every school someone could find a bureaucratically prepared document about goals, such documents were seldom vital.

Much of what occurs in the schools has a future orientation, yet students are in a period when their social and ethical values are under challenge and they need time to think about themselves and their relationships to others. They need to learn how to reflect about themselves and engage in problem solving, but they do not receive much assistance.

All of us have read a good deal about the schools' growing burdens—having to solve all of society's ills. We had little sense that the schools were being overwhelmed by increasing responsibilities. Many had breakfast programs as well as support groups for students struggling with drug problems or family difficulties, but such activities were seen as closely related to ongoing issues of teaching and learning.

*Climate*  Overall, the schools we observed were congenial places, generally displaying evidence that teachers and administrators cared about the students. The schools which tended to be the most consistent were the schools with the most carefully defined purposes—for example, the vocational schools, the selective academic schools, and one of the suburban schools. In the schools that lacked a coherent set of commonly understood and supported purposes, behavior appeared more inconsistent, and there was, overall, less commitment to the school. In settings where teachers were moved often by central bureaucracies struggling with finances and seniority issues, or where turnover was high for personal reasons, teachers chose not to give the schools much of their hearts and souls.

Physically, the buildings were clean, though it did not appear that enormous care was taken to create attractively aesthetic settings or to display curriculum imaginatively. Outside of the vocational classrooms, there was little environmental evidence of support for high-quality student work. As resources slide downward, the physical care of buildings will likely receive much less attention. Few of the schools had comfortable spaces for students and faculty to meet, and teachers had limited access to telephones. Many teachers believed that a telephone would, for example, enhance their ability to communicate with parents, establish contacts with potential community resources, and the like. Teacher interaction was generally limited, and, with only a few exceptions, the schools did not display an aura of intellectualism or reflection.

School climate is related also to issues of responsibility. Students tend not to bear much responsibility for space or activities. Teachers and administrators maintain virtually all of the significant responsibility and authority.

*Curriculum*  Structurally, curriculum appears very much as it has been for most of the last fifty years. World history is followed by American history, American government, problems of democracy, and economics. Algebra I is followed by geometry, algebra II, trigonometry, and, in a few schools, math analysis and calculus. The literature sequence also has not changed substantially. There are large numbers of electives that weren't present a decade or two ago, and one would be hard-pressed to call many of them whimsical or potentially limited intellectually. The curriculum work of the sixties—principally inquiry oriented—is apparent in very few classrooms. Textbooks have long dominated the content of most courses in the high schools. This is still the case because teachers tend not to stray too far away, even though, in many of the settings, there was little pressure on them to follow such a conventional direction. But added to the textbooks are an increasing array of supplementary materials, guides, outlines, and tests, which increase even more the grip textbooks have on the curriculum.

Little attention is given to curriculum development in the schools;

curriculum-related discussion is almost nonexistent, and efforts to reduce fragmentation through interdisciplinary activities are rare. Standards, especially in relation to expectations, are typically not uniform within the schools. The quality of questions asked and the kinds of writing completed by students varied enormously within schools and between schools. What is apparent is that teachers are not, in general, curriculum-makers or decision-makers.

The schools tend to track far more heavily than we expected, even though tracking is seldom discussed, and even though it produces a number of inequitable consequences. In part, the tracking occurs in response to teachers' frustrations in contending with the increasing levels of diversity among students. It stems also from a belief that attending to minimal levels of achievement—a common operational goal—demands special classes. The racial separation associated with the tracking that we observed is seldom discussed openly, in part because opportunities to discuss purposes and procedures just do not exist in many of the schools.

Tracking is especially prevalent in the last two years, often during the three-year period encompassing grades ten to twelve, with the ninth grade being the point at which many of the placement decisions get made. For example, ninth-grade students who are enrolled in general mathematics rather than algebra tend not to ever take geometry, chemistry, or physics. This is a serious limitation for students who, after graduation, might like to engage in specialized technical training in a community college or vocational school, or enter a four-year college or university.

Although we did not find a lot of examples of exemplary teaching or imaginative use of materials anywhere, they occurred far less frequently in the lower tracks.

Competency-testing efforts were found in several of the settings we observed. While teachers were reluctant to say they would like to get rid of the competency tests, it also was clear that these programs imposed limitations. Teachers in these particular settings organized heavily around the test; they felt pressures to gear many of the curricular offerings to a basic skills effort, to offer a less rich academic program. The schools need a larger vision of education.

Leadership is not found at high levels in the schools. Only a few of the principals viewed themselves as capable of giving leadership to discussions about curriculum. Further, they generally appeared reluctant to have external persons come in to provide this kind of assistance. Assistant principals for curriculum or curriculum-resource people, where they existed, tended to be so busy with schedule making, textbook ordering, and responding to central-office demands that they, too, were unable to provide any significant educational leadership.

*Teachers*   What stands out is a high level of isolation. Teachers have limited opportunities for interaction within their schools. There is very little discussion about teaching and learning, curriculum, purposes, and the like. In addition, teachers have very minimal opportunities for professional exchange with colleagues outside their building. This enormously limits their views of themselves as significant professionals. To participate in a professional meeting in many of the systems means losing compensation in some form. Almost nowhere did we observe productive provisions for in-service education or real concern about professional development viewed as a reflective process. Our observers were received enthusiastically in all of the schools because they provided significant contacts as stimulating outsiders interested in the teachers' work.

Teachers feel undervalued in their communities. In part, this outlook is related to compensation levels, which they feel are very low. It was surprising to us that so many—upwards of 25 percent—of the teachers held additional jobs. They felt this was essential, and they resented the necessity. But compensation, for most teachers, is not the central focus of their discontent. Of greater concern is their desire for respect, for acknowledgment by parents and others in their communities of the important role they play as teachers and decision-makers about educational matters. They feel criticized at every turn, blamed for many of the ills in society. They are especially resentful about the charge that "unemployment exists in such large numbers today because of the poor quality of education provided by teachers and schools." Teachers clearly should not have to be responsible for the lackluster performance of the American economy.

In few cases did we observe teachers actively involved in such matters as governance, decisions about the school and its curriculum, and its assessment procedures. Important decision-making, from their perspective, goes on elsewhere. There is discouragement about this, especially in the large cities.

Teachers appear, for the most part, to be teaching in areas in which they completed college university majors. This is especially the case in the sciences, mathematics, English, and foreign languages. In the social sciences, there are more people teaching in what were either minor fields in college or composite social science majors rather than majors in specific disciplines. Those teaching in minor fields tended, it appeared, to be even more tied to the textbooks than were those with more extensive academic backgrounds. But academic strength did not necessarily seem to translate into high-quality teaching. It is in the area of pedagogical skills—individualization, curriculum development, attending to the diversity of learning styles and skills—that teachers appear to need the most assistance.

Teachers could describe good teaching but did not generally feel that they were performing that role as well as they might. They believe good teaching involves caring, individualization, ideas, and intellectual challenge. They are not confident, however, that their communities view good teaching as they do.

Three other issues emerged as we observed and talked with teachers. First, they have little time for reflection and planning. If meetings are to occur, they must take place, it seems, after school, a time when many other activities—clubs, sports, planning, gathering materials, individual meetings with students—impinge on their time. There is a strong view among teachers that time ought to be made available during the school day to assist them in coming together for planning, considering curriculum, doing the staff work necessary to be of real assistance to some of the students who are struggling. Teaching loads are very heavy and becoming larger as resources decline. In most of the schools, teachers taught five and often six classes each day; they met in formal settings with 150 to 180 students per day. If they demanded serious writing on any regular basis, they were hard-pressed to keep up.

Second, the teachers in the schools are growing noticeably older. New teachers fresh out of colleges and universities have always brought new enthusiasm to schools. But there is too little room for these new teachers at the moment. In most of the schools we visited, the average age of teachers was well into the forties.

A third and last observation—one that needs more careful thought because it stands in opposition to so much of the popular discussions about generational problems—is that the teachers, in general, are able to communicate quite effectively with the students. Out of this base, there is considerable potential for rethinking, for example, school purposes and curriculum. We did not see very many efforts by administrators or teachers to actually make use of such potential.

In thinking about teachers, and having introduced the issue of leadership briefly, it might be appropriate to comment on administrators. Principals, with the exception of those in the rural settings, are, by and large, buried by obligations to other bureaucracies. They tend to be caught up in issues of discipline and order. They are not often viewed by teachers as intellectual leaders or as persons capable of exercising leadership in areas of curriculum or improved teaching. Most of the principals tended to agree with these assessments. They feel as isolated as the teachers, receive little support of consequence, and have few opportunities to reflect on their work in terms of alternatives. Our observers could have spent *all* of their time with the principals. They were, by and large, anxious to have an external person help them reflect on their practices, help them think about their schools, problems, and potential.

## Teaching and Learning

There is a sameness about how teachers approach their teaching. The format is fairly conventional, textbook oriented, information filled: twenty minutes or so of lecture and twenty to thirty minutes for students to read the assignments, respond to worksheets, answer questions at the ends of chapters, work on math problems, and write themes, while the teacher circulates around the room. We saw very little inquiry teaching, and problem-solving skills did not tend to be taught. There was virtually no team teaching and very little individualization in relation to projects or expectations, except in the vocational areas and some of the arts programs. Classroom control is not, for the most part, a serious problem; certainly it is nothing like the descriptions one often finds in the popular press. This doesn't mean that there are no difficulties. In many classrooms, we observed students who were inattentive, some even dozed (and were for the most part ignored). In relation to control—and in a number of settings there was an obsession about control—teachers often suggested that they would like to alter some of their instructional patterns, do more small-group work, and the like, but they were concerned that this could be disruptive, might result in a noisy classroom, and establish a possible external view that they had lost control.

In most of the schools, students tended not to be deeply engaged in their courses, not finding them particularly stimulating in any intellectual sense. Except for the selective academic schools, there was very little peer tutoring or student involvement in instruction. There are some experiential-education programs, but they tend to be related principally to the vocational and business education areas; hence, they engage very few students. Possibilities for more expansive educative experiences are found in urban and suburban communities, but have not been examined seriously. In the urban and suburban communities, the majority of students work, yet the schools have not found any constructive means to make use of this work experience as a catalyst for school programs or curriculum development and have not generally considered ways to integrate any of this experience into ongoing course work.

## Education Beyond the School

The schools have very limited contact with external agencies. Their level of isolation is astounding and may contribute to many of the more negative public perceptions that exist. Educating agencies abound in most urban communities, potentially providing excellent experience for high school-age students. But the working out of arrangements with these agencies tends to get bogged down when they are handled by central bureaucracies, the typical pattern. If individual schools took the responsibility, the arrangements might work far better and be more integral to the school's programs. In some settings, especially in the vocational fields, the schools have developed programs in relation to local community colleges, but the potential is larger, far beyond vocational education. In their senior years, many high school students could very well do most of their academic work in a local community college or public four-year college or university.

## Media and Technology

There is in our society a great deal of discussion about a technological revolution. The schools are not deeply involved in this revolution, however. They tend to be media poor. Little use is made of television, film, photography, and audiotape. Computers are not yet important sources of learning for students. There is little effort to systematically acquaint all students with computer use and language.

In vocational settings that are equipment dependent, equipment tends to be well behind the technology that exists outside. Given the costs, one wonders if there aren't other ways to provide vocational education.

## Some Tentative Conclusions/Recommendations

Based on the observations made in the fifteen schools in this Carnegie study sample and my own summary of those observations, as well as my longer involvement in large numbers of high schools over the past two decades, what kinds of conclusions/recommendations might I make for high school improvement? I present here *some* preliminary thoughts for discussion by the Carnegie staff. I do so with some reluctance, however, because many of the ideas are so obvious, have been discussed often, already exist as practice in some settings, and are not particularly dramatic.

The major interests in high schools revolve around social, intellectual, academic, citizenship, and pre-vocational concerns. To give these concerns vitality, high schools need to develop more explicit goals that can be clearly understood by teachers, students, and their parents. Such statements of goals should serve as a basis upon which to build common commitments; develop curricula; guide expectations; govern relationships between and among administrators, teachers, students, and parents; and give direction to public accountability. This is not to suggest that we need the sweeping goals statements prevalent in the forties and fifties that spoke of "preserving a democratic way of life" or "improving the lot of mankind"—statements that surfaced during school accreditation visits or at Fourth of July celebrations and had little, if any, real meaning for those in the schools. It is likewise not a proposal to support more minimalist statements about basic competencies of the sort that have emerged recently in some settings. The statements of purposes that now need expression must be vital statements against which *all* school practices can be judged. They must come *from* individual high schools, growing out of significant public discussion involving administrators, teachers, students, and parents.

In thinking about the foregoing, I accept the criticism that too many high schools lack a strong sense of purpose, appear to be drifting, and often latch on to an array of instructional programs that may be contradictory. Such ambivalence leads, I believe, to a lack of loyalty, solid commitment, or enthusiasm from students and staff within the high schools, and provides little encouragement for significant internal critique or constructive response to changing circumstances.

To speak of goals at the level of individual schools is also to give support to some greater form of school-site management, especially in urban centers. Such decentralization could increase the level of responsibility among teachers and administrators, encourage more vital student and parent participation, and increase accountability in an educative sense. Different schools, if they are individually concerned about particular purposes and a means of supporting these purposes, may well have unique thoughts about how best to use fiscal and human resources. Such decisions might include whether, for example, to appoint a full-time computer teacher or enter into a contract with a local computer firm; accept the offer of a local cellist to provide some specialized instruction on a voluntary basis or find a way for a local university to provide instruction in calculus; add one more counselor rather than two aides, a curriculum advisor rather than another assistant principal; or whether to use a particular text or a wide variety of alternative instructional materials. If we are to achieve this level of decentralization, those involved with particular schools need a greater voice in relation to staffing. We found little that was more debilitating to school morale than this sense of nonempowerment regarding staff appointments.

There is a need for a basic core of courses for *all* students, especially in grades nine and ten. These courses need to be untracked and built around a commitment to individualization of basic content. They should provide a common orientation toward problem solving, reading, writing, listening, and speaking. As for individualization within an untracked system, I rather like Mortimer Adler's comments in response to his "paideia" program: "Take two cartons, one holds a quart, the other a pint. Fill the quart container with cream and then fill the pint container with cream (rather than the skimmed milk and dirty water which is so often the current practice)." Students *should not* be tracked out of potential educational opportunities at these early high school levels as is now too often the case. In fact, schools have an obligation to hold and maintain high expectations for students and to provide attention to literacy in virtually every course offering.

In grades eleven and twelve (transitional years), students should be provided with more specialized opportunities that lead *principally* to postsecondary educational opportunities. While some prevocational opportunities should be available, as well as employment counseling programs that feature or support employment activities, job training in the narrow sense does not seem appropriate. Job training programs that now exist in many of our schools have served young people poorly, leaving too many with inadequate academic skills and limited postsecondary opportunities. And from the research that has been done, any initial employment advantages students in such programs have had tend to wash out within two or three years. It is at this point that this more limited academic education begins to take its toll.

In regard to more specialized opportunities, a comprehensive school might offer several specialized areas—schools within schools—as a means of building greater coherence. In the more urban communities, individual schools might feature a specialization. To suggest a higher level of specialization, however, does not mean that the common areas of study should be diminished in any way or that the individual schools must offer everything.

Students in grades eleven and twelve should be encouraged to do some of their specialized work—especially in some of the vocational fields and in advanced levels of math, science, and the arts—in settings such as community colleges and four-year colleges and universities. This might serve to blur what has been too great a demarcation line between the secondary schools and higher education institutions. There are also other community resources that could be drawn upon.

The foregoing suggestions need to be accompanied by significant curriculum development efforts, an area of education that has been seriously neglected for a number of years. Teachers have long been tied closely to textbooks and a range of materials with predetermined ends. These are exactly the kinds of materials that support passivity among students and teachers alike. In many cases, teachers have had virtually no control over such matters and, as a result, they often feel very limited responsibility for the consequences. The curriculum development we now need should support inquiry, problem solving, and more active learning—in other words, development in essentially more intellectual directions. It needs to encourage the use of a broader range of materials, teaching strategies, and teaching sites to assure that "cream" is available for *all* students. While some of the broad outlines of the secondary school's curriculum could be developed outside of the schools, the critical work needs to be carried out by individuals *within* schools. Moreover, the curriculum needs to be closely tied to the goals and commitments existing within a school to keep it vital. It might, however, be part of a collaboration between teachers in a particular school, curriculum support personnel within a school or school district, and faculty from local colleges and universities.

To address the issue of curriculum development is also to give attention to interdisciplinary studies, greater integration of students' academic and prevocational experiences, as well as to the question of what is most important for *all* students, especially in settings where tracking is to be reduced or eliminated.

We need to rethink the issue of teaching loads, and, in this connection, the length of the school day and year as well. Expecting teachers to teach five to six hours per day in formal class settings and be responsible for 150 to 180 students per day is *not* conducive to high-quality teaching as demanded in the current environment. The need for a higher level of individualization, greater attention to literacy, a greater intellectual orientation, higher expectations, a more challenging curriculum, and the like, demands as a corollary fewer hours of teaching in formal class settings and fewer students overall. Three to four classes per day with a maximum of 100 students is far more realistic, leaving teachers the time to work with individual students and small groups of students needing additional attention, and to attend to writing assignments, work on curriculum, and so on.

Teachers need a stronger sense of professionalism and a belief that they have the time and resources to be as effective as they are capable of being with students. This should be somewhat easier to accomplish in an environment where student numbers are stable or declining. It might also be accomplished, in part, by placing limits on the numbers of courses offered at the school each day and by encouraging more use of other educational centers for some of the advanced course work and vocational studies. Extending the school year from thirty-six weeks, which is the norm, to forty or forty-two weeks would also help. (European secondary schools have long gone the route of shorter school days and longer school years on the assumption that students and teachers will have more time to do their work, think, and so forth.)

While this discussion of the school day and year has focused principally on teachers, it should be clear that other educational services could improve. Counseling efforts could be qualitatively improved as students became freer during the course of an eight-hour day. Teachers could also be more easily consulted. More significant efforts to share postsecondary opportunities would be possible. At the moment, counseling activities tend to have a lackluster quality in too many places, too often involving little more than filling out postsecondary applications, checking course schedules, handling registration, and so forth. A different configuration of the school day would make it easier for students to work (as the majority now do in the urban and suburban centers) and *also* meet their academic obligations. In addition, it would create a situation where student involvement in community service activities would be more realistic.

There is a significant need for professional development of teachers *in* the schools. In the current environment, with the present organizational patterns and expectations, there is little, if any, opportunity for teachers to reflect significantly on practice; little, if any, encouragement or support for teachers to be the "students of teaching" Dewey suggested they had to be to remain vital in any professional sense. A school day that encompassed three to five hours for class instruction, individual conferring and contacts with parents and other external instructional resources, and at least two to three hours per day for planning, curriculum activity, reflection on teaching, professional development, and the like, would provide more of the opportunities that currently do not exist in very many places. Clearly, this won't diminish the continuing need for teachers to use many of their evenings, weekends, and summers for planning, reading, and thinking about teaching. But it should take enough pressure off teachers to make such continuing expectations qualitatively more interesting and productive.

As for the content of professional development efforts, it is fairly clear to those of us who spend a good deal of time in the schools—and it was a principal observation from the study of the fifteen Carnegie schools—that the needs of teachers are not, in general, for more academic courses in their teaching disciplines. (Though I would not wish to suggest that additional work in traditional academic areas should be discouraged.) Their needs are more pedagogical than academic. The resources for addressing these pedagogical-craft issues already exist within the schools, *if* the schools would organize themselves for the purpose of examining practice carefully. It would be, in this regard, helpful to have available the kinds of resources that typically exist in the colleges and universities. To *expect* colleges and universities to pair themselves to schools is clearly reasonable. There is a reciprocity of interest here with potentially enormous benefits.

There is a continuing need to attract the "best and the brightest" teachers for the schools. The conditions for attracting these kinds of individuals, however, rest more with the conditions of teaching than with salary. Rigid bureaucracies, competency testing, mandated curriculum, narrow definitions of teaching, lack of opportunities for reflection, and limited autonomy are the kinds of factors that tend to keep the "best and brightest" away or drive too many of them away after they have entered teaching. A closer tie between colleges, universities, and schools might provide a context for getting more university students involved in schools—a recruitment device that is not being tapped particularly well.

Secondary schools need to demonstrate in their organizational structures and practices their commitment to equity, democracy, and responsibility. In this regard, there is far too much failure in relation to those who are most at risk. In addition, students play too small a role in most schools; they receive too little preparation for citizenship in its broadest sense and for responsible adulthood. There are responsible roles for students within schools, some of them related to instruction, equipment maintenance, even administration. Schools with control of their own budgets—a facet of school-site management—might even devote some of their resources to paying students for certain activities. For example, as part of their curriculum, students could engage in a range of community service activities along with their teachers. We need to find more ways of integrating high school students into productive community life.

In regard to administration, all of the foregoing recommendations call attention to the need for extraordinary leadership. The efforts and energies of principals that now go toward responding to a central bureaucracy could be turned more productively toward the school. The leadership abilities we need relate to building a consensus around goals, supporting teacher growth, curriculum development, coordinating human and fiscal resources, and developing community contacts and their instructional support potential. For such roles, management training may be less important than curriculum and curriculum evaluation training.